**Scott, Foresman
Spanish Program
Book 1**

TEACHER'S ANNOTATED EDITION
VOCES Y VISTAS

Bernadette M. Reynolds
Montbello High School
Denver, Co

Carol Eubanks Rodríguez
Glen Crest Junior High School
Glen Ellyn, Il

Rudolf L. Schonfeld
Parsippany High School
Parsippany, NJ

Scott, Foresman and Company

Editorial Offices: Glenview, Illinois

Regional Offices: Sunnyvale, California · Tucker, Georgia
Glenview, Illinois · Oakland, New Jersey · Dallas, Texas

ISBN: 0-673-20721-8

12345678910 RRC 9998979695949392919089 88

CONTENTS

COMPONENTS OF THE PROGRAM

VOCES Y VISTAS is the first book in a three-book series. The student text opens with a preliminary unit *(En camino)* focusing on basic, high-frequency concepts. This is followed by sixteen chapters and an appendix offering a summary of numbers, time and calendar information, verb charts, Spanish-English and English-Spanish vocabularies, a grammar index, and maps.

This Teacher's Annotated Edition reproduces the student text with overprinted answers, teaching suggestions, and cross references to the ancillary materials. This front section also includes:

- "Organization of the Text," a description of all chapter elements with suggestions for their use
- "A Teacher's Perspective," a practical view of VOCES Y VISTAS
- "A Guide to Bridging to PASOS Y PUENTES," Book 2 of the series
- two articles, "Paired Practice: Why and How" and "Learning Spanish Through Action." The latter gives suggestions for implementing James J. Asher's methodology—most commonly known as Total Physical Response, or TPR—with VOCES Y VISTAS
- "Teacher Notes," a section of chapter-by-chapter objectives, suggestions for classroom props or materials, cultural information on the photographs and realia, additional teaching, review, and enrichment suggestions, answers to specific sections of the chapter, and oral proficiency tests
- "Index of Cultural References" for use in planning your cultural presentations to the class

Ancillary materials to accompany VOCES Y VISTAS include the following:

- *Cassette Tapes:* A set of 18 cassettes, one covering the *En camino,* one for each chapter, and a separate listening comprehension testing tape.
- *Workbook / Tape Manual:* A two-part student book. The Workbook section contains material to supplement each book chapter, plus special review sections following Chapters 4, 8, 12, and 16. The Tape Manual section contains all of the printed material necessary for students to do the listening exercises on the tapes.
- *Teacher's Edition: Workbook / Tape Manual:* The student material with overprinted answers and a complete tapescript.
- *Practice Sheet Workbook* (with separate *Teacher's Answer Key):* Worksheets designed to provide the basic-level mechanical practice for all vocabulary and grammar sections of the student text.
- *Teacher's Resource Book* (including *Testing Program):* A three-ring binder containing blackline master quizzes for all vocabulary and grammar sections, chapter tests, and four review tests (all with answers on reduced pages). The *Teacher's Edition: Workbook / Tape Manual* and a classroom wall map are also included.
- *Communicative Activity Blackline Masters:* A set of oral classroom activities for paired and group practice designed to supplement those already in the student text.
- *Overhead Transparencies:* A package of full-color overhead visuals that includes all vocabulary-teaching illustrations (with objects unlabeled), all conversation visuals *(¿Qué pasa?),* and the cartoon-strip illustrations for the *Temas* (without the captions). Also included are suggestions for use of the transparencies and an identification key.
- *Reader:* A graded reader specially designed to be used in conjunction with VOCES Y VISTAS.
- *Computer Software:* A package of computer-assisted instruction designed for use with the Scott, Foresman Spanish Program.
- *Videotape:* A tape designed to acquaint students with aspects of daily life in the Spanish-speaking world. A *Teacher's Guide* with student blackline masters is included.

ORGANIZATION OF THE TEXT

A glance at VOCES Y VISTAS will reveal an efficient predictability of format. All chapters begin with a *Prólogo cultural.* All end with a chapter vocabulary list. In between you will find the following:

> Palabras Nuevas I
>   Aplicaciones*
> Palabras Nuevas II
> Explicaciones I
>   Aplicaciones
> Explicaciones II
>   Aplicaciones

Predictability of format, however, in no way implies sameness. There is enormous variety in presentation and practice. But predictability is crucial if a book is to work truly flexibly in the classroom. If you, the teacher, are to plan well for what to emphasize or to omit, you must be able to know the organization of the text.

VOCES Y VISTAS begins with five preliminary lessons, *En camino A–E,* designed for students to talk and have fun as they begin the process of learning a second language. The *En camino* presents certain basic vocabulary sets (greetings and leave-takings, names of Spanish-speaking countries, time by the clock, numbers, the alphabet, and so on), as well as rules for the pronunciation of Spanish vowel sounds. Almost all of the *Prácticas* are communicative or activity oriented. The material in the *En camino* should not be taught for day-to-day mastery. All of these words and structures are continually and carefully re-entered throughout the text. It is recommended that you spend no more than two weeks on the *En camino.*

Sixteen chapters compose the main body of the text. What follows are some very basic suggestions for using the chapter sections. Next to each section title there are five boxes representing Listening (L), Speaking (S), Reading (R), Writing (W), and Culture (C). These show you the relative emphasis that each text section gives to each of these skills or

* The first *Aplicaciones* section focuses on listening and speaking, the second on speaking and reading, the third on writing.

areas of understanding. Red boxes represent strong emphasis; purple boxes mean some emphasis.

PRÓLOGO CULTURAL `L` `S` `R` `W` `C`

These essays give informative, curiosity-piquing glimpses into Hispanic culture. Each focuses on one of the main themes of the chapter.

We recommend that you:

- Assign the *Prólogo* as homework, with or without classroom discussion the following day.
- Help students compare and contrast what they have read with their own culture, encouraging development of a global perspective.
- Ask students to keep a cultural notebook.
- Let students use these as a point of departure for extra-credit cultural reports.
- Make as full use as possible of native speakers who may be in your class or in the school to elaborate on particular topics.
- Begin immediately to use the Teacher Notes for additional cultural information that you can share with the class.

PALABRAS NUEVAS I

Contexto visual `L` `S` `R` `W` `C`

This is new, active vocabulary presented in a visual context.

- Use the overhead transparency as the tape recites the words; have students listen and repeat.
- Identify items affirmatively / negatively (*¿Es un . . . ? / Sí. Es un . . . / No. Es un . . .*); pose either / or or open-ended questions; use gestures and pantomime; in later chapters, as students' vocabulary has increased, use synonyms / antonyms / related words / definitions in Spanish.

Contexto comunicativo `L` `S` `R` `W` `C`

This is new active vocabulary that does not lend itself

to illustration. These words are presented in the context of mini-dialogues with substitutions. New words are in boldface type and are glossed in the right-hand margin.

- Let students hear the mini-dialogues on tape.
- Let pairs of students read the mini-dialogues aloud (without the substitutions).
- Let volunteers read (or perform) the mini-dialogues for the class.
- Ask for volunteers or assign students to read the mini-dialogues with you (you might want to assume the role that has longer or more difficult speeches).*
- Redo the mini-dialogues with the class, using the *Variaciones.* Until students get the knack, explain how these work: The individual words and phrases in the text should be replaced by those to the right of the arrow. Point out that a red box represents a new *Variación.* When two or more substitutions are shown after a box, all must be made for the mini-dialogue to make sense.
- Ask simple comprehension questions, or use those provided on the tape.
- Avoid grammar discussions at this point. When you get to the *Explicaciones,* you may then want to refer to these mini-dialogues as a point of departure. Cross references appear in the on-page teacher notes.

The use of props and Total Physical Response (TPR) techniques can be very effective in presenting vocabulary. See the article entitled "Learning Spanish Through Action," page T18. Chapter-by-chapter suggestions for this technique are presented in the Teacher Notes.

En otras partes

This feature offers examples of how Spanish vocabulary differs from region to region and discourages viewing vocabulary choice as a matter of right or wrong. The words given in this feature are *not active vocabulary.* They are shown as a means of pointing out to students that they might hear variant

---

* Particularly in the early chapters, one role is generally shorter or easier than the other to encourage less verbal or performance-shy students.

forms depending on the speaker's native country or region. If you have native speakers in your class, encourage them to add any additional variants that they may use.

Práctica

These exercises are designed to help students begin to learn the new material. Many are set up for paired practice, though you may do them in a more traditional way simply by playing one of the roles yourself. (For a discussion of paired practice, see page T16.)

- You do the model and perhaps the first one or two numbered items aloud with the class before dividing them into smaller groups.
- Assign more complex exercises as homework, using in-class paired practice the following day.
- Use the *Hablemos de ti* (the final exercise) to clarify for the students the real-life, personal use of the vocabulary they are learning.

Basic vocabulary practice exercises are available in the *Practice Sheet Workbook;* higher level practice plus the written material necessary for doing tape exercises are available in the combination *Workbook / Tape Manual.* There is, in addition, a quiz on every essential chapter section as part of the testing program in the Teacher's Resource Book. This may, if you choose, be used as homework practice instead.

APLICACIONES

Diálogo

Like all of the *Aplicaciones* sections, this is discretionary. The *Diálogo* gives students an example of extended discourse, most often with explicit or underlying cultural information. Some new passive vocabulary is included for reading recognition. Words and expressions that students would not readily understand are glossed. To promote the important skill of informed guessing, cognates and more easily decodable words are not glossed.

- Play the tape as students listen.
- Interrupt the tape to ask simple factual questions (who/what/where/when/how).
- Ask for volunteers to read or perform the *Diálogo*

for the class, or divide students into small groups so that they may read together.

- Point out and discuss any cultural information mentioned or implicit in the *Diálogo.*
- Assign the *Preguntas* as written homework and then go over them in class the following day.
- In later chapters you might handle the *Preguntas* in class immediately after reading, then assign students the task of writing a third-person summary of the *Diálogo.*
- Use the additional taped oral questions either immediately after listening to the *Diálogo* the first time or, after a few days, replay the tape and let students answer them then.

Participación

This optional section provides students a controlled opportunity to create their own dialogue. Since the topic is based on the *Diálogo,* students have a model that they can follow closely.

- Assign this as an extra-credit activity for pairs of students.
- Assign the *Participación* as an oral project. In each chapter, assign it to a different pair of students. You might also ask them to prepare a written set of *Preguntas* to hand out as a listening comprehension quiz for their classmates.

Pronunciación

Over the course of using VOCES Y VISTAS, students practice the sounds of Spanish in individual words and in full sentences.

- Play the tape, asking students to repeat chorally or individually (books open or closed).
- Ask students to give additional examples of the target sound.
- Write unfamiliar words that contain the target sound, asking students to pronounce them and, when possible, to guess their meaning (try to emphasize cognates and words related to known vocabulary).
- Use the full sentences as a *dictado* a few days after students have worked with this section.

PALABRAS NUEVAS II

This is identical in format to *Palabras Nuevas I,* and recommendations for use are the same. One additional optional feature concludes *Palabras Nuevas II:*

Estudio de palabras

This section is designed to promote both linguistic and cultural awareness. Cover it quickly, but emphasize for students that an understanding of the topics discussed will help them immeasurably in their comprehension of both written and spoken Spanish. It will also help them to make educated guesses if they need to ''invent'' a word when they are speaking.

- Read the section aloud with the class or assign it as homework.
- Explain that any new words discussed or mentioned in this section will not appear on tests, but that students will be expected to recognize them when they read.
- Encourage students to look for these and additional word relationships as they read and study.
- Encourage students to examine their own language's roots, affixes, verb-noun-adjective relationships, and so on.

Actividad

One or the other of the two *Palabras Nuevas* sections includes an optional paired or small group recreational activity designed for open-ended oral practice. For some *Actividades,* props will be needed. These are listed for you in the Teacher Notes under the heading ''Suggested Materials.''

EXPLICACIONES I

These are student-oriented grammar presentations with examples and charts. Grammatical terminology is kept to a minimum, and when used it is clarified with reference to the students' experience with their native language.

To make learning the grammar easier, most structures are first introduced lexically in the *Palabras Nuevas.* Students then use the new structures in a carefully controlled context as they practice the new words. Thus by the time students come to the formal grammar presentation, they are already familiar with the structures and in many cases even have some active control of them.

To help students see the immediate practicality of what they are learning, a list of objectives appears with each grammar topic. These usually take the form of language notions and/or functions and are derived either from the basic use of the structure being studied or from the contexts and formats of the exercises in the *Práctica.*

- Begin discussion of the grammar topic by reviewing the *Palabras Nuevas* mini-dialogue(s) where the structure was initially presented (on-page notes in this teacher's edition provide cross references).
- Be sure to go over the explanations, but don't let the class get stuck there. The majority of students will learn more from the practice itself (in the book, in the *Practice Sheet Workbook,* and in the *Workbook / Tape Manual)* than from discussion of grammar points. Do not aim for immediate mastery, particularly of the more complex structures. They are continually re-entered, practiced, and reinforced in subsequent chapter elements and in subsequent chapters.
- Ask students to make up additional examples of the target structure.
- Use simple oral pattern drills before doing the text exercises.
- Use the overhead transparencies or other visuals for oral drill (short question / answer or narrative description).

Práctica
See *Palabras Nuevas I,* above, for recommendations.

Actividad
A discretionary oral activity follows one of the two *Explicaciones* sections of each chapter. See *Palabras Nuevas II*, above, for recommendations.

APLICACIONES
¿Qué pasa?
This conversation visual appears in odd-numbered chapters. It comprises an illustration with a few simple identification questions and suggestions for creating a dialogue based on it. Like other *Aplicaciones*, this section is discretionary and should be used as time permits. (Select from among the *Participación*, the *Actividades,* and the *¿Qué pasa?,* doing only one or two of the four.)

- Use the overhead transparency.
- Ask students to identify the objects and situations in the visual by naming, describing, expressing location, ownership, or by making a personal comment or observation.
- Allow students to prepare dialogues or narratives based on the visual either as homework or, as small-group work, in class. Sample dialogues appear in the Teacher Notes.
- Ask for volunteers to role play the situation.
- You may want to let students add new characters to the situation or to alter the situation suggested; encourage spontaneity, gesture, overacting, use of props, and so on; let students prepare scripts for more extended skits based on the visual.
- Emphasize performance, encouraging careful pronunciation, intonation, etc.

Lectura
This reading appears in even-numbered chapters and, like the *¿Qué pasa?* with which it alternates, is discretionary. It comprises a culturally informative extended dialogue or narration with glossed passive vocabulary followed by a series of questions. A pre-reading feature, *Antes de leer,* helps set the scene and focus the students' attention.

- Go over the *Antes de leer* in class, making sure that students understand the questions being asked.
- Play the tape as students follow along, and then review the *Antes de leer* questions to see if students understood the main idea and some of the basic information.
- Ask students to cover the glosses to see if they can understand the words from context, or go over the glossed words in advance.
- Assign the *Lectura* as homework to be gone over in class the following day (in which case, go over the *Antes de leer* when you make the assignment).
- Play the tape again, this time including the brief

oral questions that follow it; stop the tape after each question to allow for student response.
- Point out and discuss cultural information mentioned or implicit in the *Lectura.*
- Assign the *Preguntas* as written homework or do them orally in class.
- Ask students to prepare one or two true / false statements or additional questions to ask a classmate.
- Use visual aids appropriate to the *Lectura* to stimulate additional conversation.
- Ask students to summarize the *Lectura* in their own words, either orally or in writing.

EXPLICACIONES II

See *Explicaciones I,* above.

APLICACIONES

This is a four-part section designed for review and writing practice. You may choose to do all, none, or only selected portions of this material.

Repaso

The *Repaso* is a review and writing exercise closely linked to the *Tema* that follows it. It consists of a numbered series of Spanish sentences. Each is followed by English sentences which, when put into Spanish, will mirror the model sentence syntactically. The sentences in the *Repaso* are unrelated in theme and, in English, may differ greatly. But when properly rendered into Spanish, word order and part of speech will have a one-to-one relationship to the Spanish model. (Answers appear in the Teacher Notes.)

At first this may appear to the students to be a very peculiar exercise. But modeled writing is not translation for its own sake. It is guided writing that aids students in making the transition from the English thought process to the Spanish thought process. If they simply "go with the flow," they will be surprised by how much they learn from it. Above all, it will lead to their encountering an unusual degree of success in writing Spanish. (See suggestions for the *Tema.*)

The *Repaso* also reviews the vocabulary and structures presented in the chapter, as well as those from earlier chapters. The target structures are noted

for you in the on-page teacher's notes. In early chapters:
- Do the first substitution in each set for the class, emphasizing the correspondence once the sentence has been rendered into Spanish.
- Let students do the subsequent sentences as a group or working in pairs.
- Let students write what they have done on the board, with corrections being made on the spot.
- Identify areas where additional review is necessary and go over the appropriate page(s) in the text or *Practice Sheet Workbook,* or do the appropriate exercise(s) in the *Comprueba tu progreso.*
- In later chapters, assign the *Repaso* or selected sentences in it as homework to be gone over in class. Make corrections on the board or through answer sheets or transparencies that you prepare.

Tema

The *Tema* is a cartoon strip with English captions. Point out to the students that, syntactically, the Spanish version of each caption will be identical to the similarly numbered Spanish sentence in the *Repaso.* (Even if you choose not to use the *Repaso,* this should be pointed out so that students have a Spanish-language model to work from as they write.) Assign the *Tema* as written homework. (Answers appear in the Teacher Notes.)

You might also enjoy using the overhead transparency of the *Tema* cartoon strip (on which the captions do not appear) as a stimulus for in-class conversation, story-telling practice, or group composition.

Redacción

This writing exercise gives a choice of two or three additional topics for student compositions. This section is best used as an extra-credit assignment or with better classes.

Comprueba tu progreso

This section is designed for extra practice or as a pre-test before the chapter test. Answers appear in the Teacher Notes. You may want to use them to create an answer key for the students' own use.

- Assign the *Comprueba tu progreso* two days before the chapter test will be given.
- Quickly go over the material the following day, helping students identify areas of weakness either for immediate in-class review or for extra study that evening before the following day's test.
- Point out to the students the *Vocabulario del capítulo* on the following page, reminding them that these are the words they will be responsible for knowing on the test.

PHOTOS / REALIA

Throughout the program, photographs serve to illustrate the culture. Realia—tickets, menus, ads, schedules, and so forth—are provided to enrich the language-learning experience.

- Encourage students to make cultural inferences (in English) about what they see.
- Supplement the material in the student text with the additional information provided in the Teacher Notes.
- In later chapters, ask students to prepare more extensive captions than those that appear in the book or to make up questions about the pictures or realia that they can ask their classmates.
- Use the photos to stimulate narrative description, or let students use them to create a dialogue.
- Use them for spot evaluation of listening and speaking ability; for suggestions, see the oral proficiency tests in the Teacher Notes.

A TEACHER'S PERSPECTIVE

The Scott, Foresman Spanish Program provides everything you need to face the challenge of today's foreign-language classroom. Growing enrollments, the changing profile of the Spanish class, the emphasis on student communicative ability and on proficiency—all mean new teacher goals and new student expectations. Above all, it means newly designed tools for easier teaching and more active student involvement.

Here is how the Scott, Foresman Spanish Program responds to your needs and concerns and how it will help you bring your students to a realistic and rewarding level of proficiency in their new language.

"How can a book help students talk?"

VOCES Y VISTAS provides for extensive oral practice from the first page. Five preliminary units (En camino A–E) offer oral practice in some basic patterns and conversation topics. Thereafter, both the text and special ancillary materials provide abundant opportunity for growth toward oral proficiency:

- *Prácticas,* text exercises based on true-to-life contexts that students will relate to, are set up for paired practice.
- Every *Palabras Nuevas* and every *Explicaciones* section ends with *Hablemos de ti.* This series of related real-life questions practices new vocabulary and structures and reinforces for students that they are learning something practical and useful.
- *Actividades,* at least two per chapter, allow for paired or small-group oral practice.
- An oral-practice orientation in the *Contexto comunicativo* of each *Palabras Nuevas* section provides slot substitutions *(Variaciones)* to engage students actively in their learning of the new vocabulary.
- A conversation visual, *¿Qué pasa?,* encourages oral description, narration, and dialogue development. This feature appears in all odd-numbered chapters.
- A *Diálogo* in every chapter is followed by a *Participación,* in which students may create their

own conversation based on the dialogue. The *Diálogo* itself is also on tape, followed by oral questions for oral response.
- *Pronunciación* in every chapter focuses on individual sounds, stress, linking, and so on.
- The Teacher Notes provide an oral proficiency test for each chapter.

"How can we get students to learn how to really listen?"

Practice in the listening skill will occur naturally in paired exercise work and in the *Actividades,* for unless students listen to their partners, they will not be able to respond appropriately. Yet that, of course, is not the same as listening to native speakers. To better develop the listening skills needed for real-world communication, you will find the following in VOCES Y VISTAS:

- Extensive listening practice appears on the tapes. Much of it involves use of the *Tape Manual,* since paper-and-pencil activity helps ensure that attention remains focused on the listening task.
- For each chapter there is a test of listening comprehension on the separate testing tape.
- All of the *Pronunciación* sections, *Diálogos,* and *Lecturas* are on tape. So, too, are all of the visualized words and the mini-dialogues in the *Palabras Nuevas,* which offer students additional pronunciation and intonation models while helping them practice the new words. In addition, the listening skill is sharpened through the brief taped *dictados* (listen-write) and the inclusion of simple comprehension questions that follow the *Diálogo,* the *Lectura,* and the final mini-dialogue of each *Palabras Nuevas.* These have no written apparatus and call for very brief oral response (listen-speak).
- A videotape presents sixty minutes of authentic oral Spanish. Filmed in Spain and Mexico, the tape offers narration as well as unscripted, unrehearsed conversations and interviews in such locations as a department store, a school, a market, and a family home.

"I want to make sure my students learn to read"

All even-numbered chapters include a *Lectura* followed by a series of questions. The task of learning to read in a foreign language is eased through the *Antes de leer* that precedes each reading. This provides clues to a decoding of the reading, suggests things to look for while reading, and/or stimulates students to think about their own experiences in similar situations. This encouragement of basic reading strategies in the foreign language makes the overall decoding task a much less formidable one. In addition:

- The realia included in the text give students multiple opportunities to read "real" things, the types of things that they will have to read if they travel to a Spanish-speaking country. This type of reading brings special rewards as students first identify words, then phrases, and finally full sentences that they can understand.
- Beginning in Chapter 5, all *Práctica* directions are in Spanish. These give a statement of the context plus directions that explain what the student is to do. This also offers important reading practice.
- Few things give students a greater sense of accomplishment than being abe to read material outside the basic text. Thus a separate graded reader is available, specially designed for use with VOCES Y VISTAS.

"How can I help my students learn to write?"

Writing well is a problem for many students today even in their native language, so what can we expect in Spanish? With some help, we can expect quite a bit. The unique *Repaso, Tema,* and *Redacción,* found in the third *Aplicaciones* section of every chapter, carefully guide students in acquiring the writing skill.

Practice in writing is also provided in the *Workbook / Tape Manual,* in the taped *dictados,* in the *Practice Sheet Workbook,* and in any of the *Prácticas* or *Preguntas* that you choose to assign as written homework. Many of the *Actividades,* too, though oral in purpose, involve advance written preparation or a post-activity written summary.

"How do you teach the culture?"

Each chapter begins with a *Prólogo cultural,* a cultural overview of one of the main themes of the chapter. These are in English to make them fully accessible to the students. And you will discover Spanish-language captioned photographs and/or realia on any page you may open the book to. You are provided with additional cultural information on all of these in the Teacher Notes in this front section of the book. In addition:

- An Index of Cultural References cuts the time you need to spend preparing your cultural presentations.
- A videotape offers authentic cultural situations in Spain and Mexico. A *Teacher's Guide* with blackline masters for student use is included with the tape so that students can gain maximum cultural and linguistic benefit.
- Brief tests of the cultural information presented in the *Prólogo cultural* are included on each chapter and review test in the *Teacher's Resource Book.*
- The Spanish language itself, of course, is a reflection of Hispanic culture. This is made evident to the students in the *En otras partes,* where examples are given of how Spanish differs from country to country and region to region. A brief comparison of British and American English introduces the concept, so students can see that Spanish is not unique in this way.
- In the *Estudio de palabras,* students learn not only vocabulary-acquisition and reading strategies, such as an understanding of word families and affixes, but also the historical-cultural concepts of loanwords, cognates, and language roots. An understanding of how a people's language functions is a basic tool for understanding the people themselves. The Arabic and indigenous American contributions to the Spanish language reflect not only history, but also geography and ethnicity and the various world views that the three combined have fostered to create what we know as Hispanic culture.

"Is there any way to teach a little less so my students can learn a lot more?"

Yes, and to ease your and your students' task, *the*

scope of each book in the Scott, Foresman Spanish Program provides for a far more even pace than any program previously developed. Most students just cannot learn and retain the amount of new material that is presented in the typical two-year sequence. This program offers a three-year pacing that students can learn from. Because what is taught is usable and is continually reinforced, your students will almost surely master and retain more than you are accustomed to.

Since language learning is cumulative and gradual, there is strong focus here on regular re-entry and reinforcement. *We would urge you not to teach each vocabulary set and each grammar topic for immediate mastery before moving on.* Individual words and structures are frequently re-entered. Previously taught structures are continually woven into subsequent chapters' vocabulary exercises, giving students reinforcement and giving you a clear opportunity to identify areas that need additional practice. Do not let students get bogged down when they fail to grasp something immediately. Let them continue to watch for its reoccurrence. Let them continue to encounter and say it aloud in mini-dialogues. Give them the basic practice provided in the *Practice Sheet Workbook.* Soon you and they will find that they are using the structure with less hesitancy and, eventually, automatically. Language learning is, after all, a skill-mastering process far more than a data-memorizing one.

Here is how VOCES Y VISTAS will help you and your students avoid overload:

- The book always lets you and the students know what they will be held responsible for. *All structures for which they are responsible are explained and practiced in the* Explicaciones. *All active vocabulary is presented and practiced in the* Palabras Nuevas. *All other material is discretionary.*
- Most structures are presented as vocabulary items before they are taught as grammar points. This gives students an opportunity to use the language naturally and then later to have it codified. For example, the *yo / tú* forms of verbs are taught in the *Palabras Nuevas* and used conversationally in the *Práctica.* Only then, after true-to-life, contextual

practice, is the verb paradigm presented and practiced on its own. The fear of grammar is dissipated because so often the irregularities and problem areas have been made a part of the students' active language. Similarly, students are using *quiero / quieres, prefiero / prefieres,* and *puedo / puedes* long before the full paradigms of stem-changing verbs are presented.

Certain high-frequency preterite forms are also taught as lexical items with no premature, fear-inducing reference to preterite or past tense. Students learn and use *fui / fuiste / fue* knowing simply that they mean "I / you / he / she went" and "Did you / he / she go?" The concept of the preterite is presented for them to learn later.

Rather than overwhelming—and frustrating—students by presenting all of the preterite, Book 1 instead gives students gradual, solid practice in the regular preterite and in a few high-frequency irregular forms. Complete presentation of preterite irregularities is postponed to later levels. This measured presentation should increase the number of motivated, proficient second-year students. (If there are other irregular preterites that you would like to teach, a full list can be found in the verb charts in the back of the student text.)

"There's never enough practice material!"
The Scott, Foresman Spanish Program offers considerably more practice material than you will need. You shouldn't even have to devise your own practice sheets or quizzes. Here's why:

- There are book exercises to accompany not only the grammar, but also the vocabulary presentations.
- There is a *Practice Sheet Workbook* that offers students mechanical practice for all vocabulary and grammar.
- There is a *Workbook / Tape Manual* that offers higher-level writing practice for vocabulary and grammar, plus listening practice with the tapes.
- Oral practice—particularly communicative practice—is provided for through 1) the *Contexto comunicativo* in the *Palabras Nuevas,* 2) the communicatively formatted exercises in the

Prácticas, 3) the four *Hablemos de ti* sections of each chapter, 4) the *Participaciones* following the *Diálogos,* 5) the *¿Qué pasa?,* 6) the *Actividades,* and 7) the *Communicative Activity Blackline Masters* that accompany the text.

- Though any exercise can also be written, practice in the writing skill is specifically provided for in the *Repaso, Tema,* and *Redacción.*

"Do you really think I can finish this book?

Yes, but you will have to make some choices. The only material that must be covered thoroughly is in the essential chapter elements: *Palabras Nuevas I–II* and *Explicaciones I–II.* These are clearly marked for you in this Teacher's Annotated Edition. All the rest is there for you to choose among as you design lessons around your particular goals and teaching style. You may safely omit any of the three *Aplicaciones* sections knowing that there is nothing new in them that students will be held responsible for. This assurance gives you freedom and flexibility and puts you in control of the text.

You may want to use the *Aplicaciones* only occasionally (in alternate chapters, for example) or where you feel students particularly need that extra reinforcement. You may elect to omit some entirely from your teaching plans. Every chapter has a *Participación* and at least two *Actividades.* You might use only one of the three. The *Repaso* and *Tema* may be omitted, or you may assign and go through only a few of the substitution sentences in the *Repaso* and omit the *Tema.* You may use the *Tema* overhead transparency for conversation rather than writing practice. The *Diálogo* and *Lectura* include some unknown vocabulary for one-time use only. No new active material appears in them, so either or both may be skipped as often as you like.

To teach each section for immediate mastery or to follow the book assigning every exercise and activity on every page will certainly prevent your finishing the book. But that, too, is a valid choice, and careful provision has been made for the second-year teacher whose students did not finish VOCES Y VISTAS. (See the facing page for a "Guide to Bridging to PASOS Y PUENTES.")

Whatever your choices, enjoy using this program. Above all, enjoy watching your students actively engage themselves in learning Spanish.

A GUIDE TO BRIDGING TO PASOS Y PUENTES

By allowing mastery of the essential material to come gradually, and by a careful choosing from among both the ancillary practice materials and the discretionary text elements, most classes should be able to complete the essentials of VOCES Y VISTAS in one school year. If, however, you do not finish, careful provision is made for your students to move into Book 2 (PASOS Y PUENTES) at the beginning of the following year. The bridging plan assumes:

- *Mastery* (i. e., comprehension and a certain level of fluency) of all structures and vocabulary through Chapter 9 of VOCES Y VISTAS.
- *Coverage* (i.e., acquaintance and recognition) through Chapter 13.

All structures taught in Chapters 9–16 of VOCES Y VISTAS are re-presented in PASOS Y PUENTES, as are some of the more difficult concepts taught before Chapter 9 (e. g., *ser* vs. *estar,* object pronouns). In most such re-presentations, some additional new information is taught.

PASOS Y PUENTES begins with a *Repaso* that provides a series of exercises for reviewing the early grammar and lexical fields of VOCES Y VISTAS. If, for whatever reason, students do not get beyond Chapter 13 of VOCES Y VISTAS, Book 2 students will need to have the ''missed'' vocabulary presented as new words. Here is a list of the first occurrence in PASOS Y PUENTES of the vocabulary taught in Chapters 14–16 of VOCES Y VISTAS. Parenthetical numbers refer to the Book 1 chapters in which the words are taught. Book 1 overhead transparencies are excellent for introducing or reviewing vocabulary categories.

Repaso
The following would need to be taught:

el golf (14)	fantástico, -a (15)
el volibol (14)	la aventura (16)
correr (14)	

Capítulo 1
The following would need to be taught:

personal hygiene items (visual, Chap. 14)	el portugués (15)
el/la dentista (14)	la pared (15)
el despertador (14)	la tarjeta postal (15)
el equipo (14)	privado, -a (5)
atlético, -a (14)	por (15)
fuerte (14)	el/la escritor(a) (16)
hay que (14)	el/la médico(a) (16)
lo que (14)	la novela (16)
describir (15)	algo (16)
cardinal points (15)	algún, alguna (16)
la lengua (15)	lo siento (16)
	por eso (16)

Capítulo 2
The following would need to be taught:

acostarse (14)*	furniture items (visual, Chap. 15)
levantar (14)	con vista a(l) (15)
la mano (14)	de veras (15)
el/la atleta (14)	en seguida (15)
la pelota (14)	descansar (16)
débil (14)	estar de acuerdo (16)
enérgico, -a (14)	el/la enfermero(a) (16)
perezoso, -a (14)	excelente (16)
mandar (15)	adentro (16)
saber (15)	afuera (16)
el edificio (15)	

Capítulo 3
The following would need to be taught:

despertarse (14)	conocer (15)
divertirse (14)	quisiera (15)
lavarse las manos (14)	el puente (15)
perder (14)	el río (15)
quitarse (14)	el brazo (16)
el/la aficionado(a) (14)	la cabeza (16)
el/la jugador(a) (14)	el dedo (16)
despacio (14)	formidable (16)
rápidamente (14)	preferido, -a (16)

* Reflexive verbs are re-entered for meaning only. As with all structures re-presented in PASOS Y PUENTES, students are not asked to manipulate reflexives until they have been reviewed in an *Explicaciones* section.

PAIRED PRACTICE: WHY AND HOW

Paired practice is the most basic and least threatening way of increasing interaction in the foreign language classroom. Undoubtedly our classrooms have always been interactive in some ways: Teacher asks/student answers, teacher cues/student repeats or responds, students read a dialogue aloud. All of these are examples of person-to-person interaction (though some might call them parallel monologues). Paired practice, however, expands and transforms the nature of the interaction.

Paired practice is, very simply, two students practicing the language together. What are its advantages?

- *It greatly increases opportunities for student involvement and participation.* If 12 or 16 or 20 students are simultaneously saying something in the target language to their partner, that is a significantly larger number than one student at a time responding to the teacher.
- *It greatly increases meaningful, productive use of the textbook.* In paired practice, each student is practicing the entire exercise instead of only the eight or ten students called upon to do the eight or ten exercise items.
- *It promotes a level of realism and relevancy.* Paired practice simulates real-life social contact, with students having the opportunity to ask and answer questions and to initiate and engage in conversational exchanges.
- *It encourages a more natural use of language.* Face-to-face interaction encourages eye contact, proper intonation, emotional tone, rejoinders, exclamations, and so on.
- *It greatly reduces stress and reluctance to participate, thereby improving learning.* Fear of making errors in front of a whole class can be a terribly inhibiting factor, especially among teenagers, while doing so with a sympathetic peer is considerably less so. In paired practice, students can confirm what they already know and find out what they should know through a form of

cooperative learning or peer teaching that can greatly help those whom we sometimes seem unable to reach.

- *It provides variety in classroom pace with time devoted to directed skill-getting and practice.* Paired practice is a teacher-directed/student-centered activity that gives students monitored ''hands-on'' practice with the tools whose use they are acquiring.

Why are we sometimes reluctant to use paired practice? Loss of control and fear of students' getting off track are two major reasons. More general concerns about noise level and the number of student errors are also involved. But there are ways of guaranteeing successful and productive paired practice:

- *Keep the pairing simple.* Starting from a given point in the room, tell students to turn to the person to their left (right, etc.). Proximity is an easy way of pairing, and the different directions ensure that students will have at least four different partners over a period of time. (Periodic absences will increase the number.) If you change the seating plan every grading period, the number of potential partners greatly increases. (With younger students or in certain situations, it may be best to let students choose their own partners. You will find that individuals are very rarely left out in the cold.)
- *Give clear instructions.* Make sure students understand the context in which the exercise is set and the directions for what they are supposed to do. Always do the model with one of the students. If you like, you can then ask for a volunteer pair to do the first numbered item for the class as a second model.
- *Establish a time limit.* A short question-answer or statement-rejoinder exercise should be given a time limit of no more than two to three minutes, particularly at the beginning of the year. The exercises set up for paired practice in VOCES Y VISTAS are planned so that both you and your

students have an opportunity to become comfortable with the procedure. *En camino A* begins with chain drills and small-group practice. In *En camino B,* students do their first paired exercises, all controlled for one right answer. Gradually the paired exercises become more open-ended, usually with a choice of answers or exclamatory responses. For these, set a time limit of no more than five minutes.

- *Require feedback.* Ask the whole group the same questions that were just practiced in pairs. For less able students, you would ask the identical questions. For more able ones, you might pose some variation or extension of the questions. Now you will find students prepared and willing to recite in the large group because they know what is expected of them and they have gained confidence through the less threatening work with a peer.

How do you keep students from using English? Be mobile. Monitor what is going on and, if necessary, make it clear that English is not acceptable. The controlled task and time limit help eliminate the problem. When students find that feedback must be in Spanish, they will realize that using English in paired practice will not help them. Capitalize on the combination of student uncertainty and enthusiasm typical of the first few days. Model and re-model carefully rather than correcting errors, and you will almost certainly find most students eager to go along with paired practice and reluctant to jeopardize what they soon view as one of the real privileges of the foreign language classroom.

What are the alternatives for the teacher who does not want to use paired practice even though the exercise directions seem to call for it? The teacher takes the role of Student A and calls on a series of students to respond as Student B. Or, in some situations, it will work just as nicely for you to reverse the roles, calling on individuals to act as Student A while you respond or react as Student B.

Different teaching and practice formats should be used depending on the nature of the activity involved. Large-group instruction is superb for initial presentation of new concepts, i.e., for teaching and for the early stages of learning. A small-group format is good for tasks that require differentiated skills—for recombination and multi-skill practice. Individual instruction is best for remediation. Pair work, however, long the most neglected of our options, is the ideal medium for skill-getting practice and for reinforcing learning. It ensures adequate practice for everyone and helps students acquire those interactive skills so crucial to a communicative classroom and a proficiency-based curriculum.

LEARNING SPANISH THROUGH ACTION

In the Teacher Notes, you will find sections on Learning Spanish Through Action, or LSTA, which is a modified version of James J. Asher's method known as Total Physical Response (TPR). If you are not familiar with this technique, we would urge you to read Asher's *Learning Another Language Through Actions: The Complete Teacher's Guidebook,* as well as to attend one of his workshops. For more information, write to: Sky Oaks Productions, Inc., P.O. Box 1102, Los Gatos, CA 95031.

Learning Spanish Through Action closely mimics the way in which children learn their native language. In the initial stages, students follow commands, first with careful guidance, and later on their own. Speaking is not expected until students demonstrate immediate comprehension of the commands and a strong desire to begin speaking. First attempts at speaking are met with praise and little or no correction. Very gradually, more correct speech is emphasized through modeling.

LSTA is a valuable technique for teaching a foreign language. It makes the language seem more real to the students while producing a minimum of stress. Most often used as an introduction to new material, it is also appropriate at the end of a chapter as a reinforcement and practical application of the material just learned.

You will need to create an LSTA station in your classroom, consisting of at least three chairs, a table, and a chalkboard. Position the chairs side by side, with plenty of room to walk in front of them. From the chairs, there should be an uninterrupted path to both the table and the chalkboard. The entire station must be easily visible to all of the students in the room.

Most LSTA suggestions in the Teacher Notes call for props representing vocabulary groups. The most effective ones are authentic objects or toys. Photographs and drawings are also effective if they are large and free of distractors. You can collect a large supply of props by asking your students to donate items that their families might otherwise discard.

LSTA consists of five basic techniques: 1) commanding with modeling, 2) commanding without modeling, 3) role reversal, 4) narration, and 5) questioning. The first two techniques will always be used. The last three will be suggested where they best suit the material being taught.

What follows outlines the five basic techniques. It establishes a base of commands and prepositions through which you can position the students where you want them and then command them to manipulate the objects in a variety of ways. After this base has been established, you may then choose which LSTA suggestions you wish to incorporate into your curriculum. You will note that familiar commands are used in the sample lessons. You may, of course, use formal commands if you prefer.

One final note: Always remember that, in the beginning, it is normal and necessary for comprehension to exceed all other areas of mastery. Thus, if you find that you need to use a word or concept not found in the chapter being studied, do not hesitate to do so. It only means that when the word or concept is introduced later on, the students will already be acquainted with it.

SETTING THE STAGE
Lesson I: Commanding with modeling

Prop vocabulary: none

Other vocabulary: none

Staging vocabulary: levantarse, sentarse, dar la vuelta, caminar, parar
Go to the LSTA station and invite at least two students to join you. Have them sit in chairs on either side of you. Before you begin, give these instructions: "Listen to what I say. Do what I do. Don't try to speak." Then give the following commands while performing the actions with the students.

Sample
1. Levántate.
2. Siéntate.

3. Levántate.
4. Camina.
5. Para.
6. Camina.
7. Para.
8. Da la vuelta.
9. Camina.
10. Para.
11. Da la vuelta.
12. Da la vuelta.
13. Camina.
14. Para.
15. Da la vuelta.
16. Siéntate.

You will have taken the students away from the chairs and back again. The final *Siéntate* should seat them in the chairs. Perform this lesson with at least five different groups of students.

Repeat Lesson I, this time delaying the modeling until a second or two after the command is given. If the students look to you for guidance, simply encourage them with a nod or a gentle push on the elbow. If they are unable to perform without you, return briefly to modeling, and then try delaying again. When students are able to perform with the delay, proceed to Lesson II.

Lesson II: Commanding without modeling
With the students responding to your voice only, vary the order of the commands from Lesson I. If a student responds incorrectly, don't make a verbal correction. Simply move next to the student and perform the action. Stay with the group for a command or two more, then fall back again.

Sample
1. Levántate.
2. Camina.
3. Para.
4. Camina.
5. Para.
6. Siéntate *(on the floor)*.
7. Da la vuelta *(still on the floor)*.
8. Levántate.
9. Da la vuelta.
10. Da la vuelta.
11. Camina.
12. Para *(in front of the chair)*.
13. Da la vuelta.
14. Siéntate *(in the chair)*.

It is very important to be unpredictable. As vocabulary builds, one of the best ways to check for understanding is to command students to do something unexpected, such as standing on a chair or sitting under a table. The variations (and humor) hold the students' attention. Have fun! The more fun you have, the more your students will learn.

When every student is able to perform Lesson II with no prompting, proceed to Lesson III.

Lesson III: Role reversal
In role reversal, the students give the commands. Ask for two volunteers. Have one student give the commands to another. Instruct the student giving the commands not to move his or her hands so as to prevent giving clues. Also tell the student to correct errors by actions, as you have been doing, not verbally.

For you, role reversal will be a lesson in self-restraint. It would be unrealistic to expect even near-perfect pronunciation. Correct the pronunciation only if the student is failing to communicate. Your correction should be made by simply repeating the command correctly.

One of the main goals of LSTA is to instill in your students a willingness to speak Spanish. A time will come when the students ask you for help in pronunciation. At that time, give help only with the specific words they are asking about. A better time to deal with this issue is when pronunciation is itself the objective of the lesson.

When volunteers for role reversal cease to come forward, proceed to Lesson IV.

Lesson IV: Commanding with modeling, adding new vocabulary
When adding new vocabulary, a good rule of thumb is to add three new words at a time.

Prop vocabulary: bolígrafo, lápiz, libro, mesa, pizarra, tiza *(the small items arranged on a table)*

Other vocabulary: none

Staging vocabulary: tocar, señalar *(plus previously taught commands)*

Sample

1. Levántate.
2. Camina.
3. Para *(at the table).*
4. Toca la mesa.
5. Señala la mesa.
6. Toca la mesa.
7. Toca el lápiz.
8. Señala el lápiz.
9. Señala la mesa.
10. Toca la mesa.
11. Toca el lápiz.
12. Toca el bolígrafo.
13. Señala el bolígrafo.
14. Señala la mesa.
15. Señala el lápiz.
16. Toca el lápiz.
17. Toca el bolígrafo.
18. Toca la mesa.
19. Señala el bolígrafo.
20. Toca el lápiz.

Remember to delay your modeling when it seems that the students are ready. When they are responding before you model, switch to commanding without modeling. Vary the order of the commands. If you find that students are hesitating on one particular command, use it more often.

When students are responding without hesitation to commanding without modeling, you are ready to present additional vocabulary.

Sample

1. Toca el libro.
2. Señala el libro.
3. Señala la pizarra.
4. Toca la pizarra.
5. Señala el libro.
6. Señala la tiza.
7. Toca la tiza.
8. Toca la pizarra.
9. Toca el libro.

When students respond without hesitation, join together the two sample lessons in random order.

Sample

1. Toca la mesa.
2. Señala la pizarra.
3. Toca el libro.
4. Toca la tiza.
5. Señala el bolígrafo.
6. Toca el lápiz.

Next, add the original lesson—at which point the fun begins. You and your students will realize how much Spanish they understand. There should be no need to model the following.

Sample

1. Camina a la mesa.
2. Señala la pizarra.
3. Siéntate.
4. Da la vuelta.
5. Levántate y señala la tiza.
6. Siéntate en la mesa.
7. Camina a la pizarra y toca la tiza.

When students are responding quickly and correctly to the final lesson, ask for volunteers to do role reversal. You may be surprised how creative your students can be at varying the commands.

Lesson V: Narration

Using the commands from all of the previous lessons, tell the students what they are doing as they perform the commands. At this point it is appropriate to introduce plural commands. (Narration is indicated by the underscore.)

Sample

1. Juan y María, caminen a la pizarra.
2. Juan, tú caminas a la pizarra. María, tú caminas a la pizarra también.
3. Juan, toca el libro.
4. Juan, tú tocas el libro.
5. María, señala la mesa.
6. *(Point to the book yourself.)* María, tú señalas la mesa y yo señalo el libro.
7. María, señala la pizarra. Juan, señala la tiza.
8. *(Point to the table.)* Juan, tú señalas la tiza, yo señalo la mesa y María señala la pizarra.
9. Juan y María, toquen la mesa.
10. Uds. tocan la mesa, pero yo no toco la mesa.
11. María, toca el bolígrafo.

12. María, tú tocas el bolígrafo, pero no tocas la mesa.

If it is necessary to indicate to the students that they are not to respond to the narration, give them a signal to wait by holding up the palm of your hand toward them. When students understand that you are narrating and not commanding, proceed to the next lesson.

Lesson VI: Questioning

Sample

1. María, toca el libro.
   Q: María, ¿tocas el libro?
   A: Sí.
2. Sí, María. Tocas el libro.
3. Juan, señala la tiza.
   Q: Juan, ¿señalas el libro?
   A: No.
4. Muy bien, Juan. Señalas la tiza. No señalas el libro.
5. Juan y María, toquen la mesa.
   Q: Juan, ¿qué tocan Uds., la mesa o el libro?
   A: La mesa.
6. Sí, Juan. Uds. tocan la mesa.
7. María, toca el libro.
   Q: María, ¿qué tocas?
   A: El libro.
8. Sí, María. Fantástico. Tocas el libro.

Most of the time students will offer short answers. But should they use an incorrect verb form, here is a suggestion for handling the correction by using narration. (The mistakes your students make in forming a complete sentence may remind you of the mistakes a small child makes in his or her native language.)

Sample

1. Juan, toca el libro.
   Q: Juan, ¿qué tocas, el libro o la pizarra?
   A: *Tocas el libro.
2. Sí, Juan. Tú tocas el libro. Pero yo no toco el libro. *(Touch the pen.)* Yo toco el bolígrafo.
3. *(Model these actions while saying the following.)*
   Yo toco la mesa. Yo toco el libro. Yo toco el lápiz.
   Q: *(Touch the book.)* Juan, ¿qué toco, el lápiz o el libro?

A: El libro.
4. Sí, Juan. Yo toco el libro.
5. Juan, toca el lápiz.
   Q: Juan, ¿qué tocas, el libro o el lápiz?
   A: Yo toco el lápiz.
6. Estupendo, Juan. Tú tocas el lápiz.

Lesson VII: Completing the base

Prop vocabulary: *previously taught vocabulary plus* profesor(a), silla, puerta, ventana

Other vocabulary: sobre, debajo de, a la izquierda (de), a la derecha (de)

Staging vocabulary: *previously taught commands plus* poner, recoger, abrir, cerrar

Sample

1. Señalen al (a la) profesor(a).
2. Toquen al (a la) profesor(a).
3. Caminen a la silla.
4. Señalen la silla.
5. Señalen la puerta.
6. Caminen a la puerta.
7. Toquen la puerta.
8. Señalen al (a la) profesor(a).
9. Señalen la silla.
10. Señalen la puerta.
11. Toquen la silla.
12. Caminen a la silla.
13. Caminen a la puerta.
14. Toquen la puerta.
15. Toquen la ventana.
16. Caminen a la puerta.
17. Caminen a la ventana.
18. Toquen la ventana.
19. Señalen la silla.
20. Señalen la ventana.

Continue, varying the order of the commands until the students are responding without hesitation to commanding without modeling. Then add the new verbs.

Staging

1. Recojan el libro.
2. Pongan el libro sobre la mesa.
3. Recojan el bolígrafo.

4. Pongan el bolígrafo sobre la mesa.
5. Juan, recoge el lápiz.
6. Juan, pon el lápiz sobre la silla.
7. Abran el libro.
8. Cierren el libro.
9. Abran la ventana.
10. Cierren la ventana.
11. María, recoge la tiza y abre la puerta.
12. Juan, recoge el libro y camina a la mesa.
13. María, cierra la puerta.

Continue, varying the commands and re-entering the previous sample commands until the students are responding without hesitation. Then add all other vocabulary.

Sample
1. Señalen a la izquierda.
2. Señalen a la derecha.
3. Caminen a la izquierda.
4. Caminen a la derecha.
5. Caminen a la derecha y señalen a la derecha.
6. Caminen a la izquierda y señalen a la derecha.
7. Recojan el libro.
8. Pongan el libro a la derecha del lápiz.
9. Recojan el bolígrafo.
10. Pongan el bolígrafo a la izquierda del lápiz.

Practice until the students are responding without hesitation, and then continue.

11. Recojan el lápiz.
12. Pongan el lápiz sobre la silla.
13. Recojan la tiza.
14. Pongan la tiza sobre la mesa.
15. Pongan la tiza debajo de la mesa.
16. Pongan el libro sobre la silla y el bolígrafo debajo de la silla.
17. Pongan la silla debajo de la mesa.
18. Pongan la silla a la derecha de la mesa.

Continue, but frequently command only one student at a time in preparation for role reversal. When students are responding without hesitation, do role reversal, narration, and questioning.

At this point you have taught the basic commands that your students will need to know. Although others will be added, we will begin with these as we make suggestions for use of LSTA in the Teacher Notes for each chapter.

ORAL PROFICIENCY TESTING

In the Teacher Notes for each chapter you will find a suggested oral proficiency test. There are four types of test items.

- *Direct Response,* in which a statement is made in English that directs the student to ask a certain question or to make an appropriate remark.
- *Picture-Cued Response,* in which the student is shown a photograph or illustration and is asked one or more questions in Spanish.
- *Situations,* in which a context is presented in English and, given a choice of three remarks or responses, the student is directed to select the appropriate one. You might either immediately give the three choices orally and ask the student to repeat the correct one or, with better students, you might want to allow an opportunity for the testee to come up with an appropriate response. With weaker students you may want to present the three choices on a 3 × 5 card, allowing the student to read the appropriate choice.
- *Real-Life Questions,* in which the student is asked to reply conversationally to real-life or personalized questions.

The oral proficiency tests provided look for basic, minimum competency, and the suggested answers are to help you guide the student toward what you expect of him or her. Students must be free to answer creatively and spontaneously. If a response communicates correct information, no matter how it differs from what the book suggests, the answer is correct. If students respond well, you should feel free to expand with additional questions or comments to create a brief dialogue with the testee.

In using the Picture-Cued Responses, make use of the overhead transparencies (if they are available to you) instead of the visuals in the book. In those cases, hand the transparency itself to the student as you ask the questions. That will save you the trouble of covering the labels that appear in the book versions of the illustrations.

In using the Directed Response, Situations, and Real-Life Questions, adapt the items to make them as compatible as possible with the student's own experience. Use real names. That will make for real conversation. Provide appropriate props where possible and strive to use them in situations that students can identify with. This will help emphasize that speaking Spanish is not an artificial thing, but rather an important skill that is useful in real life.

Oral proficiency tests should always be administered privately, but in as relaxed and nonthreatening a setting and manner as possible. Always bear in mind that some students are uncomfortable with questions about home and family. Not all have mother, father, brothers, sisters, and pets. Not all have their own room in a single-family dwelling.

Evaluating oral proficiency and communicative progress largely involves attention to the adequacy and appropriateness of an exchange of information. Since an identifiable "perfect" score does not exist, it is simpler to give points than to subtract them from an ideal maximum. A set of three scales provides an effective and easy way to evaluate communication skills. Each scale measures a different aspect: (1) appropriateness and adequacy in carrying out the communicative intent, (2) correctness of grammar, and (3) accuracy of pronunciation. The scales are weighted differently, with the greatest importance given to the first aspect and the least to accuracy of pronunciation (though, of course, incorrect pronunciation can sometimes impede communication). You are free to modify the scale according to your own teaching objectives. You might, for example, increase the emphasis on grammatical correctness so that it matches the 0–4 scale of the communication aspect.

Here are three examples:

COMMUNICATION	GRAMMAR	PRONUNCIATION
Appropriateness	*Correctness*	*Accuracy*
Adequacy		

4 ③ 2 1 0   3 ② 1 0   ② 1 0

PICTURE-CUED RESPONSE: Chapter 8. Using the visual on p. 280 or Transparency 37, ask: *¿Qué hacen la señora y su hijo?* Student reponse: *Van compras.*

4 3 2 ① 0   ③ 2 1 0   2 ① 0

REAL-LIFE QUESTION: Chapter 6. *¿Cuántos años tienes?* Student response: *Tengo cuatro años.*

④ 3 2 1 0   3 ② 1 0   2 ① 0

SITUATION: Chapter 10. Mónica asks whether it's supposed to rain today. You think so. What might you say? Student response: *Creo sí.*

Because an exchange of information is the goal, error correction should be delayed in order to avoid interrupting the student's train of thought. It can also be helpful to correct errors by category, rather than student by student, when you find a consistency in the types of errors being made.

INDEX OF CULTURAL REFERENCES

TEACHER NOTES

TITLE PAGE

Photo

A colonial door in Guanajuato, Mexico. The legend on the wall says, ''Every man of culture loves and respects animals,'' and indicates that animals are highly regarded in Spanish-speaking countries.

The town of Guanajuato is well known for its colonial architecture, which is most prevalent in churches such as San Francisco, La Compañía, San Diego, and La Valenciana. La Valenciana is especially notable since it also reflects an architectural style known as *mudéjar,* which combines elements of Christian art with Moorish ornamentation.

PAGES IV-V

Photo

A patio in Sevilla, Spain. The vividly colored tiles *(azulejos)* shown on the left and right show the arabesque, an interlaced floral design that is one of the most common motifs in Moorish decorative art. The Moors, who arrived in Spain in 711 and dominated the country for eight centuries, left a legacy of artistic expression that is most pronounced in the architecture of the southern part of Spain. Sevilla's Torre del Oro and Giralda are notable examples of the Moorish influence. And Granada's Alhambra and Generalife, with their sumptuous courtyards, gardens, fountains, and pools, are the most outstanding examples of a style of architecture that is distinct from that of any other Western nation.

PAGE VI

Photo

Teenagers in Bogotá, Colombia.

PAGE VIII

Photo

A colorful name plate on the front of an intercity bus in San José, Costa Rica. Decorations of this type have been influenced by the designs on the traditional Costa Rican *carretas,* or oxcarts. Hand-painted leaves and flowers form colorful, distinctive patterns on the sides and wheels. This form of folk art has become extremely famous. But since the oxcart is being replaced by more modern means of transportation, Costa Ricans are seeking new ways to preserve this form of art.

PAGE IX

Photo

Día de los Muertos (Day of the Dead) in Mixquic, a small village in Mexico. The occasion for the celebration of *El Día de los Muertos* is the Roman Catholic liturgical feast known in English as All Souls' Day (November 2). On this day, Mexican families commemorate their deceased relatives by placing flowers, candles, and vigil lights around their graves. For this feast day, bakeries sell special breads called *panes de muertos.* Sugar-coated, candy *calaveras* (skulls) can be found in candy stores and pastry shops. And arts and crafts shops offer a variety of objects such as skeletons, statues, and skulls representing death and spirits from the underworld.

The Hispanic attitude toward death and the afterlife draws upon medieval and indigenous concepts that in many respects are at odds with our Anglo-Saxon traditions. We tend to overlook and even hide death, whereas in the Hispanic world death is a reality that is openly accepted. The Mexican poet and essayist Octavio Paz (1914-   ) characterized this difference in the following way in *El laberinto de la soledad:* ''Para el habitante de Nueva York, París o Londres, la muerte es la palabra que jamás se pronuncia porque quema los labios. El mexicano, en cambio, la frecuenta, la burla, la acaricia, duerme con ella, la festeja, es uno de sus juguetes favoritos y su amor más permanente.''

PAGE X

Photo

Decorations on the front of a *puesto frutero,* or fruit stand, in San José, Costa Rica. These decorations, like those shown on the bus on page VIII, have been influenced by the designs on the Costa Rican oxcarts. Most of these *carretas* are made in Sarchí, a town of about 10,000 people. Painting of the carts began in the early 1900s, and at first the patterns used were fairly simple. However, the decorations have gradually evolved into intricate designs in bold colors.

PAGE XI

Photos

(a) Peppers and mangoes being sold at a fruit stand in San José, Costa Rica. Agricultural products are the mainstay of the Costa Rican economy and generate about 65 percent of Costa Rica's export earnings. Products such as peppers and mangoes, however, are grown mainly for domestic consumption. Most of the foreign revenue that is generated in the agricultural sector comes from exporting coffee, bananas, sugar, and cacao. Historically, swings in the world prices for these commodities have greatly affected the Costa Rican economy.

(b) A food stand in Alameda Park in Mexico City. For sale are "exquisite" hot dogs and "delicious" hamburgers. On top of the stand are several bottles of a popular drink called Chaparritas. Hot dogs and hamburgers are just as popular in most of the Spanish-speaking world as they are in the U.S. The Alameda, Mexico City's beautiful central park, is almost always crowded with visitors and is, therefore, an excellent location for food stands such as this one.

PAGE XII

Photos

(a) A photo studio in Mexico.

(b) Photograph of a young Spanish woman.

PAGE XIII

Photo

A glazed pottery plate from Antigua, Guatemala. Since the sixteenth century, Antigua has been one of Latin America's main centers for this kind of Spanish pottery, which currently is used mainly by highland Mayas, descendants of the ancient Mayas, whose civilization flourished from about A.D. 300–900. The elders use the glazed plates as ceremonial dishes during meetings with *cofrades,* or community leaders. Because the *venado,* or deer, has always been important in Mayan tradition, the image of the deer on the glazed plate has a special significance for today's highland Mayas.

PAGES XIV-XV

Photo

Street dancing during the Festival of San Fermín in Pamplona, Spain. The festival honors the city's patron saint, who was also its first bishop. The highlight of the festival is the running of the bulls *(el encierro).* During this event, the streets are blocked so that the bulls can run freely from their corrals to the bullring. Ahead of them run the young men of the region (sometimes joined by a few tourists) typically dressed in white with red berets and red sashes at the waist. This spectacle, known as *los sanfermines,* attracts participants and observers from all over the world.

PAGE XVI

Photo

Stone mosaic work from the archaeological ruins in Mitla, a small village close to the city of Oaxaca in Mexico. Mitla, which probably was established long before the beginning of the Christian era, is the site of many archaeological treasures. Three different Indian civilizations—Zapotecs, Mixtecs, and Aztecs—lived in the town or had an influence on it before the Spaniards arrived there in A.D. 1521.

Mosaic work was one of the main characteristics of Mitla architecture. Involved patterns, like the ones shown in the photograph, were obtained by carefully inserting small pieces of stone into a coat of mortar.

No human or mythological figures are found in this type of architecture, but the designs are believed to symbolize beings or objects that had religious significance, such as the feathered serpent, the earth, and the sky.

PAGE XVII

Photo

This ancient Peruvian ear ornament, which is made of gold, shells, and turquoise, is a product of the Mochica, whose civilization flourished from A.D. 400–1000. The Mochica were outstanding in several respects. Skilled as architects, they built huge adobe pyramids in the deserts of northern Peru. Their ceramics are highly regarded for their realistic rendering of persons and animals. They developed advanced agricultural techniques. And they produced impressive jewelry—earrings, necklaces, and bracelets—which was worn by the men, rather than the women.

EN CAMINO A

OBJECTIVES

Communication
- to recognize first names and titles of address
- to introduce oneself and greet one another

Culture
- to distinguish between *tú* and *Ud.*

PAGE 1

Photo

Students chatting on the stairway of one of the public buildings in Andalucía, a region in southern Spain.

PAGE 2

Additions to on-page notes

Notes: Introduce the words presented in the *Contexto visual* by showing transparency 1. Ask students to listen and repeat. At first, emphasize imitation. Stress careful listening as necessary for the development of aural skills. Encourage students to speak loudly and clearly.

Introduce yourself, repeating *Me llamo* ____ several times. Ask volunteers to introduce themselves in response to the question *¿Y tú?* Encourage students to participate.

PAGE 3

Additions to on-page notes

Notes: You may want to go over the individual words presented in the *Contexto comunicativo* before you ask students to open their books. Write the words on the board for review at the end of the lesson. Recite each dialogue two or three times at a normal pace, or play the tape. Ask students to repeat and offer feedback to help them to approximate correct rhythm, intonation, and pronunciation. You may want to ask

volunteers *(voluntarios)* to act out the dialogue. Encourage students to be enthusiastic, since fostering enthusiasm will make their language-learning experience a more positive one. Ask students to practice introducing themselves.

PAGE 4

Photo

Two students at the University of Puerto Rico in San Juan. University students in Puerto Rico, like those in the United States, must complete four years of study to receive their undergraduate degree. However, in Puerto Rico most of the classes are taught in Spanish, although many of the textbooks are in English.

PAGE 5

Photo

In Spain, many elementary and secondary schools are operated by private religious groups, while most of the universities are state operated. Elementary education is mandatory for all Spaniards from ages 6 to 14. However, the Spanish Ministry of Education and Science is currently discussing several educational reforms, which include extending mandatory education to age 16.

Additions to on-page notes

Notes: You may use exercises that include *Estudiantes A* and *B* in class as chain drills or as pair work in which students alternate roles.

When working on the *Práctica* in class, make sure that students understand the directions and look at the model before beginning the exercise. Above all, make sure that students understand the directions if you expect them to do an exercise as a homework assignment. You may ask pairs of students to act out the model.

Additions to on-page notes

Notes: Model the words presented in the *Contexto visual* and *Contexto comunicativo* so that students can imitate correct pronunciation and intonation. First ask the whole class to repeat the words, and then ask for volunteers. Throughout the oral practice, encourage careful pronunciation.

Photo

Casual chats and small outdoor gatherings are typical of Spanish social life. Point out the *boina,* the beret worn by the man in the center of the photo. This is a popular article of clothing in the Basque region of northern Spain.

EN CAMINO B

OBJECTIVES

Communication
- to ask and give one's place of origin
- to identify the letters of the alphabet

Culture
- to identify various Spanish-speaking countries

SUGGESTED MATERIALS

p. 10 (Palabras nuevas I): large wall map(s) of Spain and Latin America

p. 14 (Palabras nuevas II): classroom objects

Additions to on-page notes

Notes: Before presenting the *Contexto visual,* you may want to use a large classroom map or transparency 3 to help students locate the 20 Spanish-speaking countries. One goal for this year is for students to know in which countries Spanish is the principal language spoken and where these countries are located. Avoid overemphasizing geography—we will not test students on it—but encourage an understanding of its importance to us.

Enrichment: You may want to mention that the definite article is often omitted with the names of the continents and other geographical areas.

Additions to on-page notes

Notes: You may want to go over the vocabulary thoroughly before you ask students to open their books. Read each mini-dialogue to the class, and ask students to repeat after you. You may also want to assign roles so students can act them out. Make sure that students understand that *soy* must be used with *yo; eres* with *tú; es* with *él* and *ella.* The concept of agreement of verb and subject pronoun will be taught in Chap. 2. Write the words *tú* and *él* on the board using oversize accents to remind students that accents are important.

Notes: The uses of the preposition *de* appear on p. 190.

Additions to on-page notes

Notes: Use real classroom objects to present *Palabras nuevas II.* Ask *¿Qué es esto?,* and model answers as necessary. Ask individual students to read the new words as others point to the appropriate objects. Stress the importance of learning the gender of each new noun.

Photo

These high-school students from Puerto Rico are on a field trip to El Morro, a famous sixteenth-century fortress in Old San Juan.

Additions to on-page notes

Reteach / Extra Help: To review vocabulary, point to different objects in the classroom and ask *¿Qué es esto?*

You may want to point to a boy as the class repeats *él.* Do the same with a girl: *ella.* Point to yourself as students do the same: *yo.* Do the same to review *tú.*

Write the following on the board: *soy, eres, es.* Have students copy these words and give the correct subject pronoun for each one *(yo, tú, él, ella).* Ask students to read what they wrote and to correct any mistakes.

EN CAMINO C

OBJECTIVES

Communication

■ to count from zero to 31
■ to give the days of the week and months of the year
■ to give the date

Culture

■ to define "Saint's Day"

SUGGESTED MATERIALS

pp. 20–21 (Palabras nuevas I): large wall calendar

p. 25 (Actividad): calendar for the coming year

PAGES 20–21

Additions to on-page notes

Notes: Hang a large calendar on the board, or show transparency 5. Ask students to listen and repeat as you model the words presented in the *Contexto visual:* the parts of the calendar; names of the months; and the numbers 0–31.

Enrichment: Point out to students that in Spanish the numbers 16 through 19 have alternate spellings: *diez y seis, diez y siete,* etc. And 21 through 29 also have alternates: *veinte y uno, veinte y dos,* etc.

We teach the combined forms because they are more common in modern usage.

Notes: The uses of the preposition *de* appear on p. 190.

PAGE 22

Photo

This model of the Aztec Calendar Stone is from the National Museum of Anthropology in Mexico City. The actual stone, also known as the Sun Stone *(Piedra del Sol),* is the most recognizable surviving Aztec sculpture. Carved from a 24-ton block of basalt, the stone measures about 12 feet in diameter. The face in the center of the calendar represents the sun god. And the other carvings represent religious symbols related to worship of the sun god and symbols for the days of the month.

Additions to on-page notes

Enrichment: In conjunction with mini-dialogue 6, point out to students that in addition problems, we can also say *¿Cuánto son nueve y cinco?* using *y* instead of *más* to translate "plus."

PAGE 23

Additions to on-page notes

Enrichment: In conjunction with Ex. A, you may want to mention that in subtraction problems, when the answer is "one," we say *Cuatro menos tres es uno.*

PAGE 24

Photos

(a) This Christmas light display of the Three Kings *(Los Reyes Magos)* was on exhibit in the Zócalo, Mexico City's main square. In many Spanish-speaking countries, the Three Kings bring children gifts on January 6. On Christmas day, children receive gifts from the *Niño Dios* (Jesus Child) himself, or from Santa Claus, called *Papá Noel* in many countries. Thus, children may receive presents on Christmas Day and / or on January 6, which is the Feast of the Epiphany. This day celebrates the arrival of the Three Kings in Bethlehem, where they presented the Christ Child with gifts of gold, frankincense, and myrrh.

(b) This folk dancer is dressed in traditional clothing for the annual Guelaguetza folk dance festival in Oaxaca, Mexico. The week-long festival is held at the end of July to give thanks to the corn god. Participants wear regional costumes, perform traditional music and dances, and sell local foods and handicrafts.

(c) Dancers wearing typical costumes from the La Mancha region participate in a three-day saffron harvest celebration in the small farming community of Consuegra, Spain, the world's saffron capital. The fall festival closes an intense three-week period during which the spice is harvested by hand and cured. Prepared from the crocus flower, saffron is the world's most expensive spice. The region around Consuegra produces saffron of the highest quality, called "red gold." Ninety-eight percent of the saffron the U.S. consumes annually is grown here.

PAGE 25
Photos

(a) Displays of white sugar skulls, like the one in the photo, are common throughout Mexico as part of the Day of the Dead *(Día de los Muertos)* celebration on November 2, also known as All Souls' Day. This is the day on which many Mexican families remember their deceased by spending the day at the cemetery, often bringing special food for the dead and for themselves. On this day, foods such as *panes de muertos* (bread shaped like people and animals) and *calaveras de azúcar* (white sugar skulls inscribed with people's names) are traditionally sold in Mexican bakeries.

(b) All-night vigils such as this one in the town cemetery in Pátzcuaro, Mexico, are another way in which Mexicans traditionally remember deceased family members and friends on the Day of the Dead. As part of the observance, family members clean the graves and also bring fresh flowers and offerings, which they leave at the grave.

PAGE 28
Photo
Birthday celebrations in Spanish-speaking countries resemble those in the U.S., with parties, presents, and a cake. In Mexico, family and friends sing the birthday song *Las mañanitas,* often with musical accompaniment provided by mariachis.

In some Spanish-speaking countries, saints' days rival birthdays in importance. People who are named after a saint in the Roman Catholic Church observe the day set aside to honor their particular saint with a celebration similar to that noted for birthdays.

EN CAMINO D

OBJECTIVES
Communication
- to count from 31 to 100
- to give phone numbers
- to tell time

SUGGESTED MATERIALS
pp. 33–34 (Palabras nuevas II): real clock, model of a clock with movable hands

PAGE 30
Additions to on-page notes
Notes: Model the numbers 31–100, which are presented in the *Contexto visual.* Use transparency 7, or write the numbers on the board.

To introduce the words presented in the *Contexto comunicativo,* play the tape or model the vocabulary. As students repeat, encourage them to use correct rhythm, intonation, and pronunciation.

PAGE 33

Additions to on-page notes

Notes: You may want to use a real clock to present the concept of telling time. Or you might prefer to use a model of a clock with movable hands. Make sure that students understand the difference between *es* and *son* in the expressions *Es la una, Son las dos,* etc.

PAGE 34

Photo

This flower clock *(reloj de flores)* in Viña del Mar, Chile, actually works and keeps accurate time. Flower clocks like this one are also found in other parts of Latin America.

PAGE 37

Photo

Time pressures are greater in large, modern cities such as Santiago, the capital of Chile. A city of about four million inhabitants, Santiago is the country's administrative, commercial, industrial, and cultural center. Like other Chilean cities, Santiago is vulnerable to earthquakes. In 1985 an earthquake measuring 7.4 on the Richter Scale destroyed thousands of buildings and killed hundreds of people in Santiago and the coastal towns of Valparaíso and Viña del Mar.

EN CAMINO E

OBJECTIVES

Communication

- to express likes and dislikes

PAGE 38

Additions to on-page notes

Notes: We present the expressions *me / te gusta* as a communicative whole rather than trying to explain indirect object pronouns or literal translations. Tell students that they will learn more about these phrases later. The use of *gustar* to express likes and dislikes about activities / nouns appears on p. 70; the use of *gustar* with all of the indirect object pronouns appears on p. 531.

PAGE 40

Photos

(a) This girls' secondary school basketball team is competing on an outdoor basketball court in Madrid. To enhance their own public image, private businesses often sponsor sports teams like this one.

(b) This section of the Cantabrian Mountains (also called Picos de Europa) in northern Spain provides a beautiful setting for bicycle riders. Cycling has become popular among Spaniards of all ages and economic levels partly due to the influence of the fitness movement of the last decade.

PAGE 42

Additions to on-page notes

Notes: After presenting the *Contexto visual,* point out that all of the new vocabulary items are action words, or verbs.

Make sure that students understand the difference between *tocar,* to play an instrument, and *jugar,* to play a sport / game.

PAGE 44

Photo

This shopping mall in Málaga, Spain, is the scene of a spontaneous dance demonstration. Note the traditional Spanish architectural elements—arches, tile roofs, and decorative tiles—that have been incorporated at this contemporary shopping center.

Photo

Chileans place a high premium on education. The literacy rate is higher than 90 percent, and the system of higher education is one of the best in Latin America. In high school, students may take either college preparatory courses or specialize in technical, commercial, or agricultural areas.

Photo

Guitar playing is popular among young Spaniards. Flamenco, classical, pop, or some other kind of guitar playing is sure to enliven any party.

LEARNING SPANISH THROUGH ACTION

General information about Learning Spanish Through Action appears on pp. T18–T22 of this Teacher's Edition.

EN CAMINO A

New prop vocabulary: clase, profesor(a), señor *(male student wearing old-fashioned hat and tie)*, señora *(female student wearing old-fashioned dress and / or cardigan sweater)*, señorita *(female student)*, estudiante *(one female and one male student carrying books)*

Other new vocabulary: none

New staging vocabulary: none

Sample

1. Caminen hacia la señora.
2. Toquen a la señora.
3. Caminen hacia la señorita.
4. Toquen a la señorita.
5. Toquen a la señora.
6. María, toca la silla de la señorita.
7. Toquen la silla de la señora.
8. Caminen a la silla de la señorita.
9. Caminen hacia el señor.

Continue the above until you have taught all of the new vocabulary. Narration and questioning are appropriate. Ask yes / no questions.

10. Juan, toca al señor.
    Q: Juan, ¿tocas a la señora?
    A: No.
    Q: ¿Tocas al señor?
    A: Sí.

EN CAMINO B

LESSON 1

New prop vocabulary: cuaderno, hoja de papel, dibujo

Other new vocabulary: none

New staging vocabulary: escribir

Sample
1. Toquen el cuaderno.
2. Señalen el cuaderno.
3. Señalen la hoja de papel.
4. Recojan la hoja de papel.
5. Pongan la hoja de papel a la izquierda del cuaderno.
6. Toquen el dibujo.
7. Pongan el dibujo sobre el cuaderno.
8. María, siéntate a la derecha del cuaderno.

Role reversal, narration, and questioning are appropriate.

LESSON 2

New prop vocabulary: Spanish-speaking countries. You will need an overhead or a wall map of South America, Central America, the Caribbean, and Spain. Each student will need a paper copy of the same, plus colored marking pens.

Other new vocabulary: amarillo, azul, rojo, verde

New staging vocabulary: colorear, dibujar

Sample
1. Toquen el Ecuador. *(Students will be touching the paper maps at their desks while you model, using the overhead or wall map.)*
2. Señalen España.
3. Toquen Guatemala.

Teach all of the countries in this manner, and then proceed.

4. Coloreen de azul el Paraguay.
5. Dibujen un libro en Panamá.
6. Coloreen de amarillo Bolivia.
7. Dibujen un bolígrafo en Cuba.

EN CAMINO C

LESSON 1

New prop vocabulary: 0–31. You will need 32 tennis balls with one number written on each ball. Begin with the balls set in a row on the chalktray.

Other new vocabulary: entre

New staging vocabulary: tirar, agarrar, enseñar

This lesson will work best if you direct commands to one student at a time.

Sample
1. Juan, toca el número dos.
2. Toca el número seis.
3. Señala el número seis.
4. Toca el número cinco.
5. Recoge el número dos.
6. Pon el número dos a la derecha del número seis.
7. Pon el número seis a la izquierda del número dos. *(It is already there, of course.)*
8. Recoge el número cinco.
9. Enseña el número cinco a la clase.
10. Pon el número cinco entre el dos y el seis.

Continue the above until you have taught all of the numbers, and then proceed.

11. Juan, recoge el número veinte.
12. Tírale el número veinte a Marcos.
13. Marcos, agarra el número veinte.
14. Juan, tírale el número catorce a Marcos.
15. Marcos, agarra el número catorce.
16. Marcos, enseña el número veinte a la clase, y tírale el número catorce a Juanita.

LESSON 2

New prop vocabulary: *Days of the week, numbers,* día, semana, mes. You will need to post the months of the year from a calendar on a bulletin board or tape them to the chalkboard.

Other new vocabulary: antes de, después de

New staging vocabulary: contar

Sample

1. Señalen marzo.
2. Toquen marzo.
3. Toquen noviembre.
4. Señalen febrero.

Continue the above until you have taught all of the months. Use the same method to teach the days of the week. Then add the following, working with one student at a time.

5. Pepe, toca enero.
6. Toca el mes antes de enero.
7. Señala el mes antes de diciembre.
8. Señala el mes después de diciembre.
9. Toca martes.
10. Toca el día antes de martes.
11. Señala el día después de martes.
12. Toca una semana en abril.
13. Señala una semana en octubre.

Teach this well before continuing.

14. Cuenta los días de julio. *(When modeling, use your finger to touch each day that you count.)*
15. Cuenta los días en una semana de septiembre.
16. Cuenta los días en dos semanas de noviembre.
17. Cuenta los meses.

Questioning is ideal for this lesson.

18. Juan, toca el mes antes de julio.
    Q: ¿Qué mes es?
    A: Junio.
19. Toca el veintidós de marzo.
    Q: ¿Qué día de la semana es?
    A: Martes.
20. Toca febrero.
    Q: ¿Cuántos días hay en febrero?
    A: Veintiocho.

EN CAMINO D

Teach the numbers in this lesson in the same way that you taught them in the first lesson of *En Camino C.*

EN CAMINO E

New prop vocabulary: guitarra, *balls for all sports presented*

New staging vocabulary: bailar, cantar, cocinar, comer, esquiar, hablar (por teléfono), jugar, leer, nadar, tocar, trabajar

Other new vocabulary: también, pero, inglés, español

Sample

1. Jueguen al fútbol.
2. Jueguen al básquetbol.
3. Jueguen al béisbol.

Continue the above with all sports. The students will learn them rapidly because of their close equivalents in English.

4. Canten.
5. Bailen.
6. Canten y bailen.
7. Hablen inglés.
8. Canten en inglés.
9. Canten en español.
10. Hablen español.
11. Juan, baila.
12. María, baila también.
13. Tomás, canta y baila.
14. Juan, canta pero no bailes.

Remember to re-enter sports. Narration and questioning are appropriate.

15. Tomás, canta.
16. Tú cantas, pero yo no canto. No me gusta cantar. *(Give thumbs down sign.)*
17. María, baila.
18. Tú bailas y yo bailo también. Me gusta bailar. *(Dance and gives thumbs up sign.)*
    Q: María, ¿te gusta bailar?
    A: Sí.

You may add all of the remaining actions from the staging vocabulary at any point after number 14.

CAPÍTULO 1

OBJECTIVES

Communication
- to express preferences
- to express quantity *(muchos / pocos)*
- to express likes and dislikes (activities / nouns)
- to use *hay* to ask about and identify quantity

Grammar
- to use gender and number with nouns
- to use the definite article

Culture
- to broaden students' perspectives
- to define the term "American"
- to convey the importance of Columbus and *El día de la Raza*
- to tell how America received its name
- to point out the importance of the Spanish language in understanding American culture and the cultures of the Americas

SUGGESTED MATERIALS

p. 49 (Prólogo cultural): wall map(s) of Europe, North and South America

p. 50 (Palabras nuevas I): magazine pictures of food

p. 58 (Palabras nuevas II): a record album, a newspaper, classroom objects (map, flag, chalk, books, poster, pen, pencil)

PAGES 48–49

Photo
Youths walking in front of a mural in Oakland, California. The mural was painted by Consuelo Nevel and others, and was sponsored by the Clínica de la Raza. Murals of this type, painted by Hispanics of Mexican origin, are often found in California.

While mural style can vary tremendously from abstract design to primitive realism, the subject matter most often concerns the everyday life in the *barrio* and the struggles and aspirations of the people. Recurring figures draw upon Hispanics' rich history and culture: The Aztecs and Mayas, which represent the pre-Columbian heritage; the Spanish conquistadores and personifications of the Catholic Church (often a missionary or the Virgin of Guadalupe), representative of the Spanish heritage; and the revolutionary *campesino*, a symbol of the Mexican Revolution. These figures often appear side by side with modern-day men and women in their various social and political roles.

Additions to on-page notes
Notes: You may want to assign the *Prólogo cultural* as homework or for additional outside reading. Or you may base a classroom lesson on the photograph and on questions dealing with paragraph 4. For example: What names in your area are Spanish? (If there are none, ask students to mention names of any geographical features, states, or areas that are Spanish in origin.) Are there large groups of Spanish speakers in your area? Where are they from? The *Prólogo* theme may also suggest topics for oral or written research assignments. Students will not be tested on the material in the *Prólogos;* they do, however, provide a useful overview of the chapter theme and a presentation—in English—of information students will later deal with in Spanish.

For additional suggestions for use, see p. T5.

PAGE 50

Palabras nuevas
Each lesson has two *Palabras nuevas* sections, where new active vocabulary is introduced either in visuals or in a written context—or both. Where possible, the contextual presentations are in the form of mini-dialogues, so that students can have additional exposure to communication models.

Each *Palabras nuevas* section has its own set of *Prácticas,* designed to lighten the task of vocabulary acquisition. Numerous types of exercises are used:

visual, question-answer, open-ended, which word best fits the context?, which is the logical response?, etc. Special care is given throughout the book to regular re-entry of the vocabulary presented in the *Palabras nuevas*.

For suggestions for use, see pp. T5–T6.

Alphabetical word lists by part of speech are available on the last page of each chapter.

Additions to on-page notes

Notes: Introduce the words presented in the *Contexto visual* by showing transparency 11. Ask students to listen as you model the words for them, or play the tape. Then ask them to repeat, first as a class and then individually. Stress that errors are a natural and necessary part of second-language learning. And reinforce their efforts to imitate correct pronunciation and intonation.

Culture: Find out if students are familiar with Mexican food. Explain how a *burrito* (a soft flour tortilla rolled or folded around a filling) differs from a *taco* (a fried tortilla stuffed with a filling). Tell students that the tacos served in Mexico, which are rolled into tubes and stuffed with a variety of fillings, look very different from those that we serve here.

PAGE 55

Photo

Paella is perhaps the best known of all of Spain's regional dishes. It was created in Valencia, the province that produces most of the country's rice.

Rice, saffron *(azafrán),* the spice that gives the dish its golden color, and olive oil *(aceite de oliva)* are the basic ingredients. Recipes may include meat (especially chicken and pork), fish (sea bass, bay eels, etc.), shellfish (mussels, squid, shrimp, clams, etc.), and any number of vegetables. *Paella* also refers to the shallow, two-handled pan in which the dish is cooked.

Hablemos de ti

These are questions that allow students to talk about themselves—their families, daily lives, interests, opinions, plans and ambitions. This section re-enters known vocabulary and structures in such a way that

students can readily see that Spanish, like their native language, is a tool of self-expression.

For suggestions for use, see p. T6 and the notes below.

Additions to on-page notes

Notes: The following are some suggestions for presenting the *Hablemos de ti* and other open-ended exercises where we indicate that answers will vary.

1. Draw a grid on the board that lists categories of acceptable responses. Ask one student to act as secretary and keep a tally of responses given to each question. After all answers have been given, the grid will provide a summary of the most frequently occurring responses.

2. Encourage students to offer as wide a variety of answers to the questions as possible. Appoint a secretary to copy all answers on the board. When all answers have been given, ask students to decide which answer was the most unusual, most complex, most inappropriate, funniest, etc.

3. Set a time limit and see how many possible answers students can give to individual questions within that time limit. This technique encourages fluency since the emphasis is on language production and quickness of thinking.

PAGE 56

Photo

The guitar was originally the Moorish *qítara,* a four-stringed version of the lute. Brought to Spain by the minstrels of al-Andalus, the Muslim-controlled area of the Iberian Peninsula during the Middle Ages, the guitar remains the most popular of all instruments in Spain and Latin America. It is especially popular among students.

Diálogo

Each lesson has a teen-oriented *Diálogo* that serves as a situational culmination of *Palabras nuevas I.*

For suggestions for use, see pp. T6–T7.

Additions to on-page notes

Notes: The *Diálogo* is a discretionary activity and may be skipped entirely, assigned for extra credit, or used as a classroom activity from time to time. Model the *Diálogo* for repetition, or play the tape.

Ask students to play the parts of Laura and Eduardo. Begin by asking all the girls to read Laura's part and all the boys Eduardo's. Then have individuals play the roles of Laura and Eduardo. Have students act out the dialogue. Encourage them to dramatize the conversation.

PAGE 57

Photo

These students are in the Guatemalan town of Quetzaltenango. Known to Guatemalans as *Xela* (pronounced *shay-la*), Quetzaltenango is a major industrial center.

Pronunciación

This section isolates one or more Spanish sounds and offers help in forming them.

In the interest of pedagogical simplicity and in accordance with statistical studies of prevailing speech patterns among educated native speakers of Spanish, where two differing acceptable pronunciations may exist, we offer only one.

For suggestions for use, see p. T7.

PAGE 58

Additions to on-page notes

Notes: In conjunction with transparency 12, present as many real classroom objects as possible. You may want to ask *¿Qué es esto?* Model answers as necessary. Review classroom vocabulary on pp. 14–15.

PAGE 60

Photo

José Luis Rodríguez (known as *El Puma*), Diego Verdaguer, and María Conchita Alonso are Venezuelan pop stars. Although the three singers now live in the U.S., they are popular throughout the Spanish-speaking world.

PAGE 63

Photos

(a) The municipal campgrounds sign in Córdoba, Spain, lists several prices. Included are a 78-peseta charge for children up to 10 years of age and an 84-peseta price for putting up a tent for one person.

(b) A cup of exquisite hot chocolate accompanied by a plate of *churros* is available for 100 pesetas at this cafe-bar in Madrid, Spain. *Churros,* which are long, donutlike pastries, are popular snacks in most Spanish-speaking countries and are frequently served with hot chocolate.

Realia

This Mexico City restaurant is open for breakfast. Besides featuring waffles with nuts and bananas, bacon, or strawberries and cream, it also offers a selection of house specialties catering to international tastes. Among the restaurant's egg dishes are *Petit Cluny,* with an Italian tomato sauce and cheese; *Breaccio,* with mushrooms and provolone cheese; *a la Bolognesa,* with traditional Italian meat sauce; *Colonial,* with slices of Poblano chile peppers, onion, and cream; and *Pamplona,* with Pamplona-style sausage. Also on the menu are American-style coffee, espresso, black tea, cappuccino, Dutch hot chocolate, *café au lait,* and fruit of the day.

Additions to on-page notes

Notes: Point out the differences between the Spanish loanwords and the corresponding English words; note accent marks and spellings. Tell students that loanwords and cognates are very valuable tools for learning Spanish. Encourage them to look for cognates in the *Diálogo* and *Lectura* sections and in photo captions.

Students will not be tested on material in the *Estudio de palabras.* These sections do, however, provide helpful learning tools. They help students develop an ability to recognize unfamiliar vocabulary, a useful skill as they begin to read material written exclusively in Spanish. And they also help students to recognize the interrelationship of languages.

For suggestions for use, see p. T7.

PAGE 64

Explicaciones

Every lesson has two *Explicaciones* sections, each of which presents one or more grammatical points. In the *Explicaciones,* the various aspects of a given grammar topic are presented in a series of numbered subpoints. The explanations are followed by *Prácticas,* arranged in order of difficulty and generally following the sequence of the subpoints.

For suggestions for use, see pp. T7–T8.

PAGE 66

Photo

Throughout Latin America, record stores such as this one in Colombia offer a variety of music from many areas of the world. Records and cassettes from the United States and Europe are popular sellers in Latin America, as are recordings of folk and popular Latin American music.

PAGE 67

Additions to on-page notes

Notes: Refer to the mini-dialogues on pp. 59-60 for examples of the use and omission of the definite article. To make sure students understand when to use and when to omit the definite article, give and / or elicit additional examples.

PAGE 68

Photo

Movies, particularly those from the U.S., are a very popular form of entertainment in Spanish-speaking countries. These teenagers are going to see *Jewel of the Nile (La joya del Nilo),* either dubbed in Spanish or with Spanish subtitles.

Among the movies listed in the newspaper clipping are *Young Sherlock Holmes (El secreto de la pirámide), The Purple Rose of Cairo (La rosa púrpura de El Nilo),* and *Duel in the Sun (Duelo al sol).* Notice that first-run theaters like the *Pompeya* and the *Princesa* still offer two showings a day, one before dinner (around 7:00 p.m.) and one after (around 10:00 p.m.).

PAGE 69

¿Qué pasa?

The *¿Qué pasa?* is intended to help develop conversational skills on three levels. (a) The questions encourage responses at the simplest level, and you may want to supplement these with additional questions based on the art. (b) These are followed by a suggested situation for role-playing. (c) Finally, at the highest level, you may want to have students create their own dramatizations, improvising playlets or developing scripts for more polished presentations. The use of costumes, props, and sound effects can provide added interest and enjoyment.

Depending on the capabilities of your students, you may want to select among the activities, or make individual assignments according to the varying degrees of difficulty of the activities.

The *¿Qué pasa?* appears in odd-numbered chapters only. Even-numbered chapters have a *Lectura* in which previously learned vocabulary and structures are recombined in a new context. Some new—passive—vocabulary also appears in each *Lectura.*

For additional suggestions for use, see p. T8.

Sample dialogues for *¿Qué pasa?*

Teresa and Héctor are having a conversation about what they like to do.

T: ¿Qué te gusta más, la música o los deportes?

H: Me gusta más la música. Me gusta tocar la guitarra.

T: ¡Ah, sí! Te gusta la música popular, ¿verdad?

H: ¡Sí! Me encanta la música popular. ¿Te gusta escuchar la radio?

T: Sí, pero me gusta más jugar al fútbol, o montar en bicicleta.

H: ¿Te gusta más la música clásica o la música popular?

T: Me gusta más la música popular porque me
   encanta bailar.
H: También te gustan los deportes, ¿verdad?
T: ¡Cómo no! ¿Te gusta jugar al fútbol?
H: No. Me gusta más jugar al béisbol.

PAGE 76

Photos

(a) This selection of newspapers is from the major
Colombian cities of Bogotá and Cali.

(b) In the background of this photo of Mexico City's
Alameda, so called because of the poplar trees
(álamos) that line its walks, is the Palacio de
Bellas Artes (Palace of Fine Arts), where exhibits,
plays, operas, ballets, and other cultural events
are held regularly. Begun in 1904, the Bellas
Artes was not completed until 1934.

Murals by Mexico's most famous painters
—Rufino Tamayo, José Clemente Orozco, Diego
Rivera, and David Alfaro Siqueiros—decorate the
upstairs walls. The exterior of the building is white
Italian marble; the interior is dark, reddish,
Mexican marble.

Repaso, Tema y Redacción

This section consists of a three-part summary and
review of vocabulary and structures.

1. Repaso: Here the student is given a Spanish
sentence. Beneath it are English sentences to be put
into Spanish. When correctly completed, sentences
will have been formed that are structurally identical to
the model. Each is designed to review one or more
specific grammar points.

2. Tema: This is a cartoon strip of four to six panels.
Each panel has one or more English sentences
representing the dialogue or describing the scene.
The sentences in the cartoon strip are structurally
identical to the model sentences in the *Repaso*. Upon
rendering them into Spanish, the student will have
written a unified dialogue or paragraph.

3. Redacción: This offers suggestions for more
open-ended, yet guided, writing practice.

For suggestions for use, see p. T9 and the notes for
p. 76.

Additions to on-page notes

Notes: You may want to do the *Repaso* orally in
class, or you may prefer to cover only the model
sentence and the first English sentence as
preparation for written homework. Assign the *Repaso*
to the whole class, or assign single sentences to
individuals or rows of students. Go over the
assignment in class. You may want to create additional English cues for further practice or for extra credit.

Answers to *Repaso*

1. ¿Te gustan más los sandwiches o las ensaladas? /
   ¿Te gustan más las fiestas o los exámenes?
2. ¿Te gusta el jamón? / ¿Te gusta el queso?
3. ¿Te gustan los deportes? / ¿Te gustan los mapas?
4. ¿Cuántos lápices hay? / ¿Cuántas sillas hay?
5. ¡No me gusta leer! / ¡No me gusta estudiar!

PAGE 77

Answers to *Tema*

1. ¿Te gustan más las hamburguesas o los burritos?
2. ¿Te gusta el yogur?
3. ¿Te gustan las papas fritas?
4. ¿Cuántos estudiantes hay?
5. ¡No me gusta trabajar!

PAGE 78

Additions to on-page notes

Notes: You may want to assign the *Comprueba* as
written homework. It can also function as a review of
or additional practice for specific grammar points or
vocabulary. If you prefer, assign the *Comprueba* for
at-home preparation and cover the exercises orally in
class. Other possibilities include using the *Comprueba*
as an in-class writing activity or as a self-test.

For additional suggestions for use, see pp. T9–T10.

Answers to *Comprueba tu progreso*

A
1. Me gustan (No me gustan) las hamburguesas.
2. Me gustan (No me gustan) las papas fritas.
3. Me gusta (No me gusta) el yogur.
4. Me gustan (No me gustan) los tacos.
5. Me gusta (No me gusta) la ensalada.
6. Me gusta (No me gusta) la limonada.
7. Me gustan (No me gustan) los sandwiches de queso.
8. Me gusta (No me gusta) el pan con mantequilla.
9. Me gustan (No me gustan) los refrescos.
10. Me gusta (No me gusta) el jamón.

B
1. la	4. el	7. el	10. el
2. el	5. el	8. la	11. el
3. la	6. la	9. el	12. el

C
1. las puertas
2. los meses
3. las pizarras
4. los bolígrafos
5. los lápices
6. las hojas de papel
7. los pupitres
8. las clases
9. los carteles
10. los exámenes
11. los días de fiesta
12. los lunes

D
1. Me encanta la música, pero no me gusta cantar.
2. Me encantan los deportes, pero no me gusta jugar al tenis.
3. Me encanta la clase de español, pero no me gusta hacer la tarea.
4. Me encantan los tacos, pero no me gusta cocinar.
5. Me encantan las fiestas, pero no me gusta bailar.
6. Me encanta comer, pero no me gustan los sandwiches de jamón.
7. Me encanta leer y estudiar, pero no me gusta hacer la tarea.

E
1. ¿Hay muchos profesores? No, hay pocos. ¿Cuántos hay? Nueve.
2. ¿Hay muchos estudiantes? No, hay pocos. ¿Cuántos hay? Catorce.
3. ¿Hay muchos pupitres? No, hay pocos. ¿Cuántos hay? Once.
4. ¿Hay muchas sillas? No, hay pocas. ¿Cuántas hay? Trece.
5. ¿Hay muchas mesas? No, hay pocas. ¿Cuántas hay? Dos.
6. ¿Hay muchos mapas? No, hay pocos. ¿Cuántos hay? Cuatro.
7. ¿Hay muchas ventanas? No, hay pocas. ¿Cuántas hay? Cinco.

PAGE 79

Photo

This photo shows Easter bread from Chalma, a Mexican village that is one of the country's principal places of pilgrimage, especially during *Semana Santa,* or Holy Week. Serving special kinds of bread for specific religious occasions is a widespread tradition in Mexico and in many other Spanish-speaking countries. For example, in Mexico special breads, called *panes de muertos,* are prepared for *Día de los Muertos* (Day of the Dead), which is celebrated on November 2. The basket shown in the photo comes from Pátzcuaro, a picturesque Mexican town that is the site of one of the most famous Day of the Dead celebrations.

ORAL PROFICIENCY TEST

Before administering the Oral Proficiency Test, refer to the section called Oral Proficiency Testing (on pp. T23–T24 of this Teacher's Edition), which presents guidelines for evaluating communicative progress.

Directed Response
1. How would you say that you like music very much? (*Me gusta mucho la música. OR Me encanta la música.*)
2. How would you ask a friend which he or she likes better, to cook or to wash dishes? (*¿Qué te gusta más, cocinar o lavar los platos?*)
3. What would I ask if I needed to find out how many books there are? (*¿Cuántos libros hay?*)

Picture-Cued Response

Point to the photograph on p. 60 and ask:

4. ¿Qué te gusta escuchar? *(Me gusta escuchar discos.)*
5. ¿Hay muchos discos? *(No, no hay muchos discos.)*
6. ¿Cuántos discos hay? *(Hay tres discos.)*

Situations

7. Someone says that he or she loves parties. You ask why.
   a. ¿Cómo estás?   b. ¿Qué tal?   c. *¿Por qué?*
8. A friend asks if you like yogurt. You say that you prefer ice cream.
   a. *Me gusta más el helado.*   b. Te gusta el helado.   c. No me gusta el yogur.
9. Someone asks if you like to sing. Say that you really do.
   a. Pues.   b. *¡Ah, sí!*   c. Me gusta más.

Real-Life Questions

10. ¿Te gusta más ir al cine o mirar la tele? *(Me gusta más. . . .)*
11. ¿Por qué te gusta (no te gusta) el fútbol? *(Porque me gustan (no me gustan) los deportes.)*
12. ¿Te gustan más las hamburguesas con o sin queso? *(Me gustan más las hamburguesas. . . .)*

LEARNING SPANISH THROUGH ACTION

New prop vocabulary: Food.   You will need magazine pictures or drawings of all of the foods in this chapter.

Other new vocabulary: ¿quién?, con, sin

New staging vocabulary: comer, tomar, dibujar

Sample

1. Señalen el pan.
2. Toquen el pan.
3. Toquen la leche.
4. Señalen la leche y el pan.
5. Señalen la ensalada.

Teach all of the foods in this manner, and then continue, adding *comer* and *tomar*.

6. Pongan el burrito a la derecha de la leche.
7. Pongan la hamburguesa debajo del helado.
8. Coman el helado. *(Miming.)*
9. Señalen la limonada y pongan el jamón sobre las papas fritas.
10. Tomen la limonada. *(Again, miming.)*

Now add *dibujar*, *con*, and *sin*.

11. Dibujen una hamburguesa.

12. Dibujen papas fritas a la derecha de la hamburguesa.
13. Dibujen un taco debajo de las papas fritas.
14. Dibujen pan con mantequilla.
15. Dibujen pan sin mantequilla.
16. Dibujen una hamburguesa sin pan.
17. Dibujen una hamburguesa con pan sobre el taco.

Narration and questioning are appropriate.

18. Juan, dibuja un taco. Guillermo, dibuja un burrito.
    Q: Juan, ¿quién dibuja un burrito, tú o Guillermo?
    A: Guillermo.
19. Sí, Juan. Tú dibujas un taco.
20. Guillermo, dibuja una hamburguesa con queso.
    Q: Guillermo, ¿dibujas una hamburguesa con queso o sin queso?
    A: Con queso.
21. Sí, con queso.
    Q: Juan, ¿quién dibuja una hamburguesa?
    A: Guillermo.
    Q: ¿Con queso o sin queso?
    A: Con queso.
22. Fantástico, Juan. Guillermo dibuja una hamburguesa con queso.

OBJECTIVES

Communication
- to express surprise or pleasure (*¡qué!* + adj.)

Grammar
- to describe persons and things with *ser*
- to use personal pronouns
- to express origin with *ser*

Culture
- to recognize regions, countries, and nationalities
- to focus on the diversity of backgrounds and lifestyles among Latin Americans
- to point out the Spanish language as a unifying force among Latin Americans.

SUGGESTED MATERIALS

p. 81 (Prólogo cultural): wall map(s) of South and Central America, including the Caribbean; magazine pictures of varied ethnic and racial types

pp. 82–83 (Palabras nuevas I): wall map(s) of North, South, and Central America, including the Caribbean

pp. 88–89 (Palabras nuevas II): magazine pictures of people, animals, and objects

p. 93 (Actividad): a paper bag

PAGES 80–81

Photo

This colorful market scene is in Cali, the third largest city in Colombia. Cali is a popular tourist attraction, an important industrial center and, as the photograph suggests, is located in an extremely rich agricultural area.

The people in the photograph reflect Colombia's ethnic diversity. Although most estimates of ethnic composition in Latin America are only approximations, it is believed that, within Spanish-speaking South America, Colombia has the highest percentage of people of African descent (about one-fourth of the population). However, Colombia has a very small Indian population (about one percent of the total), unlike Andean countries such as Bolivia, Peru, and Ecuador. People of direct European descent make up about one-fifth of Colombia's total population compared with over ninety percent of the total in Argentina, Costa Rica and Uruguay. *Mestizos* (people of mixed European and Indian descent) make up one-half of the Colombian population, a smaller percentage than in Mexico and Nicaragua (about three-fourths *mestizo* each), but very high compared with Argentina, Uruguay, and Costa Rica.

PAGE 82

Additions to on-page notes

Notes: Use a wall map of North, Central, and South America, or show transparency 15 to introduce this chapter. Model the Spanish names for all countries given in the *Contexto visual.* Ask students to listen first and then repeat. Ask volunteers to name the countries as you point to them.

Point out the capital of each country. Do not expect students to produce these names yet. Then say the capitals without pointing to them and ask volunteers to locate them.

PAGE 84

Additions to on-page notes

Notes: You may want to present the *Contexto comunicativo* before students open their books. Ask students to repeat, using proper rhythm, pronunciation, and intonation. Then ask them to open their books and read the dialogue in pairs. Circulate to give help where needed.

PAGE 85

Realia

Postcards showing scenes from Panama City, Caracas, and Mexico City.

PAGE 86

Photo

A portrait of the hero of Chile's independence, Bernardo O'Higgins (1778–1842), from the 10,000 peso note. O'Higgins was the son of an Irish immigrant, who with General José de San Martín, lead the army that defeated the Spanish in 1818. O'Higgins the became the first president of Chile. As president he established a navy, set up elementary schools, founded the National Library, abolished titles of nobility, and tried to break up landowners' large estates.

Realia

Passports from Chile, the U.S., and Spain. The Chilean passport bears the coat of arms of that country, which contains the motto, *Por la razón o la fuerza*—"By right or by might." To the right of the shield is the condor and to the left the huemal, a deer native to the Andes.

The Spanish passport also shows Spain's coat of arms, adopted in 1981. The central shield contains the symbols of four of Spain's ancient kingdoms— Castilla, León, Aragón, and Navarra.

Additions to on-page notes

Notes: The cognates *Irlanda,* Ireland, and *familia,* family, are not glossed. You may want to point them out to the class. Model the *Diálogo* for repetition, or play the tape. After students have heard the conversation once or twice, assign the roles of Felipe and Lolita to sections of the class. For example, the girls can play Lolita's part and the boys Felipe's. Then ask for pairs of volunteers to act out the dialogue.

PAGE 87

Photo

Passengers at the international airport in Santiago, Chile.

PAGE 88

Additions to on-page notes

Notes: You may want to present the adjectives in *Palabras nuevas II* by showing pictures from magazines. Point to each object and model the

adjective. Repeat the procedure using the illustrations on pp. 88–89 or transparency 16.

Point out the plural form of *pez (peces)*. Do students remember another word that changes in the same way? *(lápiz, lápices)*. Mention that *el pez* is used exclusively for fish that are alive. *El pescado* refers to fish caught for eating.

PAGE 92

Photos

(a) Traditionally, families in Spain and Latin America have tended to form extended families, which may include members of several generations. In extended families, parents and children, as well as grandparents, aunts, uncles, and cousins, maintain close ties and often live close to each other. However, the growth of cities and the increasingly rapid pace of life are weakening the extended family.

(b) A girl with her puppy in Mexico City, Mexico. Do students know that *cachorro* means "puppy"?

PAGE 93

Additions to on-page notes

Notes: You may want to have students do the preparation for the *Actividad* as homework. If this activity is particularly successful with your class, put students' drawings and descriptions on the bulletin board.

PAGE 94

Photo

A high school student in Puerto Rico.

PAGE 95

Photos

(a) In the background of this photo is the Cathedral of Mexico, which is one of the oldest and largest religious buildings in the Western Hemisphere. Since the cathedral took nearly three centuries to complete, it contains a mixture of architectural styles (Ionic, Doric, Corinthian, and Baroque).

(b) High school students in Spain.

PAGE 96

Additions to on-page notes

Notes: You may want to use Ex. B for pair work (having students alternate roles), as a chain drill, or as a written exercise.

Point out that *tú* is not used in the model question. The use and omission of subject pronouns is discussed further on p. 98.

PAGE 100

Photos

(a) Letter writing is an important form of communication in Madrid. Many families who live there still have relatives and friends in the small towns of Spain, and letters are a means of keeping in touch with them.

(b) To ensure faster delivery of their correspondence, letter writers can presort their own letters and packages, using the outdoor mailboxes at Madrid's central post office. All of Spain's large provinces and cities have their own boxes there.

PAGE 101

Realia

(a) This Peruvian stamp depicts regional clothing *(trajes típicos)* from the town of Tinta in the Canchis province of the department, or state, of Cuzco. The various Indian groups of the *altiplano*, or high plateau, celebrate many different religious festivals, for which they dress in a variety of elaborate and colorful costumes. These observances often date back to pre-Columbian times.

(b) Bolivia's postal service issued this stamp to promote traffic safety, advising the public that "the police are watching over you 24 hours a day."

PAGE 105

Photo

A woman and her grandchild are seen in the Mexican town of Progreso, located on the Gulf of Mexico in the state of Yucatán. Progreso is both a beach resort and a shipping center.

PAGE 106

Photo

A young man is shown mailing a letter at the post office in Madrid. An airmail letter from Madrid takes a week to ten days to reach the U.S. Letters from one part of Madrid to another usually arrive in a day or two, while mail sent from Madrid to other major cities within Spain (Barcelona, Bilbao, and Valencia, for example) takes three to five days.

Additions to on-page notes

Notes: You may use the *Repaso* as an oral exercise. As a written exercise, it is particularly helpful in reinforcing the chapter's basic grammar points. As a class activity, have volunteers offer Spanish sentences to a "secretary" at the board.

Answers to *Repaso*

1. Me llamo Irene. Soy del Canadá. / Me llamo Jaime. Somos de la América del Sur. / Me llamo Sonia. Somos de la América Central.
2. El Sr. Vilas es mi profesor. Es cubano. / Marcos es mi amigo. Es sudamericano. / Laura es mi amiga. Es norteamericana.
3. Son pequeños y rubios. / Son jóvenes y guapos(as). / Son morenas y bonitas.
4. También eres bastante viejo(a), ¿verdad? / También son demasiado jóvenes, ¿verdad? / También son muy feos, ¿verdad?

PAGE 107

Additions to on-page notes

Notes: You may assign the *Tema* as homework or as in-class work to be done orally or as a written activity. It provides additional reinforcement of the chapter's basic grammar points.

The *Redacción* is suitable for students of varying capabilities because it allows them the freedom to say as much or as little as possible while still fulfilling the requirements of the exercise. You may want to assign *Redacción 3* as pair work and ask volunteers to present their dialogues to the class.

Answers to *Tema*

1. Me llamo Ted. Soy de los Estados Unidos.
2. Rita es mi amiga. Es puertorriqueña.
3. Es alta y delgada.
4. También es muy guapa, ¿verdad?

PAGE 108

Answers to *Comprueba tu progreso*

A
1. soy
2. son
3. somos
4. es
5. eres
6. son
7. es
8. Es

B
1. Ella
2. Él
3. Ellos
4. Ella
5. Ellos
6. Ellas
7. Ellos
8. Ellos
9. Nosotros

C
1. Los pájaros son bonitos.
2. Los hombres son españoles.
3. Los profesores son puertorriqueños.
4. Los países son enormes.
5. Ella es morena.
6. Las alumnas son sudamericanas.
7. Nosotras somos bajas.
8. El escritorio es nuevo.

D
1. ¡Qué delgadas!
2. ¡Qué gordos!
3. ¡Qué cortos!
4. ¡Qué pequeños!
5. ¡Qué altos!
6. ¡Qué enormes!

E
1. larga … corta
2. alta … baja
3. delgados … gordos
4. bonito … feo
5. nuevas … viejas
6. grandes … pequeños
7. rubias … morenas
8. viejas … jóvenes

PAGE 109

Photo

These wood carvings from the southern state of Oaxaca, Mexico, like other types of Mexican folk art, incorporate both pre-Columbian and modern elements. The dogs' faces resemble those of the serpents carved in stone in the temple of Quetzalcóatl in Teotihuacán. And the use of wood and colors obtained from aniline fabric dyes reflects more modern influences.

ORAL PROFICIENCY TEST

Directed Response

1. You're almost sure that Teresa is Cuban, but you ask anyway just to see if you're right. *(Teresa es cubana, ¿verdad? OR Teresa es cubana, no?)*
2. Ask your friend what his Spanish teacher is like. *(¿Cómo es tu profesor(a) de español?)*
3. Ask Angela's parents where they are from. *(¿De dónde son Uds.?)*

Picture-Cued Response

Point to the large photograph on p. 92 and ask:
4. ¿Es la muchacha rubia or morena? *(Es morena.)*
5. ¿Cómo es el perro? *(Es bonito, joven y pequeño.)*
6. La muchacha es cubana, ¿no? *(No, la muchacha no es cubana. OR No, la muchacha es mexicana.)*

Situations

7. Someone asks you what your mother is like. Say that she's rather short.
   a. *Es bastante baja.*   b. Es demasiado baja.
   c. Es bastante alta.
8. You're really surprised that Federico's fish are so big. What would you say?
   a. ¡Hay muchos!   b. ¡Ah, son canadienses!
   c. *¡Qué grandes!*
9. You see a new student in school and want to know where she's from. What do you ask her?
   a. *¿De dónde es ella?*   b. ¿De dónde eres?
   c. ¿De dónde soy?

Real-Life Questions

10. ¿De qué país eres? *(Soy de. . . .)*
11. ¿Cuál es la capital de tu país? *(La capital de mi país es. . . .)*
12. ¿Cómo eres? *(Soy. . . .)*
13. ¿Cómo es tu compañero(a) de clase? *(Mi compañero(a) de clase es. . . .)*
14. ¿De qué origen es tu amigo(a)? *(Mi amigo(a) es de origen. . . .)*

LEARNING SPANISH
THROUGH ACTION

New prop vocabulary: gato, hombre, muchacha, muchacho, pájaro, perro, pez. You will need several magazine pictures or drawings of each item in order to demonstrate the adjectives below. Attach the pictures to the wall or to the chalkboard, with opposites next to each other: a tall man next to a short man, a long fish next to a short fish, an ugly dog next to a pretty dog. You will need groups of three pictures to demonstrate hair color and size.

Other new vocabulary: ¿cómo?; alto, bajo; bonito (guapo), feo; corto, largo; delgado, gordo; pequeño, grande, enorme; moreno, pelirrojo, rubio; joven, viejo

New staging vocabulary: borrar, dibujar

Sample
1. Toquen un perro.
2. Toquen un gato.
3. Señalen un perro.
4. Señalen un gato.
5. Señalen una mujer.
6. Toquen un perro y una mujer.

Teach all of the prop vocabulary in this manner, and then continue.

7. Toquen un perro feo.
8. Toquen un perro bonito.
9. Toquen una mujer fea.
10. Señalen una mujer bonita.
11. Señalen un perro feo y una mujer bonita.

Teach all of the adjectives, and then add *dibujar* and *borrar*.

12. Dibujen un pez.
13. Dibujen un hombre.
14. Borren el pez.
15. Borren al hombre.
16. Dibujen un pez largo y un pez corto.
17. Borren el pez corto.
18. Dibujen una muchacha fea y una muchacha bonita.
19. Borren a la muchacha fea.

Add narration and questioning.

20. Dibujen un perro gordo y un gato delgado.
21. El perro es gordo.
    Q: ¿Cómo es el gato, gordo o delgado?
    A: Delgado.
    Q: ¿Cómo es el perro?
    A: Gordo.

CAPÍTULO 3

OBJECTIVES

Communication
- to ask and tell the cost of an item
- to ask about and describe the weather
- to ask (*¿qué?, ¿cuál?, ¿quién?,* etc.) questions
- to identify clothes
- to identify colors

Grammar
- to use regular *-ar* verbs
- to recognize the use of compound nouns
- to use negative sentences

Culture
- to discuss Spain's varied climate and topography
- to dispel misconceptions about Spain's climate
- to mention the range of outdoor activities possible in Spain

SUGGESTED MATERIALS

p. 111 (Prólogo cultural): maps of the U.S. and Europe

pp. 112–113 (Palabras nuevas I): magazine and mail-order catalog pictures of clothing

p. 117 (Actividad): a paper bag

pp. 120–121 (Palabras nuevas II): magazine pictures of seasons and weather conditions

p. 132 (Actividad): index cards

p. 139 (Actividad): 12 sheets of construction paper or light cardboard

PAGES 110–111

Photo
Hiking in the Picos de Europa in Cantabria, Spain. This region, where skiing and mountain climbing are popular, has been compared to Switzerland. The most famous site in the region is the Altamira caves, with Paleolithic wall paintings and prehistoric utensils and ornaments that are over twenty thousand years old.

Additions to on-page notes
Enrichment: Using a map of the U.S., place a cutout of Spain over Texas so that students can visualize the difference in size.

On a map of Europe, have students find Spain's three closest neighbors (France, Italy, Portugal), the Atlantic Ocean, the Mediterranean, and the Pyrenees. Show Africa in relation to Spain. Elicit Spain's particular geographic formation (peninsula).

Posters can be useful to show the variety of climates and activities that are possible in Spain. The Spanish National Tourist Office (665 Fifth Avenue, New York, NY 10017) and Iberia Airlines (565 Fifth Avenue, New York, NY 10017) are good sources for maps and posters.

PAGE 112

Additions to on-page notes
Notes: In conjunction with transparency 18, you may want to use pictures of clothing from magazines and mail-order catalogs to reinforce the vocabulary presented in the *Contexto visual.*

PAGE 114

Photos
(a) The latest fashions are on sale in the skirt and blouse department of El Corte Inglés in Madrid, a famous department store chain with branches in most large Spanish cities.
(b) Two Spanish teenagers admire an oversized yellow blazer.

PAGE 118

Photo
A clothing store in Bogotá decorated for Halloween. The store advertises, "Get to know the enchantment of our low prices."

Additions to on-page notes

Culture: It is not uncommon in the Spanish-speaking world to see salesclerks stopping passers-by and trying to lure them into their shops with promises of *ropa buena y barata.*

PAGE 119

Photo

Window shoppers in front of a clothing store in Lima that advertises a summer sale.

Additions to on-page notes

Notes: You may want students to prepare the *Participación* as a written homework assignment. Ask volunteers to perform their dialogues for the class.

PAGE 123

Additions to on-page notes

Enrichment: As a homework assignment, ask students to read the weather section in the newspaper or listen to a weather report on radio or TV. They should be prepared to tell the class about the weather in five different cities. Have students limit their descriptions to the expressions on p. 121.

PAGE 126

Photo

Rock music has millions of fans among young people in Spanish-speaking countries. Teenagers are eager to buy tapes and records by British and American rock groups, in addition to those by Hispanic rock performers. Youths flock to rock concerts and listen faithfully to "top 40" radio stations. Spain, in particular, has been experiencing a rock boom. Nightclubs in Madrid feature rock music every night of the week. And you can even hear rock music mixed with a bit of flamenco, which gives it a clearly Spanish flavor. The rock boom is part of a broader cultural movement called *La Movida.* This movement, which gained strength after the end of the military government in the mid-1970s, encourages experimentation with new art forms and philosophies.

Additions to on-page notes

Reteach / Review: Remind students that they have been using verbs since the first day of class, when they learned to give their names *(Me llamo)* and ask for classmates' names *(¿Cómo te llamas?).* You may want to refer students to the glosses for mini-dialogues 2 on p. 113; 3, 4, and 5 on p. 114; and 4 on p. 122 in order to present the *yo / tú* forms or *-ar* verbs.

PAGE 127

Photo

There is a continous two-way exchange of popular music between Puerto Rico and the U.S. Rock music is heard all over the Spanish-speaking world, and the Caribbean *salsa* has been well accepted in the U.S. One Hispanic group that has been very successful in bridging the cultural gap is *Menudo,* a group of five Puerto Rican teenage boys. Menudo's popularity in the Spanish-speaking world resembles that of the Beatles in the 1960s. For years, the members of Menudo sang almost exclusively in their native Spanish; however, they crossed the language barrier in 1984, when their first record in English was released.

Additions to on-page notes

Notes: Refer students to the paradigm for *cantar* on p. 126, and then model the conjugation of several verbs from the list in section 1. Make sure that students stress the first syllable in all forms of the two-syllable verbs except the *nosotros / nosotras* and *vosotros / vosotras* forms.

   You may want to ask students to choose four verbs and write a sentence using each one. They can then compare answers with a partner.

Reteach / Review: Remind students that they shouldn't use subject pronouns with verbs—except for emphasis or for clarification—because the verb endings indicate who the subject is.

PAGE 130

Photo

Three students relax between classes at the University of Puerto Rico in San Juan. The main campus is in the Río Piedras section of San Juan, but there are regional branches throughout the island.

PAGE 131

Photo

Two girls are seen in Córdoba, a city in Andalucía.

PAGE 133

Sample dialogue for *¿Qué pasa?*

Raúl and Mercedes are discussing some of the things they like to do on Sundays when it's raining and cold.

R: ¿Qué te gusta hacer los domingos cuando llueve y hace frío?

M: Me gusta estudiar o ayudar en casa. ¿Y tú?

R: Prefiero escuchar discos. Pues a las dos de la tarde, Ramón cocina comida mexicana.

M: ¿Y ayudas tú también?

R: ¡Cómo no! ¡Me encanta comer!

PAGE 134

Additions to on-page notes

Notes: Before going over *Explicaciones II,* refer students to mini-dialogues 1–5 on pp. 112–114 and 1–6 on p. 122 to introduce questions. Make sure students understand which is the subject and which is the verb in a sentence. Say several statements and questions, or write them on the board, and ask volunteers to identify the subjects and verbs. Make up your own sentences, or use examples from the *Contexto comunicativo* (pp. 112–114 and 122).

PAGE 135

Additions to on-page notes

Reteach / Review: In connection with Ex. A, you may want to refer students to the name lists on p. 4 to help them to recall which names are masculine and which are feminine.

PAGE 136

Additions to on-page notes

Notes: You may choose to omit Exs. C and D if you feel that this summary of interrogative words will be difficult for students.

PAGE 137

Photo

A mother and daughter are shown preparing dinner in Guadalajara, México. Until recently, lunch was the most important meal of the day for most Mexican families. However, dinner has become the main meal in many homes, especially in large cities where the distances between the workplace and the home are considerable. It is often only at dinner time that families can be together for a meal.

Some basic ingredients of most meals are corn, beans, and different varieties of chili peppers. Corn has been used since ancient times to make *tortillas,* or flat pancakes, which are served with or without fillings of meat, cheese, or vegetables. Beans are found in many dishes, including *frijoles refritos,* beans fried in oil with various spices. Chili peppers are frequently used to make spicy sauces *(salsas).* However, the commonly held belief that *chile con carne* is popular in Mexico is a misconception. In fact, *chile con carne* originated in the southwestern U.S. and is not found among staple foods in Mexico.

PAGE 140

Photos

(a) A display of boots and other footwear at a Mexico City leather-goods store. Some items that are on sale are a cowhide saddlebag, Tucson and Zapata cowhide boots, Montana snakeskin boots, Oklahoma boots made of cowhide tooled to look like a turtle's shell, and kidskin shoes.

(b) Great glassware bargains at a Buenos Aires hardware store. Second row: Unheard of! Brill glasses, Rigolleau sparkling glasses, and Daniel Cristalux glasses. Third row: Impossible! Empire Cristalux glasses. Incredible! Floris-Cristalux compote bowls. Super low fixed price! Drill oil or vinegar cruets. Don't be left without yours! Super sensational offer! Three

Cadea roasting dishes. They're almost sold out! Fourth row: Impossible! Small Cristalux coffee glasses. What an offer! Nautilus 200 heat-resistant Durax glasses. Small ceramic casserole dishes. Great limited offer! Drill bottle for water-wine-juice-milk.

Tell students that the Argentine unit of currency is the *austral,* which is subdivided into 100 *centavos.*

Answers to *Repaso*

1. Hoy hace calor. Tú y ella buscan sombreros. / Ahora hace frío. Marta y yo llevamos chaquetas. / Hoy hace sol. Uds. y él compran trajes de baño.
2. Entro en la tienda y pregunto: ''¿Cuánto cuesta el vestido morado?'' / Entramos en la tienda y preguntamos: ''¿Cuánto cuesta el abrigo marrón?'' / Entran en la tienda y preguntan: ''¿Cuánto cuestan los calcetines rojos?''
3. Contestamos: ''Cincuenta pesos, señora.'' / Contestan: ''Setenta pesos, señor.'' / Contestas: ''Veinticinco pesos, señorita.''
4. ''¡Es muy vieja!'' / ''¡Son bastante cortos!'' / ''¡Son demasiado amarillas!''
5. No estudias nada. / No cocinan nada. / No cantamos nada.

PAGE 141
Answers to *Tema*

1. Hoy llueve. Elena y Clara buscan impermeables.
2. Las muchachas entran en la tienda y preguntan: ''¿Cuánto cuesta el impermeable amarillo?''
3. La vendedora contesta: ''Noventa pesos, señorita.''
4. ''Es demasiado caro.''
5. Clara y Elena no compran nada.

PAGE 142
Answers to *Comprueba tu progreso*

A 1. Leonor lleva una falda roja y blanca, una blusa amarilla, un sombrero verde y zapatos verdes.
   2. Federico lleva jeans, zapatos marrones, calcetines blancos, un abrigo marrón, una bufanda gris, guantes grises, y lleva un paraguas negro.

B 1. compra
   2. tomo
   3. entran
   4. llevas
   5. buscamos
   6. contestan
   7. bailamos
   8. mira
   9. montan
   10. escuchan

C 1. Hace calor.
   2. Hace frío.
   3. Hace sol.
   4. Hace viento.
   5. Llueve.
   6. Nieva.
   7. Hace fresco.

D 1. ¿Trabaja Ud. en el verano?
   2. ¿Escuchan los muchachos la radio?
   3. ¿Toca él la guitarra?
   4. ¿Miran Uds. el mapa?
   5. ¿Lleva Luz un paraguas?
   6. ¿Compra Ud. un traje de baño?

E 1. Ud. trabaja en el verano, ¿no?
   2. Los muchachos escuchan la radio, ¿no?
   3. Él toca la guitarra, ¿no?
   4. Uds. miran el mapa, ¿verdad?
   5. Luz lleva un paraguas, ¿verdad?
   6. Ud. compra un traje de baño, ¿verdad?

F 1. ¿Quién lleva botas?
   2. ¿Cuándo monta Eduardo en bicicleta?
   3. ¿Cómo nadas?
   4. ¿Cuántos bolígrafos hay en la mesa?
   5. ¿De dónde son Uds.?
   6. ¿Por qué cantas?
   7. ¿Cuánto cuesta el abrigo?
   8. ¿Qué prefieres?

G 1. No, la Sra. Arias no entra en la tienda.
   2. No, no tomo el sol en el invierno.

3. No, Ana no lleva pantimedias cuando hace calor.
4. No, no me gustan los zapatos rojos.
5. No, no compramos un impermeable.
6. No, los gatos no son gordos.

PAGE 143

Photo

This straw hat is from Tenejapa, a small village in southern Mexico named after the Indians who live there. The Tenejapans, along with Indians from several neighboring villages, sell crafts such as hand-woven goods and pottery in San Cristóbal de las Casas, the main market center for the area.

Despite the proximity of the villages of this region to each other, typical costumes vary greatly from village to village. The men from Tenejapa wear straw hats (like the one shown in the photograph), short white trousers and black knee-length tunics; and the women wear richly embroidered blouses, dark blue skirts with narrow stripes, broad red- and black-striped belts, and generally more colorful costumes than those worn by the men. The Chamula men, by contrast, wear white cotton shirts and trousers and white woolen cloaks, while the women's costumes consist of black wrap-around skirts with orange-, red-, or green-striped sashes, and dark blouses.

ORAL PROFICIENCY TEST

Directed Response

1. How would you tell a salesclerk that you aren't buying a blouse because it's too expensive? *(No compro la blusa porque es demasiado cara.)*
2. A friend asks you why you don't want to play tennis. Tell him because it's windy today. *(Porque hace viento hoy.)*
3. Your friend is buying a red sweater and wants to know if you like it. Tell her that you like it but that you prefer the blue one. *(Me gusta el suéter rojo, pero prefiero (me gusta más) el suéter azul.)*

Picture-Cued Response

Using the visuals on pp. 112–113 or transparency 18:

4. Point to the shoes and ask: "¿Cuánto cuestan los zapatos?" *(Treinta y cinco pesos.)*
5. Point to the salesclerk and ask: "¿Quién trabaja en la tienda?" *(La vendedora trabaja en la tienda.)*

Situations

6. You're shopping and a salesclerk sees you looking around. How would he ask if he might help you?
   a. ¿Quién es Ud.   b. *¿Qué desea Ud.?*
   c. ¿Cuánto es?
7. A friend asks you to go to a party with her. You'd love to go. What do you say?
   a. ¡Uf! No sé.   b. *¡Cómo no!*
   c. ¿Cómo es?
8. It's a sunny day, but it's very cold. A friend says he's going to play basketball. What might you say?
   a. *Hace sol pero hace mucho frío.*
   b. Llueve mucho y hace viento.
   c. Hace mal tiempo en el invierno.

Real-Life Questions

9. ¿Prefieres el verano o el invierno? *(Prefiero el. . . .)*
10. ¿Por qué prefieres el verano (el invierno)? *(Porque me gusta nadar y tomar el sol (esquiar).)*
11. ¿Qué ropa llevas cuando llueve? *(Llevo un impermeable (botas) cuando llueve.)*
12. ¿De qué color es tu impermeable? *(Mi impermeable es. . . .)*

LEARNING SPANISH THROUGH ACTION

New prop vocabulary: All items of clothing from this chapter. Doll clothes are ideal. You will need at least two samples of each item of clothing, each a different color. Arrange the items on a table, using only one color sample of each item at a time until the clothing vocabulary has been learned. Then add the differently colored items when you are teaching the adjectives of color.

Other new vocabulary: ¿de qué color?, entre, amarillo, anaranjado, azul, blanco, gris, marrón, morado, negro, rojo, verde

New staging vocabulary: buscar

Sample
1. Toquen la blusa.
2. Toquen el suéter.
3. Toquen el vestido.
4. Señalen el suéter.

Teach all of the items of clothing in this manner, and then teach the colors.

5. Toquen el suéter rojo.
6. Toquen el zapato rojo.
7. Toquen la blusa roja.
8. Toquen la blusa amarilla.
9. Señalen el suéter amarillo.

They should now be able to answer simple questions.

10. Jacobo, toca el suéter rojo y el vestido anaranjado.
   Q: ¿De qué color es el vestido?
   A: Anaranjado.
   Q: Y el suéter, ¿es anaranjado?
   A: No, es rojo.

When all of the colors have been taught, continue, adding *entre*.

11. Pongan la falda negra sobre la camisa azul.
12. Pongan el zapato blanco entre el zapato marrón y el zapato verde.

At this point you may add *buscar*. First hide several items of clothing in the room. You may want to offer a prize for finding and describing the item.

13. Carmen, busca el vestido blanco y negro.
14. Amelia y Arturo, busquen los pantalones azules que están en uno de los pupitres.

You might also have them look for items that aren't hidden.

15. Carlos, busca un alumno que lleve pantalones blancos con una camiseta morada.

CAPÍTULO 4

OBJECTIVES

Communication
- to ask and tell where someone is going
- to identify modes of transportation

Grammar
- to use the verb *ir*
- to use indefinite articles
- to describe people and things using adjectives

Culture
- to discuss the principal means of public transportation in Latin America
- to note Latin American subway systems
- to focus on the archaeological finds uncovered during the construction of Mexico City's subway

SUGGESTED MATERIALS

p. 146 (Palabras nuevas I):   magazine pictures of buildings and locations

p. 149 (Práctica B):   magazine pictures of a letter, money, an empty medicine bottle, an airline ticket, a train ticket, a doctor

p. 149 (Actividad):   colored pencils

p. 152 (Palabras nuevas II):   magazine pictures showing modes of transportation

p. 160 (Práctica D):   a wall calendar of the month of December

p. 161 (Actividad):   alphabet cards

PAGES 144–145

Photo
View of a Mexican highway, on the road to Jalapa, capital of the state of Veracruz. Mexico has many good highways, although some of them are not up to U.S. standards. The road system varies according to the population density in the different regions of the country. Thus, the road system in the northern region, where the population is relatively smaller, is less adequate than that in the central or southern regions. *Autopistas,* or superhighways, are confined mainly to the vicinity of the largest cities, such as Mexico City, Guadalajara, and Veracruz.

PAGE 146

Additions to on-page notes
Notes: As you present the *Contexto visual,* you may want to point out the following cognates: *aeropuerto, estación, hotel, hospital, banco, plaza, farmacia.*

If students ask: Other related words you may want to present: *el pueblo,* town; *el teatro,* theater; *el museo,* museum; *la calle,* street; *la librería,* bookstore.

PAGE 147

Additions to on-page notes
Notes: Present the *Contexto comunicativo* by modeling the five mini-dialogues or playing the tape. Make sure students understand that the contraction *al (a + el)* is used only with masculine singular nouns.

PAGE 150

Photo
Mexicans and foreign visitors come to enjoy the hot springs at the resort of the Balnearios de Comanjilla, located in the state of Guanajuato in central Mexico. Because of volcanic activity throughout this region, there are many spas such as this one that feature thermal and mineral waters.

Additions to on-page notes
Notes: Present the *Diálogo* by modeling the roles of Alberto and Cecilia or playing the tape. During the presentation, ask factual questions: *¿Qué?, ¿Cuándo?, ¿Dónde?, ¿Cómo?, ¿Por qué?*

PAGE 151

Photo

Some teenagers sip soft drinks while strolling down Carrera Séptima (Seventh Avenue), Bogota's eight-lane thoroughfare. On Sundays, between 8:00 a.m. and 1:00 p.m., the city closes off one side of the street to cars (for about a three-mile stretch) for use as a *ciclovía* (bicycle path). Then Carrera Séptima comes alive with cyclists, roller skaters, joggers, and pedestrians.

PAGE 152

Additions to on-page notes

Enrichment: As you present the *Contexto visual,* you may want to provide further practice by asking personalized questions such as: *¿Vas a la escuela en tren? ¿Vas a la biblioteca en autobús? ¿Te gustan las motos?*

PAGE 154

Photo

Paseo de la Reforma, named after the reform laws of former president Benito Juárez (1858–63; 1867–72), is Mexico City's major east-west artery. This broad, tree-lined boulevard was modeled after the Champs Élysées in Paris. The palm tree shown in the middle of the photo is located on one of the street's many *glorietas* (traffic circles where several streets come together). Also seen are decorations strung above the street during major holidays such as Christmas and Mexico's Independence Day, September 16.

PAGE 160

Additions to on-page notes

Reteach / Review: In preparation for Ex. D, review numbers from 1–100. Review telling time as well if your class needs additional practice.

Reteach / Extra Help: Before assigning Ex. D, you may want to provide further practice with *ir* and *ir a* + infinitive. Have students work in pairs or small groups to make up their own schedules in response to the questions in Ex. D. Students may give their answers orally or in writing.

PAGE 163

Photos

(a) Heavy traffic is a serious problem in many Latin American cities, and Mexico City is no exception. It poses a major transportation difficulty for some workers who spend hours a day commuting in their own cars or standing in line waiting for overcrowded buses. And traffic is a chief contributor to the city's air pollution problem.

Efforts to alleviate traffic congestion include using police officers (like those in the photo) to direct traffic at major intersections during rush hour. And city planners have widened a series of one-way crosstown access routes, called *ejes viales,* and installed computerized traffic signals. The city bus seen in the photo is headed toward the northern Mexico City suburb of La Villa.

(b) Buses, the most popular form of mass transportation in Latin America, are relatively inexpensive and go almost everywhere. In Mexico City first-and second-class buses are available, with the former being safer, making fewer stops, and (in theory) taking only as many as can be seated. Second-class buses have limited seating with a great deal of standing space and often crowd in as many riders as possible.

Realia

These bus tickets are from Buenos Aires, Argentina. Point out that *GRAL PAZ* on the ticket in the middle is an abbreviation for General Paz, a bus line that runs between Avenida General Paz and La Boca, the old port area of Buenos Aires and the city's Italian district.

In Buenos Aires, a bus is called an *ómnibus,* while a minibus is a *colectivo.* Together they provide extensive aboveground transportation; the *Subte* (short for *Subterráneo*) provides underground transportation. Because the streets are clogged with traffic at rush hour, most people prefer to use public transportation.

PAGE 164

Additions to on-page notes

Reteach / Review: Students were introduced to the concept of gender and number on pp. 64–65. Remind them that most nouns ending in *-o* are masculine, in *-a,* feminine. Elicit exceptions *(mapa, día).* Stress the importance of learning the definite article with new nouns.

In preparation for Exs. A and B, you may want to have students redo the *Práctica* on p. 66, using the indefinite, rather than the definite, article.

In addition, turn to pp. 146 and 152, or use transparencies 22 and 23. Ask *¿Qué es esto?* to elicit *Es un / una ____.*

PAGE 166

Photo

The clean, modern *metro* (subway) in Santiago, Chile, provides rapid crosstown transportation. By 1987, two lines (north-south and east-west) had been completed, and others were in the planning stages.

Other Latin American cities that offer subway transportation are Buenos Aires, Caracas, and Mexico City. Buenos Aires' five-line *subte* has been in service for more than 50 years. Caracas completed the first stage of its subway in 1987. Mexico City has Latin America's most extensive subway system, with ten lines and more under construction. *Fichas* (tokens) are used in Buenos Aires, while subway travelers in Santiago, Caracas, and Mexico City must buy printed tickets. Mexico also has a multiple-use ticket good for almost a month on both the subway and city buses.

Realia

This map shows Madrid's subway system, which consists of ten lines and 116 stations. The *metro* (subway) is open from 6:00 A.M. to 1:30 A.M. Proper names on the map refer to stations located on streets and squares named for important historical figures such as painters Francisco Goya (1746–1828) and Diego Velázquez (1599–1660), playwright Tirso de Molina (¿1571?–1648), and Nicaraguan poet Rubén Darío (1867–1916). Madrid's subway stations are also named for places like Plaza Colón (Columbus Square) and Puerta del Sol (Gateway to the Sun).

A symbol marks connections with the national railroad, Renfe.

PAGE 167

Realia

The first tickets are for Madrid's subway and were purchased at the entrance from a machine that marks them with the time and date. The *metro* operates on the honor system. Because inspectors periodically check tickets, passengers are advised to hold on to their tickets until the exit. *Sencillo* indicates a single-trip ticket; multiple-use tickets are also available.

Among the bus tickets from Buenos Aires is one for the General Paz bus, named for General José María Paz (1791–1854).

PAGE 168

Photo
Bicycle tour in Madrid.

Answers to *Repaso*

1. Ella y Ana van juntas al correo. / Él y yo vamos juntos a la farmacia. / Ud. y Víctor van juntos al campo.
2. Va a leer en la biblioteca. / Vamos a trabajar en el banco. / Van a esperar en la estación.
3. Viaja en coche. / Viajas en bicicleta. / Uds. viajan en tren.
4. Buscamos unas chaquetas rojas. Voy a comprar un buen traje (un traje bueno). / Esperan un autobús lento. Vas a tomar el primer tren. / Ud. escucha unos discos viejos. Vamos a buscar una buena cinta (una cinta buena).
5. Esta noche va a ir a pie de la piscina a la fiesta. / Después vamos a llevar la bandera de la escuela a la plaza. / El domingo vas a tomar el metro de la iglesia a casa.

PAGE 169

Answers to *Tema*

1. Pablo y Enrique van juntos al aeropuerto.
2. Van a estudiar en México.
3. Viajan en avión.

4. Pablo escucha unas cintas nuevas. Enrique va a leer un buen libro (un libro bueno).
5. Después van a tomar un taxi del aeropuerto al centro.

PAGE 170
Answers to *Comprueba tu progreso*

A 1. Es un aeropuerto.
   2. Son unas iglesias.
   3. Es un correo.
   4. Es una farmacia.
   5. Son unas piscinas.
   6. Es una biblioteca.

B 1. va   5. van
   2. voy   6. Vas
   3. Va   7. Van
   4. vamos

C 1. Voy al centro.
   2. Van al campo.
   3. Voy al hotel.
   4. Vamos a la ciudad.
   5. Va al hospital.
   6. Van al banco.

D 1. ¿Vas a comprar una falda nueva mañana?
   2. Ellos van a tomar el sol hoy.
   3. Vamos a esquiar en Chile el año próximo.
   4. Él va a escuchar las cintas después.
   5. No voy a cantar en la fiesta la semana próxima.
   6. ¿Ud. va a hablar por teléfono esta noche?

E 1. ¿Quieres ir en coche?
     No, prefiero ir en autobús.
   2. ¿Quieres ir en bicicleta?
     No, prefiero ir en moto.
   3. ¿Quieres ir a pie?
     No, prefiero ir en metro.
   4. ¿Quieres ir en avión?
     No, prefiero ir en barco.
   5. ¿Quieres ir en tren?
     No, prefiero ir en coche.
   6. ¿Quieres ir en moto?
     No, prefiero ir en camión.

F 1. El Sr. Marcos es un buen profesor (un profesor bueno).
   2. El lunes es el primer día de la semana.
   3. Hace mal tiempo hoy.
   4. Es un buen bolígrafo (un bolígrafo bueno).
   5. Es una mala noche (una noche mala), ¿no?
   6. Madrid es una ciudad grande (una gran ciudad).
   7. *Don Quijote* y *Lazarillo de Tormes* son grandes libros españoles (libros españoles grandes).

PAGE 171
Photo
The hand-painted clay car and truck shown in the photograph were made by Candelario Medrano, a potter from Santa Cruz de la Huerta (an area near Guadalajara, Mexico), whose work is well known in that country. The traditional Indian influence that is present in other types of Mexican pottery is not apparent in much of Medrano's work, which is often based on things he sees in today's Mexico. In addition to cars and trucks, Medrano makes diesel buses, churches, kiosks, and bulls out of clay.

ORAL PROFICIENCY TEST
Directed Response
1. Eduardo is walking out the door. Ask him where he's going tonight. *(Eduardo, ¿adónde vas esta noche?)*
2. Tell your parents that you're going to the library because you want to study. *(Voy a la biblioteca porque quiero estudiar.)*
3. Cecilia asks when your exams begin. How would you say that your first exam is tomorrow? *(Mi primer examen es mañana.)*

Picture-Cued Response
4. Using the visuals on p. 146 or transparency 22, point to the house and ask: "¿Es una casa grande o una casa pequeña?" *(Es una casa pequeña.)*

5. Point to the bottom photograph on p. 153 and ask: "¿Cómo van los estudiantes a la escuela cuando hace mal tiempo?" *(Cuando hace mal tiempo, los estudiantes van a la escuela en autobús.)*
6. Point to the photograph on p. 166 and ask: "¿Prefieres viajar en metro o en autobús?" *(Prefiero viajar en metro.)*

Situations

7. You have to mail a letter. Tell your brother where you're going.
   a. Voy al campo.   b. *Voy al correo.*
   c. Voy a pie.
8. Both you and a friend have to go downtown. Suggest that you go together.
   a. *¿Vamos juntos?*   b. ¿Adónde vamos?
   c. ¿Con quién vas?
9. Laura wants everyone to meet after school at the library. Let her know that this is fine with you.
   a. Siempre.   b. *¡Bueno!*
   c. Después.

Real-Life Questions

10. ¿Adónde van a ir tú y tu familia durante el fin de semana?
    (Durante el fin de semana vamos a ir a. . . .)
11. ¿Qué quieres hacer durante el fin de semana?
    (Durante el fin de semana quiero. . . .)
12. ¿Por qué vas al centro?
    (Porque quiero. . . .)
13. ¿Adónde vas después de ir al centro?
    (Después de ir al centro voy. . . .)

ORAL PROFICIENCY TEST   CHAPTERS 1–4

Directed Response

1. You and a friend are looking at her family photo album. Ask her who the people are. *(¿Quiénes son?)*

2. José wants to go across town by bus. Tell him that you'd rather go by subway because it's very fast. *(Prefiero ir en metro porque es muy rápido.)*
3. Elena is going to Argentina. Ask her with whom she's going to travel. *(¿Con quién vas a viajar?)*

Picture-Cued Response

4. Using the visuals on p. 58 or transparency 12, ask questions such as: ¿Cuántos libros hay en la mesa? *(Hay cinco libros en la mesa.)*
5. Point to the photograph on p. 66 and ask: "¿Va a comprar el muchacho unos libros?" *(No, (el muchacho) no va a comprar unos libros.) OR (No, (el muchacho) va a comprar unos discos.)*
6. Point to the photograph on p. 68 and ask: "¿Adónde van los muchachos hoy?" *(Los muchachos van al cine hoy.)*

Situations

7. You and Jacinta see a new girl at your school. Ask Jaime who she is.
   a. ¿Cómo es?   b. ¿Quién eres?
   c. *¿Quién es?*
8. Alicia wants to know today's date. What would she ask to find out?
   a. *¿Cuál es la fecha de hoy?*   b. ¿Qué tiempo hace?   c. ¿Qué hora es?
9. Your teacher asks you a question, and you don't know the answer. What might you say?
   a. ¡Cómo no!   b. *No sé.*
   c. No, nunca.

Real-Life Questions

10. ¿Te gusta ir al centro? *(Sí, me gusta (No, no me gusta) ir al centro.)*
11. ¿Prefieres ir al centro en autobús o a pie?
    (Prefiero ir al centro. . . .)
12. ¿Qué haces cuando vas al centro? *(Cuando voy al centro, . . .)*
13. ¿Vas solo(a) al centro? (Accept *sí, no,* or longer answers.)

LEARNING SPANISH THROUGH ACTION

New prop vocabulary: All vehicles and locations in this chapter. Representations of the locations may be drawn on the chalkboard. With some luck, you might collect toys to represent all of the vehicles. Otherwise, magazine pictures will do.

Other new vocabulary: ¿adónde?, ¿cómo?, antes, después, a pie, en + *vehicle*

New staging vocabulary: ir, correr, brincar

Sample

1. Vayan al banco.
2. Vayan al aeropuerto.
3. Vayan al banco y tóquenlo.
4. Vayan al aeropuerto y señalen el banco.
5. Vayan a la iglesia y tóquenla.
6. Joaquín, ve al banco. Mercedes, ve al aeropuerto.

Teach all of the locations in this manner, and then continue, adding *brincar* and *correr*.

7. Brinquen a la biblioteca.
8. Brinquen al correo.
9. Corran a la biblioteca.
10. Corran a la farmacia y señalen el banco.
11. Brinquen al banco.

Teach all of the locations in this manner, and then teach the names of the vehicles.

12. Toquen el coche.
13. Toquen el barco.
14. Señalen el barco y toquen el coche.

Teach all of the vehicles, and then continue, adding *a pie* and *en* + vehicle.

15. Vayan al hotel en coche. (*You may have the students pantomime driving a car or, if you prefer, they may pick up the vehicle and then walk to the location.*)
16. Vayan a la plaza en avión.
17. Vayan al hospital a pie.

Now add *antes* and *después*.

18. Vayan al banco. Pero antes, señalen la puerta.
19. Vayan a la biblioteca. Pero antes, brinquen a la iglesia.
20. Vayan a la farmacia en autobús. Después, corran al centro.

Questioning is appropriate.

21. Juan, ve a la plaza a pie.
    Q: Juan, ¿adónde vas, a casa o a la plaza?
    A: A la plaza. (*You may very likely hear* al plaza. *Remember that students are processing a lot of information, and most will not be ready to handle details such as* a la *and* al *in spontaneous responses.*)
    Q: ¿Cómo vas, en coche?
    A: No, a pie.

If you find that a student following a difficult command is unable to answer a question, it is beneficial to ask the question to an observer who does not have the added load of understanding, remembering, and carrying out the command.

CAPÍTULO 5

OBJECTIVES

Communication
- to ask and tell where someone or something is
- to ask and give one's address
- to conduct a simple phone conversation
- to ask and tell about a person's physical condition

Grammar
- to express possession with *de*
- to use *ser*
- to use *estar*
- to distinguish between the uses of *ser* and *estar*

Culture
- to present introductory information on two highly advanced Indian civilizations from Latin America—the Incas and the Mayas
- to point out the Incan postal system and the Incas' skill as road builders, architects, and engineers
- to mention the continuing Incan and Mayan influence in Latin America today

SUGGESTED MATERIALS

p. 173 (Prólogo cultural):   wall map showing the Incan Empire (from northern Ecuador to the center of Chile) and the Mayan Empire (southeastern Mexico, Guatemala, and Belize)

pp. 174–175 (Palabras nuevas I):   magazine pictures of buildings and locations

pp. 182–183 (Palabras nuevas II):   magazine pictures showing feelings and conditions (tired, sick, sad, happy, crazy, etc.); paper cups (to be used as telephones)

PAGES 172–173

Photo
View of Machu Picchu in Peru. Located high in the Andes about 70 miles northwest of Cuzco, the ruins of Machu Picchu were not discovered until 1911. The Incas strategically located this city atop the saddle of a remote mountain to provide protection from invaders. Because the Spaniards never arrived there, it is extremely well preserved.

PAGE 177

Photo
A fashionable retreat *(retiro)* for Spanish royalty in the seventeenth century, El Parque del Buen Retiro is Madrid's most beautiful public park. Located right in the center of the city, El Retiro is filled with forests, flower gardens, and dozens of monuments, statues, and fountains. Here *madrileños* enjoy open-air concerts, theater, puppet shows, book fairs, art exhibits, boat rides in the large lake, picnics, festivals, relaxing at the outdoor cafés, and strolling. The map shows the 321-acre park in its entirety. The street bordering its west side is named for Alfonso XII, king of Spain from 1874 to 1885. Along the east side, Avenida de Menéndez Pelayo bears the name of the great Spanish scholar and literary historian, Marcelino Menéndez y Pelayo (1856–1912). Cars are not allowed in the park except on the paved Paseo de Coches.

PAGE 179

Photos
(a) These buildings in Quito, Ecuador, date from the sixteenth and seventeenth centuries. Typical of Spanish colonial architecture are the simple, flat façades, the small entrances, and the second-story balconies. Small shops often occupy the first floor, while the second floor provides living quarters for shop owners or tenants. The interior courtyards are characteristic of colonial houses throughout Latin America.

(b) This Mexican house—which has been built into the hillside—has a scalloped roof, an uncommon design in Mexico, where rooftops are generally flat.

(c) This modern house, located in a suburban area of Quito, is representative of contemporary Andean architecture with its arches, large windows, open patios, and split-level design. Modern Quito encircles the colonial quarter, where one can find grandiose architecture from the past including the huge church and monastery of San Francisco, begun in 1535. Adobe houses line narrow, cobbled streets in much of Quito's colonial quarter.

(d) Mexico City is divided into 16 *delegaciones* (boroughs), which are subdivided into *colonias* (neighborhoods). This photo was taken in the Colonia Nápoles, which is located in the Delegación Benito Juárez in the Z.P., or *zona postal* (postal zone), number 18. Street names in each *colonia* follow a distinct theme; for example, in the Colonia Nápoles, streets are named after U.S. states. The cross street is Avenida de los Insurgentes, which runs the entire length of the city.

  The arrow indicates that Calle Alabama is a one-way street. *Ceda el paso* means "Yield right of way."

Additions to on-page notes

Enrichment: To reinforce new vocabulary and review associated vocabulary from p. 146, have pairs or small groups first make their own maps to show your area or an imaginary neighborhood, and then ask and answer questions based on the maps.

PAGE 180

Photo

The entrance to Old San Juan's most famous landmark, El Morro, also known as the Castle of San Felipe in honor of Philip III, former king of Spain (1578–1621). The word *morro* refers to the hill on which the structure was built at the mouth of San Juan Bay.

PAGE 181

Photo

Because of Puerto Rico's strategic location, the Spaniards used the island as a center for communication, commerce, and defense of the rest of their colonial empire in the Americas. It was, therefore, chosen as the site for the castle-fortress, El Morro. The fort requires continual repair and restoration, which is financed by the governments of Puerto Rico and the U.S.

Additions to on-page notes

Enrichment: Write these unfamiliar words on the board, and ask students to pronounce them: *baño, vago, saber, servir.*

  You may want to use the sentences in *Pronunciación* C for dictation.

PAGE 184

Additions to on-page notes

Enrichment: You may want to assign Ex. A as pair work in class and then have volunteers act out some of the conversations. Ask students to create additional practice items that follow the same pattern.

PAGE 186

Photos

(a) This teenager is talking on the telephone at home in Rota, a picturesque town on the Atlantic coast near Cádiz. In Spain, most households share one phone and, therefore, teens rarely have their own extension or private line. Spanish telephone service is modern; long-distance direct dialing within the country and abroad is simple and efficient. As indicated in the *En otras partes* on p. 183, in Spain it is customary to answer the telephone by saying *Dígame* or *Diga.*

(b) A teenager is seen talking on the phone in Puerto Rico. Although the Puerto Rican phone system has improved substantially over the past 20 years, phones in private homes are quite expensive, and residents often wait months for installation. Party lines are still very common on the island, and many rural areas have no phone service at all. Pay phones are not as prevalent in Puerto Rico as in the U.S. and are not always well maintained.

Realia

The inset lists times (according to the 24-hour clock) when reduced rates are in effect for long–distance calls from Puerto Rico to Latin America (weekdays from 8:00 A.M. to 5:30 P.M. and all day Sunday), to the continental U.S. (weekdays from 6:00 P.M. to 5:00 A.M. and all day Sunday), and to Europe (all day Sunday only). Puerto Rico's area code is 809, and calls can be direct-dialed from the U.S.

PAGE 194

Photo

Many Latin Americans traditionally pause in the late afternoon for a *merienda,* a light snack of biscuits, cookies, or pastries accompanied by tea or coffee. In Chile and Argentina, one frequently hears the expression *Vamos a tomar las once* (Let's take a coffee break). The people in the photo are seated at a café on Avenida 9 de julio, a wide boulevard named for the date in 1816 when Argentina declared its independence from Spain. The one male present will probably pay the bill unless the group has agreed to pay *a la americana* (Dutch treat).

Realia

On Padua Street in Barcelona, El Cafè del Pas (*catalán* for *El Café del Paso*) is advertised as "a new establishment *(local)* very close to you," opening extra early on weekdays *(laborables).* In Spain, *bocadillos* (literally, "little mouthfuls") are sandwiches on sliced hard rolls. *Tapas,* becoming popular in the U.S., are delicious little appetizers of astonishing variety that can be a meal in themselves. The café also offers *meriendas* (afternoon snacks) and *cenas rápidas,* simple dinners served and eaten at the counter.

PAGE 195

Sample dialogues for *¿Qué pasa?*

Pilar and Héctor are going shopping and are discussing how they'll get to the stores and what they're going to buy.

H: ¿Cómo vamos al centro? ¿En metro?
P: Prefiero ir a pie, porque hace buen tiempo.

H: ¡Bueno! ¿Quieres ir a la tienda de ropa o de música?
P: Vamos a la tienda de ropa. Quiero comprar una blusa.

P: ¿Vamos a comprar discos?
H: ¡Cómo no! ¿Dónde está la tienda de música?
P: Está entre el teatro y la farmacia.
H: No está lejos. Vamos a pie.

PAGE 197

Photo

The city of Sevilla, which is located on the Guadalquivir River (shown at the bottom), is the capital of the province of Sevilla. Because the Moors (Moslems who invaded Spain in A.D. 711) inhabited this city for hundreds of years, their influence is apparent in the architectural design of many of its buildings, including some of those seen in the photo.

In the foreground is the Torre del Oro (Tower of Gold), a structure whose name was derived from the color of its tiles, which at the time of its construction had a golden hue. The cathedral of Sevilla's 322-foot Giralda (in the background and to the right) is a tower named for the weather vane that tops it. And just to the left is the cathedral itself, the largest in Spain and the biggest Gothic building in the world.

Additions to on-page notes

Enrichment: You may want to ask students to expand their answers to Ex. B by giving reasons for everyone's feelings, using a phrase beginning with *porque.* For example: *Estamos cansados porque son las once y media de la noche.*

PAGE 198

Realia

(a) This playbill dates from the 1985 season *(temporada)* at the Teatro Colonial, located on Belgrano Avenue in Buenos Aires. The actor's surname (Di Stéfano) is of Italian origin, not unusual in Argentina where more than one-third of the population is of Italian ancestry. The translations of the titles of the two plays are "In case they ask me who I am" and "One man's truth and dream." The playbill also lists other cultural events held at the Teatro Colonial—children's theater, dance performances, concerts, and art exhibits.

(b) This playbill is from the Teatro Español in Madrid, a state-sponsored theater that shows Spanish classics.

Photo

A performance of Russian choreographer Marius Petipa's ballet *Don Quijote* (1869) at the Colón opera house in Buenos Aires. Built in the early twentieth century, it is one of the world's major opera houses and the largest in South America. The Colón hosts international concerts and ballets as well as works by its own ballet troupe, opera company, and symphony orchestra.

PAGE 199
Photo

Built at the beginning of the nineteenth century, the Teatro Español is one of the finest theaters in Madrid. High on its neoclassical façade are inscribed names of great seventeenth-century Spanish playwrights: Lope de Vega, Calderón de la Barca, and Tirso de Molina. The banner announces *La Casa de Bernarda Alba,* a modern classic by Spanish poet and dramatist García Lorca (1898–1936). The theater faces the colorful Plaza Santa Ana, where mimes, musicians, poets, and comedians often perform. Art exhibits, flea markets, and outdoor cafés can also be found there.

PAGE 200
Photos

(a) This fountain, constructed in 1981, is one of the latest additions to Paseo de la Reforma in Mexico City. The fountain's graceful forms are illuminated at night by a series of lights. This fountain stands on a traffic circle that marks the intersection with a major street called Río Mississippi to the north and Calle Sevilla to the south.

(b) The Cibeles Fountain is as symbolic of Madrid as the Eiffel Tower is of Paris. Amid the cascading water stands the eighteenth-century statue of Cibeles (Cybele), the ancient Greek goddess of fertility, riding her chariot. The Fuente de la Cibeles adorns the center of Madrid's vast traffic circle, the Plaza de la Cibeles. In the background, the massive, early-twentieth-century Palacio de Comunicaciones, the capital city's main post office, dominates much of the plaza.

(c) This fountain is in Mexico's Tomás Garrido Canabal Park in Villahermosa, capital of the southern state of Tabasco. The park, which is located within a tropical forest, includes an outdoor archaeological museum with artifacts of the Olmec culture, including the colossal heads from La Venta, the site of Olmec ruins dating back 3,000 years. Some archaeologists regard the ancient Olmecs as the first Indian civilization in Mesoamerica (the areas of Mexico and Central America where high civilizations arose in pre-Columbian times) and the forerunners of the Mayas. The park also includes a small zoo with animals indigenous to the area.

Answers to *Repaso*

1. Aquí está la oficina de Daniel. / Allí están las sillas de la Srta. Márquez. / Allá está el sombrero del policía.
2. La mujer pelirroja es la Sra. Castillo. Es profesora. / La mujer triste es la Srta. Rivera. Es policía. / La mujer loca es la Srta. González. Es vendedora.
3. Miguel es joven, pero hoy está un poco cansado. / Mis gatos son buenos, pero hoy están bastante locos. / Mi novio es inteligente, pero hoy está un poco aburrido.
4. Estás cerca del teatro nuevo. / Está enfrente del almacén grande. / Estamos detrás de la fuente alta.
5. ¿Dónde están ellas? Están entre los muchachos. / ¿Dónde están Uds.? Estamos al lado de Patricio. / ¿Dónde estás? Estoy delante de la bandera.
6. ¿Cuál es ella? Es la mujer morena y antipática, ¿verdad? (¿no?) / ¿Cuál es él? Es el muchacho tonto y aburrido, ¿verdad? (¿no?) / ¿Cuáles son ellas? Son las muchachas simpáticas y bonitas (guapas), ¿verdad? (¿no?)

Answers to *Tema*

1. Aquí está la clase de Pedro.
2. El hombre alto es el Sr. García. Es profesor.
3. Pilar es bonita (guapa), pero hoy está un poco preocupada.
4. Ricardo está al lado del muchacho moreno.
5. ¿Dónde está Pedro? Está a la derecha del profesor.
6. ¿Cuál es él? Es el muchacho alto y guapo, por supuesto.

Answers to *Comprueba tu progreso*

A
1. aburrida
2. a la derecha
3. antipático
4. lejos
5. inteligente
6. delante
7. contenta
8. detrás

B
1. El hotel está entre el restaurante y la farmacia.
2. El café está a la derecha del banco.
3. El restaurante está a la derecha del hotel.
4. El banco está enfrente del hotel.
5. El banco está entre el correo y el café.
6. La iglesia está al lado de la escuela.
7. El autobús está delante de la escuela.
8. La iglesia está enfrente del museo.
9. El teatro está al lado del museo.

C
1. Las botas son de los muchachos.
2. El coche es de las señoritas García.
3. La moto es del policía.
4. La guía telefónica es de Anita y Daniel.
5. El traje de baño es de Elena.
6. Los paraguas son de Rita y Víctor.

D
1. están
2. estoy
3. están
4. está
5. están
6. está
7. estamos
8. están
9. está
10. estás

E
1. está
2. Son
3. es
4. está
5. es
6. están
7. está
8. es

Photo

This seventeenth century *kero* from Cuzco, Peru, represents the head of a jaguar. *Kero* is the Quechua name given to wood cups, which were the most important type of Incan woodwork. At the time of the Incas, *keros* were used for toasting during special ceremonies or for entertaining guests. However, the Incan nobility preferred gold tumblers to *keros*.

The kero shown in the photograph was made by Indian artisans after the fall of the Incan empire to the Spaniards. It has brighter colors and is more imaginative than pre-Hispanic *keros*. In fact, the *keros* became a more sophisticated and innovative art form during the colonial period. Because most of the available gold was in the hands of the Spaniards, the Indian artisans were unable to provide gold tumblers to the surviving Incan aristocrats. The artisans may, therefore, have been trying to make *keros* especially attractive to compensate for the absence of gold tumblers.

ORAL PROFICIENCY TEST

Directed Response

1. There's a dog outside that you've never seen before. How would you ask whose dog it is? (*¿De quién es el perro?*)
2. Eugenio asks you why you enjoy Spanish class so much. Tell him it's because Mr. Aparicio is a good teacher. (*Porque el Sr. Aparicio es un buen profesor (profesor bueno).*)
3. As you're waiting for a bus, someone asks you where the library is. Tell her it's around the corner. (*La biblioteca está a la vuelta de la esquina.*)

Picture-Cued Response

Point to the photograph on p. 194 and ask:
4. ¿Dónde están los señores? (*Los señores están en un café.*)

Point to the photograph on p. 199 and ask:
5. ¿Cómo está la muchacha? (*La muchacha está contenta.*)
6. ¿Y están contentos los dos muchachos también? (*Sí, los dos muchachos están contentos también.*)

Situations

7. You've just found out that Cristina had a skiing accident and broke her arm. What might you say?
   a. *¡Qué lástima!*   b. ¡Por supuesto!
   c. ¡Perdón!
8. Your parents don't want to go out because they're tired. What might they say?
   a. *Estamos cansados.*   b. Estoy cansado.
   c. Están cansadas.
9. You bump into your classmate Arturo on the street. How would you greet him and ask him what's new?
   a. ¡Bueno! ¿Quién es?   b. ¿Aló? ¿Está Arturo?
   c. *¡Hola! ¿Qué pasa?*

Real-Life Questions

10. ¿Cómo estás hoy?
11. ¿Cómo es tu casa?
12. ¿Qué hay al lado de tu casa?
13. ¿Está tu casa cerca o lejos del centro?
14. ¿Cómo vas de la escuela a tu casa?

LEARNING SPANISH THROUGH ACTION

New prop vocabulary: All buildings from this chapter. You will need magazine pictures or drawings of the buildings.

Other new vocabulary: ¿dónde está?, al lado de, cerca de, lejos de, delante de, enfrente de, entre

New staging vocabulary: dibujar

Sample

1. Juana, siéntate. *(on the floor)*
2. Jacobo, siéntate detrás de Juana.
3. María, siéntate detrás de Jacobo.
4. Mario, siéntate entre Jacobo y María.
5. Roberto, siéntate cerca de Jacobo.

Teach all of the locations in this manner, and then teach the names of the buildings.

6. Toquen el museo.
7. Señalen la oficina.
8. Señalen el museo y toquen la oficina.
9. Toquen el estadio.

Teach all of the names of the buildings, and then add *dibujar*.

10. Dibujen un restaurante.
11. Dibujen un café detrás del restaurante.
12. Dibujen un teatro lejos del café.
13. Dibujen un gato enfrente del teatro y un perro a la izquierda del gato.

After they have drawn a scene, use questioning.

14. María, toca el café.
    Q: María, ¿dónde está el café?
    A: Detrás del restaurante.

CAPÍTULO 6

OBJECTIVES

Communication
- to identify rooms and parts of a house
- to express family relationships
- to ask and tell how old a person is

Grammar
- to express what one feels like doing (*tener ganas de* + inf.)
- to express obligation (*tener que* + inf.)
- to use the verb *tener*
- to use the verb *venir*
- to express ownership (possessive adjectives)

Culture
- to point out the cultural significance of the family in the Spanish-speaking world
- to discuss several family traditions

SUGGESTED MATERIALS

p. 206 (Palabras nuevas I): magazine pictures showing the interior and exterior of various types of homes and apartments

p. 212 (Diálogo): wall map of Central America showing the Caribbean island of San Andrés

p. 214 (Palabras nuevas II): magazine cutouts or photos showing family members

PAGES 204–205

Photo
A family dinner in Madrid, Spain. In the Hispanic world, as elsewhere, the nuclear family has been replacing the traditional extended family, especially in urban areas. The family, however, continues to be a person's source of well-being and security, as well as a safety zone, a controllable environment in an uncontrollable world. Loyalty to family and to friends with longstanding family ties is of prime importance.

PAGE 212

Photo
Traditionally, Spanish middle-class families have employed servants to do most of their housework. However, in modern times those families are finding it difficult to pay the higher salaries that servants have come to expect. Moreover, people who formerly would have taken jobs as servants in private homes now have better opportunities in the industrial sector. Consequently, family members, especially young people, frequently help with household chores.

PAGE 213

Photo
The two young women in the photo are doing the dishes after a meal in their parents' home. Young people in Spain often continue to live at home while attending the university or after getting jobs. And they may even continue to live there with their spouses after they get married.

Additions to on-page notes
Reteach / Review: Before students begin work on the *Participación*, you may want to review some classroom-related verbs. To elicit infinitives, ask *¿Qué (no) te gusta hacer en la clase de español?*

Enrichment: Write these unfamiliar words on the board, and ask students to pronounce them: *dedo, desde, cada, ideal, tanto, catarata, pato.* You may want to use the sentences in D for dictation.

PAGE 217

Photos
(a) This Bolivian family (top left) is eating at home in the southwestern city of Oruro. In most of the Spanish-speaking world, lunch is the largest meal of the day and usually consists of several courses. It is not uncommon for middle- and upper-class families to employ one or more

maids, who often have their own living quarters within the house.

(b) The man in the photo (top right) is helping his grandchildren with their drawings. In Hispanic communities in the U.S., as in Spanish-speaking countries, it is not unusual to find three generations living together under the same roof. Widowed parents often live with their married children and take an active role in the management of the household.

(c) This family picnic (center) takes place in a park in Bogotá. Balloon sellers in parks and on the streets are a common sight in many South American cities.

(d) This family (bottom) relaxes on their patio in the coastal city of Piriápolis in southern Uruguay. Family gatherings still play an important role in the Spanish-speaking world. Small children, teens, parents, grandparents, as well as aunts, uncles, and cousins, traditionally get together for lunch on Sunday. After the meal, family members often remain at the table to chat or play a game. This custom (known as *la sobremesa*), however, seems to be gradually disappearing in the large cities.

PAGE 219

Photo

Children in the Plaza de España in Sevilla, Spain. This semicircular plaza houses the enormous crescent-shaped Palacio Central, one of the buildings constructed for the Spanish-American Exposition held in the city in 1929–30. Near the building is a lagoon, with five arched, tiled bridges leading to it. The area is a popular meeting place for young *sevillanos*.

PAGE 225

Photo

Cyclists in Puerto Rico.

PAGE 226

Additions to on-page notes

Notes: These cognates and loanwords are not glossed: *celebrar,* to celebrate; *video,* video recorder.

Elicit the familiar verb related to *viaje (viajar),* and ask students to guess the meaning of *viaje* (trip).

Point out that *estar + guapa* means "to look pretty."

PAGE 227

Photo

In most of the Spanish-speaking world, a girl's fifteenth birthday is a major turning point in her life because she is formally presented to society. *Los quince años,* a big occasion that combines elements of the U.S. sweet-sixteen and coming-out parties, is usually celebrated with a special church service and a dinner dance. The society pages in local newspapers devote as much space to *quince años* parties as to engagements *(compromisos)* and weddings *(bodas).*

This photo shows the guest of honor and her friends pulling ribbons from the birthday cake. A ring is tied to one of the ribbons, and, according to tradition, the girl who pulls that special ribbon will be the first to get married. It is also customary for the *quinceañera* to have the first dance with her father. The greeting card reads "To my dear niece on her birthday."

PAGE 228

Additions to on-page notes

Reteach / Review: Remind students that they have been using possessive adjectives since the first week of class when they learned the expressions *¿Cómo se escribe tu nombre? (En camino B)* and *Mi cumpleaños es el ___ (En camino C).*

PAGE 229

Additions to on-page notes

Notes: In conjunction with Ex. A, remind students that some examples will require plural forms of verbs and possessive adjectives.

PAGE 232

Photo

Three Spanish sisters share a snack while one talks on the telephone. Siblings in Spanish-speaking countries are generally very close and tend to spend a lot of time together. The girls in large families often share one bedroom, and the boys share another.

Answers to *Repaso*

1. Mañana es el examen de español. Él y su prima van a estudiar en el comedor. / Hoy es el partido de béisbol. Mis amigos(as) y yo vamos a practicar en el parque. / Mañana es (la fiesta de) los quince años. Ella y sus padres van a comer en el jardín.
2. Nuestros padres vienen al centro a las cinco. / Su hermana viene a la escuela a las siete y media. / Tus tíos vienen al hotel a las dos.
3. Tengo ganas de leer en la biblioteca. / Tenemos ganas de trabajar en el garaje. / ¿Tienes ganas de cantar en la fiesta?
4. Pero no puedo hablar ahora. Tengo que comer. / Pero no puedes escuchar ahora. Tenemos que practicar. / Pero no puedo esperar ahora. Tengo que cocinar.

PAGE 233

Answers to *Tema*

1. Hoy es el cumpleaños de Silvia. Ella y sus amigos van a bailar en el patio.
2. Sus amigos vienen a la fiesta a las siete.
3. Pedro tiene ganas de nadar en la piscina.
4. Pero no puedo nadar ahora. Tengo que bailar.

PAGE 234

Answers to *Comprueba tu progreso*

A
1. abuelos
2. prima
3. madre
4. sobrinos
5. tías
6. hermano

B
1. Mi primo y yo tenemos que ayudar en casa.
2. Clara tiene que limpiar la cocina.
3. Ricardo y Lourdes tienen que lavar la ropa sucia.
4. Mi hermanito tiene que dar de comer al perro.
5. Ud. tiene que cocinar.
6. Tenemos que practicar béisbol.
7. Tengo que viajar a Chicago.
8. Héctor y tú tienen que cuidar a los niños.

C
1. No, no tengo jardín.
2. No, no tienen garaje.
3. No, no tengo oficina.
4. No, no tienes (tiene) clase a las dos.
5. No, no tenemos (tienen) examen hoy.
6. No, no tenemos apartamento.
7. No, no tiene barco.

D
1. No, no tienen ganas de cuidar a los niños.
2. No, no tengo ganas de cantar en la iglesia.
3. No, no tiene ganas de ayudar en casa.
4. No, no tenemos ganas de estudiar en la biblioteca.
5. No, no tienen ganas de limpiar la estufa.
6. No, no tengo ganas de lavar el coche.

E
1. Tiene
2. Vienes
3. tenemos
4. venimos
5. vienen
6. tiene
7. tengo

F
1. Sí, es mi tía.
2. Sí, son sus sobrinos.
3. Sí, buscamos nuestros suéteres.
4. Sí, tengo tus cuadernos.
5. Sí, es su abuela.
6. Sí, tiene mis guantes.
7. Sí, tengo su mapa.
8. Sí, tengo su dirección.

G   Answers will vary.

PAGE 235

Photo
This *retablo,* a group of figurines that represents a scene or event, is from Ayacucho, Peru, and was made from bread dough and wood. The first *retablos* originated during colonial times, when Spanish priests attempted to teach the Christian doctrine to the Indians, who would then make figurines to bring to church as gifts. The *retablo* in the photograph has no religious implications, but was made solely for decorative purposes. It seems to represent a celebration of some kind, with men and women playing various typical instruments.

ORAL PROFICIENCY TEST

Directed Response

1. Your friends are going to the movies tonight, and they want you to go. Tell them you can't go to the movies because you have to baby-sit. *(No puedo ir al cine porque tengo que cuidar a los niños.)*
2. Everyone in your family is excited because your aunt Rosa is arriving today. Ask what time your aunt is coming. *(¿A qué hora viene tía Rosa?)*
3. Paul tells you he's going to Joanne's birthday party today. Ask Paul how old she is. *(¿Cuántos años tiene?)*

Picture-Cued Response

Using the visual on p. 206 or transparency 29, ask questions such as:

4. ¿En qué piso está el apartamento? *(Está en el tercer piso.)*
5. ¿Cuántos dormitorios tiene el apartamento? *(Tiene un dormitorio.)* ¿Y baños? *(Tiene un baño.)*
6. ¿Está el comedor detrás de la sala? *(No, está a la izquierda de la sala. OR No, está detrás de la cocina.)*

Situations

7. Your new friend asks if you have any brothers or sisters. Since you don't, what might you say?
   a. Soy una hija buena.   b. *No, soy hijo(a) único(a).*   c. No, tengo una hermana.
8. Sylvia is leaving on a trip, and she can't find her jacket. You see it on the table. What might you say to her?
   a. Mi chaqueta está en la mesa.   b. Nuestra chaqueta está en el comedor.   c. *Tu chaqueta está aquí.*

Real-Life Questions

9. ¿Cuántos años tienes? ¿Tienes hermanos? ¿Cuántos años tienen?
10. ¿Tienes que limpiar tu dormitorio?
11. ¿Vienen tus abuelos a tu casa? ¿Vienen a menudo?
12. ¿Qué tienes ganas de hacer esta noche?

LEARNING SPANISH THROUGH ACTION

LESSON 1

New prop vocabulary: This is a review of the days of the week, the months, and the seasons. Post the months from a calendar as you did in the second lesson of *En camino C.*

Other new vocabulary: primero, segundo, tercero.

New staging vocabulary: none

Review the second lesson of *En camino C,* and then continue, using narration and questioning. Be sure to model until *primero, segundo,* and *tercero* have been learned.

Sample

1. Toca el primer mes del año.
   Q: ¿Qué mes es?
   A: Enero.
2. Sí, enero es el primer mes del año.
3. Toca el segundo mes del año.
   Q: ¿Es marzo?
   A: No, es febrero.
4. Ah, sí. Tienes razón. Marzo es el tercer mes del año, y febrero es el segundo.
5. Toca el primer mes de verano.
   Q: ¿Qué mes es?
   A: Es junio.

Teacher Notes   **T75**

6. Señala el tercer día de junio.
   Q: ¿Qué día es?
   A: Es jueves.
   Q: Sí, ¿y cuál es la fecha?
   A: Es el tres de junio.

You may also have them point out or touch the first, second, or third week of each month.

7. Señala la tercera semana del primer mes del año.

LESSON 2

New prop vocabulary: Family members. Draw two family trees on the chalkboard, faces only. Label them with names and ages. Be sure to include an only child in each family tree. This lesson works best if done with one student at a time.

Other new vocabulary: encima de, debajo de, hijo(a) único(a), persona, ¿quién es?, ¿cuántos años tiene?

New staging vocabulary: none

Sample
1. Señala a Antonio.
2. Antonio es el hijo de Roberto.
3. Señala a Roberto.
4. Roberto es el padre de Antonio y Anita.
5. Toca al hijo de Roberto.
6. Toca a la hija de Roberto.
7. Toca al padre de Antonio y Anita.

Teach all of the family members in this manner, and then continue.

8. Toca al tío de Antonio.
   Q: ¿Quién es?
   A: Es Rodolfo.
9. Sí, y Rodolfo es hijo único.
10. Toca al hermano de Rodolfo. (*This is impossible. The student will look puzzled.*)
11. Rodolfo no tiene hermano. Es hijo único.
12. Señala al hijo único de Mario.

You may now add *encima de, debajo de,* and *¿cuántos años tiene?*

13. Toca a la persona que está encima de Pablo.
    Q: ¿Quién es?
    A: Es María.
14. Toca a la muchacha que está debajo de María.
    Q: ¿Quién es?
    A: Es Carmen.
    Q: ¿Es la sobrina de María?
    A: No, es la hija de María.
    Q: ¿Cuántos años tiene Carmen, seis o siete?
    A: Siete.
    Q: Y María, ¿cuántos años tiene?
    A: Treinta.

The LSTA lesson from Capítulo 4 may be adapted to teach the rooms of the house.

CAPÍTULO 7

OBJECTIVES

Communication
- to identify school courses

Grammar
- to use regular *-er* and *-ir* verbs
- to use the personal *a*
- to use prepositions and prepositional pronouns

Culture
- to compare and contrast the school systems in Latin America and the U.S.

SUGGESTED MATERIALS

pp. 246–247 (Palabras nuevas II):   textbooks that your school uses for other classes

PAGES 236–237

Photo
Students at John F. Kennedy High School in Buenos Aires. Many Latin Americans admired John F. Kennedy, and numerous schools and public places throughout the region have been named after the former U.S. President.

There is often a more formal, structured atmosphere in high schools in Spanish-speaking countries than in those in the U.S. Many students are required to wear uniforms, and boys and girls still frequently attend separate schools.

PAGE 239

Additions to on-page notes
Enrichment: After presenting the *Contexto visual,* have students write two or three sentences about one of the pictures on p. 239. Then have volunteers read their sentences. You may want to check students' papers for spelling, capitalization, and punctuation.

PAGE 241

Photo
These students are attending a high school English-as-a-Foreign-Language (EFL) class in Málaga, Spain. English has surpassed French as the most important second language in Spain, and English, rather than French, is now mandatory in high school. In Spain, fewer high school students go to universities than in the U.S., but college graduates there enjoy greater prestige and more opportunities. There are fewer universities than in the U.S., and most are government operated. Admission is highly selective and competitive, and entrance exams are extremely difficult.

Additions to on-page notes
Reteach / Extra Help: Reinforce the use and omission of the definite article with names of languages by asking these questions: *¿Hablas francés? ¿Te gusta estudiar español? ¿Qué hablas ahora? Y en casa, ¿hablan Uds. en inglés o en español? ¿Quién enseña español? ¿Quiénes estudian español? ¿Tenemos un examen de español mañana?* (Answers will vary.)

PAGE 244

Photo
Students at this coeducational secondary school in Buenos Aires volunteer to respond to their teacher's questions. Argentina boasts one of the highest secondary school enrollments in all of Latin America. A large percentage of secondary school students study in the traditional *secundaria,* where they follow a *bachillerato* (college preparatory), teacher-training, or commercial curriculum. And a smaller percentage study in technical schools for careers in agriculture, industry, or health-care professions.

PAGE 245

Photo
Tourism is a major industry in Spain. It is also a

specialized career, and the government operates college-level tourism schools, called *Escuelas de Hostelería y Turismo.* In the photo, a teacher in one of these schools is giving a course in English, which has become the most important foreign language in the tourism industry. Multilingual travel brochures, guide books, and menus are usually printed with the Spanish version first, followed by English, French, German, and Italian, respectively.

Additions to on-page notes
Reteach / Extra Help: If your class finds the *Participación* difficult, ask volunteers to offer possible excuses for "the student" and suggestions for "the teacher."

PAGE 249
Photo
Computer science classes, like the one in the photo, are extremely popular in large Spanish cities like Barcelona and Madrid due to the increasing demand for people with skills in this area.

Realia
In Barcelona, as this advertisement says, there is a growing demand for employees in the field of *la palabra informática* (the computerized word, or word processing). The ad promotes an accredited course and offers a gift upon completion, a complete computer kit called "the briefcase of the future." As stated on the coupon, the information is free *(gratis).*

PAGE 252
Drawings
The drawings on this page and page 253 are adaptations of illustrations by French designer and illustrator Gustave Doré (1832–1883). They depict episodes from *Aventuras del ingenioso hidalgo Don Quijote de la Mancha,* a novel by Spanish writer Miguel de Cervantes (1547–1616). The novel, which is considered Cervantes's masterpiece, relates the adventures of the chivalrous and idealistic protagonist Don Quijote and his faithful sidekick, Sancho Panza.

Additions to on-page notes
Enrichment: To reinforce the present-tense forms of *-er* and *-ir* verbs, ask these questions. Point to yourself, a girl, a boy, and so on, changing verb forms according to the form you are eliciting. *¿Aprendes muchas palabras nuevas? ¿Comes mucho por la mañana? ¿Lees el periódico todos los días? ¿Comprendes el capítulo 7? ¿Escribes poemas? ¿Dónde vives? ¿Recibes muchas cartas? ¿Asistes a la escuela todos los días?*

PAGE 255
Photo
A chemistry teacher helps a student carry out an experiment at the Anglo-American high school in Oruro, a mining center located high in the Andes Mountains. At this private coeducational school, most classes are taught in English rather than Spanish so that students can achieve fluency in this foreign language. Students who attend such schools are usually from the middle or upper classes and pay tuition.

PAGE 256
Photo
A Spanish student studies verb forms in an English-language class in Málaga, Spain.

Realia
C.E.E. Idiomas is a language school in Madrid, located on Calle Infantas. The school offers classes in English, French, German, and Spanish—the latter, of course, for foreigners. For classes that meet for one hour daily, the school charges 3,800 pesetas per month. For an intensive two-hour-a-day course during May and June, tuition is 7,000 pesetas per month.

PAGE 261
Sample dialogues for *¿Qué pasa?*
Clara and Alberto are talking about how well prepared they are, what they have to review, and how they think they're going to do on an upcoming exam.
C: Quiero sacar una buena nota en la prueba.
A: Yo también. Pero estoy flojo en matemáticas.

C: Yo estoy bastante fuerte en matemáticas. ¿Quieres estudiar conmigo?

A: ¡Cómo no! Entonces voy a salir muy bien en la prueba.

C: ¿Qué tenemos que aprender para la prueba?

A: Tenemos que repasar dos capítulos del libro.

C: ¡Uf! No estoy preparada. ¿Y tú?

A: Yo tampoco. Vamos a estudiar juntos.

PAGE 263

Photo

Students relax between classes at this private school located in Miraflores, a modern suburb of Lima, Peru. Private schools in Miraflores tend to be small, with an average enrollment of about 600 students.

PAGE 265

Photo

Students shown here are studying in the library at the Universidad Católica de Lima. Catholic universities in Peru tend to be rather conservative, since the Church exerts considerable influence over course content. Ninety percent of the students attending Catholic universities live at home, partly because many of their families live in the main cities where those universities are located.

PAGE 266

Photo

Students enjoy free time between classes at the University of Puerto Rico's main campus. The sign lists the building's hours of operation on holidays (8:00 A.M. to 4:30 P.M.) and Sundays (10:00 A.M. to 6:00 P.M.).

Puerto Rico's university system more closely resembles that of the continental U.S. than that of other Spanish-speaking countries. Consequently, several Spanish words related to higher education are used differently on the island. *Colegio* refers to a four-year college, not to a high school; *bachillerato* is a college, rather than a high school, degree; and *dormitorio* is the term for a student dorm.

Answers to *Repaso*

1. Asisto a una escuela bilingüe. Espero la primera prueba (el primer examen). / Leemos una lección fácil. Estudio las próximas páginas. / Federico y yo escribimos un poema largo. Usamos la pequeña computadora.

2. Me gustan las lecciones de álgebra. ¿A ti te gusta el álgebra también? / Me gusta la clase de física. ¿A ti te gustan las ciencias también? / Me gusta el laboratorio de química. ¿A ti te gusta la química también?

3. Sí, cuando está ausente. Está bastante floja en geometría. / Sí, cuando estoy presente. Estoy muy fuerte en francés. / Sí, cuando está cansado. Está muy flojo en educación física.

4. Miramos nuestros dibujos, pero a veces no miramos al profesor. / Comprendemos sus preguntas, pero a veces no comprendemos a los profesores. / Busco mis notas, pero nunca busco a las profesoras.

5. ¿Quieres recibir una carta de él? ¡Ojalá! / ¿Puedo terminar la lección con Uds.? ¿Por qué no? / ¿Quieres mirar el horario conmigo? ¡Por supuesto! (¡Cómo no!)

PAGE 267

Answers to *Tema*

1. Marta y Ana asisten a un colegio (a una escuela secundaria) enorme. Esperan la próxima clase.

2. Me gusta la clase de matemáticas. ¿A ti te gustan las matemáticas también?

3. Sí, cuando estoy preparada. Estoy bastante floja en matemáticas.

4. Leo mis lecciones, pero a veces no comprendo al profesor.

5. ¿Quieres repasar el capítulo conmigo? ¡Por supuesto! (¡Cómo no!)

PAGE 268

Answers to *Comprueba tu progreso*

A 1. Lucía tiene un ocho en álgebra.
2. Agustín tiene un cinco en geometría.
3. César tiene un seis en educación física.
4. Luz tiene un tres en arte.

5. Diana tiene un diez en francés.
6. Raimundo tiene un cuatro en biología.
7. Ernesto tiene un siete en historia.
8. Olga tiene un cinco en química.
9. Héctor tiene un cuatro en computadoras.

B 1. Susana lee un horario.
2. El Sr. Rodríguez recibe una carta.
3. Marta borra la respuesta.
4. La Sra. Gómez enseña ciencias.
5. Escribo las respuestas.
6. Tenemos pruebas en mi clase de álgebra todas las semanas.
7. Carlos y Silvia repasan la lección.

C 1. vivimos   6. leen
2. Aprendes   7. asisto
3. reciben   8. escribe
4. comprenden   9. comprendemos
5. come

D 1. ¿Llamas a tu hermana?
5. ¿A quién buscas en la cocina?
6. Raquel va a esperar a Diego.
7. Él busca a su profesor de francés.

E 1. Sí, vengo contigo (con Ud.).
2. Sí, hablamos de ti (de Ud.).
3. Sí, (el refrigerador) es para Uds. (para nosotros).
4. Sí, (Enrique) trabaja para mí.
5. Sí, (los poemas) son para ella.
6. Sí, (ellos) viajan conmigo.
7. Sí, vivo cerca de ella.
8. Sí, (María) viene después de él.

PAGE 269

Photo

This clay figurine from Acatlán, Mexico, represents a cricket with very large antennae. The figurine was made by Herón Martínez, one of the most famous potters in Mexico. Martínez, who started his career making flowerpots and jars, now produces beautiful sculptures of real and imaginary animals. He also makes animal pyramids and elaborate candelabra decorated with figures of fantastic creatures. Through his work, which is called ''figural'' pottery by some experts, Martínez attempts to show things as he sees them, rather than as they are. His pottery shows his extraordinary skill as an artisan and is exhibited all over Mexico.

ORAL PROFICIENCY TEST

Directed Response

1. Roberto seems to be searching for someone in the crowd. Ask him whom he's looking for. *(¿A quién buscas?)*
2. You see your friend wrapping a shirt. Ask her whom the shirt is for. *(¿Para quién es la camisa?)*
3. Your teacher asks you a question about a poem you've just read. How would you say that you don't understand the poem? *(No comprendo el poema.)*

Picture-Cued Response

4. Using the visual on p. 249, point to the computer and ask: ''¿Qué quieres aprender a usar?'' *(Quiero aprender a usar la computadora.)*
5. Point to the photograph on p. 255 and ask: ''¿A qué clase asisten los alumnos?'' *(Los alumnos asisten a la clase de química.)*

Situations

6. Your father is walking out the door and you want to go with him. What would you say to him?
   a. Quiero ir conmigo.   b. *Quiero ir contigo.*
   c. Quiero ir con él.
7. Your aunt Marta asks whether you're a good student. What might you say?
   a. Sí, estoy floja en todo.   b. *Sí, saco buenas notas.*   c. Sí, estoy ocupada por la tarde.
8. Your parents just bought a new car, and Ana asks if they'll allow you to drive it. Tell her you hope so.
   a. *¡Ojalá!*   b. ¡Por supuesto!   c. ¡Qué suerte!

9. ¿Recibes cartas de tus primos?
10. ¿Siempre estás preparado(a) para los exámenes?

11. ¿A ti te gusta llamar a los amigos por la noche?
12. ¿Quién come contigo por la mañana?

LEARNING SPANISH THROUGH ACTION

New prop vocabulary: School subjects. You will need one textbook for each of the subjects taught in this chapter. Arrange the books on a table.

Other new vocabulary: antes, después

New staging vocabulary: none

Sample

1. Toquen el libro de álgebra.
2. Toquen el libro de biología.
3. Pongan el libro de álgebra debajo del libro de biología.
4. Abran el libro de francés.
5. Cierren el libro de francés.
6. Toquen los libros de matemáticas. *(They should touch both the algebra and the geometry books. The same would apply to science books.)*

Teach all of the subjects in this manner, and then add *antes* and *después.*

7. Toquen el libro de historia, pero antes toquen el libro de arte.
8. Toquen el libro de inglés, y después señalen el libro de química.
9. Pongan el libro de historia sobre la silla, pero antes señalen el libro de francés. Y después, abran el libro de geometría.

Dibujar and *borrar* may be used to review any vocabulary that can be drawn. See the LSTA lesson for Capítulo 2.

Escribir and *borrar* may be used to review writing skills.

CAPÍTULO 8

OBJECTIVES

Communication
- to identify foods
- to count from 100 to 1,000

Grammar
- to use the verb *hacer*
- to use the verb *poner*
- to use the verb *salir*
- to use direct object pronouns *(lo, la, los, las)*
- to use direct object pronouns with infinitives

Culture
- to note foods that originated in Latin America
- to discuss the importance of certain foods throughout the world

SUGGESTED MATERIALS

p. 271 (Prólogo cultural):   wall map(s) showing Spain, the West Indies, Mexico, and Peru

pp. 272–273 (Palabras nuevas I):   magazine pictures and / or real objects to illustrate food-related vocabulary

p. 277 (Actividad):   alphabet cards

p. 280 (Palabras nuevas II):   magazine pictures and / or real objects to reinforce names of vegetables, meat, and poultry

PAGES 270–271

Photo
View of Mercado Libertad in Guadalajara, México. This is a huge market in which many different types of products are sold, including food, regional costumes, pottery, paper flowers, and live birds.

Guadalajara, Mexico's second largest city, is the center for several of the country's most famous traditions, including *mariachis, charreadas* (Mexican rodeos), and the popular folk dance *jarabe tapatío.*

PAGE 272

Additions to on-page notes
If students ask: Other related words you may want to present: *las flores,* flowers; *la jarra,* pitcher; *la azucarera,* sugar bowl; *la cafetera,* coffeepot; *la tetera,* teapot / teakettle; *el huevo frito,* fried egg; *los huevos revueltos,* scrambled eggs.

Notes: In conjunction with transparency 36, you may want to use real objects or magazine pictures to reinforce the vocabulary presented in the *Contexto visual.*

PAGE 274

Photo
These customers are at the checkout counter of a modern supermarket *(supermercado)* in Caracas, Venezuela. Supermarkets that offer convenient one-stop shopping are becoming increasingly popular throughout Latin America, especially in large cities. Besides food, some supermarkets sell other items, including records, hardware, and even clothing. On the right is a basket filled with fresh and packaged food products. Although canned and packaged foods are common, frozen selections are very limited.

PAGE 277

Additions to on-page notes
Notes: You may want to assign letters for the *Actividad.* Refer to p.161 for additional suggestions.

PAGE 279

Photo
Four generations help to prepare dinner in Torremolinos, Spain.

Additions to on-page notes

Notes: You may want students to prepare the *Participación* as a written homework assignment. Have volunteers perform their dialogues for the class.

Enrichment: Write these unfamiliar words on the board, and ask students to pronounce them: *araña, montaña, pestaña, acompaña.* You may want to use the sentences in *Pronunciación* for dictation.

PAGE 284

Photos

(a) An ad for fresh vegetables *(verduras frescas)* appears at a store in Bogotá. Despite the growing number of modern supermarkets in Latin America, many *bogotanos* and other city dwellers buy staples at the supermarket and continue to rely on small, specialized neighborhood shops for meat, produce, bread, and dairy products.

(b) The meat department at the supermarket in Caracas. The capital of Venezuela is a contemporary, cosmopolitan city. Construction of new buildings is relatively constant, with many of the city's colonial structures, historical monuments, museums, and old churches being replaced by office buildings and enormous retail centers.

Additions to on-page notes

Reteach / Extra Help: In connection with Ex. C, have students work in pairs to create a menu for a full day. Tell them to decide what to serve at each meal and then prepare a shopping list.

PAGE 285

Photo

A pastry shop *(pastelería)* in Madrid displays a variety of tempting pastries marked with prices in pesetas. On the right are pastries that we call "elephant ears." They are essentially the same in many countries but have different names. In Spain they are called *palmeras,* or palm leaves, because of their shape. In some Latin American countries they are called *milhojas* because they crumble into thousands of little flakes.

PAGE 286

Photos

(a) An English sign is displayed at this combination bookstore and stationery shop (top) in southern Spain to attract foreign customers who don't read Spanish. Nearby is a *crepería-heladería,* a small café that serves crepes *(crepas)* and ice cream. In Spain, *crepas* are small, very thin French-style pancakes that are enjoyed as snacks. The name of the café, Pequeña Bretaña, or "Little Britain," refers to the neighboring "Big Rock" (of Gibraltar), which is governed by Great Britain *(Gran Bretaña).*

(b) This *carnicería,* or butcher shop (center), is in Union City, New Jersey. In U.S. cities and towns with large Hispanic populations, butcher shops cater to their Spanish-speaking clientele with such specialty products as *chorizo,* Spanish sausage; *morcilla,* blood sausage; and *mondongo,* tripe.

(c) This *peluquería,* or hairstyling salon (bottom left), is named *Canadá* because it is located next door to the Hotel Canadá. Barber shops *(barberías)* usually cater to men and boys only. In many Latin American countries, *peluquerías* are shops for male customers only, while *salones de belleza* are for female customers. However, in Spain *peluquerías* are for male and female customers.

(d) At this neighborhood fruit store *(frutería)* in the old section of Madrid (bottom right), people typically enjoy chatting about a variety of topics, including the prices and quality of the fruit. A varied selection of fresh fruits arrives in Madrid every day, with oranges and lemons from Valencia, strawberries from nearby Aranjuez or from Navarra in the north, and bananas from the Canary Islands off the coast of Africa being the most plentiful.

PAGE 288

Photo

A family enjoys a picnic in Mexico City's Chapultepec Park. Picnics are popular warm-weather weekend activities in Latin America. *Chapultepec* (from the *nahuatl* words meaning "grasshopper hill") is the largest and most important park in Mexico City.

PAGE 289

Additions to on-page notes

Reteach / Review: After students do Ex. B in pairs, you may want to provide practice with negative sentences. Ask questions to elicit negative responses: *¿Sales de la casa a las tres de la mañana? ¿Salen Uds. de la biblioteca a la medianoche? ¿Salimos de la escuela a las diez de la noche?*

Enrichment: In connection with Ex. C, have students write five sentences that include the verb *poner.* Ask them to bring real objects or magazine cutouts to class to illustrate their sentences.

PAGE 290

Photos
(a) These workers are harvesting cacao beans on a cocoa plantation in Villahermosa, which is located in southern Mexico. The beans are first removed from melonlike pods and then covered for several days to ferment. Once fermented, the cacao beans are dried, shelled, roasted, blended, and, finally, ground. Then the cacao is processed as cocoa butter, powdered cocoa, and sweet, bitter, bittersweet, and milk chocolate. "Cocoa" is a variant spelling of "cacao."
(b) The women in the photo are making candy at the Fenoglio chocolate factory in Bariloche, a resort city located in the region of Patagonia in southern Argentina. Bariloche—often called the Switzerland of South America—is famous for its delicious chocolate as well as for excellent skiing conditions.

Additions to on-page notes
Reteach / Review: After students do Ex. D, you may want to have them write about their own families, using the paragraph in Ex. D as a model.

PAGE 291

Photos
(a) This photograph of *churros* and cacao seeds could symbolize the blending of the Spanish and Aztec cultures. *Churros* have been a favorite pastry in Spain for centuries. And cacao is a Central American seed used to make *chocolate,* a drink of the Aztec aristocrats that was unknown to Europeans until Hernán Cortés's expedition brought it from Mexico.

Churros and *chocolate* have now become inseparable not only in Spain and Mexico, but in many other countries in the Spanish-speaking world. *Churros* are available in different varieties. For instance, in Spain and Mexico *churros* look like thin, grooved cylinders that are sometimes shaped into loops, while in Bolivia *churros* are pastries that resemble small but thick doughnuts with very small holes in the middle.
(b) *Churrerías* are *churro* bakeries and also gathering places for enjoying *chocolate con churros* in the late afternoon or after a night on the town. In Madrid some *churrerías* open as early as 5:00 A.M. to cater to early risers.

PAGE 292

Photo
The man in the photo is reading a newspaper in Lima, Peru. The headline refers to problems in the foreign currency markets.

PAGES 294–295

Photos
Various types of regional clothing from Latin America that are seen in this photo include an Andean sweater made from llama wool; a brightly colored *huipil* (a long, loose blouse from Guatemala); a long Mexican dress; and a modern-style sweater.

PAGE 297

Photo
In Spain's Basque region *(el País Vasco),* the old tradition of private cooking clubs for men only is still very much alive. Members get together to cook, dine, and socialize. Here in San Sebastián, a seaport resort city on the northern coast, two *vascos* are preparing regional dishes that they will later share with fellow club members.

Photos

(a) In Málaga, as in many European cities that enjoy a mild climate, motor scooters are a popular means of transportation for delivering various kinds of fresh food products. These scooters are a fast and economical replacement for trucks, when the quantities being delivered are small. Here a *malagueño* maneuvers his *moto* through the early morning traffic to deliver fresh bread, still warm from the ovens of the bakery where he works. His primary customers are local restaurants, cafés, *bares,* and *tabernas.*

(b) Rolls *(bolillos)* and other kinds of breads are baked fresh daily at the neighborhood bakery *(panadería).* Bakeries also sell a wide selection of sweet rolls *(pan dulce)* such as *conchas* (the bread with the crisscross topping), which are popular at breakfast or with afternoon coffee. Cakes and more elaborate baked goods are available at pastry shops *(pastelerías).*

Additions to on-page notes

Notes: Review of: 1. adverbs of past time / *fui* / *fuiste* / *fue* / *para* + infinitive 2. adverbs of frequency / *hacer* / *para* + noun 3. *poner* / prepositions 4. *hacer* / *¿quién(es)?* / direct object pronouns 5. *-ar* verbs / personal *a* / *tener que* / infinitive + direct object pronoun / *salir* / definite article with days of the week / *por la mañana* / *tarde* / *noche*

Answers to *Repaso*

1. Anoche fui al supermercado para comprar manzanas y plátanos. / Ayer por la tarde fuiste al mercado para comprar huevos y maíz. / El lunes Cecilia fue a la panadería para comprar pan.
2. A veces la Sra. Ochoa cocina pavo para la cena. / Los fines de semana hacemos sandwiches para el almuerzo. / Los domingos mis padres hacen té para el desayuno.
3. Uds. ponen las servilletas al lado de los vasos. / Ponemos los platillos debajo de las tazas. / Ponen los cuchillos a la derecha de los platos.
4. ¿Quién hace (Quiénes hacen) el pan? Lo hacemos, por supuesto. / ¿Quién quita los platos? Yo los quito, por supuesto. / ¿Quién bebe (Quiénes beben) el jugo? Lo bebemos, por supuesto.
5. Buscamos a nuestras amigas. Tenemos que buscarlas porque siempre salen con nosotros(as) los domingos por la tarde. / Llamo a mi amiga. Tengo que llamarla porque salimos contigo el sábado por la mañana. / Llaman a Sonia y Rodolfo. Tienen que llamarlos porque salen con ellos el jueves por la noche.

Answers to *Tema*

1. Ayer por la tarde fui al mercado para comprar zanahorias y papas.
2. Hoy mi hermano y yo cocinamos pollo para la cena.
3. Pongo el mantel sobre la mesa.
4. ¿Quién pone la mesa? Juanito la pone, por supuesto.
5. Esperamos a papá. Tenemos que esperarlo porque siempre sale con nuestros tíos los sábados por la tarde.

Answers to *Comprueba tu progreso*

A 1. Hay una taza sobre el platillo.
2. Hay un cuchillo y una cuchara a la derecha del plato.
3. Hay una servilleta debajo de los tenedores.
4. Hay un vaso a la izquierda de la taza y del platillo.
5. Como huevos, jamón, pan tostado y un plátano para el desayuno.
6. Pongo mantequilla y mermelada en el pan tostado.

B 1. fui 3. Fuiste 5. fue
2. fue 4. fui 6. fuiste

C 1. haces 4. hacemos 7. hace
2. pongo 5. pone 8. salgo
3. sale 6. salen 9. salimos

D
1. sales
2. haces
3. ponen
4. hacen
5. hago
6. salimos
7. pones
8. ponemos

E
1. La escucho.
2. Los pongo en el plato.
3. ¿No la compras?
4. ¿Lo busca Ud.?
5. ¿Las comen Uds.?
6. ¿Lo comprendes?
7. Las venden.
8. Los quito.

F
1. No, pero va a hacerlo más tarde.
2. No, pero van a limpiarlos más tarde.
3. No, pero voy a leerlo más tarde.
4. No, pero va a escucharla más tarde.
5. No, pero vas (va) a necesitarlo más tarde.
6. No, pero vamos a estudiarlas más tarde.
7. No, pero vamos a cocinarlos más tarde.
8. No, pero voy a lavarlos más tarde.

PAGE 301

Photo

This silver *topo* is from Bolivia. *Topo* is the Quechua name given to a large pin that was the main ornament worn by the women of the Incan empire. As shown in the photograph, *topos* have oversized heads that give them a spoonlike appearance.

The Incas, who had a good knowledge of metal craftsmanship, were able to provide *topos* made from many different metals. The *topos* could be made of gold, silver, copper, or bronze, depending on the status of the wearer. Nowadays, Bolivian Indian women wear the pins almost exclusively on festive occasions. However, *topos* are frequently sold and exhibited as examples of native craftsmanship.

ORAL PROFICIENCY TEST

Directed Response

1. Isabel is going grocery shopping and asks if you want to go along. Tell her that you went shopping yesterday afternoon. *(Fui de compras ayer por la tarde.)*

2. Your best friend is going on vacation today. How would you ask him what time he's leaving? *(¿A qué hora sales?)*

3. Eva's mother wants her to help find their dog. How does Eva tell her mother that she's going to look for the dog now? *(Voy a buscarlo ahora. OR Lo voy a buscar ahora.)*

Picture-Cued Response

Using the visual on p. 280 or transparency 37, ask:

4. ¿Qué hacen la señora y su hijo? *(Van de compras.)*

5. ¿Qué necesita la señora para la cena? *(Necesita (una docena de) huevos y un pavo.)*

6. Point to the photograph on p. 291 and ask: "¿Come el almuerzo la chica?" *(No, la chica no come el almuerzo. OR No, la chica come el desayuno.)*

Situations

7. Your family has just finished eating dinner. What might you say to your sister Elena?
   a. Tienes que poner la mesa.   b. Tengo que comer pronto.   c. *Tenemos que quitar los platos.*

8. Your father sends you to the store for lettuce. What might he say when you ask why he needs it?
   a. Lo necesito para la cena.   b. Las quiero para el almuerzo.   c. *La quiero para la ensalada.*

Real-Life Questions

9. ¿Vas de compras para comprar los comestibles?
10. ¿Compran Uds. la carne en la carnicería o la compran en el supermercado?
11. ¿Comes el desayuno con tu familia?
12. ¿A qué hora sale de casa tu padre o tu madre?

ORAL PROFICIENCY TEST   CHAPTERS 5–8

Directed Response

1. A woman asks you where the Teatro Nacional is. Tell her it's to the right of the Banco Central. *(El Teatro Nacional está a la derecha del Banco Central.)*

2. Your mother asks whose notebooks are on the

table. Tell her that the notebooks are César's. *(Los cuadernos son de César.)*

3. You see Gustavo dialing a telephone number. Ask him if he is calling María. *(¿Llamas a María?)*

Picture-Cued Response

Using the visual on p. 218 ask questions such as:

4. ¿Cuántos hermanos tiene Lola? *(Lola tiene dos hermanos. Tiene un hermano y una hermana. OR Lola tiene un hermano.)*

5. ¿Quiénes son los abuelos de Elena? *(Eduardo y Yolanda son los abuelos de Elena. OR Eduardo y Yolanda son sus abuelos.)*

6. ¿Cuál es el nombre del esposo de Sara? *(El nombre del esposo de Sara es Raúl. OR El nombre de su esposo es Raúl.)*

Situations

7. Ernesto tells you that tomorrow is his birthday. What might you say to him?
   a. *¡Felicitaciones!*   b. ¡Ojalá!   c. ¡Qué mala suerte!

8. Your sister asks if you feel like cleaning the garage. How might you answer?
   a. No, no tengo ganas de limpiarla hoy.
   b. *Sí, voy a limpiarlo ahora.*   c. ¿Va a limpiarlos también?

Real-Life Questions

9. ¿Te gusta cuidar a los niños? ¿Cuidas a los niños a menudo?

10. ¿Lees el periódico? ¿Cuándo lo lees?

11. ¿Qué prefieres comprar cuando vas de compras, ropa o comida? ¿Dónde la compras?

LEARNING SPANISH THROUGH ACTION

New prop vocabulary: Tableware items arranged on a table.

Other new vocabulary: none

New staging vocabulary: quitar

Teach the tableware items in the same manner that you taught the food items in Capítulo 1. Then add *quitar.*

Sample

1. Quiten los platos.
2. Pongan los platos sobre una silla.
3. Recojan una cuchara y pongan la cuchara a la izquierda de una servilleta.
4. Quiten las servilletas.

The foods may be taught in the same manner as those in Capítulo 1. The numbers may be taught as were those in the first lesson of *En Camino C.*

CAPÍTULO 9

SUGGESTED MATERIALS

pp. 304–305 (Palabras nuevas I): newspaper and magazine ads for various types of movies; pictures of popular television and film stars

p. 309 (Actividad): television listings from a local newspaper

pp. 312–313 (Palabras nuevas II): magazine cutouts showing people at the beach; pictures illustrating various expressions with *tener: tener miedo, tener hambre, tener sed, tener sueño,* and so on

p. 327 (Actividad): index cards

PAGES 302–303

Photo
Filming of *Su salud*, a half-hour program offered on Sundays at noon on Channel 44, a Spanish-language television station in Chicago, Illinois. *Su salud* is a talk show that features interviews with medical doctors, psychologists, social workers, and other professionals. It provides information about varied healthrelated topics that are of interest to its predominantly Hispanic audience.

Channel 44, which was founded as a full-time Spanish-language television station in July, 1985, is the only television station in Chicago that broadcasts full time in Spanish. (Channel 26 also has programs in Spanish, but it broadcasts only on a part-time basis.) Channel 44 takes great pride in its logo, *El canal de la hispanidad*. It is affiliated with a Hispanic national television network called Univisión, which provides many of the programs available on the channel. At the local level, Channel 44 broadcasts talk shows, news, variety and other entertainment programs, as well as some short-term series on current affairs. The channel offers advice to Chicago's Hispanic community, especially to newcomers who may have difficulty understanding English. It tries to provide role models for its audience by interviewing well-informed professionals and businesspeople. In 1986 a Channel 44 series, *Lo nuestro*, received an award from the Illinois Broadcasting Association naming it "the best public affairs series in the city."

PAGE 306

Photo
These two teenagers are at a video store in Spain. Although VHS has become the preferred video format in the U.S., Beta is still more popular in Europe and Latin America. Because Spain and the U.S. use different recording systems, most European-manufactured tapes are not compatible with U.S. video players and vice versa.

Realia
The inset lists titles of "Other Videos" including the British film *Burning* and three U.S. productions, among them *Divorce American Style*. The film descriptions are broken down into running time,

director, and cast *(intérpretes)*. Each movie is classified according to its suitability for children under 18 and under 13. The last listing is appropriate for all audiences.

PAGE 309

Photo
This television class is being held at the University of Puerto Rico. The communications departments of Puerto Rican universities offer a variety of television-related courses, which students may take to prepare for careers as television technicians or announcers. University-level training in the field of communications may lead to a job in what seems to be a promising field in Puerto Rico.

Television is a favorite form of entertainment on the island, and even the poorest families own a television set. Three of Puerto Rico's television stations broadcast in Spanish and offer a variety of entertainment programs, as well as the news. Many programs are Spanish-dubbed imports from the U.S.; others are local programs; and the others come from Spanish-speaking countries such as Mexico and Venezuela. In addition to these three stations, a public TV station carries both local and imported programs of higher educational value. The public station often rebroadcasts, in English, the same material offered on public television in the continental U.S. Cable television is also available; it originates in the continental U.S. and is almost entirely in English.

PAGE 310

Photos
(a) This Spanish-language television program, which is televised in New York, features a celebration of Ecuadoran Independence Day. Because Hispanics are the fastest-growing minority in the U.S., the future of Spanish-language television in this country is promising. In 1987, Hispanics comprised 7 percent of the total U.S. population, but the Census Bureau estimates that this percentage will increase to 14 percent by the year 2020 and 20 percent by 2080. Consequently, competition for the Hispanic market continues to be intense.

The largest Spanish-language television network in the country is Univisión, with over 400 affiliates in the U.S. and several in Latin America. However, a dynamic new network called Telemundo was recently created in Miami, with affiliates in Los Angeles, San Juan, Chicago, and New Jersey, and plans to expand to other cities with large Hispanic populations.

(b) This popular Spanish-language soap opera *(telenovela)*, called *Amalia Batista,* is also televised in New York. Spanish-language television stations offer a wide variety of programs, many of which come from Televisa, a gigantic Mexican network. One of the most popular programs in the Spanish-speaking world is *Siempre en domingo,* a Mexican variety show that features singers and entertainers from Latin America and Spain. Every show reaches an estimated 160 million people in the U.S. and most Spanish-speaking countries. Several *telenovelas* also have a large audience in many other countries. For the more serious-minded viewer, both Univisión and Telemundo offer high-quality international news programs on weekdays. Talk shows on the culture and politics of the Spanish-speaking world are broadcast on Sunday mornings. One of those talk shows, *Temas y debates* (Topics and debates), features interviews with personalities who analyze current events of interest to the Spanish-speaking world.

PAGE 311

Photo
A family is shown watching television in Madrid, Spain.

Additions to on-page notes
Reteach / Review: You may want students to base their *Participación* dialogues on the television listings they prepared for the *Actividad* on p. 309.

PAGE 314

Photo
Located on Spain's southeastern Costa Blanca, Benidorm was once a tranquil fishing village.

However, it has become a popular international tourist resort due to year-round tropical weather. The town is flanked by two white-sand beaches, Playa del Levante (East Beach) and Playa del Poniente (West Beach).

Additions to on-page notes
Culture: You may want students to do research on a famous beach resort in Spain (Costa Brava or Costa Blanca, for example) or in Latin America (Mar del Plata in Argentina or Viña del Mar in Chile, for example). Ask them to develop a cultural poster with information about transportation, accommodations, and other points of interest to tourists.

PAGE 315
Photo
The city of Acapulco, which is located on Mexico's southern Pacific coast, is one of the world's most famous resorts. Its three major beaches are linked by the Costera Miguel Alemán, a coastal boulevard named for a former president (1946–1952) who was instrumental in the development of Acapulco's tourist industry. Tourism is Mexico's second largest source of income after petroleum. Acapulco, which in *nahuatl* (an Indian language of southern Mexico and Central America) means "the place of thick reeds," was the main port used by the Spanish *conquistadores* for the exploration of the South Seas.

PAGE 316
Additions to on-page notes
Notes: In conjunction with the *Estudio de palabras,* tell students that Spanish words ending in *-sión* and *-ción* are always feminine.

PAGE 319
Photo
A view of the harbor and the Plaza de Toros in Málaga. Located in Andalucía, Málaga is Spain's major port city on the Costa del Sol. Málaga's principal industries include wine and olive oil production, and tourism. *Corridas de toros,* or bullfights, are held at the Plaza de Toros every Sunday from Easter through September or early October.

PAGE 320
Photos
(a) Four Colombian youngsters take time out for a snack. One of them is eating a *pincho,* a national snack (similar to a shish kebab) that is made of pieces of meat roasted on a skewer. And one of his companions is eating a hot dog.
(b) A couple drinks coffee and chats at an outdoor café in Guadalajara, Mexico's second largest city, which is located in the central state of Jalisco. Because the temperature remains in the 70s and 80s throughout the year, Guadalajarans spend a lot of time outdoors.

Additions to on-page notes
Reteach / Extra Help: Reinforce the use and meaning of *acabar de* by performing several actions. After completing each action, ask *¿Qué acabo de hacer? (Ud. acaba de borrar la pizarra / cerrar la puerta / abrir la ventana.)*

PAGE 321
Photo
Teenagers relax at a beach in Puerto Rico. Puerto Rico's Caribbean beaches are a major attraction for thousands of tourists each year, especially during the winter months. Most of the island's beaches are public, and swimming, sunbathing, and playing cards or dominoes are popular weekend activities for Puerto Ricans of all ages.

PAGE 322
Sample dialogues for *¿Qué pasa?*
Lucía and Julio are trying to decide which movie they'll see tonight, what time they'll go, and where they'll eat dinner.

L: ¿Qué película quieres ver?

J: *No veo nubes* es una película estupenda. La dan a las nueve.

L: Muy bien. Si tienes hambre, debemos comer antes de ir al cine.

J: Vamos al restaurante mexicano. Tengo ganas de comer tacos.

L: ¿Vamos a ver *Mi guitarra y yo*?

J: ¿Por qué no? ¿A qué hora la dan y cuánto dura?

L: La dan a las ocho y media y dura dos horas. Tengo hambre. ¿Quieres comer antes de ir al cine?

J: ¡Ah, sí! Vamos al restaurante enfrente del teatro. Tienen hamburguesas y papas fritas estupendas.

PAGE 324

Photo

Tourists shop for sweaters in the Andean town of San Carlos de Bariloche, Argentina. Located on the shore of Lake Nahuel Huapí, the town is usually referred to simply as Bariloche. Skiers, fishers, mountain climbers, hikers, campers, and other outdoor sports enthusiasts from North and South America, as well as Europe, flock to Bariloche throughout the year.

PAGE 326

Photo

During the Christmas season, vendors set up stalls along Barcelona's Plaza del Cristo Rey to sell holiday items such as fir trees, Christmas ornaments, and nativity scenes *(nacimientos).* The plaza is in Barcelona's Barrio Gótico, the old part of the city built during the Middle Ages.

PAGE 327

Photo

The computer has become an integral part of life in the Spanish-speaking world. Computers perform such diverse tasks as running Mexico City's subway system and regulating individual tax forms in Argentina. Computer assembly plants throughout Latin America are also important to local and national economies. Next to the computer in the photo are *El*

País, Madrid's major daily newspaper, and a pencil holder bearing a Mayan design.

PAGE 328

Photos

(a) This sidewalk café (top) is located on a narrow cobblestone street *(callejón)* in the old section of Sevilla, Spain's fourth largest city. The restaurant and bar are part of the Hostería del Laurel. *Hosterías* are government-operated restaurants that are located throughout Spain, each serving the specialties of its own region. In the past, *hosterías* also served as inns where travelers could rent lodgings.

(b) This outdoor café (bottom) is located in Salamanca's seventeenth-century Plaza Mayor. Situated 107 miles northwest of Madrid, Salamanca overlooks the Tormes River. The University of Salamanca, founded in 1219, is one of Spain's leading universities and its oldest. Because of its historical and architectural importance, the entire city has been declared a national monument.

Answers to *Repaso*

1. Son las once de la noche y acabo de arreglar el televisor de María. / Son las cinco de la tarde y acaban de ver las noticias de hoy. / Son las diez de la mañana y acabamos de limpiar la cocina de abuela.

2. Debemos ir al hotel porque tenemos mucho sueño. / Debo ir a la playa porque tengo mucho calor. / Deben ir a casa porque tienen mucho miedo.

3. ¡Cuidado! ¿Qué ves? / ¡Caramba! ¿Qué veo? / ¡Imagínate! ¿Qué vemos?

4. Es Margarita. La vemos ahora. Tiene sueño. / Es Tomás. Lo veo ahora. Tienes (Ud. tiene) razón. / Son las chicas (muchachas). ¿Las ve Ud. ahora? Tienen suerte.

5. Le damos un vaso de jugo. / Les doy una botella de agua. / Les dan un sandwich de queso.

Answers to *Tema*

1. Son las doce de la noche y Claudia y Mateo acaban de ver una película de terror.
2. Deben ir a la cocina porque tienen mucha hambre.
3. ¡Cuidado! ¿Qué ven?
4. Es el gato. Lo ven ahora. Tiene sed.
5. Mateo le da un platillo de leche.

Answers to *Comprueba tu progreso*

A
1. A las diez dan una película del oeste.
2. A las ocho y media dan una película de dibujos animados.
3. A las nueve dan una película romántica.
4. A las nueve menos cuarto dan una película policíaca.
5. A las nueve y media dan una película musical.
6. A las nueve y cuarto dan una película cómica.
7. A las ocho menos cuarto dan una película de ciencia ficción.
8. A las cinco y media dan un programa de noticias.

B
1. Ana y Paco tienen frío.
2. Beatriz tiene sed.
3. Tengo sueño.
4. Mi hermano tiene miedo.
5. Pablo y yo tenemos hambre.
6. Tienes suerte.

C
1. vemos
2. da
3. ve
4. dan
5. das
6. veo
7. ven
8. doy
9. damos
10. Ves

D
1. Acabamos de venderla.
2. Acaba de arreglarlo.
3. Acabo de mirarlas.
4. Acaban de estudiarla.
5. Acabo de leerlo.
6. Acaba de limpiarlo.

E
1. Le dan las sandalias a la niña.
2. ¿Le da Ud. el paraguas al muchacho?
3. Les damos la tarea a las profesoras.
4. Les doy las respuestas a mis compañeros de clase.
5. Les da los lápices a los estudiantes.
6. Le dan los anteojos de sol a mi hermano.
7. Le dan la leche al gato.
8. Les das la sombrilla a mis hermanas.

F
1. No. Voy a escribirle una carta más tarde.
2. No. Voy a darles el almuerzo más tarde.
3. No. Voy a leerles el periódico más tarde.
4. No. Voy a darles las notas más tarde.
5. No. Voy a arreglarle la puerta más tarde.
6. No. Voy a preguntarle cuánto cuesta más tarde.

Drawings

(a) This drawing from the Late Classic period of Mayan civilization (A.D. 600–900) is from a clay plate found in El Petén, Guatemala. It represents a man-jaguar creature playing a traditional Mayan ball game called *pok-a-tok* or *tlachtli*. Both the jaguar and the ball game were important in Mayan tradition. Jaguars, or creatures that are part jaguar, figured among the gods in the Mayan polytheistic religion. Because a jaguar god was believed to guide the dead in a canoe journey through the underworld, the image of the jaguar was often associated with death. The ball game, which was played by both the Mayas and the Aztecs, was also connected with death. Sometimes war captives were forced to play against each other, and the losing team was sacrificed. More often, however, the *pok-a-tok* was played simply as a sport with no human sacrifice involved.

This drawing and the one on the right are faithful reproductions of the drawings that decorate some of the pre-Columbian vases and plates that make up the collection of Museo Popol-Vuh, Universidad Francisco Marroquín in Guatemala.

(b) This drawing is from a vase found in El Quiché, Guatemala, and represents a Mayan nobleman. Members of Mayan nobility had several distinctive features, some of which can be observed in the drawing. For instance, it was considered fashionable to have beaklike noses, and aristocrats would build up their noses with putty to give them the desired shape. Members of the nobility also elongated the heads of their babies shortly after birth by binding each baby's head between boards. After a few days, the soft bones were flattened to give the head an elongated shape. In addition, as shown in the drawing, the Mayan aristocrats wore elaborate headdresses decorated with tail feathers from the quetzal, a sacred bird among the Mayas, and now the national bird of Guatemala.

ORAL PROFICIENCY TEST

Directed Response

1. Elena asks if you want to eat. Tell her you've just finished breakfast. *(Acabo de terminar el desayuno.)*
2. Juana asks what you're doing. Tell her you're writing a letter to your aunt. *(Le escribo una carta a mi tía.)*
3. Someone asks why Pablo didn't come to the movies tonight. Explain that horror movies scare him. *(A él le dan miedo las películas de terror.)*

Picture-Cued Response

4. Point to the photograph on p. 306 and ask: "¿Dónde ven unas películas estupendas, en casa o en el cine?" *(Ven unas películas estupendas en casa. OR Las ven en casa.)*

5. Point to the photograph on p. 327 and ask: "Los padres de Pepe le dan un televisor nuevo, ¿verdad?" *(No, los padres de Pepe (sus padres) le dan una computadora nueva. OR No, los padres de Pepe (sus padres) no le dan un televisor nuevo.)*

Situations

6. You are sunbathing at the beach, and suddenly it begins to get very cloudy. What would you be most likely to say?
   a. ¡Qué bueno!   b. *¡Caramba!*   c. ¡Cuidado!
7. Raúl wants to watch his favorite soap opera, but his brother is already watching a movie. How would he ask how long the movie lasts?
   a. ¿A qué hora dan la película?   b. *¿Cuánto dura la película?*   c. ¿Cuántos años tiene la película?
8. Your grandmother asks you to get her a sweater. What might you ask?
   a. ¿Tienes mucha sed?   b. ¿Tienes suerte?
   c. *¿Tienes frío?*

Real-Life Questions

9. ¿Cuándo es el cumpleaños de tu madre? ¿Qué le vas a comprar?
10. ¿Tienes sed cuando llegas a casa de la playa? ¿Qué te gusta beber cuando tienes mucha sed?
11. ¿Tienes que terminar la tarea antes de mirar la tele? ¿Qué programas miras después de comer la cena?

LEARNING SPANISH THROUGH ACTION

New prop vocabulary: This lesson may be used to review vocabulary of your choice.

Other new vocabulary: le, les

New staging vocabulary: dar

Sample

1. Gustavo, dale el lápiz a Marisa.
2. <u>Le das el lápiz a Marisa.</u>

3. Marisa, dale el bolígrafo a Gustavo.
   Q: ¿Qué le das a Gustavo, el libro o el bolígrafo?
   A: El bolígrafo.
4. Gustavo, dales los libros a Javier y a Roberto.
   Q: Les das los libros a Juan y a Marisa, ¿no?
   A: No, a Javier y a Roberto.
5. <u>Sí, les das los libros a Javier y a Roberto.</u>
   Q: ¿Qué les das, libros o bolígrafos?
   A: Libros.

CAPÍTULO 10

OBJECTIVES

Communication
- to identify vocabulary related to farm life
- to identify vocabulary related to the zoo

Grammar
- to use the verb *oír*
- to use the verb *traer*
- to use the verb *decir*
- to use demonstrative adjectives

Culture
- to note the importance of the llama as a pack animal in South America
- to point out various ways in which the Andean Indians use the llama
- to contrast the role of the horse in the North American society of the past with its role today

SUGGESTED MATERIALS

p. 333 (Prólogo cultural): wall map(s) showing the Andes and the southwestern U.S.; magazine pictures of llamas and / or horses

p. 334 (Palabras nuevas I): magazine pictures of farm animals

pp. 342–343 (Palabras nuevas II): magazine pictures of animals found in most zoos

p. 355 (Actividad): a paper bag

PAGES 332–333
Photo
Two Indian women are seen with their llamas in front of one of the walls of the Incan fortress Sacsahuamán, on the outskirts of Cuzco, Peru. Sacsahuamán is an outstanding example of Incan masonry. The fortress was built with huge stones, some of which weighed up to 300 tons. The Incas transported the stones and pared their edges to make them fit together securely. The job was done with such perfection that a sheet of paper cannot be inserted between most of these stones.

PAGE 335
Additions to on-page notes
Notes: After you have presented the *Contexto visual,* ask volunteers to model the animal sounds.

Remind students that *j* (in *jiii*) is pronounced like English *h;* point out that *au* (in *guau* and *miau*) is like *ow* in "how"; and make sure students are aware that the *e*'s in *meee* are not the long *e* in "me" but rather, similar to the *e* in "met."

PAGE 339
Photo
The autonomous region of Cantabria, known until recently as the province of Santander, extends along the Cantabrian Sea, which is north of Spain. Its landscape ranges from lush farmlands and forests to the snow-capped Picos de Europa, a popular ski resort in the Cantabrian Mountains.

PAGE 340
Photo
A sign advertising a clinic for horses in Argentina.

PAGE 341
Photos
(a) A veterinarian is shown giving a shot to a calf in Chile.
(b) Students are shown at a veterinary school at the University of Madrid.

Additions to on-page notes
Enrichment: In conjunction with the *Participación,* you may want to ask students to find magazine pictures at home to accompany their "interviews."

PAGE 346

Photos

(a) Mexico's tradition of *charreadas,* rodeolike contests of roping, tying, riding, and branding, originated during colonial times on the cattle ranges of Jalisco state. The *charros,* expert horsemen who participate in these contests, wear distinctive outfits that include wide-brimmed hats, embroidered shirts, loose bowties, small, tight-fitting jackets, called *boleros,* jodhphurs with metallic buttons along the sides, and boots. The largest arenas *(lienzos charros)* for *charro* performances are in Mexico City and Guadalajara, where weekly competitions are held from 11:00 A.M. to 2:00 P.M. on Sundays.

(b) Chilean cowboys, called *huasos,* are from the cattle-raising area near the city of Rancagua. Their traditional costume includes a narrow-brimmed, flat-topped hat; a short, tight-fitting jacket; a multicolored sash or cummerbund; boots; and a reversible, brightly embroidered woven poncho, called a *manta.* The official rodeo season runs from September to March, with national championships held at the end of March in Rancagua.

PAGE 351

Drawings

Two drawings from the Late Classic period of Mayan civilization, A.D. 600–900. The designs are from a vase found in Valle del Motagua, Guatemala. Like the drawings shown on page 331, they are part of the collection of Museo Popol-Vuh, Universidad Francisco Marroquín, Guatemala. The elaborate headdresses worn by the two men indicate that they were high-ranking persons among the Mayas. And the symbol drawn close to the mouth of the first figure indicates that he's engaged in conversation.

PAGE 352

Photo

These student musicians are performing in Guadalajara, Mexico. The tradition of *estudiantinas,* or student minstrels, dates back to the days when young men, dressed in ruffled shirts, cloaks, and black velvet knee britches, serenaded young noblewomen with their mandolins and guitars and were rewarded with brightly colored ribbons, which they wore proudly on their cloaks. Students at the University of Guanajuato, northwest of Mexico City, revived the tradition, which is now popular throughout Mexico.

PAGE 356

Photos

(a) This toucan is seen in El Petén, an immense, sparsely populated Guatemalan territory that was once the center of Mayan civilization. El Petén is the home of rare varieties of flowers, plants, butterflies, and hundreds of species of birds that are rare or nonexistent elsewhere. Toucan is a generic name for about 40 species of long-billed birds belonging to the *Ramphastiadae* family. Toucans are highly sociable and are among the noisiest of birds found in forests. The toucan eats by juggling pieces of fruit in its enormous bill, and then tossing its head back to swallow.

(b) Visitors to the popular Palermo Zoo in Buenos Aires are often treated to a glimpse of such strange indigenous animals as the Patagonian mara (a short-eared hare) and others, which are allowed to roam free on the grounds. In addition to the Jardín Zoológico, the Palermo park contains a racetrack, a bicycle track, a planetarium, a botanical garden, and an exquisite Japanese garden.

Realia

The inset shows a map of the zoo in Barcelona.

Answers to *Repaso*

1. Traigo a mi hermano a la panadería. / Traemos a nuestros amigos al partido. / Traen a sus alumnos(as) (estudiantes) a la biblioteca.
2. Ve la nieve. Oye los osos. / Vemos el sol. Oímos la lluvia. / Veo las gallinas. Oigo el ruido.
3. ¡Qué largo es este camino! ¡Y esa granja! ¡Qué enorme es! / ¡Qué rápidos son estos caballos! ¡Pero esas vacas! ¡Qué lentas son! / ¡Qué magníficos son estos árboles! ¡Y esas flores! ¡Qué hermosas son!

4. ¿Qué dicen Uds.? ¿Están Uds. preocupados(as)? ¿Tienen miedo de los toros? / ¿Qué dicen? ¿Están enfermos? ¿Tienen miedo del trabajo? / ¿Qué decimos? ¿Estamos cansados(as)? ¿Tenemos miedo de la prueba (del examen)?
5. Creo que no. Pero me gustan más esos corderos. / ¡Claro (que sí)! Pero me gustan estas ovejas también. / Creo que sí. Pero me gusta más ese mono.

PAGE 357

Answers to *Tema*

1. Carlos trae a su prima Rosa al zoológico.
2. "¿Ves el elefante? ¿Oyes el león?"
3. "¡Qué hermoso es este tigre! ¡Y esa jirafa! ¡Qué alta es!"
4. "¿Qué dices? ¿Estás aburrida? ¿Tienes miedo de los animales?"
5. "¡Claro que no! Pero me gustan más estos pájaros."

PAGE 358

Answers to *Comprueba tu progreso*

A
1. La vaca da leche.
2. En el invierno hay mucha nieve.
3. El cordero hace "meee."
4. Por la noche vemos la luna (Por el día vemos el sol) en el cielo.
5. Generalmente, la hierba es verde.
6. Cuando mi gato está enfermo llamo al veterinario (a la veterinaria).
7. Los peces nadan.
8. Los leones comen carne.

B
1. Oyes (Oye) un caballo.
2. Oyen una vaca.
3. Oyen (Oímos) un pato.
4. Oye un cerdo.
5. Oigo un cordero.
6. Oímos un gallo.
7. Oyen una oveja.
8. Oye un perro.

C
1. Pablo trae los churros.
   Pablo ve los churros.
2. Traigo el jugo de naranja.
   Veo el jugo de naranja.
3. Traemos la sombrilla.
   Vemos la sombrilla.
4. Traes los frijoles.
   Ves los frijoles.
5. Uds. traen las manzanas y las naranjas.
   Uds. ven las manzanas y las naranjas.
6. Daniel y Jorge traen los cuchillos y los tenedores.
   Daniel y Jorge ven los cuchillos y los tenedores.
7. Pilar trae las flores.
   Pilar ve las flores.
8. Traigo la carne.
   Veo la carne.

D
1. dice
2. Dices
3. dicen
4. decimos
5. Dicen
6. digo

E
1. esas, esta
2. este, esos
3. ese, estas
4. este, esos
5. estos, esa
6. ese, estas

PAGE 359

Photo

This eighteenth-century wood carving of a lamb is from Guatemala. Although the artist was probably a highland Maya, the sculpture shows no noticeable pre-Columbian influences. It was not solely for decorative purposes, but was also used in Church for nativity scenes.

ORAL PROFICIENCY TEST

Directed Response

1. Your brother comes into your room and asks why you're so scared. Say that you hear a noise in the living room. *(Oigo un ruido en la sala.)*
2. While shopping with a friend, you find a jacket you like. Ask your friend if he likes the jacket. *(¿A ti te gusta esta chaqueta?)*

Picture-Cued Response

Using the visual on pp. 342–343 or transparency 44, ask questions such as:

3. ¿Qué clase de animal es este animal pequeño? *(Ese animal pequeño es una iguana.)*
4. ¿Dónde están el león y el tigre? *(Están en la jaula.)*
5. ¿Qué hace el guardián? *(El guardián (le) da de comer a la llama.)*

Situations

6. You and a friend are going on a picnic tomorrow. How would you ask your friend what she's bringing?
   a. ¿Qué traen? b. *¿Qué traes?* c. ¿Qué traigo?

7. Mónica asks whether it's supposed to rain today. You think so. What might you say?
   a. Sí, por supuesto. b. Claro que sí.
   c. *Creo que sí.*
8. A classmate doesn't understand the teacher. How might he ask you what she's saying?
   a. ¿Qué dices? b. ¿Qué digo? c. *¿Qué dice?*

Real-Life Questions

9. ¿Te gustan los animales?
10. ¿Qué animales te gustan más?
11. Cuando está nublado por la mañana, ¿qué traes a la escuela?

LEARNING SPANISH THROUGH ACTION

New prop vocabulary: The vocabulary of your choice. Although we do not teach *aquel* until Book 2, we are including it in this presentation in case you would like to add it. If you prefer to delay teaching *aquel,* use only two of each object. Begin with one masculine item and one feminine item close to you, identical items at a small distance from you, and identical items much farther away from you.

Other new vocabulary: Demonstrative adjectives

New staging vocabulary: venir

Sample

1. Elisa, toca ese libro.
2. Ven aquí.
3. Toca este libro.
4. Toca aquel libro.

Repeat the above with the feminine items. Then substitute different masculine and feminine items. Finally, use plural items. Narration is appropriate, but questioning is not, because what is *that* to you becomes *this* to the person touching it.

The names of the animals may be taught in the same manner as the vocabulary in Capítulo 2.

CAPÍTULO 11

OBJECTIVES

Communication
- to identify vocabulary related to social events
- to identify vocabulary related to pastimes and hobbies

Grammar
- to use $o \rightarrow ue$ stem-changing verbs
- to use the verb *jugar*
- to use verbs followed by infinitives
- to use direct and indirect object pronouns

Culture
- to compare and contrast after-school activities, hobbies, and pastimes in the U.S. and South America

SUGGESTED MATERIALS

p. 361 (Prólogo cultural): a wall map of South America

PAGES 360–361

Photo
Two young people in front of circus posters in Spain.

PAGE 364

Additions to on-page notes
Reteach / Extra Help: You may want to reinforce the use of *e* in mini-dialogue 6. Explain that we use *e* instead of *y* to make pronunciation easier before words that begin with *i* or *hi.* Then write these pairs of words on the board, and ask volunteers to link them with *e: chaquetas / impermeables, padres / hijos, hospitales / iglesias, inteligente / interesante.*

PAGE 366

Photos
(a) Hispanic musicians are seen playing bongo drums in New York City. The base of the bongo resembles a hollow wooden barrel; the top, which players hit with the palms and fingers, is a piece of tightly stretched goatskin.

Caribbean music, a combination of Indian, Spanish, Arabic, and African elements, is popular in the New York area where nearly 80 percent of the Spanish-speaking population is of Puerto Rican, Cuban, or Dominican descent. This music is suitable for dancing, and among the most common rhythms are *la bomba* and *la plena* from Puerto Rico, *el merengue* from the Dominican Republic, and *el mambo* and *la rumba* from Cuba.

(b) A college rock band is shown here in Puerto Rico offering a *Concierto de Navidad,* or Christmas concert.

PAGE 368

Photo
A young man is shown making a phone call in Spain. The phone system in Spain is efficient in most respects. However, waiting lists for first-time applicants for phone service are usually very long, and the wait for actual phone installation is often a long one. Moreover, in many cases there are restrictions on the number of phone receivers that a given area may have. And if an area already has all of the phones it is allowed, an applicant may have to wait until another person moves out of the area before receiving his or her own phone.

PAGE 369

Photo
This rock concert takes place at the University of Puerto Rico.

Additions to on-page notes
Notes: Students who do not like rock music may prefer to create a dialogue for the *Participación* about inviting a friend to a dance.

PAGE 378

Realia
The designs on these playing cards from Spain look

very different from those found on standard playing cards used in the U.S. The photo shows some of the characteristic designs seen on Spanish cards: the straight, double-edged swords, the heavy batons or clubs, the gold coins, and the cups. The four suits in the Spanish deck of cards—*espadas* (swords), *copas* (cups), *oros* (gold coins), and *bastos* (clubs or batons)—are the equivalents of spades, hearts, diamonds, and clubs, respectively, in the standard American deck.

PAGE 379

Photo
Youngsters are seen playing tennis at Madrid's Casa de Campo Park, a recreational area located on the west side of the Río Manzanares. The park features forests, an amusement park, an outdoor theater, a zoo, swimming pools, a golf course, riding grounds, soccer fields and tennis courts.

Additions to on-page notes
Reteach / Extra Help: To reinforce the use of the infinitive right after another verb, you may want to ask students *¿Qué quieres hacer ahora?* List a number of possibilities on the board: *estudiar, cantar, bailar, jugar,* and so on. Have students answer *Quiero jugar al ajedrez ahora.* You may want to continue by asking *¿Puedes jugar al ajedrez ahora?* Accept such answers as *No, no puedo jugar ahora; tengo que estudiar español.*

To reinforce *tener que* and *acabar de,* you may want to go around the room asking students *¿Qué tienes que hacer hoy?* or *¿Qué acabas de hacer?* Students may be able to ask and answer similar questions after you have presented a model.

PAGE 381

Sample dialogue for *¿Qué pasa?*
César and Elena are having a discussion about buying tickets for a concert, about the group that's playing, and about what the concert is going to be like.

C: ¿Cuánto cuestan las entradas para el concierto de "Las Iguanas"?
E: No sé. Tal vez diez dólares.

C: El concierto va a ser fabuloso.
E: Tienes razón. ¿Pero quién va a pagar las entradas?

PAGE 382

Realia
(a) This stamp from Venezuela shows a pre-Hispanic musical instrument. Issued in 1983, the stamp is part of a series devoted to various Indian arts and crafts such as basket weaving, textiles, ceramics, and music.
(b) This stamp from Peru shows fauna from Antártida (the South Pole). Students might be interested in knowing that *pingüino* is the Spanish word for "penguin."
(c) This stamp from Bolivia was issued to commemorate the bicentenary of the birth of José Eustaquio Méndez, a guerrilla leader who fought against the Spaniards in the Bolivian war for independence.

Additions to on-page notes
Notes: In connection with the presentation of the direct and indirect object pronouns *me, te,* and *nos,* you may want to refer students to these mini-dialogues: 2, p. 363 (*me* as direct object); 6, p. 364 (*te* as direct object); 5, p. 364 and 4, p. 371 (*te* as indirect object); 7, p. 372 (*nos* as indirect object).

PAGE 383

Photo
A teenager is shown mailing a letter at the post office in Madrid. Besides receiving and dispatching mail, Spanish post offices also offer telegraph and long-distance telephone service. Stamps can be purchased at post offices, at small tobacco shops *(estancos),* and at some hotels. Spanish stamps are valued highly by stamp collectors, and the government regularly issues elaborate series featuring local festivals, historical monuments, and regional costumes.

Realia
This special delivery letter was mailed from Honduras, Central America. Can students guess what *correo aéreo* (airmail) means?

PAGE 386

Photo

This flower market is located in Mexico City's Chapultepec Park. The road signs refer to Paseo de las Lomas, a major thoroughfare that connects the neighborhoods of Las Lomas de Chapultepec (Chapultepec Heights) and Bosques Reforma (Reforma Woods), a tree-lined suburb off Paseo de la Reforma.

Flower stalls are seen in almost every neighborhood in Mexico City, where daily shopping usually includes buying fresh flowers for one's home.

PAGE 388

Photo

Soccer, the most popular game in South America, is the national pastime in Argentina. Some of the most outstanding soccer players in history have come from Argentina, a country that won the World Cup soccer championship in 1978 and 1986. Although Argentina had been competing for that prize since 1930, it was not until 1978 that it won for the first time. Argentina's victory in the 1986 World Cup championship game was due, in large part, to the efforts of Diego Maradona, an exceptional soccer player whose contribution was so significant that some people dubbed the event ''Maradona's Cup.''

Answers to *Repaso*

1. Dibujo carteles para la obra de teatro. / Sacamos fotos para el periódico del domingo. / Cristina colecciona canciones para el grupo de rock.
2. Jorge invita a Mónica a jugar al ajedrez con él. / Invitamos a Mario y a Luz a ir al centro con nosotros (nosotras). / Invito a la fotógrafa a viajar al Ecuador conmigo.
3. Pero esta noche estoy cansado (cansada). No puedo jugar. / Pero esta mañana Felipe está ausente. No pueden continuar. / Pero ese día no estás libre. No puedes ayudar.
4. Papá está aburrido, pero me cuenta un cuento. / Estamos preparados(as), y nos da la prueba (el examen). / Estás triste, pero te enseñamos un juego.

5. No volvemos. Vamos al baile con nuestros(as) amigos(as) mexicanos(as). / Ud. no duerme. Juega a las damas con su hijo enfermo. / No vuelve. Asiste al teatro con su hermana mayor.

PAGE 389

Answers to *Tema*

1. Mi hermano Paco compra entradas para un concierto de rock.
2. Invita a su novia a asistir al concierto con él.
3. Pero esa semana Paco está enfermo. No puede salir.
4. Está triste, pero me da las entradas.
5. Paco no duerme. Juega a los naipes con nuestro hermano menor.

PAGE 390

Answers to *Comprueba tu progreso*

A 1. grabadora
   2. por teléfono
   3. tomar algo
   4. fabulosa
   5. semana pasada
   6. prestar
   7. tal vez

B 1. Jugamos a los naipes.
   2. Le doy dinero.
   3. Necesitamos (Necesitan) sellos.
   4. Le di una moneda.
   5. Leemos una revista.
   6. Compramos entradas.

C 1. encuentro
   2. pueden
   3. dormimos
   4. cuenta
   5. juegan
   6. muestra
   7. podemos

D 1. Acabamos de asistir a un concierto.
   2. María puede contar del 0 al 100.
   3. El fotógrafo va a enseñarnos a usar la cámara.
   4. Los invitados tienen ganas de oír esas canciones viejas.
   5. Te invito a tomar algo mañana.
   6. Tienes que trabajar más si vas a sacar buenas notas.

E 1. nos
   2. te
   3. te
   4. nos
   5. me
   6. me

PAGE 391

Photo

This papier-mâché figure of a frog and violin from Mexico was made over copper wire by an unknown artist. The figure, made solely for decorative purposes, is an example of a popular form of contemporary urban folk art.

ORAL PROFICIENCY TEST
Directed Response
1. Ignacio is curious about what you got for your birthday. Tell him that your sister gave you a tape. *(Mi hermana me dio una cinta.)*
2. You want to go to the movies, but you have no money. Ask your mother or father if he or she can lend you ten dollars. *(¿Puedes prestarme (Me puedes prestar) diez dólares?)*
3. You run into your friends Rosa and Carlos. Say that you're inviting them to have something to drink with you. *(Los invito a tomar algo conmigo.)*

Picture-Cued Response
Point to the photograph on p. 379 and ask:
4. ¿A qué juegan los muchachos? *((Los muchachos) juegan al tenis.)*
Point to the photograph on p. 388 and ask:
5. ¿Prefieres jugar al béisbol, ¿no? *(No, prefieren jugar al fútbol. OR No, prefieren jugar al béisbol.)*

Situations
6. You see Alejandro, but he doesn't see you. What might you say to get his attention?
   a. *¡Oye, Alejandro!*   b. ¡Vámonos, Alejandro!
   c. ¡Hasta la vista, Alejandro!
7. Fernando asks Sarita why she likes Jorge so much. How might she explain that it is because he always tells her good jokes?
   a. Siempre te cuenta buenos chistes.
   b. Siempre le cuento buenos chistes.
   c. *Siempre me cuenta buenos chistes.*
8. Antonio invites you to a rock concert, and you aren't sure whether or not you want to go. What might you say to him?
   a. *Tal vez.*   b. A veces.   c. Otra vez.

Real-Life Questions
9. ¿Cuándo fue tu cumpleaños? ¿Te dio una fiesta tu familia?
10. ¿Viste un buen programa anoche en la televisión? ¿Cuál fue?
11. ¿Qué haces cuando estás libre?
12. ¿Juegan al fútbol americano los muchachos de tu escuela? ¿Juegan también las muchachas? ¿Juegas tú?

LEARNING SPANISH THROUGH ACTION

Contar may be used to review numbers and classroom items.

Sample
1. Cuenta las sillas.
   Q: ¿Cuántas sillas hay?
   A: Hay treinta.

Hacer cola may be used to review any actions that can be done in a line.

Sample
1. Hagan cola y caminen a la puerta.
2. Hagan cola y brinquen.

New prop vocabulary: The vocabulary of your choice

Other new vocabulary: otro, otra, vez, otra vez, dos / tres, etc., veces

New staging vocabulary: none

Sample
1. Toquen una camisa amarilla.
2. Toquen otra camisa.
   Q: ¿De qué color es la otra camisa?
   A: Es roja.

Teach *otro* and *otra* in this manner, and then continue, adding *vez* and *veces*.

3. Brinquen.
4. Brinquen otra vez.
5. Brinquen cuatro veces.
6. Brinquen una vez.
7. Brinquen otra vez.

CAPÍTULO 12

OBJECTIVES

Communication
- to identify vocabulary related to travel and airports
- to identify vocabulary related to buying and giving gifts (jewelry, ties, and, so on)

Grammar
- to use $e \rightarrow ie$ stem-changing verbs
- to use the comparative and superlative forms of adjectives
- to use the singular preterite forms of -ar verbs

Culture
- to present students with information about the Panama Canal

SUGGESTED MATERIALS

p. 393 (Prólogo cultural):   a wall map of Panama, including Lago de Gatún and the Gaillard Cut; magazine pictures or photos of the Panama Canal

pp. 394–395 (Palabras nuevas I):   magazine pictures of real objects to reinforce travel-related vocabulary (passport, plane ticket, and so on)

p. 401 (Actividad):   alphabet cards

p. 402 (Diálogo):   a wall map showing Buenos Aires and La Paz

pp. 404–405 (Palabras nuevas II):   costume jewelry (earring, necklace, bracelet, ring, and so on); an empty box to illustrate *abrir* and *cerrar*

p. 413 (Lectura):   a wall map showing Ecuador

PAGES 392–393

Photo
View of the Panama Canal. This 57-mile long artificial waterway connecting the Atlantic and Pacific Oceans is a rarely equalled marvel of engineering. Construction first began on a canal across the isthmus in 1882 under the direction of a Frenchman, Ferdinand de Lesseps (1805–94), who had previously overseen construction of the Suez Canal (1869). But his Panama project failed. At that time, Panama was known as *el Departamento del Istmo* and was part of Colombia. With U.S. backing, it declared its independence in 1903, and ceded the Canal Zone to the U.S. through the much-disputed Hay-Bunau Treaty. Work resumed on the canal, which was completed in 1914 at a cost of approximately $400 million. In 1978, the two countries ratified a treaty, and on October 1, 1979, the Canal Zone was officially transferred to the Panamanian government, with total transfer of ownership destined to occur on December 31, 1999.

PAGE 397

Realia
(a) The cover of a plane ticket from the government-owned Mexicana de Aviación, or Mexicana Airlines, the oldest airline in Latin America. The ticket was issued *(expedido)* at Mexicana's main office, located on Xola Street in Mexico City. The code DM2 at the top of the ticket indicates that it was issued nationally; the words across the bottom of the ticket identify it as a "passenger ticket and luggage coupon."
(b) The sticker on this boarding pass is proof that the passenger has paid the departure tax and has the "right to use the airport for international departure."
(c) The baggage-claim stubs from Mexico's other government-owned airline, Aeroméxico, bear the destination code *ACA,* designating Acapulco.

PAGE 398

Photos
(a) A Spanish woman and two teens (top left) pause on a street corner to admire the sights. The heavy wooden door and the iron grille on the window in the background are typical features of old Spanish houses.

(b) A man buying a ticket (top right) for one of Tan-Sahsa's regular flights to various U.S. cities such as Miami, as noted on the poster in the background. Tan-Sahsa (Servicios Aéreos Hondureños, Sociedad Anónima) is the Honduran national airline whose main office is located in the capital city of Tegucigalpa. Sahsa also provides domestic flights to places like San Pedro Sula, the second largest city in Honduras; Copán, an ancient Mayan city; and Puerto Cortés, the largest and most important port in Honduras.

(c) This tourist map of Costa Rica features the spa area of Ojo de Agua, ''the natural birthplace of crystalline water,'' which is located 12 miles from the capital city of San José. Over 6,000 gallons of water a minute gush from this natural spring, which supplies water for the province of Puntarenas. The resort consists of an artificial lake, several swimming pools, a soccer field, tennis, basketball, and volleyball courts, a gym, and various restaurants.

(d) A boy (bottom right) is seen waving from an intercity bus in Bogotá, Colombia. Bus drivers in Latin America often personalize their vehicles with decorations, such as the fringe hanging on the front window of the bus in this photo.

PAGE 400
Photos
(a) A departure board at Mexico City's International Airport. Major airlines such as Pan American, Eastern, KLM, American, Aeroméxico, and Mexicana provide international flights to Los Angeles, Bogotá, and Amsterdam as well as domestic flights to the Pacific beach resorts of Acapulco and Zihuatanejo, the gulf port of Veracruz, the southern cities of Mérida and Villahermosa, and the northern centers of Zacatecas and Monterrey. The departure times are listed according to the 24-hour clock; thus, 1:25 P.M. is posted as 13:25.

(b) The photo on the right shows a pilot seated at the instrument panel in the cockpit of a large jet.

PAGE 401
Additions to on-page notes
Enrichment: Additional questions you may want to ask for Ex. D: *¿Tienes planes para tus vacaciones de invierno? ¿Qué vas a hacer? ¿Te gusta viajar en avión? ¿Quién es la persona más optimista de tu familia? ¿Y quién es la más pesimista?*

PAGE 402
Photo
Bolivia's international airport at La Paz is appropriately called El Alto because it is the highest airport in the world (12,500 feet above sea level). Decorating the terminal building is a replica of the Puerta del Sol (Gateway of the Sun), a massive doorway (carved from a single piece of stone weighing 10 tons) discovered at Tiahuanaco, an archaeological site where an advanced civilization by the same name flourished until the Incas expanded their empire and seized control of much of what is now Bolivia. The airport is the home base of the country's international airline, Lloyd Aéreo Boliviano (LAB).

Additions to on-page notes
Culture: You may want to point out that Bolivia has two capitals. Sucre is the official capital, and La Paz is the administrative and financial capital. La Paz is located at an altitude of about 12,000 feet. Tell students that lack of oxygen at high altitudes causes fatigue and other symptoms of discomfort.

PAGE 403
Photo
Shepherds are shown moving sheep and a cow along Lake Titicaca. At 12,500 feet above sea level, Titicaca is the highest lake in the world, as well as the largest fresh water lake in South America. Shared by Bolivia and Peru, the 3,205-square-mile lake serves as an important avenue of transportation between cities in both countries.

Realia
A Bolivian passport with the country's coat-of-arms on the cover. Many Bolivian symbols are shown on the

coat-of-arms. Perched on top of the central shield is Bolivia's national bird, the condor. Supervising the scene below the condor is the sun, which was considered a god by the Incas. Also shown is the Cerro de Potosí, which was the center of a major silver rush during the colonial period. At that time, the Cerro was believed to have had enough silver to make a bridge that would extend from Potosí to Madrid. The llama, a pack animal that inhabits the cold eastern highlands, is shown next to the breadfruit tree, which is typical of the eastern lowland tropics. And the nine stars on the lower rim of the shield represent the nine Bolivian *departamentos,* or states.

At the top of the page is a visa (a permit to enter the country) that was stamped at Trompillo Airport in Santa Cruz, Bolivia. And to the left of the passport (on p. 402) is an exit permit from El Alto Airport in La Paz.

Additions to on-page notes
Reteach / Extra Help: Additional words you may want to use for *Pronunciación:* A: *Juan, José, juego, jalapeño;* B: *Oaxaca;* C: *gente, genio, general;* D: *vengo, engaño, ganga;* E: *traigo, jugar, enaguas.* In connection with section F, you may want to point out that some words contain the groups *güi* or *güe.* In these cases, the *u* is pronounced, as in *güiro.*

You may want to use the sentences in G for dictation.

PAGE 406
Photo
A vendor is shown displaying jewelry at a sidewalk stand in Córdoba, a city located in Andalucía. Córdoba is famous for fine filigree gold and silver jewelry, reflecting the influence of the Moors who made Córdoba their capital city during the nearly eight centuries that they occupied Spain (711–1492).

PAGE 409
Photos
(a) This gold and pearl necklace is from the Chimú culture (A.D. 1000–1476) of ancient Peru. The craft of metalworking was introduced to America as early as 900 B.C.; by A.D. 1000 several Indian civilizations had developed sophisticated techniques for working alloys, some of them unknown to the Europeans. However, the Chimú displayed a far greater volume of wealth in precious metals than any of the preceding cultures.

(b) Jewelry from the Mochica culture is represented in the photos at the top right and bottom right. At the top is a pair of ear spools, made of gold, shells, and turquoise, and at the bottom is a gold necklace. The Mochica flourished from A.D. 400–1000 on the northern coast of Peru and were excellent jewelers, potters, and architects. They were eventually conquered by the Chimú.

(c) Between the photos of the two necklaces is a mouth mask from the Nazca culture. The Nazca, who were contemporaries of the Mochica, are best known for a distinctive, polychromatic style of pottery.

PAGE 410
Additions to on-page notes
Reteach / Extra Help: You may want to use pair work or a chain drill to reinforce the forms of *e → ie* stem-changing verbs. Have students ask *¿Qué piensas de . . . ? (Pienso que . . . .)* or *¿Qué piensan Uds. de . . . ? (Pensamos que . . . .)* Ask students to make up sentences that use the verbs *cerrar, empezar, preferir,* and *querer.*

PAGE 413
Photo
Because Panama hats were named for the country from which they were first distributed in large quantities, many people think that they originated in Panama. They are, however, a product of Ecuador, and are woven of the *toquilla* straw native to the country. Cuenca, the third largest city in Ecuador, is a center of hat manufacturing.

Additions to on-page notes
Notes: You may want to point out the following cognates that are not glossed: *imaginaria, existe, productos, distancias, ponchos, famosos, instrumentos.*

Additions to on-page notes

Reteach / Extra Help: You may want to write comparative and superlative statements on the board, leaving blank spaces where nouns should be. Ask students to fill in the blanks and read the sentences aloud. For example: ____ *es más grande que* ____.

Photo

A grandfather and his grandson are seen walking in Barcelona, Spain. Barcelona, located in the northeastern region of Cataluña, is the second largest city in Spain. It is a leading commercial and industrial center, and it has the busiest seaport in the country. A major cultural hub, it is often described as cosmopolitan and sophisticated.

As in other areas of Cataluña, both Spanish and *catalán*, a Romance language that is most closely related to the Provençal of southeastern France, are spoken in Barcelona. The use of *catalán* was discouraged during Francisco Franco's presidency (1939–1975), because the government considered it divisive to have a separate language in the region. However, *catalán* is now spoken in most households, and there are plays, newspapers, television and radio programs in this language.

Barcelona has more than tripled its size since the beginning of the century, and it continues to grow at a rapid pace. Many people, attracted by higher salaries, move to Barcelona from other areas of Spain. Despite the problems of urban congestion, Barcelonans, like other people from the Mediterranean region, are warm, good-natured, and have a zest for life that manifests itself during the many song and dance festivals that are such an important part of life in Barcelona.

Photos

(a) A woman is seen on a train in Argentina. The development of the railroad in Argentina in the late nineteenth century opened up the interior of the country to the production of cattle and grain for export. Britain, formerly Argentina's chief trading partner, invested heavily in the railway, once one of the world's most extensive systems. Ferrocarriles Argentinos, the national railroad, has 27,000 miles of track and trains with diesel-powered engines, dining cars, and sleepers.

(b) This Argentine express bus is traveling through an Andean national park *(parque de turismo),* as indicated by the triangular road sign. These parks are popular among campers, fishers, and mountain climbers, and are especially abundant near the Andean Cordillera and along the Argentina-Chile border.

Additions to on-page notes

Enrichment: You may want to initiate pair work or a chain drill using sentence 1. Have students ask each other *¿Qué hiciste el mes pasado (el año pasado, el invierno pasado, el jueves pasado,* and so on)?

Answers to *Repaso*

1. ¿Qué hizo Carlos el año pasado? / ¿Qué hiciste el invierno pasado? / ¿Qué hiciste el jueves pasado?
2. Compré un anillo para mi novia. / Compraste un pañuelo para tu hermana. / Ud. compró una cartera para su abuela.
3. Pero ahora creen que Ana es más simpática (amable) que David. / Pero hoy creemos que Diego es más pesimista que Cristina. / Pero ahora crees que la cartera es mejor que el bolso.
4. Pienso cambiar diez dólares. / Queremos cerrar nuestros libros. / Quieren dejar sus maletas.
5. El piloto del avión dice que es la montaña más alta de Colombia. / Los agentes de viajes dicen que son los turistas más tacaños de la ciudad. / La auxiliar de vuelo dice que es el avión más rápido del país.

Answers to *Tema*

1. ¿Qué hizo el Sr. Ruiz la semana pasada?
2. Compró una pulsera para su esposa.
3. Pero hoy cree que el collar es más bello (hermoso) que la pulsera.
4. Piensa comprar otro regalo.
5. La Sra. Ruiz dice que es el hombre más generoso de la ciudad.

Answers to *Comprueba tu progreso*

A 1. El avión despega a las nueve.
2. ¿A qué hora empieza el programa?
3. El Sr. Torres es una persona muy optimista.
4. ¿Me esperas cerca de la entrada?
5. ¿Puede Ud. cerrar la ventana, por favor?
6. Yo soy menor (más joven) que mi hermano.
7. La familia de Ernesto es muy rica.
8. La Srta. Rosario es la cliente más tacaña de esta tienda.
9. ¿Quién es el peor piloto?

B 1. prefieren   5. piensan
2. cierran   6. empieza
3. piensas   7. cierra
4. queremos   8. preferimos

C 1. Esta corbata es más barata que ese cinturón.
2. La auxiliar de vuelo es más amable que el piloto.
3. El vuelo 807 es más rápido que el vuelo 813.
4. La Argentina es más grande que el Uruguay.
5. Graciela es más tacaña que Elisa.
6. El asiento 22C es más cómodo que el asiento 25A.
7. Esta cartera es más cara que ese bolso.
8. El fútbol es más divertido que el béisbol.

D 1. Sí, es el cine más caro del barrio.
2. Sí, es la comida más importante del día.
3. Sí, es la alumna más inteligente de la clase.
4. Sí, son los animales más hermosos del zoológico.
5. Sí, es la profesora más seria de la escuela.
6. Sí, es la persona más amable de la agencia de viajes.
7. Sí, es la ciudad más grande de España.
8. Sí, es el mejor actor de la televisión.
9. Sí, es la peor película del año.
10. Sí, es la menor niña (la niña más joven) de la escuela.

E compré, compraste, compró, pagaste, pagué, pagaste, pagó

Photo
This ceremonial gold knife from Peru was made by the Indians of the ancient Chimú culture. The Chimú rose in the year A.D. 1000 and, after years of warfare, were finally defeated and conquered by the Incas in A.D. 1476. They were outstanding architects, weavers, potters, and metal artisans, and had advanced techniques for mass production of vessels and ornaments made out of silver and gold, which seem to have been plentiful in their empire. The Incas learned much of their skill in working with metal from the Chimú.

ORAL PROFICIENCY TEST

Directed Response
1. Your friend Emilio seems distracted today. How would you ask him what he's thinking about?
(*¿En qué piensas?*)
2. Your father just returned from taking Aunt Isabel to the airport, and he was gone a long time. Ask him if the plane took off late.
(*¿Despegó tarde el avión?*)
3. Raúl asks why you're so upset. Tell him that you just got the worst grade in the class.
(*Acabo de sacar la peor nota de la clase.*)

Picture-Cued Response
Using the visual on p. 408, ask questions such as:
4. ¿Es el cinturón más barato o más caro que el reloj? (*El cinturón es más barato que el reloj.*)
5. ¿Es el bolso más barato o más caro que el collar? (*El bolso es más caro que el collar.*)
6. ¿Cuál es la cosa más cara de la tienda? (*El anillo es la cosa más cara de la tienda.*)

Situations
7. Ramón drops you off at your house, and you thank him kindly for the ride home. What might he say to you?
a. Muchísimas gracias.   b. *No hay de qué.*
c. Aquí tienes.
8. Mr. Castaño comes to your house for the first time. How might you and your family greet him?
a. *¡Bienvenido!*   b. ¡Aquí tiene Ud.!
c. ¡Está bien!

Real-Life Questions

9. ¿Qué piensas hacer después de terminar los estudios?
10. ¿Viajaste mucho el año pasado? ¿Cuál es la ciudad más interesante que visitaste? ¿Cuál es la ciudad más aburrida?
11. ¿Conoces a una persona tacaña? ¿Qué piensas de esta persona? ¿Por qué crees que esta persona es tacaña?

ORAL PROFICIENCY TEST—CHAPTERS 9–12

Directed Response

1. You're dying to know what your friend Antonia did last night. How would you ask her? (*¿Qué hiciste anoche?*)
2. David asks you if Raúl and Ramona are twins. Tell him that Ramona is younger than Raúl. (*Ramona es menor (más joven) que Raúl.*)
3. You're saving up for a new stereo. How would you tell your father that you have more than fifty dollars? (*Tengo más de cincuenta dólares.*)

Picture-Cued Response

4. Point to the photograph on p. 409 and ask: "¿Qué vas a comprarme?" (*Voy a comprarte unas joyas.*)
5. Point to the photograph on p. 418 and ask:

"¿Cuántos regalos compré hoy?" (*Ud. compró (compraste) cuatro regalos hoy.*)

Situations

6. You find out that you and Ana were at the same rock concert on Friday night. You're very surprised that you didn't see her there. What might you say to her?
   a. No la viste.   b. No te vio.   c. *No te vi.*
7. Mario has just won a trip to Spain. What might you say to him?
   a. *Tienes mucha suerte.*   b. Tienes mucha sed.
   c. Tienes mucho sueño.
8. Your neighbor asks you what you're planning to do this summer. How might you answer?
   a. Creo que es fabuloso.   b. Pienso en las vacaciones.   c. *Pienso trabajar y estudiar.*

Real-Life Questions

9. ¿Te gustan los chistes? ¿Les cuentas chistes a tus amigos? ¿Te cuentan chistes a ti? ¿Cuál es tu mejor chiste? ¿Y el peor?
10. ¿Qué piensas de la comida mexicana? Cuando vas a un restaurante mexicano, ¿qué te gusta comer?
11. ¿Eres una persona seria o chistosa? ¿Quién es la persona más chistosa de tu familia? ¿Quién es la más seria?
12. ¿Tienes un animal doméstico? ¿Cómo se llama?

LEARNING SPANISH THROUGH ACTION

New prop vocabulary: none

Other new vocabulary: abierto, cerrado

New staging vocabulary: none

Sample

1. Abran un libro.
2. Toquen el libro abierto.
3. Toquen el libro cerrado.
4. Cierren el libro.
5. Toquen la puerta.
   Q: ¿Está abierta o cerrada?
   A: Abierta.
6. Toquen todos los libros abiertos en la clase.

CAPÍTULO 13

OBJECTIVES

Communication
- to identify vocabulary related to foods and restaurants
- to identify vocabulary related to festivals and celebrations

Grammar
- to use $e \rightarrow i$ stem-changing verbs
- to use negative words
- to use the singular preterite of *comer* and *salir*

Culture
- to describe the San Fermín Festival in Pamplona, Spain

SUGGESTED MATERIALS

p. 425 (Prólogo cultural):   a wall map showing Pamplona, Spain; magazine pictures depicting the various activities that take place during the Festival of San Fermín (fireworks, parade, running of the bulls, for example)

pp. 426–427 (Palabras nuevas I):   magazine pictures of various types of food; restaurant menus

p. 431 (Actividad):   restaurant menus

p. 432 (Diálogo):   a wall map showing Cuba; a menu from a Cuban-Chinese restaurant

pp. 434–435 (Palabras nuevas II):   magazine pictures showing carnivals and other celebrations

PAGES 424–425

Photo
The running of the bulls at the *Fiesta de San Fermín* in Pamplona, Spain. These same bulls will be in the afternoon bullfight. As a safety factor, a few oxen are mixed in with the bulls. Moreover, some of the more experienced runners are expected to keep their less experienced partners from getting hurt.

PAGE 427

Additions to on-page notes
Reteach / Extra Help: You may want to reinforce the difference between *pedir* and *preguntar* by asking these questions about mini-dialogue 3: *¿Qué le pregunta Óscar a Ester? (Le pregunta: "¿Qué vas a beber?") ¿Qué pide Óscar? (Pide una naranjada fría.)*

PAGE 429

Photo
A young vendor in Portonovo, Galicia, prepares a snack for a customer. Galicia, which is located in the northwestern corner of Spain, is known for its fresh seafood.

Realia
This menu from La Pizza restaurant in Spain describes the pizza served there as "more than an ordinary pizza." The menu indicates that the restaurant's owners first introduced this pizza in England in 1977, and since then its menu and its food have been imitated by others. The owners, however, believe that theirs is still "the best." Pizza lovers are asked to wait 20 to 30 minutes for this "marvel" to be prepared, but are assured that the wait is worthwhile. Toppings available include cheese, mushrooms, several types of homemade sausages, green peppers, and anchovies. Prices include service and tax, and are comparable to those paid in the U.S. for similar fare.

PAGE 430

Photo
A chef at the Casa Botín restaurant is shown cooking one of the house specialties. Casa Botín, one of Madrid's most famous restaurants, is mentioned in Ernest Hemingway's novels *The Sun Also Rises* and *Death in the Afternoon*.

Realia

The design and lettering of the restaurant's business card (shown just above the photo) are indicative of its long history. Founded in 1725, Casa Botín, which is located at the back of Plaza Mayor, is officially known as "The ancient house of Botín's nephew."

PAGE 431

Photos

(a) A Puerto Rican man (top left) is seen eating a *bacalaíto,* codfish breaded with flour and deep-fried. He has ordered his *bacalaíto* "to go" *(para llevar)* at one of the small outdoor restaurants in Puerto Rico called *friquitines* or *fondas.* Because it has become so expensive, codfish is no longer considered a staple in Puerto Rico. The sign in the photo advertises Goya, a New Jersey-based company that manufactures a wide variety of tropical food products.

(b) A colorful window menu (bottom right) entices customers to enter a restaurant in Barcelona. Featured are *gallego con cachelo,* a hearty vegetable soup from Galicia; *parrillada,* a variety of charcoal broiled meats; and *paella.* The menu also includes octopus *(pulpo),* a delicacy in Spain.

PAGE 432

Photo

A Cuban woman in Miami is shown serving a meal. Over 60 percent of Miamians are Hispanic, and within this group, more than three-fourths are of Cuban descent. It is, therefore, not surprising that Spanish, rather than English, is the language most often heard on the streets and in stores in Miami.

Cubans are not only the most numerous but also the most influential Hispanic group in Miami. They have had a tremendous impact on the city, both economically and politically. Cubans own a large share of the business establishments in Miami; the city's mayor is Cuban; and Cubans occupy other important political positions. Cubans are also well represented in academia, with many holding teaching and administrative positions at local universities.

The success of the Cuban community in Miami has been due to a combination of factors. Many of the Cubans who came here in 1959 were well educated and had broad business experience. Several of the top businessmen brought capital with them, totaling about twenty million dollars. Moreover, Cubans came at a time of rapid expansion of trade between the U.S. and Latin America, and intermediaries with a knowledge of Spanish and the Latin American business climate were needed. Lastly, there has been a strong sense of solidarity within the Cuban community, with individuals helping each other to achieve their diverse goals.

PAGE 433

Photo

These teenagers are shown eating a snack in Buenos Aires, Argentina. Late afternoon snacks are popular in much of the Spanish-speaking world and usually consist of such snacks as fruit, pastries, and *churros,* accompanied by hot chocolate, coffee, tea, or a fruit drink.

Additions to on-page notes

Reteach / Extra Help: If your class finds the *Participación* difficult, ask volunteers to present their dialogues as models.

PAGE 436

Photo

A man dressed for the *Danza de los moros* (Dance of the Moors) in Guatemala. Variations of this dance, which dramatizes the Spaniards' struggle to drive the Moors out of their country, are performed in several areas of Mexico and Guatemala. Like other regional dances, the *Danza de los moros* originated during colonial times and reflects the early missionaries' attempts to convert the Indians to Christianity or to teach them about certain events in Spanish history.

Additions to on-page notes

Reteach / Review: In connection with mini-dialogue 3, you may want students to add two or three additional lines in which Norma asks Mónica about the color of her costume, Mónica answers appropriately, and Norma responds by telling the color of her own costume.

PAGE 437

Photo

Residents of Corrientes, located on Argentina's northern border with Paraguay, celebrate the pre-Lenten carnival, which generally occurs the first or second week in February. *Carnaval* in Corrientes is sponsored by the city's wealthy families and is modeled after the famous Río de Janeiro carnival in Brazil. During *carnaval,* the streets are filled with people of all ages who don costumes and participate in the parades and dancing. Local schools traditionally compete against each other for prizes in the costume and float contests.

Additions to on-page notes

Reteach / Extra Help: After students do Ex. A in class, you may want to assign the sentences as written homework. Vary the exercise by asking students to make their new sentences plural. For example: *Vamos vestidos(as) de toreros(as).*

PAGE 438

Photo

Representatives from the thirty-one states of the *Estados Unidos Mexicanos,* Mexico's official name, march in the annual parade held on November 20 to commemorate the Mexican Revolution. Pictured here are the state emblems of Guerrero, Morelos, Nuevo León, and Querétaro.

PAGE 439

Photos

(a) This enthusiastic observer (top right) of the annual Puerto Rican Day Parade (held in New York City in early June) proudly waves the Puerto Rican flag. Established in 1958, this is one of the largest ethnic parades in the country and the culmination of a weeklong series of events. The parade is beamed by satellite to TV viewers in the U.S., Puerto Rico, and much of Latin America.

(b) This young woman (bottom right) wears an outfit typical of those worn in Andalucía as she rides in the cavalcade at the *Feria de abril,* which is also known as the *Feria de Sevilla.*

Realia

This program advertises scheduled events for Madrid's 1986 San Isidro Festival, which is held every May in honor of the city's patron saint, Isidro. Featured at the festival are live performances by pop and rock bands, food and beverages from every region of Spain, and a series of cultural events.

The message that appears on the left-hand side of the program is from the mayor of Madrid.

PAGE 442

Realia

The check from the Casa de Valencia restaurant in Madrid describes a typical dinner for two. For less than 4,000 pesetas, the diners ate bread, salad, soup, and paella, and they drank both bottled mineral water and house wine.

Photo

This family, which is shown dining at an outdoor restaurant in Torremolinos, is drinking wine with their meal. *Frituras de pescado,* fresh seafood such as herring, clams, and shrimp deep-fried without batter, are common fare in this tourist town on Spain's Costa del Sol.

PAGE 444

Photo

This *piñata* was made in Caracas, Venezuela. A *piñata* is a brightly colored figure (usually in the shape of an animal or toy) made of tissue paper or papier-mâché that covers a clay or cardboard container filled with candy, fruit, coins, and small gifts. Although *piñatas* originated in Mexico, where they are a part of birthday and saint's day celebrations, they are popular at children's parties throughout Latin America. During such occasions, blindfolded children take turns swinging at a hanging *piñata* with a stick or a bat, and when the piñata finally breaks, the children share its contents. Children are also treated to a *piñata* on each of the nine nights of the pre-Christmas *posadas* (literally "inns"), which are a reenactment of Mary and Joseph's search for lodging.

PAGE 445

Additions to on-page notes

Enrichment: In connection with the *Actividad,* you may want to ask students to write a list of things that one should never do in the winter, in the summer, in the cafeteria, and so on.

PAGE 446

Sample dialogues for *¿Qué pasa?*

Andrea has just found David at the parade and asks him what time he got there, which costume he likes best, and whether he plans to go to the bullfight.

A: ¡Hola, David! ¿A qué hora llegaste al desfile?

D: Llegué a las cinco. ¡La celebración es muy emocionante! Me encanta mirar a la gente.

A: ¿Qué disfraz te gusta más?

D: ¡Me encanta la torera!

A: ¿Piensas ir a la corrida?

D: ¡Claro que sí!

A: Ah, David. Aquí estás. ¿A qué hora llegaste?

D: Llegué a las seis y media. ¿Y tú?

A: Llegué temprano. Es un día muy emocionante. ¿Cuál es tu disfraz favorito?

D: Me encanta la reina.

A: Sí, su disfraz es muy bonito. ¿Piensas ir a la corrida?

D: ¡Por supuesto!

PAGE 447

Additions to on-page notes

Enrichment: Reinforce the singular preterite forms of *comer* and *salir* by having students work in pairs to ask and answer *¿Qué comiste para el desayuno hoy? ¿Qué comió tu madre? ¿A qué hora saliste de la casa hoy? ¿A qué hora salió tu padre?* (Answers will vary.)

PAGE 449

Photo

A stereo equipment store in Caracas, Venezuela. Latin Americans enjoy listening to various types of popular music, such as rock and jazz. Rock has a huge audience in Latin America, especially among teenagers. Jazz is also popular, although its audience is smaller and more specialized. Some singers and groups that perform in English and Spanish (pop artist José Feliciano from Puerto Rico, jazz-rock artist Carlos Santana from Mexico, and *salsa* king Rubén Blades from Panama, for example) have become bicultural stars with fans in the U.S. and in Latin America.

PAGE 450

Photos

(a) Children (top) are shown wearing huge papier-mâché masks called *cabezudos* (literally "big heads"). *Cabezudos,* together with *gigantes* (giants), are seen in parades during the many festivals held each year in Spain.

(b) The Parade of the Giants (bottom), which is part of Toledo's solemn Corpus Christi procession, is seen in this photo. This holy day commemorates the death of Christ.

Additions to on-page notes

Notes: Review of: 1. singular preterite of *llegar* / time telling   2. singular preterite of *comer* / noun phrases with *de* / indefinite article / omission of indefinite article   3. *pedir* / indefinite article / omission of indefinite article   4. $e \rightarrow i$ stem-changing verbs / *después de* / time telling / *decir*   5. *ver* / *hay* / *no . . . nadie* / *ningún, ninguna.*

Answers to *Repaso*

1. Llegué a la salida a las once de la mañana. / Llegaste al desfile a las cuatro de la tarde. / Ud. llegó a la entrada a las diez de la mañana.

2. Comió un chile relleno y sopa. / Ud. comió una chuleta de cordero y frijoles. / Comiste un sandwich de queso y papas.

3. Ahora pides una naranjada y postre. / Luego pedimos unos pasteles y té. / Luego Ud. pide un plátano y chocolate.
4. "Nunca servimos vino antes de las cinco y media," decimos nosotros(as). "¡Nunca!" repetimos. / "Nunca sirvo paella después de las doce menos cuarto," dice el Sr. Pérez. "¿Nunca?" pregunto. / "Los camareros nunca sirven comida antes de las ocho y cuarto," dicen ellos. "¡Nunca!" repiten.
5. Veo que no hay nadie en el comedor. / Ven que no hay ningún tenedor en la mesa. / Vemos que no hay ninguna servilleta en (sobre) los platos.

PAGE 451

Answers to *Tema*
1. Miguel llegó a la cafetería a la una de la tarde.
2. Comió una chuleta de cerdo y arroz.
3. Ahora pide una manzana y leche.
4. "Nunca servimos nada después de las dos," dice el Sr. Pérez. "¡Nunca!" repite.
5. Miguel ve que no hay nadie en la cafetería.

PAGE 452

Answers to *Comprueba tu progreso*

A
1. d	5. a	9. k
2. b	6. g	10. l
3. f	7. e	11. i
4. c	8. j	12. h

B
1. pide	5. pido
2. repetimos	6. sirve
3. sirven	7. pedimos
4. repites	8. sirvo

C
1. pide	4. piden
2. pregunta	5. preguntarle
3. pregunto	6. pedimos

D
1. nunca	6. nadie
2. nadie	7. nada
3. Ningún	8. Ninguno
4. Nada (Nunca)	9. Nunca
5. ninguna	10. ninguna

E Salí, comí, comió, saliste, Salí, comiste

PAGE 453

Photos
(a) The wooden mask on the left comes from Guatemala and was made by highland Mayas in the early nineteenth century. Masks like this one are now used in the *Baile de Alvarado*, a folk dance that dramatizes events that took place in the sixteenth century during the conquest of Guatemala by Pedro de Alvarado, one of Hernán Cortés's lieutenants.
(b) The mask on the right is from Tlaxcala, Mexico, and is made out of heavily painted wood. Masks like this one are used in a popular folk dance called *Danza de la culebra*.

ORAL PROFICIENCY TEST

Directed Response
1. Your friend Armando is upset because Sofía is ignoring him. Make him feel better by telling him that Sofía never speaks to anyone. *(Sofía nunca habla con nadie.)*
2. The waiter sees that you and Elena have finished your main course. How would he ask you both what you prefer for dessert? *(¿Qué prefieren Uds. de postre?)*
3. Conchita asks you what you did on Sunday. Tell her that you went out with your family. *(Salí con mi familia.)*

Picture-Cued Response
Using the visuals on pp. 434–435 or transparency 54, ask questions such as:
4. ¿Qué llevan las personas en el desfile? *(Llevan disfraces.)*
5. ¿De qué va vestida la persona que está al lado del toro? *(Va vestida de fantasma.)*
6. ¿Qué hacen los chicos que están cerca de los toreros? *(Rompen la piñata.)*

Situations

7. The gazpacho is very spicy. How might you complain about it to the waitress?
   a. El gazpacho es muy frío.   b. El gazpacho está muy caliente.   c. *El gazpacho está muy picante.*

8. At a masquerade party, Yolanda asks Pepe if he sees any of their friends. How might he answer if he doesn't see any of them?
   a. *No veo a ninguno.*   b. No veo nada.
   c. No veo ninguna.

Real-Life Questions

9. ¿Comiste en un restaurante el sábado pasado? ¿Qué comiste? ¿Le dejaste una propina al camarero o a la camarera?
10. Si no comiste en un restaurante, ¿dónde comiste? ¿Qué comiste?
11. ¿A qué hora saliste de casa esta mañana? ¿Llegaste tarde o temprano?

LEARNING SPANISH THROUGH ACTION

The foods may be taught in the same manner as those in Capítulo 1. Preterite verb forms may be taught in the following manner:

1. Give a command.
2. Narrate in the present tense.
3. Narrate in the past tense.
4. Ask what happened.

Sample

1. Anita, sal de la clase.
2. Anita sale de la clase. *(Say this before she actually leaves.)*
3. Anita salió de la clase. *(Say this only after she has completely stopped moving.)*
   Q: ¿Quién salió de la clase?
   A: Anita.
4. Anita, corre a la pizarra.
5. Corres a la pizarra, Anita.
6. Corriste a la pizarra, Anita.
   Q: ¿Adónde corriste?
   A: A la pizarra.

CAPÍTULO 14

OBJECTIVES

Communication
- to identify vocabulary related to personal hygiene and daily routines
- to identify vocabulary related to sports

Grammar
- to use reflexive verbs
- to use infinitives after prepositions

Culture
- to note soccer as the most popular sport in Latin America and Europe
- to point out other popular sports, especially baseball, in the Spanish-speaking world
- to name various ski resorts in South America and Spain
- to discuss sports stars and champions from Spain and Latin America

SUGGESTED MATERIALS

p. 455 (Prólogo cultural): wall map(s) showing South and Central America, the Caribbean, and Spain; magazine pictures of Hispanic sports stars

pp. 456–457 (Palabras nuevas I): magazine pictures and /or real objects to reinforce hygiene-related vocabulary (comb, soap, shampoo, toothbrush, toothpaste, dental floss, and so on)

p. 461 (Actividad): magazine and newspaper ads for deodorant, toothpaste, soap, and shampoo

pp. 464–465 (Palabras nuevas II): magazine pictures of sports events

p. 470 (Explicaciones I): index cards

PAGES 454–455

Photo
A soccer game in Buenos Aires.

PAGE 458

Realia
An ad for *Suave S-3* shampoo, bath gel, and cologne. These three products, which are suitable for the entire family's daily hygiene needs, all have the same scent "so that you and your family can start out each day— so fresh."

Additions to on-page notes
Notes: After you have presented the *Contexto comunicativo,* make sure that students understand the expression *hay que.* You may want to reinforce the meaning and use of *hay que* by asking these questions: *¿Qué hay que hacer si quieres salir bien en un examen? ¿Qué hay que hacer para la clase de mañana? ¿Qué hay que hacer durante este fin de semana? ¿Qué hay que llevar cuando hace mucho frío?*

PAGE 459

Realia
(a) An ad for socks that are specially treated to eliminate odor.
(b) An ad for a deodorant that has a neutral scent, is long-lasting, and doesn't irritate the skin.

PAGE 461

Additions to on-page notes
Enrichment: For the *Actividad,* you may want students to create posters using drawings or cutouts to advertise their products.

PAGE 462

Photo
A high school class in Buenos Aires, Argentina. Students may be interested in knowing that their counterparts in Argentina take from ten to fifteen subjects, including English or French, mathematics, physics, chemistry, biological sciences, history, and others, in a single year of secondary school.

PAGE 463

Photo

Students waiting for a bus in a rural area of Latin America.

Additions to on-page notes

Enrichment: Write these unknown words on the board, and ask students to pronounce them: *colonia, genuino, estacionar, mía, período.* The sentences in C are suitable for dictation.

PAGE 467

Photos

(a) Students (top left) work out on a track in Barcelona. Sports play an important role in this city where major competitions in a number of sports such as bicycling, swimming, water polo, hockey, tennis, basketball, boxing, automobile racing, gymnastics, and track are held throughout the year. Barcelona has been chosen to host the 1992 Summer Olympics.

(b) Teenagers are seen playing soccer on the beach (bottom) in the Mexican state of Yucatán, which is located on the Gulf of Mexico.

(c) Windsurfing (top right) is one of the most popular water sports along the Mediterranean and Atlantic coasts of southern Spain. Málaga is located on the 88-mile stretch of Mediterranean coastline known as Costa del Sol, an area that is lined with cosmopolitan beach resort cities featuring some of the finest luxury hotels, golf courses, and health spas in Europe.

PAGE 468

Photo

This boy is playing soccer in the ancient ball court at the archaeological ruins in El Tajín, Mexico. El Tajín was the sacred city of the Totonac Indians, who inhabited the region north of Veracruz between the sixth and tenth centuries. Its 150-acre area includes six reconstructed temples, the ball court, and several pyramids, the most notable of which is the six-stepped Pyramid of the Niches, which has 365 niches cut into its surface of adobe and volcanic rock and resembles a huge beehive. This is one of the oldest constructions of its kind in Mexico.

Additions to on-page notes

Enrichment: Additional questions for Ex. C (pp. 468–469): *¿Qué deporte prefieres practicar? ¿Qué deporte prefieres mirar en la televisión? ¿Qué clases de equipos tiene tu escuela? ¿Cuál es el mejor equipo? ¿Y cuál es el peor?*

PAGE 469

Realia

(a) The poster on the left announces a soccer game between the teams from Manzanares and Alcobendas, two towns near Madrid.

(b) The poster on the right advertises a bicycle race in Alcobendas.

(c) The postage stamps commemorate two major international events: the 1978 World Cup soccer championship, which was hosted and won by Argentina, and the 1982 World Cup soccer championship, which was hosted by Spain and won by Italy.

PAGE 471

Photos

(a) A young woman (top) is shown brushing her teeth in Santander, Spain.

(b) Two young students (bottom) are shown grooming themselves in a school dormitory in Arcos de la Frontera, Spain.

Realia

This ad from Dercos pharmaceutical laboratories promotes a new and innovative double-action product for dry, fragile, and split hair. Made with natural vegetable oils, double-action Dercos is both a nourishing, smoothing, and strengthening hair treatment and an easy-to-rinse shampoo. It also enhances the hair's natural protection against the drying effects of the sun and sea. The results, the ad says, will surprise you.

PAGE 473

Photo

A Spanish teenager is seen brushing her hair.

PAGE 476

Photo

Gabriela ("Gaby") Sabatini, Argentina's favorite and foremost woman tennis star, is seen playing the semifinal round of the 1987 Wimbledon Championship, which she lost to Steffi Graf of West Germany. This annual two-week competition, which is held every summer at the posh All-England Lawn Tennis and Croquet Club in a London suburb called Wimbledon, is one of the world's most important tennis events. The Wimbledon tournament is the oldest—the first was held in 1877—and also one of the most difficult.

PAGE 477

Photos

(a) Baseball player Tony Armas (top left) was born in 1953 in Anzoátegui, Venezuela. An outstanding defensive outfielder, he played with the Boston Red Sox for four seasons (1983–86) until he suffered a series of leg injuries that severely affected his performance. His best season was in 1984, when he led the major leagues in home runs (43) and runs batted in (123).

(b) Soccer player Diego Maradona (top right) was born in a poor barrio of Buenos Aires, Argentina. An outstanding athlete, he has achieved fame for his significant role in Argentina's victory in the 1986 World Cup soccer championship game.

(c) Baseball great Roberto Clemente (bottom left) was born in Carolina, Puerto Rico, in 1934. At the age of 17, he played with the Santurce Cangrejos, also called Santurce Crabbers, and his batting and powerful throwing arm attracted the attention of some major-league scouts who were visiting the island. Clemente signed with the Brooklyn Dodgers in 1953 and the following year was drafted by the Pittsburgh Pirates, for whom he played for the rest of his baseball career. He led the league in hitting and maintained a .300 batting average for 13 seasons. During his career he drove in 1,305 runs and scored 1,416.

Clemente was killed in an airplane crash in 1972 while en route to Nicaragua to deliver supplies collected for earthquake victims. He was elected to the Baseball Hall of Fame in 1973.

Additions to on-page notes

Reteach / Extra Help: After students have read the *Lectura* and answered the *Preguntas,* you may want to ask them to work in pairs to prepare an imaginary description of a day in Gabriela Sabatini's life. Students may give either a first- or a third-person account: *Me levanto / Se levanta a las seis. Me lavo / Se lava la cara,* and so on.

PAGE 478

Photo

Located on the slopes of the Sierra Nevada Mountains in Spain, the Sol y Nieve ski resort (shown in the photo) provides excellent skiing conditions.

PAGE 481

Photo

Passengers boarding a plane in Santiago, Chile. Because Chile's varied terrain is composed of forests, mountains, and deserts, traveling by land is often difficult. Therefore, airplanes are the preferred form of transportation to certain areas of the country.

PAGE 482

Photos

(a) Youngsters enjoying a dive in Puerto Rico.

(b) Students at the UNAM, or Universidad Nacional Autónoma de México in Mexico City, are shown playing volleyball. Founded in 1551, the university is one of the oldest institutions of higher learning in the Western Hemisphere. The name indicates that it operates independently and is not under the control of the Ministry of Education.

Before the present campus was constructed, the schools of the university had been housed in various parts of the city. The concept of a central campus, decided upon during the administration of President Miguel Alemán (1946–1952), was a new one for Latin America.

The upper ten stories of the university library—one of the most photographed buildings in Mexico—are covered with mosaic panels, which together form the world's largest mosaic mural. The building is a monument to Mexico's heritage, with each wall being devoted to a different aspect of Mexican culture. The remainder of the campus is also noteworthy for its striking, modern buildings. The campus is one of the most popular sightseeing attractions in Mexico City.

Answers to *Repaso*

1. Ana es una jugadora fuerte pero pesimista. / Somos (unos) jugadores buenos pero perezosos. / Uds. son (unas) aficionadas simpáticas (amables) y generosas.
2. Se acuesta a las diez. / Me duermo a las nueve. / Nos despertamos a las seis.
3. Después de despertarme, me visto. Me pongo el traje y la corbata. / Después de levantarnos, nos vestimos. Nos lavamos la cara y las manos. / Después de bañarse, Uds. se visten. Se ponen el collar y los aretes.
4. Es tarde pero hay que cantar dos veces. / Es tarde y hay que regresar (volver) de prisa. / Es tarde pero hay que caminar despacio.
5. Me divierto mucho en el laboratorio de química. / Nos divertimos mucho en la clase de español. / Se divierten mucho en el partido de golf.

PAGE 483

Answers to *Tema*

1. Graciela es una atleta fuerte y enérgica.
2. Se levanta a las siete.
3. Después de bañarse, se viste. Se pone la camiseta y los pantalones.
4. Es tarde y hay que salir de prisa.
5. Graciela se divierte mucho en el partido de volibol.

PAGE 484

Answers to *Comprueba tu progreso*

A
1. a   3. a   5. a   7. a
2. b   4. b   6. a   8. a

B
1. nos lavamos
2. se divierte
3. se pone
4. cepillarme
5. nos quitamos
6. se duermen
7. levantarte
8. te vistes
9. me baño

C
1. No, se bañan con agua caliente.
2. No, me levanto a las seis.
3. No, nos despertamos tarde.
4. No, me ducho por la noche.
5. No, nos cepillamos los dientes después de comer.
6. No, me acuesto más tarde.

D
1. Uso el balón para jugar al fútbol.
2. Uso el peine para peinarme.
3. Uso el tenedor para comer.
4. Uso el champú para lavarme el pelo.
5. Uso la pasta dentífrica para cepillarme los dientes.
6. Uso el jabón para bañarme.
7. Uso el despertador para despertarme.

E
1. Después de levantarnos comemos el desayuno.
2. Mis padres necesitan un despertador para despertarme.
3. Bebo chocolate caliente para dormirme.
4. Antes de bañarme me quito la ropa.
5. Antes de divertirse hace la tarea.
6. Después de peinarme voy a salir.

F
1. Se acuesta sin decir buenas noches.
2. Recibe los regalos sin decir gracias.
3. Sube al autobús sin hacer cola.
4. Va a la escuela sin peinarse.
5. Sale del cuarto sin presentar a los invitados.
6. Empieza a comer sin esperar a nadie.

PAGE 485

Photo

A gold and turquoise mask from the Chimú culture of ancient Peru. The Chimú and the Incas used much more advanced techniques for working with metals than any of the other pre-Columbian cultures in America. They knew many of the techniques used today, including hammering, gilding, and plating.

ORAL PROFICIENCY TEST

Directed Response

1. Diana says it's time for dinner now. Say that you want to take a shower first. *(Quiero ducharme primero.)*
2. Your aunt asks why you aren't asleep yet. Say that you always read a little before you go to sleep. *(Siempre leo un poco antes de dormirme.)*
3. Your coach is afraid you'll all miss the bus if you don't hurry. How would he tell you that it's necessary for you to get dressed quickly? *(Hay que vestirse rápidamente (de prisa).)*

Picture-Cued Response

4. Point to the photograph on p. 473 and ask: "¿Qué hace el muchacho?" *(El muchacho juega al fútbol.)*
5. Point to the photograph at the bottom of p. 482 and ask: "¿A qué juegan los muchachos?" *(Los muchachos juegan al volibol.)*

Situations

6. You arrive late at the stadium and hear all of the fans cheering. What might you ask?
   a. ¿Quién gana?   b. ¿Quién se divierte?
   c. ¿A qué juega?
7. Your teacher wants to know why you're so tired today. What might you say?
   a. Me levanté tarde.   b. Te despertaste temprano.   c. *Me acosté tarde.*
8. Ana is amazed at how fast Juan can run. You agree. What might you say to her?
   a. Sí, es muy perezoso.   b. *Sí, es buen atleta.*   c. Sí, corre muy despacio.

Real-Life Questions

9. Cuando no hay clases, ¿te levantas temprano o tarde? ¿Te vistes antes o después de comer el desayuno?
10. ¿Te bañas o te duchas cada día? ¿Qué te gusta más, bañarte o ducharte?
11. ¿Cómo se llama tu atleta favorito(a)? ¿Qué deporte practica tu atleta favorito(a)?
12. ¿Qué cosas haces rápidamente? ¿Qué cosas haces más despacio? ¿Crees que lo que haces rápidamente son cosas que no te gusta hacer?

LEARNING SPANISH THROUGH ACTION

New prop vocabulary: la cara, los dientes, la mano, el pelo. To add variety, you may also use some of the parts of the body taught in Capítulo 16.

Other new vocabulary: derecho(a), izquierdo(a)

New staging vocabulary: tocarse, tocar

Sample

1. Tóquense la cara.
2. Tóquense las orejas.
3. Tóquense la mano izquierda.

Teach the parts of the body in this manner, and then continue.

4. Pedro, tócate la nariz con la mano izquierda.
5. Ana, tócate el brazo izquierdo con la mano derecha.

6. María, brinca a la puerta en el pie izquierdo.

At this point, you may demonstrate the difference between *tocarse* and *tocar* using narration.

7. Pedro, toca la mano de Luis.
8. Tocas la mano de Luis.
9. Luis, tócate la nariz.
10. Te tocas la nariz.
11. Pedro y Luis, tóquense la cabeza.
12. Uds. se tocan la cabeza, pero yo me toco la nariz. *(Touch your nose.)*
13. Pedro, toca el brazo de Luis.
14. Tocas el brazo de Luis, pero no te tocas el brazo.

See Capítulo 11 for a lesson on *veces.*

Grooming items may be taught in the same manner as the food items in Capítulo 1.

CAPÍTULO 15

OBJECTIVES

Communication
- to identify vocabulary related to travel
- to identify vocabulary related to hotel accommodations

Grammar
- to use the verb *saber*
- to use the verb *conocer*
- to distinguish between *saber* and *conocer*
- to express ongoing action *(hace . . . que)*
- to use the regular *-ar* preterite

Culture
- to note the historical and sentimental significance of Spain's *tren de la Fresa*
- to discuss the popularity of trains in Spain
- to explain why train travel is so popular in Spain

SUGGESTED MATERIALS

p. 487 (Prólogo cultural): a wall map showing Madrid and the town of Aranjuez

pp. 488–489 (Palabras nuevas I): a wall map of Europe, including northern Africa; a compass; souvenirs and post cards

p. 492 (Diálogo): a wall map showing France and Spain, including the Pyrenees; magazine pictures of the Tour de France or any international cycling event

p. 494 (Palabras nuevas II): magazine pictures of bedroom and living room furniture

p. 511 (Actividad): a paper bag

PAGES 486–487

Photo
A view of the Atocha railroad station in Madrid, Spain. Atocha is one of the two main railroad stations in Madrid; the other one is Chamartín. The Atocha station is located south of Chamartín and is the departure point for most trains to the southeast and south. The Chamartín station is located on the north side of the city and is the departure point for most trains to the northwest, north, and northeast. Trains to the eastern cities, such as Valencia and Alicante, also leave mainly from the Chamartín station. Trains to nearby points, such as El Escorial, Segovia, Guadalajara, and Alcalá de Henares, can be boarded at either station.

PAGE 492

Photo
Cyclists near Mar del Plata, Argentina. Cycling is popular in Argentina, and several cycling competitions are held there every year.

Additions to on-page notes
Culture: You may want to ask students to do research on this year's Tour de France and present brief oral reports. Students should draw a map to accompany their reports, or they should use the class map to show the route followed by Tour de France participants.

PAGE 493

Photo
A group of cyclists is seen in Spain.

PAGE 494

Additions to on-page notes
If students ask: Other related words you may want to present: *el cajón,* drawer (in furniture); *el botón,* button (for elevator).

PAGE 497

Realia
A receipt from the Hotel Cueva del Fraile, which is located in a restored sixteenth-century building in Cuenca, Spain.

Realia

A receipt from the Hotel Calipolis, a modern hotel located in Sitges, a popular seaside resort near Barcelona, Spain.

Photo

The Basílica de Nuestra Señora del Pilar is located in Zaragoza, capital of Spain's northeastern region of Aragón. This famous shrine, built during the seventeenth and eighteenth centuries, is dedicated to La Virgen del Pilar, whose feast day is celebrated on October 12 with festive parades, folk dancing, and bullfights.

Photos

(a) Seen at the top of the page is the Hotel Hacienda in Ibiza, one of the Balearic Islands (Menorca, Mallorca, and Formentera are the others), which lie off the western coast of Spain. The hotel's rooms are exquisitely decorated, and each has its own terrace with breathtaking clifftop views of the Mediterranean coastline.

(b) View from the interior of the Alhambra in Granada, Spain. The Alhambra was called the Calat Alhambra ("red castle" in Arabic) because of the color of the walls that surround it. Built in the fourteenth century as a fortified palace for the reigning dynasty of Nasrid Sultans, it stands overlooking the city and symbolizes the glory of Moorish architecture, which reached its fullest development in Granada. Organized around a series of courtyards, patios, and fountains, the Alhambra is distinctive for the ornate, geometric decoration that graces the ceilings and arches of its numerous chambers. Ceramic tiles emphasize the angularity of arabesque motifs and calligraphic decoration lining the walls. In 1526 Charles V destroyed part of the palace to make way for the construction of his royal chambers, which were financed in part by a tax levied on the Moors. It is in these rooms that Washington Irving is said to have lived while writing his *Tales from the Alhambra*.

(c) View of the exterior of the Alhambra. In contrast to the grace and delicacy of the Alhambra's interior, the exterior, with its ramparts and watchtowers, more closely resembles a military structure.

In the background of the photo are the three hills at the foot of which lies Granada. It is said that the last Moorish king, Boabdil, stopped on one of those hills to take a last look at his kingdom and palace; and since then the hill has been known as *El Suspiro del Moro* (The Sigh of the Moor).

Additions to on-page notes

Enrichment: Before students begin the *Práctica* on pp. 502–503, you may want to ask questions to reinforce the forms of *saber* and *conocer* and the differences in usage between the two verbs. For example: *¿Sabes cómo se llama la reina de Inglaterra? ¿La conoces? ¿Sabemos cuál es la capital de España? ¿La conocemos bien?* (Answers will vary.)

Photo

Barcelonans are shown dancing the *sardana*. The *sardana* of Cataluña is an example of a folk dance closely tied to the national consciousness of a people. Men and women join hands and dance in a closed circle, accompanied by drums and reed instruments. The dance, which originated in the nineteenth century as a symbol of Catalan separatism, is still performed on Sunday mornings in many of the town squares of Cataluña.

Additions to on-page notes

Enrichment: After students do Ex. D in class, ask them to write out the paragraph at home. Vary the practice by changing *yo* to *nosotros* and *Carlos* to *Carlos y Carlota*. Check students' work for correct spelling, punctuation, and capitalization.

PAGE 504
Photo

Students from all over the world visit Spain to take advantage of summer study programs that focus on language and culture as well as music and dance. Iberia Airlines of Spain offers student discount fares from the U.S., and there are special air and train fares for travel within Spain. Foreign students enjoy the hospitality at youth hostels, *pensiones,* and camping grounds throughout mainland Spain and the Balearic and Canary Islands.

Realia

The inset advertises bargain vacations for young people, offering such trips as a ''grand tour'' of Italy, a ''Swiss landscape'' trip, and a ''Viking circuit.'' Prices are given in pesetas and include transportation, hotel, breakfast, and insurance.

PAGE 505
Additions to on-page notes

Reteach / Extra Help: In preparation for Exs. A and B, ask students to work in pairs, taking turns asking and answering questions using *hace . . . que.* Circulate to give help where needed.

PAGE 506
Sample dialogues for *¿Qué pasa?*

The Girondos have just arrived in Europe, but have no hotel reservations. Mrs. Girondo makes a phone call and talks to a hotel manager about making a reservation for a room.

Sra.: Buenos días, señor. Mi esposo y yo necesitamos un cuarto, y quisiera hacer una reservación.

G: Muy bien, señora. Tengo un cuarto con baño privado y ducha.

Sra.: ¿Tiene vista al mar?

G: Sí, señora. Hay un balcón pequeño con vista al mar.

Sra.: ¿De veras? ¡Entonces vamos a salir en seguida!

Sra.: Buenos días, señor. Quisiera hacer una reservación para un cuarto con vista a la plaza.

G: Tengo un cuarto bonito, pero no tiene baño privado.

Sra.: ¿Puede Ud. describir el cuarto?

G: ¡Cómo no, señora! ¡Es magnífico! Tiene dos ventanas y también hay un balcón pequeño con vista a la plaza.

Sra.: ¿De veras? Mi esposo y yo vamos a salir en seguida.

PAGE 510
Photo

Young women at Benito Juárez International Airport in Mexico City. Of the 600 international flights entering Mexico every week, approximately three quarters of them originate in the U.S. Mexico City's airport has been expanded to accommodate the growing air traffic, which is now estimated at 10 million passengers per year and expected to double in the very near future.

Latin American airports and airlines enjoy some unique distinctions. For example, Mexico City's International Airport is the busiest in Latin America. El Alto in La Paz is the world's highest commercial airport. And Avianca, the privately owned Colombian airline founded in 1919, is the oldest in the Americas and the second oldest in the world.

PAGE 511
Photo

This souvenir shop in Sevilla displays local handicrafts, which include the colorful ceramics for which the province is famous. The ceramics produced in the various regions of Spain can be identified by their distinctive patterns and styles, and also by the techniques used in manufacturing them.

PAGE 512
Photo

Young people stroll along a street in Barcelona's Barrio Gótico.

Realia

The map and tickets seen here are issued by RENFE (Red Nacional de Ferrocarriles Españoles), Spain's state-run railroad company.

Answers to *Repaso*

1. Sabes contar chistes bastante bien. / Sabemos sacar fotos muy bien. / Saben decorar apartamentos bastante bien.
2. Hace un mes que vivo en Europa. / Hace diez días que llueve en Alemania. / Hace dos semanas que estudiamos en Inglaterra.
3. Anoche mandé un regalo. / Ayer Uds. lavaron las ventanas. / La semana pasada pagaste por las bebidas.
4. Carmen disfrutó mucho de su visita. / Disfrutaron mucho de nuestro concierto. / Disfrutamos mucho de tu cena.
5. Cree que conozco muy bien a Bárbara. / Cree que Ud. conoce muy bien el cuento. / Creo que sabemos bastante bien las respuestas (sabemos las respuestas bastante bien).

PAGE 513

Answers to *Tema*

1. Jim y Bob saben hablar español muy bien (hablar muy bien el español).
2. Hace dos meses que viajan por España.
3. Ayer visitaron Granada.
4. Disfrutaron mucho de su viaje.
5. Creen que conocen muy bien a España.

PAGE 514

Answers to *Comprueba tu progreso*

A espejo, sillón, sábanas, fundas, manta, almohadas, lámpara, alfombra, ascensor, escalera, armario, balcón

B
1. Conoce
2. Saben
3. Sabe
4. Conocen
5. Sabes
6. Conocemos
7. Conozco
8. Saben

C sabe, conoce, conoce, sé, conozco, Sabes, sé, sé, sabemos, sabemos

D
1. ¿Cuánto tiempo hace que Ud. conoce a ese guía? Hace diez años que conozco a ese guía (que lo conozco).
2. ¿Cuánto tiempo hace que miras la televisión? Hace dos horas y media que miro la televisión (que la miro).
3. ¿Cuánto tiempo hace que Felipe está enfermo? Hace una semana que está enfermo.
4. ¿Cuánto tiempo hace que Mariana sabe dibujar? Hace varios años que sabe dibujar.
5. ¿Cuánto tiempo hace que Uds. se quedan en este hotel? Hace cinco días que nos quedamos en este hotel.
6. ¿Cuánto tiempo hace que los niños viven en Inglaterra? Hace cuatro meses que viven en Inglaterra.

E llegué, estudié, ayudé, lavamos, jugué, ganó, jugaron, se acostaron, miramos, terminó, me acosté

PAGE 515

Photo

This wood niche (a recess in a wall, especially one designed for a statue) from Guatemala was made by highland Mayas in the late nineteenth century. Astatue of a saint was usually placed within the niche.

ORAL PROFICIENCY TEST

Directed Response

1. Jorge's father wants to know how long you've been living here. Tell him that you've been living here for two years. *(Hace dos años que vivo aquí.)*
2. Your teacher asks you a question. How would you tell her that you don't know the answer? *(No sé la respuesta.)*
3. Paco didn't like the movie that he and María saw together. How did he ask her what she thought of the movie? *(¿Qué pensaste de la película?)*

Picture-Cued Response

Point to the hotel receipt on p. 498 and ask:

4. ¿Sabemos quién se quedó en este hotel? *(No, no sabemos quién se quedó en ese hotel OR No, no lo sabemos.)*
5. ¿Conoces este hotel? *(No, no lo conozco.)*

Situations

6. Your cousins from Colombia are staying with you during their visit to the U.S. How would you tell a friend that they've been staying with you for a month?
   a. *Hace un mes que se quedan conmigo.*
   b. Piensan quedarse conmigo un mes.
   c. Se quedaron conmigo el mes pasado.

7. You're lost in downtown Buenos Aires. What might you say to get someone's attention so that you can ask for directions?
   a. *Discúlpeme.*   b. Con mucho gusto.
   c. Bienvenido.

Real-Life Questions

8. ¿Dónde vives? ¿Cuánto tiempo hace que vives allí?
9. ¿Haces un viaje a otra ciudad a veces? ¿Conoces a gente en otras ciudades?
10. Si vas de vacaciones a otra ciudad, ¿te quedas en casa de amigos o te quedas en un hotel? ¿Es necesario hacer una reservación?

LEARNING SPANISH THROUGH ACTION

New prop vocabulary: Countries

Other new vocabulary: este, oeste, norte, sur

New staging vocabulary: none

If you wish, teach the countries in the same manner as in the first lesson of *En Camino B,* and then continue. Use questioning.

Sample

1. Toquen el país al oeste de España.
   Q: ¿Qué país es?
   A: Portugal.
2. Señalen el país al norte de España.
   Q: ¿Qué país es?
   A: Francia.

The lesson from Capítulo 5 may be adapted to teach the items of furniture.

OBJECTIVES

Communication

■ to identify vocabulary related to the human body, illness and medical checkups

■ to identify vocabulary related to reading and book-buying

Grammar

■ to use affirmative words

■ to contrast affirmative and negative words

■ to use the regular -er / -ir preterite

Culture

■ to discuss the Spanish-language comic book

■ to point out different countries' names for "comic book" and the titles and characters of several well-known comic books in Spain and Latin America

■ to note the popularity of the *fotonovela*

SUGGESTED MATERIALS

p. 517 (Prólogo cultural): Spanish-language comic books and / or *fotonovelas;* comic strips in Spanish

p. 538 (Lectura): a wall map showing Mexico

PAGES 516–517

Photo

Comic books for rent in a poor district of Lima, Peru. The sign reads *$1.00 se alquila chiste* ($1.00 to rent a comic book). The dollar symbol ($) in this case is used to represent Peruvian money. Since the Peruvian exchange rate has fluctuated a great deal, it is difficult to tell what the exact price was in U.S. money at the time the photograph was taken; however, the price would not exceed five cents in U.S. money.

Comic books are a form of entertainment available to all social classes in Spanish-speaking countries. Most of the magazines shown are translations of comic books published in the U.S. Action and adventure heroes popular in the U.S. are represented among the titles. Cartoon-type magazines can also be found. And several horror magazines are included.

PAGE 520

Realia

(a) An ad for *Sleepover,* an inflatable neck cushion that provides head support during long trips or while relaxing in one's home or on the beach. The ad says "Don't lose your head" and adds that there's no reason to do so when you have your *Sleepover* under your arm.

The last paragraph of the ad mentions that *Sleepover* contains some excess fibers that will disappear after the first washing. It also recommends that the product be washed in plenty of lukewarm water using a mild soap product.

(b) A prescription from a doctor's office or clinic *(consultorio médico)* at Buenos Aires's Hospital Británico, which was founded in 1844.

Additions to on-page notes

Reteach / Review: After presenting the seven mini-dialogues, make sure students understand that *doler, faltar,* and *importar* function like the verbs *gustar* and *encantar.*

PAGE 522

Photos

(a) A gym class is seen in the city of Salamanca, which is located in the region of Castilla.

(b) A Spanish physician is shown checking a patient's blood pressure. In Spain, free medical care is provided. Trade guilds, employee unions, and professional associations also have their own supplementary group medical insurance. In addition, individuals and families can purchase medical policies with private insurance companies. Premiums for individual and family health insurance are much less expensive in Spain than in the U.S., and coverage is generally much more comprehensive.

PAGE 523

Photos

(a) Young handicapped men receive therapy in a gym at Hospital Pérez Carreño in Caracas. Besides private medical assistance, the Ministry of Health provides free public care at hospitals, clinics, and other facilities. The elderly and physically handicapped are aided by the Patronato Nacional de Ancianos e Inválidos (National Foundation for the Elderly and Handicapped).

(b) Students are shown exercising at the University of Chile in Santiago. Through government-run campaigns and other public-awareness programs, many Latin American countries are emphasizing the importance of a well-balanced diet and regular exercise.

PAGES 526–527

Additions to on-page notes

Notes: You may want to tell students that *poetisa* is the correct term for a female poet. However, in current usage, *poeta* is often substituted for *poetisa* and is the preferred form among female poets in the Spanish-speaking world.

PAGE 529

Photo

Students are shown browsing in a Mexico City bookstore.

PAGE 530

Photos

(a) Rush hour at the Zócalo, Mexico City's main square.

(b) View of Puerto Rico's Luquillo Beach. Located at the edge of an attractive coconut grove, Luquillo is the best-known and most visited beach on the island, attracting more than two million visitors a year.

PAGE 534

Photos

(a) Two students study at home in Panama City, Panama. All courses, textbooks, and exams are in English in about 90 percent of the private junior high and high schools in Panama. Discussions, however, are often in Spanish, which is Panama's official language. In public secondary schools, all classes are in Spanish, and English is taught as a second language.

(b) Seen here is a movie poster for a box office hit playing in Palma de Mallorca, the capital of the Balearic Islands. The title, *Un loco suelto en Hollywood,* means ''A crazy man loose in Hollywood'', and bears little resemblance to the original English title, *Down and Out in Beverly Hills.* U.S. films are extremely popular in the Spanish-speaking world, but their titles are often unrecognizable because they are usually rewritten rather than translated literally, with different versions in different countries.

PAGE 537

Photo

Two teenagers are shown chatting at an outdoor café in Viña del Mar, Chile, the country's leading summer resort.

PAGE 538

Additions to on-page notes

Culture: You may want to ask students to do research on Moctezuma. How did Cortés and his soldiers conquer the Aztecs? Ask students to present brief oral reports on their findings. Do students remember who Hernán Cortés was? (See *Lectura,* Ch. 8).

PAGE 541

Photos

(a) A city market in Cartagena, a major port and commercial center on Colombia's Caribbean coast.

(b) A woman is shown selling produce in Arcos de la Frontera, Spain. Located in the Andalusian province of Cádiz, Arcos overlooks a valley of fertile farmland irrigated by the Río Guadalete. Like other towns in the area (Jerez, Palos, Vejer, and so on), its name includes *de la Frontera* because the borders changed hands repeatedly

Teacher Notes **T125**

during two centuries of battles between the Christians and the Moors, which finally ended in 1492.

PAGE 542

Additions to on-page notes

Enrichment: Ask students to write Ex. E as a homework assignment. Check their work for correct spelling, capitalization, and punctuation.

PAGE 543

Photo

Students are shown in a classroom in Buenos Aires. Argentina, Uruguay, and Chile have the best educational programs in South America, as evidenced by a literacy rate of almost 100 percent in all three countries. Although primary education is mandatory in almost all of Latin America, literacy rates vary considerably from country to country and still tend to be lowest in rural areas. With the exception of Costa Rica, the literacy rate in Central America averages 50 percent. Most of South America and the Spanish-speaking Caribbean ranks considerably higher.

PAGE 544

Photo

Two children are shown reading a comic book in a poor district of Iquitos, Peru. Iquitos is a town of about 175,000 people on the west bank of the Amazon river.

Realia

Cover of a comic book featuring Superman. A view of Superman's exploding home planet is shown, and the words on top say, ''The Legend Begins-The Man of Steel.'' *Ejemplar de obsequio* indicates that this is a sample copy of the magazine. Superman is a popular hero all over the Spanish-speaking world. Sometimes his name is translated as *Superhombre,* but in most cases he is known simply as *Supermán.*

Answers to *Repaso*

1. Esta noche mi hermana asistió a un partido de volibol con varios(as) amigos(as). / Esa noche bebieron (tomaron) una botella de leche con sus amigos(as). / Anoche Marcos y yo comimos chuletas de cordero con nuestras novias.

2. A ella le gusta mirar a Ricardo, la persona menor (más joven) del equipo. / A ellos (ellas) les gusta escuchar a Luz, la chica (muchacha) más inteligente de la clase. / A nosotros nos gusta invitar a Pilar y a Raúl, los estudiantes más chistosos (cómicos) de la escuela.

3. Perdimos el partido, y ahora nos duelen las piernas. ¡Qué mala suerte! Escribió las cartas, y ahora le duele la mano. ¡Qué lástima! / Vi la película, y ahora me duelen los ojos. ¡Qué problema!

4. El Dr. Jiménez nos escuchó y nos dio una excusa. / El dentista me examinó y me dio un cepillo de dientes. / La enfermera las vio y les dio (unas) toallas.

5. Pablo escribió un poco. Luego, él y algunos(as) amigos(as) jugaron adentro. / Las mujeres cocinaron mucho. Luego, ellas y algunas invitadas comieron afuera. / Dormí demasiado. Más tarde, algunos chicos (muchachos) y yo corrimos afuera.

PAGE 545

Answers to *Tema*

1. Ayer Rosa asistió a un partido de fútbol con algunas amigas.
2. A Rosa le gusta mirar a Antonio, el jugador más rápido del equipo.
3. Antonio ganó el partido, y ahora le duelen las piernas. ¡Pobrecito!
4. El médico lo examinó, pero no le dio nada.
5. Antonio descansó un poco. Luego, él, Rosa y algunos amigos celebraron afuera.

PAGE 546

Answers to *Comprueba tu progreso*

A Answers will vary.

B 1. Sí, nos gusta el chocolate. No, no nos gusta el chocolate.
2. Sí, les faltan libros. No, no les faltan libros.
3. Sí, me duelen los pies. No, no me duelen los pies.
4. Sí, les gustan tus (sus) poemas. No, no les gustan tus (sus) poemas.
5. Sí, me importa recibir el dinero (recibirlo) mañana. No, no me importa recibir el dinero (recibirlo) mañana.

6. Sí, le duele el estómago. No, no le duele el estómago.

C 1. algunos   5. Algunos
  2. algo   6. algo
  3. algunas   7. Algún
  4. alguna   8. Alguien

D 1. Tienen algo en venta en esa librería.
  2. Lo hago siempre.
  3. Alguien lo conoce a él.
  4. Alguien sabe algo de él.
  5. Siempre bebo vino blanco.
  6. Tú conoces a alguien.
  7. ¿Va al baile con alguien?
  8. Tenemos algunos vestidos para la fiesta.
  9. También podemos nadar en el río.

E 1. aprendimos
  2. recibiste
  3. comieron
  4. vivió
  5. comprendieron
  6. escribí

F 1. Sí, viví en Guadalajara.
  2. Sí, aprendimos español.
  3. Sí, vendieron su casa.
  4. Sí, visité Valencia.
  5. Sí, abrió (abriste) la ventana.
  6. Sí, compré el estante.
  7. Sí, comprendí todo.
  8. Sí, disfruté mucho de esta clase.

PAGE 547

Photo

An earthenware jar from Yarinacocha, Peru. The jar was made by Indians of the Shipibo tribe, who inhabit the Amazon jungle in eastern Peru. The Shipibo are very isolated and, as a result, very little is known about them. We do know, however, that they are skilled fishermen and boatmen.

The jar shown in the photograph is used to ferment *chicha,* an alcoholic beverage made from maize. According to tradition, the jar can only be used once for that purpose. The characteristic Shipibo design on the jar is supposed to keep evil spirits away.

ORAL PROFICIENCY TEST

Directed Response

1. Say that you don't want to go to school today because your throat hurts. *(No quiero ir a la escuela hoy porque me duele la garganta.)*
2. Your little brother wakes up frightened. He hears noises. How might he ask you if there's anyone outside? *(¿Hay alguien afuera?)*
3. Diego wants to know if you've heard from Sofía. Tell him you received a letter from her yesterday. *(Recibí una carta de ella ayer.)*

Picture-Cued Response

4. Point to the bottom photograph on p. 530 and ask: "¿Adónde les gusta a Uds. ir durante el verano?" *(Nos gusta ir a la playa.)*
5. Point to the bottom photograph on p. 541 and ask: "¿Qué vieron Uds. en el mercado ayer?" *(Ayer vimos frutas en el mercado.)*

Situations

6. Your friend had a skiing accident and broke her leg. What might you say about her?
  a. ¡Ay, qué interesante!   b. ¡Tiene gripe!
  c. *¡Pobrecita!*
7. Carla just bought a new outfit and she tries it on so you can see it. What might she ask you?
  a. ¿Esperas que sí?   b. *¿Qué te parece?*
  c. ¿Te lo pido prestado?

Real-Life Questions

8. ¿Esperas ir a algún país latinoamericano algún día?
9. Muchos padres dicen que los niños no deben mirar la televisión durante la semana. ¿Estás de acuerdo? ¿Por qué?
10. ¿Qué haces cuando te duele algo? ¿Vas al médico (a la médica)?
11. ¿Te divertiste este año en la clase de español? ¿Por qué?

ORAL PROFICIENCY TEST CHAPTERS 13–16

Directed Response

1. Mariano asks you if you'd like sugar in your coffee. Tell him you never use sugar. *(Nunca uso azúcar.)*

2. Mother wants to know if you want to eat now or later. Say that it doesn't matter to you. *(No me importa.)*

3. Your teacher is getting upset because you haven't begun your exam yet. Your excuse is that you need a pencil. How would you say so? *(Me falta un lápiz.)*

Picture-Cued Response

Point to the photograph on p. 442 and ask:

4. ¿Qué hizo la familia anoche? *(La familia fue a un restaurante.)*

Using the visuals on p. 489 or transparency 60, ask questions such as:

5. Cuando haces un viaje, ¿qué mandas a tus amigos? *(Cuando hago un viaje mando tarjetas postales a mis amigos. OR Cuando hago un viaje les mando tarjetas postales.)*

6. Cuando regresas de un viaje, ¿qué les das a tus amigos? *(Cuando regreso de un viaje, les doy recuerdos a mis amigos. OR Cuando regreso de un viaje, les doy recuerdos.)*

Using the visuals on p. 494 or transparency 61, ask questions such as:

7. ¿Cómo puedes ir de un piso a otro si no quieres usar la escalera? *(Puedo usar el ascensor.)*

8. ¿Dónde pones la ropa en tu cuarto? *(La pongo en el armario (la cómoda.))*

9. ¿Qué pones en la cama cuando hace mucho frío por la noche? *(Pongo una manta en la cama cuando hace mucho frío.)*

10. ¿Qué necesitas para hacer la cama? *(Necesito sábanas, una funda y una manta.)*

Situations

11. Your father doesn't want you to use the car tonight and your mother agrees. How would she say so?
a. Lo siento.   b. *Estoy de acuerdo.*
c. No lo sé.

12. Your sister is annoyed because she wants to get into the bathroom and you're taking too long. When she asks why you're taking so long, what might you say?
a. Te lavas la cara.   b. Se lava el pelo.
c. *Me lavo las manos.*

Real-Life Questions

13. ¿Te gusta caminar? ¿Caminas rápidamente o despacio? ¿Cuánto caminas cada día?

14. ¿Eres una persona enérgica? ¿Eres perezoso(a) a veces? ¿Por qué?

15. ¿Sabes quién va a ser tu profesor(a) de matemáticas el año próximo? ¿Conoces a este(a) profesor(a)?

LEARNING SPANISH THROUGH ACTION

See Capítulo 14 for a lesson on the parts of the body.

VOCES Y VISTAS

Scott, Foresman Spanish Program Book 1

TODO HOMBRE CULTO AMA
Y PROTEGE A LOS ANIMALES

Bernadette M. Reynolds
Montbello High School
Denver, Co

Carol Eubanks Rodríguez
Glen Crest Junior High School
Glen Ellyn, Il

Rudolf L. Schonfeld
Parsippany High School
Parsippany, NJ

VOCES Y VISTAS

Scott, Foresman and Company
Editorial Offices: Glenview, Illinois

Regional Offices: Sunnyvale, California • Tucker, Georgia
Glenview, Illinois • Oakland, New Jersey • Dallas, Texas

The authors and editors would like to express their heartfelt thanks to the following team of reader consultants. Each of them read the manuscript of all three levels of the Scott, Foresman Spanish Program. Chapter by chapter, each offered suggestions and provided encouragement. Their contribution has been invaluable.

Senior Reader Consultants

Estella M. Gahala, Ph.D.
National Foreign Language
   Consultant
Scott, Foresman and Company
Glenview, IL

Barbara Snyder, Ph.D.
Parma Public Schools
Parma, OH

Reader Consultants

Sheila Starr Ashley
Radnor High School
Radnor, PA

Elaine W. Baer
Foreign Language Dept. Chairperson
John Bartram High School
Philadelphia, PA

Barbara M. Berry, Ph.D.
Foreign Language Dept. Chairperson
Ypsilanti Public Schools
Ypsilanti, MI

Anna Budiwsky
Cardinal O'Hara High School
Springfield, PA

Susan R. Cole
San Francisco USD
San Francisco, CA

J. Patricio Concha
Foreign Language Dept. Chairperson
Overbrook High School
Philadelphia, PA

Judith A. Dean
Mount Tabor High School
Winston-Salem/Forsyth Co.
   Schools
Winston-Salem, NC

Louis P. Díaz
Foreign Language Dept. Chairperson
Kirkwood High School
Kirkwood, MO

Marta Fernández, Ph.D.
Evanston Township High School
Evanston, IL

Raúl Fernández
Foreign Language Dept. Chairperson
Shiloh High School
Gwinnett Co., GA

Eugenio V. González
Eagle Pass ISD
Eagle Pass, TX

Cordelia R. Gutiérrez
Costa Mesa High School
Costa Mesa, CA

Karen L. James
Hilton Head High School
Hilton Head Island, SC

Sister Magdalena Kellner
Nazareth Academy High School
Rochester, NY

Mary Ann Kindig
Foreign Language Dept. Chairperson
Nimitz High School
Irving, TX

Walter Kleinmann
Foreign Languages Coordinator
Sewanhaka Central High School
   District
Long Island, NY

Argelia Krohn
Foreign Language Dept. Chairperson
Roosevelt High School
San Antonio, TX

Mark S. Levine
Foreign Language Dept. Chairperson
Garden City High School
Garden City, NY

Virtudes López
Foreign Language Dept. Chairperson
Miller Place High School
Miller Place, NY

María A. Montalvo-Sisneros
Albuquerque Public Schools
Albuquerque, NM

Cecilia Silva de Rodríguez, Ph.D.
Foreign Language Dept. Chairperson
Arlington ISD
Arlington, TX

Ursula F. Sihocky
Glenbard South High School
Glen Ellyn, IL

Sharon A. Smith
Frick International Studies Academy
Pittsburgh, PA

Nancy H. Strickland
Foreign Language Dept. Chairperson
Newman Smith High School
Carrollton-Farmers Branch ISD
Carrollton, TX

Susan L. Thompson
Bridgewater-Raritan Regional
   School District
Bridgewater-Raritan, NJ

Ralph P. Vander Heide, Ph.D.
Supervisor of Foreign Language
   Education
Bethlehem Central Schools
Delmar, NY

Helen P. Warriner-Burke, Ph.D.
Associate Director
Foreign Languages, ESL &
   Bilingual Education
Virginia Department of Education

Rosemary Weddington
Franklin County High School
Frankfort, KY

Gwendolyn Jones Williams
Bishop McDevitt High School
Wyncote, PA

Catherine L. Wilson
Crestwood High School
Atlanta, GA

Jo Anne S. Wilson
Foreign Language Consultant
Michigan Department of
   Education

Marcia Payne Wooten
Yadkin County Schools
Yadkin Co., NC

Jacqueline G. Yandle
Massapequa High School
Massapequa, NY

TABLA DE MATERIAS

EN CAMINO

VI

CAPÍTULO 1

CAPÍTULO 2

CAPÍTULO 5

CAPÍTULO 6

CAPÍTULO 7

CAPÍTULO 8

CAPÍTULO 9

CAPÍTULO 10

CAPÍTULO 11

CAPÍTULO 12

CAPÍTULO 13

CAPÍTULO 14

CAPÍTULO 15

CAPÍTULO 16

EN CAMINO

PALABRAS NUEVAS I

¿Cómo te llamas?

¡Hola! Me llamo Juan. ¿Y tú?

Me llamo Susana.

¿Cómo está usted?

Bien, gracias. Y tú, ¿cómo estás?

la clase de es

la profesora   el profesor

la clase de español

el estudiante

la estudiante

Culture: Explain that the important distinction between you formal *(usted)* and you familiar *(tú)* still exists in many languages.

When speaking to another person in English, we use the word "you," but in Spanish there are two words. You use *tú* when you speak to a member of your family or to anyone you call by a first name. We call this the familiar (fam.) use. You use *usted* when you speak to an adult, in formal situations, and to show respect. We call *usted* formal. Adults who do not know each other well usually use *usted*. In greeting someone you address as *tú*, you should say *¿cómo estás?* or *¿qué tal?* Otherwise, you should say *¿cómo está usted?*

Enrichment: Point out the use of accent marks (on pp. 2–3: *cómo, tú, estás, qué, sí, así, días, José, está*). Explain that accent marks in Spanish can indicate where the stress falls or serve to distinguish two words that are spelled the same. Rules for correct placement of accent marks are presented on pp. 57 and 65.

1 MARTA   **¿Cómo te llamas?**

   JUANA   Me llamo Juana. ¿Y tú?

   MARTA   Marta.

¿cómo te llamas? *what's your name?*

2 OLGA   ¿Cómo te llamas? . . . ¿Manuel?

   JOSÉ   **No,** me llamo José.

no *no*

3 JAIME   ¡Hola! **¿Qué tal? ¿Bien?**

   MARTA   **Sí, muy** bien, **gracias.**

¿qué tal? *how's it going?*
bien *well*
sí *yes*
muy *very*
gracias *thank you, thanks*
¿cómo estás? *how are you?* (fam.)
así, así *so-so*

4 CARLOS   Hola, Teresa. **¿Cómo estás?**

   TERESA   **Así, así.**

Variaciones:
■ ¿cómo estás? → ¿qué tal?
■ así, así → muy bien

5 JORGE   **Buenos días, señor*** Arias.
        ¿Cómo está usted?

   SR. ARIAS   Bien, Jorge. Y tú, ¿cómo estás?

   JORGE   Muy bien, gracias.

■ señor → profesor

buenos días *good morning*
el señor (Sr.) *Mr.; sir*
¿cómo está usted? *how are you?* (formal)

Enrichment: Explain that *¿Qué tal?* and *¡Hola!* are informal expressions used mainly in greeting close friends. Point out that *así, así* is a response that means neither very good nor very bad.

Culture: Explain that in Spanish we use punctuation marks at the beginning and end of questions and exclamations. Elicit how Spanish punctuation therefore provides a clue about the type of sentence that follows.

* The abbreviation for *señor* is *Sr.* When *señor* is used alone, without a last name, it means *sir.*

Reteach / Review: You might have students ask each other *¿Cómo te llamas?* and answer using their new Spanish names.

Here is a list of common Spanish names. If the Spanish equivalent of your name is not on the list, this is your chance to choose any name you like.

Muchachas

Alicia	Concepción	Gloria	Lucía	Raquel
Ana	Consuelo	Graciela	Luisa	Rebeca
(Anita)	Cristina	Guadalupe	Luz	Rita
Andrea	Diana	(Lupe)	Magdalena	Rosa
Ángela	Dolores	Inés	Margarita	Sara
Bárbara	(Lola)	Irene	María	Silvia
Beatriz	Elena	Isabel	Mariana	Sofía
Carlota	Elisa	Josefina	Marta	Sonia
Carmen	Emilia	Juana	Mercedes	Susana
Carolina	Esperanza	Judit	Mónica	Teresa
Catalina	Ester	Julia	Norma	Verónica
Cecilia	Eugenia	Laura	Olga	Victoria
Clara	Eva	Leonor	Patricia	Virginia
Claudia	Georgina	Lourdes	Pilar	Yolanda

En Puerto Rico

Muchachos

Agustín	Cristóbal	Gerardo	Leonardo	Raimundo
Alberto	Daniel	Gregorio	Luis	Ramón
Alejandro	David	Guillermo	Manuel	Raúl
Alfonso	Diego	Gustavo	Marcos	Ricardo
Alfredo	Eduardo	Héctor	Mario	Roberto
Andrés	Enrique	Horacio	Mateo	Rodolfo
Ángel	Ernesto	Ignacio	Mauricio	Rogelio
Antonio	Esteban	Jaime	Miguel	Samuel
Armando	Eugenio	Javier	Nicolás	Santiago
Arturo	Federico	Jesús	Oscar	Sergio
Benjamín	Felipe	Jorge	Pablo	Timoteo
Bernardo	Fernando	José (Pepe)	Patricio	Tomás
Carlos	Francisco	Juan	Pedro	Vicente
César	(Paco)	Julio	Rafael	Víctor

PRÁCTICA

A Me llamo . . . Your teacher will introduce himself or herself and ask your name. Answer in Spanish, using the name you have chosen.

> **PROFESOR(A)** *Buenos días. Me llamo ____. ¿Cómo te llamas?*
> **ESTUDIANTE** *Buenos días, profesor(a). Me llamo ____.*

B ¡Hola! In groups of three or four, take turns introducing yourself and asking each of the others what his or her name is.

> **ESTUDIANTE A** *¡Hola! Me llamo ____. Y tú, ¿cómo te llamas?*
> **ESTUDIANTE B** *Me llamo ____.*

Now practice the dialogue with the whole class. Introduce yourself to the person next to you or immediately behind you.

C ¿Qué tal? In groups of three or four, take turns asking one another how you are. You can ask either *¿Cómo estás?* or *¿Qué tal?* You can answer *Bien, Muy bien,* or *Así, así.* For example:

> **ESTUDIANTE A** *¿Qué tal?*
> **ESTUDIANTE B** *Muy bien, gracias. Y tú, ¿cómo estás?*
> **ESTUDIANTE C** *Así, así. ¿Y tú, ____? ¿Qué tal?*

Now practice the dialogue with the whole class. Ask the person next to you or immediately behind you. If you have forgotten the person's name, ask for it in Spanish.

Reteach / Extra Help: If your class needs additional examples, ask a volunteer to model the first sentence in an exercise.

Practice Sheet En Camino 1

Tape Manual Exs. 1–2 3

Reteach / Review: Ask pairs of students to practice greetings and farewells. Include the expressions introduced on pp. 2–3.

 4

**CONTEXTO
VISUAL**

Transparency 2

Buenos días

**CONTEXTO
COMUNICATIVO**   5

1 SR. CANO	**Buenas tardes.** Me llamo Rafael Cano.	**buenas tardes** *good afternoon*
SR. ÁVILA	**Mucho gusto.** Me llamo José Ávila.	**mucho gusto** *pleased to meet you*

Variaciones:

■ buenas tardes → buenos días

2 LOLITA	**Buenas noches,** señora* Toledo.	**buenas noches** *good night, good evening*
SRA. TOLEDO*	**Adiós,** Lolita.	**adiós** *good-by*

■ buenas noches → **hasta mañana**
■ adiós → **hasta luego**

hasta mañana *see you tomorrow*
hasta luego *see you later*

---

* We use *señora* when we speak to a married woman. We use *señorita* to address an unmarried woman or one whose marital status we don't know. The abbreviation for *señora* is *Sra.* The abbreviation for *señorita* is *Srta.* When they are used alone, without a last name, *señora* and *señorita* mean ''ma'am.''

Enrichment: Write *Buenos días, sí,* and *¡Hola!* on the board. Ask students for the opposite of each word or expression (*Buenas noches, no, Adiós*).

PRÁCTICA

A Mucho gusto. In groups of three or four, practice introducing yourselves. This time add that you are pleased to meet one another. When you are finished, use any of the "good-by" words to end the conversation.

B Buenos días. According to the time of day shown on the clocks, what would you say to greet the person in each picture appropriately? Follow the model.

Buenos días, Sra. Montoya.

Sra. Montoya

1. Sr. Gómez   2. Pepe   3. Mónica

4. Sra. López   5. Profesora Ruiz   6. Profesor Ávila

C Hasta luego. Your teacher will say good-by to the first person in the first row, who will respond. Then that person will turn to the next person and do the same. Continue until the last person has said good-by (to the teacher). You may use any of the "good-by" expressions you wish. For example:

PROFESOR(A)	*Buenas noches. Hasta mañana.*
ESTUDIANTE A	*Adiós. Hasta luego.*
ESTUDIANTE B	*Buenas tardes, María.*
ESTUDIANTE C	*Buenas noches, Juan. Hasta mañana.*

Práctica A
Answers will vary.
Should include *mucho gusto* and *adiós / hasta mañana / hasta luego.*

Reteach / Review: Before students form groups to do Ex. A, review the words used in introductions, greetings, and farewells, Let groups practice while you circulate to give help where needed. Pairs may volunteer to act out the conversations.

Práctica B
1. Buenos días, Sr. Gómez.
2. Buenas tardes, Pepe.
3. Buenos días, Mónica.
4. Buenas noches, Sra. López.
5. Buenas tardes, profesora Ruiz.
6. Buenas noches, profesor Ávila.

Reteach / Extra Help: If students find Ex. B difficult, write different times of day on the board. Point to each hour and ask for the appropriate Spanish greeting.

Enrichment: You may want to have students do Ex. B as a written assignment.

Reteach / Review: Follow Ex. B with a review of the use of accents and abbreviations *(Sr., Sra., Srta.)* in Spanish.

Práctica C
Answers will vary.

Tape Manual Ex. 3 6

Notes: Use Spanish in class even though the specific words or constructions have not been presented. Students will absorb a great deal in a Spanish-speaking atmosphere. Don't hesitate to use exaggerated expressions and hand signals to convey meaning.

Ask students to look at each cartoon very carefully. Go over each picture and perform the gestures until students understand. Use these expressions regularly, adding others as you need them. (Other classroom expressions are presented on pp. 18 and 46.) Repeat the gestures to reinforce the spoken words.

EXPRESIONES PARA LA CLASE

The words and phrases in these cartoons will probably be used in class by your teacher. See how many you can figure out without any help. You may not be expected to use them, but you should be able to recognize and understand them.

PRONUNCIACIÓN 7

A Spanish vowel sounds are not like English ones. First, each vowel usually has only one sound. Spanish vowel sounds are quicker and tenser than those in English, and they aren't drawn out.

B The pronunciation of the letter *a* is similar to the vowel sound in the English word "pop."

C Escucha y repite.

adiós	Esteban	mañana	gracias	así, así

¿Qué tal, Andrea?   Buenas tardes, Clara.

¿Cómo estás, Catalina?   Hasta mañana, Ana María.

Enrichment: Write unknown words containing the target sound on the board and ask students to pronounce them: *animal, habla, mamá, papá,* etc.

ACTIVIDAD

Buenas tardes, Sr. Presidente.   Work with a partner. One of you plays yourself while the other plays the role of one of the people listed below. You meet on the street, exchange greetings, ask each other how you are, and then say good-by. Then switch roles, choosing another character.

PEOPLE YOU MEET	FORMAL PHRASES	INFORMAL
Sr. García, the mail carrier	Buenos días	¡Hola!
Sra. Rodríguez, the principal	Buenas tardes	¿Qué tal?
Pepito, the boy next door	Buenas noches	¿Cómo estás?
your best friend	¿Cómo está usted?	¿Y tú?
your teacher	¿Y usted?	Adiós
Sr. Presidente	Adiós	Hasta luego
	Hasta luego	

Buenas tardes, señores.
En España

VOCABULARIO DE EN CAMINO A

Sustantivos
la clase (de español)
el/la estudiante
el profesor, la profesora
el señor
la señora
la señorita

Conjunción
y

Pronombres
tú
usted

Adverbios
bien
muy
no
sí

Expresiones
adiós
así, así
buenas noches
buenas tardes
buenos días
¿cómo está usted?
¿cómo estás?
¿cómo te llamas?

gracias
hasta luego
hasta mañana
¡hola!
me llamo
mucho gusto
¿qué tal?

PALABRAS NUEVAS I

¿De dónde eres?

8

**CONTEXTO
VISUAL**

Transparency 3

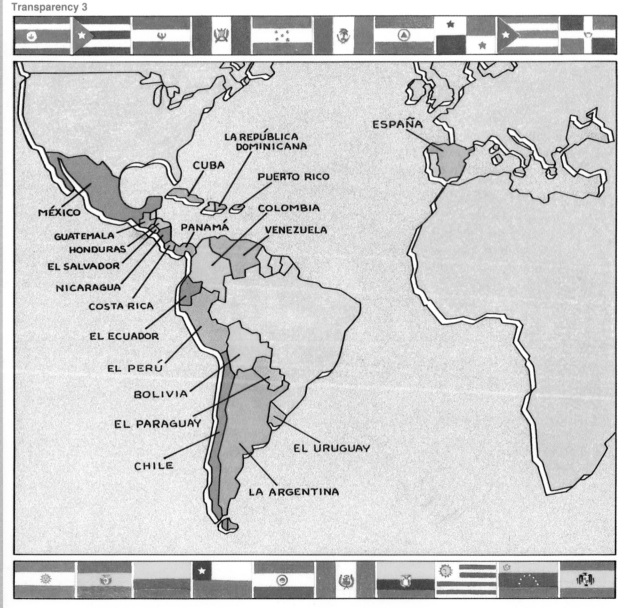

ESPAÑA

LA REPÚBLICA
DOMINICANA

CUBA

PUERTO RICO

MÉXICO

COLOMBIA

GUATEMALA

PANAMÁ

VENEZUELA

HONDURAS

EL SALVADOR

NICARAGUA

COSTA RICA

EL ECUADOR

EL PERÚ

BOLIVIA

EL PARAGUAY

EL URUGUAY

CHILE

LA ARGENTINA

CONTEXTO COMUNICATIVO 9

1 MARIO **¿De dónde eres?**
ANDREA **Soy de** México. ¿Y tú?
MARIO **Yo** soy de Costa Rica.

Variaciones:
- México → Guatemala
- Costa Rica → Honduras

Reteach / Extra Help: Go around the room and point to boys as the whole class repeats *él.* Do the same for *ella.* Point to yourself; repeat *yo.* Have students point to themselves while saying *yo* and to a friend while saying *tú.*

Enrichment: You may want to write on the board: *Yo soy _____, Tú eres _____, Ella es _____, Él es _____.* Ask volunteers to point to the appropriate person while saying the sentence. Have them add the Spanish name of the student being addressed.

¿de dónde eres? *where are you from?*
soy *I am, I'm*
de (del) *from*
yo *I*

2 LUISA **¿De dónde es** Bárbara?
JORGE **Es** de Venezuela.
LUISA ¿Y Pablo?
JORGE **Él** es de Panamá.

- Venezuela → Colombia
- ¿y Pablo → ¿y él?
- Panamá → España

¿de dónde es _____? *where is _____ from?*
es *he is (he's); she is (she's); it is (it's)*
él *he*

3 EVA **¿Eres de** Chile?
CÉSAR Sí, soy de Chile. Y tú, ¿de dónde eres?
EVA Yo soy del Ecuador.

- Chile → Bolivia
- del Ecuador → del Paraguay
- del Ecuador → de El Salvador

¿eres de _____? *are you from _____?*

4 SARA La profesora Ruiz es de la Argentina.
INÉS ¿Y Graciela Martínez? ¿Dé dónde es **ella**?
SARA **No sé.**

- la profesora → el profesor
- de la Argentina → de la República Dominicana
- Graciela → Raúl
  ella → él

ella *she*
no sé *I don't know*

Culture: You might suggest that students draw or trace their own maps and label the countries whose principal language is Spanish. You may also want to assign reports on these countries. Topics might include music, products, climate, and points of interest. Encourage students to bring to class things that they have that came from these countries.

If students ask: Explain that *de + El* doesn't form a contraction because *El* is part of the name of the country, *El Salvador*. Other uses of *del* are discussed in Chap. 5.

When we talk about someone coming from a country whose name is preceded by *el*, we say *del: de + el → del*.

José es *del* Perú.

El Salvador is the only exception.

Martín es **de** El Salvador.

When *la* comes before the name of a country, we say *de la*.

Ana es **de la** Argentina.

When we talk *about* a person whose name includes a title, such as *señor*, *señora*, or *profesor(a)*, we use *el* or *la* before the title.

¿De dónde es **la** profesora Ruiz?

El señor Ortega es de Chile.

We do not use *el* or *la* when we are talking directly *to* the person.

Buenos días, señor Ortega.

Reteach / Review: Extend the concept of *de*, *del*, and *de la* by substituting names of other countries shown on p. 10.

PRÁCTICA

A **La clase de español.**   Benjamín took a photograph of some of the exchange students at his school. Working with a partner, take turns asking and answering where each person is from.

ESTUDIANTE A   *¿De dónde es Manuel?*
ESTUDIANTE B   *Es de Honduras.*

1. Andrea   3. Mercedes   5. Ramón
2. Mateo   4. Gloria   6. Luis

Práctica A
1. ¿De dónde es Andrea? Es de Venezuela.
2. ¿... Mateo? Es de México.
3. ¿... Mercedes? Es de El Salvador.
4. ¿... Gloria? Es del Perú.
5. ¿... Ramón? Es de Puerto Rico.
6. ¿... Luis? Es de España.

B **¿De dónde eres?** It is a new semester at the International School, and everyone is getting acquainted. Working with a partner, find out where each classmate is from. Follow the model.

> Lola / el Perú   José / Chile
> JOSÉ   *¿Dé dónde eres, Lola?*
> LOLA   *Soy del Perú. ¿Y tú, José?*
> JOSÉ   *Yo soy de Chile.*

1. Carlos / Panamá   Juana / Colombia
2. Antonia / México   Ricardo / Venezuela
3. Eduardo / el Uruguay   María / el Paraguay
4. Rosa / Nicaragua   Laura / Bolivia
5. Juan / la Florida   Tomás / Colorado
6. Marta / la República Dominicana   Luis / el Ecuador

C **¿Dé dónde es?** Now, using the information from Práctica B, take turns asking a partner where each student is from. In the final response, remember to use *él* for boys and *ella* for girls.

> ESTUDIANTE A   *¿De dónde es Lola?*
> ESTUDIANTE B   *Es del Perú.*
> ESTUDIANTE A   *¿Y José?*
> ESTUDIANTE B   *Él es de Chile.*

D **El club de ajedrez.** The International School Chess Club is having a tournament between the seniors and the faculty. You recognize all of the teachers and know where they are from. But you don't know any of the older students. Working with a partner, take turns asking and answering. Use the correct words *el* or *la estudiante* and *él* or *ella*. For example:

> el profesor Ramírez / el Uruguay   Norma / Bolivia
> ESTUDIANTE A   *El profesor Ramírez es del Uruguay. Y la estudiante,*
>   *¿de dónde es ella?*
> ESTUDIANTE B   *Norma es de Bolivia.*

1. el profesor Gutiérrez / la Argentina   María / Guatemala
2. la profesora Fernández / Puerto Rico   Jorge / Chile
3. la profesora Zayas / España   Diego / el Ecuador
4. el profesor Rodríguez / Cuba   Marta / Honduras
5. la profesora Pérez / Chile   Marcos / California
6. el profesor Muñoz / Costa Rica   Isabel / El Salvador

Práctica B
1. ¿De dónde eres, Carlos? Soy de Panamá. ¿Y tú, Juana? Yo soy de Colombia.
2. ¿... Antonia? ... de México. ¿Y tú, Ricardo? ... de Venezuela.
3. ¿... Eduardo? ... del Uruguay. ¿Y tú, María? ... del Paraguay.
4. ¿... Rosa? ... de Nicaragua. ¿Y tú, Laura? ... de Bolivia.
5. ¿... Juan? ... de la Florida. ¿Y tú, Tomás? ... de Colorado.
6. ¿... Marta? ... de la República Dominicana. ¿Y tú, Luis? ... del Ecuador.

Práctica C
1. ¿De dónde es Carlos? Es de Panamá. ¿Y Juana? Ella es de Colombia.
2. ¿... Antonia? ... de México. ¿Y Ricardo? Él es de Venezuela.
3. ¿... Eduardo? ... del Uruguay. ¿Y María? Ella es del Paraguay.
4. ¿... Rosa? ... de Nicaragua. ¿Y Laura? Ella es de Bolivia.
5. ¿... Juan? ... de la Florida. ¿Y Tomás? Él es de Colorado.
6. ¿... Marta? ... de la República Dominicana. ¿Y Luis? Él es del Ecuador.

Práctica D
1. El profesor Gutiérrez es de la Argentina. Y la estudiante, ¿de dónde es ella? María es de Guatemala.
2. ... es de Puerto Rico. Y el estudiante, ¿de dónde es él? Jorge es de Chile.
3. ... es de España. Y el estudiante, ¿de dónde es él? Diego es del Ecuador.
4. ... es de Cuba. Y la estudiante, ¿de dónde es ella? Marta es de Honduras.
5. ... es de Chile. Y el estudiante, ¿de dónde es él? Marcos es de California.
6. ... es de Costa Rica. Y la estudiante, ¿de dónde es ella? Isabel es de El Salvador.

PALABRAS NUEVAS II

¿Qué quiere decir . . . ?

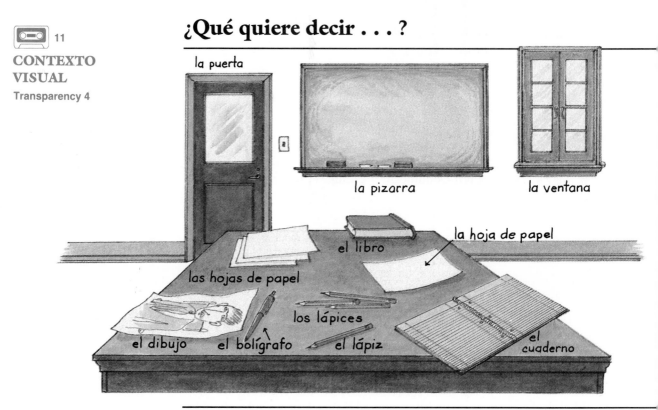

 12

1 DAVID   **¿Cómo se dice** *book* **en español?**

ELENA   Libro.

DAVID   Gracias, Elena.

ELENA   **De nada.**

Variaciones:

■ *book → chalkboard*
  libro → pizarra

■ *book → notebook*
  libro → cuaderno

¿cómo se dice ____? *how do you say ____?*

en español *in Spanish*

de nada *you're welcome*

2 TOMÁS   **No comprendo. ¿Qué quiere decir** "bolígrafo"?

PROFESORA   ¿Bolígrafo? *Ballpoint pen.*

TOMÁS   Ah, **muchas gracias.**

no comprendo *I don't understand*

¿qué quiere decir ____? *what does ____ mean?*

muchas gracias *thanks a lot*

If students ask: You may want to introduce the names of other classroom objects now: *el escritorio,* desk; *la pared,* wall; *la bandera,* flag; *la regla,* ruler; *el borrador,* eraser; *la tiza,* chalk. Some of these are taught in Chap. 1. You may want to have students draw and label these objects as a homework assignment.

If students ask: Emphasize that in the sentence *¿Cómo se escribe tu nombre?, tu* means "your." Ask what they see in the word *tú* when it means "you." Remind students that the accent mark also changes the meaning of *él* and *el*.

Reteach / Review: Remind students that in Spanish we use punctuation at the beginning and end of questions and exclamations.

El alfabeto

a (a)	h (hache)	ñ (eñe)	t (te)
b (be)	i (i)	o (o)	u (u)
c (ce)	j (jota)	p (pe)	v (ve)
ch (che)	k (ca)	q (cu)	w (doble ve)
d (de)	l (ele)	r (ere)	x (equis)
e (e)	ll (elle)	rr (erre)	y (i griega)
f (efe)	m (eme)	s (ese)	z (zeta)
g (ge)	n (ene)		

Enrichment: Tell students that the letter *y* is also called *la ye.*

3 ESTER   ¿Enrique?

ENRIQUE   ¿Sí, Ester?

ESTER   **Por favor, ¿cómo se escribe tu nombre?**

ENRIQUE   E-N-R-I-Q-U-E

■ tu nombre → Enrique

por favor *please*

¿cómo se escribe ____? *how do you spell ____?*

tu *your*

el nombre *name*

The Spanish alphabet has four more letters than the English alphabet: *ch, ll, ñ,* and *rr.* The rest of the letters are the same, but their names and sounds are different. Listen carefully as your teacher reads them to you.

When you spell words out loud, you say *acento* when a vowel has an accent mark on it. For example, when spelling the word *lápiz,* you say: *ele–a* acento–*pe–i–zeta.*

PRÁCTICA

Práctica A

1. cuaderno... ce-u-a-de-e-ere-ene-o
2. lápiz... ele-a *acento*-pe-i-zeta
3. libro... ele-i-be-ere-o
4. pizarra... pe-i-zeta-a-erre-a
5. bolígrafo... be-o-ele-i *acento*-ge-ere-a-efe-o
6. ventana... ve-e-ene-te-a-ene-a
7. dibujo... de-i-be-u-jota-o
8. lápices... ele-a *acento*-pe-i-ce-e-ese

Notes: To encourage students to participate, you may want to ask two volunteers to do Ex. A or B in front of the class. Keep the pace quick but relaxed.

A ¿Cómo se escribe . . . ?

With a partner, using the drawings as cues, take turns asking and answering. Follow the model.

ESTUDIANTE A *¿Cómo se escribe "puerta"?*
ESTUDIANTE B *P-U-E-R-T-A.*

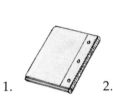 1.    2.    3.    4.

 5.    6.   7.    8.

Práctica B

1. efe-e-de-e-ere-i-ce-o
2. jota-o-ese-e-efe-i-ene-a
3. jota-a-ve-i-e-ere
4. ere-a-cu-u-e-ele
5. ce-a-ere-ele-o-te-a
6. ge-u-i-elle-e-ere-eme-o
7. te-i-eme-o-te-e-o
8. e-ese-pe-e-ere-a-ene-zeta-a
9. i griega-o-ele-a-ene-de-a
10. pe-a-te-ere-i-ce-i-o
11. Answers will vary.

B ¿Y tu nombre?

At a meeting of the Spanish Club, the faculty adviser asks each student what Spanish name he or she has selected to use and how that name is spelled. With a partner, take turns playing the roles of teacher and student. Follow the model.

PROFESOR(A) *¿Cómo te llamas?*
ESTUDIANTE *Me llamo Juanito.*
PROFESOR(A) *¿Cómo se escribe tu nombre?*
ESTUDIANTE *J-U-A-N-I-T-O.*

1. Federico
2. Josefina
3. Javier
4. Raquel
5. Carlota
6. Guillermo
7. Timoteo
8. Esperanza
9. Yolanda
10. Patricio
11. Y tú, ¿cómo se escribe tu nombre?

Enrichment: Pronunciación on pp. 119 and 463 deals with the sounds of the letters *h* and *j*. You may want to ask what English letter has the sound of the Spanish *j*, *(h)*. What sound does the letter *h* have in Spanish? *(None!)*

C No comprendo. Imagine that you and some friends are attending an international youth conference in Latin America. You tell people who you are and what states you are from. They aren't familiar with the English pronunciations of the state names, and so you must spell them in Spanish. With a partner, take turns asking and answering. For example:

> Diana / Vermont
>
> ESTUDIANTE A *¡Hola! Me llamo Diana y soy de Vermont.*
> ESTUDIANTE B *¿De dónde?*
> ESTUDIANTE A *De Vermont. V-E-R-M-O-N-T.*
> ESTUDIANTE B *¡Ah! Vermont.*

1. David / Nebraska	4. Daniel / Illinois	7. Mónica / Arizona
2. Patricia / Utah	5. Julia / Washington	8. Charles / Mississippi
3. Kate / Texas	6. Bill / Maryland	9. Y tú, ¿de dónde eres?

Práctica C
1. ... David... Nebraska...
   ene-e-be-ere-a-ese-ca-a
2. ... Patricia... Utah...
   u-te-a-hache
3. ... Kate... Texas...
   te-e-equis-a-ese
4. ... Daniel... Illinois...
   i-elle-i-ene-o-i-ese
5. ... Julia... Washington...
   doble ve-a-ese-hache-i-
   ene-ge-te-o-ene
6. ... Bill... Maryland...
   eme-a-ere-i griega-ele-a-
   ene-de
7. ... Mónica... Arizona...
   a-ere-i-zeta-o-ene-a
8. ... Charles... Mississippi...
   eme-i-ese-ese-i-ese-ese-i-
   pe-pe-i
9. Answers will vary.

Tape Manual Exs. 5–6 13

Un grupo de estudiantes en Puerto Rico

PRONUNCIACIÓN 14

A The pronunciation of the letter *e* is similar to the sound of the *e* in the word "café."

B Escucha y repite.

de   te   me   él   ella   estudiante

No sé, José.   ¿Cómo se escribe Mercedes?
Elena es del Ecuador.   Me llamo Enrique Esteban Meléndez.

ACTIVIDAD

Buena memoria. To play this memory game, form groups of four or five. One student in each group should act as secretary. The secretary begins the game by pointing to and identifying an object in the classroom. Another student points to the object, repeats the identification, and then points to another object and identifies it. Each student must remember and point to each item already identified and then point to a new one. No item can be repeated. For example, the game might begin:

SECRETARIO	*El libro.*
ESTUDIANTE A	*El libro. La ventana.*
ESTUDIANTE B	*El libro. La ventana. La hoja de papel.*

The secretary will keep a list of items in the order in which they have been called. When someone misidentifies an object, forgets the order, or repeats a word, the round ends. That person becomes the secretary for the next round.

VOCABULARIO DE EN CAMINO B

Sustantivos
el bolígrafo
el cuaderno
el dibujo
la hoja de papel,
   pl. las hojas de papel
el lápiz, *pl.* los lápices
el libro
el nombre
la pizarra
la puerta
la ventana

Países
la Argentina
  Bolivia
  Colombia
  Costa Rica
  Cuba
  Chile
el Ecuador
  El Salvador
  España
  Guatemala
  Honduras
  México
  Nicaragua
  Panamá
el Paraguay
el Perú
  Puerto Rico
la República Dominicana
el Uruguay
  Venezuela

Pronombres
él
ella
yo

Verbos
eres
es
soy

Preposición
de (del)

Adjetivo posesivo
tu

Palabra interrogativa
¿de dónde?

Expresiones
¿cómo se dice?
¿cómo se escribe?
de nada
en español
muchas gracias
no comprendo
no sé
por favor
¿qué quiere decir?

PALABRAS NUEVAS I

¿Qué día es hoy?

 15

CONTEXTO
VISUAL
Transparency 5

EL CALENDARIO

el día
el mes
la semana

lunes	martes	miércoles	jueves	viernes	sábado	domingo
1 uno	2 dos	3 tres	4 cuatro	5 cinco	6 seis	7 siete
8 ocho	9 nueve	10 diez	11 once	12 doce	13 trece	14 catorce
15 quince	16 dieciséis	17 diecisiete	18 dieciocho	19 diecinueve	20 veinte	21 veintiuno
22 veintidós	23 veintitrés	24 veinticuatro	25 veinticinco	26 veintiséis	27 veintisiete	28 veintiocho
29 veintinueve	30 treinta	31 treinta y uno				

CONTEXTO
COMUNICATIVO   16

1 EVA   ¿Qué quiere decir l-m-m-j-v-s-d?
   DAVID   **Son los** días **de** la semana: lunes, martes, miércoles, etc.

2 MARTA   **¿Qué** día es **hoy**?
   PABLO   Hoy es jueves.
   MARTA   ¿Y **mañana**?
   PABLO   Viernes.

   Variaciones:
   ■ jueves → viernes   viernes → sábado

son (they) are
el, la, los, las the
de here: of

¿qué? what?
hoy today
mañana tomorrow

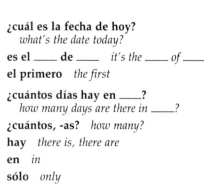

$1 - 1 = 0$
cero

3 TOMÁS   **¿Cuál es la fecha de hoy?**

    IRENE   **Es el** trece **de** enero.

- el trece de enero → **el primero** de marzo
- el trece de enero → el cinco de octubre

4 ISABEL   **¿Cuántos días hay en** septiembre?

    ANDRÉS   Hay treinta y uno.

    JOSÉ   No. Hay **sólo** treinta.

- septiembre → junio   septiembre → abril

¿cuál es la fecha de hoy?
what's the date today?

es el ____ **de** ____ *it's the ____ of ____*

el primero *the first*

¿cuántos días hay en ____**?**
how many days are there in ____?

¿cuántos, -as? *how many?*

hay *there is, there are*

en *in*

sólo *only*

5 MARÍA   ¿Cuántos meses hay en **un año**?

JUAN   Hay doce.

- meses → días
  un año → una semana
  doce → siete

6 PROFESOR   ¿Cuántos son nueve **más** cinco?

CLARITA   Catorce.

PROFESOR   ¡Muy bien!

- más → **menos**
  catorce → cuatro

un, una   *a, an; one*

el año   *year*

más   *plus*

menos   *minus*

El calendario azteca

To give today's date, we say, *Hoy es el dos de octubre.*
For the *first* day of the month we use *primero: Hoy es el primero de octubre.*
To tell what day of the week it is, we say, *Hoy es lunes.*
To say "*on* Monday," we use *el: el lunes.*

In Spanish-speaking countries, calendars usually begin the week on Monday *(lunes).* The names of the days and the months are not capitalized.

In counting, we say *uno* to mean "one." But when we use this word with a noun, *lápiz* or *puerta,* for example, we say *un* or *una:*

un lápiz $\begin{cases} a\ pencil \\ one\ pencil \end{cases}$ **una** puerta $\begin{cases} a\ door \\ one\ door \end{cases}$

The nouns that you are learning that have *el* before them are called masculine nouns. When we use a number that ends in *uno* before a masculine noun, we drop the *o: Hay **treinta y un días** en enero. Hay **veintiún días** en tres semanas.* Notice the written accent on *veintiún.*

PRÁCTICA

A Más y menos. Solve and then write in Spanish the answers to these arithmetic problems.

$2 + 1 = 3$ *Dos más uno son tres.*
$6 - 2 = 4$ *Seis menos dos son cuatro.*

1. $2 + 3$	3. $7 + 2$	5. $25 + 6$	7. $4 - 1$	9. $18 - 2$
2. $4 + 8$	4. $13 + 7$	6. $10 - 4$	8. $30 - 7$	10. $27 - 21$

B ¿Qué día es hoy? After a three-day weekend, it's sometimes hard to remember what day it is. You're apt to be a day behind all week long. Working with a partner, take turns saying what day you think it is and then correcting the mistake by giving the following day.

ESTUDIANTE A   *Hoy es martes.*
ESTUDIANTE B   *¿Martes? No, es miércoles.*

1. jueves   3. miércoles   5. lunes
2. domingo   4. viernes   6. sábado

C La fecha de hoy. When Spanish speakers use only numbers to write the date, they show the day first and then the month. For example, when we show the date as 6/10 in the United States, we mean June 10. To a Spanish speaker 6/10 means October 6. Working with a partner, take turns asking and giving the date in Spanish.

6/10
ESTUDIANTE A   *¿Cuál es la fecha de hoy?*
ESTUDIANTE B   *Es el seis de octubre.*

1. 24/10   4. 23/1   7. 29/12   10. 4/8
2. 15/3   5. 17/6   8. 13/9   11. 19/2
3. 28/4   6. 1/7   9. 31/5   12. 11/11

D Uno, dos, tres . . . Find the pattern in these numbers, and continue writing them as far as you can go.

1. dos, cuatro, seis . . .   3. tres, seis, nueve . . .
2. cero, cinco, diez . . .   4. seis, doce, dieciocho . . .

E Series y más series. Now you develop a number pattern using numbers from 1 to 30, and give it to a classmate to complete.

Práctica A
1. dos más tres son cinco
2. cuatro más ocho son doce
3. siete más dos son nueve
4. trece más siete son veinte
5. veinticinco más seis son treinta y uno
6. diez menos cuatro son seis
7. cuatro menos uno son tres
8. treinta menos siete son veintitrés
9. dieciocho menos dos son dieciséis
10. veintisiete menos veintiuno son seis

Práctica B
1. Hoy es jueves. No, es viernes.
2. ... domingo. ... lunes.
3. ... miércoles. ... jueves.
4. ... viernes. ... sábado.
5. ... lunes. ... martes.
6. ... sábado. ... domingo.

Práctica C
1. ¿Cuál es la fecha de hoy? Es el veinticuatro de octubre.
2. ... quince de marzo.
3. ... veintiocho de abril.
4. ... veintitrés de enero.
5. ... diecisiete de junio.
6. ... primero de julio.
7. ... veintinueve de diciembre.
8. ... trece de septiembre.
9. ... treinta y uno de mayo.
10. ... cuatro de agosto.
11. ... diecinueve de febrero.
12. ... el once de noviembre.

Práctica D
1. ... ocho, diez, doce, catorce, dieciséis, dieciocho, veinte, veintidós, veinticuatro, veintiséis, veintiocho, treinta
2. ... quince, veinte, veinticinco, treinta
3. ... doce, quince, dieciocho, veintiuno, veinticuatro, veintisiete, treinta
4. ... veinticuatro, treinta

Práctica E
Answers will vary.

Días de fiesta

ACTIVIDAD

Los días de fiesta. With a partner, look at a calendar for next year. In Spanish, give the day and the date on which the following special days will occur. (You may not know all of the words, but the pictures should help you.)

1. el día de San Valentín
2. el Año Nuevo
3. el día de la independencia de los Estados Unidos
4. la Navidad
5. el cumpleaños de George Washington
6. el día de San Patricio
7. tu cumpleaños
8. Hanukkah
9. el día de la Raza
10. el cumpleaños de Martin Luther King, Jr.

1.

2.

3.

4.

5.

6.

7.

8.

9.

10.

PALABRAS NUEVAS II

¡Felicidades!

CONTEXTO VISUAL
Transparency 6

18

CONTEXTO COMUNICATIVO 19

1 JOSÉ **Mi** cumpleaños es el 11 de octubre.
ELISA ¿Y **cuándo** es tu **santo**?
JOSÉ Es mañana.
ELISA ¡Felicidades!

Variaciones:
■ mañana → el viernes

mi *my*
¿cuándo? *when?*
el santo *saint's day*

2 RAMÓN ¿Cuándo es el día de **Navidad**?
MARÍA El domingo.

■ Navidad → **Año Nuevo**
■ el domingo → el martes

la Navidad *Christmas*
el Año Nuevo *New Year's Day*

3 ANITA El 31 de diciembre es un **día de fiesta**.
DAVID ¡Ah, sí! Es **el día de fin de año**.
ANITA No, es mi cumpleaños.

■ mi cumpleaños → mi santo

el día de fiesta *holiday*
el día de fin de año *New Year's Eve*

Reteach / Review: Write *cumpleaños, señor, español, mañana,* and *año* on the board. Remind students of the importance of the *tilde* on the *ñ*.

PRÁCTICA

A ¿Cuántos días hay? The math teacher has offered to forget about the last exam, because everybody failed it. But this will happen only if someone in the class can answer eight simple questions—*in Spanish.* With a partner, play the roles of student and teacher.

> PROFESOR(A) *¿Cuántos días hay en febrero?*
> ESTUDIANTE *Hay veintiocho días en febrero.*

1. ¿Cuántos días hay en octubre?
2. ¿Cuántos días hay en noviembre?
3. ¿Cuántos días hay en tres semanas?
4. ¿Cuántos meses hay en un año?
5. ¿Cuántos meses hay en dos años?
6. ¿Cuántas semanas hay en seis meses?
7. ¿Cuántas semanas hay en febrero?
8. ¿Cuántos días hay en dos semanas?

Práctica A
1. Hay treinta y un días en octubre.
2. Hay treinta días en noviembre.
3. Hay veintiún días en tres semanas.
4. Hay doce meses en un año.
5. Hay veinticuatro meses en dos años.
6. Hay veintiséis semanas en seis meses.
7. Hay cuatro semanas en febrero.
8. Hay catorce días en dos semanas.

Práctica B
1. Es el veintiuno de agosto.
2. ... cuatro de diciembre.
3. ... veinticuatro de junio.
4. ... nueve de octubre.
5. ... catorce de febrero.
6. ... veintiséis de julio.
7. ... quince de agosto.
8. ... veinticinco de abril.

B Es mi santo. You want to know when certain saint's days are. Working with a partner, take turns asking and answering the question.

> Jorge, 23/4
> ESTUDIANTE A *¿Cuándo es tu santo, Jorge?*
> ESTUDIANTE B *Es el veintitrés de abril.*

1. Mateo, 21/8
2. Bárbara, 4/12
3. Juan, 24/6
4. Inés, 9/10
5. Vicente, 14/2
6. Ana, 26/7
7. María, 15/8
8. Marcos, 25/4

In the Catholic church calendar, each day of the year is dedicated to one or more saints. In Spain and some other Spanish-speaking regions, many people celebrate both their birthday and their saint's day *(santo)*. Their saint's day is the day dedicated to the saint whose name they share. For example, a boy named Francisco would celebrate his *santo* on October 4, the feast day of San Francisco de Asís.

Práctica C

1. ¿Qué día de la semana es el primero de diciembre? Es lunes.
2. ... Es sábado.
3. ... Es miércoles.
4. ... Es jueves.
5. ... Es jueves.
6. ... Es domingo.
7. ... Es sábado.

Reteach / Extra Help: If your class needs more practice with numbers, ask volunteers to count the girls and the boys in the room. Use various classroom objects to provide further counting practice.

Practice Sheet En Camino 8

 20 Canción: Uno de enero

 21 Tape Manual Ex. 9

 22 Refrán

C Los días de la semana. December has finally arrived, and you are looking at the calendar. Working with a partner, take turns asking and answering.

ESTUDIANTE A *¿Qué día de la semana es el Año Nuevo?*
ESTUDIANTE B *Es jueves.*

diciembre

L	M	M	J	V	S	D
1 Sta. Florencia	2	3	4 Sta. Bárbara	5	6 San Nicolás	7
8	9	10	11 San Daniel	12	13 Sta. Lucía	14
15	16 Sta. Alicia	17	18	19	20	21
22	23	24 Sta. Adela	25 Navidad	26 San Esteban	27	28
29 San David	30 San Rogelio	31				

1. ¿el primero de diciembre?
2. ¿el día de San Nicolás?
3. ¿el día de fin de año?
4. ¿el día de Santa Bárbara?
5. ¿la Navidad?
6. ¿el veintiocho de diciembre?
7. ¿el día de Santa Lucía?

ACTIVIDAD

¡Felicidades! Make a chart listing the twelve months in Spanish. Then, one by one, each student asks the next student what day his or her birthday is. As each student answers, put a check mark in the appropriate month on your chart. Continue until all students have given their birthdays. Follow the model.

ESTUDIANTE A *¿Cuándo es tu cumpleaños?*
ESTUDIANTE B *Es el _____ de _____.*

When your chart is complete, answer these questions.

1. En tu clase de español, ¿hay cumpleaños en enero? ¿en febrero? etc. ¿Cuántos hay?
2. ¿Hay meses sin (*without*) cumpleaños? ¿Qué meses son?
3. ¿En qué mes hay más (*more*) cumpleaños?

PRONUNCIACIÓN 23

A The pronunciation of both the letter *i* and the word *y* is similar to the vowel sound in the English word "beet."

B Escucha y repite.

y   mi   sí   día

Mira la pizarra.

Así, así. ¿Y tú, Inés?

Hay cinco dibujos en el libro.

Mi santo es el quince de abril.

VOCABULARIO DE EN CAMINO C

Sustantivos
el año
el Año Nuevo
el calendario
el cumpleaños, *pl.* los
   cumpleaños
el día
el día de fiesta, *pl.* los días
   de fiesta
el día de fin de año
la fecha
el mes
la Navidad
el número
el primero
el santo
la semana

Verbos
hay
son

Adverbios
hoy
mañana
sólo

Preposiciones
de (del) *(of)*
en
más
menos

Días de la semana
lunes
martes
miércoles
jueves
viernes
sábado
domingo

Meses del año
enero
febrero
marzo
abril
mayo
junio
julio
agosto
septiembre
octubre
noviembre
diciembre

Números
cero
uno
dos
tres
cuatro
cinco
seis
siete
ocho
nueve
diez
once
doce
trece
catorce
quince
dieciséis
diecisiete
dieciocho
diecinueve
veinte
veintiuno (veintiún)
veintidós
veintitrés
veinticuatro
veinticinco
veintiséis
veintisiete
veintiocho
veintinueve
treinta
treinta y uno (un)

Adjetivo posesivo
mi

Artículos
un, una
el, *pl.* los
la, *pl.* las

Palabras interrogativas
¿cuándo?
¿cuántos, -as?
¿qué?

Expresiones
¿cuál es la fecha de hoy?
es el *(número)* de *(mes)*
¡felicidades!
¿qué día es hoy?

¿Cuál es tu número de teléfono?

CONTEXTO VISUAL

Transparency 7

¿Qué? and *¿cuál?* both mean "what?" But *¿qué?* usually asks for a definition or identification (*¿Qué quiere decir . . . ?*) and *¿cuál?* asks for a choice among several possibilities (*¿Cuál es la fecha de hoy?*).

If **students ask:** At this point, students may want additional vocabulary to talk about themselves. Encourage them to ask *¿Cómo se dice…?* More interrogative words will be presented on p. 134.

Culture: Dial phones are still often seen in many parts of the Spanish-speaking world.

CONTEXTO COMUNICATIVO 25

1 PILAR   ¿Cuántos **minutos** hay en una **hora**?
   PABLO   Sesenta.
   PILAR   ¿Y cuántos **segundos**?
   PABLO   ¿En una hora? No sé.

Variaciones:
■ no sé → **¡Uf!**

el minuto   *minute*
la hora   *hour*
el segundo   *second*
¡uf!   *ugh!, phew!*

2 GUSTAVO   Dolores, ¿cuál es tu **número de teléfono**?
   DOLORES   Es el 555–45–37.*

■ 555–45–37 → 414–99–58

¿cuál?   *what?*
el número de teléfono   *phone number*
el teléfono   *telephone*

PRÁCTICA

A **¿Cuántos minutos?**   The Jogging Club held a mini-marathon. Tell how many minutes and seconds it took each person to finish the race. Write your answers in order. List the fastest runner first. For example:

Magdalena: *sesenta y ocho minutos, veinticuatro segundos*

Práctica A
1. Sergio: cincuenta y siete minutos, treinta y tres segundos.
2. Sonia: sesenta y un minutos, doce segundos.
3. Susana: setenta y tres minutos, dieciocho segundos.

Isabel 92:52

Ignacio 85:39

Sonia 61:12

Sergio 57:33

Susana 73:18

Magdalena 68:24

Rafael 88:46

4. Ignacio: ochenta y cinco minutos, treinta y nueve segundos.
5. Rafael: ochenta y ocho minutos, cuarenta y seis segundos.
6. Isabel: noventa y dos minutos, cincuenta y dos segundos.

* People in Spanish-speaking countries usually pause twice when they say telephone numbers. Instead of saying 555–4537, they say 555–45–37 (*cinco, cinco, cinco, cuarenta y cinco, treinta y siete*).

Práctica B
Answers will vary.

Práctica C
1. cuarenta, cincuenta, sesenta, setenta, ochenta, noventa, cien
2. treinta y dos, cuarenta, cuarenta y ocho, cincuenta y seis, sesenta y cuatro, setenta y dos, ochenta, ochenta y ocho, noventa y seis
3. treinta y seis, cuarenta y cinco, cincuenta y cuatro, sesenta y tres, setenta y dos, ochenta y uno, noventa, noventa y nueve
4. cuarenta y cuatro, cincuenta y cinco, sesenta y seis, setenta y siete, ochenta y ocho, noventa y nueve
5. sesenta, setenta y cinco, noventa

Práctica D
Answers will vary.

Práctica E
1. Me llamo Jorge Blanco. Mi número de placa es el treinta y seis, jota i griega, veintinueve. Mi número de teléfono es el cinco uno siete, noventa y tres, noventa y uno.
2. ... María Ruiz ... veinticinco, eme te, treinta y dos ... cuatro seis cinco, cuarenta y seis, cero tres.

3. ... Gloria Benito ... treinta y nueve, be te, ochenta y siete ... tres ocho siete, cincuenta y dos, cuarenta y uno.
4. ... Luis Montoya ... cincuenta y ocho, zeta ere, noventa y seis ... dos siete siete, sesenta y ocho, cincuenta y cinco.

B El teléfono. Each student should ask the next student what his or her phone number is. One person should write the numbers on the chalkboard. If the "secretary" makes a mistake, the person whose number it is should correct it and then act as the secretary. Continue until everyone in the room has asked for and given a phone number.

ESTUDIANTE A   *¿Cuál es tu número de teléfono?*
ESTUDIANTE B   *Es el _____.*

C Uno, dos, tres . . . Find the patterns in these numbers, and continue to write them as far as you can go.

1. diez, veinte, treinta . . .
2. ocho, dieciséis, veinticuatro . . .
3. nueve, dieciocho, veintisiete . . .
4. once, veintidós, treinta y tres . . .
5. quince, treinta, cuarenta y cinco . . .

D Series y más series. Now you develop a number pattern and give it to a classmate to complete.

E Mi número de teléfono es el . . . A five-car fender-bender on an icy stretch of the Pan-American Highway! Say what each driver is telling the police officer. (There is one word you haven't learned, but you can tell from the picture what it means.) Follow the model.

Me llamo Sergio Mendoza.
Mi número de placa es el 48WX99.
Mi número de teléfono es el 555–39–71.

1. Jorge Blanco
2. María Ruiz
3. Gloria Benito
4. Luis Montoya

PALABRAS NUEVAS II

¿Qué hora es?

CONTEXTO
VISUAL   27
Transparency 8

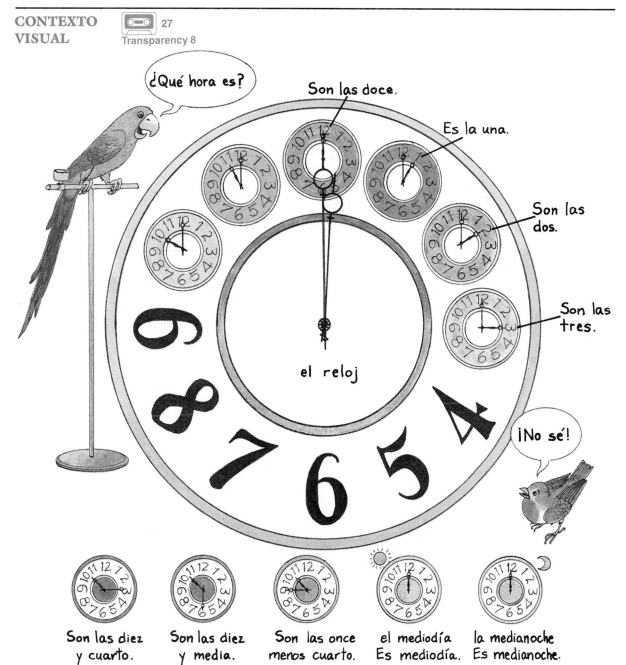

Son las diez y cuarto.

Son las diez y media.

Son las once menos cuarto.

el mediodía Es mediodía.

la medianoche Es medianoche.

 28

**CONTEXTO
COMUNICATIVO**

Enrichment: Write *la mañana, tarde, ahora,* and *medianoche* on the board, or say each word clearly. Ask for the opposite of each word (*la noche, temprano, más tarde, mediodía*).

1 GREGORIO Por favor, **¿qué hora es?**
SILVIA Son las diez y media **de la noche.**
GREGORIO ¿Las diez y media?
SILVIA Sí. Es **tarde.**

Variaciones:
■ y media → y cuarto
■ de la noche → **de la mañana**
  tarde → **temprano**

2 ANDRÉS ¿Qué hora es?
EMILIA Es mediodía.

■ es mediodía → es la una **menos diez**
■ mediodía → medianoche

3 CLARA Víctor, **¿a qué hora** es **la fiesta?**
VÍCTOR **A las** tres **de la tarde.**

■ a las tres → **a la una**

4 MARÍA ¿Qué hora es **ahora?** ¿Son las doce?
JUAN No, es **más tarde.** Es la una.

■ es la una → son las doce **y veinte**

¿qué hora es? *what time is it?*
de la noche *in the evening; P.M.*
tarde *late*

de la mañana *in the morning; A.M.*
temprano *early*

menos diez *ten (minutes) to*

¿a qué hora? *(at) what time?*
la fiesta *party*
a las ___ *at ___ (o'clock)*
de la tarde *in the afternoon, early evening; P.M.*
a la una *at one o'clock*

ahora *now*
más tarde *later*
y veinte *twenty after*

Reteach / Extra Help: If your class needs more practice with telling time, write several times of day on the board, or use a model of a clock with movable hands. Have students work in pairs to ask and answer *¿Qué hora es?*

Son las tres y veinticinco de la tarde.
Viña del Mar, Chile

34 En Camino D

ESTUDIO DE PALABRAS

In Spanish, there is only one word for both "morning" and "tomorrow": *mañana*. (Do you remember what *hasta mañana* means?) When *mañana* is preceded by the word *la*, it means "morning." Can you guess what *mañana por la mañana* means?

The word *tarde* also has two meanings. You have used it to mean "afternoon" in the expression *buenas tardes*. The other meaning is "late" (like the English word "tardy"). When *tarde* is preceded by the word *la*, it means "afternoon."

PRÁCTICA

A ¿Qué hora es? Tell what time it is. Consider morning to be from midnight to noon, afternoon from noon to 7:00 P.M., and night from 7:00 P.M. to midnight.

 Son las dos de la tarde.

 1.

 2.

 3.

 4.

 5.

 6.

 7.

 8.

 9.

 10.

 11.

12.

B ¿Tarde o temprano? One person doesn't worry about time and never hurries. Another likes to be on time for everything. With a partner, create conversations between these two people. For example:

8:10 / 8:30
ESTUDIANTE A *Son las ocho y diez. Es tarde.*
ESTUDIANTE B *No. Es temprano. La fiesta es a las ocho y media.*

1. 2:20 / 2:30   3. 6:40 / 6:45   5. 1:05 / 1:15
2. 4:45 / 5:00   4. 11:50 / 12:30   6. 5:55 / 6:15

Práctica A
1. Son las seis de la tarde.
2. Son las nueve de la noche.
3. Son las cuatro y media de la tarde.
4. Son las doce menos cuarto de la mañana.
5. Es la una de la tarde.
6. Son las diez y cuarto de la noche.
7. Es medianoche.
8. Son las cinco y cuarto de la tarde.
9. Son las tres y media de la tarde.
10. Es mediodía.
11. Son las ocho menos cuarto de la mañana.
12. Son las ocho y media de la noche.

Práctica B
1. Son las dos y veinte. Es tarde. / No. Es temprano. La fiesta es a las dos y media.
2. Son las cinco menos cuarto. Es tarde. / No. Es temprano. … a las cinco.
3. Son las siete menos veinte. Es tarde. / No. Es temprano. … a las siete menos cuarto.
4. Son las doce menos diez. Es tarde. / No. Es temprano. … a las doce y media.
5. Es la una y cinco. Es tarde. / No. Es temprano. … a la una y cuarto.
6. Son las seis menos cinco. Es tarde. / No. Es temprano. … a las seis y cuarto.

Práctica C

1. Son las tres menos veinte.
2. ... tres menos cuarto.
3. ... tres menos once.
4. ... tres menos siete.
5. ... tres menos cinco.
6. ... tres menos dos.
7. ... tres y cinco.

Práctica D

1. ¿A qué hora es la clase de música? A las nueve y cinco.
2. ¿... la clase de matemáticas? ... a las diez menos diez.
3. ¿... la clase de español? ... a las once menos veinticinco.
4. ¿... la clase de inglés? ... a las once y media.
5. ¿... la clase de dibujo? ... a la una y diez.
6. ¿... la clase de biología? ... a las dos menos cinco.
7. ¿... la clase de educación física? ... a las tres menos veinte.

Notes: Before students do Ex. D, model the names of the school subjects so that students can imitate correct pronunciation.

Practice Sheets En Camino 10, 11, 12

 29 Tape Manual Exs. 11–12

C El reloj roto. The kitchen clock is broken, and Julio's mother is baking a pie. It must come out of the oven at exactly 3:00. Every few minutes Julio's mother asks what time it is. Working with a partner, take turns playing the roles of Julio and his mother.

ESTUDIANTE A   *¿Qué hora es ahora?*
ESTUDIANTE B   *Son las tres menos veinticinco.*

1.   2.   3.   4.

5.   6.   7.

D ¿A qué hora? Pretend it's the first day of school, and you and a friend are checking your class schedule. (Though you haven't learned the names of school subjects, you should be able to understand them.) Take turns asking and answering.

ESTUDIANTE A   *¿A qué hora es la clase de historia?*
ESTUDIANTE B   *A las ocho y veinte.*

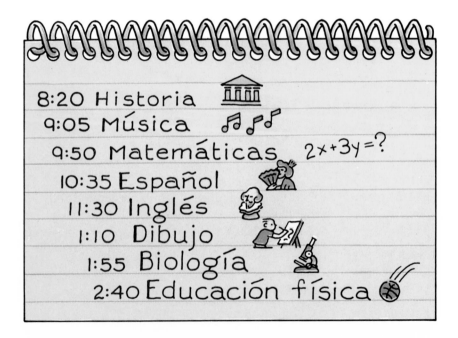

8:20 Historia
9:05 Música
9:50 Matemáticas   2x+3y=?
10:35 Español
11:30 Inglés
1:10 Dibujo
1:55 Biología
2:40 Educación física

PRONUNCIACIÓN 30

A The pronunciation of the letter *o* is similar to the vowel sound in the English word "coat."

B Escucha y repite.

yo   no   los   cómo   noche   reloj

Hola, Dolores.   Son las ocho de la noche.
Yo soy de Colombia.   Me llamo Rodolfo Olmedo.

Son las cuatro y media.

ACTIVIDAD

De diez en diez.   Get together in groups of four or five. One student should be the official scorekeeper. The student to the left of the scorekeeper begins the game by giving an addition problem with a sum of 100 or less. The first person to answer correctly gets 10 points *(puntos)*. Each time you gain 10 points, announce the *total* number of points you have. For example, if you already have 50 points and get a right answer, you might say something like this:

ESTUDIANTE A   *Treinta y dos más cuarenta y dos.*
ESTUDIANTE B   *¡Setenta y cuatro!*
ESTUDIANTE A   *¡Sí! ¡Muy bien! Diez puntos.*
ESTUDIANTE B   *Sesenta puntos en total.*

The scorekeeper should put a mark next to your name. The person who answers correctly gives the next problem. The game continues until one person earns a total of 100 points.

VOCABULARIO DE EN CAMINO D

Sustantivos	Adverbios	Números	Expresiones	
la fiesta *(party)*	ahora	cuarenta	a la una	menos cuarto
la hora	más tarde	cincuenta	a las (+ *número*)	menos (+ *número*)
la medianoche	tarde	sesenta	¿a qué hora?	¿qué hora es?
el mediodía	temprano	setenta	de la mañana	son las (+ *número*)
el minuto		ochenta	de la noche	¡uf!
el número de		noventa	de la tarde	y cuarto
teléfono	**Palabra interrogativa**	cien	es la una	y media
el reloj	¿cuál?		es medianoche	y (+ *número*)
el segundo			es mediodía	
el teléfono				

PALABRAS NUEVAS I

¿Qué te gusta hacer?

jugar al béisbol

jugar al básquetbol

montar en bicicleta

la bicicleta

nadar

jugar al fútbol americano

CONTEXTO COMUNICATIVO

🔊 32

1 ARTURO   **Me encanta** jugar al básquetbol.
    MARÍA   ¿Sí?
    ARTURO   Sí. Y **me gusta** jugar al béisbol **también**.

Variaciones:
■ básquetbol → fútbol

me encanta	*I love (to)*
me gusta	*I like (to)*
también	*too, also*

Enrichment: Point out that Spanish has borrowed and adapted the names of many English-language games: *básquetbol, fútbol, tenis, béisbol.* Other loanwords are discussed in **Estudio de palabras,** p. 63.

esquiar

jugar al tenis

jugar al fútbol

2 ELENA   ¿Qué **te gusta hacer**? ¿Te gusta nadar?
    TOMÁS   Sí, me encanta.

- nadar → montar en bicicleta
- sí, me encanta → no, **no me gusta**

3 MÓNICA   ¿Te gusta jugar al fútbol?
    LEONARDO   No, **pero** me gusta jugar al béisbol.

- fútbol → fútbol americano
- béisbol → básquetbol

¿te gusta? *do you like (to)?*
hacer *to do*

no me gusta *I don't like (to)*

pero *but*

Deportes en España

PRÁCTICA

A Me gusta o ¡me encanta! Pretend you are in a sporting goods store that has posters of different sports activities. Say whether you love, like, or don't like to play the sport or do the activity shown.

Me encanta nadar.
o: *Me gusta nadar.*
o: *No me gusta nadar.*

 1.

 2.

 3.

 4.

 5.

 6.

 7.

 8.

B No, no, no. In any group there is always disagreement. In this case, whatever sport you ask about, someone dislikes. Working in a small group, take turns asking one another *¿Te gusta _____?* The person answering should always say no to that sport and then tell what he or she does like to do. For example:

> ESTUDIANTE A *¿Te gusta jugar al béisbol?*
> ESTUDIANTE B *No, no me gusta. Pero me encanta esquiar.*

C ¿Qué te gusta hacer? Ask someone in the class *¿Qué te gusta hacer?* He or she should answer by mentioning two activities, and then ask someone else. Continue until everyone in the class has asked and answered the question. For example:

> TÚ *María, ¿qué te gusta hacer?*
> MARÍA *Me gusta nadar y jugar al tenis también. Luis, ¿qué te gusta hacer?*
> LUIS *Me gusta jugar al fútbol y al fútbol americano también. Laura, ¿qué te gusta hacer?*

Práctica A
1. ¡Me encanta (Me gusta) (No me gusta) jugar al béisbol.
2. … jugar al fútbol.
3. … jugar al tenis.
4. … jugar al fútbol americano.
5. … jugar al básquetbol.
6. … esquiar.
7. … montar en bicicleta.
8. … nadar.

Práctica B
Answers will vary, but should follow this format:
ESTUDIANTE A ¿Te gusta __?
ESTUDIANTE B No, no me gusta. Pero me encanta __.

Práctica C
Answers will vary, but the dialogue should follow this format:
ESTUDIANTE A B, ¿qué te gusta hacer?
ESTUDIANTE B Me gusta __ y __ también. C, ¿qué te gusta hacer?

PALABRAS NUEVAS II

¡Me encanta hablar por teléfono!

bailar

escuchar cintas   la cinta

comer

mirar la televisión (la tele)

escuchar la radio

el cine

escuchar discos
el disco

ir al cine

hablar por teléfono

1 SARA   ¿Qué te gusta hacer?
     LUIS   Me gusta cocinar. Y me gusta comer también.
     SARA   ¿Sí? ¿Te gusta comer **comida mexicana**?
     LUIS   Sí. Me encanta.

     Variaciones:
     ■ comida mexicana → **comida americana**

     la comida mexicana   *Mexican food*

     la comida americana   *American food*

2 ELISA   Te gusta escuchar la radio, **¿no?**
     CÉSAR   Sí, y también me gusta escuchar discos.

     ■ discos → cintas

     ¿no?   *don't you?*

3 PEPE   No me gusta **trabajar.**
     LUZ   Pero te gusta ir a la escuela, ¿no?
     PEPE   Sí, me gusta ir a la clase de español.

     ■ trabajar → leer libros

     trabajar   *to work*

En Málaga, España

PRÁCTICA

A Sí y no. Everyone likes to do some things but not others. Working with a partner, take turns asking what the other person likes to do. Follow the model.

> bailar / cantar
>
> **ESTUDIANTE A** *¿Qué te gusta hacer?*
> **ESTUDIANTE B** *Me gusta bailar.*
> **ESTUDIANTE A** *¿Y cantar?*
> **ESTUDIANTE B** *No, no me gusta cantar.*

1. comer / cocinar
2. mirar la televisión / trabajar
3. nadar / jugar al básquetbol
4. hablar por teléfono / leer
5. esquiar / montar en bicicleta
6. ir al cine / escuchar la radio

B Sí, me gusta. Imagine that a new friend is showing you pictures of his family's activities during their vacation. Work with a partner. Ask if he or she likes to do those things.

Un estudiante en Santiago, Chile

> **ESTUDIANTE A** *¿Te gusta jugar al fútbol americano?*
> **ESTUDIANTE B** *Sí, me gusta.*
> o: *No, no me gusta.*

C ¿Te gusta? Appoint a secretary to write the Spanish names of different activities on the board as class members call them out. Then your teacher will ask a student if he or she likes to do a certain thing. The student will answer yes or no and then ask another student a similar question.

> **PROFESOR(A)** *¿Te gusta jugar al béisbol?*
> **ESTUDIANTE** *Sí, me gusta jugar al béisbol. Esteban, ¿te gusta escuchar discos?*
> o: *No, no me gusta jugar al béisbol. Esteban, ¿te gusta escuchar discos?*

Práctica A
1. Me gusta comer … No, no me gusta cocinar.
2. … mirar la televisión … No, no me gusta trabajar.
3. … nadar … No, no me gusta jugar al básquetbol.
4. … hablar por teléfono … No, no me gusta leer.
5. … esquiar … No, no me gusta montar en bicicleta.
6. … ir al cine … No, no me gusta escuchar la radio.

Práctica B
1. ¿Te gusta esquiar?
2. ¿… montar en bicicleta?
3. ¿… cocinar?
4. ¿… jugar al béisbol?
5. ¿… escuchar cintas?
6. ¿… mirar la televisión?
7. ¿… hablar por teléfono?
8. ¿… tocar la guitarra?
9. ¿… leer?

Práctica C
Questions and answers will vary.

Notes: Before you introduce **Expresiones para la clase,** go over the singular **Expresiones** on p. 18. Perform the commands, and then ask students to look at the cartoons carefully.

Add students' names as you give the directions to individuals *(Ana, levanta la mano)* and to groups of students *(Miguel, Beatriz y Elena, escriban la fecha).* Model each direction so that students can repeat and perform the gesture.

Elicit what distinguishes the singular *tú* command from the plural *ustedes* form *(the endings).*

Reteach / Review: Write the singular / plural commands on the board. For example: *Levanta / Levanten.* Then write *la pregunta, en español, la ventana, el lápiz, tu nombre, en voz alta, los libros, la fecha, la mano.*

Ask for volunteers to form sentences orally by combining words from the two lists. Encourage students to come up with as many logical sentences as possible.

EXPRESIONES PARA LA CLASE

You may have noticed that your teacher gives directions one way when speaking to one person and in a slightly different way when speaking to more than one. Can you see the patterns in these commands? Again, you may not be expected to use them, but you should recognize and understand them.

A The pronunciation of the letter *u* is similar to the vowel sound in the English word "boot."

B Escucha y repite.

tú   una   lunes   fútbol   minuto   número

Mucho gusto, Julio.   Tu cumpleaños es en junio, ¿no?
Hasta el lunes, Lupe.   Arturo es el número uno en fútbol.

ACTIVIDAD

Me gusta / me encanta. The class chooses ten activities. Each student writes them on a sheet of paper with the headings *me encanta, me gusta,* and *no me gusta.* Interview one classmate, asking about all of the activities on the list. The other student answers truthfully. Then exchange roles.

ESTUDIANTE A	¿Te gusta jugar al fútbol?
ESTUDIANTE B	No, no me gusta jugar al fútbol.
ESTUDIANTE A	¿Te gusta cantar?
ESTUDIANTE B	Sí, me encanta cantar.

Mark each of your partner's answers in the appropriate space on your paper. Then, as a class, total the number of check marks under each heading for each activity.

¿Te gusta tocar la guitarra?
En Madrid, España

VOCABULARIO DE EN CAMINO E

Sustantivos
el básquetbol
el béisbol
la bicicleta
el cine
la cinta
la comida americana
la comida mexicana
el disco
la escuela
el español
el fútbol
el fútbol americano
la guitarra
la radio

la televisión (la tele)
el tenis

Adverbios
no (*not*)
también

Conjunción
pero

Verbos
bailar
cantar
cocinar
comer
escuchar
esquiar
hablar
hacer
ir a(l)
jugar al (+ *sports*)
leer
mirar
nadar
tocar (+ *musical instruments*)
trabajar

Expresiones
hablar español
hablar por teléfono
me encanta
(no) me / (no) te gusta
montar en bicicleta
¿no?

SOY AMERICANO

America is made up of many nations. In the same way that people from both Spain and England are all Europeans, citizens of Chile and Canada, of Uruguay and the United States are all Americans. To Spanish speakers, the people of the United States are *norteamericanos*. Remember, though, that Mexico and Canada are also in North America.

Ever since the time of Columbus, there has been a continuous flow of immigrants to the Americas. Spain paid for the first explorations and claimed the land as its own, so most of the early settlers were Spanish. They brought with them their language and culture. October 12, Columbus Day to us, is known as *El día de la hispanidad* in Spain and as *El día de la Raza* throughout Latin America. It is a celebration of pride in Hispanic culture.

The Americas were named for the man who first recognized them as a separate region. (Columbus, after all, had thought they were part of the Orient!) Amerigo Vespucci, an Italian navigator, used the Latin form of his name *(Americus Vespucius)* on his charts. Because they were the first ones made of the region, his name became associated with it, and so we have "America."

Many Spanish speakers live in the United States. The three largest groups have come from Puerto Rico, Mexico, and Cuba. Puerto Ricans have most often chosen to live in the Northeast. The majority of those from Mexico live in the Southwest. Most Cubans have made Florida and New York their home. Spanish speakers have a long history here. Consider the Spanish names of many of our states and cities. They stretch all the way from St. Augustine, Florida—originally called *San Agustín*—which is the oldest city in the United States, to *el Pueblo de Nuestra Señora, la Reina de Los Ángeles de Porciúncula*, in California. Today we know that city as Los Angeles.

¿Qué te gusta más?

CONTEXTO
VISUAL

Transparency 11

el helado

el pan

las papas fritas

el burrito

la leche

la limonada

el queso

la mantequilla

el yogur

el jamón

la ensalada

el sandwich de queso

el sandwich de jamón

los sandwiches

la hamburguesa

el chile con carne

el refresco

el taco

If students ask: Related vocabulary you may want to present: *la salsa de tomate*, ketchup; *la mostaza*, mustard; *la mayonesa*, mayonnaise; *la sal*, salt; *la pimienta*, pepper; *la cebolla*, onion.

Notes: When you feel confident that students understand the **Contexto visual,** present each of the five mini-dialogues, or play the tape. You may want to ask volunteers to act out the dialogues.

Culture: In Spanish-speaking countries, butter is used more often on sandwiches than mayonnaise or mustard.

CONTEXTO COMUNICATIVO 2

1 PABLO   ¿Te gustan los tacos?

LUCÍA   **¡Cómo no!** Pero **me gusta más** el chile con carne.

Variaciones:

■ los tacos → los burritos

■ me gusta más → me encanta

¡cómo no!   *of course!*
me gusta(n) más   *I prefer, I like (something) more*
más   *more*

2 PABLO   ¿Te gustan más los tacos **o** las hamburguesas?

LUCÍA   Me encantan las hamburguesas.

PABLO   **¿Con** papas fritas?

LUCÍA   ¡Cómo no!

■ los tacos → los sandwiches

■ papas fritas → queso

o   *or*

con   *with*

3 PABLO   Te gusta cocinar, **¿verdad?**

LUCÍA   Sí, **mucho.**

PABLO   **¿Por qué?**

LUCÍA   **¡Porque** me encanta comer!

■ verdad → ¿no?

■ mucho → ¡cómo no!

¿verdad?   *isn't that so? right?*
mucho   *a lot, much*
¿por qué?   *why?*
porque   *because*

4 CARLOS   Buenas tardes. Chile con carne y una limonada, por favor.

CAMARERO   ¿Y **para** la señorita . . . ?

ANITA   **Pues,** un sandwich de jamón. **Sin** mantequilla, por favor.

■ una limonada → un refresco

■ de jamón → de queso

para   *for*
pues   *well*
sin   *without*

5 MARCOS   ¿Te gusta el yogur?
    IRENE   No.
    MARCOS   ¿Te gusta el helado?
    IRENE   No.
    MARCOS   **Entonces,** ¿qué te gusta?

                                                       entonces   *then*

- el yogur → el refresco
- el helado → el queso

EN OTRAS PARTES

Though English is spoken throughout the United States, people in different parts of the country often use different words to refer to the same thing. For example, in some areas of the country, people call a soft drink a *soda.* In other areas, they call it *pop.* You may call a sandwich a *hero,* a *hoagie,* a *sub,* or a *submarine* depending on where you're from.

People in the United States and England also speak the same language, but we often use very different words to refer to the same things. For example, what we call an *apartment* the English call a *flat,* and they call an *apartment building* a *block of flats.* The English call an elevator a *lift* and a truck a *lorry.*

People who speak Spanish share the same basic language but, just as in English, there are different expressions and vocabulary used in different regions. For example, you are learning the word *el sandwich.* However, some Spanish speakers say *emparedado* to mean "sandwich." *Refresco* is understood to mean "soda" wherever Spanish is spoken, even though some people call it *gaseosa.*

The words you will learn in this book are generally understood throughout the Spanish-speaking world. But in the *En otras partes* sections, we will point out words that you might hear if you went to a particular Spanish-speaking country. All are equally correct, but you will need *to learn* only the ones we present in the *Palabras nuevas.*

Here are some words you have learned that you might hear other words for:

Se dice también *jugar al baloncesto.*

En México se dice *la nieve.*   Se dice también *la pluma.*   Se dice también *el pizarrón.*

PRÁCTICA

A En la cafetería. Imagine that you and a friend are in the cafeteria trying to decide what to have for lunch. Take turns asking each other what you like. Follow the model.

ESTUDIANTE A *Te gusta el helado, ¿verdad?*
ESTUDIANTE B *¡Sí, me encanta el helado!*
o: *¿El helado? No, no me gusta.*

Práctica A
1. Te gusta el chile con carne, ¿verdad? ¡Sí, me encanta el chile con carne! *or:* ¿El chile con carne? No, no me gusta.
2. Te gusta el jamón, ¿verdad? ¡Sí, me encanta el jamón! *or:* ¿El jamón? No, no me gusta.
3. Te gusta el queso, ¿verdad? ¡Sí, me encanta el queso! *or:* ¿El queso? No, no me gusta.
4. … el pan …
5. … la mantequilla …
6. … la ensalada …
7. … el yogur …
8. … la leche …
9. … la limonada …

Práctica B

1. ¿No te gustan las hamburguesas? ¡Cómo no! Me encantan las hamburguesas.
2. ¿No te gustan los sandwiches de queso? ¡Cómo no! Me encantan los sandwiches de queso.
3. ¿No te gustan los burritos? ¡Cómo no! Me encantan los burritos.
4. ¿… los helados? …
5. ¿… los tacos? …
6. ¿… los sandwiches de jamón? …
7. ¿… los refrescos? …

Práctica C

1. ¿Qué te gusta más, jugar al béisbol o jugar al básquetbol? Me gusta más jugar al básquetbol (al béisbol).
2. ¿Qué te gusta más, ir al cine o mirar la tele? Me gusta más …
3. ¿Qué te gusta más, escuchar discos o montar en bicicleta? Me gusta más …
4. ¿Qué te gusta más, cocinar o leer? Me gusta más …
5. ¿Qué te gusta más, cantar o tocar la guitarra? Me gusta más …
6. ¿Qué te gusta más, esquiar o escuchar cintas? Me gusta más …
7. ¿Qué te gusta más, jugar al fútbol o jugar al fútbol americano? Me gusta más …

Notes: Stress word order and intonation in Ex. B: *¿No te gustan _____?* and Ex. C: *¿Qué te gusta más, _____ o _____?* In Ex. C, make sure that students realize that they are expressing a preference for an activity, and therefore we use *te gusta / me gusta* followed by the infinitive rather than by a noun.

B ¡Me encanta comer! Some people like everything. With a partner, take turns asking and answering.

ESTUDIANTE A *¿No te gustan las papas fritas?*
ESTUDIANTE B *¡Cómo no! Me encantan las papas fritas.*

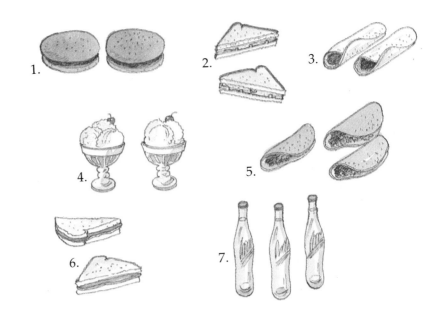

C ¿Qué te gusta más? Imagine it's Saturday morning, and you and a friend are trying to decide what to do. Take turns asking which activity the other prefers. Follow the model.

nadar / jugar al tenis
ESTUDIANTE A *¿Qué te gusta más, nadar o jugar al tenis?*
ESTUDIANTE B *Me gusta más nadar.*
o: *Me gusta más jugar al tenis.*

1. jugar al béisbol / jugar al básquetbol
2. ir al cine / mirar la tele
3. escuchar discos / montar en bicicleta
4. cocinar / leer
5. cantar / tocar la guitarra
6. esquiar / escuchar cintas
7. jugar al fútbol / jugar al fútbol americano

Reteach / Review: Before students do Ex. D on p. 55, ask them to identify the illustrations in Exs. A–B as *comida mexicana* or *comida americana.* For example: *¿Las hamburguesas? Pues, comida americana.*

D Hablemos de ti.

1. ¿Te gusta más comer comida mexicana o comida americana?
2. ¿Te gustan más las hamburguesas o los tacos?
3. ¿Te gustan más las hamburguesas con queso o los sandwiches de jamón y queso?

Sirve paella en Málaga, España

Práctica D
Answers will vary.

Enrichment: Additional questions for Ex. D: *¿Te gustan más los burritos o los tacos? ¿Te gusta más cocinar o lavar los platos?*

APLICACIONES Discretionary

Entonces, ¿qué te gusta? 4

In *Diálogos* and *Lecturas* you will see a few words that you haven't
seen before. We will give you the English equivalents for some of
those words below the dialogue or reading. You will probably be
able to understand the others without any help.

Un sábado en Laredo, Texas.

LAURA ¿Qué te gusta hacer, Eduardo? ¿Jugar al béisbol?
Me encanta el béisbol.
EDUARDO No, no me gusta el béisbol.
5 LAURA ¿Te gusta más jugar al tenis, entonces?
EDUARDO No.
LAURA ¡Ah! No te gustan los deportes.[1] ¿Te gusta ir al cine,
entonces?
EDUARDO No, no me gusta el cine.
10 LAURA No te gustan los deportes, no te gusta el cine.
Entonces, ¿qué te gusta?
EDUARDO Pues, me gusta tocar la guitarra.
LAURA Ah, me encanta la música. Te gustan los conciertos,[2]
¿verdad?
15 EDUARDO No, no me gustan.
LAURA ¡Uf!

[1]**el deporte** *sport*   [2]**el concierto** *concert*

Preguntas
Which person might say the following? *Contesta según* ("according to")
el diálogo.

1. Me gusta jugar al béisbol. ¿Laura o Eduardo?   2. No me gusta ir al
cine. ¿Laura o Eduardo?   3. No me gustan los deportes. ¿Laura o
Eduardo?   4. Me encantan los conciertos. ¿Laura o Eduardo?   5. No me
gustan los conciertos. ¿Laura o Eduardo?

Diálogo
1. Laura
2. Eduardo
3. Eduardo
4. Laura
5. Eduardo

Enrichment: Additional questions: *No me gusta jugar al tenis. (Eduardo) Me gusta la
música. (Laura)* You may vary the format by asking: *¿Es el concierto un deporte?
(No ...) ¿Es el béisbol un deporte? (Sí ...)*

Participación

Working with a partner, make up a four-line dialogue about what you like to do and don't like to do on Saturdays. The opening line of your dialogue should include the question, *¿Qué te gusta hacer los sábados?*

PRONUNCIACIÓN 5

When you speak Spanish, you stress some syllables more than others, just as you do in English. There are a few simple rules that tell you which syllable of a Spanish word to stress.

A When a word ends in a vowel or in *n* or *s*, the stress normally falls on the *next-to-last* syllable.
Escucha y repite.

taco	para	gusta	helado	hamburguesa
tenis	encantan	entonces	papas	fritas

B When a word ends in any consonant other than *n* or *s*, the stress normally falls on the *last* syllable.
Escucha y repite.

papel	hacer	yogur	español	trabajar

C There are exceptions. In those cases an accent mark indicates where the stress falls.
Escucha y repite.

lápiz	béisbol	bolígrafo	número	teléfono

D Escucha y repite.

Nicolás es del Perú.   Me gusta escuchar discos.
Mónica es de Panamá.   No me gusta trabajar el sábado.

PALABRAS NUEVAS II

En la clase

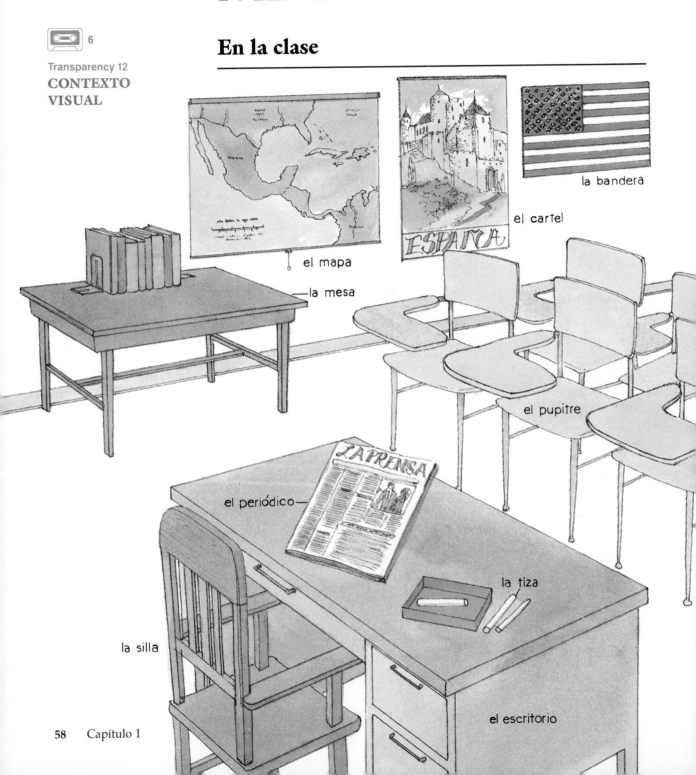

la bandera

el cartel

el mapa

la mesa

el pupitre

el periódico

la tiza

la silla

el escritorio

CONTEXTO COMUNICATIVO 7

1 JUDIT ¿Hay **muchos** estudiantes en tu clase?
  ARTURO No, hay **pocos**.
  JUDIT ¿Cuántos hay?
  ARTURO Hay sólo once.

Variaciones:
- estudiantes → pupitres
- estudiantes → libros
- once → diez

muchos, -as	*many, a lot of*
pocos, -as	*a few, not many*

2 SUSANA ¿Cuántas sillas hay?
  ANTONIO Muy pocas. Sólo dos o tres.

- sillas → mesas
- sillas → banderas

3 MARIO **¿Con quién** te gusta hacer **la tarea**? ¿Con Carlos?
  EVA No, con Isabel.

- hacer la tarea → **estudiar** para **exámenes**
- hacer la tarea → ir a la escuela
- hacer la tarea → hablar por teléfono

¿con quién?	*with whom?*
¿quién?	*who?*
la tarea	*homework*
estudiar	*to study*
el examen, *(pl.)* **los exámenes**	*test, exam*

4 PILAR ¿Te gusta **ayudar en casa**?
  CÉSAR Me gusta cocinar pero no me gusta **lavar los platos**.

- ayudar → trabajar

ayudar	*to help*
en casa	*in the house, at home*
lavar	*to wash*
el plato	*dish*

5 ANITA ¿Te gusta **practicar deportes?**
  TOMÁS **¡Ah, sí!** Me gustan mucho el tenis y el fútbol.

- ¡ah, sí! → ¡cómo no!
- el tenis → el béisbol
  el fútbol → el básquetbol

practicar	*to practice*
el deporte	*sport*
¡ah, sí!	*oh, yes!*

6 LUIS   Me encanta escuchar la radio.

      DIANA   ¿Qué **música** te gusta más?

      LUIS   La música **popular**.

- la radio → discos
- popular → **clásica**

la música   *music*

popular   *popular*

clásico, -a   *classical*

EN OTRAS PARTES

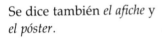

Se dice también *el afiche* y *el póster*.

Se dice también *el diario*.

Discos de música popular

PRÁCTICA

A ¿Cuántos hay? Imagine that the Board of Education has asked for an inventory of every classroom. The teacher has asked you and a partner to do that job. Using the picture, take turns asking and answering how many of each item there are.

ESTUDIANTE A *¿Cuántos periódicos hay?*
ESTUDIANTE B *Tres.*

Práctica A
1. Hay diez libros.
2. Hay seis pupitres.
3. Hay dos carteles.
4. Hay tres mapas.
5. Hay cinco sillas.

1. ¿Cuántos libros hay?
2. ¿Cuántos pupitres hay?
3. ¿Cuántos carteles hay?
4. ¿Cuántos mapas hay?
5. ¿Cuántas sillas hay?
6. ¿Cuántas banderas hay?
7. ¿Cuántos calendarios hay?
8. ¿Cuántas pizarras hay?
9. ¿Cuántos bolígrafos hay?
10. ¿Cuántos lápices hay?
11. ¿Cuántas tizas hay?
12. ¿Cuántos cuadernos hay?

6. Hay una bandera.
7. Hay un calendario.
8. Hay una pizarra.
9. Hay doce bolígrafos.
10. Hay dieciséis lápices.
11. Hay ocho tizas.
12. Hay cuatro cuadernos

B **¿Te gusta o no?** Express your preferences by saying whether you love, like, or dislike the following activities.

1. hacer la tarea
2. lavar los platos
3. hablar español
4. escuchar música popular
5. comer comida mexicana
6. bailar
7. practicar deportes
8. estudiar para exámenes
9. ayudar en casa
10. leer el periódico

C **Hablemos de ti.**
1. ¿Te gustan los deportes? ¿Qué deporte te gusta más?
2. ¿Te gusta escuchar discos y cintas? ¿Qué te gusta más, la música clásica o la música popular?
3. ¿Con quién te gusta hablar por teléfono?
4. ¿Te gusta ayudar en casa? ¿Qué te gusta más, cocinar o lavar los platos? ¿Cocinar o comer?

Practice Sheets 1–4, 1–5
Workbook Exs. C–D
Tape Manual Exs. 3–4  8
Quiz 1–2

ACTIVIDAD

Me gusta la música. Get together with a partner and ask which kinds of music and which performers he or she likes. Then switch roles. Your conversation might go like this:

ESTUDIANTE A ¿Qué música te gusta?
ESTUDIANTE B Me gusta la música popular.
ESTUDIANTE A ¿Quién te gusta?
ESTUDIANTE B Me gusta Julio Iglesias y me encanta Bruce Springsteen.
ESTUDIANTE A ¿Te gusta más Iglesias o Springsteen?

Write the name of your favorite performer on a slip of paper. Now get together as a class, and choose a secretary who will read the slips and add up votes on the chalkboard. Who is the most popular performer?

ESTUDIO DE PALABRAS

You can easily recognize some Spanish words because they look like English words. For example, *sandwich*, which the Spanish language borrowed from English, is called a loanword.

Some loanwords from English are the names of sports or activities:

béisbol   fútbol   básquetbol   camping

Some loanwords are the names of things. Can you recognize these? It will help if you say them aloud.

saxofón   suéter   champú   líder

You have also learned some Spanish words that are loanwords in English:

taco   chile

And you know others. For example:

patio   plaza   chocolate

Estudio de palabras
saxophone
sweater
shampoo
leader

¿Te gustan los waffles?

Palabras Nuevas II   **63**

EXPLICACIONES I

Los sustantivos

◆ **OBJECTIVE:**

**TO IDENTIFY
COMMON OBJECTS**

We use nouns to name people, places, and things. In Spanish, nouns have gender: some are masculine, and some are feminine. Nouns that name males are generally masculine: *el señor, el profesor.* Nouns that name females are generally feminine: *la señorita, la señora, la profesora.*

1 Almost all nouns that end in *-o* are masculine. Almost all nouns that end in *-a* are feminine.

MASCULINE	FEMININE
el disco	la música
el libro	la semana

There are very few exceptions to this rule. You know two of these: *el mapa* and *el día.*

2 Many nouns end in consonants or in vowels other than *-o* or *-a*. It is a good idea to learn a noun with its definite article, *el* or *la*, because that will always tell you the gender. *El* is used with masculine singular nouns and *la* with feminine singular nouns.

el mes   el deporte   la leche   la clase

PRÁCTICA

¿El o la?   Identify the item in each picture. Be sure to include the correct definite article.

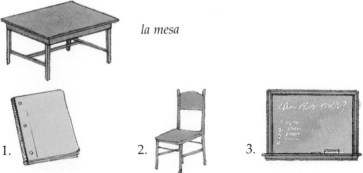

la mesa

1.

2.

3.

Notes: You may want to use mini-dialogues 1, 4, 5 on pp. 51–52 to show instances of masculine and feminine singular nouns.
   Before students do the **Práctica,** reinforce the use of *el* and *la* by asking for additional examples of masculine and feminine singular nouns.

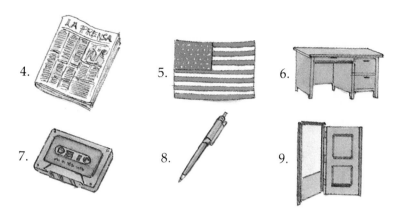

4. 5. 6.

7. 8. 9.

Práctica
1. el cuaderno
2. la silla
3. la pizarra
4. el periódico
5. la bandera
6. el escritorio
7. la cinta
8. el bolígrafo
9. la puerta

Practice Sheet 1–6

Notes: You may want to use the mini-dialogues on pp. 59–60 to show instances of masculine and feminine plural nouns.

Singular y plural

Singular = one   Plural = more than one

◆ **OBJECTIVE:**

TO IDENTIFY GROUPS OF OBJECTS

To make a noun plural we generally add:

-s to words ending in a vowel: el libro, los libro**s**
                                                      la mesa, las mesa**s**

-es to words ending in a consonant: el señor, los señor**es**
                                                              el cartel, los cartel**es**

The definite article *los* is used with masculine plural nouns. *Las* is used with feminine plural nouns.

Reteach / Review: Remind students that in Spanish the article and the noun form a unit.
    Write *-s* and *-es* on the board. Then state a series of singular nouns and articles, and ask volunteers to say the plural forms. Point to the appropriate ending on the board.

1 Singular nouns that end in the letter *z* change the *z* to *c* in the plural:

> *el lápiz → los lápi**c**es*

2 To keep the stress on the correct syllable, we sometimes have to add or take away an accent mark in the plural:

> *el **exa**men → los e**xá**menes*
> *la expli**ca**ción → las explica**cio**nes*

3 When we are talking about a mixed group of males and females, we always use the masculine plural form. For example, we would refer to a male and a female teacher together as ***los* profesores**.

Reteach / Extra Help: If your class needs more help with gender, ask students to work in pairs asking and answering *¿Qué es esto?*
    You may also want to use the chapter vocabulary lists (pp. 9, 19, 29, 37, 47, and 79) as checklists for all of the nouns presented so far. State the noun from the list and ask for the article + noun, or state the singular and ask for the plural.

Práctica

1. la guitarra, las guitarras
2. el calendario, los calendarios
3. el lápiz, los lápices
4. la bicicleta, las bicicletas
5. el mapa, los mapas
6. el profesor, los profesores
7. el cartel, los carteles
8. el mes, los meses

Practice Sheet 1–7

Una tienda de discos en Colombia

Singular y plural. Pretend that you are making flash cards to help you learn vocabulary. How would you label these flash cards?

el disco   *los discos*

1.

2.

3.

4.

5.

6.

7.

8.

Enrichment: You may want to do the **Práctica** orally before students write their answers. Then call volunteers to the board to write their flash card labels. Students can check their own answers.

El uso del artículo definido

The English equivalent of the definite article is "the." But we sometimes use definite articles in Spanish where we wouldn't use "the" in English.

1 In Spanish, when we speak about a thing in general terms, we use the definite article. In English, we do not.

> Me encanta **la música.** *I love **music.***
> ¿Te gustan **los deportes**? *Do you like **sports**?*

2 We also use the definite article with titles of respect, such as *profesor(a)*, *señor(a)*, and *señorita*, when we are talking *about* the person, *not to* the person:

> Buenos días, **señor Díaz.** *Good morning, **Mr. Díaz.***
> ¿De dónde es **el señor Díaz**? *Where is **Mr. Díaz** from?*

3 Definite articles mean "on" when we use them with days of the week.

> **El** sábado ⎫ **On** Saturday ⎫
> **Los** sábados ⎭ me gusta nadar Saturdays ⎭ I like to swim.

Days of the week that end in s have the same form in both the singular and the plural: *el lunes → los lunes.*

PRÁCTICA

A **El menú.** Pretend that you are reading a school menu. Indicate whether or not you like a particular food by saying *¡Ah, sí!* if you like it or *no* if you don't. Always include the correct definite article: *el, la, los,* or *las.* For example:

> chile con carne
> *¿El chile con carne? ¡Ah, sí! Me encanta.*
> o: *¿El chile con carne? No, no me gusta.*

1. leche
2. refrescos
3. papas fritas
4. yogur
5. sandwiches de jamón y queso
6. helado
7. tacos
8. pan con mantequilla
9. hamburguesas
10. ensalada

◆ **OBJECTIVES:**

TO EXPRESS LIKES AND DISLIKES

TO REFER TO ADULTS

TO REFER TO THINGS YOU DO ON CERTAIN DAYS

Reteach / Review: Tell students to work in pairs asking and answering *¿Qué día es hoy?, ¿Cuál es la fecha de hoy?, ¿Cuándo es tu cumpleaños?*

Enrichment: Ask students to create sentences that use either the singular or the plural article with the days of the week.

Práctica A
1. ¿La leche? ¡Ah, sí! Me encanta. *or:* No, no me gusta.
2. ¿Los refrescos? ¡Ah, sí! Me encantan. *or:* No, no me gustan.
3. ¿Las papas fritas? … Me encantan / gustan.
4. ¿El yogur? … Me encanta / gusta.
5. ¿Los sandwiches de jamón y queso? … Me encantan / gustan.
6. ¿El helado? … Me encanta / gusta.
7. ¿Los tacos? … Me encantan / gustan.
8. ¿El pan con mantequilla? … Me encanta / gusta.
9. ¿Las hamburguesas? … Me encantan / gustan.
10. ¿La ensalada? … Me encanta / gusta.

B **Los lunes me gusta . . .** Victoria asks Pedro what he likes to do on different days of the week and with whom. With a classmate, alternate roles, choosing words or expressions from the lists below.

ESTUDIANTE A *¿Qué te gusta hacer los martes?*
ESTUDIANTE B *Me gusta estudiar español.*
ESTUDIANTE A *¿Con quién?*
ESTUDIANTE B *Con el profesor Morales.*

lunes	hacer la tarea	profesor Morales
martes	jugar al *(deporte)*	señor Díaz
miércoles	practicar deportes	Francisco y Graciela
jueves	escuchar música popular	señora Álvarez
viernes	ir al cine	Guillermo
sábado	hablar por teléfono	Mónica
domingo	estudiar español	profesora Benítez
	escuchar cintas (o discos)	

C **Hablemos de ti.**
1. ¿Qué te gusta comer al mediodía?
2. ¿Qué te gusta hacer los sábados? ¿Con quién?

APLICACIONES

¿Qué te gusta hacer? Transparency 13

Pretend that you are either Héctor or Teresa. Tell what you like and don't like to do. Afterwards, work with a partner to make up a brief dialogue between Héctor and Teresa. Ask each other about what you like to do.

Notes: Sample dialogues for the **¿Qué pasa?** appear in the pre-chapter teacher pages. You may want to allow class time for pairs of students to prepare their dialogues. Circulate to give help as needed. Ask students to act out their dialogues. Encourage them to dramatize the conversations.

EXPLICACIONES II

Notes: Refer to mini-dialogues 1, 2, 3, and 5 on pp. 51–52 and 3–6 on pp. 59–60 to highlight the use of *me / te gusta(n)* and *me encanta(n)*.

Me gusta y no me gusta

We use *me gusta(n)* and *te gusta(n)* to talk about things we like.

◆ **OBJECTIVES:**

TO EXPRESS LIKES AND DISLIKES ABOUT LEISURE, SCHOOL, AND HOME ACTIVITIES

TO GIVE REASONS FOR LIKING AND DISLIKING THINGS

¿Te gusta la música popular?	*Do you like popular music?*
¿Qué deportes **te gustan**?	*What sports do you like?*
Me gustan el tenis y el béisbol.	*I like tennis and baseball.*

We use *gusta* with singular nouns and *gustan* with plural nouns or with more than one noun.

1 We use *no me gusta(n)* and *no te gusta(n)* to talk about things we don't like.

¿No te gusta la música popular?	*Don't you like popular music?*
No me gustan los deportes.	*I don't like sports.*

To answer no to a question, we say *no* twice.

¿Te gusta la música clásica?	*Do you like classical music?*
No, no me gusta (la música clásica).	*No, I don't (like classical music).*

2 We use *me encanta(n)* to express a very strong liking.

¡Me encanta el cartel!	*I love the poster!*
Me encantan las fiestas.	*I love parties.*

3 Verbs name actions or activities. For example, *jugar, estudiar, leer,* and *comer* are verbs. We always use the singular form *gusta* or *encanta* with verbs.

Me gusta cantar y **bailar.**	*I like to sing and dance.*

PRÁCTICA

A No, pero . . . Working with a partner, ask and answer according to the model.

> cantar / bailar
> ESTUDIANTE A   *¿Te gusta cantar?*
> ESTUDIANTE B   *No, pero me gusta bailar.*

los discos / la televisión
ESTUDIANTE A   *¿Te gustan los discos?*
ESTUDIANTE B   *No, pero me gusta la televisión.*

1. lavar los platos / cocinar
2. esquiar / jugar al tenis
3. tocar la guitarra / escuchar música
4. el queso / el jamón
5. los refrescos / la limonada
6. los deportes / la música
7. nadar / el béisbol y el fútbol
8. los burritos / el chile con carne

B   La fiesta.   Imagine that you and a friend are talking about what you want to buy for a party on Saturday night. Take turns asking and answering, using *gusta(n)* and *encanta(n)*.

refrescos
ESTUDIANTE A   *Te gustan los refrescos, ¿no?*
ESTUDIANTE B   *Pues sí, me encantan.*
          o: *No, no me gustan.*

1. limonada
2. música popular
3. tacos y burritos
4. discos de rock
5. sandwiches de jamón y queso
6. helado
7. hamburguesas con papas fritas
8. ensalada

C   ¿Por qué? Porque . . .   Working with a partner, ask why he or she likes certain things. Take turns asking and answering.

fiestas / bailar
ESTUDIANTE A   *Me gustan las fiestas.*
ESTUDIANTE B   *¿Por qué?*
ESTUDIANTE A   *Porque me gusta bailar.*

1. hamburguesas / comida americana
2. clase de español / profesor
3. escuchar discos / música
4. cocinar / comer
5. libros / leer
6. burritos / comida mexicana
7. ir a la escuela / estudiar
8. jugar al béisbol y al básquetbol / deportes

Práctica A
1. ¿Te gusta lavar los platos? No, pero me gusta cocinar.
2. ¿Te gusta esquiar? … me gusta jugar al tenis.
3. ¿Te gusta tocar la guitarra? … me gusta escuchar música.
4. ¿Te gusta el queso? … me gusta el jamón.
5. ¿Te gustan los refrescos? … me gusta la limonada.
6. ¿Te gustan los deportes? … me gusta la música.
7. ¿Te gusta nadar? … me gustan el béisbol y el fútbol.
8. ¿Te gustan los burritos? … me gusta el chile con carne.

Práctica B
1. Te gusta la limonada, ¿no? Pues sí, me encanta. *or:* No, no me gusta.
2. Te gusta la música popular, ¿no? Pues sí, me encanta. *or:* No, no me gusta.
3. Te gustan los tacos y los burritos, ¿no? Pues sí, me encantan. *or:* No, no me gustan.
4. Te gustan los discos de rock, ¿no? … me encantan. *or:* No, no me gustan.
5. Te gustan los sandwiches de jamón y queso, ¿no? … me encantan. *or:* No, no me gustan.
6. Te gusta el helado, ¿no? … me encanta. *or:* No, no me gusta.
7. Te gustan las hamburguesas con papas fritas, ¿no? … me encantan. *or:* No, no me gustan.
8. Te gusta la ensalada, ¿no? … me encanta. *or:* No, no me gusta.

Práctica C
1. Me gustan las hamburguesas. ¿Por qué? Porque me gusta la comida americana.
2. Me gusta la clase de español. ¿Por qué? Porque me gusta el profesor.
3. Me gusta escuchar discos. ¿Por qué? Porque me gusta la música.
4. Me gusta cocinar. ¿Por qué? … me gusta comer.
5. Me gustan los libros. ¿Por qué? … me gusta leer.
6. Me gustan los burritos. ¿Por qué? … me gusta la comida mexicana.
7. Me gusta ir a la escuela. ¿Por qué? … me gusta estudiar.
8. Me gusta jugar al béisbol y al básquetbol. ¿Por qué? … me gustan los deportes.

Práctica D

1. No me gustan los tacos.
   ¿Por qué no? Porque no me
   gusta la comida mexicana.
2. No me gusta hacer la tarea.
   ¿Por qué no? Porque no me
   gusta trabajar.
3. No me gustan los
   sandwiches. ¿Por qué no?
   Porque no me gusta el pan.
4. No me gusta jugar al fútbol
   americano. ¿Por qué no? …
   no me gustan los deportes.
5. No me gusta el libro. ¿Por
   qué no? … no me gustan los
   dibujos.
6. No me gusta cantar y bailar.
   ¿Por qué no? … no me
   gusta la música.
7. No me gustan las
   hamburguesas con queso.
   ¿Por qué no? … no me
   gusta el queso.
8. No me gustan los
   exámenes. ¿Por qué no? …
   no me gusta estudiar.

Practice Sheet 1–9

 10 Tape Manual Ex. 7
Quiz 1–4

◆ **OBJECTIVES:**

**TO ASK ABOUT
QUANTITY**

**TO EXPRESS
QUANTITIES
OF THINGS
AVAILABLE**

Notes: You may want to use
mini-dialogues 1–2 on p. 59 to
introduce *hay, ¿cuántos?,
muchos, pocos.*

D ¿Por qué no? Now it's the opposite. With a different partner, ask why he or she doesn't like certain things. Take turns asking and answering.

fiestas / bailar

ESTUDIANTE A *No me gustan las fiestas.*
ESTUDIANTE B *¿Por qué no?*
ESTUDIANTE A *Porque no me gusta bailar.*

1. tacos / comida mexicana
2. hacer la tarea / trabajar
3. sandwiches / pan
4. jugar al fútbol americano / deportes
5. libro / dibujos
6. cantar y bailar / música
7. hamburguesas con queso / queso
8. exámenes / estudiar

Hay / ¿cuántos? / muchos / pocos

Hay can mean either "there is" or "there are."

Hay helado.	*There's ice cream.*
Hay sillas.	*There are chairs.*

1 In a question, *hay* means "Is there . . . ?" or "Are there . . . ?"

¿Hay ensalada hoy?	*Is there salad today?*
¿Hay papas fritas?	*Are there French fries?*

No hay means "there isn't any" or "there aren't any." In a question it means "Isn't there any?" or "Aren't there any?"

No hay helado.	*There isn't any ice cream.*
No hay sillas.	*There aren't any chairs.*
¿No hay helado?	*Isn't there any ice cream?*
¿No hay sillas?	*Aren't there any chairs?*

2 We use *¿cuántos?* with masculine plural nouns and *¿cuántas?* with feminine plural nouns.

Reteach / Extra Help:
Reinforce *¿Cuántos ... hay? / Hay muchos (pocos) ...* by having students work in pairs to ask and answer questions based on the illustrations on pp. 53–54.

¿Cuántos libros hay?	*How many books are there?*
Hay tres.	*There are three.*
¿Cuántas banderas hay?	*How many flags are there?*
Hay dos.	*There are two.*

3 When we ask the question *¿Cuántos?* or *¿Cuántas?*, the answer will sometimes include the word *muchos, -as* or *pocos, -as.*

¿Cuántos periódicos hay?	*How many newspapers are there?*
Hay **muchos.**	*There are a lot.*
¿Cuántas guitarras hay?	*How many guitars are there?*
Hay **pocas.**	{ *There are a few.*
	{ *There aren't many.*

PRÁCTICA

Práctica A
1. Hay muchos refrescos.
2. Hay pocos sandwiches.
3. Hay muchos tacos.
4. Hay muchos burritos.
5. Hay pocas ensaladas.
6. Hay pocas cintas.
7. Hay muchos discos.
8. Hay pocas mesas.
9. Hay muchos platos.

A ¿Muchos o pocos? Pretend that you have asked your friends to help set up for a party. Tell them whether there are a lot or only a few of the items shown. (Consider anything under six as few.)

Hay pocas sillas.

Práctica B
1. ¿Cuántos refrescos hay?
   Hay veinte.
2. ¿Cuántos sandwiches hay?
   Hay cuatro.
3. ¿Cuántos tacos hay?
   Hay diez.
4. ¿Cuántos burritos hay?
   Hay doce.
5. ¿Cuántas ensaladas hay?
   Hay dos.
6. ¿Cuántas cintas hay?
   Hay cinco.
7. ¿Cuántos discos hay?
   Hay siete.
8. ¿Cuántas mesas hay?
   Hay dos.
9. ¿Cuántos platos hay?
   Hay nueve.

B ¿Cuántos hay? Working with a partner, take turns asking and answering how many of each item are shown in the picture for Práctica A.

ESTUDIANTE A *¿Cuántas sillas hay?*
ESTUDIANTE B *Hay cinco.*

C   Hablemos de ti.

1. ¿Hay carteles en tu clase de español? ¿Cuántos?
2. ¿Hay dibujos? ¿Cuántos?
3. ¿Hay mapas en tu clase? ¿Cuántos? ¿Y cuántas banderas?
4. ¿Hay muchos o pocos estudiantes en tu clase? ¿Cuántos hay?

Práctica C
Answers will vary.

Practice Sheet 1–10
Workbook Exs. G–J
Tape Manual Ex. 8   11
Refrán   12
Activity Master 1–2
Quiz 1–5

ACTIVIDAD

¡Me encantan las hamburguesas!   Take a poll to find out which foods your classmates like. The entire class should choose from a list of foods taken from the vocabulary of this chapter. Each student writes the names of the foods on a sheet of paper. Across the top, write these headings: *me encanta(n)*, *me gusta(n) mucho*, *me gusta(n)*, and *no me gusta(n)*. Then interview a classmate, asking about all of the foods on the list. Your partner should answer truthfully. Then exchange roles. For example:

Notes: You may want to have small groups respond to the poll in the **Actividad.**

ESTUDIANTE A   ¿Te gusta el pan con mantequilla?
ESTUDIANTE B   Sí, me gusta.
ESTUDIANTE A   ¿Te gusta el yogur?
ESTUDIANTE B   No, no me gusta el yogur.
ESTUDIANTE A   ¿Te gustan los burritos?
ESTUDIANTE B   ¡Cómo no! Me encantan los burritos.

Mark each of your partner's answers in the appropriate space on your chart. Then, as a class, total the number of votes for each food under each heading.

	me encanta(n)	me gusta(n) mucho	me gusta(n)	no me gusta(n)
los refrescos	IIII	II		
el helado	HHT II	III	I	
los tacos	IIII	I		
la leche	I		I	
el yogur	II			

REPASO

Look carefully at the model sentences. Then put the English cues into Spanish to form new sentences based on the models.

1. *¿Te gustan más los libros o los periódicos?*
   (Do you prefer sandwiches or salads?)
   (Do you prefer parties or exams?)

2. *¿Te gusta la música?*
   (Do you like ham?)
   (Do you like cheese?)

3. *¿Te gustan los refrescos?*
   (Do you like sports?)
   (Do you like maps?)

4. *¿Cuántas banderas hay?*
   (How many pencils are there?)
   (How many chairs are there?)

5. *¡No me gusta cocinar!*
   (I don't like to read!)
   (I don't like to study!)

Notes: Review of:
1–3. *¿Te gusta(n) (más)?*
   nouns in a general sense
   definite articles: gender and number
   noun plural formation
   4. *¿Cuántos, -as?*
   noun plural formation
   5. *no me gusta* + infinitive

En la Alameda en México

TEMA

Transparency 14

Enrichment: You may want to ask students to write new captions for the **Tema** pictures.

In conjunction with the **Redacción,** ask pairs of volunteers to act out a dialogue based on the **Tema** captions.

Now put the English captions into Spanish.

1. Do you prefer tacos or hamburgers?

2. Do you like yogurt?

3. Do you like French fries?

4. How many students are there?

5. I don't like to work!

REDACCIÓN

Notes: Answers to the **Repaso** and **Tema** appear in the pre-chapter teacher pages.

Now you are ready to write your own dialogue or paragraph. Choose one of the following topics.

1. Write a paragraph of four to six sentences about what you like and don't like about your school life and your home life. Do you like to study, to work a lot, to do homework, to speak Spanish in class? At home, do you like to wash the dishes, help around the house, watch TV, listen to records?

2. Look at the pictures in the *Tema*. Expand the poll taker's job by writing four additional questions that she might ask about the cafeteria food.

3. Using the *Tema*, imagine the answers that the students shown in the first three pictures might give the poll taker. Then write the complete dialogue, including the poll taker's questions and the students' answers.

A ¿Te gusta?
Tell whether or not you like the following food items. Use *me gusta* or *me gustan*.

Me gusta el helado.
o: *No me gusta el helado.*

1.

2.

3.

4.

5.

6.

7.

8.

9.

10.

B ¿El o la?
Write the correct definite article for each of these words.

1. puerta
2. mes
3. pizarra
4. bolígrafo
5. lápiz
6. hoja de papel
7. pupitre
8. clase
9. cartel
10. examen
11. día de fiesta
12. lunes

C ¿Los o las?
Write each word in **B** in the plural form. Be sure to include the correct definite article.

D Me encanta . . . pero . . .
Form sentences using the cues, as in the model.

escuela / estudiar para exámenes
Me encanta la escuela, pero no me gusta estudiar para exámenes.

1. música / cantar
2. deportes / jugar al tenis
3. clase de español / hacer la tarea
4. tacos / cocinar
5. fiestas / bailar
6. comer / sandwiches de jamón
7. leer y estudiar / hacer la tarea

E La clase de español
Ask and answer according to the model.

cartel / 3
¿Hay muchos carteles?
No, hay pocos.
¿Cuántos hay?
Tres.

1. profesor / 9
2. estudiante / 14
3. pupitre / 11
4. silla / 13
5. mesa / 2
6. mapa / 4
7. ventana / 5

Notes: Answers to the **Comprueba** appear in the pre-chapter teacher pages.

Reteach / Review: Ask students to give the correct definite article orally or in writing for each word in Ex. E. Then have them change the words to the plural.

Chapter 1 Test Listening Comprehension Test

VOCABULARIO DEL CAPÍTULO I

Sustantivos
la bandera
el burrito
el cartel
el chile con carne
el deporte
la ensalada
el escritorio
el examen, *pl.* los exámenes
la hamburguesa
el helado
el jamón
la leche
la limonada
la mantequilla
el mapa
la mesa
la música
el pan
las papas fritas
el periódico
el plato
el pupitre
el queso
el refresco
el sandwich (de jamón,
   de queso)
la silla
el taco
la tarea
la tiza
el yogur

Adjetivos
clásico, -a
muchos, -as
pocos, -as
popular

Verbos
ayudar
estudiar
lavar
practicar

Adverbios
entonces
más
mucho

Preposiciones
con
para
sin

Conjunciones
o
porque
pues

Palabras interrogativas
¿con quién?
¿por qué?
¿quién?

Expresiones
¡ah, sí!
¡cómo no!
en casa
me encantan
me/te gusta(n) más
¿verdad?

¿UN LATINOAMERICANO TÍPICO?

Suppose you are the casting director for a movie and the script calls for a "Latin American." What do you look for? A specific style of clothing? A particular color of hair, skin, or eyes? You'd better ask the director for a more detailed description.

Meet Mario Antonioni from Argentina, Cecilia Chang from Puerto Rico, and Lucía Díaz from Mexico. As you can tell from their names, their ancestors came from all parts of the world. Though they all share a common language—Spanish—they lead very different lives.

Mario's family originally came from Italy and Spain. Many Latin American families in Argentina, Uruguay, and Chile are of European descent. After school, Mario and his friends often sit for hours in a café on one of the wide, tree-lined avenues in Buenos Aires, talking and drinking coffee.

While Mario chats, Cecilia works through the warm Puerto Rican evening in her parents' restaurant. After the first Spaniards arrived in the Caribbean, this region became a melting pot of Europeans, Africans, and Asians. The Changs' customers are tall, short, thin, heavyset, darkest brown, and palest white. They're all Puerto Rican, and they are there for the food—the unique Caribbean cuisine that includes savory rice and beans and sweet, fried plantains.

Lucía eats at home, and her mother's recipes are hundreds of years old. The Díaz family are direct descendants of the Aztecs of Mexico. Not far from the ancient pyramids of Teotihuacán, Lucía's family grows *maíz* and grinds corn the same way her ancestors did five centuries ago. Mario, Cecilia, and Lucía are all *latinoamericanos*. Different as they are, if they were to meet they would have little trouble communicating, for they all share a basic tool—the Spanish language.

81

PALABRAS NUEVAS I

¿De qué país eres?

Transparency 15

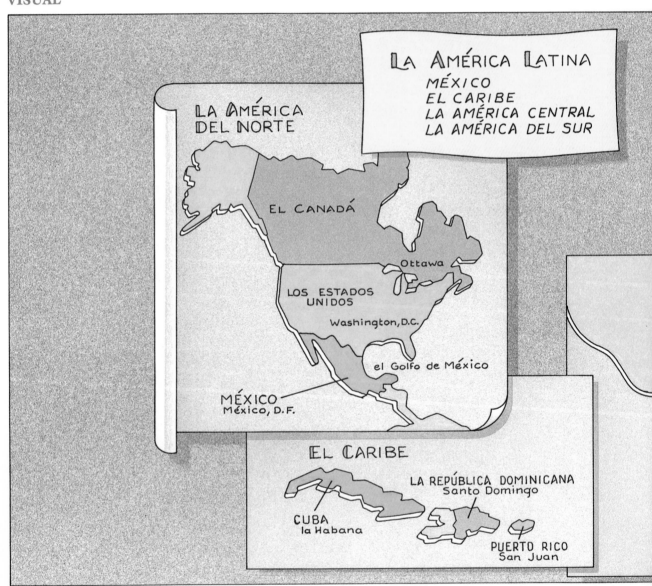

LA AMÉRICA LATINA
MÉXICO
EL CARIBE
LA AMÉRICA CENTRAL
LA AMÉRICA DEL SUR

LA AMÉRICA
DEL NORTE

EL CANADÁ

Ottawa

LOS ESTADOS
UNIDOS

Washington, D.C.

el Golfo de México

MÉXICO
México, D.F.

EL CARIBE

LA REPÚBLICA DOMINICANA
Santo Domingo

CUBA
la Habana

PUERTO RICO
San Juan

LA AMÉRICA DEL SUR

VENEZUELA
Caracas

COLOMBIA
Bogotá

EL ECUADOR
Quito

EL PERÚ
Lima

LA AMÉRICA CENTRAL

BOLIVIA
Sucre+
La Paz*

HONDURAS
Tegucigalpa

EL SALVADOR
San Salvador

EL PARAGUAY
Asunción

NICARAGUA
Managua

EL URUGUAY
Montevideo

GUATEMALA
Guatemala

CHILE
Santiago

LA ARGENTINA
Buenos Aires

COSTA RICA
San José

PANAMÁ
Panamá

* Though Sucre is the official capital of Bolivia, only the Supreme Court meets there. Most government offices were moved to La Paz in 1898, because it was less remote than Sucre and had better transportation facilities to other parts of the country.

CONTEXTO COMUNICATIVO

 2

Reteach / Review: To reinforce the *tú / usted* distinction, you may want to have students substitute *señor Valencia* for *Carlos* in the first dialogue (*¿De qué país es, señor Valencia?... ¡Ah, es cubano!*).

1 JULIA   **¿De qué país** eres, Carlos?
  CARLOS   Soy de Cuba.
  JULIA   ¡Ah, eres **cubano**! Pues, yo soy **mexicana**.

Variaciones:
- ¿de qué país? → ¿de dónde?
- Cuba → Puerto Rico
  cubano → **puertorriqueño**
- mexicana → **española**

2 TERESA   **¿Es usted norteamericano?**
  PATRICIO   Sí, de Santa Fe. Pero soy **de origen** español.

- español → **latinoamericano**

3 JORGE   ¿Es usted de los Estados Unidos?
  ANITA   No, soy del Canadá.

- de los Estados Unidos → del Caribe
- del Canadá → del Perú

4 DANIEL   Nicole es mi **compañera de clase**.
  YOLANDA   ¿Es **canadiense**?
  DANIEL   No, es **sudamericana**.

- mi compañera de clase → mi **amiga**
- mi compañera de clase → una **alumna**

5 LAURA   Honduras es un país **centroamericano**, ¿verdad?
  LUIS   Sí.
  LAURA   ¿Cuál es **la capital**?
  LUIS   Tegucigalpa.

- Honduras → Nicaragua
  Tegucigalpa → Managua
- Honduras → Costa Rica
  Tegucigalpa → San José

¿de qué país? *from what country*
el país *country*
cubano, -a *Cuban*
mexicano, -a *Mexican*

puertorriqueño, -a *Puerto Rican*
español, -a *Spanish*

¿es usted? *are you?*
norteamericano, -a *North American*
de origen *of ____ origin*
latinoamericano, -a *Latin American*

el compañero, la compañera de clase *classmate*
canadiense *Canadian*
sudamericano, -a *South American*
el amigo, la amiga *friend*
el alumno, la alumna *pupil*
centroamericano, -a *Central American*
la capital *capital*

PRÁCTICA

A De origen latinoamericano.   Tell where the following people are from and what their backgrounds are. Work with a partner. Take turns asking and answering. Follow the model.

> Marta / El Paso / Cuba
> ESTUDIANTE A   *¿De dónde es Marta?*
> ESTUDIANTE B   *Es de El Paso. Pero es de origen cubano.*

1. Lola / Philadelphia / Puerto Rico
2. José / San Diego / México
3. María / Albuquerque / América del Sur
4. Ángel / Denver / América Central
5. Eva / San Antonio / América Latina
6. Tomás / Chicago / Cuba
7. Sara / Detroit / Canadá
8. Pedro / Asunción / América del Norte
9. tu amiga / Kansas City / España

Práctica A
1. ¿De dónde es Lola? Es de Philadelphia. Pero es de origen puertorriqueño.
2. ¿De dónde es José? Es de San Diego. Pero es de origen mexicano.
3. ... de origen sudamericano.
4. ... de origen centroamericano.
5. ... de origen latinoamericano.
6. ... de origen cubano.
7. ... de origen canadiense.
8. ... de origen norteamericano.
9. ... de origen español.

B Hablemos de ti.
1. ¿De qué país eres? ¿Eres de los Estados Unidos? ¿De qué estado?
2. ¿Cuál es la capital de tu estado? ¿Eres de la capital?

Práctica B
Answers will vary.

Enrichment: Assign Ex. B for oral or written class work or as homework. Students should infer the meaning of *estado* from *los Estados Unidos*.

APLICACIONES Discretionary

¿Hay O'Briens en la América del Sur? 4

En Santiago, la capital de Chile.

FELIPE   Hola. Me llamo Felipe O'Brien. ¿Y tú?

LOLITA   Lolita Crespo.

FELIPE   Tú no eres de Chile, ¿verdad?

5   LOLITA   No, soy puertorriqueña. Y tú, ¿de qué país eres?
¿De Irlanda?

FELIPE   No. ¿Por qué?

LOLITA   Porque te llamas O'Brien.

FELIPE   Soy de Chile, pero mi familia es de origen irlandés.[1]

10   En Chile hay muchos O'Briens, O'Neils, O'Higgins,
O' . . .

LOLITA   ¿O'Higgins? ¿Como[2] Bernardo O'Higgins,* el libertador[3]
de Chile?

FELIPE   Sí, y también como Carlitos O'Higgins, mi compañero de

15   clase.

---

[1]**irlandés** *Irish*   [2]**como** *like*   [3]**el libertador** *liberator*
*Bernardo O'Higgins (1778–1842) liberated Chile from Spain in 1818.

If students ask: You may want to ask students to do research on O'Higgins or Bolívar and give brief oral reports.

Preguntas

Contesta según el diálogo.

1. ¿Cuál es la capital de Chile?   2. ¿De dónde es Lolita?   3. ¿De qué país es Felipe?   4. ¿Es Felipe de origen irlandés o puertorriqueño?   5. ¿Es Carlitos O'Higgins el libertador de Chile?

El libertador de Chile

Enrichment: Check students, understanding by asking additional questions: *¿Es Lolita de Chile? (No.) ¿Es Felipe de Chile? (Sí.) ¿Cuántos O'Higgins hay en Chile? (Hay muchos.)*

Diálogo
1. Santiago.
2. De Puerto Rico.
3. De Chile.
4. Irlandés.
5. No.

Participación

With a partner, make up a four- or five-line dialogue telling where you and one or two of your classmates are from.

PRONUNCIACIÓN ▭ 5

The pronunciation of the letter *ll* is similar to the sound of the *y* in the English word "yard."

Escucha y repite.

ella   ellos   silla   llamo   mantequilla

Ella es de Sevilla.
Me llamo Guillermo Llanos.
Hay mantequilla en la silla.

Enrichment: Write unknown words containing the target
sound on the board, and ask students to pronounce them: *llave, calle, galleta, llegar.*
You may want to use the sentences in **Pronunciación** D for dictation.   Aplicaciones   **87**

PALABRAS NUEVAS II

¿Cómo es?

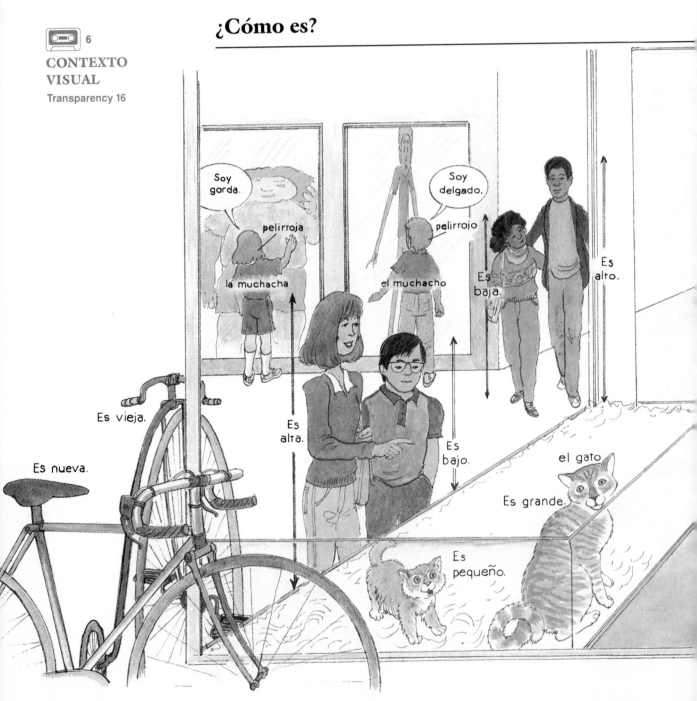

el pájaro
Es muy bonito.

el perro

Es joven.

rubio

rubia

corto, -a

Es joven.

moreno

morena

Es vieja.

Es viejo.

la mujer

el hombre

largo, -a

Es feo.

el pez
pl. los peces

Es bonito.

Es enorme.

Bajo, -a means "short" in height. *Corto, -a* means "short" in length.
So *alto/bajo* are opposites and *largo/corto* are opposites.

1 PATRICIA **¿Cómo es** tu profesor de español?

JORGE ¿Mi profesor? No es un hombre, es una mujer.

PATRICIA Pues, ¿cómo es?

JORGE Es alta y pelirroja.

Variaciones:
- alta → baja
- pelirroja → rubia

¿cómo es ____? *what's ____ like?*

2 MARTA Silvia, tu amigo Paco es moreno, ¿verdad?

SILVIA Sí, y muy **guapo.**

- moreno → rubio
- muy → **bastante**

guapo, -a *good-looking*
bastante *rather, fairly, kind of*

3 MARCO ¿Cómo es la tarea de español? ¿Corta?

ANITA **Al contrario,** es **demasiado** larga.

MARCO ¡Uf!

- la tarea → el examen
  corta → corto
  larga → largo
- demasiado → bastante

al contrario *on the contrary*
demasiado *too*

4 CECILIA Me gusta tu cartel. **¡Qué** bonito! ¿Es nuevo?

CARLOS ¿Mi cartel de España? No, es muy viejo.

- bonito → enorme

¡qué (+ adjective)! *how (+ adjective)!*

EN OTRAS PARTES

En México se dice también
güero, -a.

En Chile se dice también
colorín, colorina.

Enrichment: Use the illustrations on pp. 88–89 or magazine pictures as cues to elicit *¡Qué + adj!,* using adjectives introduced in **Palabras nuevas II.**

You may want to provide extra practice with adjectives by suggesting additional **Variaciones.**

PRÁCTICA

A ¡Qué grande! Imagine that you are trying to describe someone or something, but you're at a loss for words. A friend, however, always knows just the right adjective. Working with a partner, take turns helping each other come up with the right word. Follow the model.

> pájaro / grande
> ESTUDIANTE A *Es un pájaro muy . . . muy . . .*
> ESTUDIANTE B *¿Grande?*
> ESTUDIANTE A *¡Sí! ¡Qué grande!*

1. perro / alto
2. muchacha / guapa
3. pez / pequeño
4. mujer / rubia
5. gato / gordo
6. hombre / delgado
7. libro / enorme
8. dibujo / feo
9. guitarra / bonita

B ¿Cómo es? With a partner, take turns asking and answering the questions according to the illustrations. Follow the model.

> ESTUDIANTE A *¿Es la silla vieja o nueva?*
> ESTUDIANTE B *Es vieja.*

1. ¿rubia o morena?

2. ¿gordo o delgado?

3. ¿joven o viejo?

4. ¿bonito o feo?

5. ¿grande o pequeño?

6. ¿alto o bajo?

7. ¿corto o largo?

8. ¿nueva o vieja?

Práctica A

1. Es un perro … ¡Sí! ¡Qué alto!
2. Es una muchacha … ¡Sí! ¡Qué guapa!
3. Es un pez … ¡Sí! ¡Qué pequeño!
4. Es una mujer … ¡Sí! ¡Qué rubia!
5. Es un gato … ¡Sí! ¡Qué gordo!
6. Es un hombre … ¡Sí! ¡Qué delgado!
7. Es un libro … ¡Sí! ¡Qué enorme!
8. Es un dibujo … ¡Sí! ¡Qué feo!
9. Es una guitarra … ¡Sí! ¡Qué bonita!

Práctica B

1. ¿Es la mujer rubia o morena? Es rubia.
2. ¿Es el hombre gordo o delgado? Es gordo.
3. ¿Es el gato joven o viejo? Es joven.
4. ¿Es el pez bonito o feo? Es feo.
5. ¿Es el perro grande o pequeño? Es grande.
6. ¿Es el pájaro alto o bajo? Es alto.
7. ¿Es el lápiz corto o largo? Es corto.
8. ¿Es la guitarra nueva o vieja? Es nueva.

Práctica C

1. Al contrario, es pequeño. Y muy joven.
   No es joven. Es viejo.
2. Al contrario, es bonito. Y muy grande.
   No es grande. Es pequeño.
3. Al contrario, es rubio. Y muy delgado.
   No es delgado. Es gordo.
4. ..., es fea. Y muy baja.
   No es baja. Es alta.
5. ..., es delgado. Y muy guapo.
   No es guapo. Es feo.
6. ..., es corto. Y muy feo.
   No es feo. Es bonito.
7. ..., es grande. Y muy viejo.
   No es viejo. Es joven.
8. ..., es pequeña. Y muy fea.
   No es fea. Es bonita (guapa).

Práctica D
Answers will vary.

Practice Sheet 2–2

 8 Tape Manual Ex. 2

C Al contrario. Imagine that you and a friend are talking about people and pets you have just seen. You constantly disagree about what you saw. With another student, take turns asking and answering.

La muchacha es rubia / alta

ESTUDIANTE A *La muchacha es rubia, ¿no?*
ESTUDIANTE B *Al contrario, es morena. Y muy alta.*
ESTUDIANTE A *No es alta. Es baja.*

1. El perro es grande / joven
2. El pájaro es feo / grande
3. El hombre es moreno / delgado
4. La mujer es bonita / baja
5. El muchacho es gordo / guapo
6. El pez es largo / feo
7. El gato es pequeño / viejo
8. La muchacha es grande / fea

D Hablemos de ti.
1. ¿Qué te gustan más, los perros o los gatos?
2. ¿Cómo es tu perro (gato, pájaro, pez)?
3. ¿Cómo es tu profesor(a)?
4. Y tú, ¿cómo eres?

Workbook Exs. C–D
Quiz 2–2

En Colombia y en México

ACTIVIDAD

El hombre invisible. He may be invisible, but you can use your imagination and describe him. Write your description of the invisible man on a sheet of paper. Include at least four or five adjectives. For example: *Es rubio y muy joven. Es alto y bastante guapo, pero es demasiado delgado.* Put everyone's description in a bag, but *keep a copy of the one you wrote.* Each person then takes one of the descriptions and makes a portrait based on it.

When everyone has finished, each artist exchanges his or her drawing with another student. Then students take turns reading aloud from their own copies of the descriptions they wrote. Whoever thinks he or she has that picture of the invisible man should hold it up. Can a picture be found for every description?

Enrichment: If students have a sufficiently good grasp of adjective endings, ask them to describe *la mujer invisible.*

ESTUDIO DE PALABRAS

In Spanish, adjectives are related to the names of countries just as they are in English. For example, in English we call a person from Cuba a Cuban. In Spanish we say *cubano* or *cubana.* Notice that the adjective is not capitalized in Spanish and that it usually has an *o* ending for males and an *a* ending for females.

Many adjectives of nationality end in *-no* and *-na:*
  Perú → peru*no*, peru*na*
  Colombia → colombia*no*, colombia*na*
  Chile → chile*no*, chile*na*

Some adjectives of nationality have other endings:
  España → españ*ol*, españ*ola*
  Canadá → canad*iense*
  Guatemala → guatemal*teco*, guatemal*teca*
  Panamá → panam*eño*, panam*eña*

If you see words such as these in a dialogue or reading, look for the root—the main part of the word. It may give you a clue. For example, where do you think an *estadounidense* comes from?

EXPLICACIONES I

Los pronombres personales

◆ OBJECTIVES:

TO POINT PEOPLE
OUT

TO ASK PEOPLE
WHERE THEY ARE
FROM

Pronouns that tell us *who* is doing something are called subject pronouns. Here are the Spanish subject pronouns that you will use. You already know some of them.

Notes: You may use mini-dialogues 1–3 on p. 84 to present the use of the subject pronouns *yo* and *usted*.

Una estudiante
puertorriqueña

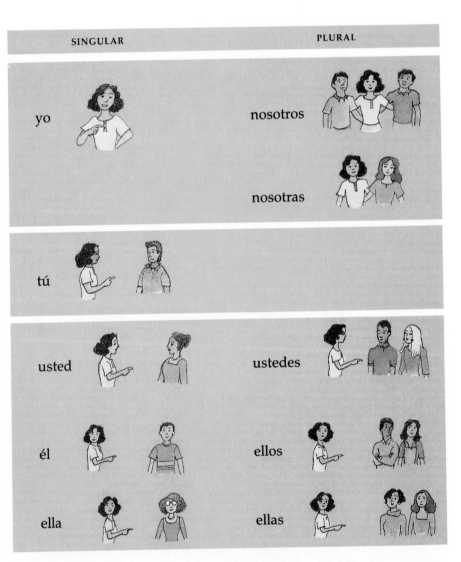

SINGULAR	PLURAL
yo	nosotros
	nosotras
tú	
usted	ustedes
él	ellos
ella	ellas

1 You have learned that we use *tú* or *usted* when speaking to one person. When speaking to more than one person we use *ustedes*. In writing we usually abbreviate *usted* as *Ud.* and *ustedes* as *Uds.* Note that the abbreviations are capitalized.

Notes: Point out that just as a *tú* or an *usted* question leads to a *yo* response, an *ustedes* question leads to a *nosotros / nosotras* response.

2 There are two forms for "we" in Spanish: *nosotros* for males or for a mixed group of males and females, and *nosotras* for females.

3 *Ellos* and *ellas* mean "they." *Ellos* refers to a group of males or to a mixed group of males and females. *Ellas* refers to a group of females only.

4 There are two other pronouns that are used in Spain: *vosotros* and *vosotras*. They are the familiar plural: *tú* + *tú* = *vosotros* or *vosotras*. We will include these pronouns when we present new verb forms, and we will use them occasionally in dialogues or readings that take place in Spain. So you should learn to recognize them.

Compañeros de clase en España y en México

PRÁCTICA

Práctica A
1. Ud.
2. yo
3. ella
4. ellos
5. él
6. nosotros
7. tú
8. ellas
9. nosotras
10. Uds.

Reteach / Extra Help: If your class needs more help with subject pronouns, do Ex. A as a class activity and then assign it as homework.

Reteach / Review: Reinforce the importance of the accent mark on *tú* and *él*. Write *el / él*, *tu / tú* on the board. Ask students to use each of the four words in a sentence. You may want them to write their sentences.

A Los amigos de Ana. What subject pronouns would Ana use to speak to or about these people?

1. 2. 3. 4. 5. 6. 7. 8. 9. 10.

Práctica B
1. ¿Eres de España?
2. ¿Es Ud. de México?
3. ¿Eres de Puerto Rico?
4. ¿Es Ud. de la República Dominicana?
5. ¿Son Uds. de los Estados Unidos?
6. ¿Es Ud. del Canadá?
7. ¿Eres de Panamá?
8. ¿Son Uds. del Uruguay?
9. ¿Son Uds. de Venezuela?

Practice Sheet 2–3

B ¿De dónde es usted? Pretend you are helping register people at the Language Fair. You must ask both students and teachers where they are from. Follow the models.

Federico / de México	¿Eres de México?
el señor Valdés / de Cuba	¿Es Ud. de Cuba?
Paco y Tomás / de la Argentina	¿Son Uds. de la Argentina?

1. Teresa / de España
2. la señora de Ruiz / de México
3. Arturo / de Puerto Rico
4. la señorita Alba / de la República Dominicana
5. Alejandro y el señor Marín / de los Estados Unidos
6. el señor Villaloz / del Canadá
7. Alfredo / de Panamá
8. Manuel y la señora Torres / del Uruguay
9. Isabel y Enrique / de Venezuela

El verbo *ser*

The verb *ser* means "to be." You already know the three singular forms.

Soy de México.	***I am*** *from Mexico.*
¿De dónde **eres**?	*Where **are you** from?*
Mi amigo **es** guapo.	*My friend **is** handsome.*

Here are all of the forms of *ser* in the present tense:

◆ **OBJECTIVES:**
TO TELL WHERE PEOPLE ARE FROM
TO EMPHASIZE OR CONTRAST

Reteach / Review: You may want to ask students to restate the first two example sentences in section 1 as questions. Have students give affirmative and negative answers.

INFINITIVO   **ser**

SINGULAR			PLURAL		
1	(yo) **soy**	*I am*	(nosotros) (nosotras) } **somos**	*we are*	
2	(tú) **eres**	*you are*	(vosotros) (vosotras) } **sois**	*you are*	
3	Ud. (él) (ella) } **es**	*you are* *he she* } *is*	Uds. (ellos) (ellas) } **son**	*you are* *They are*	

1   We use the verb *ser* to tell where someone or something is from.

Julio Iglesias **es de** España.	*Julio Iglesias **is from** Spain.*
Los carteles **son de** México.	*The posters **are from** Mexico.*
¿**Son** Uds. **del** Ecuador?	***Are you from** Ecuador?*

2   We also use *ser* with adjectives to tell what someone or something is like.

El pájaro **es bonito.**	*The bird **is pretty.***
Eres muy **bonita,** María.	***You're** very **pretty,** María.*
La mesa **es nueva.**	*The table **is new.***

Notes: In the mini-dialogues on p. 84, point out the use of *soy* (1, 2, 3), *eres* (1), and *es* (2, 3, 4, 5). The use of *ser* to tell where someone or something is from is shown in mini-dialogues 1 and 3. *Ser* + adjective is shown in mini-dialogues 1, 2, and 4.

Mini-dialogues 1–4 on p. 90 also illustrate the use of *ser* + adjective. *Somos* and *son* are presented here for the first time. Explain that the *vosotros / vosotras* form is given for recognition only.

Eres muy bonita, María.

3 We usually don't have to use subject pronouns with verbs because most Spanish verb forms indicate who the subject is.

Soy de California.	*I'm from California.*
Somos de Guatemala.	*We're from Guatemala.*
¿Cómo es el libro? **Es** largo.	*What's the book like? It's long.*

But we do use subject pronouns for emphasis or if the subject is not clear.

Tú eres joven, pero **él** es viejo.	*You're young, but he's old.*
¿De dónde son Carlos y Ana?	*Where are Carlos and Ana from?*
Él es de San Juan, y **ella** es de Los Ángeles.	*He's from San Juan, and she's from Los Angeles.*

Because several different pronouns are used with *es* and *son,* we generally do use the pronouns *usted (Ud.)* and *ustedes (Uds.).*

Notes: You may want to assign Ex. A as oral pair work in class or as written work either in class or at home. Assure students that they can answer correctly by including or excluding pronouns.

Práctica A
1. (Nosotras) somos de Costa Rica.
2. (Ellas) son de Panamá, ¿no?
3. (Ellos) son de Guatemala.
4. (Él) es de El Salvador, ¿no?

PRÁCTICA

A **¿De dónde somos?** At a large international gathering, people are telling where they and others are from. Sometimes they have to ask. Follow the models.

de Puerto Rico

Ella es de Puerto Rico.

¿de la República Dominicana?

Eres de la República Dominicana, ¿no?

1. de Costa Rica

2. ¿de Panamá?

3. de Guatemala

4. ¿de El Salvador?

5. de Honduras

6. ¿de Nicaragua?

7. de los Estados Unidos

8. ¿del Canadá?

B **Son sudamericanos.** Here is a map of South America. Working with a partner, take turns pointing to countries on the map and asking where people are from. For each country, use the pronoun shown on the map. For example, pointing to Ecuador:

ESTUDIANTE A   *¿De dónde son Uds.?*
ESTUDIANTE B   *Somos del Ecuador.*

5. (Nosotros) somos de Honduras.
6. (Uds.) son de Nicaragua, ¿no?
7. (Yo) soy de los Estados Unidos.
8. (Ud.) es del Canadá, ¿no?

Reteach / Extra Help: If students have difficulty with Ex. B, do it first as a class activity. Ask volunteers to write the sentences on the board.

Práctica B
1. ¿De dónde es él?
   Es de Colombia.
2. ¿De dónde eres (tú)?
   Soy de Venezuela.
3. ¿De dónde son Uds.?
   Somos del Ecuador.
4. ¿De dónde son ellos?
   Son del Perú.
5. ¿De dónde es ella?
   Es de Bolivia.
6. ¿De dónde son Uds.?
   Somos de Chile.
7. ¿De dónde son ellas?
   Son de la Argentina.
8. ¿De dónde eres (tú)?
   Soy del Paraguay.
9. ¿De dónde es Ud.?
   Soy del Uruguay.

Reteach / Review: Names of countries were introduced on pp. 10–11 and 82–83. Review the use of *de, del, de la.* Have students practice asking *¿Eres de / del / de la ____? +* the countries indicated on the map on p. 99.
  You may also want to use this map to cue the capitals taught on p. 83: *¿Cuál es la capital de Venezuela?* Or you might ask students to answer Ex. B by giving the capital rather than the country.

Práctica C
Answers will vary.

Practice Sheets 2–4, 2–5

Workbook Exs. E–F

 **9 Tape Manual Exs. 3–4**

Activity Master 2–1

Quiz 2–3

C Hablemos de ti.

1. ¿Hay estudiantes de origen latinoamericano en tu clase o en tu escuela?   ¿De qué países son?
2. ¿De qué país es tu profesor(a)?   ¿De qué país eres tú?

En España

APLICACIONES

Discretionary

El nuevo "Pen Pal" 10

Teresa has received a letter from Eduardo, a new pen pal.

Querida[1] Teresa:

Me llamo Eduardo Rivera. Soy puertorriqueño, de San Juan, la capital. Soy alto, delgado y bastante guapo.

Me gustan los deportes—el béisbol, el básquetbol y el tenis. También 5 me gusta nadar, pero no me gusta el fútbol americano. ¡Uf!

Me gusta ir a la escuela y tengo[2] muchos amigos. Y me encantan las fiestas. ¿Te gusta bailar, Teresa? Me gustan mucho la música popular de mi país y el rock norteamericano.

Teresa, quizás[3] soy demasiado curioso pero . . . ¿Qué te gusta hacer? 10 ¿Nadar, leer, montar en bicicleta? ¿Eres rubia o morena? ¿Gorda o delgada? ¿Alta o baja? ¿Te gusta hablar español? ¿Cómo es Chicago? Es enorme, ¿verdad?

Por favor, Teresa, contesta mis preguntas.

Hasta pronto[4]
Eduardo

---

[1]**querido, -a** *dear*   [2]**tengo** (*from* **tener**) *I have*   [3]**quizás** *perhaps*
[4]**hasta pronto** *so long*

ANTES DE LEER

Try not to look at the English equivalents of words you don't know. See how many of them you can understand from the context. As you read, look for the answers to these questions.

1. ¿De dónde es Eduardo?
2. ¿Cómo es Eduardo?
3. ¿De dónde es Teresa?

Antes de leer
1. De San Juan.
2. Es alto, delgado y bastante guapo.
3. De Chicago.

Preguntas
Choose the word or words that best complete each of these statements.

1. Me llamo Eduardo Rivera y soy ____.
   a. de Puerto Rico   b. de San José   c. de Chicago
2. Soy alto y bastante ____.
   a. gordo   b. guapo   c. bajo
3. Me gustan el tenis, el básquetbol y el ____.
   a. fútbol   b. béisbol   c. fútbol americano
4. Me gusta la música de ____.
   a. la América del Sur   b. México   c. la América del Norte
5. Quizás soy ____.
   a. enorme   b. muy gordo   c. muy curioso

Preguntas
1. a.
2. b.
3. b.
4. c.
5. c.

Notes: The following words have not been glossed: *el rock*, rock music; *curioso*, curious; *contesta*, answer (command form); *mis*, my (pl.).

EXPLICACIONES II

Sustantivos y adjetivos con el verbo *ser*

◆ **OBJECTIVES:**

TO DESCRIBE PERSONAL CHARACTERISTICS

TO DESCRIBE THINGS THAT ARE ALIKE OR OPPOSITE

Adjectives describe people and things. An adjective that describes a male or a masculine noun must have a masculine ending. An adjective that describes a female or a feminine noun must have a feminine ending. Many adjectives end in *-o* in the masculine and *-a* in the feminine.

MASCULINE	FEMININE
El hombre es rubi**o**.	La mujer es rubi**a**.
José es guap**o**.	Josefina es guap**a**.
El disco es nuev**o**.	La cinta es nuev**a**.

1   Adjectives that end in *e* or in a consonant usually have the same masculine and feminine forms.

MASCULINE	FEMININE
El Golfo de México es grand**e**.	La América del Sur es grand**e**.
Mi amigo es jove**n**.	Mi amiga es jove**n**.
<u>BUT</u>: Él es españo**l**.	Ella es españo**la**.

2   When the noun is plural, the adjective must also be plural. To make an adjective plural, we add *-s* to a final vowel or *-es* to a final consonant.

SINGULAR	PLURAL
El pez es fe**o**.	Los peces son fe**os**.
La muchacha es mexican**a**.	Las muchachas son mexican**as**.
El periódico es popular.	Los periódicos son popular**es**.

3   When an adjective is describing both a masculine and a feminine noun, we use a masculine plural ending.

El hombre y la mujer son gord**os**.
(El hombre es gord**o** y la mujer también es gord**a**. Son gord**os**.)

Reteach / Extra Help: You may want to refer students to mini-dialogues 1, 2, 4, and 5 on p. 84 and 1–4 on p. 90 to highlight masculine, feminine, singular, and plural forms of adjectives.

Reteach / Review: You may use the illustrations on pp. 88–89 or the appropriate transparency to focus attention on adjective forms. Point to specific figures and ask *¿Cómo es?*, or have pairs of students ask and answer. Circulate to help as needed.

Most adjectives have four forms.

		SINGULAR	PLURAL
MASCULINE		nuevo	nuevos
FEMININE		nueva	nuevas

Notes: Note the accent mark in *jóvenes*. Explain that it is needed to keep the stress on the correct syllable. Material on accents (stress) is presented on pp. 57 and 65.

Some adjectives have only two forms.

	SINGULAR	PLURAL
MASCULINE & FEMININE	enorme	enormes
	joven	jóvenes

Enrichment: You may want to have students do Exs. A and B as a chain drill, asking the question *¿Cómo es _____?* and answering according to the numbered items. You can also use A and B as written exercises.

PRÁCTICA

A Rubio y rubia.   These brothers and sisters are all alike. Describe them. Follow the model.

> Juan es guapo. / Alicia
> *Alicia es guapa también.*

1. María es alta. / Rafael
2. Luis es rubio. / Ana
3. José es moreno. / Marta
4. Pilar es baja. / Eduardo
5. Isabel es delgada. / Francisco
6. Clara es pelirroja. / Esteban
7. Paco es muy pequeño. / Sara
8. Guillermo es joven. / Luisa

Práctica A
1. Rafael es alto también.
2. ... rubia también.
3. ... morena también.
4. ... bajo también.
5. ... delgado también.
6. ... pelirrojo también.
7. ... pequeña también.
8. ... joven también.

B La familia García.   The Garcías are an interesting family. The boys are all like their father and the girls are like their mother. Tell what they are like, following the models.

> El señor García es alto.
> *Y los muchachos son altos también.*
> La señora García es pequeña.
> *Y las muchachas son pequeñas también*

1. El señor García es gordo.
2. La señora García es rubia.
3. El señor García es moreno.
4. La señora García es baja.
5. El señor García es grande.
6. La señora García es delgada.
7. El señor García es guapo.
8. La señora García es bonita.

Práctica B
1. Y los muchachos son gordos también.
2. Y las muchachas son rubias también.
3. Y los muchachos son morenos también.
4. Y las muchachas son bajas también.
5. Y los muchachos son grandes también.
6. Y las muchachas son delgadas también.
7. Y los muchachos son guapos también.
8. Y las muchachas son bonitas también.

C   La familia López.   The López family is different. The boys are the opposite of their father, and the girls aren't like their mother at all. Use the cues in Práctica B to describe the López family. Follow the model.

> El señor López es alto.
> *Pero los muchachos son bajos.*
> La señora López es pequeña.
> *Pero las muchachas son grandes.*

D   Los marcianos.   Martians have landed! They don't even look alike! Working with a partner, take turns asking and answering questions about the various creatures. Continue until your partner can guess which one you are describing. Your partner should guess by saying *Es el número* _____. Then switch and let the other person give a description.
For example:

ESTUDIANTE A	*¿Cómo es? ¿Es una mujer?*
ESTUDIANTE B	*No sé.*
ESTUDIANTE A	*¿Es gordo o delgado?*
ESTUDIANTE B	*Es bastante gordo.*

Notes: Ex. D works well as pair work or as written class work or homework. Students should feel free to use their imagination and have fun.

E Hablemos de ti.
1. ¿Cómo eres?
2. En tu clase de español, ¿cuántos muchachos son rubios? ¿Cuántos son morenos? ¿Pelirrojos? ¿Cuántas muchachas son rubias? ¿Morenas? ¿Pelirrojas? ¿Cuántos estudiantes en total son rubios? ¿Morenos? ¿Pelirrojos?

Práctica E
Answers will vary.

Practice Sheets 2–6, 2–7, 2–8
Workbook Exs. G–J
Tape Manual Exs. 5–6 11
Activity Master 2–2
Quizzes 2–4, 2–5

ACTIVIDAD

¿Cómo son? Five people sit in a circle. One person starts a sentence by saying a definite article—*el*, *la*, *los*, or *las*. The next person must say a noun that agrees with the article. The third person adds the correct form of the verb *ser*. The fourth person finishes the sentence by saying the correct form of an adjective. For example, a completed sentence might be like these:

Las pizarras son grandes.
El perro es gordo.

Continue until everyone has had a turn starting a sentence. Then try it with the first person saying a subject pronoun. The second person then says the correct form of *ser*. The third person says the correct form of an adjective. For example:

Yo soy grande.
Ella es pequeña.

Enrichment: Additional questions for Ex. E: *¿Cómo es tu escuela? ¿Es grande o pequeña tu clase de español?*

Enrichment: If your class enjoys this **Actividad**, continue for several rounds. If time permits, have a representative from each group write completed sentences on the board.

Dos mexicanas

REPASO

Notes: Review of:
1. *ser*
   de
   geographical terms
2. *la señora / el señor*
   adjective agreement
3. *ser*
   adjective agreement
4. *ser*
   adjective agreement
   adverbs of intensity
   tag questions

Look carefully at the model sentences. Then put the English cues into Spanish to form new sentences based on the models.

1. *Me llamo David. Soy de la América del Norte.*
   (My name's Irene. I'm from Canada.)
   (My name's Jaime. We're from South America.)
   (My name's Sonia. We're from Central America.)

2. *La señora Vilas es mi profesora. Es mexicana.*
   (Mr. Vilas is my teacher. He's Cuban.)
   (Marcos is my friend. He's South American.)
   (Laura is my friend. She's North American.)

3. *Es bajo y moreno.*
   (They (masc.) are small and blond.)
   (You (pl.) are young and good-looking.)
   They (fem.) are dark-haired and pretty.)

4. *También son demasiado pequeños, ¿verdad?*
   (You (fam.) are also rather old, right?)
   (You (pl.) are also too young, right?)
   (They (masc.) are also very ugly, right?)

TEMA

Transparency 17

Put the English captions into Spanish.

1. My name's Ted. I'm from the United States.

2. Rita is my friend. She's Puerto Rican.

3 She's tall and thin.

4. She's also very good-looking, right?

REDACCIÓN

Now you are ready to write your own dialogue or paragraph. Choose one of the following topics.

1. Write a four-sentence paragraph about yourself. Give your name, say where you are from, and describe yourself.

2. In the *Tema,* suppose that Rita is describing Ted instead of the other way around. Write the three or four sentences that she might use to describe him.

3. Create a six-line dialogue between Ted and Rita. Pretend that Rita has just arrived from Puerto Rico. She and Ted are telling each other a little about their likes and dislikes.

Notes: Answers to the **Comprueba** appear in the pre-chapter teacher pages.

A   Somos amigos
Complete each sentence with the correct form of the verb *ser*.

1. (Yo) _____ norteamericana.
2. (Ellos) _____ mexicanos.
3. (Nosotros) _____ compañeros de clase.
4. (Ella) _____ puertorriqueña.
5. (Tú) _____ cubano, ¿no?
6. Uds. _____ amigas.
7. (Él) _____ centroamericano.
8. ¿ _____ Ud. canadiense?

B   ¿Y usted?
Substitute one pronoun for the words in italics.

1. *Elena* es bonita.
2. *El hombre* es grande.
3. *Los alumnos* son muy populares.
4. *La muchacha* es española.
5. *El señor Gómez y las muchachas* son morenos.
6. *Las señoritas* son de Cuba, ¿verdad?
7. *Los señores* son de Puerto Rico.
8. *Las mujeres y los hombres* son bastante jóvenes.
9. *Luis y yo* somos muy guapos, ¿no?

C   ¿Cómo es?
Form sentences using these words. Follow the model.

   la mujer / rubio
   La mujer es rubia.

1. los pájaros / bonito
2. los hombres / español
3. los profesores / puertorriqueño
4. los países / enorme
5. ella / moreno
6. las alumnas / sudamericano
7. nosotras / bajo
8. el escritorio / nuevo

D   ¡Qué bonito!
Based on who or what is being described, complete each exclamation with the correct form of the adjective. Follow the model.

bonito
¡Qué bonitas!

1. delgado   2. gordo   3. corto

4. pequeño   5. alto   6. enorme

E   Al contrario
Complete each question using the correct form of the adjective in parentheses. Then answer, using the correct form of the adjective that means the opposite.

1. (largo)   ¿Es _____ la tarea?
   Al contrario, es _____.
2. (alto)   ¿Es _____ tu amiga?
   Al contrario, es _____.
3. (delgado)   ¿Son _____ los muchachos?
   Al contrario, son _____.
4. (bonito)   ¿Es _____ el perro?
   Al contrario, es _____.
5. (nuevo)   ¿Son _____ las sillas?
   Al contrario, son _____.
6. (grande)   ¿Son _____ los peces?
   Al contrario, son _____.
7. (rubio)   ¿Son _____ las muchachas?
   Al contrario, son _____.
8. (viejo)   ¿Son _____ las mujeres?
   Al contrario, son _____.

Chapter 2 Test

Listening Comprehension Test

VOCABULARIO DEL CAPÍTULO 2

Sustantivos
el alumno, la alumna
el amigo, la amiga
la capital
el compañero, la compañera
  de clase
el gato
el hombre
el muchacho, la muchacha
la mujer
el país
el pájaro
el perro
el pez, *pl.* los peces

Pronombres
ellos, ellas
nosotros, nosotras
ustedes (Uds.)

Países y regiones
 la América Central
 la América del Norte
 la América del Sur
 la América Latina
 el Canadá
 el Caribe
los Estados Unidos
 el Golfo de México

Adjetivos
alto, -a
bajo, -a
bonito, -a
canadiense
centroamericano, -a
corto, -a
cubano, -a
delgado, -a
enorme
español, -a
feo, -a
gordo, -a
grande
guapo, -a
joven, *pl.* jóvenes
largo, -a
latinoamericano, -a
mexicano, -a
moreno, -a
norteamericano, -a
nuevo, -a
pelirrojo, -a
pequeño, -a
puertorriqueño, -a
rubio, -a
sudamericano, -a
viejo, -a

Verbo
ser

Adverbios
bastante
demasiado

Expresiones
al contrario
¿cómo es____?
de origen
¿de qué país?
¡qué + *adjective!*

ESPAÑA, PAÍS DE CONTRASTES

If you could pick up the entire country of Spain and put it on top of the state of Texas, there would still be a lot of space left around the edges. Spain is only about three-quarters the size of Texas, but it is a land full of surprises.

In northern Spain, the land is green with forests. There are mountains, too: the Pyrenees *(los Pirineos)*, which form the border between Spain and France. On the eastern coast, along the Mediterranean Sea, you will find some of the world's most beautiful beaches. The central part of Spain is flat, brown, and dry, while in the southern part there are areas of sandy desert that are somewhat like the American Southwest. Filmmakers often take advantage of this fact and make westerns or shoot desert scenes there. Somewhere in Spain you can find a landscape that resembles just about any place on earth.

We don't usually think of Spain as being cold. After all, in Madrid the average temperature in the *coldest* month of the year is 4.5° Celsius. That would seem quite warm to most North Americans in January. But the *madrileños*—the people of Madrid—think that during the winter their city is almost unbearable to live in. They do realize, however, that it is nice to be able to ski all winter long in the Sierra de Guadarrama, only an hour's drive away.

How, then, did Spain get a reputation for being a land of warmth and sunshine? Because it is very close to Africa, separated from the African nation of Morocco only by the very narrow Strait of Gibraltar. Winds that blow across the Sahara Desert carry dry heat into Spain and keep the southern coastline sunny and pleasant all year long. Why else would that area be called *la Costa del Sol* (the Sun Coast)?

PALABRAS NUEVAS I

1

CONTEXTO VISUAL

¿Qué desea Ud., señorita?

la blusa $11

$20

la falda

el zapato

la vendedora

el vestido

las pantimedias

La Tienda de Ropa

CONTEXTO COMUNICATIVO

2

1

VENDEDORA	¿**Qué desea Ud.**, señor?
FRANCISCO	¿**Cuánto cuestan** los jeans?
VENDEDORA	Cien pesos.*
FRANCISCO	Son muy **caros.**

Variaciones:

- los jeans → los pantalones
- cien → ochenta
- caros → **baratos**

¿**qué desea Ud.?**   *may I help you?*

¿**cuánto?**   *how much?*

¿**cuánto cuesta(n)?**   *how much is (are)?*

caro, -a   *expensive*

barato, -a   *cheap, inexpensive*

* The *peso* is the monetary unit in seven Spanish-speaking countries: Bolivia, Chile, Colombia, Cuba, the Dominican Republic, Mexico, and Uruguay.

If students ask: Other related words you may want to present: *dólares*, dollars; *la corbata*, tie; *el cinturón*, belt; *la gorra*, cap; *rosado*, pink.

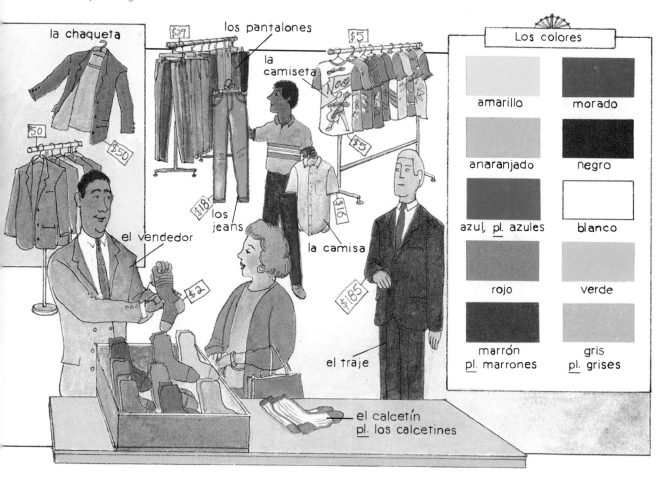

la chaqueta

los pantalones

la camiseta

los jeans

el vendedor

la camisa

el traje

el calcetín
pl. los calcetines

Los colores

amarillo	morado
anaranjado	negro
azul, <u>pl</u>. azules	blanco
rojo	verde
marrón <u>pl.</u> marrones	gris <u>pl.</u> grises

2 MAGDALENA **La ropa aquí** es muy bonita. Me gusta mucho el vestido blanco.

ALICIA Pues, ¿por qué no **preguntas** cuánto cuesta?

■ blanco → verde
■ el vestido blanco → la chaqueta blanca

la ropa *clothing*
aquí *here*
preguntar (yo pregunto, tú preguntas) *to ask*

3 CARLOS   **Busco** zapatos.

VENDEDOR   **¿De qué color?**

CARLOS   **Prefiero** zapatos negros.

- zapatos → calcetines
- negros → marrones

buscar (yo busco, tú buscas) *to look for*

¿de qué color? *what color?*

(yo) prefiero, (tú) prefieres (from preferir) *to prefer*

4 ELENA   Rosa, ¿por qué no **contestas la pregunta**?

ROSA   ¿Quién, yo?

ELENA   Sí, tú. ¿Qué blusa prefieres **llevar** con la falda gris?

ROSA   No sé, Elena. No sé.

- la falda → el traje
- gris → azul

contestar (yo contesto, tú contestas) *to answer*

la pregunta *question*

llevar (yo llevo, tú llevas) *to wear; to carry*

5 EVA   Me encanta **comprar** ropa.

LUIS   ¿Por qué no **entras en la tienda,** entonces?

EVA   Porque aquí la ropa es muy cara.

- cara → fea

comprar (yo compro, tú compras) *to buy*

entrar (en) (yo entro, tú entras) *to go in, to enter*

la tienda *store*

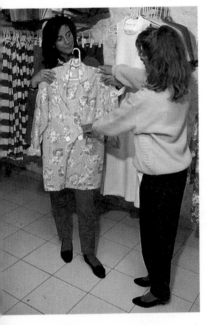

Almacenes grandes en Madrid

EN OTRAS PARTES

En la Argentina y el Perú se dice *la media*.

En la América Latina se dice también *el saco*, y en España se dice también *la americana*.

En Puerto Rico y la República Dominicana se dice *los mahones*, en España se dice *el pantalón vaquero* o *los vaqueros*.

En la Argentina y el Uruguay se dice *la pollera*.

En España se dice *los panty*. También se dice *la media pantalón* y *las medias pantalón*.

En México y en partes de la América del Sur se dice *de color café*.

PRÁCTICA

A   ¿De qué color?   Pretend that you are shopping with a friend who has difficulty telling colors apart. Ask and answer according to the model.

ESTUDIANTE A   *¿De qué color son los pantalones?*
ESTUDIANTE B   *Son marrones.*

1.

2.

3.

4.

5.

6.

7.

8.

9

Palabras Nuevas I   **115**

1. ¿Qué desea Ud., señor(ita)?
   ¿Cuánto cuestan los
   calcetines? Dos pesos.
2. ¿Qué desea Ud., señor(ita)?
   ¿Cuánto cuesta la
   camiseta? Cinco pesos.
3. ¿Qué desea Ud., señor(ita)?
   ¿Cuánto cuestan las
   pantimedias? Tres pesos.
4. ¿Qué desea Ud., señor(ita)?
   ¿Cuánto cuesta la blusa?
   Once pesos.
5. ¿Qué desea Ud., señor(ita)?
   ¿Cuánto cuesta la falda?
   Veinte pesos.
6. ¿Qué desea Ud., señor(ita)?
   ¿Cuánto cuestan los
   zapatos? Treinta y cinco
   pesos.
7. ¿Qué desea Ud., señor(ita)?
   ¿Cuánto cuestan los jeans?
   Dieciocho pesos.
8. ¿Qué desea Ud., señor(ita)?
   ¿Cuánto cuesta el vestido?
   Veinticinco pesos.
9. ¿Qué desea Ud., señor(ita)?
   ¿Cuánto cuesta el traje?
   Ochenta y cinco pesos.

Notes: Before students do
Ex. B, make sure they
understand the use of *cuesta*
with singular nouns and
cuestan with plural nouns.

Reteach / Extra Help: If your
class needs more help with
numbers, have students review
asking and answering *¿Cuál es
tu número de teléfono?* Remind
students to pause twice
(421–68–75) rather than once
(421–6875) as they recite
phone numbers.

B   ¿Cuánto cuesta?   Imagine that you are shopping in Mexico and
need to ask the salesclerk how much things cost. With a partner, take
turns playing the roles of the salesclerk and the customer.

ESTUDIANTE A   *¿Qué desea Ud., señor(ita)?*
ESTUDIANTE B   *¿Cuánto cuesta la camisa?*
ESTUDIANTE A   *Dieciséis pesos.*

ESTUDIANTE A   *¿Qué desea Ud., señor(ita)?*
ESTUDIANTE B   *¿Cuánto cuestan los pantalones?*
ESTUDIANTE A   *Veintinueve pesos.*

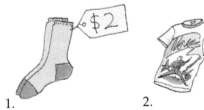  

1.   2.   3.

4.   5.   6.

7.   8.   9.

C ¿Cuál prefieres?
In each case, tell which color item of clothing you prefer. Follow the model.

Prefiero los pantalones azules.

o: *Prefiero los pantalones negros.*

1.   2.   3.

4.   5.   6.

 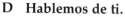 

7.   8.   9.

D Hablemos de ti.
1. ¿Qué ropa llevas hoy?
2. ¿De qué color es?

Enrichment: Additional questions for Ex. D: *¿Qué color prefieres? ¿Qué lleva tu amigo(a) hoy?*

ACTIVIDAD

¿Quién soy? On a sheet of paper, write a description of what the person to your right or immediately behind you is wearing. Begin the description, *Hoy llevo . . .* End the description, *¿Quién soy?* When everyone in the room has finished writing, put the papers into a bag. Each student then takes one out. One by one, each person reads aloud the description he or she has picked. The rest of the class guesses whose clothing is being described.

APLICACIONES Discretionary

Aquí no hay polleras 4

San Juan, Puerto Rico, delante de[1] una tienda de ropa.

VENDEDOR	¡Ropa bonita y barata! ¡Hay blusas, faldas, chaquetas! ¡Ah! ¿Qué desea Ud., señorita?
CECILIA	Una pollera.
5 VENDEDOR	¿Una pollera? Aquí no hay polleras. Hay blusas, faldas, chaquetas . . .
CECILIA	¿No hay polleras aquí? Entonces, ¿qué es esto?[2]
VENDEDOR	Es una falda, señorita. Hay faldas de toda clase:[3] cortas y largas, blancas y negras, rojas y azules. Muy bonitas y baratas.
10 CECILIA	Pero esto es una pollera. ¿Cuánto cuesta?
VENDEDOR	¿Una pollera? Es una *falda*, señorita. ¿Es Ud. de los Estados Unidos?
CECILIA	No, soy de la Argentina. En la Argentina las mujeres llevan polleras.
15 VENDEDOR	Pues en Puerto Rico llevan faldas.

---

[1]**delante de**   *in front of*   [2]**esto**   *this*   [3]**de toda clase**   *of all kinds*

Notes: If students do not see the humor in the situation, tell them to imagine the salesclerk's reaction if a customer came into a store that sold "hoagies" and asked for a "submarine." Explain that the clerk probably thought Cecilia wanted to buy a chicken coop.

Preguntas
Contesta según el diálogo.

1. ¿Cómo es la ropa?   2. ¿Hay ropa cara?   3. ¿Qué desea Cecilia?
4. ¿Cómo se dice pollera en Puerto Rico?   5. ¿De dónde es Cecilia?
6. ¿Qué llevan las mujeres en Puerto Rico?

Enrichment: Additional questions you may want to ask:
¿Qué hay en la tienda? (Hay blusas, faldas y chaquetas.)
¿Qué clase de faldas hay? (Hay faldas de toda clase /
Hay faldas cortas, largas, blancas,
negras, rojas y azules.)

Una venta en Bogotá, Colombia

Diálogo
1. Bonita y barata.
2. No, no hay ropa cara.
3. Una pollera.
4. En Puerto Rico se dice falda.
5. Es de la Argentina.
6. Llevan faldas.

Participación

Work with a partner to make up a four- to six-line dialogue in Spanish between a clothing store salesclerk and a customer. Be sure to mention what the customer wants to buy, the color, the price, and perhaps the customer's likes and dislikes in clothing.

PRONUNCIACIÓN 5

In Spanish, the letter *h* is never pronounced.
Escucha y repite.

hoy	hasta	hablar	helado

¡Hasta luego!   Héctor es de Honduras.
Hoy no hay helado.   Me encanta hablar con Horacio.

Enrichment: Write these words on the board, and ask
students to pronounce them: *hago, huevo, hambre, hermana.*
You may use the sentences in **Pronunciación** for dictation.

PALABRAS NUEVAS II

¿Qué tiempo hace?

Las cuatro estaciones

la primavera

el verano

If students ask: Other related words you may want to present: *la flor*, flower; *el árbol*, tree; *la playa*, beach.

Notes: In conjunction with transparency 19, you may want to show magazine pictures depicting activities, clothing, and weather conditions associated with the seasons.

el otoño

el invierno

¿Qué tiempo hace?

Hace fresco.

Hace mal tiempo.

Hace calor.

Hace sol.

el suéter

la bota

el guante

el sombrero

el traje de baño
pl. los trajes de baño

la bufanda

el abrigo

el paraguas

el impermeable

Hace buen tiempo.

Hace frío.

Nieva.

Llueve.

Hace viento.

CONTEXTO COMUNICATIVO 7

1 CONSUELO ¿**Qué tiempo hace** hoy?
ROBERTO Hace mal tiempo. Llueve.
CONSUELO ¿Hace viento también?
ROBERTO No, pero hace fresco.

Variaciones:
- mal → muy mal
- hace viento → hace mucho frío

Culture: In connection with mini-dialogue 2, make sure students understand that when it is summer in the Northern Hemisphere, it is winter in the Southern Hemisphere.

2 EVA **Cuando** es verano aquí, es invierno en Chile.
MATEO ¿En qué meses hace calor, entonces?
EVA En enero y febrero.

- es verano → hace calor
- es invierno → hace frío

3 FELIPE ¿En qué estación llueve mucho aquí?
JORGE En la primavera. Pero llueve **a menudo** en el otoño también.

- la primavera → el verano
- a menudo → **a veces**

4 OLGA ¿Qué **haces** en el verano?
SERGIO Me gusta ir **de vacaciones.** Y tú, ¿qué haces?
OLGA **Nada. Tomo el sol** y **no hago nada.**

- ir de vacaciones → jugar al tenis

5 JAIME Me gustan los días de fiesta de diciembre.
LUISA ¿**Cuáles?**
JAIME Oh, la Navidad . . . el fin de año . . . mi cumpleaños . . .

- diciembre → enero
la Navidad → el Año Nuevo
el fin de año → el cumpleaños de M. L. King

6 TOMÁS ¿**Quiénes** son Mariana y Laura?
ÁNGELA Son estudiantes de Guatemala.

- estudiantes → muchachas

---

el tiempo *weather*
¿qué tiempo hace? *what's the weather like?*

cuando *when*

a menudo *often*

a veces *sometimes*

(yo) hago, (tú) haces (from hacer) *to do*
de vacaciones *on vacation*
(no...) nada *nothing, not anything*
tomar el sol (yo tomo, tú tomas) *to sunbathe*

¿cuál?, ¿cuáles? *which one(s)?*

Reteach / Review: Point out the double negative in mini-dialogue 4. The use of *no... nada* is explained on p. 137.

¿quién?, ¿quiénes? *who?*

EN OTRAS PARTES

En España se dice *el jersey*, y en Bolivia, Chile y el Perú se dice *la chompa*.

En España se dice *el bañador*, en la Argentina se dice *la malla*, en Cuba se dice *la trusa*, y en el Perú se dice *la ropa de baño*.

En España se dice *la gabardina*.

En la Argentina se dice *el sobretodo*.

PRÁCTICA

A ¿Qué tiempo hace? Tell what the weather is according to the picture.

1.

2.

3.

4.

5.

6.

7.

8.

Notes: In preparation for Ex. A, you may want to show magazine pictures, ask *¿Qué tiempo hace?*, and have students answer with *Llueve / Nieva / Hace buen / mal tiempo*, etc. To extend the exercise, have students answer the question *¿En qué estación llueve?*, using picture cues 1–8.

Práctica A
1. Llueve.
2. Hace sol. *or:* Hace buen tiempo.
3. Hace viento.
4. Hace calor.
5. Hace mal tiempo.
6. Nieva.
7. Hace fresco.
8. Hace frío.

Palabras Nuevas II   **123**

Práctica B

1. Llevo un abrigo.
2. Llevo un traje de baño.
3. Llevo un suéter.
4. Llevo un impermeable.
5. Llevo una chaqueta.
6. Llevo un abrigo y un sombrero.
7. Llevo un paraguas.
8. Llevo botas y guantes cuando nieva (llueve, hace frío, etc.).

Notes: Before students do Ex. B, make sure that they understand the *llevas* → *llevo* transformation. You may also want to contrast the use of *cuando* without an accent with its use in B8 with an accent.

Reteach / Review: As a follow-up to Ex. B, ask students to name the seasons and months of the year. Elicit the names of the seasons, and write them on the board. Ask volunteers to give the months that correspond to each season.

B   La ropa y el tiempo.   Different weather conditions influence your choice of clothes. Ask and answer based on the pictures.

cuando nieva

ESTUDIANTE A   *¿Qué llevas cuando nieva?*
ESTUDIANTE B   *Llevo botas y una bufanda.*

1. cuando hace frío

2. cuando hace calor

3. cuando hace fresco

4. cuando llueve

5. cuando hace mal tiempo

6. cuando hace frío

7. cuando llueve

8. Y tú, ¿cuándo llevas botas y guantes?

124   Capítulo 3

C ¿En qué estación? With a partner, discuss in which season or seasons you prefer to do the following activities. Take turns asking and answering.

> nadar
> ESTUDIANTE A *¿En qué estación te gusta nadar?*
> ESTUDIANTE B *En el verano.*

1. esquiar
2. montar en bicicleta
3. jugar al fútbol americano
4. jugar al tenis
5. jugal al béisbol
6. tomar el sol
7. jugar al básquetbol
8. ir de vacaciones

D ¿Cuándo llueve? Imagine that a pen pal has asked about the weather in your hometown. Answer the questions based on the weather where you live.

1. ¿Qué tiempo hace en el verano?
2. ¿Qué tiempo hace en el invierno?
3. ¿En qué estación hace buen tiempo?
4. ¿Nieva mucho?
5. ¿Hace mucho calor en el verano?
6. ¿Hace mucho frío en el invierno?
7. ¿Llueve mucho? ¿Cuándo?
8. ¿Qué tiempo hace en la primavera y en el otoño?

E Hablemos de ti.
1. ¿Qué tiempo hace hoy?
2. ¿Qué estación del año te gusta más? ¿Por qué?
3. ¿Qué estaciones o meses no te gustan? ¿Por qué?
4. ¿Cuándo te gusta ir de vacaciones?

ESTUDIO DE PALABRAS

There are many words that are similar in Spanish and English. They usually have the same meaning. Some are loanwords, but some came into both Spanish and English from other languages. Words in different languages that come from the same source are called *cognates*.

1. Some cognates are spelled alike but are pronounced differently.

> capital   popular   radio   color

2. Some are less similar but are still recognizable.

> clase   plato   tenis   música   teléfono   guitarra

Práctica C
1. En el invierno.
2. Answers will vary: En la primavera/el verano/el otoño.
3. En el otoño.
4. Answers will vary: En la primavera/el verano/el otoño.
5. Answers will vary: En la primavera/el verano.
6. En el verano.
7. Answers will vary.
8. Answers will vary.

Práctica D
Answers will vary.

Enrichment: Have students do Ex. D as a pair or small-group activity, and then assign it as written homework. Refer students to the letter on p. 101 for the salutation and closing of a letter.

Práctica E
Answers will vary.

Enrichment: Additional questions for Ex. E: *¿Qué haces en el verano / invierno? ¿Qué día de la semana te gusta más? ¿Por qué?*

Reteach / Review: In connection with the **Estudio de palabras,** you may want to point out additional cognates: *enorme, examen, mapa, practicar.*

EXPLICACIONES I

Verbos que terminan en -ar

◆ **OBJECTIVES:**

**TO EXPRESS WHAT
YOU AND OTHERS
DO REGULARLY OR
ARE DOING NOW**

**TO EXPLAIN WHY
OR WHY NOT**

Most verbs name actions. To sing, to talk, to dance are all verbs. If you look up a verb in a Spanish dictionary, the form you will find is called the infinitive. In English, the infinitive has the word "to" in front of the verb. In Spanish, the infinitive always ends in -ar, -er, or -ir. *Cantar, hablar, bailar* are all infinitives.

Ser, which you learned in Capítulo 2, is called an irregular verb. No other verb is like it. But many Spanish verbs are regular, that is, they follow a pattern. There are three groups of regular verbs. The infinitive of the first group ends in -ar. For example:

$$cantar \ = \ cant \ + \ ar \qquad hablar \ = \ habl \ + \ ar$$

Here are all of the forms of *cantar* in the present tense. The main part of the verb—the stem—does not change. But notice how the endings change according to which person does the action.

Un concierto de rock
en Madrid, España

INFINITIVO		cantar			
SINGULAR				**PLURAL**	
1	(yo)	cant**o**	*I sing* *I'm singing*	(nosotros) } cant**amos** (nosotras)	*we sing* *we're singing*
2	(tú)	cant**as**	*you sing* *you're singing*	(vosotros) } cant**áis** (vosotras)	*you sing* *you're singing*
3	Ud. }		*you sing* *you're singing*	Uds. }	*you sing* *you're singing*
	(él) }	cant**a**	*he sings* *he's singing*	(ellos) } cant**an**	*they sing* *they're singing*
	(ella) }		*she sings* *she's singing*	(ellas) }	*they sing* *they're singing*

Look at the English equivalents.

A veces **canta**.   *Sometimes he **sings**.*
Canta ahora.   *He's **singing** now.*

The Spanish present tense is equivalent to *both* "I sing, you sing, he or she sings," etc., *and* to "I'm singing, you're singing, he's or she's singing," etc.

1 Here are all of the regular *-ar* verbs that you know:

ayudar	*to help*	**hablar**	*to speak, to talk*
bailar	*to dance*	**lavar**	*to wash*
buscar	*to look for*	**llevar**	*to wear; to carry*
cantar	*to sing*	**mirar**	*to look at, to watch*
cocinar	*to cook*	**montar (en)**	*to ride*
comprar	*to buy*	**nadar**	*to swim*
contestar	*to answer*	**practicar**	*to practice*
entrar (en)	*to enter, to go in (to)*	**preguntar**	*to ask*
escuchar	*to listen (to)*	**tocar**	*to play (an instrument)*
esquiar	*to ski*	**tomar el sol**	*to sunbathe*
estudiar	*to study*	**trabajar**	*to work*

2 The verb *esquiar* has an accent mark in all its present-tense forms except the *nosotros* form.

esquío	esquiamos
esquías	esquiáis
esquía	esquían

Reteach / Extra Help:
Remind students that they have already seen the *yo / tú* forms of these verbs. To review, ask students to give the *yo / tú* forms for each verb in the list.

Enrichment: Call attention to the bold type used to highlight the endings in the *cantar* paradigm. You may want volunteers to write the forms of different verbs on the board. Ask them to underline or circle the endings.

Before students do the **Práctica** on pp. 128–129, have them practice using various *-ar* verbs in familiar contexts. For example, you might write these phrases on the board: *estudiar español, mirar la tele, tocar la guitarra.* Do a chain drill or have students work in pairs to ask and answer questions that use all of the verb forms.

Un concierto de música popular en San Juan, Puerto Rico

Práctica A

1. Bailo.
2. Estudio.
3. Cocino.
4. Lavo los platos.
5. Esquío.
6. Monto en bicicleta.
7. Toco la guitarra.
8. Nado.
9. Miro la televisión.

Práctica B

1. ¿Por qué no hablas? Porque prefiero escuchar música.
2. ¿Por qué no nadas? Porque prefiero tomar el sol.
3. ¿Por qué no entras en la tienda? Porque prefiero hablar con mi amiga.
4. ¿Por qué no compras comida mexicana? Porque prefiero cocinar.
5. ¿Por qué no preguntas? Porque prefiero buscar en el libro.
6. ¿Por qué no esquías? Porque prefiero mirar la tele.
7. ¿Por qué no ayudas en casa? Porque prefiero jugar al fútbol.
8. ¿Por qué no cantas? Porque prefiero tocar la guitarra.

Práctica C

1. Canto en español. Ester canta en español también.
2. Nado cuando hace calor. Él nada cuando hace calor también.
3. Trabajo en casa. Manuel trabaja en casa también.
4. Estudio español. Ella estudia español también.
5. Busco una bicicleta. Teresa busca una bicicleta también.
6. Compro zapatos grises. Tomás compra zapatos grises también.
7. Bailo mucho. Ella baila mucho también.
8. Llevo un suéter. Él lleva un suéter también.

PRÁCTICA

A ¿Qué haces? Imagine that every Saturday you do the activities shown in each picture. Ask and answer based on the picture.

ESTUDIANTE A *¿Qué haces los sábados?*
ESTUDIANTE B *Canto.*

B ¿Por qué? Ask and answer based on the model.

bailar / escuchar la radio
ESTUDIANTE A *¿Por qué no bailas?*
ESTUDIANTE B *Porque prefiero escuchar la radio.*

1. hablar / escuchar música
2. nadar / tomar el sol
3. entrar en la tienda / hablar con mi amiga
4. comprar comida mexicana / cocinar
5. preguntar / buscar en el libro
6. esquiar / mirar la tele
7. ayudar en casa / jugar al fútbol
8. cantar / tocar la guitarra

C **Ellos también.** Imagine that someone else always does the same things as you. Follow the model.

> tocar la guitarra / Juan
> ESTUDIANTE A   *Toco la guitarra.*
> ESTUDIANTE B   *Juan toca la guitarra también.*

1. cantar en español / Ester
2. nadar cuando hace calor / él
3. trabajar en casa / Manuel
4. estudiar español / ella
5. buscar una bicicleta / Teresa
6. comprar zapatos grises / Tomás
7. bailar mucho / ella
8. llevar un suéter / él

D **¿Y Ud., profesor(a)?** How do you think your teacher would answer these questions? With a partner, take turns playing the roles of student and teacher. Give any answers you choose, but say more than just *sí* or *no*.

> cocinar sólo comida mexicana
> ESTUDIANTE   *Ud. cocina sólo comida mexicana, ¿verdad?*
> PROFESOR(A)   *Sí. (Me encanta la comida mexicana.)*
>   o: *No. (Cocino comida americana también.)*

1. llevar un paraguas cuando llueve
2. trabajar mucho
3. hablar español muy bien
4. tocar la guitarra
5. escuchar sólo música clásica
6. practicar deportes los sábados
7. tomar el sol cuando hace calor
8. mirar la tele a menudo
9. contestar muchas preguntas

E **¿Y Uds.?** Now pretend the tables are turned and the teacher is asking the class the questions in Práctica D. With a partner, take turns playing the roles of teacher and student. The "student" should answer according to how he or she thinks the majority of the class would answer.

> cocinar sólo comida mexicana
> PROFESOR(A)   *Uds. cocinan sólo comida mexicana, ¿verdad?*
> ESTUDIANTE   *Sí. (Cocinamos sólo comida mexicana.)*
>   o: *No. (Cocinamos comida americana también.)*
>   o: *No, no cocinamos.*

Reteach / Extra Help: If your class needs more help with negative sentences, before students do Exs. D and E, ask questions to elicit negative responses: *¿Esquías en el verano? ¿Tomamos el sol en el invierno? ¿Montas en bicicleta cuando llueve? ¿Bailamos en la clase de español?* You might also have students redo Ex. C in the negative.
  Negative sentences will be explained in detail on p. 137.

Práctica D
Answers to each question will vary. Questions are:
1. Ud. lleva un paraguas cuando llueve, ¿verdad? ...llevo...
2. Ud. trabaja mucho, ¿verdad? ...trabajo...
3. Ud. habla español muy bien, ¿verdad? ...hablo...
4. Ud. toca la guitarra, ¿verdad? ...toco...
5. Ud. escucha sólo música clásica, ¿verdad? ...escucho...
6. Ud. practica deportes los sábados, ¿verdad? ...practico...
7. Ud. toma el sol cuando hace calor, ¿verdad? ...tomo...
8. Ud. mira la tele a menudo, ¿verdad? ...miro...
9. Ud. contesta muchas preguntas, ¿verdad? ...contesto...

Práctica E
Answers to each question will vary. Questions are:
1. Uds. llevan paraguas cuando llueve, ¿verdad? ...llevamos...
2. Uds. trabajan mucho, ¿verdad? ...trabajamos...
3. Uds. hablan español muy bien, ¿verdad? ...hablamos...
4. Uds. tocan la guitarra, ¿verdad? ...tocamos...
5. Uds. escuchan sólo música clásica, ¿verdad? ...escuchamos...
6. Uds. practican deportes los sábados, ¿verdad? ...practicamos...
7. Uds. toman el sol cuando hace calor, ¿verdad? ...tomamos...
8. Uds. miran la tele a menudo, ¿verdad? ...miramos...
9. Uds. contestan muchas preguntas, ¿verdad? ...contestamos...

F ¿Qué verbo? Complete the sentences using the correct form of the appropriate verb in parentheses.

1. Los muchachos de Colombia *(escuchar, hablar)* español.
2. Cuando llueve, tú *(cocinar, llevar)* botas, pero yo sólo *(llevar / mirar)* un paraguas.
3. ¿Qué *(escuchar, mirar)* Uds.? ¿Música clásica?
4. Hace buen tiempo. ¿Por qué no *(entrar / montar)* nosotros en bicicleta?
5. Los profesores *(comprar / entrar en)* la tienda a menudo pero no *(comprar / contestar)* discos.
6. Él *(lavar / llevar)* un traje de baño cuando *(tocar / tomar)* el sol.
7. Cuando yo *(buscar / preguntar)* cuánto cuesta el vestido, la vendedora no *(contestar / practicar)*.
8. Los sábados las muchachas *(estudiar / trabajar)* en una tienda de ropa.
9. Aquí nieva mucho y los estudiantes *(esquiar / nadar)* a menudo.

Estudiantes en la Universidad de Puerto Rico

Sujetos compuestos

In Spanish, just as in English, we can use two subject pronouns together or a subject pronoun with a noun. For example, when you are talking about yourself and someone else, you really mean "we," and in Spanish we use the *nosotros* form of the verb.

Tomás y yo (= nosotros) estudiamos. *Tomás and I (= we)* } *study.* *are studying.*

Tú y yo (= nosotros) escuchamos. *You and I (= we)* } *listen.* *are listening.*

1 When you are speaking to more than one person—even if you call one of them *tú*—you use the *ustedes* form of the verb.

Tú y Luz (= ustedes) trabajan aquí, ¿no? *You and Luz (= you pl.) work here, don't you?*

2 When you are talking about more than one person or thing, you use the *ellos / ellas* form.

María y él (= ellos) hablan. *María and he (= they) are talking.*
María y ella (= ellas) hablan. *María and she (= they) are talking.*
La blusa y la falda (= ellas) son azules. *The blouse and skirt (= they) are blue.*

PRÁCTICA

A **¿Quiénes?** Complete each sentence using the correct form of the verb. Follow the model.

> Roberto, Ana y yo _____ en casa. *(ayudar)*
> *Roberto, Ana y yo ayudamos en casa.*

1. Arturo y yo _____ con José. *(hablar)*
2. María, Ana y tú _____ a menudo. *(bailar)*
3. Ella y yo _____ en la fiesta. *(cantar)*
4. Tú y Lucía _____ básquetbol. *(practicar)*
5. Luis, Carmen y yo _____ zapatos rojos. *(llevar)*
6. Esteban y él _____ guantes. *(comprar)*
7. Usted, Olga y yo _____ en el cine. *(entrar)*
8. Ella y Luisa _____ en la tienda de ropa. *(trabajar)*

En Córdoba, España

Práctica A
1. hablamos
2. bailan
3. cantamos
4. practican
5. llevamos
6. compran
7. entramos
8. trabajan

◆ OBJECTIVES:

TO EXPRESS WHAT MORE THAN ONE SPECIFIC PERSON IS DOING

TO CONTRADICT

Explicaciones I   131

B ¿Qué hacen Uds. los sábados? With a partner, take turns asking what each of you might do with a friend on Saturdays. Use the verbs in the list below. Follow the model.

ESTUDIANTE A *Tú y tu amigo(a) cocinan los sábados, ¿no?*
ESTUDIANTE B *Sí, cocinamos.*
o: *No, no cocinamos. Estudiamos.*

ayudar en casa
cocinar
comprar (discos, etc.)
esquiar
estudiar (para exámenes)
tocar la guitarra
lavar (la ropa, etc.)

mirar la tele
montar en bicicleta
nadar
practicar (básquetbol, etc.)
tomar el sol
escuchar (cintas, etc.)
trabajar (en la tienda o en casa)

Práctica C
Answers will vary.

Practice Sheet 3–6

Workbook Exs. E–F

9 Tape Manual
Exs. 5–6

Activity Master 3–1

Quiz 3–3

C Hablemos de ti.
1. ¿Qué haces en el verano?
2. ¿Qué haces los sábados?

Reteach / Review: In conjunction with Ex. C, have students practice asking and answering questions about what they do when it's cold, hot, and so on: *¿Qué haces cuando llueve / nieva / hace frío / hace calor / hace mal tiempo?*

ACTIVIDAD
Ustedes y yo hablamos . . . Get together in groups of three or four to play this sentence-building card game. First write all of the 22 regular *-ar* verbs that you know on separate index cards. Write them in the infinitive form. (The complete list is on page 127.) On another set of 22 cards write 10 subject pronouns (*yo, tú, Ud., él, ella, nosotros, nosotras, Uds., ellos, ellas*) plus 12 compound subjects, such as *Ana y yo.*

Take turns drawing one card from each set and making up a sentence of at least four words. A player who makes up a correct sentence keeps those two cards. Otherwise, he or she puts those cards at the bottom of the appropriate pile. When all of the cards have been taken, the person who has the most cards wins.

APLICACIONES

Discretionary

¿Qué tiempo hace? Transparency 20

¿Qué pasa en el dibujo? ¿Qué tiempo hace? ¿Qué haces tú cuando hace mal tiempo?

Make up a four- to six-line dialogue in which two students talk about what they like to do on Sundays when it's raining and cold.

Notes: Sample dialogues for the **¿Qué pasa?** appear in the pre-chapter teacher pages.

Aplicaciones **133**

Reteach / Review: To review
question words with your class,
ask questions such as *¿Quién
nada bien? ¿Cuántos
muchachos / cuántas
muchachas hay en la clase?*
Review familiar questions, too:
¿Qué tiempo hace? etc.

EXPLICACIONES II

◆ **OBJECTIVES:**

**TO REQUEST
INFORMATION**

**TO ASK FOR
CLARIFICATION**

**TO EXPRESS
OPINIONS**

Preguntas

1   When we ask a question in Spanish, we usually put the subject after
the verb, or sometimes at the end of the sentence. An upside down
question mark indicates where the question begins.

¿Lleva Norma una blusa azul?	*Is Norma wearing a blue blouse?*
¿Es rojo el vestido?	*Is the dress red?*
¿Trabaja mucho Luis?	*Does Luis work a lot?*

2   You can also ask a question by adding *¿verdad?* or *¿no?* at the end of
a statement. We usually do that when we expect the answer to be
yes.

Hace calor, ¿verdad?	*It's hot, isn't it?*
Él estudia mucho, ¿no?	*He studies a lot, doesn't he?*

3   Here is a list of question words that you know.

¿Qué?	*What?, Which?*	**¿Quién? ¿Quiénes?**	*Who?, Whom?*
¿Por qué?	*Why?*	**¿Cuál?**	*Which one?, What?*
¿Cuándo?	*When?*	**¿Cuáles?**	*Which ones?, What?*
¿Dónde?	*Where?*	**¿Cuánto?**	*How much?*
¿Cómo?	*How?*	**¿Cuántos? ¿Cuántas?**	*How many?*

Notice that all of the words have accent marks. When we are not using
them in a question, we do not use the accent mark.

Cuando es verano aquí, es invierno en Chile.	*When it's summer here, it's winter in Chile.*

4   Notice that Spanish has a plural word for "who?"—*¿quiénes?* We use
the plural form when we know or are pretty sure that the answer will
be plural.

¿Quiénes bailan?	*Who is dancing?*
¿Con quiénes te gusta jugar al básquetbol?	*Whom do you like to play basketball with?*

Reteach / Extra Help: Have each student make up two questions to ask a partner.
Encourage students to elicit information they really want to know.

PRÁCTICA

A ¿Y ellos? Gabriela is telling a friend how well and how often she does things. Ask and answer based on the model. Choose your final comment from the list at the right.

> bailar bien / Carlos
> **ESTUDIANTE A** *Bailo bien.*
> **ESTUDIANTE B** *¿Y Carlos? ¿Baila bien él?*
> **ESTUDIANTE A** *Bastante bien.*

1. estudiar mucho / Leonor
2. cocinar a veces / Raúl
3. cantar bien / Consuelo y Elena
4. ayudar en casa / Olga
5. esquiar bien / Andrés
6. nadar a menudo / Daniel y Raquel
7. tocar bien la guitarra / Gustavo
8. trabajar mucho / Antonio y Diego

¡Ah, sí!
Bastante bien.
¡Cómo no!
No sé.
¡Uf!

Práctica A
Final comment will vary.
1. Estudio mucho. ¿Y Leonor? ¿Estudia mucho ella?
2. Cocino a veces. ¿Y Raúl? ¿Cocina a veces él?
3. Canto bien. ¿Y Consuelo y Elena? ¿Cantan bien ellas?
4. Ayudo en casa. ¿Y Olga? ¿Ayuda en casa ella?
5. Esquío bien. ¿Y Andrés? ¿Esquía bien él?
6. Nado a menudo. ¿Y Daniel y Raquel? ¿Nadan a menudo ellos?
7. Toco bien la guitarra. ¿Y Gustavo? ¿Toca bien la guitarra él?
8. Trabajo mucho. ¿Y Antonio y Diego? ¿Trabajan mucho ellos?

B Te gusta, ¿verdad? Pretend that you and a friend are in a store, pointing out things you like. Use any adjectives that make sense.

> **ESTUDIANTE A** *El vestido es bonito, ¿verdad?*
> **ESTUDIANTE B** *Sí, y la chaqueta también.*

 1.

 2.

 3.

 4.

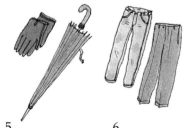 5.

 6.

 7.

8.

Práctica B
Adjectives may vary. Might include *barato, bonito, caro, feo, grande, guapo.*
1. El traje de baño es ____, ¿verdad? Sí, y la camiseta también.
2. La blusa es ____, ¿verdad? Sí, y la falda también.
3. La chaqueta es ____, ¿verdad? Sí, y la bufanda también.
4. Los zapatos son ____, ¿verdad? Sí, y las botas también.
5. Los guantes son ____, ¿verdad? Sí, y el paraguas también.
6. Los jeans son ____, ¿verdad? Sí, y los pantalones también.
7. El sombrero es ____, ¿verdad? Sí, y el abrigo también.
8. El traje es ____, ¿verdad? Sí, y la camisa también.

Reteach / Extra Help: If your class finds Ex. B difficult, review items of clothing and noun–adjective agreement.

1. ¿Qué toca ahora Carolina? La guitarra.
2. ¿Con quién canta ella? Con César.
3. ¿Cómo es César? Guapo y simpático.
4. ¿Cómo cantan César y Carolina? Muy bien.
5. ¿Cuándo practican ellos? Los lunes.
6. ¿Dónde trabajas los sábados? En una tienda (muy grande).
7. ¿Cuántas vendedoras hay? Hay cinco.
8. ¿Cómo es la ropa? Muy bonita y barata.
9. ¿Dónde hace mal tiempo? Aquí.
10. ¿Por qué prefieres el invierno? Porque me gusta esquiar.

1. ¿Quién toca (ahora) la guitarra? Carolina.
2. ¿Quién canta con César? Ella.
3. ¿De dónde es César? De Colombia.
4. ¿Quiénes cantan muy bien? César y Carolina.
5. ¿Dónde practican ellos los lunes? En la escuela.
6. ¿Cómo es la tienda? Muy grande.
7. ¿Dónde hay cinco vendedoras? En la tienda.
8. ¿Qué es muy bonita y barata? La ropa.
9. ¿Qué tiempo hace hoy? (Hace) mal tiempo.
10. ¿Qué (estación) prefieres? El invierno.

Practice Sheets 3–7, 3–8

🔲▭ 10 Tape Manual Ex. 7

Quiz 3–4

C Por teléfono.   Imagine that you are talking on the phone and the connection is very bad. You must keep asking your friend to repeat certain words. Follow the model.

ESTUDIANTE A *Carolina y yo estudiamos español.* (¿Quiénes?)
ESTUDIANTE B *¿Quiénes estudian español?*
ESTUDIANTE A *Carolina y yo.*

1. Carolina toca ahora la guitarra.   (¿Qué?)
2. Ella canta con César.   (¿Con quién?)
3. César es un muchacho guapo y simpático de Colombia.   (¿Cómo?)
4. César y Carolina cantan muy bien.   (¿Cómo?)
5. Ellos practican en la escuela los lunes.   (¿Cuándo?)
6. Los sábados trabajo en una tienda muy grande.   (¿Dónde?)
7. En la tienda hay cinco vendedoras.   (¿Cuántas?)
8. La ropa es muy bonita y barata.   (¿Cómo?)
9. Hoy hace mal tiempo aquí.   (¿Dónde?)
10. Prefiero el invierno porque me gusta esquiar.   (¿Por qué?)

D Otra vez, por favor.   The telephone connection was so bad during the previous conversation that you couldn't concentrate on what your friend was saying. Ask new questions about the parts of each statement that are in italics. Follow the model.

Carolina y yo estudiamos *español.*
¿Qué estudian Uds.?
Español.

1. *Carolina* toca ahora la guitarra.
2. *Ella* canta con César.
3. César es un muchacho guapo y simpático *de Colombia.*
4. *César y Carolina* cantan muy bien.
5. Ellos practican *en la escuela* los lunes.
6. Los sábados trabajo en una tienda *muy grande.*
7. *En la tienda* hay cinco vendedoras.
8. *La ropa* es muy bonita y barata.
9. *Hace mal tiempo* hoy.
10. Prefiero *el invierno* porque me gusta esquiar.

Notes: Make sure students use proper intonation and word order when forming questions in Exs. C and D.

Enrichment: You may want to assign Ex. D as written work. You might also ask students to form questions based on elements in the sentence that are not italicized: 1. *¿Qué toca Carolina? ¿Cuándo toca Carolina la guitarra?*

Frases negativas

To make a sentence negative, we put *no* before the verb.

Ana María **no** trabaja.	*Ana María does**n't** work.*
No busco los guantes.	*I'm **not** looking for the gloves.*

OBJECTIVES:
TO SAY NO
TO EXPLAIN WHY NOT
TO CONTRADICT

1 To answer no to a question in Spanish, we usually use the word *no* twice. The first *no* answers the question, and the second *no* makes the sentence negative.

¿Es española tu profesora?	*Is your teacher Spanish?*
No, no es española. Es cubana.	*No, she is**n't** Spanish. She's Cuban.*
¿No llevas un abrigo?	*Aren't you wearing a coat?*
No, no hace frío.	*No, it's **not** cold.*

2 We also put *no* before the verb when we use *nada*.

No hago **nada**.	*I'm **not** doing **anything**.*
No estudiamos **nada**.	*We aren't studying **anything**.*

Enrichment: Go over mini-dialogue 4 on p. 122 as an example of a negative sentence with *nada*. Extend the presentation of negative sentences by having students work in pairs, taking turns asking each other questions that will elicit negative responses. For example: *¿Entramos en la clase a las seis de la mañana? ¿Trabaja el (la) profesor(a) en una tienda de ropa?* Encourage students to be as creative as possible. Refer them to the list of *-ar* verbs on p. 127.

Reteach / Review: Make sure that students understand the use of the double negative in the expression *No hago nada*.
  More information about negative words and structures is given in Chap. 13.

Una mujer mexicana y su hija cocinan en Guadalajara.

Práctica A

1. ¿No llevas botas? No, no llueve (no nieva; no hace frío).
2. ¿No llevas un abrigo? No, no hace frío.
3. ¿No llevas pantalones cortos? No, no hace calor.
4. ¿No llevas un suéter? No, no hace fresco (frío).
5. ¿No llevas una bufanda? No, no hace frío (viento, etc.).
6. ¿No llevas un impermeable? No, no llueve.
7. ¿No llevas guantes? No, no hace frío.
8. ¿No llevas un sombrero? No, no hace frío.

Práctica B

Affirmative answers should include *a veces* or *a menudo*.

1. ¿Trabajas los sábados? Sí (No, no) trabajo los sábados.
2. ¿Tocas música clásica? Sí (No, no) toco música clásica.
3. ¿Miras la tele a las tres de la mañana? Sí (No, no) miro la tele a las tres de la mañana.
4. ¿Esquías en el invierno? Sí (No, no) esquío en el invierno.
5. ¿Montas en bicicleta cuando nieva? Sí (No, no) monto en bicicleta cuando nieva.
6. ¿Compras helados cuando hace frío? Sí (No, no) compro helados cuando hace frío.
7. ¿Llevas un paraguas cuando hace viento? Sí (No, no) llevo paraguas cuando hace viento.
8. ¿Tomas el sol cuando hace calor? Sí (No, no) tomo el sol cuando hace calor.

Práctica C

1. ¿No cocinas comida mexicana? No, no cocino nada.
2. ¿No tocas la guitarra? No, no toco nada.
3. ¿No miras la televisión? No, no miro nada.
4. ¿No cantas "Cielito lindo"? No, no canto nada.

PRÁCTICA

A Hoy no. Adults never seem to think teenagers are dressed right for the weather. Ask and answer in the negative, giving a reason based on the weather. Follow the model.

> paraguas
> ESTUDIANTE A *¿No llevas el paraguas?*
> ESTUDIANTE B *No, no llueve.*

1. ¿botas?
2. ¿un abrigo?
3. ¿pantalones cortos?
4. ¿un suéter?
5. ¿una bufanda?
6. ¿un impermeable?
7. ¿guantes?
8. ¿un sombrero?

B ¿Sí o no? Some of your friends do certain things but not others. With a partner, ask each other and answer truthfully whether you do the following sometimes, often, or not at all. Follow the model.

> ESTUDIANTE A *¿Trabajas los domingos?*
> ESTUDIANTE B *Sí, trabajo a veces los domingos.*
> o: *No, no trabajo los domingos.*

1. trabajar los sábados
2. tocar música clásica
3. mirar la tele a las tres de la mañana
4. esquiar en el invierno
5. montar en bicicleta cuando nieva
6. comprar helados cuando hace frío
7. llevar un paraguas cuando hace viento
8. tomar el sol cuando hace calor

C Hoy no hago nada. Some people don't do anything. Ask and answer in the negative based on the model.

> estudiar español
> ESTUDIANTE A *¿No estudias español?*
> ESTUDIANTE B *No, no estudio nada.*

1. cocinar comida mexicana
2. tocar la guitarra
3. mirar la televisión
4. cantar "Cielito lindo"
5. comprar discos
6. lavar las ventanas
7. preguntar cuánto cuesta
8. hacer la tarea

Notes: You may want small groups to do Exs. A and C on p. 138 as chain drills.

D Hablemos de ti.

1. ¿Qué tiempo hace hoy?
2. ¿Qué ropa llevas cuando hace mal tiempo? ¿Qué llevas cuando hace mucho calor?
3. ¿Practicas deportes? ¿Cuáles? ¿Cuál te gusta más?

ACTIVIDAD

¿Por qué? ¡Porque . . . ! Divide the class into two teams. The teacher assigns each student one of the question words: *qué, por qué, cuándo, dónde, cómo, quién, quiénes, cuál, cuáles, cuánto, cuántos,* or *cuántas*. Students then take turns asking members of the other team questions using the words they have been given. For example, if you are given the word *¿qué?*, you might ask *¿Qué tiempo hace?* or *¿Qué llevas hoy?* or *¿Qué día es hoy?* A student on the other team must answer your question. Teams get one point for a correct question and one point for a correct answer. If a student forms an incorrect question or makes a mistake in answering, the other team gets a chance to try for the point. The game continues until everyone has had at least one turn. The team that has the most points wins.

5. ¿No compras discos? No, no compro nada.
6. ¿No lavas las ventanas? No, no lavo nada.
7. ¿No preguntas cuánto cuesta? No, no pregunto nada.
8. ¿No haces la tarea? No, no hago nada.

Práctica D
Answers will vary.

Practice Sheet 3–9
Workbook Exs. G–J
Tape Manual Ex. 8 11
Activity Master 3–2
Quiz 3–5

APLICACIONES Discretionary

Notes: Answers to the **Repaso** and **Tema** appear in the pre-chapter teacher pages. Have students work on the cues orally or in writing before they go on to the **Tema**.

REPASO

Look carefully at the model sentences. Then put the English cues into Spanish to form new sentences based on the models.

1. *Hoy nieva. Rogelio y yo escuchamos discos.*
   (*It's hot today. You* (fam.) *and she are looking for hats.*)
   (*It's cold now. Marta and I are wearing jackets.*)
   (*It's sunny today. You* (formal) *and he are buying bathing suits.*)

Tiendas en la Ciudad de México y en Buenos Aires

2. *Una mujer entra en la tienda y pregunta: "¿Cuánto cuestan las faldas blancas?"*
   (*I go into the store and ask: "How much does the purple dress cost?"*)
   (*We go into the store and ask: "How much does the brown coat cost?"*)
   (*They go into the store and ask: "How much do the red socks cost?"*)

3. *Ud. contesta: "Ochenta pesos, señor."*
   (*We answer: "Fifty pesos, ma'am."*)
   (*They* (fem.) *answer: "Seventy pesos, sir."*)
   (*You* (fam.) *answer: "Twenty-five pesos, miss."*)

4. *"¡Es bastante barato!"*
   (*"It's very old* (fem.)*!"*)
   (*"They're rather short* (masc.)*!"*)
   (*"They're too yellow* (fem.)*!"*)

5. *Los hombres no escuchan nada.*
   (*You* (fam.) *don't study anything.*)
   (*You* (pl.) *don't cook anything.*)
   (*We don't sing anything.*)

Notes: Review of:
1. weather expressions
   compound subject
   -ar verbs
2. -ar verbs
   ¿cuánto cuesta(n)?
   adjectives of color
3. -ar verbs
   numbers
   terms of address
4. adjective agreement
   adverbs of intensity
5. -ar verbs
   no ... nada

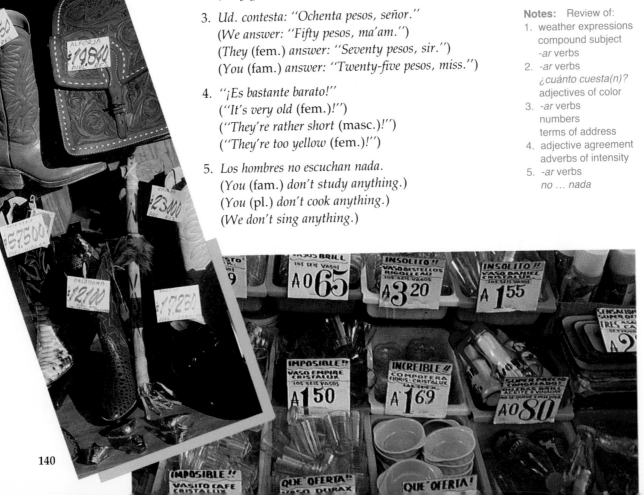

140

Put the English cues into Spanish to form a paragraph.

1. It's raining today. Elena and Clara are looking for raincoats.

2. The girls go into the store and ask, "How much does the yellow raincoat cost?"

3. The salesclerk answers, "Ninety pesos, miss."

4. "It's too expensive."

5. Clara and Elena don't buy anything.

REDACCIÓN

Now you are ready to write your own dialogue or paragraph. Choose one of the following topics.

1. Write a brief paragraph of four to six lines based on the *Tema*. Describe Clara and Elena. What do they look like? What are they wearing?

2. Write a four- to six-line paragraph describing the items in the store pictured on pages 112–113. Tell what some of them are, what colors they are, their prices, and which ones you like.

3. Write a four- to six-line dialogue between a teenager and his or her parent in a clothing store.

A La ropa
Write sentences that tell what each person is
wearing and the color of each item of clothing.

1.   Leonor   2.   Federico

B Los verbos -*ar*
Complete each sentence using the correct form of
the verb in parentheses.

1. Elena _____ muchas blusas. *(comprar)*
2. (Yo) _____ el sol en el verano. *(tomar)*
3. Las señoras _____ en la escuela. *(entrar)*
4. ¿No _____ (tú) un abrigo? *(llevar)*
5. (Nosotros) _____ el gato. *(buscar)*
6. Tú y Jaime _____ el teléfono. *(contestar)*
7. Pepe y yo _____ muy bien. *(bailar)*
8. Ud. _____ la televisión. *(mirar)*
9. David y Luisa _____ en bicicleta. *(montar)*
10. Ud. y Ana _____ discos. *(escuchar)*

C ¿Qué tiempo hace?
Tell what the weather is like in each picture.

1.   2.   3.   4.   5.   6.   7.

D Pregúntas
Make each statement into a question.

María habla español.
¿Habla María español?

1. Ud. trabaja en el verano.
2. Los muchachos escuchan la radio.
3. Él toca la guitarra.
4. Uds. miran el mapa.
5. Luz lleva un paraguas.
6. Ud. compra un traje de baño.

E ¿Verdad?
Now, using the items in Exercise D, form
questions using ¿no? for the first three and
¿verdad? for the last three.

F Más preguntas
For each statement, form a question asking about
the part of the sentence that is in italics.

Estudio *español.*
¿Qué estudias?

1. *La profesora* lleva botas.
2. Eduardo monta en bicicleta *ahora.*
3. Nado *muy bien.*
4. Hay *dos* bolígrafos en la mesa.
5. Somos *de los Estados Unidos.*
6. Canto *porque me gusta la música.*
7. El abrigo cuesta *cien pesos.*
8. Prefiero *los gatos negros.*

G No
Answer each question in the negative using a
complete sentence.

1. ¿Entra la Sra. Arias en la tienda?
2. ¿Tomas el sol en el invierno?
3. ¿Lleva pantimedias Ana cuando hace calor?
4. ¿Te gustan los zapatos rojos?
5. ¿Compran Uds. un impermeable?
6. ¿Son gordos los gatos?

Chapter 3 Test
Listening Comprehension Test

Notes: Answers to the **Comprueba**
appear in the pre-chapter teacher pages.

VOCABULARIO DEL CAPÍTULO 3

Sustantivos

el abrigo
la blusa
la bota
la bufanda
el calcetín, *pl.* los calcetines
la camisa
la camiseta
el color
la chaqueta
la estación, *pl.* las estaciones
la falda
el guante
el impermeable
el invierno
los jeans
el otoño
los pantalones
las pantimedias
el paraguas
el peso
la pregunta
la primavera
la ropa
el sombrero
el suéter
el tiempo
la tienda (de + *noun*)
el traje
el traje de baño
el vendedor, la vendedora
el verano
el vestido
el zapato

Pronombres

(no…) nada

Adjetivos

amarillo, -a
anaranjado, -a
azul
barato, -a
blanco, -a
caro, -a
gris, *pl.* grises
marrón, *pl.* marrones
morado, -a
negro, -a
rojo, -a
verde

Verbos

buscar
comprar
contestar
entrar (en)
llevar
preguntar
llueve
nieva

(yo) hago
(tú) haces

(yo) prefiero
(tú) prefieres

Adverbios

a menudo
a veces
aquí
cuando

Palabras interrogativas

¿cuál, -es?
¿cuánto?
¿quién, -es?

Expresiones

¿cuánto cuesta(n)?
¿de qué color…?
de vacaciones
hace buen tiempo
hace calor
hace fresco
hace frío
hace mal tiempo
hace sol
hace viento
¿qué desea Ud.?
¿qué tiempo hace?
tomar el sol

CAPÍTULO 4

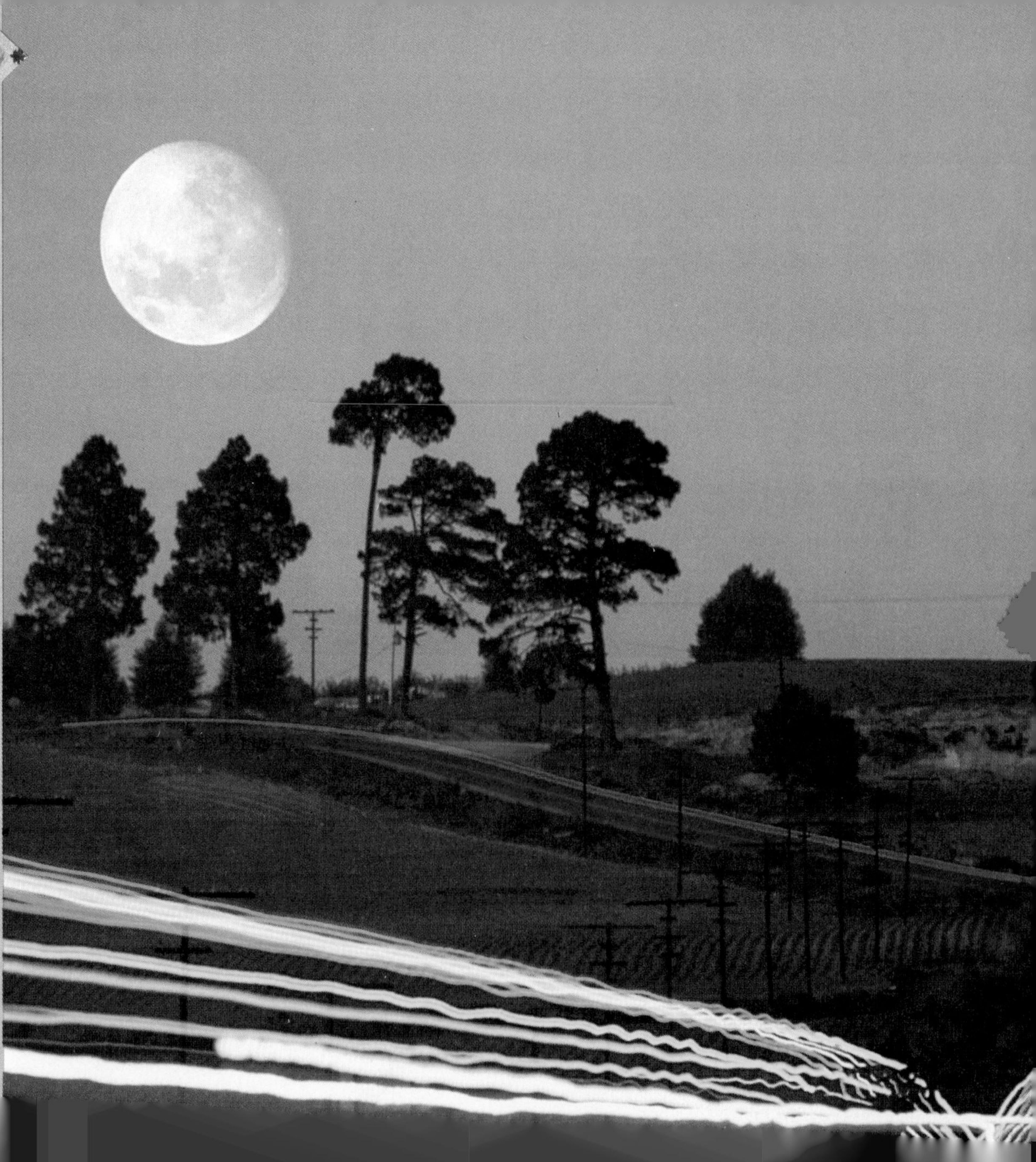

EL TRANSPORTE PÚBLICO

Getting around in Latin America can be more of an adventure than you might imagine. It can mean hanging on to your seat as the train barrels down the mountain pass known as *La nariz del diablo* (the Devil's Nose) on the way to Guayaquil, Ecuador. Or it can mean sharing your seat with a crate of chickens on a bus ride through rural areas. If you travel by plane, you will find that some airports are located in regions so mountainous that planes are forced to make almost vertical takeoffs and landings.

The bus is by far the most popular means of travel in Latin America. Buses go wherever there are roads—and even a few places where roads probably won't ever be built.

In large cities, public transportation is usually very good. Countless taxis zoom along the crowded streets, but they are too expensive for most people. Collective taxis—*colectivos*—operate in many cities. These are vans or minibuses that pick up and drop off passengers along a fixed route. Because they are shared by several travelers, *colectivos* are very inexpensive.

There are up-to-date subway systems in Buenos Aires, Santiago, Caracas, and Mexico City. Mexico City's subway is one of the most interesting in the world. Construction was begun during preparations for the 1968 Olympic Games. When workers began to dig, they struck buried treasure: artifacts and ruins of the ancient Aztec civilization whose capital had stood there centuries before. Archeologists, engineers, and builders worked night and day to complete the subway while preserving this fantastic discovery. Today some subway stations are mini-museums. If you used the Pino Suárez station, for example, you would pass right by a temple dedicated to the Aztec god of the wind.

PALABRAS NUEVAS I

¿Adónde vas?

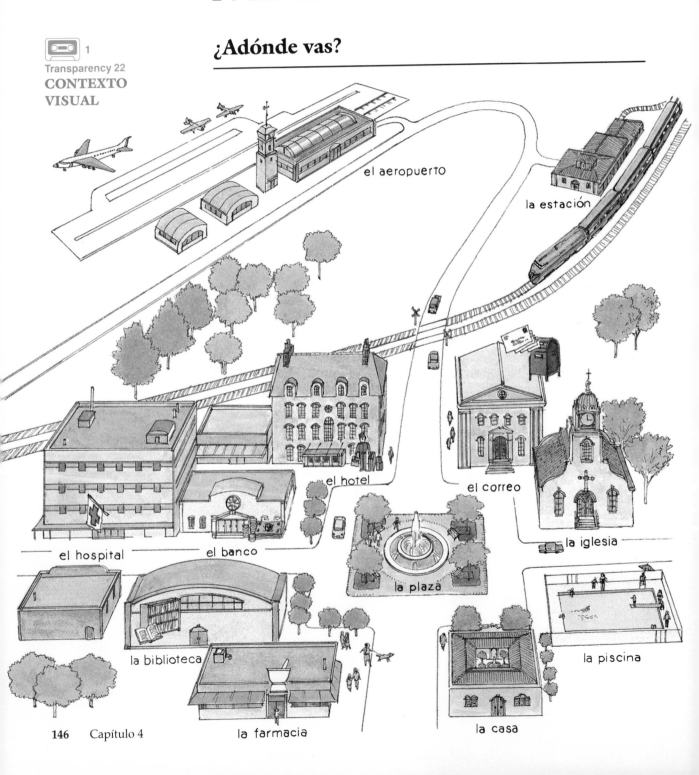

el aeropuerto

la estación

el hotel

el correo

la iglesia

el hospital

el banco

la plaza

la piscina

la biblioteca

la farmacia

la casa

Enrichment: To reinforce the use of the preposition *a*, use the **Contexto visual** illustration or transparency, and ask individual students *¿Adónde vas?* to elicit the answer *Voy + a la/al + a place name.* Model *Voy a casa, al centro, a la estación* as examples.

Ask for the opposites of new vocabulary words *juntos, –as (solo, –a)* and *nunca (siempre).* Other pairs of opposites appear on p. 153.

CONTEXTO COMUNICATIVO 2

1 JUDIT   ¿Qué haces **durante el fin de semana**?

ALFREDO   A veces **voy al** cine. Pero prefiero ir **a la** piscina.

JUDIT   ¿Con quién vas al cine?

ALFREDO   Con **mis** amigos.

Variaciones:
- el fin de semana → el verano
- a la piscina → **al campo**

2 ENRIQUE   ¿**Quieres** jugar al fútbol?

DANIEL   Ahora no. Voy **al centro.**

ENRIQUE   ¿Al centro? ¿Por qué?

DANIEL   Porque quiero comprar una camisa.

ENRIQUE   ¿Y **después**?

DANIEL   Después voy **a casa.**

- al centro → a **la ciudad**
- a casa → al correo
- después → más tarde

3 JORGE   ¿**Adónde** vas **esta noche**?

PILAR   Voy a una fiesta. ¿Y tú?

JORGE   Yo también. Voy a tocar mi guitarra.

PILAR   ¡Ah! Y la semana **próxima** hay una fiesta en la escuela.

- esta noche → mañana
- la semana próxima → el viernes
- la semana próxima → el mes próximo
- en la escuela → en la plaza

4 MARGARITA   **Vamos juntas** a la biblioteca, Laura.

LAURA   No, no quiero. Prefiero estudiar más tarde en casa.

---

durante   *during*

el fin de semana, *pl.* **los fines de semana**   *weekend*

(yo) voy, (tú) vas (from **ir**)   *to go*

a   *to*

a la, al (a + el)   *to the*

mis (with pl. nouns)   *my*

el campo   *country, countryside*

(yo) quiero, (tú) quieres (from **querer**)   *to want*

el centro   *downtown*

al centro   *(to) downtown*

después   *afterwards, later*

a casa   *(to one's) home*

la ciudad   *city*

¿adónde?   *(to) where?*

esta noche   *tonight*

próximo, -a   *next*

vamos   *let's go*

juntos, -as   *together*

5 **ELISA** ¿**Siempre** vas a la escuela con **tus** amigas?

JUANA No, **nunca.** Prefiero ir **sola.**

■ a la escuela → al centro

siempre *always*
tus (with pl. nouns) *your*
nunca *never*
solo, -a *alone*

EN OTRAS PARTES

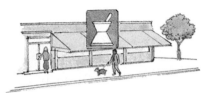

Práctica A

1. ¿Adónde vas ahora?
   Voy a la farmacia.
   ¿Y después?
   Al correo.
2. Voy al cine. …
   Al aeropuerto.
3. Voy a la iglesia. …
   Al hotel.
4. Voy a la piscina. …
   Al banco.
5. Voy a la estación. …
   A la biblioteca.
6. Voy al aeropuerto. …
   Al hospital.

También se dice *la botica.*

En la Argentina se dice *la pileta* y en México, *la alberca.*

Reteach / Extra Help: In preparation for Ex. A, have students identify the place shown in each illustration, including the definite article.

PRÁCTICA

A ¿Adónde vas? Imagine that you have a list of places you must go. Ask and answer each question according to the model. Be careful! With masculine nouns use *al*, and with feminine nouns use *a la.*

ESTUDIANTE A	*¿Adónde vas ahora?*
ESTUDIANTE B	*Voy al banco.*
ESTUDIANTE A	*¿Y después?*
ESTUDIANTE B	*A la biblioteca.*

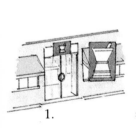

1.

2.

3.

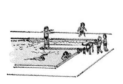

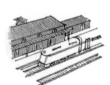

4.

5.

6.

B **¿Por qué?** Working with a partner, take turns asking and answering why you go to a certain place. Choose your reasons from the column at the right (or give other reasons if you can).

¿Por qué vas . . .
a la biblioteca?
a la piscina?
a la estación?
a la tienda?
a la escuela?
al centro?
al aeropuerto?
al campo?
a casa?

Porque quiero . . .
ir de vacaciones
mirar la tele
trabajar
ir a (*nombre de un país*)
ir a la clase de español
hacer la tarea
leer (libros, el periódico)
estudiar
nadar
comprar ropa (o una chaqueta, discos, etc.)
tomar el sol

C **Hablemos de ti.**
1. ¿Te gusta ir al centro? ¿Por qué? ¿Qué haces cuando vas al centro?
2. ¿Hay muchos o pocos hoteles en tu ciudad? ¿Hay muchas o pocas iglesias? ¿Sabes ("do you know") cuántas bibliotecas hay? ¿Hay una estación o un aeropuerto? ¿Es pequeño o grande el aeropuerto?
3. ¿Qué quieres hacer esta noche?
4. ¿Adónde quieres ir durante el fin de semana? ¿Con quién?
5. ¿Qué quieres hacer durante el verano próximo?

Práctica B
Answers will vary.

Practice Sheet 4–1
Workbook Exs. A-B
Tape Manual Exs. 1–2 3
Quiz 4–1

Reteach / Review: In preparation for Ex. B, you may want to use magazine pictures to reinforce the vocabulary on p. 146.

Práctica C
Answers will vary.

Enrichment: Additional questions for Ex. C: *¿Te gusta ir a la biblioteca? ¿Por qué? ¿Prefieres estudiar en casa o en la biblioteca? ¿Te gusta nadar?*

ACTIVIDAD

¿Adónde quieres ir? Working with a partner, draw a map of an imaginary town. In the center put *la plaza*. Then use symbols, not words, for the various locations. Include at least ten of the buildings and locations that you have learned.

When you have finished, tell your partner where you are going. Begin at the *plaza* and name at least four places. For example:

Voy al cine. Después quiero ir a la farmacia. Más tarde voy a la estación y después a casa.

As you tell where you are going, your partner should use a colored pencil to draw your route on the map. Check to make sure your partner drew the route correctly. Then switch roles and use a different color to draw the route your partner describes. Remember: Use *al* with masculine nouns and *a la* with feminine nouns.

Notes: You may want to ask volunteers to show and describe the routes they prepared for the **Actividad**.

APLICACIONES Discretionary

Diálogo
1. Es sábado
2. Son las tres de la tarde.
3. Es pequeña, pero muy bonita.
4. Es enorme y muy feo.
5. Va a la piscina de Andrea.
6. Va al cine porque allí no hay perros.

En México

Vamos a la piscina 4

El sábado a las tres de la tarde en Miami, Florida.

ALBERTO   Hola, Cecilia, ¿adónde vas?

CECILIA   Voy a nadar en la piscina de Andrea.[1] ¿Quieres ir?

ALBERTO   ¿A la piscina de Andrea? ¡Nunca!

CECILIA   ¿Por qué no? Su[2] piscina es pequeña, pero muy bonita.

ALBERTO   Sí, pero su perro es enorme y muy feo.

CECILIA   Entonces, voy sola.

ALBERTO   Pues, yo voy al cine. Allí[3] no hay perros.

———————

[1]**de Andrea**   *Andrea's*   [2]**su** *her*   [3]**allí** *there*

Enrichment: Additional questions: *¿Qué no hay en el cine? (No hay perros.) ¿De dónde son Alberto y Cecilia? (Son de Miami.)* You may assign the questions as written homework.

Preguntas

Contesta según el diálogo.

1. ¿Qué día es?   2. ¿Qué hora es?   3. ¿Cómo es la piscina de Andrea?   4. ¿Cómo es su perro?   5. ¿Adónde va Cecilia?   6. Y Alberto, ¿adónde va? ¿Por qué?

Participación

Working with a partner, make up a dialogue of four to six lines in which one of you wants to do one thing and the other doesn't. You end up going to different places. Where does each of you want to go? Why doesn't the other want to go there?

PRONUNCIACIÓN 5

A Except at the beginning of a word or after *l* or *n*, you pronounce the letter *r* by tapping the tip of your tongue once on the ridge behind your upper teeth. The sound is similar to the *dd* in the English word "ladder."
Escucha y repite.

para	tarea	número	americano	periódico
grande	centro	abrigo	pupitre	escritorio
ser	color	leer	hablar	popular

B To make the sound of the letter *rr*, you tap your tongue several times on the ridge behind your front teeth.
Escucha y repite.

churro	perro	burrito	pizarra	guitarra

C When *r* is the first letter of a word or comes after *l* or *n*, it is pronounced like the *rr*.
Escucha y repite.

rojo	ropa	radio	rubio	reloj
Enrique	enrolar	alrededor		

D Escucha y repite

El hombre es rubio.   Enrique compra un abrigo amarillo.
El aeropuerto es enorme.   El pájaro es rojo, pero el perro es negro.

Aplicaciones   **151**

PALABRAS NUEVAS II

¿Cómo vas?

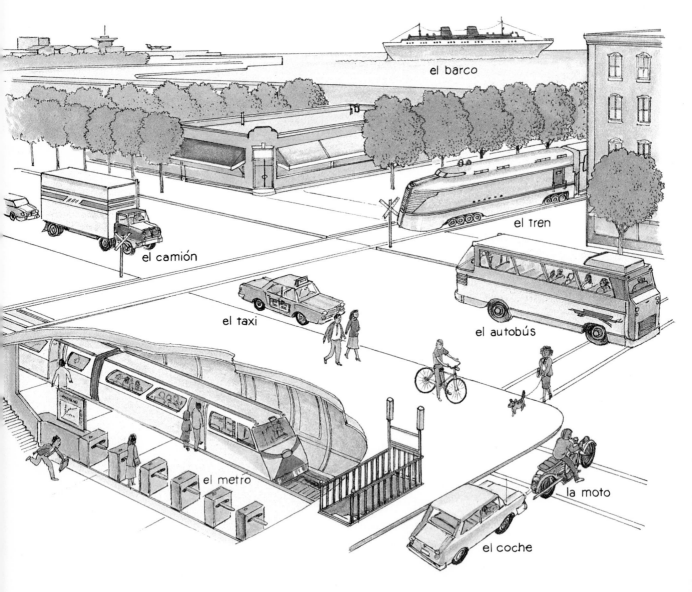

el avión

el barco

el tren

el camión

el taxi

el autobús

el metro

la moto

el coche

Reteach / Review: Go over the plural forms of the nouns presented on p. 152. Remind students that *avión, camión,* and *autobús* form their plurals like *estación* and *lección*, that is, they lose their accent mark in the plural. The rule appears on p. 65.

Point out that *buen/mal* in mini-dialogue 1 and *buenos/malos* in 2 are different forms of the same words. Highlight *bueno/malo* and *rápido/lento* as pairs of opposites. See mini-dialogues 4 and 5 on pp. 147–148 for other antonyms presented in Chap. 4.

Remind students that they first used *primero* when talking about dates. Refer to mini-dialogue 3 on p. 21.

CONTEXTO COMUNICATIVO 7

1 Cuando hace buen tiempo, siempre voy a la escuela **a pie.** Cuando hace mal tiempo, voy **en** autobús. Y tú, ¿cómo vas a la escuela?

   Variaciones:
- a pie → en bicicleta
- a pie → en moto
- hace buen tiempo → hace sol
- hace mal tiempo → llueve

a pie	*on foot, walking*
en + vehicle	*by*

2 SR. GÓMEZ   En España los trenes son muy **buenos,** ¿no?
   SRA. COLÓN   Sí, y muy **rápidos** también.
   SR. GÓMEZ   Aquí son **malos** y demasiado **lentos.**

- los trenes → los autobuses

bueno (buen), -a	*good*
rápido, -a	*fast*
malo (mal), -a	*bad*
lento, -a	*slow*

3 GLORIA   ¿Vas a **viajar** a España?
   RAFAEL   Sí, mañana voy a **tomar** el **primer** avión.
   GLORIA   **¡Bueno!**

- España → México
- primer → próximo

viajar	*to travel*
tomar	*to take*
primero (primer), -a	*first*
¡bueno!	*okay, fine*

4 GLORIA   ¿Vamos a tomar el autobús del aeropuerto al centro?
   RAFAEL   No quiero **esperar** el autobús.
   GLORIA   Entonces vamos en metro. Es muy rápido.

- del aeropuerto → de la estación
- en metro → en taxi

esperar	*to wait (for)*

5 JAIME   Quiero comprar **unos** libros clásicos.
   LUCÍA   ¿Por qué no compras *Don Quijote?* Es un **gran** libro.

unos, unas	*some, a few*
gran	*great*

EN OTRAS PARTES

También se dice *el auto* (*el automóvil*) y *el carro*.

En México se dice *el camión;* en Puerto Rico y Cuba, *la guagua;* en la Argentina, *el ómnibus* o *el colectivo;* en Bolivia y el Perú, *el microbús* o *el micro.*

También se dice *el subte* (*el subterráneo*).

Una calle en México, D.F.

PRÁCTICA

A ¿Cómo quieres ir? Two people are talking about their preferred ways of getting places. Ask and answer according to the model.

> al centro / autobús / coche
> ESTUDIANTE A   *¿Quieres ir al centro en autobús?*
> ESTUDIANTE B   *No, prefiero ir en coche.*

1. al banco / taxi / metro
2. a la escuela / pie / bicicleta
3. a la biblioteca / moto / coche
4. al aeropuerto / autobús / tren
5. a la tienda / coche / taxi
6. a la estación / metro / moto
7. a la iglesia / pie / autobús
8. a Puerto Rico / barco / avión

B ¿Cómo vas tú? Ask and answer based on the pictures. Follow the model.

> a la escuela
> ESTUDIANTE A   *¿Cómo vas a la escuela?*
> ESTUDIANTE B   *Siempre voy a pie. ¿Y tú?*
> ESTUDIANTE A   *Yo nunca voy a pie. Voy en autobús.*

1. a la tienda   2. al centro   3. al aeropuerto

4. a la plaza   5. a la farmacia   6. al correo

Práctica A

1. ¿Quieres ir al banco en taxi? No, prefiero ir en metro.
2. ¿Quieres ir a la escuela a pie? No, prefiero ir en bicicleta.
3. ¿Quieres ir a la biblioteca en moto? No, prefiero ir en coche.
4. ¿Quieres ir al aeropuerto en autobús? No, prefiero ir en tren.
5. ¿Quieres ir a la tienda en coche? No, prefiero ir en taxi.
6. ¿Quieres ir a la estación en metro? No, prefiero ir en moto.
7. ¿Quieres ir a la iglesia a pie? No, prefiero ir en autobús.
8. ¿Quieres ir a Puerto Rico en barco? No, prefiero ir en avión.

Práctica B

1. ¿Cómo vas a la tienda? Siempre voy a pie. ¿Y tú? Yo nunca voy a pie. Voy en coche.
2. ¿Cómo vas al centro? Siempre voy en camión. ¿Y tú? Yo nunca voy en camión. Voy en metro.
3. ¿Cómo vas al aeropuerto? Siempre voy en moto. ¿Y tú? Yo nunca voy en moto. Voy en taxi.
4. ¿Cómo vas a la plaza? Siempre voy a pie. ¿Y tú? Yo nunca voy a pie. Voy en metro.
5. ¿Cómo vas a la farmacia? Siempre voy en coche. ¿Y tú? Yo nunca voy en coche. Voy en autobús.
6. ¿Cómo vas al correo? Siempre voy en bicicleta. ¿Y tú? Yo nunca voy en bicicleta. Voy en taxi.

Práctica C
1. La blusa verde y amarilla / La camisa azul y blanca
2. Los pantalones blancos / Los jeans grises
3. La falda marrón / El vestido anaranjado
4. La chaqueta negra / El abrigo azul
5. Las botas blancas / Los zapatos morados
6. Los calcetines rojos / Las pantimedias negras

Reteach / Extra Help: To prepare for Ex. C, use the illustration on pp. 112–113 or show the transparency. Have students work in pairs, taking turns asking and answering *¿De qué color es/son____?* Circulate to give help where needed.

Práctica D
Answers will vary.

Enrichment: Additional questions for Ex. D: *¿Cómo prefieres viajar, en tren o en autobús? ¿Por qué? ¿Hay metro en tu ciudad? ¿Es rápido o lento? ¿Te gusta viajar en moto? ¿Quieres un coche grande o pequeño?*

Reteach / Review: You may want to use the **Estudio de palabras** as the basis for a written homework assignment. Ask students to write sentences with each of the words discussed in the text.

C   ¿Cuál prefieres?   Pretend that you and a friend are window-shopping. Working with a partner, take turns saying which items you prefer.

ESTUDIANTE A	*¿Cuál prefieres?*
ESTUDIANTE B	*El coche rojo y negro.*
o:	*La moto negra.*

D   Hablemos de ti.
1. ¿Cómo vas a la escuela? ¿Cómo prefieres ir cuando hace mal tiempo?
2. ¿Cómo prefieres ir al centro?
3. ¿Hay autobuses en tu ciudad? ¿Cómo son? ¿Buenos o malos? ¿Rápidos o lentos?
4. Cuando vas de vacaciones, ¿cómo prefieres viajar? ¿Por qué? ¿Adónde vas de vacaciones?

Practice Sheet 4–2   Workbook Exs. C–D

🔲 **8 Tape Manual Ex. 3   Quiz 4–2**

ESTUDIO DE PALABRAS

You already know several words that have more than one meaning. For example: *mañana* ("morning" and "tomorrow") and *tarde* ("afternoon" and "late"). Some words have an accent mark to show a difference in meaning:

tu	*your*	el	*the*	solo, -a	*alone*
tú	*you*	él	*he*	sólo	*only*

Estación has two very different meanings: "season" and "station." The **verb** *llevar* means both "to wear" and "to carry."

Sometimes there are two Spanish words where in English we usually use only one. For example, *el país* means "country" or "nation." The Spanish word for *country* meaning "countryside" or "rural area" is *el campo*. We cannot use *el país* and *el campo* interchangeably.

EXPLICACIONES I

El verbo *ir*

The verb *ir* ("to go") is irregular. Here are its present-tense forms.

SINGULAR		PLURAL	
1	(yo) **voy** — *I go / I'm going*	(nosotros) (nosotras) } **vamos** — *we go / we're going*	
2	(tú) **vas** — *you go / you're going*	(vosotros) (vosotras) } **vais** — *you go / you're going*	
3	Ud. } **va** — *you go / you're going* (él) *he goes / he's going* (ella) *she goes / she's going*	Uds. } **van** — *you go / you're going* (ellos) *they go / they're going* (ellas) *they go / they're going*	

1. When we use the preposition *a* with verbs of motion such as *ir* or *viajar*, it means "to." With the masculine definite article *el*, it contracts to *al*: *a + el = al*.

   Nunca van **al** cine. — *They never go **to the** movies.*
   Voy **a** Quito con Eduardo. — *I'm going **to** Quito with Eduardo.*
   ¿Vas **a** la estación? — *Are you going **to** the station?*

2. Just as we say "going to" in English to talk about the future, we can use a form of *ir + a +* infinitive in Spanish.

   Van a tomar el avión mañana. — ***They're going to take** the plane tomorrow.*
   ¿Cuándo **vas a ir** al centro? — *When **are you going to go** downtown?*

3. *Vamos a +* infinitive means "let's."

   Vamos a bail**ar**. — *Let's dance.*
   Vamos a com**er**. — *Let's eat.*

◆ OBJECTIVES:

TO TALK ABOUT WHAT YOU AND OTHERS ARE GOING TO DO

TO EXPRESS INTENTIONS

TO MAKE PLANS

TO MAKE SUGGESTIONS

Notes: You may want to use mini-dialogues 1, 3, and 4 on p. 147 to introduce *ir*; refer to mini-dialogues 1 and 2 for further examples of *ir + a la/al +* place. Mini-dialogue 4 on p. 153 illustrates *ir a +* infinitive.

Práctica A

1. Van a jugar al béisbol. ¡Vamos a jugar al béisbol también!
2. Raquel va a esperar el tren. ¡Vamos a esperar el tren también!
3. Alejandro va a comer. ¡Vamos a comer también!
4. Los alumnos van a bailar. ¡Vamos a bailar …!
5. Los hombres van a viajar a España. ¡Vamos a viajar…!
6. Carlos y ella van a nadar. ¡Vamos a nadar …!
7. Gloria va a tomar el metro. ¡Vamos a tomar…!
8. Van a cantar. ¡Vamos a cantar…!

Práctica B

1. ¿Adónde va Ud.? Voy a la plaza.
2. ¿Adónde van Uds.? Vamos al hotel.
3. ¿Adónde va Ud.? Voy al cine.
4. ¿Adónde va Ud.? Voy a la biblioteca.
5. ¿Adónde van Uds.? Vamos a la iglesia.
6. ¿Adónde van Uds.? Vamos a la piscina.
7. ¿Adónde va Ud.? Voy al banco.
8. ¿Adónde van Uds.? Vamos al correo.

PRÁCTICA

A **Nosotros también.** Some people always want to do what someone else is doing, no matter what it is. With a partner, take turns making statements about what others are going to do and suggesting that the two of you do the same.

David / estudiar

ESTUDIANTE A   *David va a estudiar.*

ESTUDIANTE B   *¡Vamos a estudiar también!*

1. (ellos) / jugar al béisbol
2. Raquel / esperar el tren
3. Alejandro / comer
4. los alumnos / bailar
5. los hombres / viajar a España
6. Carlos y ella / nadar
7. Gloria / tomar el metro
8. (ellas) / cantar

B **¿Adónde van Uds.?** Imagine that you are on a tour and have some free time. The tour leader wants to know where everyone is going. Ask and answer according to the model.

Uds. / el centro

ESTUDIANTE A   *¿Adónde van Uds.?*

ESTUDIANTE B   *Vamos al centro.*

Ud. / la farmacia

ESTUDIANTE A   *¿Adónde va Ud.?*

ESTUDIANTE B   *Voy a la farmacia.*

1. Ud. / la plaza
2. Uds. / el hotel
3. Ud. / el cine
4. Ud. / la biblioteca
5. Uds. / la iglesia
6. Uds. / la piscina
7. Ud. / el banco
8. Uds. / el correo

C **¿Cómo van?** Using the picture cues, tell how each person or group goes to certain places.

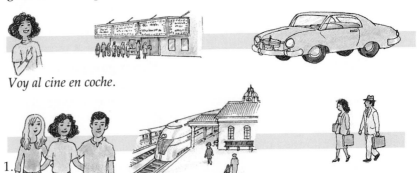

Voy al cine en coche.

1.

Práctica C
1. (Nosotros) vamos a la estación a pie.
2. (Ella) va al correo en bicicleta.
3. (Ellos) van al aeropuerto en camión.
4. Uds. van al hotel en taxi.
5. (Él) va a Puerto Rico en barco.
6. (Nosotras) vamos a la plaza en metro.
7. (Tú) vas al banco en autobús.
8. (Yo) voy a México en avión.
9. Ud. va a la biblioteca a pie.
10. (Ellas) van al hospital en moto.

Explicaciones I **159**

Práctica D
1. Voy a ir a la iglesia.
2. Voy a comprar una chaqueta y guantes.
3. Voy a lavar el coche el 11.
4. Voy a mirar la tele *(or: España de hoy)* a las ocho de la noche.
5. Voy a hablar con mi profesora de español. (El próximo día) voy a estudiar para mis exámenes.
6. Voy a cocinar para la Navidad.
7. Voy a ir a la fiesta en casa de Luz a las siete y media.
8. Vamos a viajar a Nevada.

D **¿Qué haces durante el mes de diciembre?** December looks like a busy month. Pretend that this is your calendar. Write sentences telling what you are going to be doing. Then, working with a partner, take turns asking and answering the questions.

1. ¿Qué vas a hacer el 8 de diciembre a las 8 de la mañana?
2. ¿Qué vas a hacer el 17?
3. ¿Cuándo vas a lavar el coche?
4. ¿Qué vas a hacer el 1 de diciembre? ¿A qué hora?
5. ¿Con quién vas a hablar el 5? ¿Qué vas a hacer el próximo día?
6. ¿Qué vas a hacer el 24?
7. ¿Adónde vas a ir el día de fin de año? ¿A qué hora?
8. ¿Qué van Uds. a hacer del 19 al 23?

E Hablemos de ti.

1. ¿Qué vas a hacer mañana?
2. ¿Adónde vas a ir durante el fin de semana? ¿Van a ir al cine tú y tus amigos? ¿Cuándo?
3. ¿Cuántas horas vas a estudiar esta noche?
4. ¿Te gusta viajar? ¿Viaja mucho tu familia? ¿En qué estación del año viajan Uds.? ¿Adónde van Uds.?

ACTIVIDAD

Frases fantásticas.   Get together in groups of three or four students. Your teacher will give three letters of the alphabet to each group. Your group's job is to make up as many correct alliterative sentences as you can. A group secretary should write the sentences on a piece of paper. (In alliterative sentences, most of the words begin with the same sound.) For example, if your group has the letters *A*, *G*, and *V*, some of your sentences might be:

Ahora no hay abrigos aquí.
El gato grande lleva guantes.
Víctor y Verónica van a viajar a Venezuela.

After a time your teacher will ask groups to exchange papers. Take turns reading the other group's sentences aloud. Choose two or three favorites and read them to the class.

Práctica E
Answers will vary.

Enrichment: Additional questions for Ex. E: *¿Cuándo vas a la biblioteca? ¿Vas a viajar en avión durante el verano? ¿Adónde vas a ir? ¿Con quién vas a viajar?*

Practice Sheets 4–3, 4–4, 4–5
Workbook Exs. E–F
Tape Manual Exs. 4–5   9
Activity Master 4–1
Quizzes 4–3, 4–4

Notes: When assigning letters for the **Actividad,** omit *K, X, Y, Z, Ll,* and *Ch.* At this point, students are not familiar with enough words beginning with these letters.

APLICACIONES   Discretionary

Un día muy largo 10

ANTES DE LEER

As you read, look for the answers to these questions.

1. ¿Qué quiere decir *taxista* en inglés?

2. ¿Por qué a veces va la Sra. López a su ("her") trabajo a las siete de la mañana? (Note that *el trabajo* is related to a word you already know. What do you think it means?)

3. ¿Cómo va Pablo a su "trabajo"?

El señor López es taxista. A las seis de la mañana va al garaje en moto, busca su[1] taxi y empieza a[2] trabajar. Durante el día muchas personas viajan en su taxi. Van a diferentes partes de la ciudad: al centro, al aeropuerto, a los hoteles, a las dos estaciones de tren, etc. El señor López
5 vuelve[3] a casa a las ocho y media de la noche.

La señora López trabaja en el centro. Va a su trabajo en autobús. ¡Cuántas personas hay en el autobús a las ocho de la mañana! ¡Viajan como[4] sardinas! A veces la señora López toma el autobús a las siete de la mañana, porque hay pocas personas en el autobús cuando es temprano.
10 A las cinco de la tarde toma el autobús otra vez[5] y vuelve a casa. Pero siempre hay muchas personas en el autobús.

Pablo López trabaja también. Él trabaja en la escuela y en casa. Es estudiante. Pero Pablo no toma el autobús. Va a la escuela a pie. A las tres de la tarde vuelve a casa, donde hace la tarea y a veces mira la
15 televisión. Su mamá vuelve alrededor de[6] las seis menos cuarto y Pablo y ella cocinan. Después esperan juntos al señor López.

---

[1]**su** *his, her*   [2]**empieza a** *(from* **empezar***) begins*   [3]**vuelve** *(from* **volver***) returns*
[4]**como** *like*   [5]**otra vez** *again*   [6]**alrededor de** *around*

Preguntas

Contesta según la lectura.

1. ¿Cómo va el señor López a su trabajo?
2. ¿Cuál es su trabajo?
3. ¿Adónde va el señor López durante el día?
4. ¿A qué hora vuelve a casa?
5. ¿Dónde trabaja la señora López?
6. ¿Cómo va ella a su trabajo?
7. ¿Cómo viajan las personas en los autobuses a las ocho de la mañana y a las cinco de la tarde?
8. ¿Adónde va Pablo?
9. ¿Cómo va él?
10. ¿A qué hora vuelve Pablo a casa?
11. ¿Qué hace entonces?

Notes: These cognates have not been glossed: *garaje,* garage; *personas,* persons; *diferentes,* different; *partes,* parts; *sardinas,* sardines; *mamá,* mother.

Unas policías en la capital
mexicana

Un estudiante mexicano
toma el autobús.

EXPLICACIONES II

Notes: You may want to use mini-dialogue 5 on p. 153 to introduce the indefinite article.

El artículo indefinido

◆ **OBJECTIVES:**

TO IDENTIFY PEOPLE AND THINGS

TO PLAN A SHOPPING TRIP

The singular indefinite articles in Spanish are *un* and *una*. Their English equivalents are "a" and "an." *Un* is used with masculine singular nouns, *una* with feminine singular nouns.

un aeropuerto	*an airport*
una estación	*a station*

The plural indefinite articles are *unos* and *unas*. They mean "some" or "a few."

Quiero **unas** papas fritas.	*I want **some** French fries.*
Vamos a esperar **unos** minutos.	*Let's wait **a few** minutes.*

Práctica A

1. Quiero comprar un abrigo. Y yo quiero comprar unos guantes.
2. una falda / unos pantalones
3. un traje / unos zapatos
4. un suéter / unas camisas
5. una chaqueta / unos vestidos
6. un vestido / unas camisetas
7. un traje de baño / unos calcetines
8. un impermeable / unas blusas

Práctica B

1. Son unos trenes.
2. Es un camión.
3. Son unos aviones.
4. Es una moto.
5. Son unos barcos.
6. Son unos autobuses.
7. Es un aeropuerto.
8. Son unas iglesias.
9. Son unas farmacias.
10. Es un banco.
11. Es una estación.
12. Son unos hospitales.

PRÁCTICA

A Yo quiero. Two people are planning a shopping trip. What do they want to buy?

blusa / camisetas

ESTUDIANTE A   *Quiero comprar una blusa.*
ESTUDIANTE B   *Y yo quiero comprar unas camisetas.*

1. abrigo / guantes
2. falda / pantalones
3. traje / zapatos
4. suéter / camisas
5. chaqueta / vestidos
6. vestido / camisetas
7. traje de baño / calcetines
8. impermeable / blusas

B ¿Qué es . . . ? Imagine that you are baby-sitting for two small Spanish-speaking children. They have a new picture book. Can you help them identify the objects on page 165? Use *es* or *son*, the correct indefinite article, and the noun.

Practice Sheet 4–6
Tape Manual Ex. 6 11
Quiz 4–5

◆ **OBJECTIVES:**

TO DESCRIBE PEOPLE AND THINGS

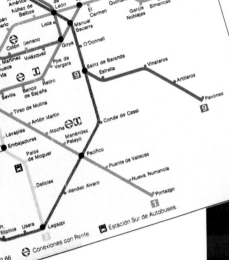

El metro en Santiago, Chile

La posición de los adjetivos

You have been using adjectives of color with nouns. You may have noticed that these adjectives came *after* the nouns. In Spanish, adjectives usually come after the noun they describe.

un barco **amarillo**	unos camiones **verdes**
una moto **blanca**	unas bicicletas **rojas**

1 *Bueno* and *malo* come either before or after the noun. *Primero* almost always comes before. Before a masculine singular noun we drop the final *-o* of these three adjectives.

un **buen** profesor	unos **buenos** profesores
una **buena** profesora	unas **buenas** profesoras
un **mal** día	unos **malos** días
una **mala** noche	unas **malas** noches
el **primer** examen	los **primeros** exámenes
la **primera** clase	las **primeras** clases

2 *Grande* may come either before or after a noun. But the meaning is different depending upon its position. After a noun it means "large" or "big." Before a noun it means "great." We shorten *grande* to *gran* before *both* masculine and feminine singular nouns.

Es un hombre **grande**.	Son hombres **grandes**.
Es una ciudad **grande**.	Son ciudades **grandes**.
Es un **gran** hombre.	Son **grandes** hombres.
Es una **gran** ciudad.	Son **grandes** ciudades.

PRÁCTICA

A **¿Cómo es?**   Ask and answer according to the model. Always use the correct masculine or feminine form of the adjective—and be careful! Some adjectives will go before the noun, and some will follow the noun.

> un autobús / lento / rápido
> ESTUDIANTE A   *¿Es un autobús lento?*
> ESTUDIANTE B   *No, es un autobús rápido.*

1. una tienda / nuevo / viejo
2. una profesora / malo / grande
3. una moto / caro / barato
4. el tren / primero / próximo

5. un libro / malo / bueno
6. una cinta / largo / corto
7. un barco / pequeño / grande
8. una casa / blanco / rojo

B **Mi tienda de ropa.**   Pretend that you are writing a radio commercial for a clothing store called *Así, Así*. Rewrite the commercial using the correct forms of the adjectives.

(Bueno) días, señoras y señores. Me llamo Manolo Mentiroso. Yo trabajo en la *(grande)* tienda de ropa *Así, Así*. En mi tienda *(grande)* hay ropa *(bonito)* y muy *(barato)*. En mi tienda hay jeans *(negro, gris, marrón y azul)*. ¡Y sólo cuestan 99 pesos! Para el invierno hay *(bueno)* suéteres
5 *(canadiense)* para las noches *(largo)* cuando hace mucho frío. ¡Y no son *(caro)*! ¿Esquían Uds.? En mi tienda hay bufandas *(largo)* y guantes de muchos colores. Hay ropa para muchachos y muchachas *(alto y bajo)*. Para *(bueno)* ropa *(bonito y barato)*, la tienda *Así, Así* es la *(primero)* tienda de la ciudad.

C **Hablemos de ti.**
1. ¿Qué ropa llevas hoy? ¿Qué ropa lleva tu profesor(a)?
2. ¿Qué tiempo hace? ¿Hace mal tiempo?
3. ¿Cómo es tu escuela?
4. ¿Eres un(a) buen(a) estudiante? ¿Siempre haces la tarea o sólo a veces?   .

Práctica A
1. ¿Es una tienda nueva? No, es una tienda vieja.
2. ¿Es una mala profesora? *or:* ¿Es una profesora mala? No, es una gran profesora.
3. ¿Es una moto cara? No, es una moto barata.
4. ¿Es el primer tren? No, es el tren próximo.
5. ¿Es un libro malo? *or:* ¿Es un mal libro? No, es un libro bueno. *or:* un buen libro.
6. ¿Es una cinta larga? No, es una cinta corta.
7. ¿Es un barco pequeño? No, es un barco grande.
8. ¿Es una casa blanca? No, es una casa roja.

Práctica B
line 1: Buenos
line 2: gran / grande
line 3: bonita / barata / negros, grises, marrones y
line 4: azules / buenos
line 5: canadienses / largas
line 6: caros / largas
line 7: altos y bajos
line 8: buena / bonita y barata / primera

Práctica C
Answers will vary.

REPASO

Notes: Answers to the
Repaso and **Tema** appear in
the pre-chapter teacher pages.

Notes: Review of:
1. compound subject
   ir a(l)
2. *ir a* + infinitive
3. *–ar* verbs
   en + vehicle
4. *–ar* verbs
   indefinite article
   adjective agreement and
   position
   use of subject
   pronoun for emphasis or
   contrast
5. Adverbs of time
   ir a + infinitive
   de(l) . . . a(l)

Look carefully at the model sentences. Then put the English cues into Spanish to form new sentences based on the models.

1. *Tú y yo vamos juntos a la escuela.*
   (She and Ana are going to the post office together.)
   (He and I are going to the drugstore together.)
   (You (formal) *and Víctor are going to the country together.)*

2. *Va a nadar en la piscina.*
   (He's going to read in the library.)
   (We're going to work in the bank.)
   (They're going to wait in the station.)

3. *Viajo en barco.*
   (He's traveling by car.)
   (You're (fam.) *traveling by bike.)*
   (You're (pl.) *traveling by train.)*

4. *Busco unos periódicos viejos. Él va a comprar un gran libro.*
   (We're looking for some red jackets. I'm going to buy a good suit.)
   (They're waiting for a slow bus. You (fam.) *are going to take the first train.)*
   (You (formal) *are listening to some old records. We're going to look for a good tape.)*

5. *Mañana voy a tomar un autobús del hotel a la estación.*
   (Tonight she's going to go on foot from the swimming pool to the party.)
   (Afterwards we're going to carry the flag from the school to the plaza.)
   (On Sunday you (fam.) *are going to take the subway home from church.)*

TEMA

Transparency 24

Enrichment: You may want to expand the practice in the **Tema** by having students prepare two questions based on each of the five illustrations. The preparation can be done in class as oral pair work or as written homework.

Put the English captions into Spanish to form a paragraph.

1. Pablo and Enrique are going to the airport together.

2. They're going to study in Mexico.

3. They're traveling by plane.

4. Pablo is listening to some new tapes. Enrique is going to read a good book.

5. Later they're going to take a taxi from the airport to downtown.

REDACCIÓN

Now you are ready to write your own dialogue or paragraph. Choose one of the following topics.

1. Expand the *Tema* by adding four to six sentences about Pablo and Enrique. What are they like? Where are they from? What are they going to do on weekends in Mexico?

2. Imagine a conversation between Pablo and Enrique, and create a series of talk balloons for pictures 1 through 5.

3. Write a four- to six-sentence paragraph about what you are going to do next summer. Are you going to travel? Are you going to go to the country? Tell some of the things you want to do during the summer. Do you like vacations? Or do you prefer to go to school?

A ¿Qué es . . . ?

Identify each of the following places. Use *es* or *son* and the correct indefinite article.

1.   2.   3.

4.   5.   6

B Ir a la ciudad

Complete each sentence using the correct form of the verb *ir*.

1. Ella _____ a la estación.
2. Después (yo) _____ a casa.
3. ¿_____ Ud. a la piscina ahora?
4. Paco y yo _____ a la farmacia.
5. Ellos nunca _____ al centro.
6. (Tú) _____ a la biblioteca, ¿no?
7. ¿_____ Uds. a llevar botas?

C ¿Adónde vas?

Answer each question by writing a complete sentence. Follow the model.

> ¿Adónde van Uds.? (iglesia)
> *Vamos a la iglesia.*

1. ¿Adónde va Ud.? (centro)
2. ¿Adónde van tus amigas? (campo)
3. ¿Adónde vas? (hotel)
4. ¿Adónde van Luis y tú? (ciudad)
5. ¿Adónde va la muchacha? (hospital)
6. ¿Adónde van tus compañeros de clase? (banco)

D Mañana

Rewrite each sentence, changing it from the present to the future using *ir a*. Follow the model.

> Entro en la escuela. (más tarde)
> *Voy a entrar en la escuela más tarde.*

1. ¿Compras una falda nueva? (mañana)
2. Ellos toman el sol. (hoy)
3. Esquiamos en Chile. (el año próximo)
4. Él escucha las cintas. (después)
5. No canto en la fiesta. (la semana próxima)
6. ¿Ud. habla por teléfono? (esta noche)

E ¿Cómo vas?

Ask and answer. Follow the model.

> ¿Quieres ir a pie?
> *No, prefiero ir en taxi.*

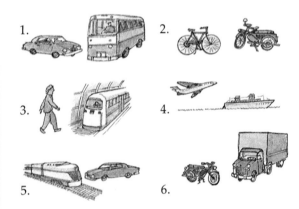

1.   2.

3.   4.

5.   6.

F Bueno y malo

Rewrite the sentences using the correct form of the adjective either before or after the noun.

1. El señor Marcos es un *profesor*. (bueno)
2. El lunes es el *día* de la semana. (primero)
3. Hace *tiempo* hoy. (malo)
4. Es un *bolígrafo*. (bueno)
5. Es una *noche*, ¿no? (malo)
6. Madrid es una *ciudad*. (grande)
7. Don Quijote y Lazarillo de Tormes son *libros* españoles. (grande)

Sustantivos

el aeropuerto
el autobús, *pl.* los autobuses
el avión, *pl.* los aviones
el banco
el barco
la biblioteca
el camión, *pl.* los camiones
el campo
la casa
el centro
la ciudad
el coche
el correo
la estación, *pl.* las estaciones
    (*station*)
la farmacia
el fin de semana, *pl.* los fines de
    semana
el hospital
el hotel
la iglesia
el metro
la moto
la piscina
la plaza
el taxi
el tren

Adjetivos

bueno (buen), -a
gran
juntos, -as
lento, -a
malo (mal), -a
primero (primer), -a
próximo, -a
rápido, -a
solo, -a

Adjetivos posesivos

mis
tus

Artículos indefinidos

unos, -as

Verbos

esperar
tomar
viajar

(yo) quiero
(tú) quieres

Adverbios

después
nunca
siempre

Preposiciones

a(l)
durante

Palabra interrogativa

¿adónde?

Expresiones

a casa
a pie
¡bueno!
en + *vehicles*
esta noche
ir a + *infinitive*
vamos a + *infinitive*

DOS CULTURAS INDIAS

A thousand years ago the Incan emperor could send a message from Cuzco, in the south of Peru, to northern Colombia in just one week. Today it might even take a bit longer. The Incan postal service was a lot like the pony express of the American West—but without ponies. A runner carried the information for a short distance and passed it on to another runner. They traveled along a highly developed system of roads and bridges that extended for 2,000 miles, most of it high in the Andes Mountains.

The Incas were not only excellent road builders, but they were also marvelous architects and engineers. They built gigantic fortresses and palaces using carefully cut boulders, many of which were the size of trucks. They fit these huge boulders together so perfectly and so tightly that today—many hundreds of years later—you cannot slip a piece of paper between one boulder and the next.

The Mayas of Central America lived in an entirely different kind of world—the hot, dense rain forests of Guatemala, Belize, and southeastern Mexico. Every foot of the land had to be hacked out of the jungle. As soon as a space had been cleared, the jungle began to overrun it again. After the Mayas were conquered by neighboring tribes around 1450, their cities disappeared under thick vegetation. Many of them were not seen again until the nineteenth century, and others may still lie hidden.

The Incan civilization suffered the impact of the Spanish conquest and was finally destroyed around 1572. And yet even today something of those worlds remains. Go to the modern city of Cuzco, with its automobiles and tall buildings, and you can still find people who speak Quechua, the language of the Incas. Go to the jungles of the Yucatán, a few miles from popular tourist resorts, and you will still hear Maya being spoken.

PALABRAS NUEVAS I

¿Dónde está?

el estadio

el almacén
pl. los almacenes

el restaurante

la oficina

el museo

el policía

el teatro

el parque

la fuente

Yo estoy aquí.

Ud. está allí.

Él está allá.

el café

If students ask: Related vocabulary you may want to present: *el edificio*, building; *la acera*, sidewalk; *el camarero / la camarera*, waiter / waitress; *la película*, movie.

Es divertido.

Es aburrido.

inteligente

Está aburrido.

tonto, –a

CONTEXTO COMUNICATIVO 2

1 RAÚL   Perdón, señor. ¿**Dónde está** el Teatro Colón?

POLICÍA   Allí **en** la esquina, **a la izquierda de** la biblioteca.

Variaciones:
- a la izquierda de → **a la derecha de**
- de la biblioteca → **del** restaurante

¿dónde está?	*where is?*
en	here: *on*
(a) la izquierda (de)	*(to) the left (of)*
(a) la derecha (de)	*(to) the right (of)*
de(l)	*of the, from the*

2 LUIS   Hay una **obra de teatro** bastante divertida en el Teatro Colón.

ESTER   Al contrario. Es muy aburrida.

- divertida → **interesante**
- bastante divertida → nueva
  aburrida → vieja

la obra de teatro   *play*

interesante   *interesting*

3	SERGIO	¿Cuál es **la dirección** del museo?	**la dirección,** *pl.* **las direcciones** *address*
	RAQUEL	**Avenida** Juárez 89. **Está** allá, **a la vuelta de la esquina.**	**la avenida** *avenue*
	SERGIO	¿**Enfrente del** parque?	**está** *it's*
	RAQUEL	Sí.	**a la vuelta de la esquina** *around the corner*

- enfrente de → **al lado de**
- enfrente de → **cerca de**

enfrente de *across from, opposite*
al lado de *next to, beside*
cerca de *near, close to*

4	PEDRO	¿Quieres ir al parque?
	NORMA	¿Está **lejos de** aquí?
	PEDRO	Pues, está **detrás del** hotel, **entre** el museo y el estadio.
	NORMA	Entonces, prefiero ir al **partido de** fútbol.

- lejos de → cerca de
- detrás del → enfrente del
- partido de fútbol → partido de tenis

lejos de *far from*
detrás de *behind*
entre *between*
el partido (de + deporte**)** *game; match*

5	ARTURO	¿**De quién** es el coche nuevo?
	ANITA	Es **de la señorita Miranda.**
	ARTURO	¿Quién es ella?
	ANITA	Es mi profesora de español. Es muy **simpática.**

- nuevo → azul y blanco
- la señorita → la señora
- simpática → interesante

¿de quién? *whose?*
de + noun ___'s; ___s'
simpático, -a *nice, pleasant*

6	CARMEN	Nunca voy a la tienda San José.
	OSCAR	¿Por qué no?
	CARMEN	Porque los vendedores allí son **antipáticos.**

- a la tienda → al almacén
- antipáticos → tontos
- antipáticos → lentos

antipático, -a *unpleasant, not nice*

7	ANITA	¿Dónde está tu moto?
	PABLO	Está allí, **delante de** la farmacia.

- delante de → detrás de
- de la farmacia → del café

delante de *in front of*

Enrichment: Write *aburrido, a la derecha, cerca de, simpático, delante de* on the board. Ask for the opposite of each (*interesante / divertido, a la izquierda, lejos de, antipático, detrás de*). Practice the new prepositions by asking questions about the location of classroom objects and where students are sitting.

En El Retiro en Madrid

PRÁCTICA

A **¿Dónde están?** Mira el mapa. Pregunta y contesta según el modelo.

ESTUDIANTE A *¿Está la farmacia al lado o enfrente del museo?*
ESTUDIANTE B *Está al lado del museo.*

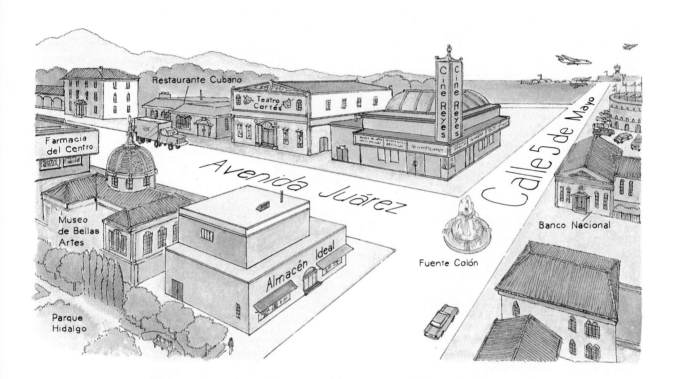

Práctica A
1. cerca
2. entre el restaurante y el cine
3. enfrente
4. cerca
5. detrás
6. enfrente
7. en la esquina
8. entre la farmacia y el almacén
9. enfrente
10. enfrente
11. delante

1. ¿Está el almacén cerca o lejos de la fuente?
2. ¿Está el teatro enfrente del restaurante o entre el restaurante y el cine?
3. ¿Está el cine enfrente o detrás del almacén?
4. ¿Está el estadio lejos o cerca del centro?
5. ¿Está el parque detrás o enfrente del almacén?
6. ¿Está el banco enfrente o al lado del cine?
7. ¿Está el cine en la esquina o al lado del restaurante?
8. ¿Está el museo detrás de o entre la farmacia y el almacén?
9. ¿Está el museo al lado o enfrente del teatro?
10. ¿Está la farmacia enfrente o detrás del restaurante?
11. ¿Está el camión delante o detrás del restaurante?

Reteach / Extra Help: If your class needs more help with directions and locations, before doing Ex. A, have students work in pairs asking and answering *¿Dónde está _____?* with the visuals on pp. 146 and 174. Then go over the map in Ex. A with the class before assigning the exercise as written class work or homework.

B ¿Qué hay? Contesta según el mapa.

1. ¿Qué hay al lado del museo?
2. ¿Qué hay enfrente de la farmacia?
3. ¿Qué hay entre el restaurante y el cine?
4. ¿Qué hay lejos del centro?
5. ¿Qué hay cerca del estadio?
6. ¿Qué hay detrás del almacén?
7. ¿Qué hay al lado del teatro?
8. Estás en el teatro. ¿Qué hay a la izquierda del museo?
9. ¿Qué hay enfrente del teatro?
10. Estás en el museo. ¿Qué hay a la derecha del restaurante?
11. ¿Qué hay en la esquina de la Calle 5 de Mayo y la Avenida Juárez?

C Hablemos de ti.

1. ¿Cómo es tu casa?
2. ¿Cuál es tu dirección?
3. ¿En qué calle está tu escuela? ¿Está tu casa cerca o lejos de la escuela? ¿Qué hay enfrente de la escuela? ¿Hay una bandera delante de la escuela? ¿De qué color es?
4. ¿Te gusta ir a partidos de fútbol americano o de béisbol? ¿Con quién vas? ¿Cómo vas?

Practice Sheet 5–1   Workbook Exs. A–B

3 Tape Manual Exs. 1–2   Quiz 5–1

Casas en Quito y en México

Práctica B
1. el almacén o la farmacia
2. el restaurante
3. el teatro
4. el aeropuerto o el estadio
5. el aeropuerto o el banco
6. el parque
7. el cine o el restaurante
8. el almacén
9. el museo
10. el teatro
11. la fuente, el cine, el almacén

Práctica C
Answers will vary.

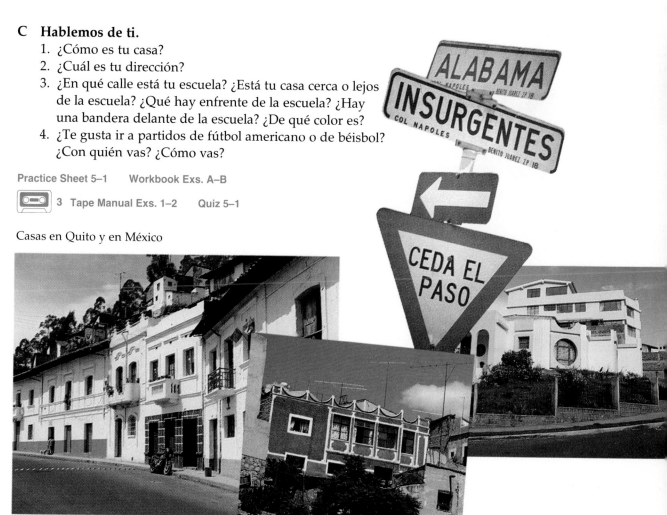

APLICACIONES

Discretionary

¿Dónde está El Morro?* 4

Notes: Make sure students understand the meanings of cognates that have not been glossed: *aventuras*, adventures; *famoso*, famous.

Diálogo
1. de Nuevo México
2. a El Morro
3. San Juan
4. No está muy lejos.
5. no; porque está (demasiado) lejos
6. Van a ir en taxi.

Las aventuras de dos estudiantes de Nuevo México en Puerto Rico.

LAURA   Allí hay un policía. Vamos a preguntar dónde está el famoso Morro de San Juan.

5   ANDRÉS   No, voy a mirar el mapa.

LAURA   Prefiero hablar con el policía. Buenas tardes, señor, ¿dónde está El Morro?

POLICÍA   No muy lejos, señorita. A la vuelta de la esquina.

ANDRÉS   ¿Cómo vamos? ¿A pie?

10   POLICÍA   ¡Por supuesto![1] Sigan por[2] aquí. En la esquina, a la izquierda, está la calle San Sebastián. Sigan por San Sebastián. Al lado del café, van a la derecha. Después, a la izquierda y después a la derecha. El Morro está allí, junto al mar.[3]

15   ANDRÉS   Muchas gracias, señor.

LAURA   ¡Taxi, taxi! ¿Cuánto cuesta ir de aquí a El Morro?

[1]**por supuesto**   *of course*   [2]**sigan por**   *follow along*
[3]**junto al mar**   *by the sea*

* El Morro is a fortress built by the Spaniards between 1539 and 1787 to guard the Bay of San Juan against attacks by English, French, and Dutch pirates.

Preguntas

Contesta según el diálogo.
1. ¿De dónde son los estudiantes?   2. ¿Adónde van?   3. ¿En qué ciudad está El Morro?   4. Según el policía, ¿está El Morro cerca o lejos? 5. ¿Van a ir a El Morro a pie? ¿Por qué?   6. ¿Cómo van a ir?

Culture: As a research project, have students find out more about El Morro and the pirates who plundered the Caribbean in the sixteenth and seventeenth centuries.

Participación

Working with a partner, prepare directions describing how to get to a nearby place. Use your school as a starting point. For example:

ESTUDIANTE A   Perdón, señor(ita). ¿Dónde está el parque?
ESTUDIANTE B   A la vuelta de la esquina y enfrente del museo.
ESTUDIANTE A   Muchas gracias.

PRONUNCIACIÓN 5

In Spanish the letters *b* and *v* are pronounced alike.

A Except after a vowel, both are pronounced like the *b* in the English word "mob."
Escucha y repite.

| bien | bailar | vamos | ¿verdad? |

B When *b* and *v* come after a vowel, make the sound by bringing your lips together until they *almost* touch. This sound is softer than *b* or *v* in English.
Escucha y repite.

hablar	rubio	Cuba	sábado	autobús
nuevo	joven	avión	lavar	primavera
la blusa	la bicicleta	a veces	ella va	

C Escucha y repite.

Llevan un vestido nuevo. El autobús blanco es nuevo.
Vamos a viajar en avión. A veces bailamos los sábados.

El Morro en San Juan,
Puerto Rico

PALABRAS NUEVAS II

¿Cómo estás?

la cabina telefónica

555–12-12

la guía
telefónica

cansado, -a

triste

loco, -a

enfermo, -a

contento, -a

preocupado, -a

**CONTEXTO
COMUNICATIVO**

7

1 ALICIA **¿Qué pasa,** Jorge?

JORGE Quiero hablar con mi **novia,** pero **la línea** está
ocupada.

ALICIA **¡Qué mala suerte!**
(*Un poco* más tarde)

JORGE **¡Qué lástima!** La línea **todavía** está ocupada.

Variaciones:

■ novia → amiga

If students ask: Related vocabulary you
may want to present: *enojado, -a,* angry; *la
llamada telefónica,* phone call; *llamar por
teléfono,* to telephone.

¿qué pasa? *what's going on?,*
what's happening?

el novio, la novia *boyfriend,*
girlfriend

la línea *line*

ocupado, -a *busy*

¡qué (mala) suerte! *what (bad)*
luck!

un poco *a little*

¡qué lástima! *that's too bad!,*
that's a shame!

todavía *still*

---

2 SRA. MUÑOZ **¿Aló?**

RICARDO Buenos días, señora. ¿Está Tomás en casa?

SRA. MUÑOZ Sí, **un momento,** por favor. . . . Tomás está ocupado. ¿Quieres esperar?

RICARDO Sí, señora. **Por supuesto.**

- buenos días → buenas tardes
- por supuesto → ¡cómo no!

¿aló?	*hello? (on phone)*
un momento	*just a moment*
por supuesto	*of course*

3 PATRICIA ¿Aló?

ÁNGEL ¡Hola, Pati! ¿Qué tal? ¿Cómo estás?

PATRICIA **Estoy mal,** Ángel.

ÁNGEL **¡No me digas!** ¿Qué pasa?

PATRICIA Hay un examen mañana y estoy muy preocupada.

- ¡no me digas! → ¡qué lástima!

estar (yo estoy, tú estás) *to be*
mal *not well*
¡no me digas! *you don't say!*

EN OTRAS PARTES

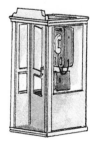

También se dice *la cabina de teléfono* o *la casilla telefónica.*

También se dice *la guía de teléfonos.*

¿Aló?

También se dice *Bueno* (México), *Diga* o *Dígame* (España), *Hola* (Argentina y Uruguay), *Oigo* (Cuba y Puerto Rico) y *A ver* (Colombia).

Enrichment: After going over the mini-dialogues, ask for volunteers to act them out, using paper cups as "telephones."

Palabras Nuevas II **183**

PRÁCTICA

A **¿Cómo estás?** Imagina que hablas por teléfono con varios amigos. Pregunta y contesta según el modelo.

> **ESTUDIANTE A** *¿Cómo estás, Luisa?*
> **ESTUDIANTE B** *Estoy enferma. No voy a ir a la escuela mañana.*

1. Cristina
2. Ernesto
3. Vicente
4. Ángela
5. Federico
6. Eduardo
7. Teresa
8. Pedro

B **¿Quieres comer tacos?** Imagina que tú y un(a) amigo(a) son turistas y que miran una guía turística (*tourist guide*). Pregunta y contesta según el modelo.

¿Quieres comer comida mexicana?
ESTUDIANTE A *Quiero comer comida mexicana.*
ESTUDIANTE B *Vamos a buscar el número de El Taco Picante.*
ESTUDIANTE A *Bueno. Es el dos ocho tres, cero cinco, veintitrés.*

1. ¿Quieres leer un libro de horror?
2. ¿Quieres comprar zapatos?
3. ¿Quieres comer comida cubana?
4. ¿Quieres comprar un vestido?
5. ¿Quieres tomar un taxi al museo?
6. ¿Quieres ir al hotel donde hablan inglés?
7. ¿Quieres ir al Canadá en autobús?

Práctica B
1. … de La Librería El Misterio.
   … Es el siete uno tres, cuarenta, veinte.
2. … de La Zapatería El Zócalo.
   … Es el cinco cuatro cuatro, treinta, treinta y seis.
3. … del Restaurante La Habana.
   … Es el ocho cero tres, diecisiete, diecisiete.
4. … de la Tienda San José.
   … Es el siete dos cero, veinte, diecinueve.
5. … de El Taxi Lento.
   … Es el cuatro ocho ocho, cero siete, cero siete.
6. … del Hotel Internacional.
   … Es el ocho cero uno, quince, quince.
7. … de Autobuses Día y Noche.
   … Es el tres dos siete, diez, once.

Práctica C

1. … ¿Cuál es la dirección de la Librería El Misterio?
   Avenida José Martí cincuenta y siete.
2. … ¿Cuál es la dirección de la Zapatería El Zócalo?
   Calle Cinco de Febrero dieciocho.
3. ¿ … del Restaurante La Habana?
   Calle Bolívar ocho.
4. ¿ … de la Tienda San José?
   Avenida Díaz diecisiete.
5. ¿… de El Taxi Lento?
   Avenida Santa Fe veintidós.
6. ¿ … del Hotel Internacional?
   Avenida Veinticinco de Mayo noventa.
7. ¿ … de Autobuses Día y Noche?
   Calle Córdoba trece.

Práctica D
Answers may include:
1. ¡Qué suerte! o ¡No me digas!
2. ¡Por supuesto! o ¡Cómo no!
3. ¡Uf!
4. ¡No me digas!
5. ¡Qué mala suerte! o ¡Qué lástima!
6. ¡Al contrario! o ¡Uf!
7. ¡Felicidades!
8. ¡No me digas! o ¡Qué mala suerte!
9. ¡Qué mala suerte! o ¡Uf! o ¡No me digas!

C **¿Y la dirección?** Ahora busca en la guía turística de la Práctica B para indicar *(tell)* la dirección. Pregunta y contesta según el modelo.

> ¿Quieres comer comida mexicana?
>
> ESTUDIANTE A   *Quiero comer comida mexicana. ¿Cuál es la dirección de El Taco Picante?*
>
> ESTUDIANTE B   *Calle Santa Marta 9.*

D **¡Qué suerte!** ¿Cómo reaccionas *(do you react)*? Escoge *(choose)* una expresión de la lista. Contesta según el modelo.

> Mario está enfermo.
>
> ESTUDIANTE A   *Mario está enfermo.*
>
> ESTUDIANTE B   *¡Qué mala suerte!*

1. Mis amigas(os) van a viajar al Caribe.
2. Vamos a la fiesta, ¿no?
3. No me gusta estudiar para exámenes.
4. Pablo va a ir al aeropuerto a pie.
5. La línea todavía está ocupada.
6. Soy muy guapo(a), ¿no?
7. Mañana es mi cumpleaños.
8. No hay pan.
9. El restaurante está muy lejos de aquí.
10. Nieva.
11. Voy a casa. Es tarde y estoy muy cansado(a).
12. El tren está todavía en la estación.
13. Mi novio(a) está enfermo(a).

¡Al contrario!
¡Cómo no!
¡Felicidades!
¡No me digas!
¡Por supuesto!
¡Qué lástima!
¡Qué mala suerte!
¡Qué suerte!
¡Uf!

Practice Sheet 5–2

Workbook Exs. C–D

Tape Manual Exs. 3–4 8

Quiz 5–2

E **Hablemos de ti.**

1. ¿Cómo estás hoy? ¿Estás contento(a)? ¿Triste? ¿Estás preocupado(a)? ¿Por qué?
2. ¿Te gusta hablar por teléfono? ¿Hablas mucho por teléfono? ¿Con quién hablas?

10. ¡No me digas! o ¡Qué (mala) suerte!
11. ¡Uf! o ¡Qué lástima!
12. ¡Qué suerte! o ¡Por supuesto!
13. ¡Qué lástima! o ¡No me digas!

Práctica E
Answers will vary.

Horas de rebaja para América Latina:
Días de la semana, de 08:00 a 17:30 horas, y domingos todo el día.

Para Estados Unidos:
Días de la semana, de 18:00 a 05:00 horas, y domingos todo el día.

Para Europ…

ACTIVIDAD

¡No me digas!   You and a partner should imagine that a friend has called to tell you something surprising or exciting. Without conferring, each of you should write down *your* half of the conversation. Write only your responses to what the caller is saying. Write three or four questions or exclamations. Begin with *¿Qué pasa?* For example:

TÚ	¿Qué pasa?
TÚ	¡Qué mala suerte!
TÚ	¡No me digas!

Show your surprise or excitement by saying such things as *¡Felicidades!, ¡Por supuesto!,* and *¡Cómo no!* Leave two blank lines between responses. Now exchange papers with your partner. Each of you will then fill in what the person who called might have said. For example:

TÚ	¿Qué pasa?
TU AMIGO	*Hay un gato negro en la piscina.*
TÚ	¡Qué mala suerte!
TU AMIGO	*¡Sí! Pero nada muy bien.*
TÚ	¡No me digas!
TU AMIGO	*Sí. Él y yo vamos a nadar juntos. Hasta luego.*

Afterward you may want to read your conversations to the class.

ESTUDIO DE PALABRAS

Many words that begin with *s* + a consonant in English begin with *es* in Spanish.

estadio	*stadium*	España	*Spain*	estación	*station*
estudiante	*student*	escuela	*school*	estudiar	*to study*

Can you guess what these Spanish words mean?

estricto   espléndido   especial   espectacular

Words that are spelled with a double *s* in English are spelled with a single *s* in Spanish.

clase   clásico   profesor

What do you think these words mean?

profesión   pasar   pasaporte   pesimista   necesario

EXPLICACIONES I

Usos del verbo *ser*

◆ **OBJECTIVES:**

TO DESCRIBE PEOPLE AND TELL WHO THEY ARE

TO GIVE REASONS

You already know that the verb *ser* means "to be" and many of the ways it is used.

1 To tell the time of day and the date.

Son las dos.	*It's two o'clock.*
Es el 3 de julio.	*It's July 3.*

2 To tell where someone or something comes from.

Somos de los Estados Unidos.   *We're from the United States.*

3 To tell what someone's nationality is.

Carlos **es** puertorriqueño.   *Carlos is Puerto Rican.*

Reteach / Review: Refer to each of the mini-dialogues where the first five uses of *ser* were introduced: (1) time of day: p. 34, date: pp. 20–21; (2) p. 11; (3) p. 84; (4) p. 90; (5) p. 84. All the forms of *ser* are given on p. 97.

4 To describe characteristics that are usually associated with a certain person or thing.

Laura **es** muy simpática.	*Laura is very nice.*
Los camiones **son** grandes.	*The trucks are big.*

5 To connect a noun or a pronoun to another noun or pronoun.

Carlota **es** mi amiga.	*Carlota is my friend.*
¿**Son** ellas tus profesoras?	*Are they your teachers?*

6 After the verb *ser*, we usually do not use the indefinite article (*un, una*) with occupations or professions unless we are using an adjective.

El Sr. Cárdenas **es profesor.**	*Mr. Cárdenas is a teacher.*
Soy estudiante.	*I'm a student.*

But:

El Sr. Cárdenas **es un buen profesor.**	*Mr. Cárdenas is a good teacher.*
Soy un estudiante inteligente.	*I'm a smart student.*

Reteach / Extra Help: Before students do the three exercises in the **Práctica**, you may want to review the forms of *ser*. Do a chain drill or have pairs do Ex. B on p. 99. Circulate to give help where needed.

PRÁCTICA

A ¿Quién eres? Contesta las preguntas.

1. ¿Cuál es la fecha de hoy?
2. ¿Qué día es hoy?
3. ¿Qué hora es?
4. ¿De dónde eres?
5. ¿Eres español(a)?
6. ¿Eres pelirrojo(a)?
7. ¿Cuántos estudiantes son morenos en tu clase de español?
8. ¿Cómo eres?
9. ¿Eres profesor(a) o estudiante?
10. ¿Eres un(a) buen(a) estudiante?
11. Y ahora, ¿qué hora es?

Práctica A
Answers will vary.

B ¿Cómo es? Imagina que tú no recuerdas *(remember)* cómo son estas personas *(these people)*. Pregunta y contesta según el modelo.

> ¿David? / alto
> **ESTUDIANTE A** *¿Es alto David?*
> **ESTUDIANTE B** *No. Es bajo.*

1. ¿la señorita Díaz? / fea
2. ¿Pedro? / rubio
3. ¿Bárbara? / joven
4. ¿Leonardo? / delgado
5. ¿el señor Torres? / tonto
6. ¿Alicia? / antipática

Práctica B
1. ¿Es fea la señorita Díaz? No. Es guapa (bonita).
2. ¿Es rubio Pedro? No. Es moreno (pelirrojo).
3. ¿Es joven Bárbara? No. Es vieja.
4. ¿Es delgado Leonardo? No. Es gordo.
5. ¿Es tonto el señor Torres? No. Es inteligente.
6. ¿Es antipática Alicia? No. Es simpática.

C ¿Por qué? Imagina que tú y un(a) amigo(a) hablan de *(about)* unos compañeros. Pregunta y contesta según el modelo. Usa la forma correcta del adjetivo.

aburrido	bonito	inteligente	simpático
antipático	guapo	joven	tonto

> estudiar / Pedro
> **ESTUDIANTE A** *¿Por qué estudias con Pedro?*
> **ESTUDIANTE B** *Porque es muy inteligente.*

1. hablar por teléfono / Tomás
2. ir a la fiesta / Andrea y Sara
3. trabajar / Carmen
4. no hablar / Ramón y Víctor
5. no ir al cine / Pilar
6. no ir a jugar al tenis / Silvia y Esteban
7. ir a comer / Victoria
8. no bailar / Raúl
9. no ir al centro / Beatriz y Sonia

Practice Sheet 5–3   Quiz 5–3

Práctica C
The responses may vary, and some students might replace *muy* with *demasiado* or *bastante*. They might include:
1. ¿Por qué hablas por teléfono con Tomás? Porque es muy inteligente (simpático).
2. ¿ ... vas a la fiesta con ...? ... son muy simpáticas.
3. ¿ ... trabajas con ... ? ... es muy inteligente.
4. ¿ ... no hablas con ... ? ... son muy tontos (aburridos).
5. ¿ ... no vas al cine con ...? ... es muy aburrida.
6. ¿... no vas a jugar al tenis con ... ? ... son muy tontos (jóvenes).
7. ¿ ... vas a comer con ... ? ... es muy guapa (simpática).
8. ¿ ... no bailas con ... ? ... es muy antipático (joven).
9. ¿ ... no vas al centro con ...? ... son muy aburridas.

La preposición *de*

◆ **OBJECTIVE:**

TO IDENTIFY OWNERSHIP

Reteach / Review: It may be helpful to refer back to the mini-dialogues where some of the uses of *de* were introduced: (1) prepositions: 1, 3, 4, and 7 on pp. 175–176; (2) 5 on p. 176; (3) 3 on p. 11; (4) 5 on p. 176.

You know that we use *de* to mean "from" or "of."

¿**De** dónde es Ud.?	*Where are you **from**?*
Viajan **de** México al Canadá.	*They're traveling **from** Mexico to Canada.*
Hoy es el primer día **de** la semana.	*Today is the first day **of** the week.*

1 We use *de* in many expressions

la América del Norte (del Sur)	el número de teléfono
la clase de español	la obra de teatro
el día de fiesta	el partido de fútbol
el fin de semana	la tienda de ropa
la hoja de papel	el traje de baño

and as part of many prepositions: *al lado de, cerca de, detrás de,* and so forth.

2 We also use *de* with nouns to show possession. If there are two nouns we usually repeat *de.*

Es la casa **de Luis y de Ana.**	*It's **Luis and Ana's** house.*
Las botas **de la profesora** son nuevas.	*The **teacher's** boots are new.*

3 Remember that *de + el → del.*

¿Son Uds. **del** Perú?	*Are you **from** Peru?*
La oficina **del** Sr. Cabrera es grande.	*Mr. Cabrera's office is large.*

4 To ask "whose?" we say *¿de quién es?* or *¿de quién son?* If we think something belongs to more than one person, we say *¿de quiénes son?*

¿**De quién es** la guitarra?	*Whose guitar is it?*
Es de Juan.	*It's Juan's.*
¿**De quién son** los carteles?	*Whose posters are they?*
Son de Silvia.	*They're Silvia's.*
¿**De quiénes son** las motos?	*Whose motorcycles are they?*
Son de los profesores.	*They're the teachers'.*

Reteach / Extra Help: In preparation for the **Práctica,** have students work in pairs to ask and answer *¿De quién / quiénes es / son ____?* about classmates' clothing and classroom objects.

PRÁCTICA

A Después de la fiesta. The party is over,
but a lot of guests have left things behind.
The hosts are trying to figure out what belongs
to whom. *Pregunta y contesta según el modelo.*
Usa "¿de quién . . . ?" o "¿de quiénes . . . ?"

ESTUDIANTE A	*¿De quién es el abrigo?*
ESTUDIANTE B	*Es de Silvia.*

Silvia

1. Bárbara 2. Tomás y Luz 3. Roberto 4. Beatriz

5. Susana y Jorge 6. Guillermo 7. Eduardo 8. Julia

B A limpiar la clase. Pretend that you and a classmate are
straightening up the classroom. One of you recognizes to whom
various things belong. *Pregunta y contesta según el modelo. Usa "¿de
quién . . . ?" o "¿de quiénes . . . ?"*

los periódicos / los muchachos

ESTUDIANTE A	*¿De quiénes son los periódicos?*
ESTUDIANTE B	*¿Los periódicos? Son de los muchachos.*

1. los lápices / el Sr. Vera
2. el mapa / la Sra. Díaz
3. las hojas de papel / Ana
4. el bolígrafo / el Sr. Arias
5. los cuadernos / Elena y Luz
6. las cintas / María y Pepe
7. el calendario / Luis
8. los dibujos / Pedro y Juan

Práctica A

1. ¿De quién es la guitarra?
   Es de Bárbara.
2. ¿De quiénes son los
   paraguas?
   Son de Tomás y de Luz.
3. ¿De quién es el disco?
   Es de Roberto.
4. ¿De quién es el guante?
   Es de Beatriz.
5. ¿De quiénes son las botas?
   Son de Susana y de Jorge.
6. ¿De quién es el sombrero?
   Es de Guillermo.
7. ¿De quién son las cintas?
   Son de Eduardo.
8. ¿De quién es la bufanda?
   Es de Julia.

Práctica B

1. ¿De quién son los lápices?
   ¿Los lápices? Son del
   Sr. Vera.
2. ¿De quién es el mapa?
   ¿El mapa? Es de la
   Sra. Díaz.
3. ¿De quién son las hojas de
   papel? ¿Las hojas de papel?
   Son de Ana.
4. ¿De quién es el bolígrafo?
   ¿El bolígrafo? Es del
   Sr. Arias.
5. ¿De quiénes son los
   cuadernos? ¿Los
   cuadernos? Son de Elena y
   de Luz.
6. ¿De quiénes son las
   cintas? ¿Las cintas? Son de
   María y de Pepe.
7. ¿De quién es el calendario?
   ¿El calendario? Es de Luis.
8. ¿De quiénes son los
   dibujos? ¿Los dibujos? Son
   de Pedro y de Juan.

El verbo *estar*

◆ **OBJECTIVES:**

TO TELL WHERE THINGS ARE LOCATED

TO TELL WHERE PEOPLE ARE

TO GIVE AND UNDERSTAND DIRECTIONS

You know that *ser* means "to be." But Spanish has another verb—*estar*—that also means "to be." They are used differently, though. Here are all of the forms of *estar* in the present tense. Note that the *yo* form is irregular and that the letter *a* has a written accent in all except the *nosotros* form.

INFINITIVO **estar**

	SINGULAR		PLURAL	
1	(yo)	**estoy**	(nosotros) (nosotras) }	**estamos**
2	(tú)	**estás**	(vosotros) (vosotras) }	**estáis**
3	Ud. (él) (ella) }	**está**	Uds. (ellos) (ellas) }	**están**

Notes: You may want to use mini-dialogues 1 and 4 on p. 175 and 1–3 on pp. 182–183 to show the singular forms of *estar*.

Enrichment: Reinforce the use of *estar* to express location by having volunteers move around the room asking *¿Dónde estoy?* The rest of the class will answer *Estás ___*.

One of the ways we use the verb *estar* is to tell where someone or something is located.

Estoy en la escuela. *I'm at school.*
San Juan **está** en Puerto Rico. *San Juan **is** in Puerto Rico.*

Here are some of the words you know that are used with the verb *estar* to show location.

en *in, at, on*
cerca de *near, close to*
lejos de *far from*
al lado de *next to, beside*
enfrente de *across from, opposite*

delante de *in front of*
detrás de *behind*
entre *between*
a la izquierda de *to the left of*
a la derecha de *to the right of*

SAN JUAN

PUERTO RICO

PRÁCTICA

A **¿Dónde están?** Mira el dibujo. Pregunta y contesta según el modelo.

> ¿el cine? / el parque
>
> **ESTUDIANTE A** *¿Dónde está el cine?*
> **ESTUDIANTE B** *Está al lado (a la derecha o cerca) del parque.*

1. ¿la escuela? / la biblioteca y el museo
2. ¿la biblioteca? / la escuela
3. ¿la moto? / el teatro
4. ¿el autobús? / el parque
5. ¿el autobús? / el coche
6. ¿la cabina telefónica? / la esquina
7. ¿la cabina telefónica? / el teatro
8. ¿los muchachos? / el parque
9. ¿tu oficina? / el parque

Práctica A
1. Está entre la biblioteca y el museo.
2. Está al lado (a la derecha) de la escuela.
3. Está delante del teatro.
4. Está delante del parque.
5. Está detrás del coche.
6. Está en la esquina.
7. Está al lado (a la izquierda) del teatro.
8. Están en el parque.
9. Está enfrente del parque.

Reteach / Extra Help: If your class finds Ex. A difficult, have volunteers model the first two items for the rest of the class. Alert students to the plural subject in 8 *(los muchachos).*

Explicaciones I   **193**

1. ¿Dónde está Cecilia? Está en Guadalajara. ¿Y dónde está Guadalajara? Está en México.
2. ¿Dónde están Luis y Marcos? Están en La Paz. ¿Y dónde está La Paz? Está en Bolivia.
3. ¿Dónde están los amigos de Luz? Están en Bogotá. ¿Y dónde está Bogotá? Está en Colombia.
4. ¿Dónde está Georgina? Está en Laredo. ¿Y dónde está Laredo? Está en Texas.
5. ¿Dónde está el señor Santos? Está en Las Vegas. ¿Y dónde está Las Vegas? Está en Nevada.
6. ¿Dónde están las amigas de Julia? Están en Tegucigalpa. ¿Y dónde está Tegucigalpa? Está en Honduras.
7. ¿Dónde está tu novio(a)? Está en San José. ¿Y dónde está San José? Está en Costa Rica.
8. ¿Dónde está Yolanda? Está en Viña del Mar? ¿Y dónde está Viña del Mar? Está en Chile.
9. ¿Dónde estamos (nosotros)? Estamos (or: Uds. están) en ... ¿Y dónde está ...? Está en ...

Práctica C
Answers will vary.

B ¿Dónde? ¿Dónde? Imagina que cuidas a un niño (baby-sitting). El niño pregunta dónde están estas personas y ciudades. Pregunta y contesta según el modelo.

Diego y Andrés / Madrid / España

ESTUDIANTE A *¿Dónde están Diego y Andrés?*

ESTUDIANTE B *Están en Madrid.*

ESTUDIANTE A *¿Y dónde está Madrid?*

ESTUDIANTE B *Está en España.*

1. Cecilia / Guadalajara / México
2. Luis y Marcos / La Paz / Bolivia
3. los amigos de Luz / Bogotá / Colombia
4. Georgina / Laredo / Texas
5. el señor Santos / Las Vegas / Nevada
6. las amigas de Julia / Tegucigalpa / Honduras
7. tu novio(a) / San José / Costa Rica
8. Yolanda / Viña del Mar / Chile
9. (nosotros) / _____ / _____

C Hablemos de ti.
1. Describe dónde estás en la clase de español con relación a dos o tres compañeros. Por ejemplo, ¿entre qué estudiantes estás? ¿Hay un estudiante a tu izquierda? ¿Quién es?
2. ¿Qué te gusta hacer cuando estás solo(a) en casa?
3. ¿A veces estás aburrido(a)? ¿Qué haces cuando estás aburrido(a) o triste?

Practice Sheets 5–5, 5–6   Workbook Exs. E–F   Tape Manual Ex. 7 [cassette] 10

Activity Master 5–1   Quiz 5–5

Un café en Buenos Aires

EL CAFÈ DEL PAS

Un nou local, molt a prop de Vostè.
Obert els diumenges i festius.
Laborables desde les 7,30 del matí.

Sandvitxos. Tapes. Entrepans.
Esmorzars i berenars.
Dinars i sopars ràpids.

Pàdua, 104 - Barcelona-6.

APLICACIONES

Discretionary

Notes: Sample dialogues for the **¿Qué pasa?** appear in the pre-chapter teacher pages.

El centro   Transparency 27

La plaza está en el centro de la ciudad. ¿Dónde está la farmacia?
¿Dónde está la cabina telefónica? ¿Cuántas tiendas hay en el dibujo?

Pilar and Héctor want to go shopping. Create a dialogue in which they
talk about what they are going to buy and how they are going to get to
the stores. You may want to use these words or phrases:

la tienda de ropa o de música	¿Cómo vamos?	en la calle
¿Vamos a comprar . . . ?	¿Dónde está?	prefiero

Aplicaciones   **195**

EXPLICACIONES II

Ser y estar

Notes: Refer to mini-dialogues 1–3, 5, and 6 on pp. 175–176 for examples of the different uses of *ser* and *estar*.

◆ **OBJECTIVES:**

TO DESCRIBE HOW PEOPLE ARE FEELING

TO DESCRIBE ORIGIN AND LOCATION

Reteach / Extra Help: Use the visuals on p. 174 or transparency 25 to reinforce the different uses of *ser* and *estar*. Point to the different places and ask *¿Qué es?* Then ask *¿Y dónde está?*

Práctica A
1. David es de Nueva York, ¿verdad? Sí, pero ahora está en Santo Domingo.
2. Diana y Julia son de Denver, ¿verdad? Sí, pero ahora están en Bolivia.
3. Gloria y Sara son de Chicago, ¿verdad? Sí, pero ahora están en Costa Rica.
4. Claudia es de Tampa, ¿verdad? Sí, pero ahora está en la Argentina.
5. Samuel y Patricia son de Richmond, ¿verdad? Sí, pero ahora están en el Ecuador.
6. Norma es de Albuquerque, ¿verdad? Sí, pero ahora está en Panamá.
7. Mario y Virginia son de San Francisco, ¿verdad? Sí, pero ahora están en el Uruguay.
8. Daniel es de Cleveland, ¿verdad? Sí, pero ahora está en Colombia.

You have a pretty good idea when to use *ser*, and you know that we use *estar* to talk about location: *Pedro es de Madrid, pero ahora está en Sevilla.* You also know that we use *ser* with adjectives to describe characteristics that are usually associated with a certain person or thing: tall, short, pretty, ugly, fat, thin, intelligent, and so on. We use *estar* to describe conditions that are *not* usually associated with that person or thing. It is often the equivalent of "to be" in the sense of "to feel."

Carmen está enferma.	*Carmen is sick. (She feels sick.)*
Pedro está muy contento.	*Pedro is very happy. (He feels happy.)*
Estás un poco triste hoy.	*You're a little sad today. (You feel sad.)*

Notice how the following sentences differ depending on whether we use *ser* or *estar*.

¿Cómo es Clara?	*What's Clara like? (her usual characteristics)*
¿Cómo está Clara?	*How is Clara? (how she feels)*
Tomás es aburrido.	*Tomás is boring. (He's a boring person.)*
Tomás está aburrido.	*Tomás is bored. (He feels bored.)*

PRÁCTICA

A Un año en la América Latina. Estos *(these)* estudiantes de los Estados Unidos pasan *(are spending)* el año en otros *(other)* países. Pregunta y contesta según el modelo.

> Laura / San Antonio / Venezuela
> ESTUDIANTE A *Laura es de San Antonio, ¿verdad?*
> ESTUDIANTE B *Sí, pero ahora está en Venezuela.*

1. David / Nueva York / Santo Domingo
2. Diana y Julia / Denver / Bolivia
3. Gloria y Sara / Chicago / Costa Rica
4. Claudia / Tampa / la Argentina
5. Samuel y Patricia / Richmond / el Ecuador
6. Norma / Albuquerque / Panamá
7. Mario y Virginia / San Francisco / el Uruguay
8. Daniel / Cleveland / Colombia

B **Un fin de semana largo.** Es lunes por la noche después de *(after)* un fin de semana largo. ¿Cómo están estas personas? Usa adjetivos de la lista. No uses ningún adjetivo más de dos veces. *(Don't use any adjective more than twice).* Sigue el modelo.

aburrido   contento   ocupado   triste
cansado   enfermo   preocupado

    (tú y yo)
    Estamos cansados.

1. Susana
2. Tomás
3. Carlos y César
4. Luisa y Alicia
5. tú y Alberto
6. Anita
7. (nosotras)
8. Uds.
9. (yo)
10. Ud.
11. Olga y yo
12. tú y ella

La ciudad de Sevilla al lado del Guadalquivir

C **En la agencia de viajes.** Completa la conversación con la forma correcta de *ser* o *estar*.

SR. PÉREZ   Buenos días, señor Díaz. ¿Cómo _____ Ud.?

SR. DÍAZ   Muy bien, gracias. ¿_____ Ud. ocupado?

SR. PÉREZ   No. ¿Qué desea Ud.?

SR. DÍAZ   Quiero ir a España. Me gusta mucho viajar.

5 SR. PÉREZ   Bueno. Madrid y Barcelona _____ ciudades muy grandes y bonitas.

SR. DÍAZ   Prefiero ir a Madrid.

SR. PÉREZ   El Hotel Cervantes _____ muy popular y no _____ demasiado caro. _____ en el centro, cerca de las tiendas y

10   los museos.

SR. DÍAZ   Y los teatros, ¿dónde _____? Me encantan las obras de teatro españolas.

SR. PÉREZ   Muchos teatros también _____ cerca del hotel.

SR. DÍAZ   ¡Qué suerte! (Yo) _____ muy contento. Muchas gracias,

15   señor Pérez.

D **Hablemos de ti.**

1. ¿Cómo es tu ciudad? ¿Hay muchos parques? ¿Hay fuentes bonitas en los parques? ¿Hay muchos almacenes en tu ciudad? ¿Están cerca de tu casa?

2. ¿Cómo son los restaurantes en tu ciudad? ¿Hay buenos restaurantes cerca de tu casa? ¿Dónde están?

3. ¿Vas al teatro a veces? ¿Te gustan las obras de teatro? ¿Hay un teatro o un cine muy cerca de tu casa? ¿Dónde está?

Un ballet en el Teatro Colón de Buenos Aires

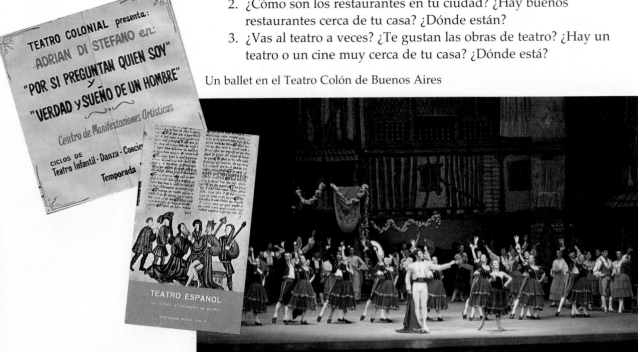

Soy guapo y estoy contento.

Soy guapo y estoy contento. Divide the class into groups of four of five. The first person should describe himself or herself accurately or imaginatively by making one statement that includes *ser* and one that includes *estar*. For example:

Soy guapo(a) y estoy contento(a).

The next person must repeat that person's self-description and then give his or her own. For example:

Tú eres guapo(a) y estás contento(a).
Yo soy inteligente y estoy preocupado(a).

After each person has had a turn, begin a new round.

El Teatro Español
en Madrid

Enrichment: For the **Actividad,** appoint a secretary within each group to keep a record of the group's descriptions. One way to do this is by making two columns: *ser* and *estar*. The group secretary should write the speaker's initials and each of the two adjectives in the appropriate column.

You may want the secretaries or other volunteers to present the groups' descriptions. Make sure students use the proper forms of *ser* and *estar*.

REPASO

Notes: Answers to the **Repaso** and **Tema** appear in the pre-chapter teacher pages.

Look carefully at the model sentences. Then put the English cues into Spanish to form new sentences based on the model.

1. *Aquí están los amigos de la profesora.*
   (*Here is Daniel's office.*)
   (*There are Miss Márquez's chairs.*)
   (*Over there is the police officer's* (masc.) *hat.*)

2. *La mujer baja es la Sra. Martínez. Es estudiante.*
   (*The red-haired woman is Mrs. Castillo. She's a teacher.*)
   (*The sad woman is Miss Rivera. She's a police officer.*)
   (*The crazy woman is Miss González. She's a salesclerk.*)

3. *Roberto es simpático, pero hoy está muy ocupado.*
   (*Miguel is young, but today he's a little tired.*)
   (*My cats are good, but today they're rather crazy.*)
   (*My boyfriend is smart, but today he's a little bored.*)

4. *Uds. están lejos de la iglesia vieja.*
   (*You* (fam.) *are near the new theater.*)
   (*It's across from the large department store.*)
   (*We're behind the tall fountain.*)

5. *¿Dónde están María y Jorge? Están a la izquierda de Jaime.*
   (*Where are they* (fem.)? *They're between the boys.*)
   (*Where are you* (pl.)? *We're next to Patricio.*)
   (*Where are you* (fam.)? *I'm in front of the flag.*)

6. *¿Cuál es ella? Es la policía rubia y joven, por supuesto.*
   (*Which one is she? She's the dark-haired, unpleasant woman, right?*)
   (*Which one is he? He's the dumb, boring boy, isn't he?*)
   (*Which ones are they* (fem.)? *They're the nice, pretty girls, aren't they?*)

Notes: Review of:
1. *aquí / allí / allá*
   estar
   possessive *de*
2. adjective agreement
   ser + profession
   definite article with titles of respect
3. adjective agreement
   ser vs. *estar*
4. *estar* with prepositions
   forms of *de*
   adjective agreement
5. *estar* with prepositions
6. *¿Cuál(es)?*
   ser + profession + adjective
   adjective agreement
   tag questions

Fuentes en México y España

TEMA

Transparency 28

Enrichment: In connection
with the **Tema**, students can
work in pairs to prepare new
captions based on their own
class.

Put the English captions into Spanish.

1.

Here's Pedro's class.

2.

The tall man is
Mr.García. He's
a teacher.

3.

Pilar is pretty, but
today she's a little
worried.

4.

Ricardo is next
to the dark haired
boy.

5.

Where is Pedro? He's to the
right of the teacher.

6.

Which one is he?
He's the tall,
handsome boy,
of course.

REDACCIÓN

Now you are ready to write your own dialogue or paragraph. Choose one
of the following topics.

1. Write four to six more lines based on the *Tema*. How many students
   are there in the class? What is the teacher like? Is he nice? Describe
   Pilar. Describe Ricardo. Why is he tired? Does he work a lot?

2. Write a six- to eight-line paragraph about your town or city. Is it big or
   small, old or new? Is there a stadium? Are there many movie theaters?
   Museums? Where are they? Do you go to restaurants? Are they good?
   Are they cheap or expensive?

3. Write a four- to six-line phone conversation between a new student
   and someone who has been in the Spanish class all year. The new
   student wants to know what you are like or what someone else in the
   class is like and how you (or they) are today.

COMPRUEBA TU PROGRESO CAPÍTULO 5 Discretionary

Notes: Answers to the **Comprueba** appear in the pre-chapter teacher pages.

A Al contrario
Complete each sentence with a word or expression to make it mean the opposite of the first sentence.

1. La obra de teatro no es divertida. Es muy ____.
2. El restaurante no está a la izquierda de la oficina. Está ____ de la oficina.
3. José no es muy simpático. Es ____.
4. El estadio no está cerca de la esquina. Está ____ de la esquina.
5. Elena no es tonta. Al contrario, es muy ____.
6. El museo no está detrás del café. Está ____ del café.
7. La profesora no está triste. Está ____.
8. La farmacia no está enfrente del almacén. Está ____ del almacén.

B ¿Qué está . . . ?
Look at the picture and answer the questions according to the model.

> ¿Qué está a la izquierda del banco?
> *El café está a la izquierda del banco.*

1. ¿Qué está entre el restaurante y la farmacia?
2. ¿Qué está a la derecha del banco?
3. ¿Qué está a la derecha del hotel?
4. ¿Qué está enfrente del hotel?
5. ¿Qué está entre el correo y el café?
6. ¿Qué está al lado de la escuela?
7. ¿Qué está delante de la escuela?
8. ¿Qué está enfrente del museo?
9. ¿Qué está al lado del museo?

C ¿De quién es?
Answer each question according to the model.

> ¿De quién es el lápiz? (profesora)
> *El lápiz es de la profesora.*

1. ¿De quiénes son las botas?   (los muchachos)
2. ¿De quién es el coche?   (las señoritas García)
3. ¿De quién es la moto?   (el policía)
4. ¿De quién es la guía telefónica?   (Anita y Daniel)
5. ¿De quién es el traje de baño?   (Elena)
6. ¿De quiénes son los paraguas?   (Rita y Víctor)

D El verbo *estar*
Complete each sentence with the correct form of *estar*.

1. Ignacio y David ____ muy cansados.
2. (Yo) ____ en la cabina telefónica.
3. Los policías ____ en la esquina.
4. María ____ triste.
5. Las señoras ____ muy ocupadas.
6. Paco ____ enfermo.
7. (Nosotros) ____ en la escuela.
8. (Uds.) ____ en el aeropuerto.
9. (Ud.) ____ preocupada.
10. Y tú, ¿cómo ____?

E ¿*Ser* o *estar*?
Complete each sentence with the correct form of *ser* or *estar*.

1. La iglesia ____ enfrente de la plaza.
2. ¿____ Uds. de Cuba?
3. Ella ____ muy bonita.
4. La línea ____ ocupada.
5. Luisa ____ la novia de Eduardo.
6. Las muchachas ____ un poco preocupadas.
7. Ramón no ____ en casa.
8. El hotel ____ demasiado pequeño.

Reteach / Review: Have students ask a question with *¿Cómo?* or *¿Dónde?* for items 1–9 in Ex. D.

Chapter 5 Test Listening Comprehension Test

Sustantivos
el almacén, *pl.* los almacenes
la avenida
la cabina telefónica
el café
la calle
la dirección, *pl.* las direcciones
la esquina
el estadio
la fuente
la guía telefónica
la línea
el museo
el novio, la novia
la obra de teatro
la oficina
el parque
el partido (de + *deporte*)
el/la policía
el restaurante
el teatro

Adjetivos
aburrido, -a
antipático, -a
cansado, -a
contento, -a
divertido, -a
enfermo, -a
inteligente
interesante
loco, -a
ocupado, -a
preocupado, -a
simpático, -a
tonto, -a
triste

Verbos
estar

Adverbios
allá
allí
mal
todavía
un poco

Preposiciones
a la derecha de
a la izquierda de
al lado de
cerca de
delante de
detrás de
en *(on)*
enfrente de
entre
lejos de

Expresiones
a la vuelta de la esquina
¿aló?
¿de quién?, ¿de quiénes?
¿dónde está?
¡no me digas!
¡perdón!
¡por supuesto!
¡qué lástima!
¡qué (mala) suerte!
¿qué pasa?
un momento

LA FAMILIA

Imagine that you're attending a teenager's party in Latin America. You might be surprised to see a ten-year-old girl dancing with her grandfather, or two school friends chatting with the host's aunt. Both school friends and family members are often invited to the same party, because the Spanish-speaking world places greater importance on family ties than on age.

To most people in the United States, the word "family" means parents and children. But in Spanish-speaking countries, the family includes cousins, aunts and uncles, grandparents, and godparents as well. Older children help take care of younger ones, and as a rule, sons and daughters continue to live at home until they marry and set up their own households.

One of the daily traditions in many Spanish-speaking homes is the gathering of the family for the midday meal. The largest meal of the day is usually served between 1:00 and 2:00 P.M. Schoolchildren come home to eat, and many businesses still provide a two-hour break so that working parents can join their families. Because of modern business schedules, however, this tradition is dying out in many large cities.

Family celebrations of all kinds are important events in the Spanish-speaking world. Birthdays, saints' days, weddings, and first communions are joyous occasions with plenty of food and fun. A baptism (*bautizo*) is another important family celebration. A godmother (*madrina*) and godfather (*padrino*) are selected to be responsible for the child in case anything happens to the parents. The godparents help to make sure that the child has a good religious upbringing, and they often help with the cost of education as well. It is a great honor to be chosen godparents, who then become members of the extended family.

PALABRAS NUEVAS I

El apartamento

If students ask: Other related words you may want to present: *el sótano*, basement; *el desván*, attic; *el pasillo*, hall.

1

Transparency 29
**CONTEXTO
VISUAL**

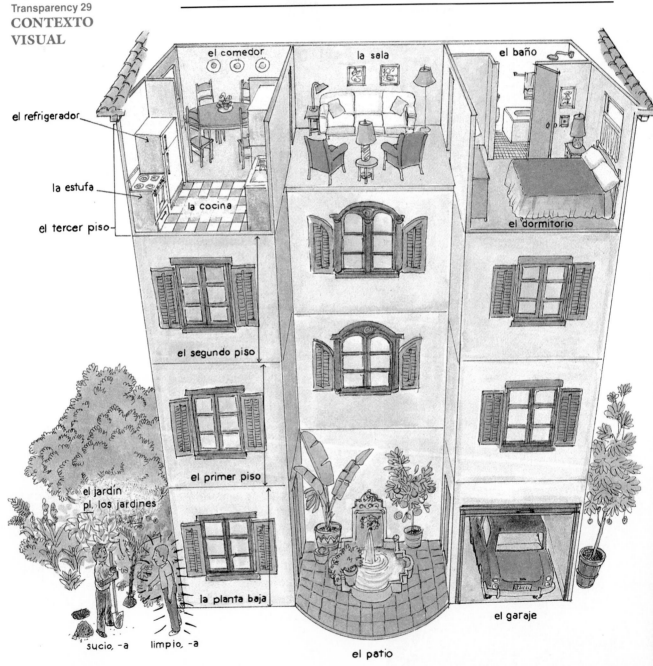

el comedor

la sala

el baño

el refrigerador

la estufa

la cocina

el tercer piso

el dormitorio

el segundo piso

el primer piso

el jardín
pl. los jardines

la planta baja

el garaje

sucio, -a   limpio, -a

el patio

Enrichment: Ask students to vary mini-dialogue 1 by describing their own houses or apartments. Suggest additional **Variaciones** for 2: *ir al cine → jugar al tenis; ayudar en casa → estudiar.*

Reteach / Extra Help: In connection with mini-dialogue 2, reinforce the difference between *tener ganas de* and *tener que* by asking *¿ Tienes que ir a una fiesta el viernes? (No, pero tengo ganas de ir.) ¿ Tienes ganas de limpiar la casa el sábado? (No, pero tengo que limpiar la casa.)*

CONTEXTO COMUNICATIVO 2

1 **Tengo** una casa grande y muy **cómoda**. En la planta baja* hay una sala, un comedor y una cocina. En el primer piso hay tres dormitorios y un baño.

Variaciones:
- grande → pequeña
  cómoda → **incómoda**
  tres dormitorios → sólo un dormitorio

tener (yo tengo, tú tienes) *to have*

cómodo, -a *comfortable*

incómodo, -a *uncomfortable*

2 ERNESTO **Tengo ganas de** ir al cine, pero no **puedo**.
   ISABEL ¿Por qué no?
   ERNESTO **Tengo que** ayudar en casa.
   ISABEL ¡Qué lástima! Pero puedes ir mañana, ¿no?
   ERNESTO ¡Por supuesto! Pero quiero ir hoy.

- ayudar en casa → **ayudar a** cocinar
- ayudar en casa → **limpiar** la cocina
- mañana → esta noche
- hoy → ahora

tener ganas de + infinitive *to feel like (doing something)*

(yo) puedo, (tú) puedes (from **poder**) *to be able to, can*

tener que + infinitive *to have to (do something)*

ayudar a + infinitive *to help to*

limpiar *to clean*

3 DIEGO **¿Vienes** a la fiesta, Gloria?
   GLORIA No, no puedo ir. Tengo que limpiar el apartamento. Está sucio.
   DIEGO ¿Y después?
   GLORIA **Tampoco** puedo ir después. Tengo que **cuidar a los niños** de Emilia y Pablo.

- a la fiesta → al partido de básquetbol
- el apartamento → mi dormitorio
- cuidar a los niños → **dar de comer al** gato

venir (yo vengo, tú vienes) *to come*

tampoco *neither, not either*

cuidar a los niños *to baby-sit, to take care of the children*

dar de comer a(l) *to feed*

Notes: Point out the use of *venir* in the question and *ir* in the response in mini-dialogue 3. Make sure students understand the meaning and use of *tampoco* in mini-dialogue 3.

---

* Spanish speakers refer to the first floor as the ground floor (*la planta baja*). What we call the second floor, they call the first floor (*el primer piso*), and so on.

EN OTRAS PARTES

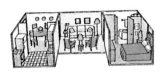

También se dice *el departamento*. En España se dice *el piso*.

También se dice *la alcoba* y *la habitación*. En Puerto Rico se dice *el cuarto (de dormir)*. En México se dice *la recámara*.

En España y en otros países también se dice *la nevera*. En la Argentina se dice *la heladera*.

PRÁCTICA

Práctica A
1. Juan Carlos limpia el comedor.
2. Yo limpio el baño.
3. Teresa limpia la cocina.
4. La señora García y Bernardo limpian la sala.
5. Diego y yo limpiamos la estufa.
6. Bernardo y Francisco limpian el dormitorio.

A ¿Quieres limpiar la casa? Imagina que ayudas a la familia García a limpiar la casa. ¿Qué hace cada persona? *(What is each person doing?)* Sigue *(Follow)* el modelo.

el señor García y Daniel
El señor García y Daniel limpian el garaje.

1. Juan Carlos

2. (Yo)

3. Teresa

4. La señora García y Bernardo

5. Diego y yo

6. Bernardo y Francisco

B Una casa nueva. Imagina que tu familia compra una casa muy grande. ¿Puedes describir la casa? Contesta según el dibujo.

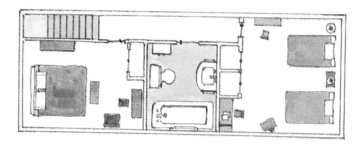

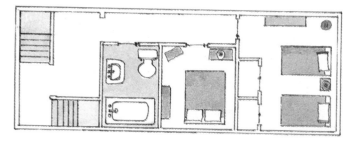

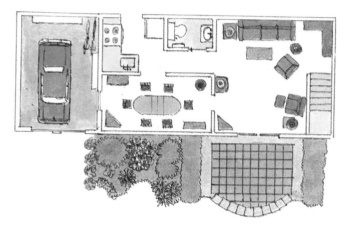

Reteach / Review: In preparation for Ex. B, you may want to review some of the prepositions covered in Chap. 5 by asking these questions: *En el tercer piso, ¿dónde está el baño? (Está entre los dormitorios.) En el segundo piso, ¿están los dormitorios a la derecha o a la izquierda del baño? (Están a la derecha del baño.) ¿Está el comedor delante o detrás de la cocina? (Está delante de la cocina.) ¿Está el garaje delante de la casa? (No, está al lado de la casa.)*

Enrichment: After students have done Ex. B in class, ask them to draw a floor plan of their own house or apartment (or of their dream home) as a homework assignment. Tell students to label the rooms in Spanish and to be prepared to answer classmates' questions (similar to those in Ex. B) about their drawings.

Práctica B
Some answers may vary.
1. Hay tres pisos.
2. Hay cuatro dormitorios. Dos (dormitorios) están en el primer piso y dos están en el segundo piso.
3. Hay tres baños.
4. Está entre los dormitorios.
5. Está en la planta baja (a la derecha del comedor).
6. Está en la planta baja (a la izquierda de la sala).
7. la cocina
8. Está al lado (a la izquierda) de la casa.
9. Está al lado (a la izquierda) del patio (*or:* delante de la casa).

1. ¿Cuántos pisos hay?
2. ¿Cuántos dormitorios hay? ¿En qué pisos están?
3. ¿Cuántos baños hay?
4. ¿Dónde está el baño del segundo piso?
5. ¿Dónde está la sala?
6. ¿Dónde está el comedor?
7. ¿Qué hay detrás del comedor?
8. ¿Dónde está el garaje?
9. ¿Dónde está el jardín?

Palabras Nuevas I   **209**

C **Ahora no puedo.** Imagina que no puedes ir con tus amigos porque siempre tienes que hacer algo (*something*). Escoge (*Choose*) una expresión de la izquierda para preguntar y otra (*another*) de la derecha para contestar. Sigue el modelo.

ESTUDIANTE A *¿Puedes ir al cine?*
ESTUDIANTE B *Ahora no puedo. Tengo que hacer mi tarea.*

1. ir al cine	cuidar a los niños
2. ir a la biblioteca	limpiar los dormitorios
3. ir al centro	ayudar a lavar el coche
4. ir al partido de fútbol	estudiar para exámenes
5. ir al teatro	practicar la guitarra
6. ir a la casa de Jorge	lavar la ropa
7. ir al campo	hacer mi tarea
8. ir al museo	dar de comer al perro de (*nombre*)
9. ir a la fiesta	ayudar en la cocina

D **Yo tampoco / yo también.** Hay personas que siempre están de acuerdo (*in agreement*). Sigue los modelos.

no ir al teatro
ESTUDIANTE A *No tengo ganas de ir al teatro.*
ESTUDIANTE B *Yo tampoco.*

mirar la tele
ESTUDIANTE A *Tengo ganas de mirar la tele.*
ESTUDIANTE B *Yo también.*

1. comer burritos	5. tomar el sol
2. no ir a la piscina	6. hablar español
3. jugar en el parque	7. no hacer la tarea
4. no escuchar cintas españolas	8. no viajar en metro

E El fin de semana. Es sábado y estás aburrido(a). Un(a) amigo(a) quiere hacer algo que *(something that)* tú no quieres hacer. Con un(a) compañero(a) de clase, pregunta y contesta según el modelo.
(The questioner should choose activities that he or she thinks are undesirable.)

ESTUDIANTE A *¿Tienes ganas de ____?*
ESTUDIANTE B *No, no tengo ganas de ____. Prefiero ____.*

ir a la plaza	montar en bicicleta
trabajar en el jardín	lavar las ventanas
ir a bailar	ir a esquiar
limpiar el garaje	ayudar a limpiar la casa
ir a nadar	jugar al tenis
limpiar el refrigerador	ir a comer en el centro
escuchar música clásica	ir al museo
tomar el sol	mirar la tele

F Hablemos de ti.
1. ¿Tienes que hacer mucha tarea? ¿Cuándo haces la tarea?
2. ¿Tienes que ayudar en casa los fines de semana? ¿Qué tienes que hacer?
3. ¿Cómo es tu dormitorio?

Practice Sheet 6–1   Workbook Exs. A–B

 3 Tape Manual Exs. 1–2   Quiz 6-1

Práctica E
Answers will vary.

Enrichment: Additional questions for Ex. F: *¿Tienes ganas de hacer la tarea o tienes ganas de mirar la tele? ¿Tienes que estudiar mucho para los exámenes? ¿Tienes que hablar mucho en la clase de español?*

Práctica F
Answers will vary.

Notes: Students may do the **Actividad** using magazine pictures rather than drawing a floor plan.

ACTIVIDAD

Un apartamento cómodo With one or more classmates, draw a picture or a floor plan of *un apartamento cómodo* and of *un apartamento incómodo.* For instance, the comfortable apartment might have a big kitchen, and the uncomfortable apartment might have very small bedrooms; one might have three telephones and the other might have only one. Label in Spanish all the rooms, appliances, and furniture that you can name. Exchange your drawings with another group. Ask *¿Por qué es cómodo tu apartamento?* and *¿Por qué es incómodo?* about the two apartments that the other group drew. They will answer and then ask the same questions about your drawings.

DIÁLOGO

APLICACIONES

Discretionary

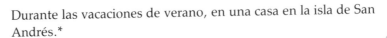

Sonia, la Cenicienta[1]

4

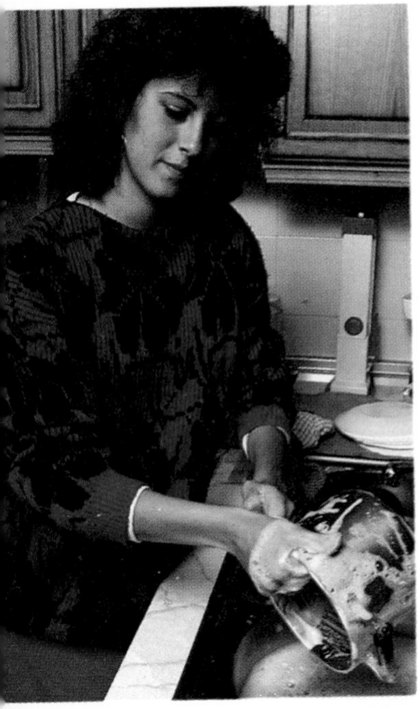

En España

Durante las vacaciones de verano, en una casa en la isla de San Andrés.*

SONIA Mamá, voy a nadar. Hasta luego.

MAMÁ ¡Un momento! Primero tienes que ayudar aquí en casa. La criada[2] está enferma hoy.

SONIA Más tarde, mamá. Ahora tengo que ir a nadar con mis amigas.

MAMÁ No, Sonia. Tienes ganas de ir a nadar, pero tienes que ayudar a limpiar. Primero tu dormitorio y después la sala. Luego[3] puedes ir a nadar.

SONIA ¿Más tarde, mamá? ¿Mañana?

MAMÁ Mañana, no. Más tarde, no. Ahora, sí. Y también tienes que dar de comer al perro.

SONIA Bueno, mamá. Limpiar mi dormitorio . . . la sala . . . dar de comer al perro. Entonces puedo ir a nadar. Ya[4] estoy cansada. Soy Sonia, la Cenicienta . . .

---

[1]**Cenicienta** *Cinderella* [2]**la criada** *maid* [3]**luego** *then* [4]**ya** *already*

* San Andrés is a Caribbean island and a popular beach resort. It is about 150 miles northeast of Nicaragua and belongs to Colombia.

Notes: Make sure students understand the cognate that has not been glossed: *isla*, island.

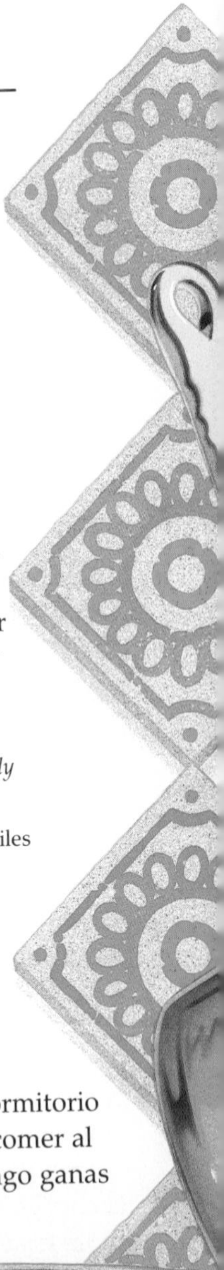

Preguntas

¿Quién habla, Sonia o Mamá? Contesta según el diálogo.

1. Quiero ir a nadar. 2. Tengo que ayudar en casa. 3. Tu dormitorio está sucio. 4. Puedo nadar más tarde. 5. Tengo que dar de comer al perro. 6. No tengo ganas de limpiar la casa. 7. Tampoco tengo ganas de dar de comer al perro. 8. Tú nunca ayudas en casa.

Diálogo
1. Sonia
2. Sonia
3. Mamá
4. Sonia
5. Sonia
6. Sonia
7. Sonia
8. Mamá

Enrichment: Additional questions you may want to ask: *¿Dónde está Sonia? (Está en San Andrés.) ¿Qué tiene ganas de hacer Sonia? (Tiene ganas de nadar.) ¿Puede ir ahora? (No.) ¿Por qué? (Tiene que limpiar su dormitorio y la sala. También tiene que dar de comer al perro.)*

Participación

Working with a partner, make up a dialogue of four to six lines in which you play the roles of student and teacher. Using the expression *tener que*, the teacher says what the student should do. The student responds and says what he or she feels like doing instead.

PRONUNCIACIÓN 5

A Except after a vowel, the letter *d* is pronounced almost like the English *d*, but the tip of the tongue touches the inside of the upper teeth.
Escucha y repite.

de   día   después   donde   segundo   dormitorio

B After a vowel, *d* is pronounced almost like the "th" in the English word "mother."
Escucha y repite.

adiós   ayudar   cómodo   cuidar   mediodía   refrigerador

C When we pronounce the letter *t* in English, it is often followed by a little puff of air. In Spanish, the letter *t* is pronounced without this puff of air. The tongue is right behind the upper teeth.
Escucha y repite.

tengo   triste   hotel   estufa   tampoco

D Escucha y repite.

Todavía tengo que estudiar.
¿Dónde están los vendedores?
El dormitorio de David está en el tercer piso.

6
Transparency 30
CONTEXTO VISUAL

La familia

mi abuelo   mi abuela
mis abuelos

mi madre   mi padre
mis padres

mi tía   mi tío
mis tíos

mi hermano   mi hermana
mis hermanos

yo

mi primo   mi prima
mis primos

If students ask: Other related words you may want to present: *el padrastro*, stepfather; *la madrastra*, stepmother; *el hermanastro*, stepbrother; *la hermanastra*, stepsister; *el/la pariente*, relative; *el cuñado*, brother-in-law; *la cuñada*, sister-in-law.

Mi familia

CONTEXTO COMUNICATIVO 7

1 CECILIA   **Los quince años*** es una fiesta muy **especial.**
    ANDRÉS   ¿Y quién es **la quinceañera**?
    CECILIA   Alejandra. Aquí está.
    ANDRÉS   ¡**Felicitaciones,** Alejandra!

Variaciones:
- una fiesta → un cumpleaños
- especial → **importante**
- la quinceañera → **la chica**

los quince años	*fifteenth birthday (party)*
especial	*special*
la quinceañera	*fifteen-year-old birthday girl*
felicitaciones	*congratulations*
importante	*important*
el chico, la chica = el muchacho, la muchacha	

2 MARÍA   ¿Quién es la señora rubia?
    HÉCTOR   Es mi **esposa.**
    MARÍA   Y **el niño** rubio, ¿es tu **hijo**?
    HÉCTOR   No, él es mi **sobrino.**

- la señora → la mujer
- el niño → el chico

el esposo, la esposa	*husband, wife*
el niño, la niña	*little boy, little girl*
el hijo, la hija	*son, daughter*
el sobrino, la sobrina	*nephew, niece*

3 DAVID   Tus abuelos están aquí, ¿verdad?
    EVA   Sí, y mis tíos también.
    DAVID   ¿Con **sus hijos**?
    EVA   ¡Por supuesto!

- tus abuelos → tus padres
- sus hijos → tus primos

su, sus	*his, her, your* (formal), *their*
los hijos	*sons, son(s) and daughter(s), children*

4 ANA   ¿Dónde están los padres de Alejandra?
    PEDRO   Allí están sus padres.
    ANA   Y los **niños** pelirrojos, ¿quiénes son?
    PEDRO   Sus primos.

- sus padres → su **papá** y su **mamá**
- los niños → los chicos
- primos → **sobrinos**

los niños	*children*
el papá	*dad*
la mamá	*mom*
los sobrinos	*nephews, nephew(s) and niece(s)*

* In a Spanish-speaking country, when a girl reaches her fifteenth birthday *(los quince años),* her parents often throw a huge party to celebrate. This is a girl's most important birthday. After her *quince años,* she won't be considered a child any longer, but a young woman.

5 OLGA	¿Tienes hermanos?	**mayor** *older*
FELIPE	Sí, tengo dos. Una hermana **mayor** y un hermano **menor.** ¿Y tú?	**menor** *younger*
OLGA	Soy **hija única.**	**el hijo único, la hija única** *only child*

■ hermano menor → **hermanito**

el hermanito, la hermanita *little brother, little sister*

6 PROFESOR	¿Cuál es tu nombre?	
ESTUDIANTE	Elisa María.	
PROFESOR	¿Y tu **apellido**?	**el apellido** *last name*
ESTUDIANTE	Velázquez Díaz.* Soy Elisa María Velázquez Díaz.	

■ ¿cuál es tu nombre? → ¿cómo te llamas?

7 SARA	**¿Cuántos años tienes,** Luis?	**¿cuántos años tienes?** *how old are you?*
LUIS	**Tengo** veinte **años.**	**tener** ____ **años** *to be ____ years old*
SARA	¡Ay, qué viejo eres! Yo sólo tengo dieciséis.	

■ veinte → veintiún
■ veinte → treinta y un

Enrichment: After presenting the **Contexto comunicativo**, ask students to work in pairs, asking and answering the questions in mini-dialogues 5–7. Encourage students to personalize their responses. You may want them to change the order of the mini-dialogues, practicing 5 after 6 and 7.

EN OTRAS PARTES

También se dice *el marido*.   También se dice *la mujer*.

Culture: In connection with mini-dialogue 6, note that in Spanish-speaking countries, when a woman marries, she adds *de* plus her husband's last name. For example, if Elisa Velázquez Díaz marries Mateo Arias, she becomes Elisa Velázquez de Arias.

* In Spanish-speaking countries people frequently use two last names. The first is the father's last name, and the second is the mother's maiden name. In this case, Elisa's father is Sr. Velázquez, and her mother's maiden name is Díaz.

Familias latinoamericanas en:
(arriba, izquierda) Oruro,
Bolivia; (arriba, derecha)
St. Paul, Minnesota; (derecha)
Bogotá, Colombia; (abajo)
Piriápolis, Uruguay

PRÁCTICA

Reteach / Extra Help: In preparation for Ex. A, you may want to reinforce the vocabulary presented on pp. 214–216 by making these statements and asking volunteers to complete them: *La hermana de mi mamá es mi ___. (tía) El esposo de tu tía es tu ___. (tío) La mamá de mi papá es mi ___. (abuela) Los hijos de tus tíos son tus ___. (primos) La hija de tus tíos es la ___ de tus padres. (sobrina)*

A   Mi familia.   Me llamo Lola. Aquí está mi familia. ¿Quién es quién? Completa las frases.

Práctica A
1. hija
2. hijo
3. padre
4. tía
5. hermanas, hijas
6. abuelo
7. sobrinos
8. tíos
9. hermanos
10. primas
11. sobrina
12. hijos

1. María es la _____ de Eduardo y Yolanda.
2. Marcos es el _____ de Raúl y Sara.
3. Sergio es el _____ de Claudia.
4. Lupe es mi _____.
5. Ana y yo somos las _____ de Marcos y las _____ de Sara y Raúl.
6. Eduardo es el _____ de Andrés.
7. Andrés, Claudia y Elena son los _____ de Sara y Raúl.
8. Sergio y Lupe son mis _____.
9. María y Sergio son los _____ de mi madre.
10. Claudia y Elena son mis _____.
11. Elena es la _____ de mis padres.
12. Sara, María y Sergio son los _____ de mis abuelos.

B La familia de Sergio. Mira el dibujo de la Práctica A. Imagina que tú eres Sergio. Contesta según el modelo.

María *María es mi hermana.*

1. Lupe
2. Sara
3. Lola
4. Eduardo y Yolanda
5. Elena
6. Marcos y Ana
7. Andrés
8. María y Sara

C ¿Cuántos años tienes? Quieres saber *(to know)* cuántos años tienen los niños de la familia Díaz. Pregunta y contesta según el modelo.

Juan (7)

ESTUDIANTE A *Juan, ¿cuántos años tienes?*
ESTUDIANTE B *Tengo siete años.*

1. Teresa (16)
2. Bernardo (17)
3. Miguelito (3)
4. Francisco (19)
5. Diego (14)
6. Daniel (21)

D Hablemos de ti.

Puedes contestar según tu familia o según una familia ideal o imaginaria.

1. ¿Cuál es tu apellido? ¿Cuál es tu nombre? ¿Cuántos años tienes? ¿Cuál es tu dirección? ¿Cuál es tu número de teléfono?
2. ¿Tienes una familia grande o eres hijo(a) único(a)?
3. ¿Tienes hermanos? ¿Cuántos? ¿Cómo son? ¿Cuáles son sus nombres? ¿Cuántos años tienen ellos?
4. ¿Tienes hermanas? ¿Cuántas? ¿Cómo son? ¿Cuáles son sus nombres? ¿Cuántos años tienen ellas?
5. ¿Tienes muchos tíos y primos? ¿Cuáles son sus nombres?

ACTIVIDAD

Tu árbol genealógico. Work with a partner to create a family tree like the one on page 214. You can base it on your own family, on an ideal family, or on a famous family that you know of. Name each of the relatives—for example, *mi abuelo Carlos, mi tía Elena,* and so forth—and then practice asking and answering questions such as *¿Quién es tu abuela? ¿Quiénes son tus primos?*

Next, each of you should pick a different relative to describe. For example: *¿Cómo es tu primo Paco? Es alto, moreno y guapo. Toca la guitarra. Es muy inteligente y simpático.* You can make up anything you would like to about this relative.

Notes: In conjunction with the **Actividad**, ask students to bring in photos of their relatives or magazine pictures depicting their ideal families.

ESTUDIO DE PALABRAS

We can use the endings *-ito, -ita* with nouns to show affection or to indicate that someone or something is small. If the word ends in *-o* or *-a,* we drop the final vowel before adding *-ito, -ita.*

hermano → hermanito	abuela → abuelita
brother → little brother	*grandmother → grandma*
perro → perrito	muchacha → muchachita
dog → little dog, puppy	*girl → little girl*
momento → momentito	casa → casita
moment → a tiny moment	*house → cozy little house*

If the word ends in *-co* or *-ca,* we change the *c* to *qu: chico → chiquito.*

How would you say *grandpa, little cat, little table* in Spanish?

Reteach / Review: You may want to expand on the **Estudio de palabras**. Call out or write these words on the board, and ask for the *-ito/-ita* forms: *libro, Juana, barco, taco (librito, Juanita, barquito, taquito).*

EXPLICACIONES I

El verbo *tener*

The verb *tener* means "to have." You already know two forms of *tener*:
(yo) tengo and *(tú) tienes*. Here are all of the present-tense forms.

◆ **OBJECTIVES:**

**TO TELL WHAT
PEOPLE HAVE**

**TO TELL WHAT
PEOPLE HAVE TO
DO AND WHAT
THEY FEEL LIKE
DOING**

TO MAKE EXCUSES

INFINITIVO: **tener**

	SINGULAR		PLURAL	
1	(yo)	**tengo**	(nosotros) (nosotras) }	**tenemos**
2	(tú)	**tienes**	(vosotros) (vosotras) }	**tenéis**
3	Ud. (él) (ella) }	**tiene**	Uds. (ellos) (ellas) }	**tienen**

1   In a negative sentence, we generally don't use the indefinite article
after the verb *tener* unless there is an adjective.

> No tenemos **jardín.**   *We don't have **a garden.***
> *But:* No tengo **un perro negro.**   *I don't have **a black dog.***

2   We use *tener* in many common expressions. For example:

> ¿Cuántos años tienes?   *How old are you?*
> Tengo catorce años.   *I'm fourteen (years old).*
> Tienen ganas de mirar la tele.   *They feel like watching TV.*
> Tenemos que estudiar ahora.   *We have to study now.*

Notes: You may want to use mini-dialogues 1–3 on p. 207 and 5 and 7 on p. 216 to
introduce *tener*. Refer to mini-dialogue 7 on p. 216 for further examples of *tener* ____ *años*,
2 on p. 207 for *tener ganas de*, and 2 and 3 on p. 207 for *tener que*.

   If students need extra help with any of these expressions, initiate a chain drill: ¿*Cuántos
años tienes?* or ¿*Qué tienes ganas de hacer hoy?* or ¿*Qué tienes que hacer?*

Práctica A

1. Ud. tiene una camisa.
2. Paco y Jaime tienen discos.
3. María y yo tenemos cuadernos.
4. Ana tiene una bufanda.
5. (Yo) tengo un reloj.
6. Uds. tienen un teléfono.
7. (Él) tiene un traje de baño.
8. (Tú) tienes un paraguas.
9. (Ella) tiene botas.

Práctica B

1. María tiene que estudiar para un examen.
2. Ud. tiene que ir a la farmacia.
3. Jorge y tú tienen que lavar las ventanas.
4. Héctor y Ana tienen que trabajar en el jardín.
5. Uds. tienen que cuidar a sus hermanitos.
6. Las chicas tienen que hacer la tarea.
7. (Tú) tienes que limpiar el garaje.
8. Answers will vary.

PRÁCTICA

A Algo nuevo.   Todo el mundo tiene algo nuevo. (*Everyone has something new.*) ¿Qué tienen? Sigue el modelo.

José
José tiene un suéter.

1. Ud.

2. Paco y Jaime

3. María y yo

4. Ana

5. (yo)

6. Uds.

7. (él)

8. (tú)

9. (ella)

B ¿Qué tienen que hacer?   Yo no puedo cocinar. ¿Por qué estoy solo(a) aquí en la cocina? Sigue el modelo.

Cristóbal / ir a su oficina
Cristóbal tiene que ir a su oficina.

1. María / estudiar para un examen
2. Ud. / ir a la farmacia
3. Jorge y tú / lavar las ventanas
4. Héctor y Ana / trabajar en el jardín
5. Uds. / cuidar a sus hermanitos
6. las chicas / hacer la tarea
7. (tú) / limpiar el garaje
8. Y tú, ¿qué tienes que hacer en casa?

C ¿Qué tienen ganas de hacer? Hoy es domingo. Cada miembro (*each member*) de la familia de Pedro quiere hacer algo especial. Escoge (*choose*) actividades de la columna a la derecha. Sigue el modelo.

> ¿Y su mamá?
> **ESTUDIANTE A** *Su hermano tiene ganas de _____.*
> **ESTUDIANTE B** *¿Y su mamá?*
> **ESTUDIANTE A** *Su mamá tiene ganas de _____.*

1. ¿Y su abuelo?
2. ¿Y sus tíos?
3. ¿Y su hermana Luz?
4. ¿Y el esposo de Luz?
5. ¿Y su hermana menor?
6. ¿Y su sobrino?
7. ¿Y su hermano mayor y su esposa?
8. ¿Y Uds.?
9. Y tú, Pedro, ¿qué tienes ganas de hacer?

montar en bicicleta
jugar en el parque
ir al museo
escuchar música clásica
estar en casa
jugar al tenis
cocinar en el patio
ir al partido de béisbol
ir al café
nadar en la piscina
ir al cine
viajar al campo
no hacer nada

Práctica C
Answers will vary.

Notes: Point out the negative structure in the last item of the second column in Ex. C. Elicit or note the two possible ways to phrase answers with *no hacer nada*. For example: *Su hermano tiene ganas de no hacer nada.* or *Su hermano no tiene ganas de hacer nada.*

Enrichment: In connection with Ex. B on p. 222 and Ex. C on p. 223, you may want to ask students to write five sentences at home about themselves and four relatives, using the expressions *tener que* and *tener ganas de*. For example: *Mi hermana tiene ganas de ir al cine, pero tiene que trabajar en el jardín.*

Practice Sheet 6–3

Tape Manual Ex. 5 9

El verbo *venir*

The verb *venir* means "to come." Here are its present-tense forms.

INFINITIVO	**venir**		
	SINGULAR		**PLURAL**
1	(yo) **vengo**	(nosotros) (nosotras)	**venimos**
2	(tú) **vienes**	(vosotros) (vosotras)	**venís**
3	Ud. (él) (ella) **viene**	Uds. (ellos) (ellas)	**vienen**

◆ **OBJECTIVES:**
TO TELL OR FIND OUT WHO IS (OR IS NOT) COMING TO AN EVENT
TO MAKE EXCUSES

Notes: You may want to use mini-dialogue 3 on p. 207 to introduce *venir*. Elicit or suggest additional examples to illustrate all of the forms of *venir*.

Explicaciones I   **223**

Práctica A

1. Elena viene en tren.
2. Javier y Laura vienen en coche.
3. Uds. vienen a pie.
4. (Tú) vienes en moto.
5. Patricia y José vienen en bicicleta.
6. Ellos vienen en metro.
7. Los hermanos Mendoza vienen en autobús.
8. (Nosotras) venimos en taxi.
9. Answers will vary.

Reteach / Review: In preparation for Ex. A, you may want to review the means of transportation presented on pp. 152–153. Ask *¿Vienes a la escuela a pie / en _____?* about each of the drawings in Ex. A.

PRÁCTICA

A ¿Cómo vienen a la escuela? ¿Cómo vienen los estudiantes a la escuela? Contesta según los dibujos.

Pablo
Pablo viene a pie.

1. Elena   2. Javier y Laura   3. Uds.

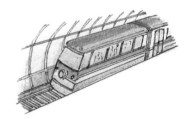

4. (tú)   5. Patricia y José   6. ellos

7. los hermanos Mendoza   8. (nosotras)   9. Y tú, ¿cómo vienes?

B **¿Quiénes vienen?** Imagina que estás en el estadio. Los miembros de tu familia y tus amigos están todos *(all)* ocupados y no pueden venir al partido. ¿Por qué no? ¡Tú puedes inventar el porqué *(reason)*! Pregunta y contesta según el modelo.

> Catalina
> ESTUDIANTE A ¿Viene Catalina al partido?
> ESTUDIANTE B No, no viene.
> ESTUDIANTE A ¿Por qué?
> ESTUDIANTE B Porque tiene que ____.

1. Ángela
2. Juana y Norma
3. Rogelio
4. tú y Sonia
5. Rodolfo y Ester
6. Esperanza y su hermano
7. tú
8. Uds.
9. tus padres
10. tus primos

C **Hablemos de ti.**
1. ¿Qué tienes ganas de hacer esta noche? ¿Qué tienes que hacer?
2. ¿Quién tiene que limpiar tu casa o apartamento? ¿Tienes que ayudar a limpiar la casa? ¿Cuándo?
3. ¿Quién cocina en tu casa? ¿Quién lava la ropa? ¿Ayudas a cocinar y a lavar la ropa?
4. ¿A qué hora vienes a la escuela? ¿Cómo vienes? ¿Con quién?

Practice Sheets 6–4, 6–5   Workbook Exs. E–F

 10 Tape Manual Ex. 6   Activity Master 6–1   Quiz 6–3

ACTIVIDAD

¿Qué tenemos que hacer? Work with a partner to make two lists, one headed *Tenemos que hacer . . .* and the other headed *Tenemos ganas de hacer . . . .* Share ideas about things you have to do and things you feel like doing. The first list might include such things as *Tenemos que lavar la ropa . . . ayudar en casa . . . .* The second list might begin with *Tenemos ganas de escuchar discos de música popular . . . montar en bicicleta . . . .* Write at least ten activities on each list. When you have finished, join another pair of students. Take turns pantomiming activities from your lists. Can you guess all of the activities on each other's lists?

APLICACIONES Discretionary

¡Feliz cumpleaños, Julia! 11

La familia Hernández está en la sala—los padres de Julia y su hermanito Jorge, sus abuelos, sus tíos, sus primos y su hermana mayor. Todos hablan a la vez.[1] ¿Qué pasa?

5 El mes próximo van a celebrar los quince años de Julia, pero, ¿qué desea la quinceañera para su cumpleaños? Su tía sugiere[2] un viaje a Acapulco. Su mamá sugiere un collar de perlas,[3] y su hermana un video.

¿Y dónde está Julia? ¿Qué quiere ella? Julia está sola en su dormitorio. Quiere tener una gran fiesta. Tiene ganas de cantar y bailar con su familia y con sus amigos. Quiere llevar un bonito vestido blanco y zapatos de 10 tacón alto.[4] ¡Y tienen que ser de tacón muy alto! Va a ser un día importante, un día muy especial, y Julia quiere estar muy guapa. ¡Una muchacha celebra sus quince años sólo una vez![5]

---

[1]**todos hablan a la vez** *they're all talking at once* [2]**sugiere** (*from* **sugerir**) *suggests*
[3]**el collar de perlas** *pearl necklace* [4]**de tacón alto** *high-heeled* [5]**una vez** *once*

Preguntas

Escoge la palabra (*word*) o expresión correcta para completar cada frase (*each sentence*).

1. La familia de Julia está _____.
   a. en el dormitorio   b. en la sala   c. en la cocina
2. Jorge es el _____ de Julia.
   a. hermano mayor   b. primo   c. hermano menor
3. La mamá de Julia tiene ganas de comprar un _____.
   a. collar de perlas   b. video   c. vestido blanco
4. Julia está _____.
   a. con su familia   b. en la sala   c. en su dormitorio
5. Julia prefiere _____.
   a. viajar a Acapulco   b. mirar videocintas   c. tener una fiesta
6. Julia tiene ganas de llevar _____.
   a. un collar de perlas   b. un vestido blanco   c. botas de tacón alto
7. Julia tiene ahora _____.
   a. 14 años   b. 15 años   c. 16 años

 12 Canción: Las mañanitas

Fiesta de cumpleaños en
Buenos Aires, Argentina

Para Mi
Sobrina Querida
En Su Cumpleaños

227

EXPLICACIONES II

Adjetivos posesivos

You know that we use *de* + a noun to show possession.

Es el cuaderno **de** María.   *It's Maria's notebook.*

Another way to show possession is by using possessive adjectives. You already know some of them.

Aquí está **tu** bicicleta.   *Here's **your** bike.*
Mi hermanita tiene diez años.   ***My** little sister is ten years old.*

Here are all of the possessive adjectives. Like other adjectives, they always agree with the nouns that follow them.

POSSESSIVE ADJECTIVE + SINGULAR NOUN							
mi { tío / tía	my { uncle / aunt			**nuestro** tío / **nuestra** tía	our { uncle / aunt		
tu { tío / tía	your { uncle / aunt			**vuestro** tío / **vuestra** tía	your { uncle / aunt		
su { tío / tía	your / his / her { uncle / aunt			**su** { tío / tía	your / their { uncle / aunt		

POSSESSIVE ADJECTIVE + PLURAL NOUN							
mis { tíos / tías	my { uncles / aunts			**nuestros** tíos / **nuestras** tías	our { uncles / aunts		
tus { tíos / tías	your { uncles / aunts			**vuestros** tíos / **vuestras** tías	your { uncles / aunts		
sus { tíos / tías	your / his / her { uncles / aunts			**sus** { tíos / tías	your / their { uncles / aunts		

1. Only the *nuestro* and *vuestro* forms have different masculine and feminine endings. Like the *vosotros* form of verbs, *vuestro(s), -a(s)* is used in Spain.

2. Both *tu/tus* and *su/sus* mean "your." Use *tu/tus* when speaking with someone you call *tú*. Use *su/sus* with someone you call *usted* or with more than one person *(ustedes)*.

PRÁCTICA

A ¿Dónde está? Imagina que estás muy distraído(a) *(absent-minded)*. Pregunta y contesta según el modelo.

ESTUDIANTE A *¿Dónde está mi sombrero?*
ESTUDIANTE B *¿Tu sombrero? Está en la sala, ¿no?*

1.
2.
3.
4.
5.
6.
7.
8.
9.

Reteach / Extra Help: In preparation for the **Práctica**, do a chain drill or ask students to work in pairs asking and answering *¿De quién(es) es / son ____?* using classroom objects and items of clothing. Students should use all forms of the possessive adjectives except *vuestro*.

Práctica A
1. ¿Dónde está mi guitarra?
   ¿Tu guitarra? Está en el patio, ¿no?
2. ¿Dónde está mi camiseta?
   ¿Tu camiseta? Está en el jardín, ¿no?
3. ¿Dónde están mis guantes?
   ¿Tus guantes? Están en el comedor, ¿no?
4. ¿Dónde están mis hojas de papel?
   ¿Tus hojas de papel? Están en el pupitre, ¿no?
5. ¿Dónde está mi hamburguesa?
   ¿Tu hamburguesa? Está en la estufa, ¿no?
6. ¿Dónde están mis botas?
   ¿Tus botas? Están en el baño, ¿no?
7. ¿Dónde está mi refresco?
   ¿Tu refresco? Está en el refrigerador, ¿no?
8. ¿Dónde está mi traje de baño?
   ¿Tu traje de baño? Está en el dormitorio, ¿no?
9. ¿Dónde está mi chaqueta?
   ¿Tu chaqueta? Está en el garaje, ¿no?

Práctica B

1. ¿Es su coche? Sí, es nuestro primer coche.
2. ¿Es su perro? Sí, es nuestro perro Camilo.
3. ¿Son sus bicicletas? Sí, son nuestras bicicletas viejas.
4. ¿Es su casa? Sí, es nuestra casa de verano cerca del Cabo San Juan.
5. ¿Son sus primos? No, son nuestros compañeros de clase.
6. ¿Es su abuela? No, es nuestra profesora de guitarra.
7. ¿Es su apartamento? Sí, es nuestro apartamento en Ponce.
8. ¿Es su barco? Sí, es nuestro barco ''El Colón.''

Práctica C

1. Profesora Díaz, ¿de qué color es su paraguas? ¿Verde?
   No, no tengo un paraguas verde.
2. Sofía, ¿...es tu impermeable? ¿Morado?
   No, no tengo un impermeable morado.
3. Julia, ¿... son tus botas? ¿Amarillas?
   No, no tengo botas amarillas.
4. Profesor Marín, ¿... es su bufanda? ¿Gris?
   No, no tengo una bufanda gris.
5. Jaime, ¿... es tu abrigo? ¿Marrón?
   No, no tengo un abrigo marrón.
6. Rebeca, ¿... son tus calcetines? ¿Anaranjados?
   No, no tengo calcetines anaranjados.
7. Profesor Suárez, ¿... son sus guantes? ¿Negros?
   No, no tengo guantes negros.
8. Arturo, ¿... son tus camisetas? ¿Azules?
   No, no tengo camisetas azules.

B **¿Quiénes son?** Imagina que miras el álbum de fotos de dos chicos puertorriqueños que acaban de llegar *(who just arrived)* a tu ciudad. Pregunta y contesta según el modelo.

> ¿padres? / no / tíos de San Juan
> **ESTUDIANTE A** *¿Son sus padres?*
> **ESTUDIANTE B** *No, son nuestros tíos de San Juan.*

1. ¿coche? / sí / primer coche
2. ¿perro? / sí / perro Camilo
3. ¿bicicletas? / sí / bicicletas viejas
4. ¿casa? / sí / casa de verano cerca del Cabo San Juan
5. ¿primos? / no / compañeros de clase
6. ¿abuela? / no / profesora de guitarra
7. ¿apartamento? / sí / apartamento en Ponce
8. ¿barco? / sí / barco ''El Colón''

C **¿De qué color es . . . ?** Hay mucha ropa en el Depósito de objetos perdidos *(Lost and Found)*. ¿De quién es? Pregunta y contesta según el modelo. ¡Cuidado! *(Watch out!)* ¿Usas su o tu?

> Pedro / suéter / rojo
> **ESTUDIANTE A** *Pedro, ¿de qué color es tu suéter? ¿Rojo?*
> **ESTUDIANTE B** *No, no tengo un suéter rojo.*

1. profesora Díaz / paraguas / verde
2. Sofía / impermeable / morado
3. Julia / botas / amarillas
4. profesor Marín / bufanda / gris
5. Jaime / abrigo / marrón
6. Rebeca / calcetines / anaranjados
7. profesor Suárez / guantes / negros
8. Arturo / camisetas / azules

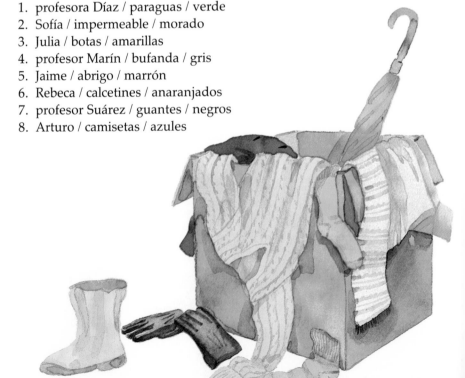

D Nuestra familia. Imagina que tu tarea para mañana es entrevistar a *(to interview)* la familia Pérez. Pregunta y contesta según el modelo.

ESTUDIANTE A Sra. García de Pérez, ¿es la Sra. Pérez de Enríquez su sobrina?
ESTUDIANTE B *No, es mi hija.*

1. Marta, ¿es el Sr. Pérez García tu abuelo?
2. Ignacio e Isabel, ¿es el Sr. Pérez López su tío?
3. Sr. Enríquez, ¿es Luisa su hermana?
4. Sra. Pérez Enríquez, ¿es el Sr. Pérez García su primo?
5. Isabel, ¿es Marta tu hermana?
6. Marta e Ignacio, ¿es la Sra. García de Pérez su tía?
7. Sra. Pérez de Enríquez, ¿son Ignacio e Isabel sus hijos?
8. Ignacio e Isabel, ¿son Marta y Mateo sus hermanos?

E Hablemos de ti.
1. Cuando tienes que estudiar para exámenes, ¿dónde estudias? ¿Estudias a veces en la biblioteca? ¿Prefieres estudiar en casa o en la biblioteca?
2. ¿Tienes un perro, un gato o un pájaro? ¿Cuál es su nombre? Si tienes peces, ¿tienen nombres? ¿Cuáles son?

Practice Sheets 6–6; 6–7   Workbook Exs. G–J

 13 Tape Manual Exs. 7–8   Activity Master 6–2   Quizzes 6–4, 6–5

Práctica D
1. No, es mi tío.
2. No, es nuestro abuelo.
3. No, es mi esposa.
4. No, es mi hermano.
5. No, es mi prima.
6. No, es nuestra abuela.
7. No, son mis sobrinos.
8. No, son nuestros primos.

Notes: Point out the conjunction *e* in 2, 6, 7, and 8 in Ex. D. Tell students that *y* (and) becomes *e* when the word following it begins with *i* or *hi*.

Enrichment: In connection with Ex. D, you may want to reinforce the various meanings of *su / sus* by making statements about the drawing and asking students for clarification. For example: *Luisa es su esposa. (Es la esposa de Enrique.); Ignacio e Isabel son sus primos. (Son los primos de Marta y Mateo.); El Sr. Pérez López es su abuelo. (Es el abuelo de Ignacio e Isabel.); La Sra. García de Pérez es su mamá. (Es la mamá de Luisa.).*
  Then ask questions about objects that students can identify as yours: *¿Es / Son mi / mis ____? (Sí, es / son su / sus ____.).*

Práctica E
Answers will vary.

APLICACIONES

REPASO

Notes: Answers to the
Repaso and **Tema** appear in
the pre-chapter teacher pages.

Look carefully at the model sentences. Then put the English cues into Spanish to form new sentences based on the models.

1. *Hoy es la fiesta de Carmen. Mi hermano y yo vamos a ayudar en la cocina.*
   (Tomorrow is the Spanish test. He and his cousin (f.) are going to study in the dining room.)
   (Today is the baseball game. My friends and I are going to practice in the park.)
   (Tomorrow is the fifteenth birthday party. She and her parents are going to eat in the garden.)

2. *Sus abuelos vienen al estadio a las ocho.*
   (Our parents are coming downtown at 5:00.)
   (His sister comes to school at 7:30.)
   (Your (fam.) aunt and uncle are coming to the hotel at 2:00.)

3. *Los niños tienen ganas de comer en el restaurante.*
   (I feel like reading in the library.)
   (We feel like working in the garage.)
   (Do you (fam.) feel like singing at the party?)

Hermanas españolas
en Madrid

4. *Pero no puedes jugar ahora. Tienes que trabajar.*
   (But I can't talk now. I have to eat.)
   (But you (fam.) can't listen now. We have to practice.)
   (But I can't wait now. I have to cook.)

Notes: Review of:
1. possessive adjectives
   ir a + infinitive
   en + noun
2. possessive adjectives
   venir
   a(l)
   telling time
3. *tener ganas de* + infinitive
   en + noun
4. *puedo / puedes*
   tener que + infinitive

Put the English captions into Spanish.

1. Today is Silvia's birthday. She and her friends are going to dance on the patio.

2. Her friends are coming to the party at 7:00.

3. Pedro feels like swimming in the pool.

4. "But I can't swim now. I have to dance."

REDACCIÓN

Now you are ready to write your own dialogue or paragraph. Choose one of the following topics.

1. Write a paragraph of four to six sentences about the pictures. How many friends are coming to the party? What are they wearing? What do Pedro and Silvia look like?

2. Expand the story in the *Tema* by writing four to six sentences describing three or four of Silvia's friends and telling what they want to do at the party.

3. Write a brief dialogue of six to eight lines between Silvia and some of her guests.

A   La familia
Complete each sentence with the correct word.

1. Los padres de mi padre son mis _____.
2. La hija de mi tía es mi _____.
3. La esposa de mi padre es mi _____.
4. Los hijos de mi hermana son mis _____.
5. Las hermanas de mi madre son mis _____.
6. El hijo de mis padres es mi _____.

B   ¿Qué tienen que hacer?
Write sentences describing what different people have to do. Follow the model.

  Arturo / ir a la tienda
  Arturo tiene que ir a la tienda.

1. mi primo y yo / ayudar en casa
2. Clara / limpiar la cocina
3. Ricardo y Lourdes / lavar la ropa sucia
4. mi hermanito / dar de comer al perro
5. Ud. / cocinar
6. (nosotros) / practicar béisbol
6. (yo) / viajar a Chicago
8. Héctor y tú / cuidar a los niños

C   No, no tengo
Answer negatively in a complete sentence.

1. ¿Tienes un jardín?
2. ¿Tienen ellos un garaje?
3. ¿Tiene Ud. una oficina?
4. ¿Tengo una clase a las dos?
5. ¿Tenemos un examen hoy?
6. ¿Tienen Uds. un apartamento?
7. ¿Tiene Alicia un barco?

D   No tengo ganas
Answer each question according to the model.

  ¿Vas a lavar los platos?
  No, no tengo ganas de lavar los platos.

1. ¿Van a cuidar ellos a los niños?
2. ¿Va a cantar Ud. en la iglesia?
3. ¿Va a ayudar Pablo en casa?

4. ¿Van a estudiar Uds. en la biblioteca?
5. ¿Van a limpiar ellas la estufa?
6. ¿Vas a lavar el coche?

E   *¿Tener o venir?*
Complete each sentence with the correct form of *tener* or *venir*.

1. ¿_____ Ud. los periódicos de hoy?
2. ¿_____ tú en autobús o a pie?
3. (Nosotros) _____ que limpiar el baño.
4. (Nosotras) _____ a la escuela en coche.
5. Juan y María no _____ a mi casa.
6. Nuestro apartamento no _____ comedor.
7. (Yo) _____ dos hermanas.

F   Los adjetivos posesivos
Answer each question with a complete sentence. Use a possessive adjective.

  ¿Tienes el libro de Julia?
  Sí, tengo su libro.

1. ¿Es Alicia tu tía?
2. ¿Son Inés y Paco los sobrinos de la señora Hernández?
3. ¿Buscan Uds. sus suéteres?
4. Mamá, ¿tienes mis cuadernos?
5. ¿Es la señora alta la abuela de Gloria?
6. ¿Tiene Jorge tus guantes?
7. ¿Tienes el mapa de los chicos?
8. Marta, ¿tienes nuestra dirección?

G   ¿Qué haces allá?
Write logical answers to each question.

1. ¿Qué tienes ganas de hacer hoy?
2. ¿Qué haces en la cocina?
3. ¿Cuántos dormitorios tiene tu casa o apartamento?
4. ¿Cuántos baños tiene?
5. ¿Cuántas sillas hay en tu sala?
6. ¿Qué tienes en tu garaje?
7. ¿Tiene tu familia un jardín?
8. ¿Tienen tú y tu familia una casa o un apartamento?

VOCABULARIO DEL CAPÍTULO 6

Sustantivos

el abuelo, la abuela
los abuelos
el apartamento
el apellido
el baño
la cocina
el comedor
el chico, la chica
el dormitorio
el esposo, la esposa
la estufa
la familia
el garaje
el hermanito, la hermanita
el hermano, la hermana
los hermanos
el hijo, la hija
los hijos
el jardín, *pl.* los jardines
la madre
la mamá
el niño, la niña
los niños
el padre
los padres
el papá
el patio

el piso
la planta baja
el primo, la prima
la quinceañera
los quince años
el refrigerador
la sala
el sobrino, la sobrina
los sobrinos
el tío, la tía
los tíos

Adjetivos

cómodo, -a
especial
importante
incómodo, -a
limpio, -a
mayor
menor
sucio, -a
único, -a

Adjetivos posesivos

nuestro, -a, -os, -as
su, sus

Verbos

ayudar a + *inf.*
limpiar
tener
venir
(yo) puedo
(tú) puedes

Adverbio

tampoco

Expresiones

¿cuántos años tienes?
cuidar a los niños
dar de comer a(l)
el primer (segundo, tercer) piso
¡felicitaciones!
tener ____ años
tener ganas de + *inf.*
tener que + *inf.*

LA EDUCACIÓN SECUNDARIA

I f you got a grade of 10 on your report card, you'd probably be very upset! But many Latin American *escuelas secundarias* or *colegios* use a grading system that goes from 1 to 10.

An *escuela secundaria* has a lot in common with your high school, but there are some important differences. For example, in many Spanish-speaking countries, the year is divided into three terms, or trimesters, of three months each. The classes in your school are probably held in different rooms. In an *escuela secundaria*, students usually stay in the same room and a different teacher comes in for each subject. School is often more formal than in the United States. In many countries, such as Mexico and Nicaragua, students may be required to wear uniforms.

An even bigger difference is that the course of study in an *escuela secundaria* takes five years rather than four. The first three years are called the *ciclo básico* or *ciclo común*. During those three years students take basic courses, just as you do: national and world history, literature, grammar, mathematics, science, and another language, usually English or French. Unlike schools in the United States, there are no elective courses.

Students spend their last two years in specialized training. If they want to become teachers, they attend an *escuela normal*. If they want to go into business or become skilled laborers, they go to an *escuela técnica*. Students who plan to go to college continue taking courses leading to a *bachillerato* (an academic high school degree).

Students graduate only after they have passed a certain number of required courses. In addition, they often have to take a series of difficult oral and written exams. And after all that hard work it still isn't party time. Big graduation parties are not usual in Spanish-speaking countries.

PALABRAS NUEVAS I

El colegio

If students ask: Other related words you may want to present: *el signo interrogativo*, question mark; *el punto*, period; *la coma*, comma.

borrar

¿Cómo está Ud.?

el borrador

3 de marzo de 1989
Querida María

la carta

escribir

dibujar

la papelera

la página

el inglés

I think that
I shall never
see
A poem lovely
as a tree.

el acento

la palabra

¿Cómo está Ud.?
Estoy muy bien.

la frase

el poema

el colegio

llamar

¡Juanita!

llamar

la cafetería

el laboratorio

el francés

* The word for "high school" *(escuela secundaria)* varies throughout the Spanish-speaking world. In Spain *el colegio* is a public high school, while in Latin America it often refers to a private school. The word for a public high school in Latin America might be *la escuela, la escuela secundaria, la escuela preparatoria, el instituto,* or *el colegio.*

Palabras Nuevas I **239**

CONTEXTO COMUNICATIVO

 2

Enrichment: Have students vary mini-dialogue 2: *México → Miami, Nueva York, Santa Fe*; 3: *aprender → leer, escribir.* You may want students to suggest additional **Variaciones** for *cafetería* in 5.

1 PROFESORA ¿Quién está **ausente** hoy?

PABLO **Nadie. Todos** los estudiantes están **presentes.**

PROFESORA Muy bien. Es importante **asistir a** la clase de español **todos los días.**

Variaciones:

- presentes → aquí
- a la clase de español → al colegio

2 MARÍA **Vivo** en México, pero en mi casa hablamos inglés y español.

LUIS ¡Ah! Tu familia es **bilingüe.** ¿Qué te gusta más, el inglés o el español?

MARÍA Prefiero hablar inglés, pero me gusta escribir en español.

- México → San Antonio
- escribir → leer

3 ANA ¿Qué tenemos que **aprender** para mañana?

JORGE **Según** Marta, tenemos que **aprender** todo el poema **de memoria.**

- aprender para mañana → estudiar para el lunes
- todo el poema → toda la página

4 ANDREA Aquí hay una carta de mi primo Carlitos.

FELIPE ¡Sólo hay dibujos! ¿Dónde están las palabras?

ANDREA Pues, Carlitos sólo tiene cinco años. Pero dibuja muy bien, ¿no?

FELIPE ¡Ah! Ahora **comprendo** por qué te gusta **recibir** sus cartas. Son muy divertidas.

- primo Carlitos → prima Elenita
  Carlitos → Elenita

5 JUAN ¿Tiene acento la palabra *cafetería*?

EMILIA ¡Por supuesto!

JUAN Gracias. Ahora tengo **la respuesta correcta.**

- cafetería → página
- ¡por supuesto! → ¡cómo no!

---

ausente *absent*

nadie *no one, nobody, not anyone*

todo, -a, -os, -as *every; all; the whole*

presente *present*

asistir a *to attend*

todos los días *every day*

vivir (yo vivo, tú vives) *to live*

bilingüe *bilingual*

aprender (yo aprendo, tú aprendes) *to learn*

según *according to*

aprender ___ de memoria *to memorize*

comprender (yo comprendo, tú comprendes) *to understand*

recibir (yo recibo, tú recibes) *to receive, to get*

la respuesta *answer*

correcto, -a *correct*

Reteach / Review: Point out the use of diminutives in mini-dialogue 4 *(Carlitos, Elenita).* Elicit Carlitos and Elenita's real names *(Carlos, Elena).* You may want to refer students to the **Estudio de palabras** on p. 220.

6 GLORIA   Tengo un examen de francés mañana y no estoy **preparada.** Tengo que estudiar dos **capítulos** del libro.

LOLA   ¿Por qué no llamas a mi tía Norma?

GLORIA   **¿A quién?**

LOLA   A mi tía Norma. Ella **enseña** francés y es muy simpática.

GLORIA   ¡Qué suerte! Muchas gracias, Lola.

- capítulos → **lecciones**
- ¡qué suerte! → **¡no me digas!**

preparado, -a   *prepared, ready*
el capítulo   *chapter*

¿a quién(es)?   *(to) who(m)*
enseñar   *to teach*

la lección, *pl.* **las lecciones**
   lesson

NOTE: We use the definite article with the names of languages except after *en, de,* and the verbs *aprender, enseñar, estudiar,* and *hablar.* We also usually use the definite article with the names of school subjects except after those same words.

Lecciones de inglés en España

PRÁCTICA

A ¿Qué hacen? Contesta las preguntas según el dibujo.

1. ¿Qué dibuja el muchacho?
2. ¿Con qué dibuja?
3. ¿En qué dibuja?
4. ¿Dibuja también la muchacha?
5. ¿Qué palabras en la pizarra tienen acento?
6. ¿A quién llama la profesora?
7. ¿Qué capítulo estudia Andrés? ¿Qué página?
8. ¿Hablan francés o español en la clase?
9. ¿Qué hay en la papelera?
10. ¿Cuántos estudiantes están presentes?
11. ¿Quién está en la puerta?

Práctica A
1. una bandera
2. con una tiza
3. en la pizarra
4. No, borra una frase.
5. lección y páginas
6. a Andrés
7. el capítulo 7, página 39
8. español
9. hojas de papel
10. seis
11. nadie

B ¿Cuál es la tarea? Imagina que tú enseñas la clase de español hoy. ¿Qué tarea vas a dar *(to give)* a los estudiantes? Escoge palabras de las dos columnas. Sigue el modelo.

> *Uds. tienen que aprender la página 75 de memoria.*

aprender	un poema corto
aprender ___ de memoria	unas frases en inglés
buscar	el periódico en casa
contestar	todas las preguntas en español
dibujar	un mapa de España
escribir	una carta en español
estudiar	la lección 7
leer	la página 75
practicar	un capítulo aburrido
	un cartel tonto
	todas las respuestas correctas
	la bandera española
	las palabras nuevas
	unos libros en la biblioteca

C Hablemos de ti.

1. ¿Te gusta dibujar? ¿Qué dibujas? ¿Son buenos tus dibujos? ¿Qué estudiantes en tu clase dibujan bien?
2. ¿Están todos presentes en tu clase de español hoy? ¿Quién(es) está(n) ausente(s)?
3. ¿Quiénes enseñan español en tu escuela? ¿Quiénes enseñan francés?

Práctica B
Answers will vary.

Notes: You may want to do Ex. B as a class activity after giving students a few minutes to study the lists.

Práctica C
Answers will vary.

Enrichment: Additional questions for Ex. C: *¿Te gusta hablar por teléfono? ¿A quién llamas a menudo? ¿Estás ausente a veces o asistes a la escuela todos los días? ¿Te gusta leer poemas? ¿Siempre comprendes los poemas?*

Practice Sheet 7–1

Workbook Exs. A–B

Tape Manual Exs. 1–2   3

Quiz 7–1

ACTIVIDAD

Cadenas *(chains)* Play this association game with two or three other students. One person starts by saying a noun or a verb: *dibujar,* for example. Another person must say a word that is connected in some way to the first word. For example:

> el dibujo / el lápiz / la hoja de papel / etc.

See how many words you can link together logically in a chain. When no one can think of another word, someone else should begin a new chain. Here are some words you might use to begin chains:

el almacén	la familia	limpiar
la ciudad	comer	llamar
el deporte	escribir	
la escuela	leer	

la nota

la prueba

el horario

la escuela

la clase

APLICACIONES

Discretionary

Señorita, no comprendo 4

En un colegio de San José, Costa Rica.

PROFESORA	Buenos días, alumnos. ¿Están todos preparados hoy?
ALUMNOS	Sí, Sra. Rivera.
5 PROFESORA	Muy bien . . . Carlos, ¿quieres escribir la palabra *bilingüe* en la pizarra?
CARLOS	No comprendo. ¿Qué quiere decir *bilingüe*?
PROFESORA	¿Cómo? ¿Y dónde está tu tarea? La palabra *bilingüe* está en la lección de hoy.
10 CARLOS	No tengo mi tarea, señora.
PROFESORA	¿Por qué no?
CARLOS	Porque ahora no tengo tiempo.[1] Mi abuela de California está en casa.
PROFESORA	¡Ah! Tu abuela es de los Estados Unidos. ¿Habla inglés?
15 CARLOS	¡Por supuesto, señora!
PROFESORA	¿Y habla español también?
CARLOS	¡Cómo no!
PROFESORA	Entonces, tu abuela es bilingüe. Habla dos lenguas,[2] el inglés y el español. ¿Comprendes ahora?
20 CARLOS	¡Ah, sí! ¡Ahora comprendo! Una persona que[3] habla dos lenguas es bilingüe.

Estudiantes en Buenos
Aires

---

[1] **el tiempo** here: *time*   [2] **la lengua** *language*   [3] **que** *who*

Culture: Have students find Costa Rica on a map. You may want students to do research on Costa Rica and present brief oral reports to the class.

Preguntas

Contesta según el diálogo.

1. ¿Dónde están la profesora y Carlos?   2. ¿Qué palabra tiene que escribir Carlos?   3. ¿Por qué no tiene Carlos su tarea?   4. ¿Quién está en la casa de Carlos?   5. ¿De dónde es su abuela?   6. ¿Cuántas lenguas habla ella? ¿Cuáles son?   7. ¿Qué quiere decir la palabra *bilingüe*? (Quiere decir que . . . .)

Enrichment: Additional questions you may want to ask: ¿Quién es la profesora? (la Sra. Rivera) ¿Está preparado Carlos? (No.) ¿Por qué está ocupado Carlos? (Porque su abuela está en casa y él tiene que estar con ella.)

Diálogo

1. En un colegio de San José, Costa Rica.
2. *bilingüe*
3. Porque no tiene tiempo. (Su abuela de los Estados Unidos está en casa y él tiene que estar con ella.)
4. su abuela
5. de los Estados Unidos (de California)
6. dos lenguas: (el) inglés y (el) español
7. . . . una persona habla dos lenguas

244   Capítulo 7

Participación

Work with a partner to make up a four- to six-line dialogue in Spanish between a teacher and a student who is not prepared for class. For example, the student might say *Mi madre está enferma* or *No tengo un lápiz.* What does the teacher say? It might begin *Tienes que . . . .*

PRONUNCIACIÓN 5

A The pronunciation of the letter *p* in English is often followed by a little puff of air. If you put your hand close to your mouth, you can feel the air when you say the word "popular." In Spanish, *p* is pronounced without this puff of air.
Escucha y repite.

por	papa	palabra	poema	papelera

B Escucha y repite.

Pablo siempre está preocupado.
¿Por qué no aprendes el poema?
Pepe está preparado para el partido.
No comprendo las palabras del primer capítulo.

PALABRAS NUEVAS II

¿Qué materias tienes hoy?

la química

la biología

la física

el arte

la nota

el álgebra

sacar una buena nota

Reteach / Review: Reinforce the vocabulary presented in the **Contexto visual** by asking students to work in pairs asking and answering *¿Te gusta la clase de ____?* and adding the names of school subjects. Tell students to answer *No sé* if they've never taken the subject.

If students ask: Other related words you may want to present: *el bolso*, purse; *el peine*, comb; *el cepillo*, brush; *el lápiz de labios*, lipstick; *el cesto*, basket.

la educación física

la geometría

la historia

la computadora

la computadora

las computadoras

sacar una mala nota

el horario

1 LUIS ¿Cuál es tu **materia favorita**?

ESTER La química o la física. **Estoy** muy **fuerte en las ciencias.**

Variaciones:
- física → biología
- estoy muy fuerte → saco buenas notas

la materia *school subject*
favorito, -a *favorite*
estar fuerte en *to be good in*
las ciencias *science*

2 RAÚL Sacas muy buenas notas en geometría. ¡Qué **lista** eres!

ANDREA Sí, pero **estoy floja en** historia. Es muy **difícil** para **mí.** Voy a **salir mal en** el examen.

- ¡qué lista eres! → ¡qué suerte tienes!
- historia → inglés
- es muy difícil → no es muy **fácil**
- salir mal → sacar una mala nota

listo, -a *smart, clever*
estar flojo, -a en *to be poor in*
difícil *hard, difficult*
mí *me*
salir mal en *to do badly on (exams)*

fácil *easy*

3 JAVIER No voy a **salir bien en la prueba** de biología.

SONIA ¿Quieres **repasar** el capítulo 14 **conmigo**?

JAVIER **¿Contigo?** ¡Nunca! Siempre sacas malas notas.

SONIA ¡Qué antipático eres!

- salir bien → sacar una buena nota
- repasar → estudiar

salir bien en *to do well on (exams)*
la prueba = el examen
repasar *to review*
conmigo *with me*
contigo *with you* (fam.)

4 MATEO ¿Tienes biología **por la mañana**?

INÉS Sí. A las diez.

MATEO ¿Cuándo tienes **matemáticas**?

INÉS **Después de** biología.

MATEO ¿Y a qué hora **terminan** tus clases?

INÉS A las doce.

- biología → ciencias
- por la mañana → **por la tarde**
  a las diez → a las dos
  a las doce → a las cuatro

por la mañana *in the morning*

las matemáticas *mathematics*
después de (+ noun) *after;* (+ infinitive) *after* + verb + *-ing*
terminar *to end, to finish*

por la tarde *in the afternoon*

5

LUIS	¿Quieres **aprender a usar** la computadora?
JUDIT	¡Cómo no! ¿Cuándo es la clase? ¿Por la mañana?
LUIS	No, es por la tarde. A las 4:30.
JUDIT	¡Qué lástima! Estoy ocupada por la tarde.

- por la tarde → **por la noche**
  a las 4:30 → a las 7:45
  la tarde → la noche

aprender a + inf.   *to learn (how) to*

usar   *to use*

por la noche   *in the evening, at night*

6

BEATRIZ	**¿Para quién** es el libro de arte? ¿Para **ti**?
CÉSAR	**¡Ojalá!** Pero no sé para quién es.

- ti → él
- ti → Ud.
- ti → mí

¿para quién?   *for whom?*
ti   *you (object)*
¡ojalá!   *I hope so!, let's hope so!*

Culture: In mini-dialogue 6, point out that *¡ojalá!* is derived from Arabic and literally means "Allah grant that. . . ." This loanword is among many that made their way into Spanish during the Moorish occupation of Spain (711–1492).

EN OTRAS PARTES

En España se dice
el ordenador.

la materia

En España se dice
la asignatura.

Una clase de computadoras
en España

PRÁCTICA

Práctica A
1. A las nueve.
2. A las diez menos cuarto.
3. A las once y cuarto.
4. A las diez y media.
5. A las ocho y cuarto.
6. A las ocho y cuarto.
7. A las trece (*or*: a la una) y cuarto.
8. A las doce (*or*: al mediodía).

Reteach / Extra Help:
Expand the practice in Ex. A by asking students to talk about their own class schedules.

Enrichment: For a written homework assignment, ask students to prepare their own class schedules, using the one on p. 36 as a model.

A El horario. Mira el horario. Pregunta y contesta según el modelo.

HORARIO

HORA	MATERIA	PROFESOR(A)
8:15–8:55	computadoras	Srta. Burgos
9:00–9:40	química (laboratorio)	Sra. Pedernera
9:45–10:25	historia (biblioteca)	Sr. Galván
10:30–11:10	álgebra	Srta. Burgos
11:15–11:55	español	Sra. Fernández
12:00–12:25	hora de comer (cafetería)	
12:30–13:10	inglés	Sr. Castro
13:15–13:55	educación física (gimnasio)	Sra. Herrera (muchachas) Sr. González (muchachos)

ir a la clase de historia
ESTUDIANTE A *¿A qué hora tienes que ir a la clase de historia?*
ESTUDIANTE B *A las diez menos cuarto.*

1. ir al laboratorio de química
2. estar en la biblioteca
3. asistir a la clase de español
4. ir a la prueba de álgebra
5. ir a la clase de computadoras
6. estar en la escuela para tu primera clase
7. ir al gimnasio
8. ir a comer

* In Spanish-speaking countries, schedules and timetables often use a 24-hour clock rather than A.M. and P.M. Therefore, 13:15 is the equivalent of 1:15 P.M., and 14:00 is the equivalent of 2:00 P.M.

B ¿A qué clase van? ¿A qué clase va cada (*each*) estudiante? ¿Cuándo es la clase? ¿Por la mañana, por la tarde o por la noche? Contesta según el modelo.

la muchacha
La muchacha va a la clase de física por la mañana.

1. Miguel

2. sus amigas

3. la profesora

4. Ana

5. el primo de José

6. la tía de Nicolás

7. el hermano de Lucía

8. el sobrino del profesor

9. Pepe

Práctica B

1. Miguel va a la clase de álgebra por la mañana.
2. Sus amigas van a la clase de historia por la tarde.
3. La profesora va a la clase de español por la mañana.
4. Ana va a la clase de química por la tarde.
5. El primo de José va a la clase de francés por la mañana.
6. La tía de Nicolás va a la clase de educación física por la noche.
7. El hermano de Lucía va a la clase de biología por la tarde.
8. El sobrino del profesor va a la clase de geometría por la tarde.
9. Pepe va a la clase de arte por la noche.

Práctica C

Answers will vary.

C Hablemos de ti.

1. ¿En qué materias estás fuerte? ¿En cuáles estás flojo(a)?
2. ¿Quién es tu profesor(a) favorito(a)? ¿Por qué?
3. ¿Te gustan o no te gustan las pruebas de español? ¿Por qué? ¿Siempre sales bien? ¿Por qué?
4. ¿Estás siempre preparado(a) para tus clases? ¿Para tus pruebas? ¿Qué nota sacas cuando no estás preparado(a)?

Practice Sheet 7–2   Workbook Exs. C–D

 8 Tape Manual Exs. 3–4   Quiz 7–2

ESTUDIO DE PALABRAS

Many Spanish words that end in -*ia* and -*ía* have English equivalents that end in -*y*.

la farmacia	*pharmacy*	la biología	*biology*
la historia	*history*	la geografía	*geography*
la comedia	*comedy*	la geometría	*geometry*

What do you think the following words mean?

memoria	democracia	filosofía
tragedia	compañía	psicología

Enrichment: Additional questions for Ex. C: *¿Vas a la clase de español por la mañana o por la tarde? ¿Estudias a veces con un(a) compañero(a)? ¿Quién repasa contigo? ¿Cuál es tu materia favorita?*

Palabras Nuevas II   **251**

EXPLICACIONES I

Verbos que terminan en *-er* y en *-ir*

◆ **OBJECTIVE:**

TO TELL WHAT YOU DO IN SCHOOL

Notes: You may want to refer students to the glosses on p. 240 for the *yo / tú* forms of some *-er* and *-ir* verbs.

You already know the present tense of *-ar* verbs. There are two other groups of regular verbs—one with infinitives ending in *-er*, the other in *-ir*. Here are the present-tense forms of the *-er* verb *aprender* ("to learn").

INFINITIVO   **aprender**

	SINGULAR		PLURAL	
1	(yo)	aprend**o**	(nosotros) (nosotras) }	aprend**emos**
2	(tú)	aprend**es**	(vosotros) (vosotras) }	aprend**éis**
3	Ud. (él) (ella) }	aprend**e**	Uds. (ellos) (ellas) }	aprend**en**

Aprendemos muchas palabras.   *We learn a lot of words.*
¿Aprendes a hablar español?   *Are you learning to speak Spanish?*

Other regular *-er* verbs that you know are *comer, leer,* and *comprender.*

Now look at the present tense of verbs that end in *-ir*. *Escribir* ("to write") is an example:

INFINITIVO   **escribir**

	SINGULAR		PLURAL	
1	(yo)	escrib**o**	(nosotros) (nosotras)	escrib**imos**
2	(tú)	escrib**es**	(vosotros) (vosotras)	escrib**ís**
3	Ud. (él) (ella)	escrib**e**	Uds. (ellos) (ellas)	escrib**en**

Mi amigo **escribe** poemas.   *My friend **writes** poems.*
¿Qué **escriben** Uds.?   *What **are you writing**?*

Other regular *-ir* verbs that you know are *vivir, recibir,* and *asistir*.

Regular *-er* and *-ir* verbs have identical endings in the present tense except in the *nosotros* and *vosotros* forms.

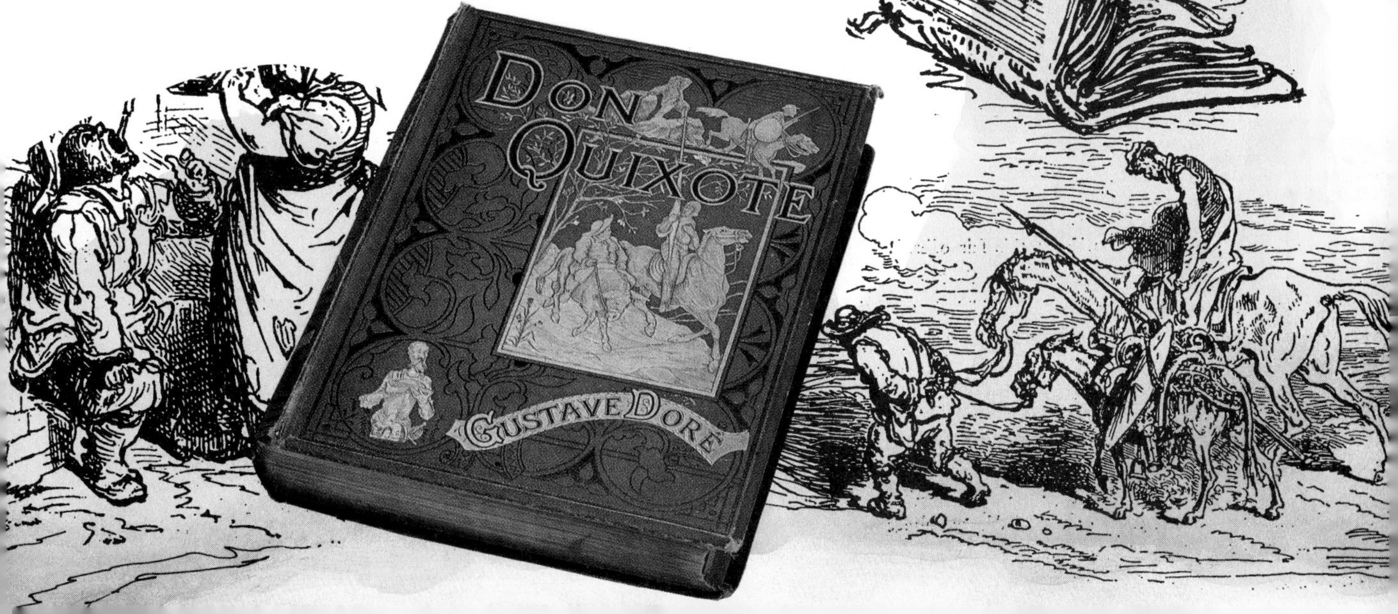

Práctica A
1. Graciela comprende las palabras.
2. Uds. comprenden la frase.
3. Nosotros no comprendemos el capítulo.
4. Los muchachos no comprenden las lecciones.
5. Yo comprendo el poema.
6. Tú no comprendes la respuesta.
7. Nadie comprende la pregunta.
8. Ud. no comprende la tarea.
9. Mis hermanas comprenden el horario.
10. Anita y tú comprenden la lección.

Reteach / Extra Help: When students have completed Ex. A, you may want to extend the practice by asking students to change the affirmative sentences (1, 2, 5, 7, 9, 10) to negative sentences using *no*.

Práctica B
1. ¿Qué reciben tus hermanas?
   Siempre reciben bufandas.
2. ¿Qué recibes?
   Siempre recibo un impermeable.
3. ¿Qué recibe tu prima Luz?
   Siempre recibe calcetines.
4. ¿Qué recibe tu hermano mayor?
   Siempre recibe libros.
5. ¿Qué recibes?
   Siempre recibo un traje.
6. ¿Qué reciben Uds.?
   Siempre recibimos carteles.
7. ¿Qué reciben tus abuelos?
   Siempre reciben bolígrafos.
8. ¿Qué recibe tu mamá?
   Siempre recibe una falda.
9. ¿Qué recibe tu papá?
   Siempre recibe zapatos.

PRÁCTICA

A ¿Quién no comprende? Di *(tell)* quién comprende y quién no comprende. Sigue el modelo.

> Arturo / no / la frase
> *Arturo no comprende la frase.*

1. Graciela / las palabras
2. Uds. / la frase
3. nosotros / no / el capítulo
4. los muchachos / no / las lecciones
5. yo / el poema
6. tú / no / la respuesta
7. nadie / la pregunta
8. Ud. / no / la tarea
9. mis hermanas / el horario
10. Anita y tú / la lección

B Regalos de Navidad. Cada *(each)* miembro de la familia Herrera recibe la misma clase de regalo *(the same kind of present)* todos los años. Pregunta y contesta según el modelo.

tu hermano Carlitos

ESTUDIANTE A   *¿Qué recibe tu hermano Carlitos?*
ESTUDIANTE B   *Siempre recibe un reloj.*

1. tus hermanas   2. (tú)   3. tu prima Luz

4. tu hermano mayor   5. (tú)   6. Uds.

7. tus abuelos   8. tu mamá   9. tu papá

C Tengo muchas preguntas. Imagina que hablas con unos amigos que asisten a otro *(another)* colegio. Pregunta y contesta según el modelo.

> aprender a hablar inglés / francés
> ESTUDIANTE A   *¿Aprenden Uds. a hablar inglés?*
> ESTUDIANTE B   *No, aprendemos a hablar francés.*

1. vivir cerca de la escuela / lejos de
2. escribir mucho en su clase de inglés / muy poco
3. aprender poemas de memoria / nada de memoria
4. leer periódicos en inglés / periódicos en español
5. comer en la cafetería / en casa
6. recibir notas muy buenas / notas buenas y malas
7. asistir al colegio por la tarde / sólo por la mañana

Práctica C
1. ¿Viven Uds....?
   No, vivimos lejos.
2. ¿Escriben Uds....?
   No, escribimos muy poco.
3. ¿Aprenden Uds....?
   No, no aprendemos nada de memoria.
4. ¿Leen Uds....?
   No, leemos…
5. ¿Comen Uds....?
   No, comemos…
6. ¿Reciben Uds....?
   No, recibimos…
7. ¿Asisten Uds....?
   No, asistimos…

En Oruro, Bolivia

D **Para sacar buenas notas.** Escribe la forma correcta de cada verbo entre paréntesis para completar este anuncio (*this advertisement*).

¿(Recibir) tú malas notas en el colegio, y no (*comprender*) por qué? Nosotros (*tener*) la respuesta. Con nuestro libro *El estudiante perfecto*, puedes (*aprender*) todas las materias en sólo una semana. Nuestros estudiantes (*aprender*) ciencias, matemáticas, historia y muchas
5 lenguas. Después de una semana, ellos (*comprender*) las lecciones, (*escribir*) las respuestas correctas a preguntas muy difíciles y (*leer*) en inglés, francés y español. ¿Por qué no (*aprender*) tú con nosotros?

En un colegio español

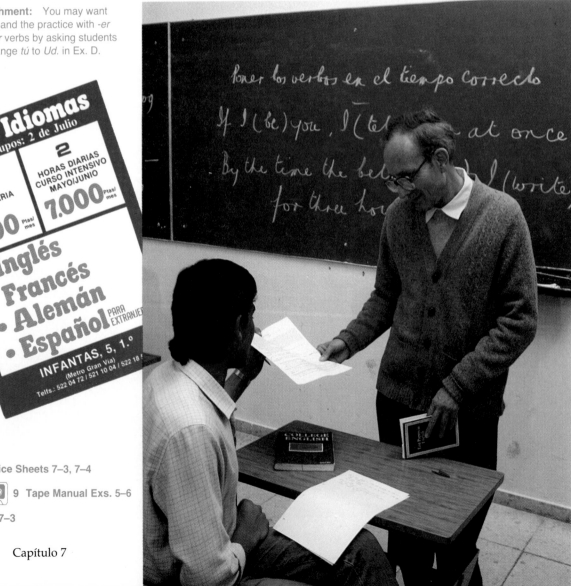

La a personal

Notes: Point out that the personal *a* is first presented in mini-dialogue 6 on p. 241.

A direct object is the person or thing that receives the action of a verb. The following sentences have direct objects. They tell *what* and *who* I understand.

Comprendo **mi libro de matemáticas.**	*I understand **my math book.***
Comprendo $\begin{cases} \textbf{al profesor.} \\ \textbf{a la profesora.} \end{cases}$	*I understand **the teacher.***

In Spanish we use *a* before the direct object when it is a specific person or group of people. That's why it's called the personal *a*. Remember that *a + el → al*.

¿A quién miras?	***Whom** are you looking at?*
Miro **a mi hermana.**	*I'm looking at **my sister.***
¿Qué miras?	***What** are you looking at?*
Miro **el reloj.**	*I'm looking at **the clock.***

1 We use the personal *a* before *¿quién?* and *¿quiénes?* when they are direct objects.

¿A quién esperas?	***Whom** are you waiting for?*
¿A quiénes dibujan?	***Whom** are they drawing?*

2 When more than one person is mentioned, we usually repeat the *a*.

Esperamos **a Graciela y a su mamá.**	*We're waiting for **Graciela and her mother.***

3 We can also use the personal *a* when the direct object is a pet.

Busco **a mi perro.**	*I'm looking for **my dog.***

4 We usually do not use the personal *a* after the verb *tener*.

Tengo muchos tíos.	*I have a lot of aunts and uncles.*

◆ **OBJECTIVES:**

TO DESCRIBE DOING THINGS THAT INVOLVE OTHER PEOPLE— LOOKING FOR, WAITING FOR, WATCHING THEM, AND SO FORTH

Enrichment: You may want to initiate a chain drill asking *¿A quién miras? (Miro a _____.)* Contrast this with *¿Qué miras? (Miro _____.)* using classroom objects.

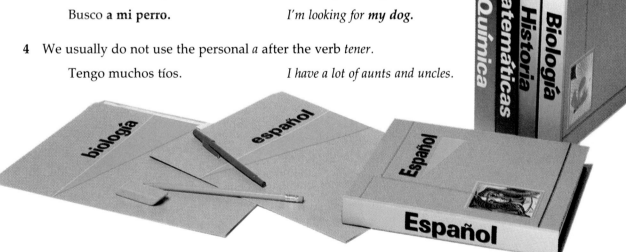

PRÁCTICA

A **¿A quién buscan?**   En el aeropuerto hay muchas personas que buscan a sus amigos o a sus parientes *(relatives)*. ¿Cómo van a encontrarlos *(to find them)*? Pregunta y contesta según el modelo.

Ricardo Profesora Díaz

Rita Pedro Yolanda Lucía y su mamá Rosa Sr. Muñoz Sra. Cruz y Sr. Cruz

Andrea / su hermana Rita

ESTUDIANTE A   *¿A quién busca Andrea?*
ESTUDIANTE B   *Busca a su hermana Rita. Lleva zapatos rojos.*

1. el Sr. García / su hijo Ernesto
2. Roberto y David / Pedro y Yolanda
3. la Sra. Marín / su sobrina Rosa
4. Julio Cruz / sus padres
5. Sofía / Lucía y su mamá
6. los estudiantes / la profesora Díaz
7. (tú) / mi primo Ricardo
8. la Sra. Muñoz / su esposo

B **Un viaje interesante.** Felipe está en México, su ciudad favorita. Está delante del hotel—y está muy contento. ¿Qué mira él? Sigue el modelo.

una chica pelirroja
Mira a una chica pelirroja.

1. los chicos en el parque
2. una avenida grande
3. los estudiantes del colegio
4. el museo de historia
5. el policía en la esquina
6. la fuente de la plaza
7. una niña y su mamá
8. muchos autobuses y taxis
9. Gloria, su prima
10. un vendedor de ropa

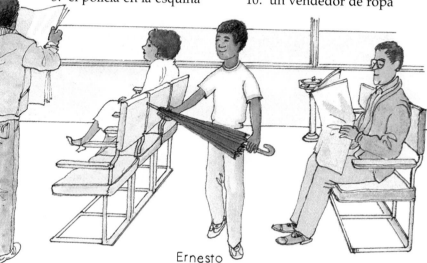

Ernesto

C **Tienes mucho que hacer.** Imagina que cuando llegas a casa hay muchos recados (*messages*) para ti. Escribe ocho de los recados que recibes. Usa una palabra o expresión de cada columna. Sigue el modelo.

Tienes que llamar a tu padre a las ocho.

buscar	tus primos	a las ocho
mirar	el autobús	por la tarde
esperar	tu padre	esta noche
llamar	la carta	para mañana
dibujar	tu gato	ahora
contestar	la lección	en el laboratorio
repasar	tu hermanita	en el libro de francés
escuchar	las preguntas	en casa
ayudar	Isabel y Luis	enfrente del colegio
tomar	los profesores	al centro
escribir	las respuestas	de la profesora

D Hablemos de ti.

1. ¿Cuál es tu materia favorita? ¿Por qué? ¿Es fácil o difícil para ti? ¿Sacas buenas o malas notas?
2. ¿Te gustan todas tus clases? ¿Qué materias no te gustan? ¿Por qué?
3. ¿Tiene tu escuela una cafetería? ¿Es buena la comida? ¿Comes allí todos los días? ¿Qué comes al mediodía?
4. ¿A veces tienes que aprender poemas de memoria? ¿Escribes poemas? ¿Son largos o cortos tus poemas? ¿Escribes poemas en español?
5. ¿Recibes muchas cartas? ¿De quiénes?
6. ¿Escribes cartas? ¿A quiénes? ¿Contestan ellos tus cartas?
7. ¿Usan tú y tus compañeros computadoras? ¿Te gustan las computadoras? ¿Por qué?
8. ¿Vives en la ciudad o en el campo? ¿Cuál es tu dirección?

ACTIVIDAD

¿A qué hora comes? Get together in groups of three or four students to ask one another questions. One person begins by picking a question word or a phrase from the left-hand column. The next person picks a verb from the right-hand column that continues the question and addresses it to *tú*. The third person thinks up an ending to the question, and the fourth person must answer the question. For example:

ESTUDIANTE A ¿De quién . . . ?
ESTUDIANTE B ¿De quién recibes . . . ?
ESTUDIANTE C ¿De quién recibes cartas?
ESTUDIANTE D Recibo cartas de mis abuelos.

¿de quién(es)?	asistir a
¿a quién(es)?	comer
¿dónde?	contestar
¿por qué?	escribir
¿con quién(es)?	hablar
¿cuándo?	ir
¿a qué hora?	recibir
	ser
	terminar
	usar
	vivir

APLICACIONES

Discretionary

En la escuela
Transparency 34

Los alumnos asisten a sus clases. ¿Qué materias estudian hoy?
¿Qué hacen? ¿Qué clases son difíciles? ¿Cuáles son fáciles?

Clara and Alberto are studying for a mathematics exam. Make up a four–
to six-line dialogue in which they talk about how well prepared they are,
what they have to review, and how they think they are going to do on
the exam. You may want to use some of these words or phrases:

aprender (de memoria)   ¡ojalá!
estar flojo, -a en   sacar una buena / mala nota
estar fuerte en   salir bien / mal en la prueba

Notes: Sample dialogues for
the **¿Qué pasa?** appear in the
pre-chapter teacher pages. You
may want volunteers to present
their dialogues to the class.

Notes: Mini-dialogues 2 and 3 on p. 248 and 6 on p. 249 illustrate prepositions used with prepositional pronouns.

Remind students that *de* does not contract with the pronoun *él*. You may want to explain that the accent on the pronoun *mí* differentiates it from the possessive adjective *mi*.

◆ **OBJECTIVES:**

TO EXPRESS DOING THINGS WITH AND FOR OTHER PEOPLE

TO COMPARE LIKES AND DISLIKES

EXPLICACIONES II

Las preposiciones y los pronombres prepositivos

Here is a list of prepositions that you have learned so far:

a	*at, to*	detrás de	*behind*
de	*of, from*	delante de	*in front of*
en	*in, on, at*	enfrente de	*opposite, across from*
para	*for*	cerca de	*near*
con	*with*	lejos de	*far away from*
sin	*without*	después de	*after*
al lado de	*next to, beside*	según	*according to*
entre	*between*		

Pronouns that come after prepositions are called "prepositional pronouns." You have already used most of them.

SINGULAR	PLURAL
para **mí** *for me*	para { **nosotros** / **nosotras** } *for us*
para **ti** *for you*	para { **vosotros** / **vosotras** } *for you*
para **usted (Ud.)** *for you*	para **ustedes (Uds.)** *for you*
para **él** *for him, it* para **ella** *for her, it*	para { **ellos** / **ellas** } *for them*

Note that these pronouns are identical to the subject pronouns except for *mí* and *ti*. Remember that *mí* has an accent, but *ti* does not.

1 After the preposition *con,* there are special forms for *mí* and *ti: conmigo* and *contigo.*

¿Viene Ud. **conmigo**?	*Are you coming **with me**?*
¿Puedo ir **contigo**?	*May I go **with you**?*

2 You know the expressions *me/te gusta(n)* and *me encanta(n)*. To emphasize the *me* and *te* we add the phrase *a mí* and *a ti*.

No me gusta el álgebra. ¿**A ti** te gusta?
¡Ah, sí! **A mí** me gusta mucho.

*I don't like algebra. Do **you** like it?*
*Oh, yes! **I** like it a lot.*

Notes: Refer students to mini-dialogues 6 on p. 241 and 6 on p. 249 for further examples of word order with prepositions and question words.

3 When we ask a question using a preposition we put the preposition before the question word.

¿**Con quién** repasas el capítulo?

Con Uds.

¿**Para quién** es el vestido largo?
Es para mí.

***With whom** are you reviewing the chapter?*
With you.

***Whom** is the long dress **for**?*
It's for me.

Enrichment: Provide practice with *a mí me gusta(n)* and *a ti te gusta(n)* by asking pairs to work with the example given here in **Explicaciones II**. Encourage students to substitute personalized information.

Delante de la escuela en el Perú

PRÁCTICA

Práctica A
1. ¿Para quién es el libro?
   Es para ella.
2. ¿Para quién es el refrigerador? Es para Uds.
3. ¿Para quién(es) son las
   blusas? Son para nosotras.
4. ¿Para quién es la bufanda?
   Es para él.
5. ¿Para quién es la mesa?
   Es para mí.
6. ¿Para quién es la guitarra?
   Es para ti.

A Es para ti.   Después de la subasta del barrio (*neighborhood auction*), buscas a las personas que compraron estos artículos (*who bought these items*). Pregunta y contesta según el modelo.

ESTUDIANTE A   *¿Para quién son los bolígrafos?*
ESTUDIANTE B   *Son para él.*

1.

2.

3.

4.

5.

6.

Reteach / Extra Help: After students do Ex. A in class, you may want to assign it as written homework. Vary the practice by asking students to substitute *de* for *para.*

Práctica B
Final comment will vary.
1. ¿Con quién dibuja Julia el
   cartel? Conmigo.
   ¿Contigo?…
2. ¿Con quién(es) escribes la
   tarea?… ¿Con ellos?…
3. ¿Con quién entra Diana en
   la clase?… ¿Con él?…
4. ¿Con quién(es) usan
   Federico y Norma la
   computadora?…
   ¿Con Uds.? (*or:* ¿Con
   nosotros?)…
5. ¿Con quién borra Judit la
   pizarra?… ¿Con ella?…
6. ¿Con quién(es) vienen los
   muchachos aquí?… ¿Con
   ellas?…

B ¿Con quién?   Jorge es una persona muy curiosa. Tiene muchas preguntas sobre (*about*) todos sus compañeros de clase. Pregunta y contesta según el modelo. Usa una de las expresiones de la lista a la derecha.

María / repasar el capítulo / con Juan
ESTUDIANTE A   *¿Con quién repasa María el capítulo?*
ESTUDIANTE B   *Con Juan.*
ESTUDIANTE A   *¿Con él? ¡Qué suerte!*

1. Julia / dibujar el cartel / conmigo   ¡Qué lástima!
2. (tú) / escribir la tarea / con Julio y Silvia   ¡Qué bueno!
3. Diana / entrar en la clase / con Pedro   ¡Qué suerte!
4. Federico y Norma / usar la computadora / con   ¡No me digas!
   nosotros   ¡Ojalá!
5. Judit / borrar la pizarra / con Rosa
6. los muchachos / venir aquí / con sus novias

7. Uds. / hablar del horario / con nuestro profesor
8. Timoteo / leer el libro de biología / con Olga y Sonia
9. (tú) / comer al mediodía / contigo
10. Ud. / tomar el metro / con Ud.

C Hablemos de ti.

1. ¿Quién vive contigo?
2. ¿Quiénes de tus amigos viven cerca de ti?
3. ¿Qué hay enfrente de ti en este *(this)* momento?
4. ¿A qué hora termina la clase de español? ¿Adónde vas después de la clase? ¿Está cerca o lejos de aquí? ¿Cuántos minutos hay entre tus clases?
5. Te gusta sacar buenas notas, ¿verdad? ¿Por qué? ¿Quieres sacar buenas notas para tus profesores, tus padres o para ti?

7. ¿Con quién hablan Uds. del horario?... ¿Con él?...
8. ¿Con quién(es) lee Timoteo el libro de biología?... ¿Con ellas?...
9. ¿Con quién comes al mediodía? Contigo. ¿Conmigo?...
10. ¿Con quién toma Ud. el metro?... ¿Conmigo?...

Práctica C
Answers will vary.

Enrichment: Additional questions for Ex. C: *¿Dónde viven tus abuelos? ¿Viven cerca o lejos de ti? ¿Vienes solo(a) a la escuela o viene un amigo contigo?*

En la Universidad Católica de Lima

APLICACIONES

REPASO

Notes: Answers to the **Repaso** and **Tema** appear in the pre-chapter teacher pages.

Notes: Review of:
1. *-ar / -er / -ir* verbs agreement and position of adjectives
2. *me / te gusta(n)* with prepositional pronouns definite article as "the" and use with nouns in a general sense noun phrases with *de*
3. *estar* adjective agreement
4. *-ar* and *-er* verbs possessive adjectives direct object nouns and personal *a*
5. *puedo / puedes quiero / quieres* prepositional pronouns exclamations

Look carefully at the model sentences. Then put the English cues into Spanish to form new sentences based on the models.

1. *Julio asiste a una clase difícil. Comprende las primeras lecciones.*
   (I attend a bilingual school. I'm waiting for the first test.)
   (We're reading an easy lesson. I'm studying the next pages.)
   (Federico and I are writing a long poem. We're using the small computer.)

2. *Me gusta el libro de historia. ¿A ti te gusta la historia también?*
   (I like the algebra lessons. Do you like algebra too?)
   (I like the physics class. Do you like science too?)
   (I like the chemistry laboratory. Do you like chemistry too?)

3. *Sí, cuando estamos ocupados. Estamos muy ocupados en abril.*
   (Yes, when she's absent. She's rather poor in geometry.)
   (Yes, when I'm present. I'm very good in French.)
   (Yes, when he's tired. He's very poor in phys. ed.)

4. *Escucho mis cintas, pero a menudo no escucho a la profesora.*
   (We look at our drawings, but sometimes we don't look at the teacher (m.).)
   (We understand their questions, but sometimes we don't understand the teachers (m.).)
   (I look for my grades, but I never look for the teachers (f.).)

5. *¿Puedes escribir las palabras para nosotros? ¡Cómo no!*
   (Do you want to get a letter from him? I hope so!)
   (Can I finish the lesson with you (pl.)? Why not?)
   (Do you want to look at the schedule with me? Of course!)

Biblioteca de la
Universidad de Puerto Rico

Put the English captions into Spanish.

REDACCIÓN

Now you are ready to write your own dialogue or paragraph. Choose one
of the following topics.

1. Expand your story by writing four to six sentences about the pictures
   in the *Tema*. Describe Marta and Ana. What subjects are they good in?
   Which ones are they poor in? Do they get good grades? Are they going
   to do well on the algebra test?

2. Write a paragraph of four to six sentences about your school. What
   time does your first class begin? How many classes do you have?
   Which classes are easy? Which ones are hard? What's your favorite
   class? Is there a science lab in your school? A gym? A cafeteria? Do you
   like your school? Why?

COMPRUEBA TU PROGRESO   CAPÍTULO 7   Discretionary

Notes: Answers to the **Comprueba** appear in the pre-chapter teacher pages.

A   Notas buenas y malas

What are these students' grades in each subject.

Alberto: 6 *Alberto tiene un seis en español.*

1. Lucía: 8   2. Agustín: 5   3. César: 6

4. Luz: 3   5. Diana: 10   6. Raimundo: 4

7. Ernesto: 7   8. Olga: 5   9. Héctor: 4

B   Contesta las preguntas

Answer the questions in complete sentences using the correct word.

1. ¿Qué lee Susana?   *(un horario / un laboratorio / una papelera)*
2. ¿Qué recibe el Sr. Rodríguez? *(una carta / un colegio / la materia)*
3. ¿Qué borra Marta? *(el capítulo / el borrador / la respuesta)*
4. ¿Qué enseña la Sra. Gómez? *(ciencias / notas / pruebas)*
5. ¿Qué escribes? *(el dibujo / la papelera / las respuestas)*
6. ¿Cuándo tienen pruebas en tu clase de álgebra? *(nadie / ojalá / todas las sᴇmanas)*
7. ¿Qué repasan Carlos y Silvia? *(la cafetería / la computadora / la lección)*

C   Completa, por favor

Complete the sentences with the correct form of the verb in parentheses.

1. Elena y yo _____ en el primer piso.   *(vivir)*
2. ¿_____ (tú) a esquiar? *(aprender)*
3. Ellos _____ muchas cartas.   *(recibir)*
4. Uds. _____ bien la materia.   *(comprender)*
5. Ud. no _____ mucho.   *(comer)*
6. Luis y tú _____ la página 11.   *(leer)*
7. (Yo) siempre _____ a la clase de educación física.   *(asistir)*
8. Mi padre _____ poemas muy bonitos. *(escribir)*
9. Tú y yo _____ todo el capítulo.   *(comprender)*

D   La *a* personal

Rewrite those sentences that require the personal *a*.

1. ¿Llamas (?) tu hermana?
2. Tenemos (?) muchos amigos.
3. Espero (?) el autobús de la escuela.
4. No comprendo (?) todas las respuestas.
5. ¿(?) quién buscas en la cocina?
6. Raquel va a esperar (?) Diego.
7. Él busca (?) su profesor de francés.
8. ¿Miras (?) el horario?
9. ¿(?) quién termina la prueba?
10. Dibujo (?) mi guitarra.

E   ¿Qué haces?

Answer each question with *sí* and the correct pronoun.

   ¿Hablas de Pepe?
   Sí, hablo de él.

1. ¿Vienes conmigo?
2. ¿Hablan Uds. de mí?
3. ¿Es para nosotros el refrigerador?
4. ¿Trabaja Enrique para Ud.?
5. ¿Son para María los poemas?
6. ¿Viajan ellos contigo?
7. ¿Vives cerca de la profesora?
8. ¿Viene María después de Gustavo?

Chapter 7 Test   Listening Comprehension Test

Sustantivos

el acento
el álgebra *(f.)*
el arte
la biología
el borrador
la cafetería
el capítulo
la carta
las ciencias
el colegio
la computadora
la educación física
la física
el francés
la frase
la geometría
el gimnasio
la historia
el horario
el inglés
el laboratorio
la lección, *pl.* las
    lecciones
las matemáticas
la materia
la nota
la página
la palabra
la papelera
el poema
la prueba
la química
la respuesta

Pronombres

conmigo
contigo
mí
nadie
ti
todos, -as

Adjetivos

ausente
bilingüe
correcto, -a
difícil
fácil
favorito, -a
listo, -a
preparado, -a
presente
todo, -a

Verbos

aprender (a + *inf.*)
asistir a
borrar
comprender
dibujar
enseñar
escribir
llamar
recibir
repasar
terminar
usar
vivir

Preposiciones

después de (+ *noun* / *inf.*)
según

Expresiones

aprender _____ de
    memoria
¿a quién(es)?
estar flojo, -a en
estar fuerte en
¡ojalá!
¿para quién?
por la mañana (la noche /
    la tarde)
sacar una buena / mala
    nota
salir bien / mal en (*un
    examen* / *una prueba*)
todos los días

CAPÍTULO 8

COMIDA AMERICANA

King Ferdinand and Queen Isabella of Spain were disappointed by the results of Columbus's first voyage. They had not sent him to look for new lands, not even for gold and silver. What they had *really* wanted were spices from the Orient.

In those days, without refrigeration, meat was preserved by drying or salting. Spices that would hide the taste were very valuable. A pound of pepper cost as much as the average farmer earned in several weeks.

What Columbus *did* bring back from the Americas was a great variety of foods that no European had ever seen: Indian corn, sweet potatoes, papayas, and pineapples. On his later trips, he did the reverse: he brought European wheat, chickpeas, and sugar cane to the Caribbean. In time, other important crops were brought to America, including bananas from India and coffee from Arabia.

Within fifty years, many more Spanish explorers followed Columbus's route. And they, too, discovered new and exotic foods. The first Spaniard to explore Mexico, Hernán Cortés, was the first European to taste tomatoes, avocados, turkey, chili peppers, vanilla, and chocolate. The Aztecs of Mexico even knew about chewing gum. In Peru, another Spaniard, Francisco Pizarro, found potatoes, squash, and lima beans.

In the end, the foods of Latin America have proved more valuable than all the gold and silver that were found there. Chocolate, the beverage of the Aztec aristocracy, soon became the preferred drink of European royalty. Potatoes became a staple of the European diet, and today corn, peppers, and tomatoes are grown throughout the world. So when you eat your next Thanksgiving dinner, remember that turkey, mashed potatoes, corn, tomatoes, cranberries, and pumpkins really are *comida americana*.

PALABRAS NUEVAS I

1

La comida

las frutas
el limón
pl. los limones
la manzana
el plátano

el café con leche
el café

la naranja

el huevo

el té
el chocolate
los churros*

el azúcar

el pan tostado

la mermelada

el mantel

el jugo de manzana

el jugo de naranja

el jugo
el vaso
la taza

la servilleta
el tenedor

el plato

el platillo

el cuchillo
la cuchara

* *Churros* are deep-fried pastries that are similar to doughnuts. They are often eaten for breakfast, usually with hot chocolate.

poner
la mesa

quitar
los platos

beber

sobre la mesa

debajo
de la mesa

CONTEXTO COMUNICATIVO 2

1 CLARA Vamos a poner la mesa para **la cena.**

TOMÁS ¿Dónde **pongo** la servilleta?

CLARA Sobre el plato.

TOMÁS ¿Y el platillo?

CLARA ¡Debajo de la taza, por supuesto!

Variaciones:

■ sobre el → al lado del

la cena *dinner; supper; evening meal*

poner (yo pongo, tú pones) *to put, to place*

2 MAMÁ ¿Qué quieres para **el desayuno** hoy?

PEDRO Chocolate con churros, por favor.*

■ chocolate → café con leche

■ churros → pan tostado

el desayuno *breakfast*

3 GLORIA ¿Qué hay en el refrigerador?

JAIME Tenemos hamburguesas, queso, ensalada, frutas. ¿Cuál prefieres?

GLORIA **Un poco de todo.**

■ en el refrigerador → para **el almuerzo**

■ un poco de todo → una hamburguesa con queso

un poco (de) *a little*

todo (pron.) *everything*

el almuerzo *lunch*

* In Spain and some Latin American countries, *el desayuno* traditionally consists of *café con leche* with churros, a roll, or bread.

4	MATEO	Hola, Marta. Ahora **salgo de** la oficina.
	MARTA	¿Cuándo **llegas** a casa?
	MATEO	**Pronto,** ¿por qué?
	MARTA	Porque tengo que salir **para** comprar comida.* No tenemos nada en casa.

salir (de) (yo salgo, tú sales)
  to leave, to go out, to come out
llegar *to arrive*
pronto *soon*
para + inf. *to, in order to*

- salgo de → voy a salir de
- no tenemos → no hay
- en casa → aquí

5	PILAR	Laura, ¿qué **haces** hoy **al mediodía**?
	LAURA	No hago nada especial.
	PILAR	¿Quieres ir conmigo a un restaurante mexicano? Tengo ganas de comer burritos.
	LAURA	¡Bueno! Hasta luego entonces.

hacer (yo hago, tú haces)
  to make, to do
al mediodía *at noon*

- hoy al mediodía → después de clase

* The names of the meals vary from country to country. In Spain and Mexico, for example, *la comida* means "lunch." We will use *la comida* to mean "food" or "meal" in general. *El desayuno* is "breakfast," *el almuerzo* is "lunch," and *la cena* is "supper" or "dinner"—the evening meal.

Enrichment: To reinforce the use of the present tense for an action that will take place in the near future, elicit or suggest additional **Variaciones** for mini-dialogues 4 and 5.

Una señora compra comestibles en Caracas, Venezuela.

EN OTRAS PARTES

También se dice *la banana*.
En Colombia, el Ecuador y
Panamá se dice *el guineo*.

En Puerto Rico y la
República Dominicana se
dice *la china*.

En España se dice *el zumo*.

PRÁCTICA

A **¿Dónde pongo todo?**   Imagina que los sábados trabajas en un
restaurante. Tienes que poner las mesas. El gerente quiere ver si
sabes hacerlo. *(The manager wants to see if you know how.)* Pregunta
y contesta según el modelo.

> **ESTUDIANTE A**   *¿Qué pones sobre el plato?*
> **ESTUDIANTE B**   *¿Sobre el plato? Pongo la servilleta.*

Práctica A
1. ¿Debajo de todo?
   Pongo el mantel.
2. ¿Sobre el platillo?
   Pongo la taza.
3. ¿A la izquierda del plato?
   Pongo los tenedores.
4. ¿Al lado del cuchillo?
   Pongo las cucharas.

1. ¿Qué pones en la mesa debajo de todo?
2. ¿Qué pones sobre el platillo?
3. ¿Qué pones a la izquierda del plato?
4. ¿Qué pones al lado del cuchillo?
5. ¿Qué frutas pones delante del plato?
6. ¿Qué pones al lado de la taza y del platillo?
7. ¿Qué pones a la derecha del plato?

5. ¿Delante del plato?
   Pongo manzanas, naranjas
   y plátanos.
6. ¿Al lado de la taza y del
   platillo? Pongo el vaso.
7. ¿A la derecha del plato?
   Pongo el cuchillo y las
   cucharas.

Palabras Nuevas I   **275**

Práctica B
Answers will vary but should
follow the model.

B **¿Qué quieres?** ¿Qué vas a comer para el desayuno o el almuerzo? Usa el menú para escoger dos cosas *(to choose two things)*. Pregunta y contesta cinco veces *(times)*. Sigue el modelo.

ESTUDIANTE A   *¿Qué vas a comer para el almuerzo?*
ESTUDIANTE B   *Un sandwich de jamón y queso y un té. ¿Y tú?*
ESTUDIANTE A   *Carne con papas fritas y un jugo de naranja.*

MENÚ

DESAYUNO

Huevos con jamón
Pan tostado con mantequilla
y mermelada
Pan tostado con queso

ALMUERZO

Sandwich de queso
Sandwich de jamón
Hamburguesa
Hamburguesa con queso
Carne con papas fritas

BEBIDAS

Limonada
Jugo de naranja
Jugo de manzana
Leche
Té (con leche o con limón)
Café
Café con leche
Chocolate

POSTRES

Ensalada de frutas
Plátanos
Manzanas
Yogur de limón
Helado

C Hablemos de ti.

1. ¿Qué prefieres comer para el desayuno?
2. ¿Qué te gusta beber para el desayuno? ¿Para el almuerzo? ¿Para la cena?
3. ¿Te gusta el té? ¿El café? ¿Prefieres el té con limón? ¿Con leche? ¿Pones azúcar en el té o en el café?
4. ¿A qué hora llegas a la escuela por la mañana? ¿A qué hora sales de la escuela por la tarde? ¿A qué hora llegas a casa?

ACTIVIDAD

Aliteración.   Alliteration is the repetition of initial consonant sounds in a sentence. For example, if you use the letters *c*, *m*, and *t*, you can create sentences such as these:

> Clara y Carmen comen carne con cucharas.
> Mamá, hay mermelada de manzanas en el mantel.
> Todavía tengo tres tazas de té.

With a partner, make up ten sentences that use alliteration. Then get together with another pair of students and read your sentences to each other.

APLICACIONES

La cena es a las nueve 4

Kevin, un chico de los Estados Unidos, está en Sevilla para estudiar español. Hoy es su primer día en casa de los Martín,* su nueva "familia."

SRA. MARTÍN ¡Arturo, Kevin! Son las dos y media. Tenéis que
5 poner la mesa para la comida.[1] Ya[2] llega vuestro padre.

ARTURO Sí, mamá. Kevin, tú pones los platos, las servilletas y los vasos y yo pongo los cuchillos, los tenedores y las cucharas. Aquí está todo. Y después de la
10 comida quitamos los platos.

KEVIN Pero, Arturo, si[3] comemos ahora, ¿cuándo vamos a comer la cena?

ARTURO Kevin, aquí la cena es a las nueve o las diez de la noche. En la cena no comemos mucho.

15 KEVIN ¡A las diez! ¿El desayuno a las nueve, la comida a las tres y la cena a las diez?

ARTURO Sí, hombre, es así[4] aquí en España.

KEVIN ¡Entonces vamos a comer!

---

[1]En España *la comida* quiere decir el almuerzo.   [2]**ya**   *already*   [3]**si**   *if*
[4]**es así**   *it's that way*

* In Spanish we do not use a plural form for people's last names:
la familia García = los García.

Enrichment: Additional questions: *¿De dónde es Kevin? (Es de los Estados Unidos.) ¿Son hermanos Kevin y Arturo? (No, no son hermanos.) ¿Es la Sra. Martín la mamá de Arturo o de Kevin? (Es la mamá de Arturo.)*

Preguntas

Contesta según el diálogo.
1. ¿En qué ciudad está el chico norteamericano?   2. ¿Por qué está en España?   3. ¿Quiénes tienen que poner la mesa para la comida? ¿A qué hora?   4. ¿Quién llega?   5. ¿Quiénes van a quitar los platos? ¿Cuándo?   6. ¿A qué hora es la comida en España?   7. ¿A qué hora es la cena?   8. ¿Cuál es la comida más importante del día en los Estados Unidos?   9. ¿A qué horas comes tú las tres comidas del día?

Notes: Point out the *vosotros* form of *tener (tenéis)* and the possessive adjective *vuestro*. Remind students that *vosotros / vosotras* are familiar plural pronouns used in Spain. You may want to refer to number 4 on p. 95.

Diálogo
1. Sevilla
2. para estudiar español
3. Arturo y Kevin; a las dos y media
4. el padre de Arturo (*or*: el Sr. Martín)
5. Arturo y Kevin; después del almuerzo
6. a las tres (de la tarde)
7. a las nueve o las diez de la noche
8. Answers may vary, though most will say *la cena.*
9. Answers will vary.

Culture: Ask students to locate Sevilla on a map. You may want students to do research on Sevilla and give brief oral reports.

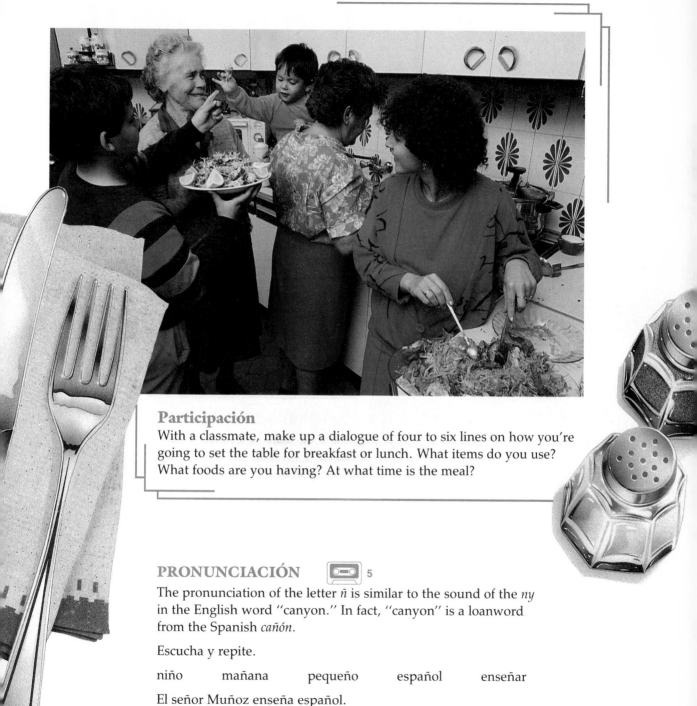

Participación

With a classmate, make up a dialogue of four to six lines on how you're going to set the table for breakfast or lunch. What items do you use? What foods are you having? At what time is the meal?

PRONUNCIACIÓN 5

The pronunciation of the letter *ñ* is similar to the sound of the *ny* in the English word "canyon." In fact, "canyon" is a loanword from the Spanish *cañón*.

Escucha y repite.

niño   mañana   pequeño   español   enseñar

El señor Muñoz enseña español.
Mañana es el cumpleaños del niño.
Mi compañera de clase es puertorriqueña.

PALABRAS NUEVAS II

Ir de compras

El Mercado

la panadería · la carnicería · el supermercado

Las Verduras

el agua
la zanahoria
la papa · el tomate
la lechuga
la docena
los guisantes · el cebolla
los frijoles
el maíz
la botella
el pollo · el pavo
la carne
el litro $10
el agua mineral

280   Capítulo 8

If students ask: Other related words you may want to present: *el puesto,* stand; *la balanza,* scales; *el mostrador,* counter.

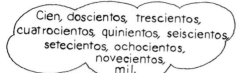

Cien, doscientos, trescientos, cuatrocientos, quinientos, seiscientos, setecientos, ochocientos, novecientos, mil.

Notes: Make sure students recognize that mini-dialogue 2 contains past-tense forms of *ir*. More work with irregular preterites will be presented in Chap. 12.

1000 gramos = 1 kilo

cien (pesetas)   doscientas   trescientas

cuatrocientas   quinientas   seiscientas   setecientas

ochocientas   novecientas   mil

CONTEXTO COMUNICATIVO

 7

1 MAMÁ ¿Cuándo vas **de compras**, hija? **Necesito** unas **cosas**.

LUZ Yo **las** compro, mamá. ¿Qué necesitas?

MAMÁ Quinientos gramos† de café y una docena de huevos.

LUZ Bien, mamá. Salgo ahora.

Variaciones:

- unas cosas → unos **comestibles**
  las → **los**

2 EVA ¿Quieres ir al supermercado?

FELIPE **Ya fui** al mercado del **barrio.**

EVA ¿Cuándo **fuiste**?

FELIPE **Ayer por la tarde.** Y Tomás **fue** conmigo.

- ayer por la tarde → ayer por la noche
- ayer por la tarde → **anoche**

de compras *shopping*
necesitar *to need*
la cosa *thing*
las *you (f. pl.); them (f. pl.)*
los comestibles *groceries*
los *you (m. pl. / m. & f. pl.); them (m. pl. / m. & f. pl.)*
ya *already*
(yo) fui *I went*
el barrio *neighborhood*
(tú) fuiste *you went; did you go?*
ayer *yesterday*
ayer por la tarde (mañana / noche) *yesterday afternoon (morning / evening)*
Ud. (el / ella) fue *you (formal) / he / she went*
anoche *last night*

---

* The *peseta* is the monetary unit of Spain.

† All Spanish-speaking countries use the metric system. They measure food in grams and kilograms and liquids in liters.

3 SRA. ROCHA   ¿Cuánto cuestan los frijoles?
VENDEDOR   Los **vendo a ciento dos** pesetas el kilo.
SRA. ROCHA   ¡Ay, qué caros son!

■ los frijoles → las zanahorias
los → las
caros → caras
■ ciento dos pesetas → **ciento una** pesetas

4 MAMÁ   ¿Qué haces con el pan, Pepe?
PEPE   **Lo** necesito, mamá. Voy a hacer un sandwich.

■ el pan → la mantequilla
lo → **la**

vender (a + amount of money)
to sell (for)
ciento dos   *102*

ciento uno, -a   *101*

lo   *you* (m. formal) / *him* / *it*
(m. sing.)
la   *you* (f. formal) / *her* / *it*
(f. sing.)

EN OTRAS PARTES

En España se dice *la patata*.

También se dice *los chícharos*
y *las arvejas*.

También se dice *las habichuelas*. En la Argentina,
el Perú y Chile se dice *los porotos*.

En México se dice *el guajolote*; en Cuba, *el guanajo*
y en la América Central, *el chompipe*.

También se dice *las legumbres*
y *las hortalizas*.

En México se dice *el jitomate*.

PRÁCTICA

A ¿Cuánto necesito?
Imagina que vas de compras con un(a) amigo(a). Sigue el modelo.

gramos de jamón / 250 / 400 pesetas

ESTUDIANTE A *¿Cuántos gramos de jamón necesitamos?*
ESTUDIANTE B *Doscientos cincuenta gramos. ¿Cuánto cuestan?*
ESTUDIANTE A *Cuatrocientas pesetas el kilo.*

1. kilos de carne / 2 / 600 pesetas
2. kilos de papas / 3 / 50 pesetas
3. gramos de frijoles / 300 / 100 pesetas
4. kilos de cebollas / 2 / 60 pesetas
5. kilos de zanahorias / 1 / 75 pesetas
6. gramos de café / 500 / 250 pesetas
7. gramos de azúcar / 750 / 125 pesetas
8. kilos de manzanas / 3 / 120 pesetas
9. kilos de naranjas / 4 / 80 pesetas
10. kilos de plátanos / 1 / 135 pesetas

B ¿Adónde fuiste?
Imagina que preguntas a tu amigo(a) adónde fue —y con quién. Escoge *(choose)* una expresión de cada columna. Pregunta y contesta según el modelo.

ESTUDIANTE A *¿Adónde fuiste ayer por la tarde?*
ESTUDIANTE B *Fui al cine.*
ESTUDIANTE A *¿Quién fue contigo?*
ESTUDIANTE B *Mi hermana mayor.*

anoche	a la panadería	mis tíos
el viernes por la noche	a casa	mi amigo(a) *(nombre)*
ayer por la mañana	a la fiesta de *(nombre)*	mi mamá
el sábado por la tarde	a la iglesia	mi hermano(a) mayor
el domingo por la mañana	a la biblioteca	mi padre
	al supermercado	mi tía *(nombre)*
ayer por la tarde	de compras	mi hermanito(a)
el domingo por la noche	al campo	mi novio(a)
	al gimnasio	mis primos
el sábado por la noche	al teatro	mi primo(a) *(nombre)*
después de la fiesta	al partido de ____	nadie

Reteach / Review: To provide additional practice with numbers, you may want students to compute the total price of the items in Ex. A. For example: *Doscientos cincuenta gramos de jamón a cuatrocientas pesetas el kilo cuestan cien pesetas.*

Práctica A

1. ¿Cuántos kilos de carne necesitamos?
   Dos kilos. ¿Cuánto cuestan?
   Seiscientas pesetas el kilo.
2. ¿Cuántos kilos de papas necesitamos?
   Tres kilos. ¿Cuánto cuestan?
   Cincuenta pesetas el kilo.
3. ¿...?
   Trescientos gramos. ¿...?
   Cien pesetas el kilo.
4. ¿...?
   Dos kilos. ¿...?
   Sesenta pesetas el kilo.
5. ¿...?
   Un kilo. ¿...?
   Setenta y cinco pesetas el kilo.
6. ¿...?
   Quinientos gramos. ¿...?
   Doscientas cincuenta pesetas el kilo.
7. ¿...?
   Setecientos cincuenta gramos. ¿...?
   Ciento veinticinco pesetas el kilo.
8. ¿...?
   Tres kilos. ¿...?
   Ciento veinte pesetas el kilo.
9. ¿...?
   Cuatro kilos. ¿...?
   Ochenta pesetas el kilo.
10. ¿...?
   Un kilo. ¿...?
   Ciento treinta y cinco pesetas el kilo.

Práctica B
Answers will follow the model pattern.

En Bogotá, Colombia

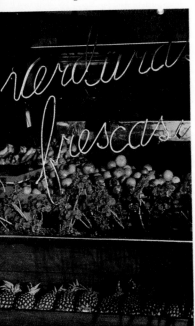

C   El menú.   Imagina que escribes los menús para tu familia para el fin de semana. Usa los dibujos para completar las frases.

1. Para la comida del domingo, necesito . . .

2. Para los sandwiches, necesito . . .

3. Para la cena del sábado, necesito . . .

4. Para la ensalada del mediodía, necesito . . .

5. Para la carne, necesito . . .

6. Para la cena del viernes, necesito . . .

Practice Sheet 8–2   Workbook Exs. C–D

 8 Canción: Los pollos de mi cazuela

D   Hablemos de ti.
1. ¿Adónde fuiste ayer por la tarde? ¿Quién fue contigo?
2. ¿Te gusta ir de compras con tus amigos? ¿Adónde van Uds.? ¿Qué buscan Uds.? Cuando vas al supermercado, ¿qué compras?
3. ¿Hay una panadería cerca de tu casa o de tu escuela? ¿Es buena? ¿A veces compras pan en la panadería o siempre lo compras en el supermercado?
4. ¿Te gustan las verduras? ¿Cuál es tu verdura favorita?
5. ¿Te gustan las ensaladas? ¿Qué pones en tu ensalada favorita?

 9 Tape Manual Exs. 2, 3, 4, 5   Quiz 8–2

En Caracas, Venezuela

284   Capítulo 8

ACTIVIDAD

Buscapalabras With a partner, create a *buscapalabras* puzzle. Include at least 15 words from this chapter. You will probably have to make a box 20 letters wide by 20 high. *Buscapalabras* look like the illustration. (But do not, of course, circle the words when you create the puzzle.) When you have finished, exchange puzzles with another team and try to solve them.

Notes: Remind students to include the tilde on the *ñ* and accent marks on any vowels that require them. You may want to post completed puzzles on the bulletin board.

Chicos españoles delante de una pastelería

ESTUDIO DE PALABRAS

The noun ending *-ería* usually means a place where certain items are sold. For example, you buy *carne* in a *carnicería*. Here are some other items and the names of the stores in which they are sold.

Puedes comprar **leche** en una **lechería**.
Puedes comprar **libros** en una **librería**.
Puedes comprar **papel** en una **papelería**.
Puedes comprar **frutas** en una **frutería**.

English has borrowed this ending for some words. Think of "pizzeria." The meaning of *cafetería*, on the other hand, has changed. It was originally a store where coffee was sold.

¿En qué tienda puedes comprar helado?

EXPLICACIONES I

Los verbos *hacer, poner* y *salir*

You have already used the *yo* and *tú* forms of *hacer, poner* and *salir*.

¿Qué **haces**?   *What **are you doing**?*
Pongo los platos en la mesa.   *I'm **putting** the plates on the table.*
¿A qué hora **sales**?   *What time **are you leaving**?*
Salgo a las ocho.   *I'm **leaving** at eight.*

1 Here are the forms of *hacer* and *poner* in the present tense.

INFINITIVO   **hacer**

SINGULAR		PLURAL	
1	(yo) **hago**	(nosotros) (nosotras) } **hacemos**	
2	(tú) **haces**	(vosotros) (vosotras) } **hacéis**	
3	Ud. (él) (ella) } **hace**	Uds. (ellos) (ellas) } **hacen**	

INFINITIVO   **poner**

SINGULAR		PLURAL	
1	(yo) **pongo**	(nosotros) (nosotras) } **ponemos**	
2	(tú) **pones**	(vosotros) (vosotras) } **ponéis**	
3	Ud. (él) (ella) } **pone**	Uds. (ellos) (ellas) } **ponen**	

Hacer and *poner* take the same endings as regular *-er* verbs. The only difference is the *g* in the *yo* form.

◆ **OBJECTIVES:**

TO ARRANGE FOR PICNICS AND MEALS AT HOME

TO DESCRIBE DAILY ROUTINE

Notes: You may want to refer students to mini-dialogues 4 on p. 122, 5 on p. 274, and 4 on p. 282 for more examples of the *yo / tú* forms of *hacer*. Use mini-dialogue 1 on p. 273 to illustrate *pongo* and 4 on p. 274 to show *salgo.*

Enrichment: In pairs, students can take turns putting classroom objects on or under tables, chairs, and desks as they ask each other ¿Qué *haces?* and answer *Pongo* _____ *sobre / debajo de* _____.

2 Here are the forms of *salir* in the present tense.

INFINITIVO **salir**

	SINGULAR		PLURAL	
1	(yo)	sal**go**	(nosotros) (nosotras) }	sal**imos**
2	(tú)	sal**es**	(vosotros) (vosotras) }	sal**ís**
3	Ud. (él) (ella) }	sal**e**	Uds. (ellos) (ellas) }	sal**en**

Salir takes the same endings as regular *-ir* verbs. Again, the only difference is the *g* in the *yo* form.

Reteach / Extra Help: Before students do Ex. A, have them practice using *hacer, poner,* and *salir*. Do a chain drill or have students work in pairs to ask and answer questions that use all the verb forms. You may want to base the practice on the four example sentences at the top of p. 287.

Una familia mexicana

Práctica A
1. Ud. hace la limonada.
2. (Yo) hago los churros.
3. Emilia y yo hacemos el café.
4. Tú y yo hacemos el helado.
5. Uds. hacen los tacos.
6. Mamá y Esteban hacen la ensalada.
7. Raquel y Dolores hacen el té.
8. Answers will vary.

PRÁCTICA

A En el campo. Los Ramírez van a comer en el campo. ¿Qué hace cada persona? Sigue el modelo.

Papá  *Papá hace los sándwiches.*

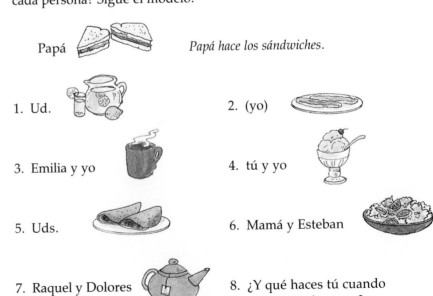

1. Ud.

2. (yo)

3. Emilia y yo

4. tú y yo

5. Uds.

6. Mamá y Esteban

7. Raquel y Dolores

8. ¿Y qué haces tú cuando comes en el campo?

B **¿A qué hora salen?** ¿Cuándo salen estas (*these*) personas? Con un(a) compañero(a) de clase, pregunta y contesta según el modelo. Añade (*add*) una hora apropiada (*appropriate*).

> (tú) de casa / siempre
> ESTUDIANTE A *¿A qué hora sales de casa?*
> ESTUDIANTE B *Siempre salgo a las ocho y cuarto.*

1. los estudiantes de la escuela / siempre
2. Uds. del almacén / a veces
3. tú y Olga de la oficina / siempre
4. (tú) del gimnasio / a menudo
5. tu hermana de la tienda de comestibles / a veces
6. el profesor Vidal de la biblioteca / siempre
7. tus padres de la tienda / a menudo
8. (él) del museo / a veces

C **¿Qué hacen Uds.?** Imagina que tu familia espera a invitados (*guests*). Toda la familia ayuda a preparar la cena y a poner la mesa. Usa la forma correcta de los verbos *hacer* y *poner*. Escoge (*choose*) una palabra o expresión de cada columna para preguntar y contestar. Sigue el modelo.

> Uds.
> ESTUDIANTE A *¿Qué hacen Uds.?*
> ESTUDIANTE B *Ponemos la limonada en la mesa.*

1. ¿Jorge?
2. ¿mamá?
3. ¿tu abuela?
4. ¿papá?
5. ¿tus hermanas?
6. (¿tú?)
7. ¿Uds.?
8. ¿Ud.?

la botella de leche
los platos
las cucharas
las servilletas
los tenedores
las frutas
los vasos
los guisantes
el mantel
el pavo

a la derecha de los platos
a la izquierda de los platos
entre los tenedores y el
  cuchillo
en la mesa
en la estufa

Práctica B
1. ¿A qué hora salen los estudiantes de la escuela? Siempre salen a (*answers will vary*).
2. ¿A qué hora salen Uds. del almacén? / A veces salimos…
3. ¿A qué hora salen tú y Olga de la oficina? / Siempre salimos…
4. ¿… sales (tú) del gimnasio? / A menudo salgo…
5. ¿… sale tu hermana de la tienda de comestibles? / A veces sale…
6. ¿… sale el profesor Vidal de la biblioteca? / Siempre sale…
7. ¿… salen tus padres de la tienda? / A menudo salen…
8. ¿… sale (él) del museo? / A veces sale…

Práctica C
Answers will follow the model pattern.
1. ¿Qué hace Jorge? Pone…
2. ¿Qué hace mamá? Pone…
3. ¿Qué hace tu abuela? Pone…
4. ¿Qué hace papá? Pone…
5. ¿Qué hacen tus hermanas? Ponen…
6. ¿Qué haces (tú)? Pongo…
7. ¿Qué hacen Uds.? Ponemos…
8. ¿Qué hace Ud.? Pongo…

D En mi casa. Usa la forma correcta de cada verbo entre paréntesis para completar el párrafo *(paragraph)*.

En mi casa, nosotros *(salir)* todos los días para *(ir)* a la escuela o al trabajo. Por la mañana, mamá *(cocinar)* huevos, yo *(poner)* la mesa, y mi hermanita *(ir)* a la panadería. Entonces papá *(hacer)* pan tostado con mermelada para todos. Yo *(salir)* a las 7:30 y mi hermana *(salir)* a

5 las 7:45. ¡Ella siempre *(llegar)* tarde! Mis padres *(salir)* a las ocho. Mi papá *(trabajar)* en una oficina en el centro y mamá en una tienda bastante cerca de nuestra casa. Ella *(vender)* ropa para niños. Mi hermana y yo *(llegar)* a casa a las cuatro de la tarde. Yo *(hacer)* mi tarea, pero generalmente mi hermana y su amiga Elena *(salir)* para jugar en

10 el parque. Más tarde, cuando mis padres *(llegar)* a casa, la primera cosa que ellos *(hacer)* es ir a la cocina. Yo *(ayudar)* a mi hermana a *(poner)* el mantel en la mesa, y entonces nosotros *(poner)* juntos la mesa. Después de la comida, yo *(quitar)* los platos y mi hermanita y yo *(lavar)* todo.

E Hablemos de ti.

1. ¿Qué haces para ayudar en casa? ¿Quién pone la mesa en tu casa?
2. ¿Qué hacen tú y tus amigos después de las clases? ¿Qué hacen Uds. juntos los fines de semana? Cuando Uds. salen juntos, ¿adónde van? ¿Cómo van allí?
3. ¿Cómo es tu barrio? ¿Hay muchas tiendas? ¿Hay supermercados? ¿Hay farmacias? ¿panaderías?

Una plantación de cacao en México

Dulces de chocolate en la Argentina

APLICACIONES

Discretionary

¿Qué es el chocolate? 11

Piensa en¹ la taza de chocolate que bebes por la mañana o cuando hace mucho frío. Piensa en el helado de chocolate que comes en el verano. Usamos el chocolate todos los días, pero ¿qué es el chocolate? ¿Y de dónde viene?

5   Imagina que estás en el siglo² XVI. El conquistador Hernán Cortés llega a México. Él descubre³ que los aztecas combinan agua con las semillas⁴ del cacao (una planta tropical de la América Central) para preparar una bebida que ellos llaman *chocolate*. En azteca, la palabra *chocolate* quiere decir "agua amarga,"⁵ porque la bebida de los aztecas es muy diferente
10 del chocolate dulce⁶ de hoy.

    Cortés lleva unas semillas del cacao a España y muy pronto el chocolate es la bebida favorita de los españoles. Pero el chocolate que ellos preparan no es dulce tampoco. Son los ingleses quienes, en el siglo XVIII, preparan el chocolate con leche y azúcar que bebemos ahora.

---

¹**piensa en** (from **pensar**) *think about*   ²**el siglo** *century*   ³**descubrir** *to discover*   ⁴**la semilla** *seed*   ⁵**amargo, -a** *bitter*   ⁶**dulce** *sweet*

Notes: Make sure students understand these cognates: *imagina*, imagine; *combinan*, combine; *planta tropical*, tropical plant; *diferente*, different.

Culture: You may want to ask students to do research on Hernán Cortés and then give brief oral reports.

Preguntas

Contesta según la lectura.

1. ¿De dónde viene el chocolate?
2. ¿Qué es el cacao?
3. Cuando Cortés llega a México, ¿quiénes ya usan el chocolate?
4. ¿Cómo preparan los aztecas el chocolate?
5. ¿Cómo es la bebida de los aztecas?
6. ¿Quién lleva unas semillas del cacao a España?
7. ¿Cómo es el chocolate que preparan entonces en España?
8. ¿Quiénes aprenden a preparar el chocolate con leche y azúcar?
9. ¿Qué bebes tú cuando hace mucho frío? ¿Qué te gusta beber cuando hace mucho calor?

ANTES DE LEER

1. The word *bebida* is related to the verb *beber*. What do you think *bebida* means?
2. What do you think of when you hear the word "chocolate"?

Preguntas
1. de las semillas del cacao (*or*: de la América Central / de México)
2. una planta tropical
3. los aztecas
4. Combinan las semillas del cacao con agua.
5. amarga
6. Cortés
7. No es dulce. Es amargo.
8. los ingleses
9. Answers will vary.

EXPLICACIONES II

El complemento directo:
Los pronombres *lo, la, los, las*

◆ **OBJECTIVES:**

TO AGREE AND DISAGREE

TO CLARIFY AND EXPLAIN

Notes: Do students remember why the second sentence includes *a?* You may want to refer to mini-dialogue 6 on p. 241 and to **Explicaciones I** on p. 257 for examples of direct objects and the personal *a*; mini-dialogues 1, 3, and 4 on pp. 281–282 illustrate the use of direct object pronouns.

You already know what a direct object is. It tells who or what receives the action of the verb. For example, in these sentences the direct object tells who or what I understand.

Comprendo **la pregunta.**	*I understand **the question.***
Comprendo **a la profesora.**	*I understand **the teacher.***

To avoid repeating a direct object noun, we often replace it with a direct object pronoun.

¿Comprendes **la pregunta**?	*Do you understand **the question**?*
Sí, **la** comprendo.	*Yes, I understand **it.***
¿Comprendes **a la profesora**?	*Do you understand **the teacher**?*
No, no **la** comprendo.	*No, I don't understand **her.***

The direct object pronoun comes right before the verb and we don't use the personal *a* with it. Here are the direct object pronouns meaning "him," "her," "it," "you" (formal and plural), and "them."

lo	*him, it, you* (formal)	**los**	
la	*her, it, you* (formal)	**las**	*them, you* (pl.)

1 Direct object pronouns can refer to people or things. They agree in gender and number with the nouns they replace. *Lo* replaces a masculine singular noun, and *la* replaces a feminine singular noun. *Los* replaces a masculine plural noun, and *las* replaces a feminine plural noun.

¿Lees **el periódico**?	*Do you read **the newspaper**?*
Sí, **lo** leo.	*Yes, I read **it.***
¿Necesitas **la dirección**?	*Do you need **the address**?*
Sí, **la** necesito.	*Yes, I need **it.***
¿Prefieres **los trajes grises**?	*Do you prefer **the gray suits**?*
Sí, **los** prefiero.	*Yes, I prefer **them.***
¿Esperas **a tus hermanas**?	*Are you waiting for **your sisters**?*
Sí, **las** espero.	*Yes, I'm waiting for **them.***

Reteach / Extra Help: Expand the presentation of direct object pronouns by having students work in pairs to ask and answer *¿Compras _____? Sí, lo / la / los / las compro* using the visuals on p. 280 as cues. Circulate to give help where needed.

2 When the pronoun replaces both a masculine and feminine direct object noun, *los* is used.

¿Compras **el vestido y las dos faldas**?
Sí, **los** compro.

*Are you buying **the dress and the two skirts**?*
*Yes, I'm buying **them**.*

¿Ayudas **a Eva y a Juan**?
No, no **los** ayudo.

*Are you helping **Eva and Juan**?*
*No, I'm not helping **them**.*

PRÁCTICA

A   Sí, lo quiero.   Imagina que tienes un(a) hermano(a) que va a la universidad. Él o ella pregunta si *(if)* quieres algunas *(some)* de sus cosas. Sigue el modelo.

ESTUDIANTE A   *¿Quieres mi cartel?*
ESTUDIANTE B   *Sí, gracias, lo quiero.*
          o: *No, gracias, no lo quiero.*

1.
2.
3.
4.
5.
6.
7.
8.
9.

B   ¿Por qué no?   Hay personas que nunca están de acuerdo *(in agreement)*. Sigue el modelo.

escribir la tarea / es demasiado difícil
ESTUDIANTE A   *¿Qué haces?*
ESTUDIANTE B   *Escribo la tarea.*
ESTUDIANTE A   *Yo no la escribo. Es demasiado difícil.*

1. escuchar música clásica / no me gusta
2. usar la computadora / es aburrida
3. repasar la lección / es muy fácil
4. esperar a Claudia / siempre llega tarde
5. mirar la televisión / me gusta más leer
6. llamar a Gloria / es muy antipática
7. terminar la tarea / tengo que hacer muchas cosas

Enrichment: After students do Ex. A in class, you may want to assign it as written homework. Vary the exercise by having students change the singular objects to plural. Elicit or point out the spelling change in 6 *(pez → peces)*.

Práctica A
1. ¿Quieres mi calendario? Sí (no), gracias, (no) lo quiero. *(Format: lo quiero throughout.)*
2. ¿... mi teléfono?
3. ¿... mi reloj?
4. ¿... mi sombrero?
5. ¿... mi escritorio?
6. ¿... mi pez?
7. ¿... mi suéter?
8. ¿... mi mapa?
9. ¿... mi dibujo?

Práctica B
1. ¿Qué haces? / Escucho música clásica. / Yo no la escucho. No me gusta.
2. ¿...? / Uso la computadora. / Yo no la uso. Es aburrida.
3. ¿...? / Repaso la lección. / Yo no la repaso. Es muy fácil.
4. ¿...? / Espero a Claudia. / Yo no la espero. Siempre llega tarde.
5. ¿...? / Miro la televisión. / Yo no la miro. Me gusta más leer.
6. ¿...? / Llamo a Gloria. / Yo no la llamo. Es muy antipática.
7. ¿...? / Termino la tarea. / Yo no la termino. Tengo que hacer muchas cosas.

Práctica C

1. Busco a mi mamá. / No está aquí. ¿Por qué la buscas? / Porque vamos juntos(as) a casa.
2. Busco a mi amigo Ernesto. / No está aquí. ¿Por qué lo buscas? / Porque vamos juntos a la escuela.
3. Busco al hijo del Sr. Díaz. / ¿... lo buscas? / ... vamos juntos al cine.
4. Busco a la profesora Millán. / ¿... la buscas? / ... Vamos juntos(as) a la biblioteca.
5. Busco a mi abuelo. ¿... lo buscas? / ... vamos juntos a la panadería.
6. Busco al esposo de Marta. / ¿... lo buscas? / ... vamos juntos al gimnasio.
7. Busco a mi tío Federico / ¿... lo buscas? / ... vamos juntos al mercado.
8. Busco a mi hermano. / ¿... lo buscas? / ... vamos juntos al laboratorio.
9. Busco a tu sobrina. / ¿... la buscas? / ... vamos juntos(as) a la cafetería.
10. Busco a Yolanda. / ¿... la buscas? / ... vamos juntos(as) a una fiesta de cumpleaños.

Práctica D

1. ¿Quieres los zapatos negros? / Sí (*or*: No, no) los necesito. All will follow the model. Format: *los necesito* throughout.

C ¿A quién buscas? Tantas (*so many*) personas buscan a tantas otras (*other*) personas. Pregunta y contesta según el modelo.

mi primo Mateo / al partido de fútbol
ESTUDIANTE A *Busco a mi primo Mateo.*
ESTUDIANTE B *No está aquí. ¿Por qué lo buscas?*
ESTUDIANTE A *Porque vamos juntos al partido de fútbol.*

1. mi mamá / a casa
2. mi amigo Ernesto / a la escuela
3. el hijo del Sr. Díaz / al cine
4. la profesora Millán / a la biblioteca
5. mi abuelo / a la panadería
6. el esposo de Marta / al gimnasio
7. mi tío Federico / al mercado
8. mi hermano / al laboratorio
9. tu sobrina / a la cafetería
10. Yolanda / a una fiesta de cumpleaños

D ¿Qué llevas? Imagina que vas a hacer tu maleta (*to pack your suitcase*). Tu hermanito(a) mira toda tu ropa. Quiere ver (*to see*) qué ropa vas a poner en la maleta. Pregunta y contesta según el modelo.

los pantalones verdes
ESTUDIANTE A *¿Quieres los pantalones verdes?*
ESTUDIANTE B *Sí, los necesito.*
o: *No, no los necesito.*

1. los zapatos negros
2. los guantes morados
3. los calcetines rojos
4. el paraguas y el impermeable
5. el traje gris y la camisa blanca
6. los jeans nuevos
7. los pantalones cortos
8. el suéter y la bufanda
9. los zapatos marrones
10. las camisetas y el suéter

Ropa de la América Latina

E **¿Dónde las venden?** Imagina que trabajas en un almacén. Tienes que contestar muchas preguntas. Pregunta y contesta según el modelo.

> cintas / primer piso
> ESTUDIANTE A *¿Venden Uds. cintas?*
> ESTUDIANTE B *Sí, las vendemos en el primer piso.*

1. botas / la planta baja
2. mermeladas / el segundo piso
3. estufas / la planta baja
4. guitarras / el tercer piso
5. mesas y sillas / el primer piso
6. faldas para las niñas / el tercer piso
7. bicicletas / la planta baja
8. papeleras / el segundo piso

F **¿Qué haces?** Imagina que tú y un(a) amigo(a) hablan de lo que (*what*) Uds. no hacen durante las vacaciones. Siempre usa el complemento directo correcto. Sigue el modelo.

> leer libros de matemáticas
> ESTUDIANTE A *¿Lees libros de matemáticas?*
> ESTUDIANTE B *No, nunca los leo.*

1. mirar la televisión
2. tocar la guitarra
3. beber té y café
4. escribir cartas
5. llamar a tus amigos
6. cuidar a tus hermanitas
7. limpiar tu dormitorio
8. escuchar música clásica
9. leer el periódico
10. llevar una camisa blanca y un traje

Practice Sheets 8–5, 8–6

📼 12 Tape Manual Ex. 7   Quiz 8–4

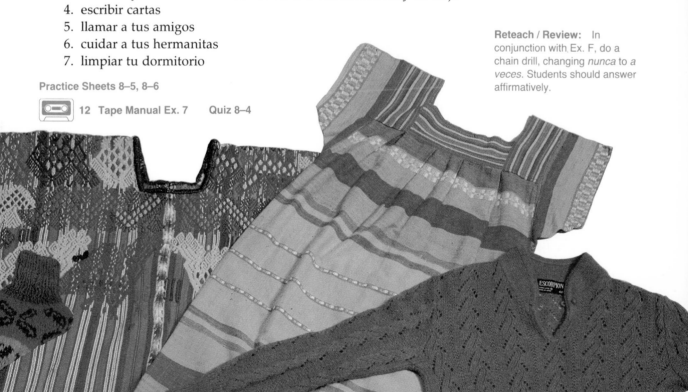

Los complementos directos con el infinitivo

◆ **OBJECTIVES:**
TO EXPRESS
INTENTIONS
TO MAKE PLANS

Look at the position of the direct object pronouns in the answers to this question.

¿Puedes lavar **los platos**?   *Can you wash **the dishes**?*
Sí, puedo lavar**los**.
Sí, **los** puedo lavar.   *Yes, I can wash **them**.*

When we use direct object pronouns with infinitives, we can either attach them to the end of the infinitive or put them before the main verb.

PRÁCTICA

A En el mercado. Felipe y su padre están de compras en el supermercado. Pregunta y contesta según el modelo.

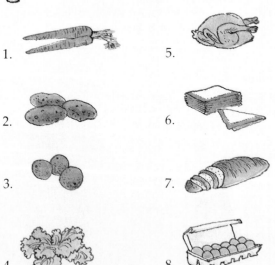

ESTUDIANTE A *Necesitamos una botella de agua mineral.*
ESTUDIANTE B *Muy bien, voy a buscarla.*

1.

2.

3.

4.

5.

6.

7.

8.

B ¿Qué desea Ud.? Mira los dibujos de la Práctica A y sigue el modelo.

ESTUDIANTE A *Quiero comprar una botella de agua mineral.*
ESTUDIANTE B *La voy a buscar.*

Notes: Before students begin the **Práctica**, expand the presentation by asking these questions and eliciting responses with pronouns attached to the infinitive and also placed before the main verb: *¿Necesitas estudiar la lección 8? ¿Puedes hablar bien el español? ¿Tenemos que comer verduras? ¿Vamos a estudiar los capítulos 9 y 10?*

Práctica A
1. Necesitamos zanahorias. Muy bien, voy a buscarlas.
2. ... papas. ... buscarlas.
3. ... naranjas. ... buscarlas.
4. ... lechuga. ... buscarla.
5. ... (un) pollo. ... buscarlo.
6. ... servilletas. ... buscarlas.
7. ... pan. ... buscarlo.
8. ... huevos. ... buscarlos.

Práctica B
1. Quiero comprar zanahorias. Las voy a buscar.
2. ... papas. Las voy a buscar.
3. ... naranjas. Las voy a buscar.
4. ... lechuga. La voy a buscar.
5. ... (un) pollo. Lo voy a buscar.
6. ... servilletas. Las voy a buscar.
7. ... pan. Lo voy a buscar.
8. ... huevos. Los voy a buscar.

Reteach / Extra Help: If your class needs more help with direct object pronouns, do Ex. B as a class activity and then assign it as homework.

C Voy a hacerlo mañana. ¿Siempre esperas hasta *(until)* mañana?
Pregunta y contesta según el modelo.

> ESTUDIANTE A *Necesito estudiar la lección 15.*
> ESTUDIANTE B *¿Tienes que estudiarla hoy?*
> ESTUDIANTE A *No, la puedo estudiar mañana.*

1. Necesito escribir unas cartas.
2. Necesito limpiar el garaje.
3. Necesito repasar el poema.
4. Necesito terminar la tarea.
5. Necesito buscar la guía telefónica.
6. Necesito comprar comestibles.
7. Necesito llamar a José.
8. Necesito ayudar a papá.

D Hablemos de ti.

1. ¿Tienes muchos discos o cintas? Aproximadamente *(About)* ¿cuántos discos o cintas tienes? ¿Tienes discos o cintas favoritos? ¿Cuáles son? ¿Cuándo los escuchas? ¿Vas a escucharlos esta noche?
2. Cuando tienes tarea, ¿dónde la haces? ¿Cuándo la haces? ¿Tienes tarea para mañana? ¿En qué materias? ¿Cuándo vas a hacerla?
3. Después de la cena, ¿quién quita los platos en tu casa? ¿Quién los lava? ¿Quién va a lavarlos esta noche?

Practice Sheet 8–7   Workbook Exs. G–J

 13 Tape Manual Ex. 8   Activity Master 8–2   Quizzes 8–5, 8–6

Práctica C
1. ¿Tienes que escribirlas hoy? No, las puedo escribir mañana.
2. ¿Tienes que limpiarlo hoy? No, lo puedo limpiar mañana.
3. ¿... repasarlo hoy? No, lo puedo repasar mañana.
4. ¿... terminarla hoy? No, la puedo terminar mañana.
5. ¿... buscarla hoy? No, la puedo buscar mañana.
6. ¿... comprarlos hoy? No, los puedo comprar mañana.
7. ¿... llamarlo hoy? No, lo puedo llamar mañana.
8. ¿... ayudarlo hoy? No, lo puedo ayudar mañana.

Práctica D
Answers will vary.

Enrichment: Additional questions for Ex. D: *¿Te gustan los huevos? ¿Cuándo los comes? ¿Te gusta comprar ropa? ¿Dónde la compras?*

ACTIVIDAD

Quince preguntas. Divide the class into two teams. Each team makes up 15 questions. Afterwards, members of each team take turns asking and answering one another's questions. Every answer should include a direct object pronoun. Continue playing until both teams have asked and answered 15 questions. Here are some verbs you may want to use:

aprender	comprar	hacer	ir a
beber	contestar	lavar	necesitar
borrar	cuidar	limpiar	prefiero / prefieres
buscar	dibujar	mirar	puedo / puedes
cocinar	escuchar	poner	quiero / quieres
comer	esperar	recibir	tener que

Notes: You may want to ask students to prepare three or four questions at home for the **Actividad.** When the teams assemble, they can choose the questions they want to use.

Explicaciones II   **297**

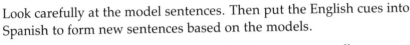
REPASO

Notes: Answers to the **Repaso** and **Tema** appear in the pre-chapter teacher pages.

El señor lleva pan a las tiendas en España.

Look carefully at the model sentences. Then put the English cues into Spanish to form new sentences based on the models.

1. *Ayer por la mañana, Raúl fue a la carnicería para comprar pollo y carne.*
   (Last night I went to the supermarket to buy apples and bananas.)
   (Yesterday afternoon you (fam.) went to the market to buy eggs and corn.)
   (On Monday Cecilia went to the bakery to buy bread.)

2. *A menudo cocino huevos para el desayuno.*
   (Sometimes Mrs. Ochoa cooks turkey for dinner.)
   (On weekends we make sandwiches for lunch.)
   (On Sundays my parents make tea for breakfast.)

3. *Diego pone el tenedor a la izquierda del plato.*
   (You (pl.) put the napkins next to the glasses.)
   (We put the saucers under the cups.)
   (They put the knives to the right of the plates.)

4. *¿Quiénes hacen la tarea? Ellos la hacen, por supuesto.*
   (Who's making the bread? We're making it, of course.)
   (Who's clearing the table? I'm doing it, of course.)
   (Who's drinking the juice? We're drinking it, of course.)

5. *Busco a María. Tengo que buscarla porque siempre sale conmigo los viernes por la noche.*
   (We're looking for our friends (f.). We have to look for them because they always go out with us on Sunday afternoons.)
   (I'm calling my girlfriend. I have to call her because we're going out with you (fam.) on Saturday morning.)
   (They're calling Sonia and Rodolfo. They have to call them because they're going out with them on Thursday night.)

TEMA

Transparency 38

Notes: You may want to assign the **Tema** as written homework.

Students can work in pairs to complete their **Redacción** dialogues and paragraphs. Ask volunteers to read their work aloud.

Put the English captions into Spanish.

Yesterday afternoon I went to the market to buy carrots and potatoes.

Today my brother and I are cooking chicken for dinner.

I put the tablecloth on the table.

Who sets the table? Juanito sets it, of course.

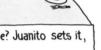

We're waiting for Dad. We have to wait for him because he always goes out with our uncles on Saturday afternoons.

REDACCIÓN

Now you are ready to write your own dialogue or paragraph. Choose one of the following topics.

1. Expand the *Tema* by writing four to six sentences about the pictures. For example, in picture 1, what fruits and vegetables do they sell in the market? What don't they sell? In picture 2, what else do you think they are going to eat? What are they doing in picture 3? In picture 4, what does Juanito say as he sets the table? In picture 5, what are they doing? What are they going to do after their father arrives?

2. Write a paragraph of four to six sentences about a weekend lunch. Do you eat alone? Do you and your family eat together? Where do you eat? What do you eat and drink?

3. Write a dialogue of four to six lines between a shopkeeper and a shopper that might take place in the market shown in picture 1. What does the shopper want to buy? What does it cost per kilo? Is it expensive or cheap? Is the shopper going to buy it?

COMPRUEBA TU PROGRESO   CAPÍTULO 8   Discretionary

Notes: Answers to the **Comprueba** appear in the pre-chapter teacher pages.

A   La comida

Answer the questions according to the picture. Use complete sentences.

1. ¿Qué hay sobre el platillo?
2. ¿Qué hay a la derecha del plato?
3. ¿Qué hay debajo de los tenedores?
4. ¿Qué hay a la izquierda de la taza y del platillo?
5. ¿Qué comes para el desayuno?
6. ¿Qué pones en el pan tostado?

B   ¿Adónde fuiste?

Complete the sentences using the correct form: *fui, fuiste,* or *fue.*

1. (Yo) _____ a la panadería ayer por la tarde.
2. Laura _____ al mercado ayer.
3. ¿_____ (tú) al supermercado con Jorge anoche?
4. (Yo) no _____ a la carnicería ayer.
5. Él no _____ a casa ayer por la mañana.
6. (Tú) _____ al barrio de Pablo anoche.

C   ¿Qué haces?

Complete the sentences with the correct verb form.

1. *(hacer)* ¿Qué _____ (tú) en la cocina?
2. *(poner)* (Yo) _____ los churros en la cocina.
3. *(salir)* José _____ conmigo los domingos.
4. *(hacer)* (Nosotros) _____ pan.
5. *(poner)* ¿Dónde _____ María las tazas?
6. *(salir)* Uds. _____ mucho por la noche.
7. *(hacer)* Ud. _____ dibujos muy bonitos.
8. *(salir)* (Yo) _____ del estadio a las dos.
9. *(salir)* (Nosotros) _____ de casa juntos.

D   ¿Cuál es el verbo?

Complete each sentence with the correct form of *salir, poner,* or *hacer* according to the meaning.

1. ¿(Tú) _____ para el aeropuerto a las seis?
2. ¿Qué _____ (tú) los lunes por la tarde?
3. ¿Quiénes _____ la mesa esta noche?
4. Mis hermanos _____ té para el desayuno.
5. (Yo) _____ el almuerzo para mis amigos.
6. Manuel y yo _____ del café después de las ocho.
7. ¿(Tú) _____ los comestibles en el refrigerador?
8. ¿Por qué (nosotros) _____ los platos en el agua? Para lavarlos, ¡por supuesto!

E   ¿Lo buscas?

Rewrite the sentences, replacing the italicized words with the correct direct object pronoun.

    Busco *a mi hermano.*
    Lo busco.

1. Escucho *a mi hermana.*
2. Pongo *los plátanos y las manzanas* en el plato.
3. ¿No compras *la botella de agua mineral?*
4. ¿Busca Ud. *su libro de álgebra?*
5. ¿Comen Uds. *las zanahorias?*
6. ¿Comprendes *al vendedor?*
7. Venden *las lechugas.*
8. Quito *mis platos.*

F   ¿Lo haces?

Answer the questions according to the model.

    ¿Compras la blusa ahora?
    No, pero voy a comprarla más tarde.

1. ¿Hace Roberto jugo de naranja?
2. ¿Limpian ellos los baños?
3. ¿Lee Ud. el periódico?
4. ¿Escucha la radio?
5. ¿Necesito mi abrigo ahora?
6. ¿Estudian Uds. las lecciones?
7. ¿Cocinan Uds. el pollo y las verduras?
8. ¿Lavas las tazas y los platillos?

Sustantivos
el agua (*f.*)
el agua mineral
el almuerzo
el azúcar
el barrio
la botella
el café (*coffee*)
el café con leche
la carne
la carnicería
la cebolla
la cena
los comestibles
la comida (*meal*)
la cosa
la cuchara
el cuchillo
el chocolate
los churros
el desayuno
la docena
los frijoles
la fruta
el gramo
los guisantes
el huevo
el jugo
el jugo de naranja /
    de manzana / de tomate
el kilo
la lechuga
el limón, *pl.* los limones
el litro
el maíz
el mantel
la manzana
el mercado
la mermelada

la naranja
la panadería
el pan tostado
la papa
el pavo
la peseta
el plátano
el platillo
el plato
el pollo
la servilleta
el supermercado
la taza
el té
el tenedor
el tomate
el vaso
la verdura
la zanahoria

Pronombre
todo

Pronombres de complemento
directo
lo, la, los, las

Verbos
beber
hacer
llegar
necesitar
poner
salir (de)
vender

(yo) fui
(tú) fuiste
Ud. (él / ella) fue

Adverbios
anoche
ayer
pronto
ya

Preposiciones
debajo de
para + *inf.*
sobre

Números
ciento uno, -a
ciento dos
doscientos, -as
trescientos, -as
cuatrocientos, -as
quinientos, -as
seiscientos, -as
setecientos, -as
ochocientos, -as
novecientos, -as
mil

Expresiones
al mediodía
ayer por la mañana / noche /
    tarde
de compras
un poco (de)
poner la mesa
quitar los platos
vender a + (*amount of money*)

CAPÍTULO 9

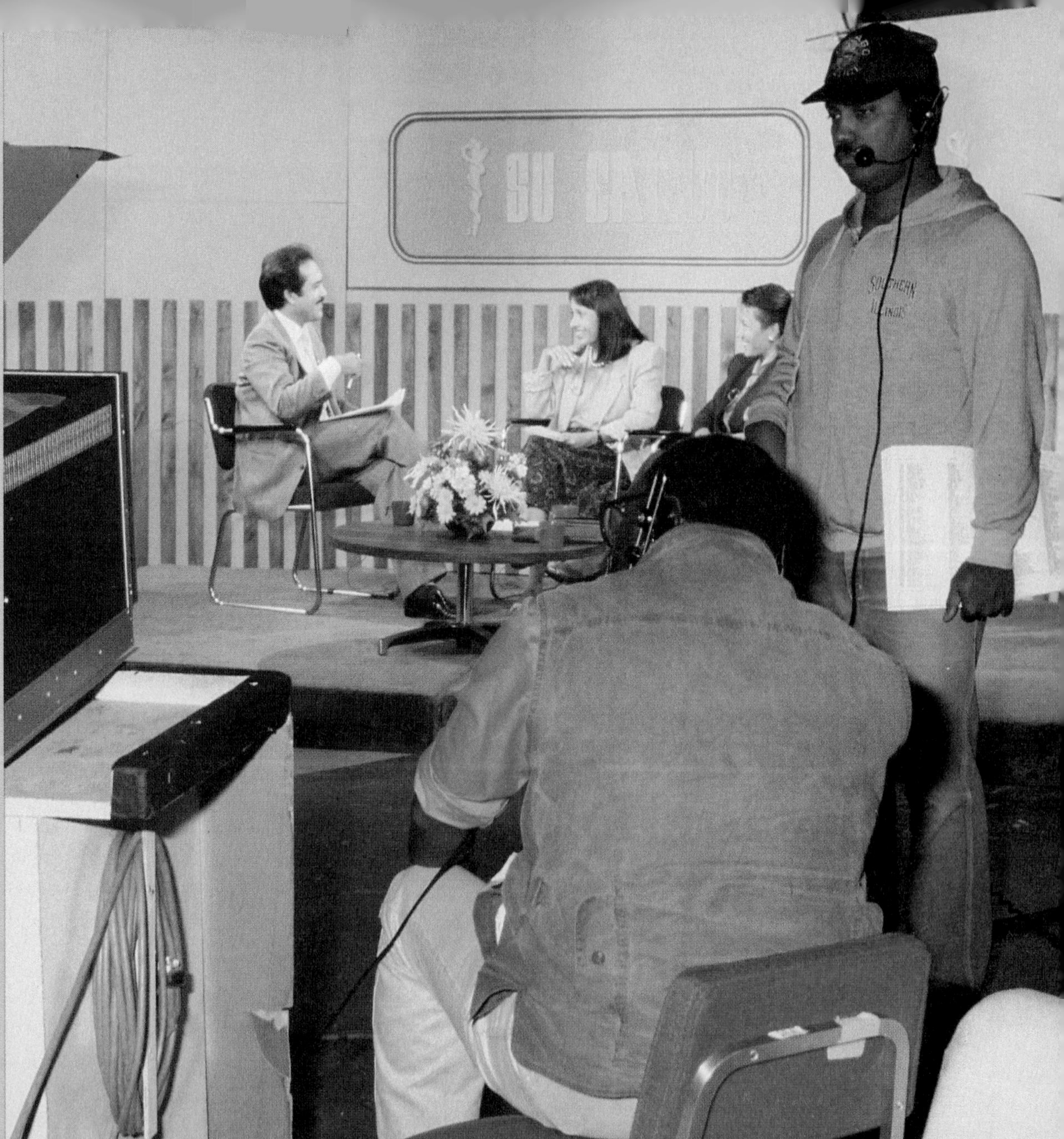

LA TELE EN LOS ESTADOS UNIDOS

The best way to practice Spanish is to go to a Spanish-speaking country. But if you can't do that, you may be able to bring the Spanish-speaking world into your own home simply by turning on your television set. In most parts of the United States you can find at least one local cable channel or television station that features Spanish-language programming. The Spanish International Network, now called Univision, celebrated its twenty-fifth anniversary in 1986. This national network imports and produces programs for more than 400 stations in the United States. In some places, these stations broadcast 24 hours a day.

Spanish-language television features four main types of programs: movies, *telenovelas* (soap operas), variety shows, and sports. As in all soap operas, *telenovelas* feature many characters and various story lines going on at the same time. But unlike the ones you are familiar with, *telenovelas* usually run for a period of only a few months. Families and friends often gather to watch the final episodes of their favorite *telenovelas* together.

Variety shows feature musicians and dancers along with comedians, magicians, and acrobats. Sometimes even the superstars of the Spanish-speaking world appear on these shows.

If you are a soccer fan, you may have already watched some Spanish-language sports programs. They present the best games from around the world and are often the only programs to cover international soccer tournaments such as the World Cup competition.

Even if you've studied Spanish for only a short time, you can enjoy these sports and variety shows. You might even be surprised to discover how much you understand. If there's a Spanish channel in your area, try it—it's like opening a window onto another world.

PALABRAS NUEVAS I

El cine y la tele

película de ciencia ficción

película cómica

¿QUÉ HAY DETRÁS DE LA PUERTA?

película de terror

La mujer misteriosa

película romántica

Mi Primo Tonto

Ellos vienen del AÑO 3000

dibujos animados

El Autobús inteligente

película policíaca

EL AGENTE 0991

JUSTICIA AL MEDIODÍA

película del oeste

¿QUIERES BAILAR CONMIGO?

película musical

If students ask: Other related words you may want to present: *las palomitas de maíz,* popcorn; *la estrella de cine,* movie star.

Notes: Make sure students understand the difference between *el televisor* (TV set—the appliance itself) and *la televisión* (the programming that we watch).

Enrichment: You may want to reinforce the use of *desde* and *hasta* in mini-dialogue 3 by asking *¿Cuánto dura la clase de español? ¿Cuánto dura el almuerzo? ¿Cuánto duran las vacaciones de verano?*

el televisor

las noticias

el anuncio
comercial

el actor

la actriz
pl. las actrices

CONTEXTO COMUNICATIVO 2

1 EVA   ¿Qué **programa** vas a **ver** esta noche?

   LUIS   Una película cómica muy vieja.

   EVA   ¿Es **en colores**?

   LUIS   Sí.

   EVA   ¿Y quiénes son los actores?

   LUIS   No sé. No son **muy conocidos**.

Variaciones:
- cómica → musical
- en colores → en blanco y negro

el programa	*program*
ver (yo veo, tú ves)	*to see*
en colores	*in color*
(muy) conocido, -a	*(well-) known*

2 DIANA   **¡Imagínate! Acabo de** ver a Daniel Vadías en **el canal** 17.

   RAÚL   ¿En qué **clase de** programa?

   DIANA   **Bueno . . . ,** en un anuncio comercial.

- ¡imagínate! → ¡qué suerte!

¡imagínate!	*imagine!*
acabar de + infinitive	*to have just (done something)*
el canal	*TV channel*
la clase (de)	here: *kind (of), type (of)*
bueno	here: = pues

3 EDUARDO **¿Cuánto dura** el programa **sobre** México?

   ÁNGELA   Tres horas. **Desde** las nueve **hasta** las doce. Y **continúa*** mañana por la noche.

   EDUARDO ¿Vas a ver todo el programa?

   ÁNGELA   ¡Ojalá!

- las doce → la medianoche
- continúa → no termina hasta

¿cuánto dura?	*how long does (something) last?*
durar	*to last*
sobre	here: *about*
desde	*from*
hasta	*until*
continuar	*to continue*

* Note the written accent on the *ú* in all present-tense forms of *continuar* except for the *nosotros* and *vosotros* forms: *continúo, continúas, continúa, continuamos, continuáis, continúan.*

4 EVA   Hola, Carlos. Esta noche **doy** una fiesta en mi casa. ¿Quieres venir?

CARLOS   ¡Cómo no! ¿A qué hora es?

EVA   A las siete.

- ¡cómo no! → ¡por supuesto!
- siete → ocho y media

dar (yo doy, tú das)   *to give*

Reteach / Review: Ask students to add the final line for Carlos in mini-dialogue 4, including a farewell.

5 DOLORES   ¿Vienes al cine conmigo, Antonio?

ANTONIO   **Hoy no.** Tengo que **arreglar** mi bicicleta.

DOLORES   ¡Qué mala suerte! **Dan una película estupenda** en el cine Luxor.

- hoy no → no puedo
- estupenda → muy interesante

hoy no   *not today*
arreglar   *to fix, to repair*
dar una película / un programa   *to show a movie / a program*
estupendo, -a   *fantastic, great*

6 LUZ   En el canal 38 dan una película del oeste. ¿Quieres verla conmigo?

JORGE   ¿Cuándo? ¿Ahora?

LUZ   No, en una hora **y media.**

JORGE   Muy bien, pero tengo que terminar la tarea **antes de** mirar la tele.

- del oeste → de ciencia ficción
- del oeste → de terror
- en una hora y media → en **media hora**
- antes de → después de
- terminar la tarea → repasar mis lecciones

y media   *and a half*
antes de   *before*
antes de + infinitive   *before (doing something)*

media hora   *half an hour*

Enrichment: You may want to reinforce the expression *media hora* in mini-dialogue 6 by asking *¿Cuánto dura ____?* with the title of a popular half-hour TV show. Make sure students omit the indefinite article *una*.

Una tienda de videocintas en España

PRÁCTICA

A **¿Qué película dan?** Mira los anuncios. Con un(a) compañero(a) de clase, discute *(discuss)* las películas. Sigue el modelo.

> ESTUDIANTE A *¿Qué clase de película dan en el cine Colón?*
> ESTUDIANTE B *Una película de terror. ¿Quieres verla?*
> ESTUDIANTE A *Sí. Vamos a verla.*
> o: *No. No quiero verla.*

Práctica A
1. Una película de ciencia ficción.
2. Una película musical.
3. Una película cómica.
4. Una película romántica.
5. Una película policíaca.
6. (Una película de) dibujos animados.
7. Una película del oeste.

B **¿Cuáles te gustan?** Mira los anuncios de la Práctica A, y discute qué clases de películas te gustan. Sigue el modelo.

> ESTUDIANTE A *¿Te gustan las películas de terror?*
> ESTUDIANTE B *Sí, me gustan mucho. ¿A ti te gustan?*
> o: *No, no me gustan. ¿A ti te gustan?*
> ESTUDIANTE A *Sí. Mucho.*
> o: *No.*

Práctica B
Answers will vary but should follow the model.

Práctica D
1. ¿Cuánto dura el programa de preguntas y respuestas (para niños)? Media hora. Desde las seis hasta las seis y media.
2. ¿Cuánto dura el programa de noticias? Media hora. Desde las seis y media hasta las siete.
3. ¿Cuánto dura el programa de ciencias populares? Una hora. Desde las siete hasta las ocho.
4. ¿Cuánto dura el programa sobre la comida mexicana? Media hora. Desde las ocho hasta las ocho y media.
5. ¿Cuánto dura la película de terror? Una hora y media. Desde las ocho y media hasta las diez.
6. ¿Cuánto dura el programa de deportes? Media hora. Desde las diez hasta las diez y media.
7. ¿Cuánto dura la película romántica? Una hora y media. Desde las diez y media hasta las doce (medianoche).
8. ¿Cuánto dura el programa de noticias y música? Quince minutos. Desde las doce (medianoche) hasta las doce y cuarto.

C Me gusta mucho la tele. Di *(Tell)* qué clases de programas te gustan, cuáles no te gustan y por qué. Puedes usar también las palabras *muy*, *bastante* o *demasiado* antes del adjetivo. Sigue el modelo.

> *Me gustan los dibujos animados. Son (muy) divertidos.*

1. los anuncios comerciales
2. los programas policíacos
3. los programas en el canal *(número)*
4. los programas cómicos
5. las noticias
6. las películas románticas
7. los programas de deportes
8. los dibujos animados
9. los programas musicales
10. los programas de ciencia ficción
11. los programas sobre las ciencias

aburrido
bueno
divertido
estupendo
interesante
malo

D Mi programa favorito. Dos amigos hablan sobre cuánto duran los programas en el canal 9. Pregunta y contesta según el modelo.

ESTUDIANTE A *¿Cuánto dura el programa de dibujos animados?*
ESTUDIANTE B *Media hora. Desde las cinco y media hasta las seis.*

Tv guía

MIÉRCOLES   3

17:30.—**Los tres peces pequeños:** Programa de dibujos animados
18:00.—**¿Cuándo es nunca?:** Programa de preguntas y respuestas para niños
18:30.—**Hoy en la ciudad:** Programa de noticias
19:00.—**¿Por qué llueve?:** Programa de ciencias populares
20:00.—**Frijoles y maíz:** Programa sobre la comida mexicana
20:30.—**La casa sin ventanas:** Película de terror
22:00.—**Los deportes de hoy:** Programa de deportes
22:30.—**El viento triste:** Película romántica
24:00.—**¡Hasta mañana!:** Programa de noticias y música (15 minutos)

-22:30 (☆☆☆) —*El viento triste.* 1988. 90 minutos. Director: Osvaldo Petrera. Actores: Ana Moreno, Daniel Salcedo. Carmen, una chica bonita de Nueva York, viaja a Puerto Rico para ver a su novio Manolo, hombre con un

4

E Hablemos de ti.

1. ¿Qué programas de televisión te gustan más? ¿Por qué?
2. ¿Qué clases de películas te gustan menos? ¿Por qué? ¿Ves muchas películas?
3. ¿Quiénes son tu actor y tu actriz favoritos? ¿Por qué?
4. ¿Qué películas dan ahora en tu ciudad?
5. ¿Te gustan las películas viejas? ¿Dónde las ves?
6. ¿Te gustan las películas en blanco y negro o prefieres las películas en colores? ¿Por qué?
7. ¿Qué programas ves los sábados por la noche? ¿Vas a mirar la televisión esta noche? ¿Qué programas vas a ver?

Enrichment: Additional questions for Ex. E: *¿Miras la televisión antes de venir a la escuela? ¿Qué programas prefieres mirar? ¿Tienes un anuncio comercial favorito? ¿Cuál es?*

Práctica E
Answers will vary.

Practice Sheet 9–1

Workbook Exs. A–B

Tape Manual Exs. 1–2   3

Quiz 9–1

ACTIVIDAD

¿Qué programas dan?   Form seven groups. Your teacher will assign a day of the week to each group. Work together to make up a TV listing for all of the programs being shown on that night on a particular channel between 6:00 and 10:00 P.M. Give each program a title, and prepare a brief description of what it is about. You might use words or phrases from the list below. Afterwards, you might get back together as a class and take turns reading your TV listings, or you might post them for others to look at.

el actor / la actriz	durar
los anuncios	estupendo, -a
el canal	las noticias
conocido, -a	una película
continuar	un programa
desde . . . hasta	sobre

Reteach / Extra Help: If your class finds the **Actividad** difficult, ask students to bring in TV listings from a local newspaper or magazine to use as a model for their own listings.

Palabras Nuevas I   **309**

APLICACIONES

Discretionary

Notes: Remind students that *fútbol* is soccer, not football (*fútbol americano*).

¿Qué programa vamos a ver?

 4

Todo el mundo[1] tiene su programa favorito, pero hay sólo un televisor en la casa.

MARÍA	Alfonso, ¿vas a mirar la tele esta noche?
ALFONSO	Sí. Quiero ver un partido de fútbol a las siete. Ciudad
	Juárez contra[2] Mérida.* ¡Va a ser estupendo!
MARÍA	¡Esta noche no! A las siete dan *Todos los sábados*, mi
	programa favorito.
ALFONSO	Tú siempre ves esos[3] programas musicales.
MARÍA	Y tú ves programas de deportes todos los días. Béisbol
	ayer, fútbol hoy, básquetbol mañana.
ALFONSO	Papá, yo quiero ver el partido de fútbol. Tú quieres
	verlo también, ¿no?
PAPÁ	No, Alfonso. Vamos todos a ver las noticias hasta las
	7:30. Después, yo voy a leer el periódico y Uds. van a
	hacer su tarea. Más tarde dan una gran película
	policíaca en el canal 33. Tu mamá y yo tenemos ganas
	de verla y dura hasta las 10:30.
ALFONSO	Entonces yo voy a escuchar el partido de fútbol en mi
	dormitorio. Y tú, María, ¿qué vas a hacer?
MARÍA	No sé. Pero yo no voy a escuchar el partido de fútbol.
	¡Qué aburrido!

5

10

15

20

---

[1]**todo el mundo** *everybody*   [2]**contra** *against, versus*   [3]**esos, esas** *those*

* Ciudad Juárez is located in the northernmost part of Mexico, and Mérida is located in the south.

Enrichment: Additional questions: *¿De qué país son los equipos de fútbol? (Son de México.) ¿Cómo va a escuchar Alfonso el partido? (Va a escucharlo en la radio.) Según María, ¿cómo son los partidos de fútbol? (Son aburridos.)*

Preguntas

Contesta según el diálogo.

1. ¿Qué programa tiene ganas de mirar Alfonso?   2. ¿Cuál es el programa favorito de María? ¿Qué clase de programa es?   3. ¿A qué hora tiene Alfonso ganas de mirar la televisión? ¿Qué clase de programa prefiere Alfonso?   4. ¿Quiénes van a mirar las noticias? ¿Qué van a hacer después?   5. ¿Qué clase de película van a ver los padres?   6. ¿A qué hora termina la película?   7. ¿Qué va a hacer Alfonso entonces?   8. ¿Por qué no pueden mirar todos su programa favorito?

Diálogo
1. el partido de fútbol
2. *Todos los sábados*; un programa musical
3. a las siete; programas de deportes
4. todos; Papá va a leer el periódico y María y Alfonso van a hacer su tarea.
5. una película policíaca
6. a las diez y media
7. Va a escuchar el partido de fútbol en su dormitorio.
8. Porque hay sólo un televisor en la casa.

Participación

Working with a partner, make up a dialogue of four to six lines in which you decide what programs to watch this evening and why.

PRONUNCIACIÓN 5

A In Spanish we pronounce the letter combination *qu* like the letter *c* in the English word "cat." In English, that sound is usually followed by a puff of air. In Spanish it is not.
Escucha y repite.

que   queso   quiero   porque   esquina   esquiar

B When the letter *c* comes before *a, o, u,* or a consonant, it is also pronounced like the *c* in "cat." Again, there is no puff of air.
Escucha y repite.

casa   contento   cuando   cuchara
poco   acabar   claro   creo

C When *c* comes before *e* or *i*, most Spanish speakers pronounce it like the *s* in the English word "sand."
Escucha y repite.

cero   cinco   ciudad   ciencias   conocido

D Escucha y repite.

Dan una película cómica.
Quiero mirar el canal cinco.
Hay quince anuncios comerciales.
Es una película de ciencia ficción en colores.

PALABRAS NUEVAS II

La playa

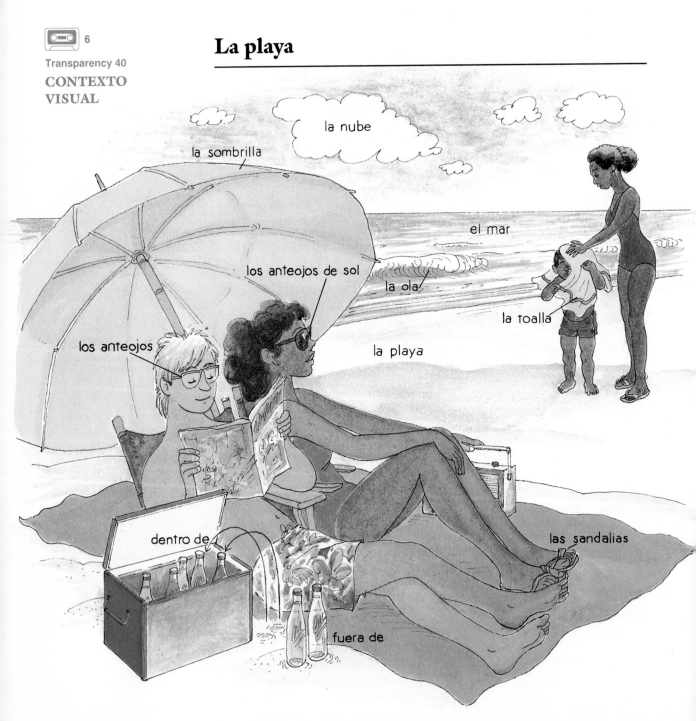

la nube

la sombrilla

el mar

los anteojos de sol

la ola

la toalla

los anteojos

la playa

dentro de

fuera de

las sandalias

If students ask: Other related words you may want to present: *la arena*, sand; *la loción bronceadora*, suntan lotion; *la manta*, blanket; *secar*, to dry.

tener frío (m.)

tener calor (m.)

tener razón (f.)

tener sed (f.)

tener hambre (f.)

no tener razón (f.)

tener sueño (m.)

tener miedo (de) (m.)

tener suerte (f.)

CONTEXTO COMUNICATIVO 🔊 7

1 PABLO Hola, Rosa, ¿quieres ir a la playa conmigo?

ROSA Pero, ¿por qué vas a la playa? **Está nublado.**

PABLO **¿Qué importa?** No puedo tomar el sol, pero puedo nadar.

Variaciones:

■ está nublado → no hace sol

■ no puedo tomar el sol → no hace **mucho** calor

está nublado *it's cloudy*
¿qué importa? *so what?*
mucho, -a here: *very*

Palabras Nuevas II **313**

2	CÉSAR	¿**Todo el mundo** va a la playa?
	MARCOS	**Casi** todo el mundo. José no va.
	CÉSAR	¿Por qué no?
	MARCOS	**A** él **le dan miedo** las olas.

■ a la playa → al parque
  las olas → los perros

todo el mundo   *everybody*

casi   *almost*

le   *here: him; see p. 323.*

dar miedo a   *to frighten, to scare (someone)*

3	ANITA	¿Dónde está Jaime?
	HÉCTOR	Fue a comprar hamburguesas y refrescos.
	ANITA	**¡Qué bueno!**
	HÉCTOR	**¡Cuidado,** Anita! **Si** vas a nadar, no **debes** comer.
	ANITA	Tienes razón, pero tengo mucha hambre.

■ refrescos → limonada
■ tienes razón → sí, debo **tener cuidado**

¡qué bueno!   *great!*

¡cuidado!   *watch out! careful!*

si   *if*

deber   *should, ought to*

tener cuidado (m.)   *to be careful*

4	JORGE	Tienes mucha suerte, Felipe.
	FELIPE	¿Por qué?
	JORGE	Porque nunca estudias mucho y siempre sacas buenas notas.
	FELIPE	**Ya no.** Acabo de recibir un cero en mi prueba de geometría.
	JORGE	**¡Caramba!**

■ estudias → repasas las lecciones
■ sacas → recibes
■ un cero → una "F"
■ ¡caramba! → ¡qué lástima!

ya no   *not anymore*

¡caramba!   *gosh!, gee!*

Reteach / Extra Help: For mini-dialogue 3, elicit or provide additional suggestions with *debes.* For example: *Si vas a tomar el sol, debes tener cuidado. Si quieres salir bien en un examen, debes estudiar.*

EN OTRAS PARTES

En España se dice *las gafas.*
En el Caribe se dice *los espejuelos.*

En España se dice *el parasol.*

PRÁCTICA

A ¿Cómo están? Tell how each of these people feels.

(él)
Tiene suerte.

1. Todo el mundo

2. Ud.

3. (tú)

4. Uds.

5. (ellos)

6. (nosotros)

B ¡Ay, tengo . . . ! Imagina que estás en cada (*each*) una de estas (*these*) situaciones. Usa la expresión apropiada con *tener* y *mucho, -a* para describir cómo te sientes (*how you feel*).

Estás en Alaska durante el mes de enero y no llevas abrigo.
Tengo mucho frío.

1. Estás en la playa de Acapulco en el verano. Hace mucho sol y no tienes sombrilla.
2. Es mediodía. Acabas de llegar al hotel y quieres comer.
3. Es medianoche. Estás solo(a) en una casa vieja. No puedes ver nada.
4. Tienes un traje de baño nuevo y quieres tomar el sol, pero siempre está nublado.
5. Es *muy* tarde, después de la medianoche. Y todavía debes estudiar para un examen de álgebra.
6. Montas en bicicleta en una ciudad grande y hay muchos coches en la calle. Pero tú no tienes miedo. ¿Por que?
7. Acabas de jugar al tenis. Hace mucho calor y no hay nada para beber.

Práctica A
1. Todo el mundo tiene hambre.
2. Ud. tiene sueño.
3. Tienes miedo.
4. Uds. tienen sed.
5. Tienen calor.
6. Tenemos frío.

Práctica B
1. Tengo mucho calor.
2. Tengo mucha hambre.
3. Tengo mucho miedo.
4. No tengo mucha suerte.
5. Tengo mucho sueño.
6. Tengo mucho cuidado.
7. Tengo mucha sed.

Acapulco, México

C ¡Qué problema! Escoge *(choose)* la palabra o expresión apropiada para completar cada frase.

1. _____ vamos al parque los domingos. *(hoy no / mañana / siempre)*
2. _____ Tengo sed y no hay agua en el refrigerador. *(¡Caramba! / ¡Qué bueno! / ¡Cuidado!)*
3. Es mayo y en los Estados Unidos _____ hace mucho frío. *(casi / ya no / siempre)*
4. Debemos buscar _____ antes de ir a la playa. *(una sombrilla / un anuncio comercial / una nube)*
5. _____ Las olas son muy grandes hoy. ¿No tienes miedo de nada? *(¡Imagínate! / ¡Cuidado! / ¿Qué importa?)*
6. _____ No puedo ir al mar contigo. *(¡Qué bueno! / ¡Cuidado! / ¡Caramba!)*
7. Si no llevo mis _____, no puedo ver la pizarra. *(anteojos de sol / anteojos / vasos)*
8. ¡Qué lástima! _____ dan mi programa favorito. *(Siempre / Ya no / A menudo)*

D Hablemos de ti.
1. ¿Hay una playa en tu ciudad o cerca de ella? ¿Vas allí en el verano? ¿Con quiénes vas? ¿Qué hacen Uds. cuando van a la playa?
2. ¿Qué haces cuando tienes hambre? ¿Y cuando tienes sed?
3. ¿Qué llevas cuando hace frío? ¿Y cuando hace mucho calor? ¿Tienes frío o calor ahora?
4. ¿De qué tienes miedo? ¿De los perros grandes o de los gatos negros? ¿O no tienes miedo de nada?

Practice Sheets 9–2, 9–3   Workbook Exs. C–D

 8 Tape Manual Exs. 3–4   Quiz 9–2

ESTUDIO DE PALABRAS

Spanish words that end in *-sión* or *-ción* often have English equivalents that end in *-sion* or *-tion*.

la televisión	*television*
la expresión	*expression*
la ficción	*fiction*
la pronunciación	*pronunciation*
la participación	*participation*

You shouldn't have any trouble understanding the following words.

la confusión	la visión	la tensión
la acción	la loción	la fracción

EXPLICACIONES I

Los verbos *dar* y *ver*

The verb *dar* means "to give." Except for the *yo* form—*doy*—it takes the same present-tense endings as a regular *-ar* verb.

INFINITIVO **dar**

	SINGULAR		PLURAL	
1	(yo)	**doy**	(nosotros) (nosotras)	**damos**
2	(tú)	**das**	(vosotros) (vosotras)	**dais**
3	Ud. (él) (ella)	**da**	Uds. (ellos) (ellas)	**dan**

The verb *ver* means "to see." Like *dar*, only its *yo* form is irregular: *veo*. Otherwise it takes the same present-tense endings as a regular *-er* verb.

INFINITIVO **ver**

	SINGULAR		PLURAL	
1	(yo)	**veo**	(nosotros) (nosotras)	**vemos**
2	(tú)	**ves**	(vosotros) (vosotras)	**veis**
3	Ud. (él) (ella)	**ve**	Uds. (ellos) (ellas)	**ven**

Notes: Point out the use of *dar* in mini-dialogues 4 and 5 on p. 306 and of *ver* in 1–3 on p. 305 and 6 on p. 306.

◆ **OBJECTIVES:**

TO REPORT WHAT YOU SEE

TO DISCUSS GIVING THINGS TO OTHERS

Reteach / Extra Help: In preparation for the **Práctica** on pp. 318–319, ask students to work in pairs or do a chain drill to practice the forms of *dar* and *ver*: ¿Doy una fiesta el sábado? ¿Qué / A quién veo todos los días en la clase de español?

Remind students to use the personal *a* with *ver* when the direct object is a person.

PRÁCTICA

A ¿Qué damos? Usa la forma correcta de *dar* para formar frases. Sigue el modelo.

> (tú) / una computadora al colegio
> *Das una computadora al colegio.*

1. (yo) / las respuestas correctas
2. (tú) / una cena mañana
3. tus padres / casi todos sus libros a la biblioteca
4. mi profesor de matemáticas / buenas notas
5. Uds. / un televisor a la escuela, ¿verdad?
6. (nosotros) / de comer al perro
7. todo el mundo / muchas pruebas
8. (nosotras) / una fiesta esta noche
9. Yolanda y tú nunca / nada a nadie

B ¿Qué vemos aquí? Imagina que vas de compras con unos amigos. ¿Qué ve cada persona? Usa cualquier *(any)* adjetivo apropiado en tu respuesta. Sigue el modelo.

Luis y Teresa
ESTUDIANTE A   *¿Qué ven Luis y Teresa?*
ESTUDIANTE B   *Ven una computadora muy cara.*

1. Mónica

2. César y Pablo

3. (tú)

4. ellas

5. yo

6. Roberto

Uds. ven a personas también. Usa *¿a quién?* para preguntar. ¡Cuidado! No olvides *(don't forget)* la *a* personal cuando contestas.

7. (nosotros)

8. Uds.

9. Elena y tú

10. todos

C El diario (diary) de Cristóbal. Cristóbal mira su diario viejo, pero no puede leer unas palabras. Usa la forma correcta de *dar* o *ver* para ayudarlo a leer su diario.

Enrichment: After students do Ex. C in class, you may want to ask them to find a photo or magazine picture and write an imaginary diary entry about it at home. Students should be prepared to ask and answer questions about their entries.

DIARIO

fecha: *martes, 28 de agosto*

Estamos en Valencia. Nosotros ——— a mi primo Juan todos los días. ¡Qué aburrido! Es un niño muy tonto. Tía Luisa ya no ——— muy bien. Tiene anteojos nuevos pero no quiere llevarlos. El canal 7 ——— dos películas interesantes esta noche, pero no puedo ———las porque duran cuatro horas y debo ir a un restaurante con mis tíos. ¡Caramba! Pero anoche fui al cine para ——— una película sobre un hombre que vive en el mar.

Málaga, España

DIARIO

fecha: *jueves, 30 de agosto*

Ahora estoy en Málaga y ——— el mar desde mi ventana. ¡Es estupendo! En el hotel hay un pájaro de muchos colores. Mis padres ——— de comer al pájaro todos los días, pero todavía no canta. El pájaro le ——— mucho miedo al gato que vive en el hotel. Es muy divertido. Estoy fuera del hotel casi todo el día. Todavía está nublado. ¿Cuándo vamos a ——— un día sin nubes?

DIARIO

fecha: *lunes, 3 de septiembre*

Acabamos de salir de Málaga. Tenemos que estar en casa mañana. La semana próxima nosotros ——— una fiesta y nuestros amigos van a ——— todas las películas de nuestras vacaciones. Ellos tienen suerte, ¿no?

Practice Sheets 9–4, 9–5

Tape Manual Exs. 5–6 9

Quiz 9–3

Práctica C
vemos
ve
da
ver
ver
veo
dan
da
ver
damos
ver

Acabar de + infinitivo

◆ OBJECTIVES:

TO DESCRIBE OR
REPORT THINGS
THAT JUST
HAPPENED

TO GIVE REASONS
OR EXCUSES

Acabar is a regular *-ar* verb. We use *acabar de* + an infinitive to talk about something that has *just taken place*.

Ellos **acaban de** salir.   *They've **just** left.*
Acabamos de llegar.   *We've **just** arrived.*

PRÁCTICA

A ¿Qué tienes?   Paco habla por teléfono. Pregunta y contesta según el modelo. Usa expresiones de la lista para contestar.

tener hambre

ESTUDIANTE A   *¿Tienes hambre?*
ESTUDIANTE B   *No, acabo de terminar el desayuno.*

1. tener calor
2. tener hambre
3. tener frío
4. tener suerte
5. tener sed
6. tener miedo

beber una botella de agua mineral
beber una taza de té
comer una tortilla
comprar un perro grande
ver a un policía
sacar una mala nota
salir del mar
terminar el desayuno

Práctica A
Answers will vary.

Notes.   You may want to refer students to mini–dialogues 2 on p. 305 and 4 on p. 314 for further examples of *acabar de* + infinitive.

(abajo, izquierda) En un café en Guadalajara, México; (abajo, derecha) Amigos en Bogotá, Colombia

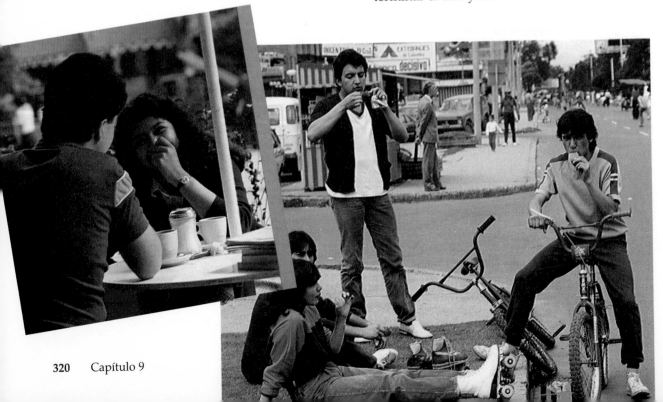

B ¿Y qué pasa ahora? Imagina que cuidas a unos niños. Tú miras una película policíaca en la tele. De vez en cuando *(from time to time)* uno de los niños entra en la sala y pregunta "¿Qué pasa ahora?" Pregunta y contesta según el modelo.

> la actriz morena / ver un gato negro
> ESTUDIANTE A   *¿Qué hace la actriz morena?*
> ESTUDIANTE B   *Acaba de ver un gato negro.*

1. la tía simpática / llamar a sus padres
2. la novia del muchacho / escribir una carta
3. el actor muy bajo / bailar con la chica alta
4. el señor delgado / salir de su oficina
5. sus abuelos / contestar el teléfono
6. el chico latinoamericano / llegar en taxi
7. el sobrino / recibir una carta
8. los policías / llegar a casa

C Hablemos de ti.

1. ¿Das muchas fiestas? ¿Cuándo las das? ¿Por qué?
2. ¿Da muchas pruebas tu profesor(a) de español? ¿Siempre sales bien?
3. ¿Da buenas notas tu profesor(a) de español?
4. ¿Qué acaban de aprender tú y tus compañeros en la clase de español?
5. ¿Qué acabas de hacer?

Práctica B
1. ¿Qué hace la tía simpática? Acaba de llamar a sus padres.
2. ¿Qué hace la novia del muchacho? Acaba de escribir una carta.
3. ¿Qué hace el actor muy bajo? Acaba de bailar con la chica alta.
4. ¿Qué hace el señor delgado? Acaba de salir de su oficina.
5. ¿Qué hacen sus abuelos? Acaban de contestar el teléfono.
6. ¿Qué hace el chico latinoamericano? Acaba de llegar en taxi.
7. ¿Qué hace el sobrino? Acaba de recibir una carta.
8. ¿Qué hacen los policías? Acaban de llegar a casa.

Práctica C
Answers will vary.

Enrichment: Additional questions for Ex. C; *¿Ves a tus primos a menudo? ¿Cuándo los ves? ¿Dan películas a veces en tu escuela? ¿Qué clases de películas dan?*

Una playa en Puerto Rico

Practice Sheets 9–6, 9–7

Workbook Exs. E–F

Tape Manual Ex. 7 10

Activity Master 9–1

Quiz 9–4

APLICACIONES

Discretionary

Notes: Sample dialogues for the **¿Qué pasa?** appear in the pre-chapter teacher pages. If students prepare their dialogues in pairs, ask volunteers to act them out for the class.

¿Qué película vemos?   Transparency 41

Julio y Lucía acaban de llegar al centro. ¿Qué van a hacer? ¿Qué películas dan esta noche? ¿Qué clase de película es *Mi guitarra y yo?*

Lucía thinks that she and Julio should have dinner before going to the movies. Make up a dialogue in which they decide which movie they will see, what time they will go, and where they will eat. You might want to use these words or phrases:

tener hambre   durar
comer   media hora
antes de   estupendo, -a

EXPLICACIONES II

El complemento indirecto: Los pronombres *le* y *les*

An indirect object tells *to whom* or *for whom* an action is performed. An indirect object pronoun replaces an indirect object noun. Here are the indirect object pronouns meaning "to (or for) him, her, you" (formal and plural), and to (or for) "them."

Le doy los libros.   *I'm giving the books* $\begin{cases} \textbf{\textit{to him.}} \\ \textbf{\textit{to her.}} \\ \textbf{\textit{to you.}} \text{ (Ud.)} \end{cases}$

or: *I'm giving **him (her, you)** the books.*

Les compro suéteres.   *I'm buying sweaters* **for** $\begin{cases} \textbf{\textit{them.}} \\ \textbf{\textit{you.}} \text{ (Uds.)} \end{cases}$

or: *I'm buying **them (you)** sweaters.*

Notice that like direct object pronouns, indirect object pronouns come directly before the verb.

1 When we use a noun as an indirect object, we usually also use the indirect object pronoun.

> **Le** doy los libros **a Teresa.**   *I'm giving the books **to Teresa.***
> **Les** compro suéteres **a mis padres.**   *I'm buying sweaters **for my parents.***

2 You can see that *le* and *les* can have more than one meaning. To make the meaning clear, we can add the preposition *a* + a prepositional pronoun.

le $\begin{cases} \text{a él} \\ \text{a ella} \\ \text{a Ud.} \end{cases}$ les $\begin{cases} \text{a ellos} \\ \text{a ellas} \\ \text{a Uds.} \end{cases}$

> **Le** doy los libros **a ella.**   *I'm giving the books **to her.***
> **Les** compro suéteres **a Uds.**   *I'm buying sweaters **for you.***

◆ **OBJECTIVES:**

TO EXPRESS DOING THINGS FOR OTHERS

TO DESCRIBE GIVING THINGS TO OTHERS

Notes: Mini-dialogue 2 on p. 314 illustrates the indirect object pronoun *le* and the use of *a* + the prepositional pronoun *él*.

Make sure students can distinguish between direct and indirect objects by asking these questions about the examples in (1) under **Explicaciones** II:
¿Qué das? (los libros)
¿A quién? (a Teresa)
¿Qué compras? (suéteres)
¿A quiénes? (a mis padres).

3 We can also add *a* + noun or prepositional pronoun for emphasis.

Le doy los libros **a ella,** (no **a él.**)	*I'm giving the books **to her,** (not **to him**).*
Le escribo una carta **a David,** (no **a Miguel**).	*I'm writing a letter **to David,** (not **to Miguel**).*

4 We can attach an indirect object pronoun to an infinitive or put it before the main verb, just as we do with direct object pronouns.

Voy a comprar**les** suéteres. ⎫
Les voy a comprar suéteres. ⎭ *I'm going to buy sweaters **for them.***

5 To ask the question "to whom" or "for whom" we use *¿a quién?* + *le* or *¿a quiénes?* + *les*.

¿A quién le das el libro?	***To whom** are you giving the book?*
¿A quiénes les escribes cartas?	***To whom** do you write letters?*

Una tienda en Bariloche, Argentina

PRÁCTICA

A ¿A quién le escribes? Imagina que un estudiante de España pasa (*is spending*) el año con tu familia. Casi todas las noches escribe cartas. Tú le preguntas a quién le escribe. Pregunta y contesta según el modelo.

> mi abuelo
> ESTUDIANTE A *¿A quién le escribes?*
> ESTUDIANTE B *A mi abuelo. Le escribo a menudo.*

1. mi hermana
2. mi padre
3. mi profesor de inglés
4. mi sobrina
5. mi tío Alberto
6. mi prima Luz
7. mi amigo Carlos
8. mi tía Alicia

B ¿Qué haces para tu familia? Imagina que hablas con un(a) amigo(a) sobre lo que (*what*) hace—o no hace—para los otros (*others*). Pregunta y contesta según el modelo.

> arreglarles el coche a tus padres
> ESTUDIANTE A *¿Les arreglas el coche a tus padres?*
> ESTUDIANTE B *Sí, les arreglo el coche.*
> o: *No, no les arreglo el coche.*

1. darles el almuerzo a tus hermanitas
2. enseñarles español a tus hermanos
3. darles el chocolate a los niños
4. comprarles los anteojos de sol a tus padres
5. leerles el periódico a tus abuelos
6. darles de comer a tus peces
7. cocinarles el pavo a ellas
8. comprarles limonada a las chicas

C ¿A quién le da las cosas viejas? Cecilia acaba de ganar la lotería (*won the lottery*). Les da todas sus cosas viejas a sus amigos porque compra cosas nuevas. Sigue el modelo.

> los trajes de baño / sus hermanas
> *Les da los trajes de baño a sus hermanas.*

1. la toalla de Disneyland / Felipe
2. los discos de rock / sus amigos
3. las sandalias / su madre
4. las cartas de actrices conocidas / Carlota y Eva
5. la moto / el novio de Leonor
6. las cucharas de Bolivia / el hijo del Sr. Piñera
7. las faldas de primavera / las chicas
8. los libros policíacos / el profesor de inglés

Práctica A
1. A mi hermana. Le escribo….
2. A mi padre. Le escribo….
3. A mi profesor de inglés. Le escribo….
4. A mi sobrina. Le escribo….
5. A mi tío Alberto. Le escribo….
6. A mi prima Luz. Le escribo….
7. A mi amigo Carlos. Le escribo….
8. A mi tía Alicia. Le escribo….

Práctica B
1. ¿Les das el almuerzo a tus hermanitas? Sí, (*or:* No, no) les doy el almuerzo.
2. ¿Les enseñas español a tus hermanos? …les enseño español.
3. ¿Les das el chocolate a los niños? …les doy el chocolate.
4. ¿Les compras los anteojos de sol a tus padres? …les compro los anteojos de sol.
5. ¿Les lees el periódico a tus abuelos? …les leo el periódico.
6. ¿Les das de comer a tus peces? …les doy de comer.
7. ¿Les cocinas el pavo a ellas? …les cocino el pavo.
8. ¿Les compras limonada a las chicas? …les compro limonada.

Práctica C
1. Le da la toalla de Disneyland a Felipe.
2. Les da los discos de rock a sus amigos.
3. Le da las sandalias a su madre.
4. Les da las cartas de actrices conocidas a Carlota y a Eva.
5. Le da la moto al novio de Leonor.
6. Le da las cucharas de Bolivia al hijo del Sr. Piñera.
7. Les da las faldas de primavera a las chicas.
8. Le da los libros policíacos al profesor de inglés.

Práctica D

1. ¿Qué van a comprarle a Silvia? Le van a comprar toallas.
2. ¿Qué van a comprarle a tía Mercedes? Le van a comprar una sombrilla.
3. ¿Qué van a comprarle a abuelita? Le van a comprar un televisor.
4. ¿Qué van a comprarle a tío Jaime? Le van a comprar un teléfono.
5. ¿Qué van a comprarles a las hijas de Silvia? Les van a comprar un pájaro.
6. ¿Qué van a comprarle a Antonio? Le van a comprar un reloj.
7. ¿Qué van a comprarles a Luz y a Luis? Les van a comprar un perro.
8. ¿Qué van a comprarle a tío Pablo? Le van a comprar una estufa.
9. ¿Qué van a comprarle a la novia de tío Pablo? Le van a comprar guantes.

Reteach / Review: After students finish Ex. D, expand the practice by asking volunteers for the alternate form of each of the questions and responses. For example: *¿Qué le van a comprar a Rosa? (Van a comprarle sandalias.)*

Una calle en Barcelona, España

Enrichment: You may want students to write several sentences at home about what they are going to give friends and / or relatives on their birthdays. They may use Ex. D as a model.

326 Capítulo 9

D ¿Qué le compran? Imagina que es diciembre y que dos niños hablan de lo que *(what)* sus padres van a darles a los otros miembros de la familia. Sigue el modelo.

Rosa

ESTUDIANTE A   *¿Qué van a comprarle a Rosa?*
ESTUDIANTE B   *Le van a comprar sandalias.*

1. Silvia

2. tía Mercedes

3. abuelita

4. tío Jaime

5. las hijas de Silvia

6. Antonio

7. Luz y Luis

8. tío Pablo

9. la novia de tío Pablo

E Hablemos de ti.

1. ¿Tienes amigos en otras ciudades o países? ¿Les escribes a menudo? ¿Cuándo los ves?
2. ¿Qué les das a tus padres para sus cumpleaños? Si tienes hermanos, ¿qué les das a ellos?
3. Si tienes hermanos menores, ¿los ayudas a hacer la tarea? ¿En qué materias?
4. ¿Te gustan los anuncios comerciales en la televisión? ¿Cuáles son tus favoritos? ¿Cuáles no te gustan?
5. ¿Te gustan los dibujos animados? ¿Cuándo los miras? ¿Cuáles son tus favoritos?
6. ¿Cuidas a los niños a veces? ¿Qué te gusta hacer cuando cuidas a los niños? ¿Les lees libros? ¿Miran juntos la tele?
7. ¿Cuándo deben tener cuidado los niños pequeños? Y tú, ¿cuándo debes tú tener mucho cuidado?

Práctica E
Answers will vary.

Practice Sheets 9–8, 9–9, 9–10

Workbook Exs. G–J

Tape Manual Ex. 8   11

Activity Master 9–2

Quizzes 9–5, 9–6

Notes: Make sure students understand the directions for the **Actividad.** Explain that this is a variation on the card game called "Concentration" or "Memory."

ACTIVIDAD

Le doy el borrador a él. Get together with two or three other students. Write each of the words listed below on separate cards. Place them face up on a desk, and take half a minute to memorize where each item is. Then turn the cards over. One person starts by picking up a card (without looking at it) and giving it to someone while saying what he or she is giving that person. For example, if you think the card you are picking up says *el borrador*, say:

Le doy el borrador a *(nombre)*.

You get a point for each card you identify correctly. Take turns picking cards until none are left. The person who has the most points wins.

los bolígrafos	el cuaderno	las papeleras
el borrador	los dibujos	el periódico
los carteles	los lápices	el pupitre
la computadora	el mapa	la tiza

APLICACIONES

Discretionary

Notes: Answers to the **Repaso** and **Tema** appear in the pre-chapter teacher pages.

REPASO

Look carefully at the model sentences. Then put the English cues into Spanish to form new sentences based on the models.

1. *Son las nueve de la mañana y Paco acaba de leer el periódico de anoche.*
   (It's 11:00 in the evening, and I've just fixed María's TV set.)
   (It's 5:00 in the afternoon, and you've (pl.) just seen today's news.)
   (It's 10:00 in the morning, and we've just cleaned Grandmother's kitchen.)

2. *Debe ir al café porque tiene mucha sed.*
   (We should go to the hotel because we're very sleepy.)
   (I should go to the beach because I'm very hot.)
   (They should go home because they're very scared.)

3. *¡Uf! ¿Qué ve Roberto?*
   (Watch out! What do you (fam.) see?)
   (Gosh! What do I see?)
   (Imagine! What do we see?)

4. *Son los perros. ¿Los ves ahora? Tienen frío.*
   (It's Margarita. We see her now. She's sleepy.)
   (It's Tomás. I see him now. You're right.)
   (It's the girls. Do you (formal) see them now? They're lucky.)

5. *Héctor le da una taza de té.*
   (We give her a glass of juice.)
   (I give them a bottle of water.)
   (They give you (pl.) a cheese sandwich.)

Notes: Review of:
1. telling time
   acabar de
   de as possessive and in noun phrases
2. *deber*
   a(l)
   tener expressions
3. exclamations
   ver
4. *ver*
   direct object pronouns
   tener expressions
5. *dar*
   indirect object pronouns
   noun phrases with *de*

(arriba) Una esquina en Sevilla; (derecha) Un café en Salamanca

Put the English captions into Spanish.

It's twelve o'clock at night, and Claudia and Mateo have just seen a horror film.

They should go to the kitchen because they are very hungry.

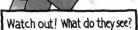

Watch out! What do they see?

It's the cat. They see him now. He's thirsty.

Mateo gives him a saucer of milk.

REDACCIÓN

Now you are ready to write your own dialogue or paragraph. Choose one of the following topics.

1. Expand the *Tema* by writing four to six new sentences about the pictures. What are the young people watching? (Invent a name for the film.) What channel is it on? How is the movie? After feeding the cat, what are Claudia and Mateo going to eat?

2. Write a paragraph of four to six sentences about a favorite television program. What kind of program do you like to watch? Cartoons? News programs? Sports? When do you watch the program? How long does it last? A half hour? An hour? Who are the actors in it? Do you like or dislike commercials? Why?

3. Write talk balloons for each picture. What are Claudia and Mateo saying to each other?

COMPRUEBA TU PROGRESO   CAPÍTULO 9   Discretionary

Notes: Answers to the **Comprueba** appear in the pre–chapter teacher pages.

A ¿A qué hora?
At what time are these programs being shown?

   6:00
A las seis dan una película de terror.

1. 10:00   2. 8:30

3. 9:00   4. 8:45

5. 9:30   6. 9:15

7. 7:45   8. 5:30

B ¿Qué pasa?
Based on the drawings, tell how the following people feel.

1. Ana y Paco   2. Beatriz   3. (yo)

4. mi hermano   5. Pablo y yo   6. (tú)

C ¿*Dar* o *ver*?
Use the correct form of *dar* or *ver*.

1. Nosotros nunca _____ los dibujos animados.
2. El Sr. Taboada le _____ una prueba a la clase.
3. Luis _____ a Patricio todos los días.
4. Pedro y Teresa _____ una fiesta esta noche.
5. (Tú) les _____ pan a los pájaros.
6. Desde el avión (yo) _____ el mar.

7. ¿Qué programa _____ Uds.?
8. (Yo) no les _____ muchos refrescos a los muchachos.
9. (Nosotros) ya no les _____ nada a ellos.
10. ¿_____ (tú) la ola·estupenda?

D Acaban de hacerlo
Answer according to the model. Use a direct object pronoun in your answer.

¿Terminas el capítulo?
Acabo de terminarlo.

1. ¿Venden Uds. su casa?
2. ¿Arregla papá tu reloj?
3. ¿Miras las noticias?
4. ¿Estudian los alumnos la lección 4?
5. ¿Lees tu cuaderno?
6. ¿Limpia Lisa el apartamento?

E ¿A quiénes?
Form sentences using *dar* and the cues given. Follow the model.

(yo) / la manzana / el profesor
Le doy la manzana al profesor.

1. (ella) / sandalias / la niña
2. ¿Ud. / el paraguas / el muchacho?
3. (nosotros) / la tarea / las profesoras
4. (yo) / las respuestas / mis compañeros de clase
5. (él) / lápices / los estudiantes
6. (ellos) / anteojos de sol / mi hermano
7. (ellas) / leche / el gato
8. (tú) / la sombrilla / mis hermanas

F Voy a hacerlo más tarde
Answer in the negative. Follow the model.

¿Le arreglas la moto a tu papá?
No. Voy a arreglarle la moto más tarde.

1. ¿Le escribes una carta a tu padre?
2. ¿Les das el almuerzo a las niñas?
3. ¿Les lees el periódico a tus hermanas?
4. ¿Les das las notas a los estudiantes?
5. ¿Le arreglas la puerta a tu mamá?
6. ¿Le preguntas cuánto cuesta al vendedor?

Chapter 9 Test   Listening Comprehension Test

Sustantivos
el actor, la actriz
los anteojos
los anteojos de sol
el anuncio comercial
el canal
la clase (de) *(kind)*
los dibujos animados
el mar
la media hora
las noticias
la nube
la ola
la película
la playa
el programa
las sandalias
la sombrilla
el televisor
la toalla

Pronombres de complemento indirecto
le, les

Adjetivos
cómico, -a
(muy) conocido, -a
estupendo, -a
mucho, -a *(very)*
musical
policíaco, -a
romántico, -a

Conjunción
si

Verbos
acabar de + *inf.*
arreglar
continuar
dar
deber
durar
ver

Adverbio
casi

Preposiciones
antes de
dentro de
desde
fuera de
hasta
sobre *(about)*

Expresiones
bueno *(well)*
¡caramba!
¿cuánto dura?
¡cuidado!
dar miedo a
dar una película / un programa
de ciencia ficción
del oeste
de terror
en colores
está nublado
hoy no
¡imagínate!
¡qué bueno!
¿qué importa?

tener { calor
cuidado
frío
hambre
miedo (de)
sed
sueño
suerte

tener (no tener) razón
todo el mundo
ya no
y media *(and a half)*

DOS ANIMALES DE LAS AMÉRICAS

Have you ever heard the expression "ship of the desert"? It describes the camel, the only pack animal that can endure the harsh desert conditions. Another member of the camel family—though one without humps—is one of the best pack animals of the Andes. High on the mountain trails, where travel is difficult or impossible for horses, the sure-footed llama can carry up to 100 pounds for distances up to 20 miles.

The Indians of the Andes use the llama in a variety of ways. It is a topnotch pack animal because of the heavy loads it can carry and because it can survive at high altitudes and live for weeks without water. The Indians use its meat for food, its wool for clothing, and its fat for candles.

Although the llama is native to the Americas, the horse is not. You may be surprised to learn that there were no horses in the Western Hemisphere before the Spaniards came to Mexico in 1519. The Mexican Indians, who had never seen riders on horseback, believed that the Spaniards were strange beasts, half man and half animal.

As time passed, of course, horses became a familiar sight in North America. Mustangs and broncos, descendants of the first Spanish horses, roamed wild in Mexico and what is now the southwest United States. The Indians used horses in battle and in hunting buffalo.

As recently as the early 1900s, horses pulled carriages through our cities and towns. They were our primary means of transportation. Today we use horses mainly for recreation, but they still play an important role in the North American way of life, just as llamas do in South America.

1

Transparency 43
CONTEXTO VISUAL

La granja

If students ask: Other related words you may want to present: *la cabra*, goat; *la lana*, wool; *la cerca*, fence.

CONTEXTO COMUNICATIVO 2

1 SOFÍA   ¿Quieres **caminar** cerca del lago? Es un día muy **hermoso.**

    TOMÁS   Sí, vamos. Me gusta mucho caminar cuando hace buen tiempo.

Variaciones:
- hermoso → **agradable**
- hace buen tiempo → hace sol

caminar   *to walk*
hermoso, -a   *beautiful*

agradable   *pleasant*

2 SARA   La veterinaria viene hoy.

    LUIS   ¿Están enfermos los **animales**?

    SARA   Los caballos, sí.

- la veterinaria → el veterinario
- los caballos → las vacas
- los animales → **los animales domésticos**
  los caballos → nuestro perro viejo

el animal   *animal*

el animal doméstico   *pet*

3 PEDRO   ¿Ves los patos?

    JULIA   No, pero los **oigo.**

    PEDRO   Yo también. ¡Cua, cua!

- los patos → los cerdos
  ¡cua, cua! → ¡oinc, oinc!
- los patos → los caballos
  ¡cua, cua! → ¡jiiii!
- los patos → las ovejas
  los oigo → las oigo
  ¡cua, cua! → ¡meee!

oír (yo oigo, tú oyes)   *to hear*

Palabras Nuevas I   **335**

4 **ANA** ¿Adónde vas, José? ¿No tienes que dar de comer a las gallinas?

JOSÉ Acabo de hacerlo.

ANA ¿Por qué llevas tu mochila entonces?

JOSÉ Le **traigo** unos huevos a mamá.

ANA ¡En tu mochila!

■ mamá → mi abuela

Reteach / Extra Help: Ask students to substitute *mis abuelos* for *mamá* in mini-dialogue 4. Did they remember to change *le* to *les*?

traer (yo traigo, tú traes)
to bring

EN OTRAS PARTES

También se dice *la finca*.

También se dice *el finquero / la finquera* y *el agricultor / la agricultora*.

En muchos países de la America Latina se dice *el chancho*. También se dice *el puerco*.

Práctica A
Answers may vary.

1. ¿Dónde pongo el sol? En el cielo, detrás de la nube.
2. ¿Dónde pongo la nube? En el cielo, al lado (delante) del sol / a la izquierda del pájaro / sobre la lluvia / entre el sol y el pájaro.
3. ¿Dónde pongo la lluvia? En el cielo, debajo de la nube / sobre las flores.
4. ¿Dónde pongo las flores? En la tierra, debajo de la nube.
5. ¿Dónde pongo el lago? En la tierra, a la izquierda (al lado) del camino.
6. ¿Dónde pongo la hierba? En la tierra, a la izquierda (al lado) del camino / debajo del lago.
7. ¿Dónde pongo el camino? En la tierra, a la derecha del lago / a la izquierda del árbol / entre el lago y el árbol / entre el día y la noche.

PRÁCTICA

A **¿En el cielo o en la tierra?** Imagina que tú y un(a) amigo(a) ayudan a preparar el escenario *(stage)* para una obra de teatro. Usa el dibujo para indicar *(tell)* dónde debe estar cada *(each)* cosa—en el cielo o en la tierra. Usa también la lista de preposiciones para indicar la posición de cada cosa en relación con otra cosa *(something else)*. Sigue el modelo.

ESTUDIANTE A *¿Dónde pongo el pájaro?*

ESTUDIANTE B *En el cielo, a la derecha de la nube.*

a la derecha	sobre	entre	detrás de
a la izquierda	debajo de	al lado de	delante de

B ¿Qué oyes en la granja? Pregunta y contesta según el modelo.

ESTUDIANTE A *¿Oyes los patos?*
ESTUDIANTE B *Sí, los oigo. Hacen "cua-cua."*

1.  muuu

2.  jiii

3.  guau, guau

4.  oinc, oinc

5.  quiquiriquí

6.  cloc, cloc

7.  meee

8.  miau

9.  muuu

8. ¿Dónde pongo las estrellas? En el cielo, a la izquierda y a la derecha de la luna.
9. ¿Dónde pongo la luna? En el cielo, entre las estrellas / sobre la nieve.
10. ¿Dónde pongo la nieve? En el cielo, debajo de la luna y las estrellas.
11. ¿Dónde pongo el árbol? En la tierra, a la derecha del camino.
12. ¿Dónde pongo las hojas? En la tierra, debajo (al lado) del árbol.

Práctica B
1. ¿Oyes la vaca? Sí, la oigo. Hace "muu."
2. ¿Oyes el caballo? Sí, lo oigo. Hace "jiii."
3. ¿Oyes los perros? Sí, los oigo. Hacen "guau."
4. ¿Oyes el cerdo? Sí, lo oigo. Hace "oinc, oinc."
5. ¿Oyes el gallo? Sí, lo oigo. Hace "quiquiriquí."
6. ¿Oyes las gallinas? Sí, las oigo. Hacen "cloc, cloc."
7. ¿Oyes la oveja? Sí, la oigo. Hace "meee."
8. ¿Oyes los gatos? Sí, los oigo. Hacen "miau."
9. ¿Oyes el toro? Sí, lo oigo. Hace "muu."

Notes: If students enjoy Ex. B, expand on it by asking them to change 1, 2, 4, 5, 7, and 9 to plural and 3, 6, and 8 to singular.

1. ¿Qué tiene la muchacha? Una botella. ¿Qué bebe el cordero? Leche.
2. ¿Cómo están las vacas? Contentas. ¿Qué comen las vacas? Hierba.
3. ¿Qué hace el gallo? Quiquiriquí. ¿Cuándo? Por la mañana.
4. ¿Qué hacen los pájaros? Cantan. ¿Dónde están? En el árbol.
5. ¿Qué hacen los niños? Nadan. ¿Dónde nadan? En el lago.
6. ¿Qué hacen las niñas? Les dan de comer a los patos. ¿Cómo son los patos? Amarillos.
7. ¿Qué hace el niño? Dibuja un caballo. ¿De qué color es el caballo? Blanco.
8. ¿Adónde va la niña? A la escuela. ¿Qué lleva? Una mochila.
9. ¿Qué trae el granjero? Huevos. ¿Para qué? Para el desayuno.

Notes: Encourage students to look carefully at each of the drawings in Ex. C.

Point out the short answer in the model *(Maíz)*, and tell students to omit verbs in their own answers to the second question in each group.

Reteach / Extra Help: If your class finds Ex. C difficult, ask volunteers to model the first few items.

C En la granja. Pregunta y contesta según los dibujos.

¿Qué hace . . . ?
¿Qué comen . . . ?

ESTUDIANTE A	*¿Qué hace la granjera?*
ESTUDIANTE B	*Les da de comer a las gallinas.*
ESTUDIANTE A	*¿Qué comen las gallinas?*
ESTUDIANTE B	*Maíz.*

1. ¿Qué tiene . . . ?
   ¿Qué bebe . . . ?

2. ¿Cómo están . . . ?
   ¿Qué comen . . . ?

3. ¿Qué hace . . . ?
   ¿Cuándo . . . ?

4. ¿Qué hacen . . . ?
   ¿Dónde . . . ?

5. ¿Qué hacen . . . ?
   ¿Dónde . . . ?

6. ¿Qué hacen . . . ?
   ¿Cómo son . . . ?

7. ¿Qué hace . . . ?
   ¿De qué color . . . ?

8. ¿Adónde va . . . ?
   ¿Qué lleva . . . ?

9. ¿Qué trae . . . ?
   ¿Para qué . . . ?

D Hablemos de ti.

1. ¿Vives en una granja o en una ciudad? ¿Te gustan las granjas o prefieres las ciudades grandes? ¿Por qué?
2. ¿Qué animales viven en una granja?
3. ¿Tienes un jardín? ¿Es grande o pequeño? ¿Hay muchas flores en tu jardín? ¿Hay árboles?
4. ¿Qué tiempo hace hoy? ¿De qué color es el cielo? ¿Hay nubes? ¿Llueve o nieva? ¿Te gusta la lluvia? ¿Por qué? ¿Te gusta la nieve? ¿Por qué?

ACTIVIDAD

Estaciones Work with a partner to make up a poem of four to five lines about your impressions of a season. The lines don't have to rhyme, nor do they have to be complete sentences. For example:

> **EL VERANO**
> Me gusta el verano.
> Árboles grandes
> Con hojas verdes,
> Flores y sol.

When you've finished writing the poem, you may want to read it aloud to the class.

Práctica D
Answers will vary.

Enrichment: Additional questions for Ex. D: *¿Caminas a la escuela? ¿Caminas solo(a) o con un(a) hermano(a) o un(a) amigo(a)? ¿Te gusta caminar cuando llueve? ¿Tienes un animal doméstico en casa? ¿Qué es? ¿Cuál es su nombre? ¿Hay un lago cerca de tu casa? ¿Ves patos allí a veces?*

Practice Sheet 10–1

Workbook Exs. A–B

Canción: La pájara pinta 3

Tape Manual Exs. 1–2 4

Quiz 10–1

Reteach / Review: Before students begin the **Actividad,** elicit the names of the seasons *(el verano, el otoño, el invierno, la primavera).*

APLICACIONES Discretionary

La profesión de veterinario 5

Un estudiante del Colegio Superior de Puerto Rico habla con la doctora* Estela Torres, veterinaria.

PABLO   Dra. Torres, me llamo Pablo Guzmán. Escribo para el periódico del colegio. Quiero hablar con Ud. sobre su profesión.

5

DRA. TORRES   ¡Cómo no!

PABLO   ¿Trabaja Ud. con animales de la granja o con animales domésticos?

DRA. TORRES   Bueno, prefiero los animales de la granja: caballos, vacas, cerdos, ovejas . . .

10

PABLO   ¿Cuáles son sus animales favoritos?

DRA. TORRES   Todos, me gustan todos. Por eso[1] soy veterinaria.

PABLO   ¿Y tiene Ud. un gato o un perro en su casa?

DRA. TORRES   ¿*Un* gato? ¿*Un* perro? ¡Tengo cuatro gatos hermosos y dos buldogs!

15

PABLO   ¿Y qué hace Ud. cuando están enfermos?

DRA. TORRE   Llamo al veterinario, por supuesto. Una buena médica nunca cuida a los miembros de su propia[2] familia.

---

[1]**por eso**   *that's why*   [2]**propio, -a**   *own*

* We use *el doctor / la doctora* as the title when we speak to or about a doctor. The term for the profession of doctor is *el médico / la médica*. For example: *Nuestro médico es el Dr. Sánchez.*

Notes: Make sure students understand these words that have not been glossed: *la profesión*, profession; *los buldogs*, bulldogs; *los miembros*, members.

Preguntas

Contesta según el diálogo.

1. ¿Con quién habla Pablo? ¿Por qué?   2. ¿Cuál es la profesión de la Dra. Torres?   3. ¿Con qué clase de animales prefiere trabajar?
4. ¿Cuáles son sus animales favoritos?   5. ¿Tiene animales domésticos? ¿Cuáles? ¿Cuántos?   6. ¿Qué hace cuando sus animales están enfermos? ¿Por qué?   7. ¿Qué haces tú cuando tus animales están enfermos?

Diálogo
1. Con la Dra. Torres. Porque va a escribir sobre ella para su periódico.
2. Es veterinaria.
3. Con los animales de la granja.
4. Todos.
5. Sí; cuatro gatos y dos buldogs.
6. Llama al veterinario. Porque una buena médica nunca cuida a los miembros de su propia familia.
7. Answers will vary.

Enrichment: Ask students to suggest alternate ways to say the following expressions from the **Diálogo:** line 1: *me llamo (mi nombre es)*, line 6: *¡Cómo no! (¡Por supuesto!)*, line 9: *prefiero (me gustan más)*.

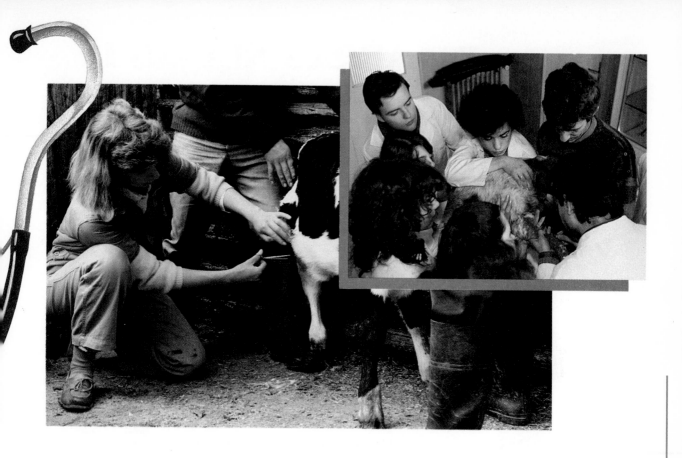

Participación

Work with a partner to make up a dialogue of six to eight lines in which a student who writes for the school newspaper interviews a farmer.

PRONUNCIACIÓN 🎞 6

A In Spanish, the letter *s* usually has the same sound as the *s* in the English word "sand."
Escucha y repite.

sol siete después casas física televisión

B The letter *z* in Spanish is usually pronounced like the *s*.
Escucha y repite.

pez diez tiza plaza almuerzo izquierda

C Escucha y repite.

El museo está en la esquina.
¿Te gustan los zapatos azules?
Hay seis pizarras en esta clase.

Aplicaciones **341**

PALABRAS NUEVAS II

CONTEXTO
VISUAL

If students ask: Other related words you may want to present: *la cola,* tail; *la trompa,* trunk; *el cuello,* neck; *las manchas,* spots; *las orejas,* ears.

Enrichment: You may want to point out the cognates in the **Contexto visual.** Elicit or note the spelling differences between the English and Spanish words. For example, *elefante: ph → f; jirafa: g → j, ff → f; hipopótamo: pp → p; cebra: z → c.*

Una visita al zoológico

el leopardo · la cebra · el elefante · la jirafa · la guardiana (de zoológico) · el zoológico · el hipopótamo

CONTEXTO
COMUNICATIVO

 8

1 ALFREDO	Una **visita** al zoológico es siempre muy agradable.	**la visita** *visit*
LAURA	¿Qué animales te gustan más?	
ALFREDO	**Generalmente,** voy para ver los tigres y los leones. ¡Son **magníficos**!	**generalmente** *generally, usually* **magnífico, -a** *magnificent*
LAURA	Yo prefiero los monos. Son muy listos.	

Variaciones:

■ agradable → divertida

■ los tigres y los leones → las jirafas y las cebras
magníficos → magníficas

■ listos → inteligentes

el oso

el rinoceronte

la jaula

el tigre

la serpiente

la iguana

el mono

el guardián
(de zoológico)

el león
pl. los leones

la llama

el caimán
pl. los caimanes

2 ELENA   ¿Puedes **visitar** el zoológico conmigo hoy?

DIEGO   **¡Claro!** Y tu hermano, ¿viene con nosotros?

ELENA   **Creo que no.** Tiene que trabajar.

■ claro → por supuesto
■ hermano → primo

visitar   *to visit*
claro (que sí) = por supuesto
creo que no   *I don't think so*
creer   *to think, to believe*

3 MAMÁ   ¿Te dan miedo los **ruidos que** hacen los leones?

BENJAMÍN   **Claro que no,** mamá. Todos están en sus jaulas.

■ te dan miedo → tienes miedo de
■ los leones → esos animales

el ruido   *noise*
que   *that; who*
claro que no   *of course not*

Palabras Nuevas II   **343**

4	JORGE	Luz, ¿**cómo se llaman esos** animales?	¿**cómo se llama(n)?** *what is (are) the name(s) of?*
	LUZ	**Este** animal pequeño es una iguana.	**esos, -as** *those*
	JORGE	¿Y **ese** animal grande allí? ¿Es un caimán?	**este, -a** *this*
	LUZ	No sé. Pero **creo que sí.**	**ese, -a** *that*

- esos → **estos**
  ese → este
  allí → aquí
- creo que sí → creo que no

creo que sí *I think so*

estos, -as *these*

Notes: Make sure students understand the difference between *este* (this) and *ese* (that) in mini-dialogue 4. Demonstrative adjectives are explained on p. 353.

5	NORMA	¿Qué hace un guardián de zoológico?
	PEPE	**Varias** cosas. Es **la persona** que les da de comer a los animales, los cuida y limpia sus jaulas.
	NORMA	¡Uf! ¡Qué aburrido!
	PEPE	¡Al contrario, es un **trabajo** muy interesante!

varios, -as *several*

la persona *person*

el trabajo *job; work*

- un guardián → una guardiana
- varias → muchas

6	TÍA MÓNICA	¿Por qué no **dices la verdad**, Sergio?
	SERGIO	¡Siempre digo la verdad!
	TÍA MÓNICA	¿Siempre?
	SERGIO	Bueno, . . . a veces.

decir (yo digo, tú dices) *to say, to tell*

la verdad *truth*

- no → nunca
- dices la verdad → **dices que sí**
  digo la verdad → digo que sí
- a veces → casi siempre

decir que sí / no *to say yes / no*

EN OTRAS PARTES

También se dice *la culebra.*

En México se dice *el chango.*
También se dice *el mico.*

También se dice *el lagarto.*

PRÁCTICA

A **¿Cómo son?** Imagina que estás en el zoológico con un(a) amigo(a) y que Uds. hablan de los animales. Pregunta y contesta según el modelo. Usa adjetivos apropiados *(appropriate)* de la lista.

| ESTUDIANTE A | *Los hipopótamos son grandes, ¿no?* |
| ESTUDIANTE B | *Yo creo que son muy gordos.* |

aburrido	estupendo	hermoso	lento	pequeño
alto	feo	inteligente	limpio	rápido
bonito	gordo	interesante	listo	sucio
enorme	grande	largo	magnífico	tonto

Práctica A
Adjectives will vary.
1. Las llamas…
2. Los elefantes…
3. Los osos…
4. Las jirafas…
5. Las cebras…
6. Las serpientes…
7. Los caimanes…
8. Los monos…
9. Los leopardos…
10. Los rinocerontes…
11. Los tigres…
12. Los leones…

1.
2.
3.
4.
5.
6.
7.
8.
9.
10.
11.
12.

B **Una visita al zoológico.** Susana visita el zoológico de Chapultepec con su hermano mayor. Ella tiene muchas preguntas. Completa el diálogo con la palabra o expresión correcta.

| claro que no | creo que sí | iguana | persona | se llama |
| creo | guardián | jaula | ruido | verdad |

SUSANA ¿Cómo _____ ese animal verde, Francisco?

FRANCISCO Es una _____.

SUSANA ¡Ay! ¿Oyes el _____ que hacen los leones?

FRANCISCO Sí. _____ que tienen hambre. ¿Te dan miedo?

5 SUSANA ¡_____!

FRANCISCO ¿Por qué no dices la _____?

SUSANA Bueno, tengo un poco de miedo. Mira, Francisco, ¿quién es esa _____ que entra en la _____ de los leones?

FRANCISCO Es el _____, por supuesto.

10 SUSANA ¿Les va a dar de comer ahora?

FRANCISCO _____.

Práctica B
se llama
iguana
ruido
Creo
Claro que no
verdad
persona / jaula
guardián
Creo que sí

Práctica C
Answers will vary.

Enrichment: Additional
questions for Ex. C: ¿Te dan
miedo los animales en el
zoológico? ¿Cuáles te dan
mucho miedo? ¿Por qué?

C Hablemos de ti.

1. ¿Hay un buen zoológico en tu ciudad o cerca de ella? ¿Cómo es? ¿Te gusta visitarlo? ¿Por qué?
2. ¿Qué animales del zoológico son tus favoritos? ¿Por qué?
3. Cuando vas al parque, ¿a veces les das de comer a los patos? ¿Qué les das? ¿Les das de comer a los animales cuando visitas el zoológico? ¿Por que?
4. ¿Qué animales comen carne? ¿Cuáles comen hojas y hierba? ¿Qué comen los monos? ¿Y las gallinas?

Practice Sheet 10–2   Workbook Exs. C–D   9 Tape Manual Exs. 3–4   Quiz 10-2

ESTUDIO DE PALABRAS

Many English words have come from Spanish. This is partly because Spanish-speaking people had settled in the western and southwestern United States long before English-speaking settlers arrived. These newcomers adopted many Spanish words that were already in use. *Patio, plaza, fiesta, adobe,* and *burro* are some of those. Naturally, many of our loanwords from Spanish are associated with the West. Here are some of them.

buckaroo, from *vaquero,* cowboy
canyon, from *cañón,* a deep valley with steep slopes
corral, from *corral,* a yard or pen for animals
lariat, from *la reata,* a rope for leading animals
lasso, from *lazo,* a loop or noose
mesa, from *mesa,* a flat-topped hill, like a table
palomino, from *paloma* (''dove''), a dove-colored, light gray horse
savvy, from the question *¿sabes?* (''you know''), common sense or know-how
stampede, from *estampida,* the hurrying away of a frightened herd of animals

(arriba) Un mexicano;
(derecha) Dos chilenos

EXPLICACIONES I

Los verbos *oír* y *traer*

Here are all of the present-tense forms of *oír* ("to hear").

INFINITIVO   **oír**

	SINGULAR		PLURAL
1	(yo) **oigo**	(nosotros) (nosotras) } **oímos**	
2	(tú) **oyes**	(vosotros) (vosotras) } **oís**	
3	Ud. (él) (ella) } **oye**	Uds. (ellos) (ellas) } **oyen**	

Notice that the *yo* form ends in *-go*. The *nosotros* and *vosotros* forms have an accent on the *i*: *oímos, oís*. In all other forms, the *i* changes to *y*.

Here are all of the present-tense forms of *traer* ("to bring").

INFINITIVO   **traer**

	SINGULAR		PLURAL
1	(yo) **traigo**	(nosotros) (nosotras) } **traemos**	
2	(tú) **traes**	(vosotros) (vosotras) } **traéis**	
3	Ud. (él) (ella) } **trae**	Uds. (ellos) (ellas) } **traen**	

Like several other verbs, *traer* has only one irregular present-tense form: *traigo*. All of the other forms are like those of regular *-er* verbs.

◆ **OBJECTIVES:**
TO TELL WHAT YOU HEAR
TO PLAN A PICNIC
TO GO OVER A CHECKLIST

Notes: Mini-dialogue 3 on p. 335 illustrates the *yo* form of *oír;* 4 on p. 336 provides an example of the *yo* form of *traer.*
Before students use the forms of *oír* and *traer*, make sure they can pronounce them correctly.

Enrichment: Reinforce the present-tense forms of *oír* and *traer* by asking these questions. Change verb forms and point to yourself, a girl, two boys, and so on according to the form you are eliciting: *¿Qué oyes en la calle? ¿Qué oyes en el parque? ¿Qué oyes en la biblioteca? ¿Qué traes a la escuela? ¿Qué traes a una fiesta?* (Answers will vary.)

Práctica A

1. Oigo los patos. ¿Los oyes tú? Sí, los oigo, pero no los veo.
2. ...los monos. ¿Los ...? ...los... ...los...
3. ...el oso... ¿Lo ...? ...lo... ...lo...
4. ...el elefante. ¿Lo ...? ...lo... ...lo...
5. ...el tigre. ¿Lo ...? ...lo... ...lo...
6. ...los cerdos. ¿Los ...? ...los... ...los...
7. ...la oveja. ¿La ...? ...la... ...la...
8. ...los leopardos. ¿Los ...? ...los... ...los...

Notes: Before students begin Ex. B, you may want to point out that the subject for 8 *(todos)* refers to "all of us."

Práctica B

1. Oigo el gallo. Hace "Quiquiriquí."
2. Marta y Jorge oyen el caballo. Hace "Jiii."
3. Elena y yo oímos el cerdo. Hace "oinc, oinc."
4. María oye el pato. Hace "Cua, cua."
5. Pedro y tú oyen la vaca. Hace "Muuu."
6. Oyes la gallina. Hace "Cloc, cloc."
7. Oímos la lluvia. Hace "¡Plin, plin!"
8. Todos oímos al granjero. Hace "Zzzz."

Reteach / Extra Help: After students do Ex. B in class, assign the sentences as written homework. You may want to vary the practice by asking students to substitute subject pronouns for the nouns in 2–5.

PRÁCTICA

A En el zoológico. Imagina que vas al zoológico con un(a) amigo(a). A veces Uds. oyen unos animales, pero no los ven. Pregunta y contesta según el modelo.

> ESTUDIANTE A *Oigo el león. ¿Lo oyes tú?*
> ESTUDIANTE B *Sí, lo oigo, pero no lo veo.*

1. los patos	3. el oso	5. el tigre	7. la oveja
2. los monos	4. el elefante	6. los cerdos	8. los leopardos

B Los ruidos de la granja. Imagina que tú y unos estudiantes de la ciudad están en una granja. Durante la noche, es muy difícil dormir *(to sleep)* porque Uds. oyen muchos ruidos. ¿Qué oyen Uds.? Sigue el modelo.

Rafael

Rafael oye la oveja. Hace "¡Meee!"

1. (yo)

2. Marta y Jorge

3. Elena y yo

4. María

5. Pedro y tú

6. (tú)

7. (nosotros)

8. todos

C ¿Qué traen? Imagina que tu clase va a tener un picnic. Tú y un(a) compañero(a) repasan una lista de lo que *(what)* traen las personas. Sigue el modelo.

> ¿Jorge? / la ensalada
> ESTUDIANTE A *¿Qué trae Jorge?*
> ESTUDIANTE B *Creo que trae la ensalada.*

1. ¿Jaime? / los refrescos
2. ¿Yolanda y Roberto? / el chile con carne
3. ¿Anita? / el pan y el queso
4. ¿Ricardo y tú? / los platos y los vasos
5. ¿Emilia y Ramón? / la mantequilla y la mermelada
6. ¿(tú)? / las frutas
7. ¿la profesora? / los manteles y las servilletas

Práctica C
1. ¿Qué trae Jaime? Creo que trae los refrescos.
2. ¿Qué traen Yolanda y Roberto? Creo que traen el chile con carne.
3. ¿...trae Anita? ...trae el pan y el queso.
4. ¿...traen Ricardo y tú? ...traemos los platos y los vasos.
5. ¿...traen Emilia y Ramón? ...traen la mantequilla y la mermelada.
6. ¿...traes? ...traigo las frutas.
7. ¿...trae la profesora? ...trae los manteles y las servilletas.

Practice Sheet 10–3   Workbook Exs. E–F   10 Tape Manual Exs. 5–6   Activity Master 10–1   Quiz 10–3

D Hablemos de ti.
1. ¿Traes tu almuerzo a la escuela? ¿Qué traes?
2. ¿Tienes una mochila? ¿Qué traes a la escuela en ella?
3. ¿Oyes muchos ruidos desde la ventana de tu dormitorio? ¿Qué oyes generalmente?

Práctica D
Answers will vary.

ACTIVIDAD

¿Qué traes a la fiesta? Pretend that your Spanish class is going to have a party during a vacation. Everyone has to bring something. What will each person bring? Choose someone to write the list on the chalkboard. He or she begins by saying *Traigo* ____, writes it on the board, and then asks, *¿Qué traes, Inés?* Each person adds something and asks another student until everyone has signed up to bring something. Can your class make up a list that has everyone bringing something different?

APLICACIONES Discretionary

Pecosa y yo 11

Graciela Sandoval, una muchacha de 16 años, trabaja en el zoológico durante los fines de semana. Aquí habla de su trabajo en la casa de las serpientes. Graciela dice: "Las serpientes son magníficas. La boa, por ejemplo, es una serpiente muy grande y muy larga. Generalmente las
5 boas viven en la América del Sur, especialmente en el Brasil y las Guayanas. Comen pequeños animales, pero pueden vivir varios meses sin comida. Las boas no son venenosas,[1] pero debes tener cuidado porque pueden morder."[2]

Yo tengo una boa que tiene dos años. Vive conmigo en Brooklyn.
10 Se llama Pecosa, que quiere decir "freckled," porque es marrón y roja. Pecosa no es muy inteligente, pero es muy hermosa y muy limpia. Vive en una jaula grande en mi dormitorio y nunca hace ruido. Le doy de comer cada[3] dos semanas. A veces cuando hace buen tiempo la llevo al parque. Muchas personas tienen miedo de Pecosa. No sé por qué. Todo
15 el mundo me pregunta si es difícil cuidarla. Yo les digo que sólo tengo que darle de comer y darle mucho cariño.[4] En mi barrio Pecosa es muy conocida y muy popular."

---

[1]**venenoso, -a** *poisonous*   [2]**morder** *to bite*   [3]**cada** *every*   [4]**cariño** *affection*

Antes de leer   1. Una serpiente muy grande y muy larga 2. Generalmente en la América del Sur, especialmente en el Brasil y las Guayanas 3. Es marrón y roja, hermosa y muy limpia.

Preguntas
Contesta según la lectura.

1. ¿Dónde trabaja Graciela? ¿Cuándo trabaja allí?
2. ¿Qué dice Graciela de las serpientes?
3. ¿De dónde son las boas?
4. ¿Qué comen las boas? ¿Comen a menudo?
5. ¿Por qué tienes que tener cuidado con las boas?
6. ¿Dónde vive Pecosa?
7. ¿Qué tiene que hacer Graciela para cuidar a Pecosa?
8. ¿De qué color es Pecosa?
9. ¿Te dan miedo las serpientes? ¿Por qué?

Notes: These words have not been glossed: *boa*, boa constrictor; *por ejemplo*, for example; *especialmente*, especially.
Make sure students understand that Brooklyn is a borough of New York City.

EXPLICACIONES II

El verbo *decir*

The verb *decir* means "to say" or "to tell." Here are all of its forms in the present tense.

INFINITIVO **decir**

SINGULAR		PLURAL	
1	(yo) **digo**	(nosotros) (nosotras) } **decimos**	
2	(tú) **dices**	(vosotros) (vosotras) } **decís**	
3	Ud. (él) } **dice** (ella)	Uds. (ellos) } **dicen** (ellas)	

Notice that the *yo* form ends in *-go* and that the *e* changes to *i* in all except the *nosotros* and *vosotros* forms.

When another verb comes after *decir* or *creer*, we must use *que*. In English, after verbs like "say" and "think" we can leave out the word "that." But in Spanish we can't. For example:

Dicen que ella no viene.
Él **cree que** hay muchas gallinas en la granja.

*They **say (that)** she isn't coming.*
*He **thinks (that)** there are a lot of hens on the farm.*

◆ **OBJECTIVES:**
TO REPORT WHAT PEOPLE SAY ABOUT SOMETHING

Notes: Refer to mini-dialogue 6 on p. 344 for the *yo* and *tú* forms of *decir*. Can students name other verbs whose *yo* forms end in *-go*? (*hacer, oír, poner, salir, tener, traer, venir.*)

Reteach / Extra Help: Before students begin the **Práctica** on p. 352, ask them to work in pairs or do a chain drill to practice all the forms of *decir*. For example: *¿Qué digo cuando entro en la clase por la mañana? ¿Qué dices cuando sales de una fiesta? ¿Qué dice Raquel cuando sale mal en un examen? ¿Qué decimos cuando tenemos hambre? ¿Qué dicen Tomás y Elena cuando no les doy tarea?* (Answers will vary.)

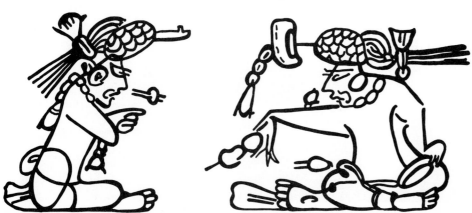

Práctica A

1. ¿Qué dice María? Dice que no.
2. ¿Qué dicen Uds.? Decimos que sí.
3. ¿...dicen Ana y Susana? Dicen...
4. ¿...decimos nosotros? Dicen (*or:* Decimos)...
5. ¿...dice Julia? Dice...
6. ¿...dicen Leonor y tú? Decimos...
7. ¿...dicen los buenos estudiantes? Dicen...
8. Digo que sí / no.

Práctica B

1. ¿Qué dice Juan? Dice que es muy inteligente.
2. ¿...dicen Marta y Julia? Dicen...
3. ¿...dices? Digo...
4. ¿...dice Ana? Dice...
5. ¿...dice Leonor? Dice...
6. ¿...dice Antonio? Dice...no es...
7. ¿...dicen Uds.? Decimos... no es...
8. ¿...dice Ud.? Digo...no es...

PRÁCTICA

A ¿Crees que sí? El profesor de inglés dice que el inglés es muy fácil. ¿Qué dicen sus estudiantes? Pregunta y contesta según el modelo.

> ¿Felipe? / sí
>
> **ESTUDIANTE A** *¿Qué dice Felipe?*
> **ESTUDIANTE B** *Dice que sí.*

1. ¿María? / no
2. ¿Uds.? / sí
3. ¿Ana y Susana? / sí
4. ¿nosotros? / no
5. ¿Julia? / sí
6. ¿Leonor y tú? / no
7. los buenos estudiantes / sí
8. Y tú, ¿qué dices?

B ¿Cómo es el nuevo profesor? Imagina que hay un nuevo profesor de música. Todos los alumnos tienen una opinión. ¿Qué dicen de él? Sigue el modelo.

> ¿Miguel? / no . . . muy alto
>
> **ESTUDIANTE A** *¿Qué dice Miguel?*
> **ESTUDIANTE B** *Dice que no es muy alto.*

1. ¿Juan? / muy inteligente
2. ¿Marta y Julia? / bilingüe
3. ¿(tú)? / muy joven
4. ¿Ana? / aburrido
5. ¿Leonor? / bastante interesante
6. ¿Antonio? / no . . . muy simpático
7. ¿Uds.? / no . . . muy agradable
8. ¿Ud.? / no . . . tonto

En Guadalajara, México

Practice Sheet 10–4 **12 Tape Manual Ex. 7**

Adjetivos demostrativos

We use demonstrative adjectives to point out people and things.

Este elefante es grande. Ese elefante es pequeño.

◆ **OBJECTIVES:**
TO POINT THINGS OUT
TO CLARIFY
TO FIND OUT PRICES IN A STORE

Notes: Point out the use of demonstrative adjectives in mini-dialogue 4 on p. 344.

Enrichment: Expand on the presentation by eliciting additional examples using each of the demonstrative adjectives. Write *este / ese, esta / esa, estos / esos, estas / esas* on the board. Then ask students to write an appropriate noun in each of the four columns.
   Students may work in pairs or small groups to ask and answer questions about classroom objects and items of clothing, using demonstrative adjectives.

Demonstrative adjectives come before the noun and agree with it in number and gender.

SINGULAR		PLURAL	
m. **este** granjero f. **esta** granjera } *this farmer*		m. **estos** granjeros f. **estas** granjeras } *these farmers*	
m. **ese** granjero f. **esa** granjera } *that farmer*		m. **esos** granjeros f. **esas** granjeras } *those farmers*	

We use forms of *este* to refer to people or things that are *near the speaker*. We use forms of *ese* to refer to people or things that are *near the person being spoken to*.* We also, of course, use *este / esta* when we are not actually pointing something out: *este año, esta noche,* for example.

---

* There is a third demonstrative adjective—*aquel, aquella, aquellos, aquellas*—that refers to things that are far away from *both* the speaker *and* the person being spoken to. For now, we will concentrate on the words presented in the chart.

PRÁCTICA

Práctica A

1. ¿Cuánto cuestan estos frijoles?
   Trescientos pesos el kilo.
2. ¿...estas zanahorias?
   Doscientos pesos el kilo.
3. ¿...este pavo?
   Seiscientos pesos el kilo.
4. ¿...esta (botella de) agua mineral?
   Cincuenta pesos la botella.
5. ¿...estos limones?
   Setenta y cinco pesos el kilo.
6. ¿...estos plátanos?
   Ciento veinte pesos el kilo.
7. ¿...estas manzanas?
   Trescientos pesos el kilo.
8. ¿...estos churros?
   Ciento ochenta pesos la docena.
9. ¿...este pollo?
   Cuatrocientos pesos el kilo.

Práctica B

1. ¿Cuánto cuestan esos frijoles?
   Trescientos pesos el kilo.
2. ¿...esas zanahorias?
   Doscientos pesos el kilo.
3. ¿...ese pavo?
   Seiscientos pesos el kilo.
4. ¿...esa (botella de) agua mineral?
   Cincuenta pesos la botella.
5. ¿...esos limones?
   Setenta y cinco pesos el kilo.
6. ¿...esos plátanos?
   Ciento veinte pesos el kilo.
7. ¿...esas manzanas?
   Trescientos pesos el kilo.
8. ¿...esos churros?
   Ciento ochenta pesos la docena.
9. ¿...ese pollo?
   Cuatrocientos pesos el kilo.

A En el supermercado. Imagina que estás de compras en el supermercado del barrio y que le preguntas al vendedor cuánto cuestan las cosas. Pregunta y contesta según el modelo.

ESTUDIANTE A *¿Cuánto cuestan estas naranjas?*
ESTUDIANTE B *Doscientos cincuenta pesos el kilo.*

B Todavía en el supermercado. Imagina que un(a) amigo(a) entra en el supermercado y le pregunta al vendedor cuánto cuestan las cosas. Usa los dibujos de la Práctica A para preguntar y contestar. Sigue el modelo.

ESTUDIANTE A *¿Cuánto cuestan esas naranjas?*
ESTUDIANTE B *Doscientos cincuenta pesos el kilo.*

C   En el almacén.

Imagina que estás en un almacén y que quieres ver varias cosas. Pregunta y contesta según el modelo.

> sombrilla: 800 pesetas

> ESTUDIANTE A   *Quiero ver esa sombrilla, por favor.*
> ESTUDIANTE B   *¿Esta sombrilla?*
> ESTUDIANTE A   *Sí. ¿Cuánto cuesta?*
> ESTUDIANTE B   *Ochocientas pesetas.*

1. toallas: 500 pesetas
2. anteojos de sol: 600 pesetas
3. sombrero: 800 pesetas
4. camiseta: 320 pesetas
5. sandalias: 750 pesetas
6. calcetines: 100 pesetas
7. traje de baño: 940 pesetas
8. chaqueta: 870 pesetas
9. pantalones: 460 pesetas
10. bufanda: 280 pesetas
11. blusas: 650 pesetas
12. vestido: 990 pesetas

D   Hablemos de ti.

1. ¿Qué vas a hacer esta noche? ¿Qué vas a hacer este fin de semana? ¿Qué haces generalmente durante los fines de semana?
3. ¿Te gusta este libro de español? ¿Por qué?
3. ¿Crees que aprendes mucho este año? ¿Qué aprendes en tu clase de historia? ¿En tu clase de español?

ACTIVIDAD

¿Tienes suerte?   Work in pairs or groups of three. Each group will write unusual fortune cookie messages. Every message will end with a question. Working together, think up six fortunes, and write each one on a separate slip of paper. The fortunes should begin with *Decimos que.* Here are some examples:

> Decimos que mañana vas a traer un pato a la escuela. ¿Para quién es?
> Decimos que hay un caimán en tu pupitre. ¿Qué vas a hacer?

When you have finished writing the fortunes, fold them and put them into a bag. Then exchange bags with another group. Take turns drawing fortunes from the bag. Read them aloud, changing *decimos* to *dicen* and changing the statement and question to the *yo* form. For example:

> Dicen que mañana *voy* a traer un pato a la escuela. ¿Para quién es?
> Dicen que hay un caimán en *mi* pupitre. ¿Qué *voy* a hacer?

After you have read each fortune, answer the question.

Práctica C

1. Quiero ver esas toallas, por favor. ¿Estas toallas? Sí. ¿Cuánto cuestan? Quinientas pesetas.
2. Quiero ver esos anteojos de sol. ¿Estos anteojos de sol? Sí. ¿Cuánto cuestan? Seiscientas pesetas.
3. Quiero ver ese sombrero. ¿Este sombrero? Sí. ¿Cuánto cuesta? Ochocientas pesetas.
4. Quiero ver esa camiseta. ¿Esta camiseta? Sí. ¿Cuánto cuesta? Trescientas veinte pesetas.
5. ...esas sandalias. ¿Estas sandalias? Sí. ¿Cuánto cuestan? Setecientas cincuenta pesetas.
6. ...esos calcetines. ¿Estos calcetines? Sí. ¿Cuánto cuestan? Cien pesetas.
7. ...ese traje de baño. ¿Este traje de baño? Sí. ¿Cuánto cuesta? Novecientas cuarenta pesetas.
8. ...esa chaqueta. ¿Esta chaqueta? Sí. ¿Cuánto cuesta? Ochocientas setenta pesetas.
9. ...esos pantalones. ¿Estos pantalones? Sí. ¿Cuánto cuestan? Cuatrocientas sesenta pesetas.
10. ...esa bufanda. ¿Esta bufanda? Sí. ¿Cuánto cuesta? Doscientas ochenta pesetas.
11. ...esas blusas. ¿Estas blusas? Sí. ¿Cuánto cuestan? Seiscientas cincuenta pesetas.
12. ...ese vestido. ¿Este vestido? Sí. ¿Cuánto cuesta? Novecientas noventa pesetas.

Práctica D
Answers will vary.

APLICACIONES Discretionary

Notes: Answers to the **Repaso** and **Tema** appear in the pre-chapter teacher pages.

REPASO

Notes: Review of:

1. *traer*
   personal *a*
   possessive adjectives
2. *ver*
   oír
3. *¡qué* + adjective + *ser!*
   demonstrative adjectives
4. *decir*
   estar + adjective
   tener miedo de
5. *... que sí / no*
   me gusta(n) más
   demonstrative adjectives

Look carefully at the model sentences. Then put the English cues into Spanish to form new sentences based on the models.

1. *El granjero trae a su hijo al hospital.*
   (I'm bringing my brother to the bakery.)
   (We're bringing our friends to the game.)
   (They're bringing their students to the library.)

2. *Uds. ven los trenes. Oyen los aviones.*
   (He sees the snow. He hears the bears.)
   (We see the sun. We hear the rain.)
   (I see the hens. I hear the noise.)

3. *¡Qué guapo es este muchacho! ¡Y esa muchacha! ¡Qué bonita es!*
   (How long this road is! And that farm! How enormous it is!)
   (How fast these horses are! But those cows! How slow they are!)
   (How magnificent these trees are! And those flowers! How beautiful they are!)

4. *¿Qué dice Ud.? ¿Está Ud. cansado? ¿Tiene miedo de los rinocerontes?*
   (What do you (pl.) say? Are you worried? Are you afraid of the bulls?)
   (What do they (m.) say? Are they sick? Are they afraid of the job?)
   (What do we say? Are we tired? Are we afraid of the test?)

5. *¡Claro que no! Pero me gustan más estas cebras.*
   (I don't think so. But I like those lambs more.)
   (Of course! But I like these sheep too.)
   (I think so. But I like that monkey more.)

(arriba) Un tucán en Guatemala; (derecha) Un zoológico en Buenos Aires

Put the English captions into Spanish.

1. Carlos is bringing his cousin Rosa to the zoo.

2. "Do you see the elephant? Do you hear the lion?"

3. "How beautiful this tiger is! And that giraffe! How tall it is!"

4. "What do you say? Are you bored? Are you afraid of the animals?"

5. "Of course not! But I like these birds more."

REDACCIÓN

Now you are ready to write your own dialogue or paragraph. Choose one of the following topics.

1. Expand the story in the *Tema* by writing four to six new sentences. Tell what day of the week it is. How does Rosa feel? Is she happy? Sad? Is she thirsty? Hungry? What does Carlos buy her to eat or drink? Is Rosa happy then?

2. Write a paragraph of four to six sentences about a farm. Is it small or large? Are there animals? Many or few? What kinds? What are they like? Who takes care of them? What does he or she do to take care of them?

3. Make up a dialogue of four to six lines between two people at the zoo. What do they see and hear? Which animals does each one like? Why?

COMPRUEBA TU PROGRESO   CAPÍTULO 10   Discretionary

Notes: Answers to the **Comprueba** appear in the pre-chapter teacher pages.

A   ¿Verdad?
Rewrite each sentence, correcting the false information.

1. El toro da leche.
2. En el verano hay mucha nieve.
3. La gallina hace "meee."
4. Por la noche vemos el sol en el cielo.
5. Generalmente, la hierba es roja.
6. Cuando mi gato está enfermo llamo al granjero.
7. Los peces caminan.
8. Los leones comen verduras.

B   Los ruidos de la granja
Answer each question according to the model.

¿Qué oye Ud.? (una gallina)
Oigo una gallina.

1. ¿Qué oigo? (un caballo)
2. ¿Qué oyen Marcos y Teresa? (una vaca)
3. ¿Qué oímos? (un pato)
4. ¿Qué oye Elena? (un cerdo)
5. ¿Qué oyes? (un cordero)
6. ¿Qué oyen Uds.? (un gallo)
7. ¿Qué oyen los niños? (una oveja)
8. ¿Qué oye el veterinario? (un perro)

C   ¿Qué traes?
Form sentences using the verbs *traer* and *ver*.

Pilar / la mochila
Pilar trae la mochila.
Pilar ve la mochila.

1. Pablo / los churros
2. (yo) / el jugo de naranja
3. (nosotras) / la sombrilla
4. (tú) / los frijoles
5. Uds. / las manzanas y las naranjas
6. Daniel y Jorge / los cuchillos y los tenedores
7. Pilar / las flores
8. (yo) / la carne

D   ¿Quién dice . . . ?
Complete each question with the appropriate form of *decir*.

1. ¿Siempre _____ Ud. la verdad?
2. ¿_____ tú que oyes un ruido?
3. Mamá y papá _____ que no.
4. (Nosotros) _____ que vamos a traer los caballos.
5. ¿_____ Uds. que sí?
6. (Yo) _____ que la película es magnífica.

E   ¿Cuál prefieres?
Complete each question according to the art. Follow the model.

¿Prefieres _____ sandwich o _____ hamburguesa?
¿Prefieres este sandwich o esa hamburguesa?

1. ¿Prefieres _____ naranjas o _____ manzana?
2. ¿Prefieres _____ helado o _____ plátanos?
3. ¿Prefieres _____ maíz o _____ zanahorias?
4. ¿Prefieres _____ jamón o _____ huevos?
5. ¿Prefieres _____ tomates o _____ lechuga?
6. ¿Prefieres _____ pan o _____ papas?

VOCABULARIO DEL CAPÍTULO 10

Sustantivos

el animal
el animal doméstico
el árbol
el caballo
el caimán, *pl.* los caimanes
el camino
la cebra
el cerdo
el cielo
el cordero
el elefante
la estrella
la flor
la gallina
el gallo
la granja
el granjero, la granjera
el guardián, la guardiana
(de zoológico)
la hierba
el hipopótamo
la hoja
la iguana
la jaula
la jirafa
el lago
el león, *pl.* los leones
el leopardo
la luna
la llama

la lluvia
la mochila
el mono
la nieve
el oso
la oveja
el pato
la persona
el rinoceronte
el ruido
la serpiente
el sol
la tierra
el tigre
el toro
el trabajo
la vaca
la verdad
el veterinario, la veterinaria
la visita
el zoológico

Pronombre relativo

que

Adjetivos

agradable
hermoso, -a
magnífico, -a
varios, -as

Adjetivos demostrativos

ese, -a, -os, -as
este, -a, -os, -as

Verbos

caminar
creer
decir
oír
traer
visitar

Adverbio

generalmente

Expresiones

claro (que sí / no)
cómo se llama(n)
creo que sí / no
decir que sí / no

PASATIEMPOS POPULARES

Imagine that you are visiting friends in South America. School is over, and you and your friends want to have some fun. What will you do for entertainment? You'll find that young people in South America do many of the same things for entertainment that you do. They might take you to a party or a movie, or you might go bicycle riding or to a soccer game. But whatever you do there, you will probably not do it alone; teenagers in South America generally spend a lot of time in group activities.

The most popular sport throughout the Spanish-speaking world is *fútbol*. You can usually find a *fútbol* game being played at any hour of the day wherever there is room in a park or courtyard or on the grassy slope of a steep hill.

You may not be familiar with a variation of *fútbol*, called *fulbito* (minisoccer), which is often played in the street by two teams of five players each. Whenever a car comes, the game stops, and the players frantically move the goals out of the way. On the beach a vigorous game of *fulbito* is usually followed by a refreshing swim.

One sport you might never have heard of is *esquí sobre arena*—sand skiing! This is popular along the coast of Peru, where the rippling dunes of the desert and beaches offer a warm alternative to skiing in the mountains. In mountainous regions, school or city mountain-climbing clubs are also popular, as is snow skiing.

South American teenagers go out on dates, too. But occasionally an older or younger brother or sister or another relative comes along. During the evening a few friends might join them at the town's central plaza, and before you know it, a spontaneous party is underway. In Spanish-speaking countries free time is time for being with friends and socializing.

PALABRAS NUEVAS I

Transparency 46
CONTEXTO VISUAL

Una fiesta fabulosa

If students ask: Other related words you may want to present: *el regalo*, gift; *los audífonos*, earphones; *la silla de ruedas*, wheelchair.

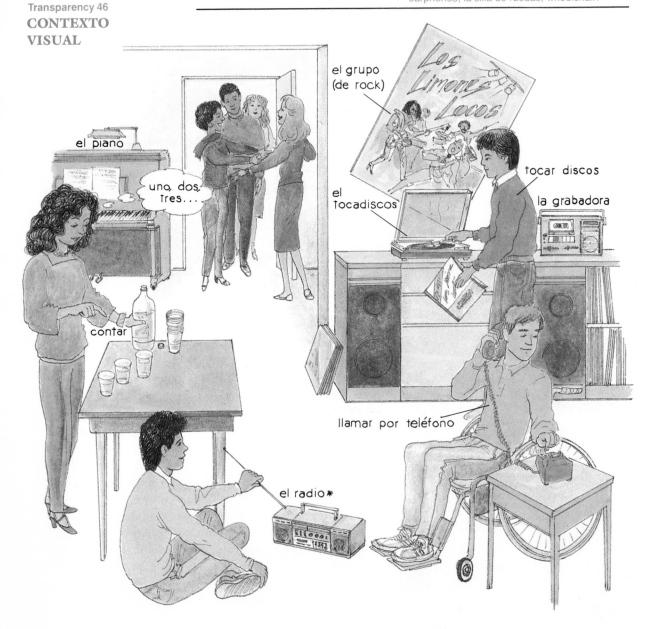

el grupo (de rock)

el piano

uno, dos, tres...

contar

tocar discos

el tocadiscos

la grabadora

llamar por teléfono

el radio*

* In most Spanish-speaking countries a distinction is made between *el radio*, meaning radio set, and *la radio*, meaning the broadcast you listen to.

CONTEXTO COMUNICATIVO   2

1 ÁNGEL   La semana **pasada** la mamá de Pedro le **dio** una
              fiesta de cumpleaños **fabulosa.**

   LOLA   ¿Y qué le **diste** tú para su cumpleaños?

   ÁNGEL   Le **di** unos discos de rock.

Variaciones:

- la semana pasada → el mes pasado
- fabulosa → estupenda
- unos discos de rock → un libro de ciencia ficción

pasado, -a	*last; past*

**(yo) di, (tú) diste, (Ud., él,
   ella) dio** (from **dar**) *gave*

fabuloso, -a *fabulous*

2 GREGORIO   ¿Qué haces?

   TERESA   Escribo **las invitaciones** para **el baile** de fin de
              año.

   GREGORIO   ¿Cuántos **invitados** vas a tener?

   TERESA   Entre treinta y cuarenta personas.

   GREGORIO   ¿**Me** vas a **invitar**?

   TERESA   Claro. **Aquí tienes** tu invitación.

- el baile → la fiesta
- claro.→ ¡cómo no!

**la invitación, pl. las
   invitaciones** *invitation*

el baile *dance*

el invitado, la invitada *guest*

me *me*

invitar *to invite*

aquí tienes / tiene Ud. *here is,
   here are*

3 RAMÓN   ¡**Oye,** Carmen! ¿Quieres ir conmigo al cine esta
              noche?

   CARMEN   Gracias, pero no **puedo.** Ya tengo un **plan** para
              esta noche. **Tal vez otro** día.

- cine → baile
- otro día → la semana próxima

¡oye! *listen!, hey!*

**poder (o → ue) (yo puedo, tú
   puedes)** *can, to be able to*

el plan *plan*

tal vez *maybe, perhaps*

otro, -a *other, another*

Notes: Make sure students understand that *¡Oye!* in mini-dialogue 3 is a command.

4 RAQUEL   Buenos días, señor. Busco el disco nuevo del
                 grupo "Las Iguanas." ¿Dónde lo puedo
                 encontrar?

    VENDEDOR   **Aquí lo tiene Ud.**

    RAQUEL   Gracias. ¿Cuánto **cuesta**?

    VENDEDOR   Mil pesos.

- buenos días → buenas tardes
- mil → 700

**encontrar (o → ue) (yo
    encuentro, tú encuentras)**
    to find
**aquí lo (la, los, las) tienes /
    tiene Ud.**   *here it is, here they
    are*
costar (o → ue)   *to cost*

---

5 JAIME   Voy a tocar **otra vez** esa **canción** de "Las
                 Iguanas."

    CATALINA   Sí, me gusta mucho. Es muy **chistosa.**

    JAIME   Si quieres, **te presto** el disco.

- presto → **muestro**

otra vez   *again*
la canción, pl. **las canciones**
    song
chistoso, = a   *funny*
te   *you* (familiar)
prestar   *to lend*
**mostrar (o → ue) (yo muestro,
    tú muestras)**   *to show*

---

6 REBECA   Te quiero **presentar** a mis amigas Inés **e*** Isabel.

    GUILLERMO   ¡Mucho gusto! Si están **libres,** las invito a **tomar
                 algo.**

- están libres → no están ocupadas

presentar   *to introduce*
e = y
libre   *not busy, free*
tomar   here: = beber
tomar algo   *to have something to
    drink*

NOTE: In Spanish we sometimes use the present tense to express
an idea in the future. For example:

Si quieres, te **presto** el disco.   *If you want, **I'll lend** you the record.*
¿Me **presentas** a tus amigas?   *Are you **going to introduce** me
                                    to your friends?*

EN OTRAS PARTES

En España se dice *el
magnetofón* y *el magnetófono*.

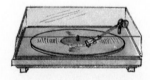

También se dice *el fonógrafo*.

También se dice *telefonear*.

* The Spanish word *y* becomes *e* before a word beginning with *i* or *hi*.

PRÁCTICA

A ¿Con quiénes fuiste? Imagina que tienes un(a) amigo(a) muy
curioso(a). Siempre quiere saber (*to know*) quiénes van de excursión
(*on outings*) contigo. Sigue el modelo.

> el lago / Marta, Inés
> ESTUDIANTE A   *¿Con quiénes fuiste al lago?*
> ESTUDIANTE B   *Con Marta e Inés.*

1. la granja / Mario, Pedro
2. el gimnasio / Ana, Ignacio
3. el campo / Patricia, Isabel
4. la panadería / Virginia, Luz
5. el zoológico / Pilar, Irene
6. la playa / Jorge, Elena

Práctica A
1. ¿Con quiénes fuiste a la granja? Con Mario y Pedro.
2. ¿Con quiénes fuiste al gimnasio? Con Ana e Ignacio.
3. ¿... al campo? Con Patricia e Isabel.
4. ¿... a la panadería? Con Virginia y Luz.
5. ¿... al zoológico? Con Pilar e Irene.
6. ¿... a la playa? Con Jorge y Elena.

B ¿Qué le diste? Consuelo recibió (*received*) muchos regalos (*gifts*) para
sus quince años. Todo el mundo pregunta qué recibió. Sigue el
modelo.

 / Manuel /

> ESTUDIANTE A   *¿Qué le diste a Consuelo para su cumpleaños?*
> ESTUDIANTE B   *Le di una bufanda.*
> ESTUDIANTE A   *¡Qué fabuloso! ¿Y qué le dio Manuel?*
> ESTUDIANTE B   *Unas cintas.*

1.  / Cecilia /
2.  / Mario /
3.  / Elena /
4.  / Eduardo /
5. 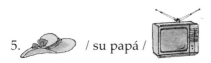 / su papá /
6. 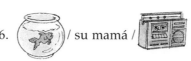 / su mamá /
7.  / Irene /
8. / Juanito /

Práctica B
1. ¿Qué le diste a Consuelo para su cumpleaños? Le di un disco. ¡Qué fabuloso! ¿Y qué le dio Cecilia? Unas flores.
2. ¿Qué le diste...? Le di un tocadiscos. ¡Qué fabuloso! ¿Y qué le dio Mario? Unos anteojos de sol.
3. ¿Qué le diste...? Le di un suéter. ¡Qué fabuloso! ¿Y qué le dio Elena? Una blusa.
4. ¿Qué le diste...? Le di una mochila. ¡Qué fabuloso! ¿Y qué le dio Eduardo? Un paraguas.
5. ¿Qué le diste...? Le di un sombrero. ¡Qué fabuloso! ¿Y qué le dio su papá? Un televisor.
6. ¿Qué le diste...? Le di un pez. ¡Qué fabuloso! ¿Y qué le dio su mamá? Una grabadora.
7. ¿Qué le diste...? Le di un radio. ¡Qué fabuloso! ¿Y qué le dio Irene? Unas sandalias.
8. ¿Qué le diste...? Le di un reloj. ¡Qué fabuloso! ¿Y qué le dio Juanito? Una papelera.

Reteach / Review: Ask
students to work in pairs to
come up with two or three
additional situations for Ex. C.

C **Una conversación.** Si un(a) amigo(a) dice estas cosas, ¿qué contestas? Escoge *(Choose)* una frase apropiada de la lista.

1. Mario lleva su libro de química al baile.
2. Creo que voy a poner el helado en la estufa.
3. Tengo que escribir 50 invitaciones hoy.
4. Esta noche voy al baile con tu novio(a).
5. No encuentro el tocadiscos.
6. Te presento a Victoria.
7. Mi hermana me presta su coche este sábado.
8. No estoy libre para ir al cine.
9. La línea ya no está ocupada.
10. Tengo los horarios. Aquí los tienes.

Aquí lo tienes.
Mucho gusto.
¡Oye! ¿Estás loco(a)?
¡Qué aburrido!
¡Qué bueno!
¡Qué chistoso!
¡Qué fabuloso!
¡Qué lástima!

(arriba) En Nueva York; (abajo) En Puerto Rico

D Hablemos de ti.

1. ¿Hay bailes en tu escuela? ¿Cuándo? ¿Te gustan los bailes? ¿Van a ellos tú y tus amigos?
2. ¿Qué clase de música prefieres escuchar? ¿Tienes un tocadiscos? ¿Una grabadora? ¿Tienes muchos discos y cintas?
3. ¿Qué clase de música escuchan tus padres? ¿Hay un radio en el coche de tus padres? En su coche, ¿puedes escuchar tu música favorita o tienes que escuchar la música favorita de tus padres?
4. ¿Cuál es tu grupo de rock favorito?
5. ¿Tocas la guitarra o el piano? ¿Tocas a veces canciones españolas en la guitarra o el piano? ¿Cuáles?
6. ¿Qué dices cuando presentas a un amigo(a) a otro(a)?

Práctica D
Answers will vary.

Practice Sheet 11–1

Workbook Exs. A–B

Canción: La bamba 3

Tape Manual Exs. 1–2 4

Quiz 11–1

ACTIVIDAD

El teléfono   Work in groups of three. Choose one person to be the caller, one to be the person being called, and one to be the "telephone." The caller chooses one of the dialogue topics listed below and then "calls" to invite the second person. Each person must talk to the "telephone," who then passes on the message. For example, the caller might ask, *¿Quieres ir al cine?*, and the "telephone" would say, *(Nombre) pregunta si quieres ir al cine.* When the other person answers the question, the "telephone" will relay the message. In your conversation, you might discuss where you want to go, when, what you need, how much money you have, etc. After each brief conversation, switch roles and conversation topics.

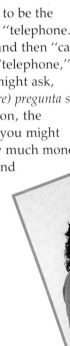

ir a un restaurante	ir al parque
ir a un café	ir a un partido de ____
ir al cine o al teatro	ir de compras
ir al zoológico	ir al centro

Reteach / Review: If your class enjoys this activity, you may want to vary the **Actividad** by dividing the class into larger groups. Then ask the first student to whisper a message to the second, who passes it on to the third, and so on. How much does the message change by the time it gets to the last student in each group?

APLICACIONES Discretionary

Caimán, Caimán 5

Rafael llama a Mariana por teléfono.

RAFAEL ¿Aló, Mariana? Habla Rafael. ¿Qué planes tienes para este sábado? ¿Estás libre?

MARIANA Pues . . . hay un baile en el centro juvenil.[1]

5 RAFAEL ¡Ay, Mariana! ¡Qué aburrido! Oye, yo tengo un plan. Hay un concierto[2] de rock en el Coliseo. ¿Por qué no vamos juntos? Yo te invito.

MARIANA ¡Qué bueno! Me encanta el rock. ¿Quiénes tocan?

RAFAEL Un grupo mexicano fabuloso: "Caimán, Caimán." ¿Te gusta?

10 MARIANA ¡Claro que sí! Es mi grupo favorito. Tengo casi todos sus discos.

RAFAEL ¡Magnífico! Hasta el sábado, entonces.

[1] **el centro juvenil** *youth center*   [2] **el concierto** *concert*

Notes: Make sure students understand the unglossed word *coliseo*, coliseum.

Preguntas

Contesta las preguntas según el diálogo.

1. ¿Qué hacen Mariana y Rafael?   2. ¿Cuándo es el baile? ¿Dónde es?   3. ¿Qué dice Rafael del plan de Mariana?   4. ¿Cuál es el plan de Rafael?   5. ¿Qué es "Caimán, Caimán"?   6. ¿Por qué tiene Mariana casi todos sus discos?   7. ¿Puedes inventar unos títulos (*titles*) de canciones para ese grupo?

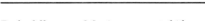

Un muchacho llama por teléfono en España.

Diálogo
1. Hablan por teléfono.
2. el sábado; en el centro juvenil
3. Dice que es aburrido.
4. Quiere ir a un concierto de rock en el Coliseo.
5. Es un grupo de rock mexicano.
6. Porque es su grupo de rock favorito.
7. Answers will vary.

Enrichment: Additional questions you may want to ask: *¿A Rafael le gustan los bailes en el centro juvenil? (No, no le gustan.) ¿Hay un centro juvenil en tu ciudad? ¿Dan bailes allí? ¿Te gusta ir a esos bailes? (Answers will vary.)*

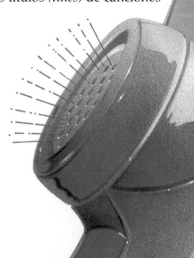

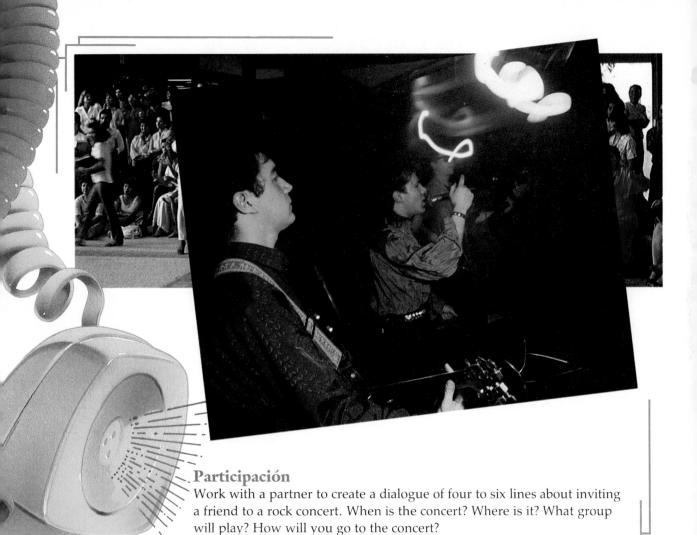

Participación

Work with a partner to create a dialogue of four to six lines about inviting a friend to a rock concert. When is the concert? Where is it? What group will play? How will you go to the concert?

PRONUNCIACIÓN 6

A In Spanish the letter *ch* has the same sound as the *ch* in the English word "check."

Escucha y repite.

chica   chistoso   mucho   coche   leche   derecha

B Escucha y repite.

Buenas noches, Conchita.
La chica bebe mucha leche.
Bebemos chocolate a las ocho de la noche.

Enrichment: Write these unknown words on the board, and ask students to pronounce them: *chiflado, hecho, gaucho, ficha.* The sentences in B are suitable for dictation.

7
Transparency 47
CONTEXTO VISUAL

Los pasatiempos

If students ask: Other related words you may want to present: *los juegos de tablero—Monopolio, Bingo,* board games—Monopoly, Bingo; *una baraja,* deck of cards.

jugar a los naipes

jugar al ajedrez

el ajedrez

los naipes

jugar a las damas

las damas

la moneda

la cámara

coleccionar monedas

el fotógrafo

dormir (o—ue)

la foto

la fotógrafa

sacar fotos

la revista

el concierto

el dinero

el sello

hacer cola

la entrada

coleccionar sellos

Notes: Make sure students remember to use the preposition *a* + definite article with expressions with *jugar*.

Enrichment: Ask students to vary mini-dialogue 1 by describing how they usually spend Sundays.
  In connection with mini-dialogue 5, you may want to expand on the *o* → *u* note by providing further examples: *siete u ocho, septiembre u octubre, mujer u hombre*.

CONTEXTO COMUNICATIVO 8

1 DANIEL   Oye, Graciela, ¿cómo **pasas** los domingos?
     GRACIELA   Leo revistas y **juego** a los naipes.
     DANIEL   ¡Esos **pasatiempos** son muy aburridos!
     GRACIELA   Tal vez para ti. A mí me gustan.

Variaciones:
- revistas → **cuentos**
- aburridos → tontos

pasar   *to spend (time)*
jugar (u → ue) (yo juego, tú juegas)   *to play*
el pasatiempo   *pastime, hobby*

el cuento   *story*

2 GLORIA   ¿Puedo ir al cine, papá?
     PAPÁ   ¿A qué hora vas a **volver**?
     GLORIA   Si veo sólo la primera película, vuelvo a las diez.
     PAPÁ   **Está bien, hasta pronto.**

- primera película → película policíaca
- hasta pronto → **hasta la vista**

volver (o → ue) (yo vuelvo, tú vuelves)   *to return, to go back, to come back*
está bien   *okay, all right*
hasta pronto   *see you soon*
hasta la vista   *see you later*

3 NORMA   Acabo de ver a José.
     RAÚL   ¿Dónde lo **viste**?
     NORMA   Lo **vi** en el concierto, pero él no me **vio.**

- en el concierto → delante del teatro

(yo) vi, (tú) viste, (Ud., él, ella) vio (from **ver**)   *saw*

4 DAVID   Quiero ir al concierto, pero no puedo **pagar** las entradas.
     SERGIO   ¡Qué lástima! Si quieres, te presto unos pesos.

- pagar → comprar
- pagar → **pagar** 500 pesos **por**
- ¡qué lástima! → **¡qué problema!**

pagar   *to pay (for)*

pagar + sum of money + **por**   *to pay ... for*
¡qué + noun!   *what a(n)...!*
el problema   *problem*

5 MARCOS   ¿Cuál prefieres, el ajedrez **u*** otro **juego**?
     GEORGINA   Me encanta jugar a las damas.
     MARCOS   ¿Jugamos un partido, entonces?

u = o
el juego   *game*

---

* The Spanish word *o* becomes *u* before a word beginning with *o* or *ho*.

6	MAMÁ	**Vámonos,** chicos. Estoy cansada.	**vámonos** *let's leave, let's go*
	HIJOS	¿No **nos** compras un juego?	**nos** *us*
	MAMÁ	Hoy no.	

- un juego → una cámara
- un juego → unas revistas

7	EVA	¡Qué aburrido! Pedro sólo habla **de** sus problemas.	**de** *here: about*
	JORGE	Yo creo que es muy divertido. Siempre me **cuenta**	**contar (o → ue)** *here: to tell*
		chistes.	**el chiste** *joke*

- problemas → sellos

EN OTRAS PARTES

También se dice *la estampilla* y en México se dice *el timbre.*

También se dice *tomar fotos.*

También se dice *jugar a las cartas.*

Práctica A

1. ¿Qué hace Sara? Busca (los) naipes.
2. ¿Qué hacen Uds.? Jugamos al ajedrez.
3. ¿Qué hacen (ellos)? Leen revistas.
4. ¿Qué haces? Saco fotos.
5. ¿Qué hace mamá? Escucha un (*or:* el) concierto
6. ¿Qué hacen Uds.? Jugamos a las damas.
7. ¿Qué haces? Cuento monedas.
8. ¿Qué hacen (ellas)? Miran (los) sellos.
9. ¿Qué hace tu abuelo? Toca el piano.

Reteach / Extra Help: In preparation for Ex. A, you may want to ask questions to review the forms of *hacer*, *-ar* verbs, and *-er* verbs.

PRÁCTICA

A ¿Qué hacen? Hoy llueve, y todo el mundo está en casa. Pregunta y contesta según el modelo.

(tú) / arreglar

ESTUDIANTE A *¿Qué haces?*
ESTUDIANTE B *Arreglo la cámara.*

1. Sara / buscar

2. Uds. / jugar

3. (ellos) / leer

4. (tú) / sacar

5. mamá / escuchar

6. Uds. / jugar

7. (tú) / contar

8. (ellas) / mirar

9. tu abuelo / tocar

B **¿Lo viste?** Imagina que le cuentas a un(a) amigo(a) las cosas que viste ayer. Pregunta y contesta según el modelo.

> las noticias en el canal 5
> ESTUDIANTE A *¿Viste las noticias en el canal 5?*
> ESTUDIANTE B *Sí, las vi. ¡Qué interesantes!*

Puedes usar estas expresiones:

¡Qué aburrido, -a!	¡Qué fabuloso, -a!	¡Qué hermoso, -a!
¡Qué chistoso, -a!	¡Qué feo, -a!	¡Qué interesante!
¡Qué divertido, -a!	¡Qué grande!	¡Qué largo, -a!

1. el coche nuevo de mis padres
2. la cola delante del estadio
3. las fotos de la fiesta
4. la nueva película de terror
5. las revistas que tiene mi amiga
6. las monedas viejas del profesor
7. mi tocadiscos nuevo
8. el piano blanco en la tienda de discos
9. los sellos nuevos que venden en el correo
10. el programa de música española

C **Hablemos de ti.**
1. ¿Cuáles son tus pasatiempos favoritos?
2. ¿Coleccionas sellos o monedas? ¿Coleccionas discos o libros? ¿Crees que es un pasatiempo divertido e interesante? ¿Es caro? ¿Puedes mostrar tu colección a la clase y hablar un poco de ella?
3. ¿Coleccionan cosas tus hermanos o tus padres? ¿Qué coleccionan?
4. ¿Qué juegos te gustan? ¿Te gusta jugar al ajedrez o a las damas? ¿Juegas a menudo? ¿Juegas bien? ¿Con quién juegas?
5. ¿A veces les prestas cosas a tus amigos? ¿Qué les prestas? Y ellos, ¿te prestan cosas? ¿Qué te prestan?
6. ¿Viste una buena película la semana pasada? ¿Cuál? ¿Con quién fuiste al cine? ¿Cuánto cuesta una entrada de cine?
7. Cuando vas al cine con tu novio(a), ¿quién paga?

ESTUDIO DE PALABRAS

Many Spanish words have the letter *f* where English words use *ph*.

Felipe	*Philip*	la geografía	*geography*	el teléfono	*telephone*
la foto	*photo*	Josefina	*Josephine*	el elefante	*elephant*
la farmacia	*pharmacy*	la física	*physics*		

What do you think these words mean:

la fobia   fotocopiar   la filosofía   las Filipinas

EXPLICACIONES I

Verbos con el cambio o → ue

◆ OBJECTIVES:

TO INDICATE
LOCATION

TO EXPRESS
CURFEWS

TO RELATE A DAY'S
EVENTS AND
ACTIVITIES

In the present tense of certain verbs, like *contar*, the *o* in the stem changes to *ue* in all except the *nosotros* and *vosotros* forms. We call these *stem-changing* verbs. Sometimes we call them *shoe* verbs, because we can draw a shoe around the four forms that change. Here are all of the forms of *contar* ("to count; to tell") in the present tense. Notice that although the stem changes, the endings are regular.

INFINITIVO   **contar**

	SINGULAR		PLURAL
1	(yo) **cuento**	(nosotros) (nosotras) } **contamos**	
2	(tú) **cuentas**	(vosotros) (vosotras) } **contáis**	
3	Ud. (él) (ella) } **cuenta**	Uds. (ellos) (ellas) } **cuentan**	

Luis **cuenta** muchos chistes.   *Luis **tells** a lot of jokes.*
Pablo y yo **contamos** las monedas.   *Pablo and I **are counting** the coins.*

Here are the other verbs you know that have the stem change *o → ue*.

-AR verbs		-ER / -IR verbs	
costar	*to cost*	poder	*to be able, can*
encontrar	*to find*	volver	*to return, to go back, to come back*
mostrar	*to show*	dormir	*to sleep*

NOTE: That *encontrar* is often equivalent to "can find" in English:

No encuentro mi dinero.   *I **can't find** my money.*

Notes: Refer to these mini-dialogues for examples of *o → ue* stemchanging verbs: *contar:* 7 on p. 372; *costar:* 4 on p. 364; *mostrar:* 5 on p. 364; *poder:* 3 on p. 363, 4 on p. 364, 2 and 4 on p. 371; *volver:* 2 on p. 371.

Reteach / Extra Help: In preparation for the **Práctica** on pp. 375–378, ask students to work in pairs or do a chain drill to reinforce the forms of *o → ue* verbs: *¿A quién encuentras en casa por la tarde? ¿Puedes contar hasta cien en español? ¿A qué hora vuelves a casa de la escuela? ¿Duermes bien antes de un examen?*

PRÁCTICA

A ¿Dónde lo encuentran? Escoge (*choose*) elementos de las tres columnas para describir qué cosas encuentran estas personas y dónde las encuentran. Sigue el modelo.

Francisco encuentra el gato detrás del piano.

Francisco	pan	cerca del teléfono
la Sra. Molina	sellos	detrás del televisor
(yo)	el coche	debajo de la silla
(tú)	revistas	delante de la puerta
Ud.	naipes	detrás del piano
(nosotras)	el pájaro	en el refrigerador
Uds.	el gato	en la mochila
Ana y yo	fotos	en el árbol
las chicas	anteojos de sol	sobre la mesa
	la guía telefónica	dentro del garaje
	cartas	en la calle
		fuera de su jaula

Práctica A
Answers will vary.
1. Francisco encuentra…
2. La Sra. Molina encuentra…
3. Encuentro…
4. Encuentras…
5. Ud. encuentra…
6. Encontramos…
7. Uds. encuentran…
8. Ana y yo encontramos…
9. Las chicas encuentran…

B ¿A qué hora vuelven? Di (*tell*) a qué hora estas personas vuelven a casa los sábados. Sigue el modelo.

Juan

ESTUDIANTE A *¿A qué hora vuelve Juan?*
ESTUDIANTE B *Vuelve a las nueve y media.*

1. (tú)

2. Ricardo y tú

3. María y Elena

4. tú y tu tío

5. Uds.

6. Inés

7. Ud.

8. Ramón y yo

Práctica B
1. ¿A qué hora vuelves? Vuelvo a las once.
2. ¿A qué hora vuelven Ricardo y tú? Volvemos a la una y cuarto.
3. ¿A qué hora vuelven María y Elena? Vuelven a la medianoche (a las doce).
4. ¿A qué hora vuelven tú y tu tío? Volvemos a las once y media.
5. ¿A qué hora vuelven Uds.? Volvemos a las dos menos cuarto.
6. ¿A qué hora vuelve Inés? Vuelve a las diez y veinte.
7. ¿A qué hora vuelve Ud.? Vuelvo a las once menos veinte.
8. ¿A qué hora volvemos Ramón y yo? (Uds.) Vuelven a las dos y media.

Reteach / Review: You may want to expand on Ex. A by asking students to work in pairs to ask questions using *buscar* and answer using *encontrar*. For example: *¿Qué busca Francisco?* (*Busca el gato y lo encuentra detrás del piano.*)

Práctica C
1. encuentras / podemos
2. cuenta / puede
3. encontramos / cuesta
4. cuentan / puedo
5. muestro / encuentro
6. volvemos / pueden
7. puedes / cuestan
8. podemos / dormimos
9. vuelve / muestra
10. duermo / duermen

C ¿Qué dicen?   Completa las frases con la forma correcta del verbo.

1. Si tú no _____ el tocadiscos, nosotros no _____ bailar.
   (*encontrar / poder*)
2. Cuando Pablo _____ chistes, nadie _____ hablar. (*contar / poder*)
3. Cuando (nosotras) _____ un vestido bonito, siempre _____
   mucho. (*encontrar / costar*)
4. Si ellas me _____ sus problemas, (yo) _____ tal vez ayudarlas.
   (*contar / poder*)
5. (Yo) no te _____ la foto de mi novia porque no la _____.
   (*mostrar / encontrar*)
6. ¡Vámonos! Si (nosotros) _____ a casa temprano, Uds. _____ ver
   la película de medianoche en la tele. (*volver / poder*)
7. ¡Oye, Esteban! ¿Nos _____ decir otra vez cuánto _____ las
   entradas para ese concierto? (*poder / costar*)
8. Los domingos, si (nosotros) _____, siempre _____ hasta las diez.
   (*poder / dormir*)
9. Cuando ella _____ de su país, siempre nos _____ las revistas que
   trae. (*volver / mostrar*)
10. Yo _____ nueve horas todas las noches, pero mis hermanos sólo
    _____ siete. (*dormir / dormir*)

Práctica D
encuentra / muestra
pueden
volvemos
podemos
vuelven
cuenta
pueden / vuelven

Notes: You may want to
assign Ex. D as written
homework, asking students to
write out the entire paragraph.
Check students' work for
correct spelling, capitalization,
and punctuation.

D Planes para el domingo.   Usa la forma correcta de cada (*each*) verbo
para completar el párrafo (*paragraph*).

El domingo por la mañana, Alicia llama por teléfono a su nueva
amiga Gloria para invitarla a ir a nadar en el lago. Gloria busca su
traje de baño, pero no lo _____ (*encontrar*). Su mamá le _____ (*mostrar*)
dónde está. Ella lo pone en su mochila y sale para ir a la casa de
5 Alicia. Cuando llega allí, Alicia la presenta a su mamá. Después, las
muchachas toman el autobús y van al lago, pero cuando llegan no
_____ (*poder*) nadar porque ahora hace demasiado fresco y está
nublado. "Oye," dice Alicia, "¿por qué no _____ (*volver*) (nosotras) a
mi casa? (Nosotras) _____ (*poder*) ir al cine más tarde. Dan una
10 fabulosa película cómica en el Aragón." "Está bien," contesta Gloria.
"¡Vámonos!" Las chicas esperan el autobús y _____ (*volver*) a la casa
de Alicia. Alicia le _____ (*contar*) a su mamá sus planes nuevos. Su
mamá les dice que (ellas) _____ (*poder*) ir al cine si no _____ (*volver*)
demasiado tarde.

El verbo *jugar* (*u* → *ue*)

Jugar is a stem-changing verb. In the present tense, the *u* of the stem changes to *ue* except in the *nosotros* and *vosotros* forms. The endings are regular.

INFINITIVO **jugar**

	SINGULAR		PLURAL	
1	(yo)	**juego**	(nosotros) (nosotras)	**jugamos**
2	(tú)	**juegas**	(vosotros) (vosotras)	**jugáis**
3	Ud. (él) (ella)	**juega**	Uds. (ellos) (ellas)	**juegan**

Notes: Mini-dialogues 1 and 5 on p. 371 illustrate some of the stem-changing forms of *jugar*.

PRÁCTICA

A ¿A qué juegan? Pregunta y contesta según el modelo.

Ramón y Carlos

ESTUDIANTE A *¿A qué juegan Ramón y Carlos?*
ESTUDIANTE B *Juegan al fútbol.*

1. Silvia e Inés

2. (tú)

3. Martín

4. los padres e hijos

5. Uds.

6. Alicia y tú

Práctica A
1. ¿A qué juegan Silvia e Inés? Juegan al ajedrez.
2. ¿A qué juegas? Juego a los naipes.
3. ¿A qué juega Martín? Juega al béisbol.
4. ¿A qué juegan los padres e hijos? Juegan a las damas.
5. ¿A qué juegan Uds.? Jugamos al tenis.
6. ¿A qué juegan Alicia y tú? Jugamos al básquetbol.

Reteach / Extra Help: Before students begin Ex. A, ask volunteers to suggest sentences using the forms of *jugar*. Refer students to the **Contexto visual** on p. 370 if they need help.

Práctica B

1. ¿Cuentas muchos chistes?
   Sí, (No, no) cuento muchos
   chistes.
2. ¿Juegas al ajedrez? Sí, (No,
   no) juego al ajedrez.
3. ¿Vuelves a casa después de
   medianoche? Sí, (No, no)
   vuelvo…
4. ¿Cuentas las horas hasta el
   examen? Sí, (No, no)
   cuento…
5. ¿Puedes ir a conciertos de
   rock? Sí, (No, no) puedo…
6. ¿Juegas a los naipes? Sí,
   (No, no) juego…
7. ¿Duermes ocho horas? Sí,
   (No, no) duermo…
8. ¿Vuelves a la biblioteca para
   estudiar? Sí, (No, no)
   vuelvo…

Enrichment: To reinforce the
o → ue stem-changing verbs
and *jugar*, you may want to ask
students to redo Ex. B using
the third person singular:
¿Duerme bien? You may want
students to use the name of
someone in the class for each
of the eight items.

Práctica C

1. ¿Cuentan Uds.…?
   …contamos…
2. ¿Juegan Uds.…?
   …jugamos…
3. ¿Vuelven Uds.…?
   …volvemos…
4. ¿Cuentan Uds.…?
   …contamos…
5. ¿Pueden Uds.…?
   …podemos…
6. ¿Juegan Uds.…?
   …jugamos…
7. ¿Duermen Uds.…?
   …dormimos…
8. ¿Vuelven Uds.…?
   …volvemos…

B Antes del examen. Habla con un(a) amigo(a) de las cosas que haces
o no haces antes de un examen. Sigue el modelo.

> dormir bien
>
> ESTUDIANTE A *¿Duermes bien?*
> ESTUDIANTE B *Sí, duermo bien.*
>   o: *No, no duermo bien.*

1. contar muchos chistes
2. jugar al ajedrez
3. volver a casa después de medianoche
4. contar las horas hasta el examen
5. poder ir a conciertos de rock
6. jugar a los naipes
7. dormir ocho horas
8. volver a la biblioteca para estudiar

C ¿Y qué hacen Uds.? Haz *(do)* Práctica B con dos compañeros o
compañeras de clase. Sigue el modelo.

> dormir bien
>
> ESTUDIANTE A   *¿Duermen Uds. bien?*
> ESTUDIANTES B-C *Sí, dormimos bien.*
>   o: *No, no dormimos bien.*
>   o: *Yo duermo bien, pero él (ella) no.*

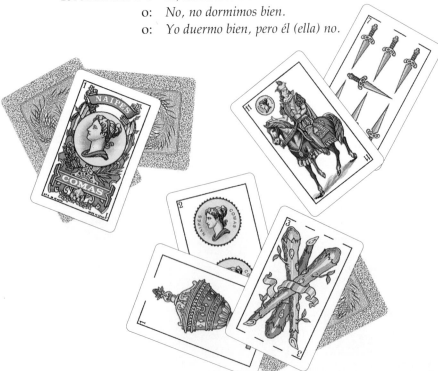

Practice Sheet 11–3   10 Tape Manual Ex. 4   Quiz 11–3

El infinitivo con otro verbo

We often use an infinitive right after another verb. Some of these verbs are *gustar, deber, encantar, necesitar, poder, preferir (prefiero),* and *querer (quiero).*

◆ **OBJECTIVES:**
TO ASK FOR PERMISSION
TO EXPRESS OBLIGATION
TO ANSWER A SURVEY

Pueden salir para México ahora.	*They can leave for Mexico now.*
¿Quieres jugar al tenis?	*Do you want to play tennis?*
Necesitamos abrir esta puerta.	*We need to open this door.*
Prefiero estudiar solo.	*I prefer to study alone.*

1 Some verbs require *a* before an infinitive. For example: *aprender, ayudar, enseñar, invitar, ir,* and *venir.*

Aprendemos a tocar el piano.	*We're learning to play the piano.*
Ella les **enseña a leer**.	*She's teaching them to read.*
Siempre **ayudo a lavar** los platos.	*I always help wash the dishes.*
Vienen a arreglar el radio.	*They're coming to fix the radio.*
Los **invito a tomar** algo.	*I'm inviting them to have something to drink.*

2 *Tener* requires *que* before an infinitive and *acabar* requires *de*.

Acabamos de pagar la entrada.	*We just paid for the ticket.*
Tengo que volver pronto.	*I have to return soon.*

Tenis en Madrid, España

379

PRÁCTICA

Práctica A
1. ¿Puedo tomar algo? Sí, pero después tienes que lavar el vaso.
2. ¿Puedo tocar unos discos? Sí, pero después tienes que terminar la tarea.
3. ¿Puedo invitar a María a comer? Sí, … tienes que ayudar en la cocina.
4. ¿Puedo contar un chiste? Sí, … tienes que decirlo en español.
5. ¿Puedo pasar el día con Jaime? Sí, … tienes que trabajar en el jardín.
6. ¿Puedo mostrar mi bicicleta nueva a Eva? Sí, … tienes que ponerla en el garaje.
7. Puedo llevar mi juego nuevo a la casa de Pepe? Sí, … tienes que traerlo a casa.
8. ¿Puedo visitar a Graciela? Sí, … tienes que estudiar.

Práctica B
Answers will vary.

Práctica C
Answers will vary.

A ¿Qué puedo hacer? Los niños quieren hacer muchas cosas, pero primero tienen que preguntarle a su mamá. Pregunta y contesta según el modelo.

> jugar al ajedrez / tocar el piano
> ESTUDIANTE A   *¿Puedo jugar al ajedrez?*
> ESTUDIANTE B   *Sí, pero después tienes que tocar el piano.*

1. tomar algo / lavar el vaso
2. tocar unos discos / terminar la tarea
3. invitar a María a comer / ayudar en la cocina
4. contar un chiste / decirlo en español
5. pasar el día con Jaime / trabajar en el jardín
6. mostrar mi bicicleta nueva a Eva / ponerla en el garaje
7. llevar mi juego nuevo a la casa de Pepe / traerlo a casa
8. visitar a Graciela / estudiar

B ¿Te gusta hablar español? Usa frases completas para contestar las preguntas de esta encuesta *(survey)*.

1. ¿Qué aprendes a hacer en la clase de español?
2. ¿Crees que puedes aprender a hablar bien el español?
3. ¿Qué acabas de aprender en tu clase de español?
4. ¿Tienes que leer un diálogo muchas veces para comprenderlo?
5. ¿Cuántas horas de tarea debes hacer por la noche para tu clase de español?
6. ¿Prefieres estudiar español con un(a) amigo(a) o solo(a)? ¿Dónde prefieres estudiar?
7. ¿Qué prefieres estudiar, el español u otra materia? ¿Cuál?
8. ¿Con quién puedes hablar español?
9. ¿Quién te ayuda a repasar para las pruebas de español?
10. ¿Puedes contar chistes en español?
11. ¿Quieres visitar países donde hablan español? ¿Cuáles?
12. ¿Vas a estudiar español el año próximo? ¿Dónde?

C Hablemos de ti.
1. ¿Te gusta sacar fotos? ¿De qué o de quién sacas fotos?
2. ¿En qué estaciones del año juegas al béisbol? ¿Al fútbol americano? ¿Al básquetbol?
3. ¿Estás cansado(a)? Generalmente, ¿cuántas horas duermes por la noche?
4. Cuando sales los viernes o los sábados por la noche, ¿a qué hora tienes que volver a casa? ¿Siempre vuelves a esa hora? ¿Qué pasa cuando vuelves después de esa hora?

APLICACIONES Discretionary

Notes: Sample dialogues for the **¿Qué pasa?** appear in the pre-chapter teacher pages.

Pasatiempos Transparency 48

Casi todo el mundo tiene un pasatiempo favorito. ¿Cuáles son los pasatiempos favoritos de estas personas? ¿Por qué hacen cola?

Make up a dialogue of four to six lines in which two people discuss buying the tickets, the group that's playing, and what the concert is going to be like. Here are some words you may want to use:

| la canción | pagar | tocar (discos) | tal vez |
| la entrada | pasar | costar | otra vez |

Enrichment: You may want to ask students to work in pairs to describe the picture. Volunteers may present their descriptions to the class.

EXPLICACIONES II

Los complementos directos e indirectos: *me, te, nos*

◆ **OBJECTIVES:**

TO ASK OTHERS TO DO THINGS FOR YOU

TO REFUSE OR PUT PEOPLE OFF

TO OFFER TO DO FAVORS

TO BARGAIN

You already know the direct and indirect object pronouns that mean "him," "her," "you" (*Ud., Uds.*), "it," and "them." The pronouns *me, te,* and *nos* mean "me," "you" (familiar), and "us." We use them as both direct and indirect object pronouns.

Me ven en la cola.	*They see **me** in line.*
¿**Me** das el dinero?	*Are you giving **me** the money?*
No **te** creen.	*They don't believe **you**.*
No **te** escribo.	*I don't write **to you**.*
¿**Nos** oyen?	*Do they hear **us**?*
Nos muestran las entradas.	*They're showing **us** the tickets.*

Instrumento Musical Prehispánico

VENEZUELA

Bs. 2

1 Remember that direct and indirect object pronouns go right before the verb or can be attached to an infinitive.

Anita **me** da un sello.	*Anita is giving **me** a stamp.*
No **te** llaman por teléfono.	*They aren't phoning **you**.*
Nos esperan en la esquina.	*They're waiting for **us** on the corner.*
Te quiero contar un chiste.	*I want to tell **you** a joke.*
Quiero contar**te** un chiste.	
David **me** debe llamar.	*David should call **me**.*
David debe llamar**me**.	

2 Remember that we can emphasize the indirect object pronouns *le* and *les* by using the preposition *a* + *Ud.* / *Uds.* / *él* / *ella* / *ellos* / *ellas*. We can emphasize the indirect object pronouns *me, te,* and *nos* by adding *a mí, a ti,* or *a nosotros, -as.*

¿A quién le escriben?	*To whom are they writing?*
Me escriben **a mí**.	*They're writing **to me**.*
¿A quién le cantas?	*For whom are you singing?*
Te canto **a ti**.	*I'm singing **for you**.*
¿A quiénes les hablan?	*To whom are they talking?*
Nos hablan **a nosotros**.	*They're talking **to us**.*

3 Here is a summary of the direct and indirect object pronouns.

DIRECT OBJECT PRONOUNS				INDIRECT OBJECT PRONOUNS			
SINGULAR		**PLURAL**		**SINGULAR**		**PLURAL**	
me	*me*	**nos**	*us*	**me**	*(to / for) me*	**nos**	*(to / for) us*
te	*you*	**os***	*you*	**te**	*(to / for) you*	**os***	*(to / for) you*
lo	*you* *him* *it*	**los**	*you* *them*	**le**	*(to / for)* *you* *him* *her* *it*	**les**	*(to / for)* *you* *them*
la	*you* *her* *it*	**las**	*you* *them*				

* Like *vosotros, os* is used mainly in Spain. You should recognize it when you see it.

En el correo en Madrid,
España

PRÁCTICA

Práctica A

1. ¿Me crees? Siempre (No, no) te creo.
2. ¿Me esperas? Siempre (No, no) te espero.
3. ¿Me escuchas? Siempre (No, no) te escucho.
4. ¿Me llamas antes de salir? Siempre (No, no) te llamo (antes de salir).
5. ¿Me comprendes? Siempre (No, no) te comprendo.
6. ¿Me ayudas con la tarea? Siempre (No, no) te ayudo (con la tarea).
7. ¿Me presentas a los otros invitados? Siempre (No, no) te presento (a los otros invitados).
8. ¿Me buscas después del concierto? Siempre (No, no) te busco (después del concierto).

Práctica B

1. ¿Te muestra sus fotos? Sí, a menudo (No, nunca) me muestra sus fotos.
2. ¿Te cuenta chistes? Sí, a menudo (No, nunca) me cuenta chistes.
3. ¿Te presta su coche? Sí, a menudo (No, nunca) me presta su coche.
4. ¿Te canta canciones románticas? Sí, a menudo (No, nunca) me canta…
5. ¿Te escribe poemas? Sí, a menudo (No, nunca) me escribe…
6. ¿Te habla de sus planes? Sí, a menudo (No, nunca) me habla…
7. ¿Te cuenta sus problemas? Sí, a menudo (No, nunca) me cuenta…
8. ¿Te dice cosas bonitas? Sí, a menudo (No, nunca) me dice…

A ¿Me invitas? Imagina que hablas por teléfono con un(a) amigo(a). Pregunta y contesta según el modelo.

> invitar al baile
> **ESTUDIANTE A** *¿Me invitas al baile?*
> **ESTUDIANTE B** *¡Claro! Siempre te invito.*
> o: *No, no te invito.*

1. creer
2. esperar
3. escuchar
4. llamar antes de salir
5. comprender
6. ayudar con la tarea
7. presentar a los otros invitados
8. buscar después del concierto

B El novio de Julia. Julia tiene un novio nuevo y todas sus amigas le preguntan cómo es. Pregunta y contesta según el modelo.

> traer flores
> **ESTUDIANTE A** *¿Te trae flores?*
> **ESTUDIANTE B** *Sí, a menudo me trae flores.*
> o: *No, nunca me trae flores.*

1. mostrar sus fotos
2. contar chistes
3. prestar su coche
4. cantar canciones románticas
5. escribir poemas
6. hablar de sus planes
7. contar sus problemas
8. decir cosas bonitas

C Ahora no. Imagina que cuidas a dos niños que quieren muchas cosas. Tú no tienes ganas de hacer nada. Pregunta y contesta según el modelo.

> querer hacer un dibujo
> **ESTUDIANTE A** *¿Quieres hacernos un dibujo?*
> o: *¿Nos quieres hacer un dibujo?*
> **ESTUDIANTE B** *Ahora no. Tal vez más tarde.*

1. poder cantar otra canción
2. poder mostrar tus revistas
3. ir a prestar tu cámara
4. poder comprar helados
5. poder contar un cuento
6. ir a tocar otro disco
7. ir a leer unos libros
8. poder traer un vaso de agua

 12 Tape Manual Ex. 6

D Una visita a los abuelos.   Emilia va a pasar un mes en la granja de sus abuelos. Su hermanito tiene muchas preguntas. Pregunta y contesta según el modelo.

llevar la carta de mamá

ESTUDIANTE A *¿Vas a llevarles la carta de mamá?*
ESTUDIANTE B *Claro que sí.*
          o: *Claro que no.*

1. prestar tu cámara

2. traer fotos

3. dar mis dibujos

4. escribir cartas

5. traer maíz y papas

6. hablar de tu novio

7. contar de tu visita

8. mostrar tus notas

9. decir muchas gracias

Práctica C
1. ¿Puedes cantarnos (Nos puedes cantar) otra canción?
2. ¿Puedes mostrarnos (Nos puedes mostrar) tus revistas?
3. ¿Vas a prestarnos (Nos vas a prestar) tu cámara?
4. ¿Puedes comprarnos (Nos puedes comprar) helados?
5. ¿Puedes contarnos (Nos puedes contar) un cuento?
6. Vas a tocarnos (Nos vas a tocar) otro disco?
7. ¿Vas a leernos (Nos vas a leer) unos libros?
8. ¿Puedes traernos (Nos puedes traer) un vaso de agua?

Práctica D
1. ¿Vas a prestarles tu cámara?
2. ¿Vas a traernos fotos?
3. ¿Vas a darles mis dibujos?
4. ¿Vas a escribirnos cartas?
5. ¿Vas a traernos maíz y papas?
6. ¿Vas a hablarles de tu novio?
7. ¿Vas a contarnos de tu visita?
8. ¿Vas a mostrarles tus notas?
9. ¿Vas a decirles muchas gracias?

E Una buena amiga. María hace muchas cosas para sus amigos. Sigue el modelo.

> a él / prestar su radio
> *A él le presta su radio.*

1. a mí / traer sellos de otros países
2. a Uds. / enseñar canciones nuevas
3. a ella / leer libros de cuentos
4. a ti / contar chistes divertidos
5. a él / dar revistas de deportes
6. a nosotros / traer flores del campo
7. a ellas / mostrar los dibujos animados
8. a todos nosotros / prestar sus cintas de rock

Una mujer vende flores en México.

F **¿Y qué me das tú?** Si una persona te hace un favor, tú debes hacerle uno a ella. Completa las frases con los pronombres correctos.

1. Si tú _____ prestas tu tocadiscos, yo _____ toco mi disco nuevo.
2. Si Uds. _____ cocinan la cena, nosotros _____ lavamos los platos.
3. Si tú _____ ayudas a limpiar el garaje, yo _____ pago.
4. Si ellos _____ dan el dinero, nosotras _____ compramos las entradas.
5. Si tú _____ traes el libro, yo _____ leo un cuento.
6. Si Ud. _____ espera esta tarde, yo _____ enseño a usar la computadora.
7. Si Uds. _____ dan la guitarra, yo _____ toco una canción.
8. Si ella _____ arregla la grabadora, nosotros _____ damos cien pesos.

Práctica F
1. me, te   5. me, te
2. nos, les   6. me, le
3. me, te   7. me, les
4. nos, les   8. nos, le

Enrichment: After completing Ex. F, you may want to have pairs of students extend the pattern by saying to each other *Si tú me prestas tu _____, yo te presto mi _____* and *Si tú me ayudas con _____, yo te ayudo con _____.*

G **Hablemos de ti.**
1. ¿Cuánto dinero te dan tus padres durante la semana? ¿Qué compras?
2. ¿A veces les prestas dinero a tus amigos? ¿Por qué? ¿Qué cosas te prestan tus amigos a ti?
3. ¿Quiénes te escriben cartas? ¿Te escriben cartas tus amigos cuando van de vacaciones? ¿De qué cosas te escriben?
4. ¿Te esperan tus amigos después de las clases? ¿Dónde? ¿Adónde van Uds. entonces?
5. ¿Tienes planes para el próximo verano? ¿Puedes contarle a la clase tus planes?

Práctica G
Answers will vary.

Practice Sheets 11–5, 11–6

Workbook Exs. G–J

Tape Manual Ex. 7 13

Refrán 14

Activity Master 11–2

Quiz 11–5

ACTIVIDAD

¡Oye! Working in pairs, take turns choosing a verb from the list and saying what you are going to do for your partner. Your partner will interrupt, and then rephrase and complete your offer, saying what he or she would like you to do.

ESTUDIANTE A   Voy a darte . . .
ESTUDIANTE B   Vas a darme dinero para el almuerzo.

comprar	enseñar (a)	mostrar	presentar
contar	escribir	pagar	prestar
dar	leer		

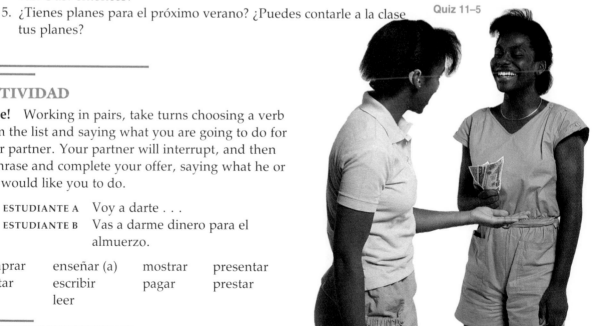

APLICACIONES

Discretionary

Notes: Answers to the **Repaso** and **Tema** appear in the pre-chapter teacher pages.

REPASO

Notes: Review of:
1. *-ar* verbs
   para
   noun phrases with *de*
2. *invitar a* + infinitive
   personal *a*
   con + prepositional pronoun
3. demonstrative adjectives
   estar + adjective
   poder + infinitive
4. *estar* + adjective
   indirect object pronouns
5. *o → ue* stem-changing verbs
   jugar
   verb + *a* + noun
   possessive adjectives
   adjective agreement

Look carefully at the model sentences. Then put the English cues into Spanish to form new sentences based on the models.

1. *Mis padres hacen cola para el partido de fútbol.*
   (I'm drawing posters for the play.)
   (We're taking pictures for Sunday's newspaper.)
   (Cristina collects songs for the rock group.)

2. *Invitan a sus primos a ir al estadio con ellos.*
   (Jorge invites Mónica to play chess with him.)
   (We invite Mario and Luz to go downtown with us.)
   (I invite the photographer (f.) to travel to Ecuador with me.)

3. *Pero ese sábado estamos ocupadas. No podemos trabajar.*
   (But tonight I'm tired. I can't play.)
   (But this morning Felipe is absent. They can't continue.)
   (But that day you (fam.) aren't free. You can't help.)

4. *Luis está preocupado, pero te presta las fotos.*
   (Dad is bored, but he tells me a story.)
   (We're prepared, and he gives us the test.)
   (You're (fam.) sad, but we teach you (fam.) a game.)

5. *No duermo. Juego al ajedrez con mi primo favorito.*
   (We're not coming back. We're going to the dance with our Mexican friends.)
   (You (formal) aren't sleeping. You're playing checkers with your sick son.)
   (She isn't coming back. She's attending the theater with her older sister.)

Un partido de fútbol en
Buenos Aires, Argentina

Put the English captions into Spanish.

1. My brother Paco is buying tickets for the rock concert.

2. He invites his girlfriend to attend the concert with him.

3. But that week Paco is sick. He can't go out.

4. He's sad, but he gives me the tickets.

5. Paco doesn't sleep. He plays cards with our younger brother.

REDACCIÓN

Now you are ready to write your own dialogue or paragraph. Choose one of the following topics.

1. Expand the *Tema* by writing five more sentences, giving the following information. Your father returns home. He plays cards with your brothers. You return from the concert and tell Paco that you saw his girlfriend at the concert with another boy. Now Paco is very sad!

2. Pretend that you are the brother or sister to whom Paco gave the tickets. Write a dialogue of four to six lines, giving the phone conversation between you and the friend you are inviting to go with you. Explain that your brother is sick and cannot go to the rock concert and that he gave you the tickets. Invite your friend to go with you. He or she either accepts the invitation or makes an excuse not to go.

3. Create talk balloons for the five pictures in the *Tema*. What are the characters saying or thinking?

COMPRUEBA TU PROGRESO   CAPÍTULO 11   Discretionary

Notes: Answers to the **Comprueba** appear in the pre-chapter teacher pages.

A   Pasatiempos

In each blank write the word from the list below that best completes each sentence.

chistoso	tal vez	tomar algo
fabulosa	por teléfono	semana pasada
prestar	grabadora	

1. Tengo un tocadiscos muy viejo, pero no tengo _____.
2. Quiero invitar a Marta. Voy a llamarla _____.
3. ¿Tienes sed? Pues, vamos a _____.
4. ¡Tu nueva canción es _____!
5. No voy a verlo hoy porque lo vi la _____.
6. ¿Me puedes _____ dinero?
7. No puedo ir contigo hoy; _____ mañana.

B   ¿Y aquí qué pasa?

Answer the questions according to the pictures. Use complete sentences.

1. ¿A qué juegan Uds.?   2. ¿Qué le das a Pedro?

3. ¿Qué necesitamos?   4. ¿Qué le diste a él?

5. ¿Qué leen Uds.?   6. ¿Qué compran Uds.?

C   ¿Qué hacen?

Complete the sentences with the correct form of the verb.

1. Yo no _____ la nueva tienda de ropa. (*encontrar*)
2. ¿Por qué no _____ Uds. ir al teatro? (*poder*)
3. Nosotros no _____ mucho. (*dormir*)
4. Pepito _____ chistes muy buenos. (*contar*)
5. Ellos _____ a las damas. (*jugar*)
6. Ella me _____ sus dibujos. (*mostrar*)
7. ¿Por qué no _____ continuar nosotros? (*poder*)

D   ¿Qué pueden hacer?

Form complete sentences using the words given. Use *a*, *de*, or *que* when necessary.

1. (nosotros) / acabar / asistir / un concierto
2. María / poder / contar / del 0 al 100
3. el fotógrafo / ir / enseñarnos / usar / la cámara
4. los invitados / tener ganas / oír / esas canciones viejas
5. (yo) / te / invitar / tomar algo / mañana
6. (tú) / tener / trabajar más / si / ir / sacar / buenas notas

E   ¿A quién?

Complete the sentence with the correct pronoun: *me*, *te*, or *nos*.

> Si no me das tu número de teléfono, no _____ puedo llamar.
> *Si no me das tu número de teléfono, no te puedo llamar.*

1. Cuando jugamos al tenis, ellos _____ miran.
2. Tú me invitas a tomar algo y yo _____ invito a mi casa.
3. ¿Por qué le hablas al perro, Paco? Él no _____ comprende.
4. Le damos discos a Ernesto, y él _____ presta sus cintas.
5. Mi amiga Leonor siempre _____ llama por teléfono.
6. Para mi cumpleaños mis padres _____ van a dar un radio nuevo.

Chapter 11 Test   Listening Comprehension Test

VOCABULARIO DEL CAPÍTULO 11

Sustantivos
el ajedrez
el baile
la cámara
la canción, *pl.* las canciones
el concierto
el cuento
el chiste
las damas
el dinero
la entrada
la foto
el fotógrafo, la fotógrafa
la grabadora
el grupo
la invitación, *pl.* las invitaciones
el invitado, la invitada
el juego
la moneda
los naipes
el pasatiempo
el piano
el plan
el problema
el radio
la revista
el rock
el sello
el tocadiscos, *pl.* los tocadiscos

Pronombres de complemento directo e indirecto
me
nos
te

Adjetivos
chistoso, -a
fabuloso, -a
libre
otro, -a
pasado, -a

Verbos
coleccionar
contar (o → ue) *(to count; to tell)*
costar (o → ue)
dormir (o → ue)
encontrar (o → ue)
invitar
mostrar (o → ue)
pagar (+ *sum of money* + por)
pasar
poder (o → ue)
presentar
prestar
tocar (discos)
tomar *(to drink)*
volver (o → ue)

di, diste, dio
vi, viste, vio

Conjunciones
de *(about)*
e
u

Expresiones
aquí tienes / tiene Ud.
está bien
hacer cola
hasta la vista
hasta pronto
jugar al ajedrez
jugar a las damas
jugar a los naipes
llamar por teléfono
otra vez
¡oye!
sacar fotos
tal vez
tomar algo
¡qué + *noun!*
¡vámonos!

EL CANAL DE PANAMÁ

A huge ocean liner moves slowly through the water. Passengers on deck take pictures of the thick, green, tropical jungle that surrounds them. Is this a scene from an adventure movie? No, just another day on the Panama Canal, where every year some 12,000 ships cross from one sea to another.

After a ship enters the canal from the Caribbean, it travels through a series of locks that gradually raise the level of water to a height of 85 feet above sea level. Then it moves through Lago de Gatún, an enormous lake that was created by building a dam on the tiny Río Chagres.

At about the halfway point, the mountains begin to close in and the canal becomes much narrower. Soon the ship enters the Gaillard Cut, an eight-mile section carved out of solid rock. This part alone took six years to build.

Finally, the ship reaches the Miraflores locks, where it begins to make the trip back down to sea level. Powerful electric engines are hitched alongside to pull the ship into each lock. Then, a few miles farther on, the ship enters the Pacific Ocean. To the east rise the skyscrapers of Panama City, the nation's capital and one of the first cities the Spanish founded on this continent.

The 50-mile trip takes at least 24 hours to complete, roughly two thirds of it spent waiting to enter locks. It costs about $26,000 for a ship to travel through the canal. But that's a bargain if you consider the time and expense it would require to go all the way around South America to reach that same point on the Pacific coast of Central America. Those 50 miles are nothing compared with the alternative, which is a trip of 13,000 miles!

Although it was completed over 70 years ago, the canal continues to serve the world's needs, and it remains one of the most important and amazing feats of engineering ever accomplished.

PALABRAS NUEVAS I

En el aeropuerto

la montaña

la piloto

el piloto

la ventanilla

bajar (de)

el asiento

subir (a)

el auxiliar de vuelo

la auxiliar de vuelo

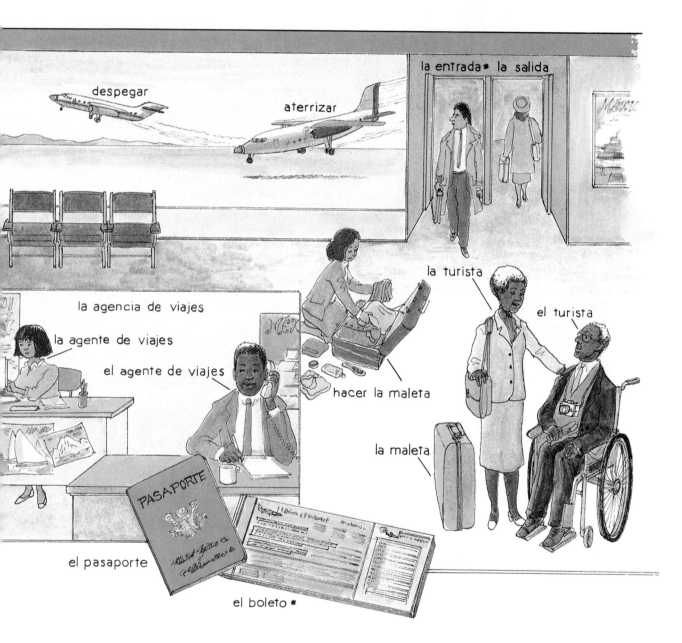

despegar

aterrizar

la entrada* la salida

la agencia de viajes

la agente de viajes

el agente de viajes

hacer la maleta

la turista

el turista

la maleta

el pasaporte

PASAPORTE

el boleto *

* *Un boleto* is a ticket for traveling. *Una entrada* is an admission ticket to a performance or an event, or to a public building such as a museum. What do you think is the literal meaning of *entrada*? What verb is it related to?

Palabras Nuevas I   **395**

1 ESTELA   ¿**En** qué **piensas**?
ANDRÉS   En mi trabajo nuevo. **Empiezo** el lunes.
ESTELA   Estás contento, ¿verdad?
ANDRÉS   Sí. Va a ser un trabajo muy agradable.

Variaciones:
- empiezo → empiezo a trabajar
- el lunes → la semana próxima

pensar en (e → ie) (yo pienso, tú piensas)   *to think about*
empezar (a + inf.) (e → ie) (yo empiezo, tú empiezas)   *to start, to begin*

2 CATALINA   ¿De quién es esta **guía** del Perú?
ENRIQUE   De mi papá. Trabaja para una agencia de viajes.

- esta guía → este mapa
- del Perú → de Puerto Rico

la guía   *guidebook*

3 ROSA   ¿Dónde **piensas** pasar **las vacaciones**?
DANIEL   En Chile, ¿y tú?
ROSA   Papá y yo **queremos** ir a Costa Rica.

- piensas → quieres
- queremos → **preferimos**
- Costa Rica → las montañas

pensar + inf.   *to plan to, to intend to*
las vacaciones   *vacation*
querer (e → ie) (yo quiero, tú quieres)   *to want*
preferir (e → ie) (yo prefiero, tú prefieres)   *to prefer*

4 CLARA   ¿Puedo **dejar** esta maleta contigo? Tengo que llamar a mi mamá.
MARIO   Sí, cómo no.
CLARA   Muchas gracias. Vuelvo muy pronto.

- maleta → mochila
- muy pronto → en un momento

dejar   *to leave (something behind)*

5 AUXILIAR DE VUELO   **Bienvenida** al **vuelo** 425. ¿Cuál es el número de su asiento?
TURISTA   El 16-F.
AUXILIAR DE VUELO   Aquí está, al lado de la ventanilla.
TURISTA   ¡Qué suerte! Puedo ver las montañas durante el vuelo.

- las montañas → los Andes
- el vuelo → **el viaje**

bienvenido, -a   *welcome*
el vuelo   *flight*

el viaje   *trip*

Notes: An additional variation you may want to use in mini-dialogue 5: *las montañas → las nubes.*

6 ALICIA   El avión va a aterrizar en **menos de** 45 minutos.
   CARLOS   No vamos a llegar **a tiempo.**
   ALICIA   Claro que sí. Eres muy **pesimista,** Carlitos.
   CARLOS   ¡Y tú eres demasiado **optimista**!

■ aterrizar → despegar
■ 45 minutos → media hora

menos de + número   *less than*
a tiempo   *in time, on time*
pesimista   *pessimistic*
optimista   *optimistic*

7 GUILLERMO   **¿Cuánto tiempo** dura el viaje?
   ROSA   Un poco **más de** dos horas.

■ más de → menos de

¿cuánto tiempo?   *how long?*
el tiempo   here: *time*
más de + número   *more than*

NOTE: The verb *pensar* has several English equivalents. When *pensar* is followed by an infinitive, it means ''to plan, to intend (to do something).'' With *en*, it means ''to think about.'' With *de*, it means ''to think of, to have an opinion about.''

¿Piensas empezar ahora?	*Do you **plan to** start now?*
¿Piensas en Elisa?	*Are you **thinking about** Elisa?*
¿Qué **piensas de** la guía?	*What do you **think of** the guidebook?*

Spanish speakers often use the verb *creer* to express an opinion.

¿Qué **piensas de** la guía?	*What do you **think of** the guidebook?*
Creo que es fabulosa.	*I **think** it's fabulous.*

PASE PARA ABORDAR
BOARDING PASS

VUELO 502
FLIGHT

FECHA 19
DATE

DESTINO
DESTINATION

ASIENTO 6A
SEAT No.

ROGAMOSLE PASAR
DE INMEDIATO A
LA SALA

PLEASE PROCEED
AT ONCE TO
GATE B

DERECHO DE
USO DEL
AEROPUERTO
$1600 00
PESOS
SALIDA
INTERNACIONAL
SERIE "B"

06977

DM2 1 089 231

MEXICANA

ACA

AEROMEXICO

Expedido por Cia. Mexicana de Aviación, S.A. de C.V.
Xola 535, México, D.F. 03100

boleto de pasajero y cupón de equipaje

EN OTRAS PARTES

También se dice *la valija*.
En México también se dice
la petaca.

También se dice *el aeromozo*.

También se dice *la azafata* y
la aeromoza.

En España se dice *el billete*.
En México, la América
Central y Colombia también
se dice *el tiquete*.

(arriba, izquierda) Turistas
en España; (arriba, derecha)
Una agencia de viajes
en Costa Rica; (derecha)
Un viaje en autobús
en Bogotá, Colombia

PRÁCTICA

A ¿Quién lo dice? Decide cuál de estas personas dice *(says)* cada *(each)* frase.

un(a) agente de viajes   una persona optimista   un(a) turista
un(a) auxiliar de vuelo   una persona pesimista

1. Está nublado. Siempre llueve cuando dejo mi paraguas en casa.
2. Señores y señoras, el piloto nos dice que el avión va a despegar en diez minutos.
3. Si Ud. va a viajar en agosto, debe comprar el boleto en mayo.
4. Ahora llueve, pero creo que más tarde va a hacer buen tiempo.
5. Vamos a llegar tarde al aeropuerto otra vez.
6. San Juan tiene playas bonitas y muchos hoteles muy cómodos.
7. Buenos días, Sr. Suárez. Aquí está su asiento.
8. Estoy siempre muy contenta con todo.
9. Pienso sacar muchas fotos durante el viaje.
10. Bienvenidos al vuelo número 507.

Práctica A
1. pesimista
2. auxiliar de vuelo
3. agente de viajes
4. optimista
5. pesimista
6. agente de viajes
7. auxiliar de vuelo
8. optimista
9. turista
10. auxiliar de vuelo

Enrichment: Students may enjoy creating other statements for the people listed in Ex. A.

B ¿Qué pasa en el aeropuerto? Contesta según los dibujos.

Práctica B
1. Lleva (dos) maletas.
2. Busca su (*or:* el) pasaporte.
3. La auxiliar de vuelo
4. El piloto

¿Adónde vas de vacaciones?
Voy a las montañas.

1. ¿Qué lleva la Sra. Muñoz?   2. ¿Qué busca el Sr. Muñoz?

3. ¿Quién espera en la entrada?   4. ¿Quién espera en la salida?

Palabras Nuevas I   **399**

5. Aterriza a las dieciséis (*or:* las cuatro de la tarde).
6. Despega. A las once (de la mañana)
7. Hay una ventanilla.
8. Hace la (*or:* su) maleta.

LLEGADAS

VUELO	DE	HORA
300	Acapulco	10:15
467	Lima	14:00
727	Los Ángeles	16:00

SALIDAS

VUELO	A	HORA
243	Nueva York	9:30
224	Toronto	11:00
777	Madrid	15:35

5. ¿A qué hora aterriza el vuelo 727?
6. ¿Aterriza o despega el vuelo 224? ¿A qué hora?

Práctica C
hago / pienso / pongo
prefiero / subimos
despega / empiezo
aterriza / bajamos

7. ¿Qué hay al lado del asiento?   8. ¿Qué hace?

Enrichment: You may want to use Ex. C as a dictation or as oral reading practice.

C En avión a San Luis. Completa cada (*each*) frase con la forma correcta del verbo apropiado (*appropriate*) de la lista.

aterrizar	empezar	poner
bajar	hacer	preferir
despegar	pensar	subir

Cuando visito a mi abuela, voy en avión. Mamá me compra el boleto, pero yo _____ las maletas. Si _____ estudiar, también _____ varios libros en la maleta. Mi mamá siempre quiere ir conmigo al aeropuerto, pero yo _____ ir solo. Los otros turistas y yo _____ al
5 avión y un poco después el avión _____. Ya en el avión, _____ a leer una revista de deportes. Menos de dos horas más tarde, el avión _____ en San Luis y todos (nosotros) _____.

Un horario de vuelos
en México

VUELO FLIGHT VOL.	SALIDA DEPARTURE DEPART	ABORDAR BOARDING EMBARON	SALA LOUNGE SALLE	PUERTA GATE SORTIE	DESTINO DESTINA
623	10:50	10:20	B	8	VERACRUZ
646	10:55	10:25	D	16	LOS ANGELES
503	11:10	10:40	B	5	ACAPULCO
481	11:20	10:50	D	17	BOGOTA --------
498	11:30	11:00	D	13	MIAMI
734	11:35	11:05	B	8	GUADALAJARA-MAZ
					MONTERREY
936	11:45	11:15	B		HERMOSILLO
688	11:45	11:15	D	15	HOUSTON-AMSTER
966	11:45	11:15	B	7	ZACATECAS-TIJUA
541	11:55	11:25	B		MERIDA-CHETUMAL
517	11:55	11:25	B		VILLAHERMOSA-T
					GUTIERREZ
804	12:00	11:30	B		GUADALAJARA-PTO
					CHICAGO
720	12:20	11:50	B		MONTERREY-SAN
201	12:30	12:00	B		ZIHUATANEJO
601	12:30	12:00	B		MERIDA
102	13:00	12:30	B		GUADALAJARA-HER
667	13:00	12:30	B		VILLAHERMOSA
309	13:05	12:35	B		ACAPULCO
904	13:05	12:35	D		ATLANTA-PROVIDE
802	13:10	12:40	B		ACAPULCO-CHICA
748	13:25	12:55	B		TAMPICO
240	13:45	13:15	B		REYNOSA
976	13:55	13:25	B		ZIHUATANEJO-PT
					SAN FRANCISCO

D Hablemos de ti.

1. ¿Tienes planes para tus vacaciones de verano? ¿Qué piensas hacer? ¿Adónde piensas ir de vacaciones este año? ¿Ayudas a hacer los planes cuando viajas con tu familia?
2. ¿Adónde fuiste de vacaciones el verano pasado? ¿Fuiste en avión? ¿Con quién fuiste?
3. ¿Qué dicen los auxiliares de vuelo cuando subes al avión? ¿Siempre son simpáticos? ¿Crees que su trabajo es interesante o aburrido? ¿Por qué?
4. ¿Eres una persona pesimista u optimista? ¿Puedes darnos ejemplos *(examples)* de tu pesimismo u optimismo?

Notes: Ask students to prepare vocabulary for this **Actividad** for homework. You may want to vary the game by having one student give the person's name, another the city, and a third the object.

Point out to students that there are places named *Florida* in Colombia, Chile, and Uruguay.

Práctica D
Answers will vary.

Practice Sheet 12–1

Workbook Exs. A–B

Tape Manual Exs. 1–2 3

Quiz 12–1

ACTIVIDAD

¡Un viaje rápido!   Form groups of four to play this word game. Players take turns saying:

(Nombre) viaja a *(ciudad)*. Lleva *(cosa)*.

Each of the three words must begin with the same letter of the alphabet. For example:

Verónica viaja a *Valencia*. Lleva una *vaca*.

A player who has difficulty thinking of something may look up a word in the *Vocabulario español-inglés* in the back of this book. Do not use the letters *Ch, K, LL, Ñ, Q, U, W, X, Y,* or *Z*. Here is a list of cities and towns you may want to use, but feel free to use others.

Asunción	Florida	La Paz	Rosario
Bogotá	Guayaquil	Montevideo	San José
Caracas	Hermosillo	Nogales	Tegucigalpa
Durango	Ibiza	Oviedo	Valparaíso
El Paso	Jaén	Pamplona	

VALENCIA

APLICACIONES Discretionary

En el aeropuerto más alto del mundo 4

El Alto, La Paz, Bolivia

El avión de Buenos Aires acaba de aterrizar en El Alto, el aeropuerto de La Paz, Bolivia. Es el aeropuerto más alto del mundo.[1] La familia Ayala baja del avión.

	SR. AYALA	¡Uf! Estas maletas son pesadísimas.[2] ¡Qué cansado
5		estoy!
	SRA. AYALA	Yo también. Esta guía de Bolivia dice que el aire aquí
		no tiene mucho oxígeno.
	LUISA	Papá, ¿es verdad que estamos en el aeropuerto más
		alto del mundo?
10	SR. AYALA	Sí, hija, no hay otro más alto.
	LUISA	Y ahora, ¿adónde vamos?
	SR. AYALA	A La Paz, la capital más alta del mundo.
	SRA. AYALA	Y mañana vamos a ir al lago Titicaca,* el . . .
	LUISA	Ya sé, mamá. El lago más alto del mundo, ¿verdad?
15	SR. AYALA	Hijita, ¿cómo adivinaste?[3]

[1]**más alto del mundo** *highest in the world*   [2]**pesadísimo, -a** *very heavy*
[3]**¿cómo adivinaste?** *how did you guess?*

* Lake Titicaca, which forms part of the boundary between Bolivia and Peru, lies at the highest point above sea level of any major lake in the world.

Notes: You may want to point out the following cognate that has not been glossed: *el oxígeno.* You may want to mention that the endings *-ísimo, -ísima* are added to emphasize an adjective. Further explanation and examples appear on p. 409.

Diálogo
1. Buenos Aires
2. en La Paz, Bolivia
3. El Alto
4. Porque el aire en La Paz no tiene mucho oxígeno (*or:* porque tiene que llevar maletas pesadísimas).
5. el lago Titicaca / entre Bolivia y el Perú
6. Answers will vary.

Preguntas

1. ¿De dónde viene la familia Ayala?   2. ¿En qué ciudad y en qué país están ellos ahora?   3. ¿Cómo se llama el aeropuerto?   4. ¿Por qué está cansado el Sr. Ayala?   5. ¿Cómo se llama el lago más alto del mundo? ¿Dónde está?   6. Imagina que escribes una guía sobre La Paz. ¿Qué vas a decir? Puedes empezar: "Bienvenidos a La Paz. Después de bajar del avión . . ."

Enrichment: Additional questions you may want to ask: *¿Qué hace la familia Ayala? (La familia baja del avión.) ¿Quién lleva las maletas? (el Sr. Ayala).*

Participación

Work with a partner to create a dialogue of six to eight lines. Imagine that you are two strangers waiting for a plane at an airport (or for a train at a station). Why is each of you traveling? Where are you going? What time does your plane take off (or your train leave)? What time will you arrive? Do you think your plane (or train) is going to be on time? Why or why not?

PRONUNCIACIÓN 5

A Pronunciation of the Spanish *j* is not like any English sound. It is a breathy sound, something like the *h* in the English word "hay," but it is made very far back in the mouth—almost in the throat.
Escucha y repite.

jamón	junio	joven	jueves
viaje	dejar	mujer	flojo

B In a few words the letter *x* has the same sound.
Escucha y repite.

Texas   México

C Before *e* and *i*, the letter *g* is pronounced just like the *j*.
Escucha y repite.

agencia   página   gimnasio   inteligente

D After *n*, the letter *g* is pronounced like the *g* in the English word "get."
Escucha y repite.

tengo   pongo   inglés

E In all other cases the letter *g* has a softer sound. The back of your tongue almost touches the roof of your mouth.
Escucha y repite.

amiga	pagar	digo	abrigo
agosto	agua	iguana	Olga

F In the groups *gue* and *gui* the *u* is not pronounced.
Escucha y repite.

guía   guitarra   Guillermo   guisantes

G Escucha y repite.
El abrigo de Jorge es rojo.
Me gusta el jugo de naranja.
Tengo un amigo en Guatemala.
Guillermo es guapo, joven, grande e inteligente.

PALABRAS NUEVAS II

CONTEXTO VISUAL

¿Quieres comprar un regalo?

If students ask: Other related words you may want to present: *el anillo de compromiso,* engagement ring; *el anillo de bodas,* wedding ring; *el diamante,* diamond; *el zafiro,* sapphire; *el rubí,* ruby; *la plata,* silver; *el oro,* gold.

8

CONTEXTO COMUNICATIVO

1 TERESA ¿Qué regalo le compro a mamá?

DAVID Esta pulsera es muy **bella.**

TERESA Pero cuesta **demasiado.**

DAVID Entonces, ¿por qué no le compras ese collar? Es **más** barato **que** la pulsera.

TERESA Tienes razón. ¿Me prestas el dinero?

bello, -a *beautiful*

demasiado here: *too much*

más + adj. + **que**
  more + adj. + *than*

Variaciones:

- muy bella → **bellísima**
- cuesta demasiado → es **carísima**
- más barato que → **menos** caro **que**

bellísimo, -a *very beautiful*

carísimo, -a *very expensive*

menos + adj. + **que**
  less + adj. + *than*

Enrichment: You may want to ask students to vary mini-dialogue 1 by changing *pulsera* to any of the other gift items pictured. Make sure all gender changes are correct.

abrir abierto, -a cerrar (e → ie) cerrado, -a

generoso, -a tacaño, -a

pobre rico, -a

2 MARIO Pedrito, ¿**qué hiciste** cuando fuiste al centro?

PEDRO Le **compré** a Sara **el** anillo **más** bonito **de** la tienda.

MARIO ¿Cuánto **pagaste**?

PEDRO Imagínate, menos de **un dólar.** Sólo pagué 99 **centavos.**

MARIO ¡Chico! ¡Qué tacaño eres!

■ hiciste → compraste
■ anillo → collar
■ ¡chico! → ¡caramba!

¿qué hiciste? *what did you (fam.) do?*

(yo) compré, (tú) compraste (from **comprar**) *bought*

el / la / los / las más + adj. + **de** *the most* + adj. + *in*

(yo) pagué, (tú) pagaste (from **pagar**) *paid*

el dólar *dollar*

el centavo *cent*

3   JUAN   ¿Cuándo van a abrir el banco?

   ELISA   Mañana. Hoy es día de fiesta. Los bancos están
           cerrados.

   JUAN   ¡Pero tengo que **cambiar** dinero!   **cambiar**   *to change, to exchange*

   ELISA   Te puedo prestar diez dólares.

   JUAN   Eres muy **amable**, Elisa. Muchas gracias.   **amable**   *kind, nice*

   ELISA   **No hay de qué**, Juan.   **no hay de qué** = de nada

■ están cerrados → no están abiertos

■ amable → generosa

■ no hay de qué → de nada

4   RAÚL   El Sr. Saldaña es **el peor** profesor de esta escuela.   **peor**   *worse*

   MAMÁ   ¿Por qué? **¿Qué hizo?**   **el / la peor** + noun   *the worst*

   RAÚL   Me dio una mala nota en geometría.   **¿qué hizo?**   *what did he / she /*
                                                     you (formal) *do?*
   MAMÁ   Pues, Raúl, tú eres el estudiante menos **serio** de la
           clase.   **serio, -a**   *serious*
                                                     mejor   *better*
■ peor → **mejor**   **el / la mejor** + noun   *the best*

   mala nota → buena nota

   menos serio → más listo

(abajo) Una vendedora de joyas en Andalucía, España

EN OTRAS PARTES

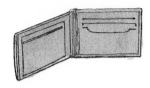

En varios países de la América del Sur se dice *la billetera*.

También se dice *la cartera*. En México se dice *la bolsa*.

En la Argentina y en el Perú se dice *los aritos* y en Venezuela se dice *los zarcillos*. También se dice *los pendientes*.

También se dice *el brazalete*.

También se dice *la sortija*.

PRÁCTICA

A ¿Qué palabra falta (is missing) aquí? Completa las frases con la palabra correcta.

1. Cuando hace calor prefiero dormir con la ventana (*abierta* / *cerrada*).
2. Martín siempre ayuda a los clientes. Es un vendedor muy (*antipático* / *amable*).
3. El tío de Elena nunca le da regalos. Es muy (*generoso* / *tacaño*).
4. Las joyas en esta tienda cuestan demasiado. Son (*bellísimas* / *carísimas*).
5. El papá de Inés tiene una casa grande en Madrid y una casa de verano en la playa. Es un hombre muy (*pobre* / *rico*).
6. Es domingo y no puedo cambiar dinero. Los bancos están (*abiertos* / *cerrados*).
7. Mi amigo Pablo siempre me presta dinero. Es una persona muy (*generosa* / *tacaña*).
8. Tomás siempre saca ceros en física. Es el (*peor* / *mejor*) alumno de la clase.
9. Después del partido, Uds. deben poner los naipes en (*la cartera* / *la caja*).
10. No puedo (*bajar del* / *subir al*) avión porque no tengo (*entrada* / *boleto*).

Práctica A
1. abierta
2. amable
3. tacaño
4. carísimas
5. rico
6. cerrados
7. generosa
8. peor
9. la caja
10. subir al / boleto

Práctica B

1. un collar / veinticinco dólares y treinta centavos
2. un anillo / ochenta y siete dólares y quince centavos
3. aretes / cincuenta y tres dólares y setenta y cinco centavos
4. (dos) pañuelos / trece dólares y setenta centavos
5. una corbata / cinco dólares y veinticinco centavos
6. un cinturón / doce dólares y cincuenta centavos
7. una cartera / cuarenta y ocho dólares y noventa y nueve centavos
8. un bolso / setenta y tres dólares y sesenta y ocho centavos
9. un reloj / catorce dólares y ochenta y cinco centavos

B ¿Qué compraste ayer?   Imagina que ayer fuiste a una tienda para comprar regalos. Pregunta y contesta según el modelo.

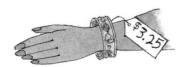

ESTUDIANTE A	*¿Qué compraste ayer?*
ESTUDIANTE B	*Compré una pulsera.*
ESTUDIANTE A	*¿Cuánto pagaste?*
ESTUDIANTE B	*(Sólo) tres dólares y veinticinco centavos.*

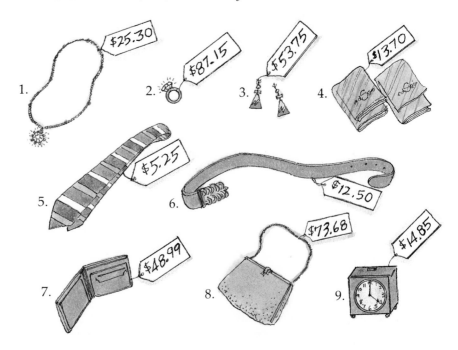

Práctica C
Answers will vary.

Practice Sheet 12–2

Workbook Exs. C–D

 9 Tape Manual Exs. 3–4

Quiz 12–2

C Hablemos de ti.

1. ¿Qué clase de regalos te gusta recibir? ¿Qué quieres recibir para tu próximo cumpleaños?
2. ¿Qué clase de regalos te gusta comprar? ¿Para quién(es) los compras? ¿Qué regalos les diste a tus padres o a tus amigos para la Navidad pasada? ¿Pagaste mucho?
3. ¿Qué haces cuando abres un regalo que no te gusta? ¿Qué le dices a la persona que te dio el regalo?
4. ¿Te gusta llevar joyas? ¿Qué joyas llevas? ¿A veces llevan corbata los muchachos de tu clase? ¿Cuándo?
5. ¿Qué hacen las personas generosas? ¿Y las personas tacañas? ¿Eres tú generoso(a) o tacaño(a)? ¿Por qué?

ESTUDIO DE PALABRAS

In Spanish we can emphasize an adjective by adding the endings *-ísimo(s)* or *-ísima(s)*. A racing car is more than *un coche rápido*; it is *un coche rapidísimo*. Because *gracias* means "thanks" and *muchas gracias* means "thanks a lot," *muchísimas gracias* means "thank you *very* much."

Enrichment: In connection with the **Estudio de palabras**, you may want to have students create original statements using the examples given.

Here are some other examples. Notice that in English we can use a lot of different words to make an adjective stronger.

un collar bellísimo	*a very beautiful necklace*
una joya carísima	*an extremely expensive jewel*
unos programas aburridísimos	*some really boring programs*
unas montañas altísimas	*some fantastically high mountains*
un chiste divertidísimo	*a terribly funny joke*
una película tontísima	*an awfully silly movie*

To retain the right pronunciation, an adjective whose last consonant is *c* or *g* changes to *qu* or *gu* before adding the *-ísimo(a)* ending: *rico, -a → riquísimo, -a; largo → larguísimo, -a.*

How do you think you might say the following in Spanish?

> It's a terribly easy test.
> It's a very fat hen.
> They're incredibly generous men.

Estudio de palabras
Es un examen facilísimo.
Es una gallina gordísima.
Son hombres generosísimos.

Joyas peruanas

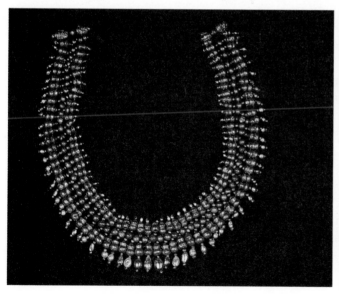

EXPLICACIONES I

Verbos con el cambio e → ie

Notes: Some forms of e → ie stem-changing verbs appear in mini-dialogues 1 and 3, p. 396.

◆ OBJECTIVES:

TO TELL ABOUT
PLANS & WHAT
YOU WANT TO DO

TO FIND OUT
WHEN SOMETHING
BEGINS

TO ARRANGE TO
BE ON TIME

You have already learned about stem-changing verbs whose stem vowel changes from *o* to *ue*. In another group of verbs the stem vowel changes from *e* to *ie* in all of the present-tense forms except *nosotros* and *vosotros*. Here are the present-tense forms of *pensar*.

INFINITIVO	**pensar**		
SINGULAR		**PLURAL**	
1	(yo) pienso	(nosotros) (nosotras) } pensamos	
2	(tú) piensas	(vosotros) (vosotras) } pensáis	
3	Ud. (él) } piensa (ella)	Uds. (ellos) } piensan (ellas)	

Notice that the endings are the same as for regular *-ar* verbs. Here are other *e* → *ie* stem-changing verbs that you know.

-AR	-ER / IR
cerrar	preferir
empezar	querer

PRÁCTICA

A ¿Qué piensan ser? Varios estudiantes hablan de sus futuras carreras (*careers*). Indica qué piensan ser. Sigue el modelo.

(tú)
Piensas ser veterinaria, ¿verdad?

1. Patricia

2. Esteban y Armando

3. Ud.

4. Horacio

5. Rosa y tú

6. Miguel y Diana

7. Ana y Gabriela

8. (tú)

9. Uds.

Práctica A

1. Piensa ser actriz.
2. Piensan ser agentes de viaje.
3. Ud. piensa ser policía.
4. Piensa ser profesor.
5. Piensan ser guardianas de zoológico.
6. Piensan ser auxiliares de vuelo.
7. Piensan ser pilotos.
8. Piensas ser fotógrafo.
9. Uds. piensan ser granjeros.

Práctica B

1. ¿Qué quiere ser (Patricia)? Creo que quiere ser actriz.
2. ¿Qué quieren ser (Esteban y Armando)? …quieren ser agentes de viaje.
3. ¿Qué quiere ser Ud.? …quiero ser policía.
4. ¿Qué quiere ser (Horacio)? …quiere ser profesor.
5. ¿Qué quieren ser (Rosa y tú)? …queremos ser guardianas de zoológico.
6. ¿Qué quieren ser (Miguel y Diana)? …quieren ser auxiliares de vuelo.
7. ¿Qué quieren ser (Ana y Gabriela)? …quieren ser pilotos.
8. ¿Qué quieres ser? …quiero ser fotógrafo(a).
9. ¿Qué quieren ser Uds.? …queremos ser granjeros.

Práctica C

Answers will vary but should follow the model.

B **¿Qué quieren ser?** Usa los elementos de la Práctica A para preguntar y contestar según el modelo.

> ESTUDIANTE A *¿Qué quieres ser?*
> ESTUDIANTE B *Creo que quiero ser veterinaria.*

C **Mucho más.** Ester siempre exagera *(exaggerates)* todo. Escoge *(choose)* de la lista un adjetivo apropiado *(appropriate)* para preguntar y contestar. Sigue el modelo.

> mi trabajo
> ESTUDIANTE A *¿En qué piensas?*
> ESTUDIANTE B *Pienso en mi trabajo.*
> ESTUDIANTE A *¿Es difícil?*
> ESTUDIANTE B *Dificilísimo.*

1. mis notas de álgebra
2. los chistes de Mario
3. mi perro Bruno
4. mi película favorita
5. el novio de Silvia
6. la canción nueva de los "Rockeros"
7. mis aretes nuevos
8. los árboles de mi jardín
9. el anillo que vi en la tienda
10. los dibujos animados que vi anoche

alto
bello
bueno
caro
difícil
divertido
guapo
inteligente
malo
tonto

Práctica D
1. ¿Cuándo empieza el partido de fútbol? A las cinco y media. Pero nosotros preferimos llegar a las cinco.
2. ¿Cuándo empiezan las clases? A las ocho y media. Pero los estudiantes prefieren llegar a las ocho.
3. ¿Cuándo empieza...? A las tres. Pero prefiero llegar a las dos y media.
4. ¿Cuándo empieza...? A las diez y media. Pero... prefiere llegar a las diez.
5. ¿Cuándo empieza...? A las nueve y media. Pero... prefieren llegar a las nueve.
6. ¿Cuándo empieza...? A las diez. Pero...prefiere llegar a las nueve y media.
7. ¿Cuándo empiezan...? A la una y media. Pero... preferimos llegar a la una.
8. ¿Cuándo empieza...? A las cuatro. Pero...prefiere llegar a las tres y media.
9. ¿Cuándo empiezan (ellos)? A la una. Pero prefiero llegar a las doce y media.
10. ¿Cuándo empezamos...? A las ocho. Pero...prefieren llegar a las siete y media.

Práctica E
Answers will vary.

Practice Sheet 12–3

Workbook Exs. E–F

 10 Tape Manual
Ex. 5

 11 Refrán

Activity Master 12–1

Quiz 12–3

D Siempre temprano. Hay personas que siempre quieren llegar media hora antes. Pregunta y contesta según el modelo.

> el concierto / 8:30 / Elena y yo
> ESTUDIANTE A   ¿Cuándo empieza el concierto?
> ESTUDIANTE B   A las ocho y media. Pero Elena y yo preferimos llegar a las ocho.

1. el partido de fútbol / 5:30 / (nosotros)
2. las clases / 8:30 / los estudiantes
3. la obra de teatro / 3:00 / (yo)
4. la película de terror / 10:30 / todo el mundo
5. la fiesta / 9:30 / las chicas
6. la cena / 10:00 / Esperanza
7. los exámenes / 1:30 / Rafael y yo
8. el baile / 4:00 / Cristóbal
9. (ellos) / 1:00 / (yo)
10. (nosotros) / 8:00 / unos invitados

E Hablemos de ti.

1. ¿Qué piensas de las materias que estudias este año? ¿Cuáles prefieres? ¿Por qué?
2. ¿Dan nuevos programas de televisión este año? ¿Qué piensas de ellos? ¿Son estupendos? ¿Son aburridos? ¿Cuáles prefieres?
3. ¿A qué hora empieza tu programa de televisión favorito? ¿Cuánto tiempo dura? ¿Hay muchos anuncios comerciales durante el programa?
4. ¿A qué hora abren los almacenes en tu ciudad? ¿A qué hora cierran? ¿Están abiertos los domingos? ¿Hay tiendas o supermercados que nunca cierran? ¿Cuáles?
5. ¿Qué piensas hacer esta noche?

ACTIVIDAD

¿Qué piensas hacer?   Form groups of three or five students. (If possible, groups should be of uneven numbers.) One person begins by saying what he or she plans to do, and why. The next person responds with a sentence that expresses a different point of view. For example:

> ESTUDIANTE A   Pienso viajar a las montañas porque allí hace fresco.
> ESTUDIANTE B   Prefiero viajar a la playa porque hace calor.

The next person makes up a new sentence. For example:

> ESTUDIANTE C   Pienso comer en un buen restaurante porque soy rico.
> ESTUDIANTE D   Prefiero comer en casa porque soy tacaño.

APLICACIONES

Discretionary

¡Bienvenidos al Ecuador! 12

Ver para creer.[1] Pero a menudo creemos en cosas que no podemos ver. El ecuador[2] es una de ellas, porque es una línea imaginaria. Pero nadie dice que no existe. El Ecuador es también el nombre de un país de la América del Sur. Tiene ese nombre
5 porque esa línea imaginaria pasa por[3] él. El ecuador pasa cerca de Quito, la capital, y también pasa por la ciudad de San Antonio.

En la ciudad de San Antonio está el museo Solar. En este museo hay instrumentos para estudiar el sol y el ecuador. Una entrada del museo está en el hemisferio sur,[4] y la otra está en el
10 hemisferio norte. ¡Imagínate! Dentro de un momento puedes caminar de un hemisferio al otro.

¿Hay otras atracciones en el Ecuador? ¡Por supuesto! Por ejemplo, puedes visitar muchos mercados indios.[5] El mercado más conocido e importante está en Otavalo. Todos los sábados los
15 indios caminan grandes distancias para vender sus productos allí. Llevan trajes de muchos bellos colores. Los hombres llevan ponchos azules y rojos y las mujeres, faldas rojas, anaranjadas, verdes o moradas.

También debemos hablar de los famosos "sombreros de
20 Panamá," esos sombreros que empezaron[6] a ser populares en los Estados Unidos durante la construcción del canal de Panamá. Pues no son de Panamá. Los hacen aquí, en el Ecuador.

---

[1]**ver para creer** *seeing is believing* [2]**el ecuador** *equator* [3]**pasar por** *to pass through* [4]**el hemisferio sur / norte** *Southern / Northern Hemisphere* [5]**indio, -a** *Indian* [6]**empezaron** *began*

Preguntas

1. ¿Qué es el ecuador?
2. ¿Dónde está el museo Solar?
3. ¿Qué encuentras allí?
4. ¿Dónde están las entradas del museo?
5. ¿Por qué es conocida la ciudad de Otavalo?
6. ¿En qué día hay mercado allí?
7. ¿Por qué los "sombreros de Panamá" tienen ese nombre?
8. ¿Qué quiere decir "ver para creer"? ¿Qué crees tú? ¿Es difícil creer en una cosa si no puedes verla?

ANTES DE LEER

As you read, look for the answers to these questions.
1. ¿De dónde viene el nombre del país?
2. ¿Cuál es la gran atracción del museo Solar?
3. ¿De dónde vienen los "sombreros de Panamá"?

Preguntas
1. una línea imaginaria
2. en San Antonio, Ecuador
3. instrumentos para estudiar el sol y el ecuador
4. Una (entrada) está en el hemisferio sur y la otra en el hemisferio norte.
5. Porque un mercado indio importante está allá.
6. (todos) los sábados
7. Porque empezaron a ser populares durante la construcción del canal de Panamá.
8. Answers will vary.

Antes de leer
1. del ecuador, una línea imaginaria que pasa por él
2. Hay instrumentos para estudiar el sol y el ecuador allí.
3. del Ecuador

Aplicaciones **413**

EXPLICACIONES II

Notes: You may want to point out that comparisons appear in mini-dialogues 1, p. 404; 2, p. 405; and 4, p. 406.

Comparativos y superlativos

◆ **OBJECTIVES:**

TO MAKE COMPARISONS

TO STATE OPINIONS

TO TAKE AN OPINION POLL

Note how we make comparisons in Spanish.

Ana   Luz   Eva

Ana es **alta.**   Luz es **más alta que** Ana.   Eva es **la** chica **más alta.**

Remember that adjectives must agree with their nouns. For example:

Marco   Luz   Inés   Eva

Marco es **alto.**   Luz e Inés son **más altas que él.**   Eva es **la más alta.**

1 To say that someone or something is the "most" or the "best" in a group, we use *de.*

Eva es **la** muchacha **más lista de** la clase.	Eva is **the smartest** girl **in** the class.
Jorge e Inés son **los** estudiantes **más listos de** la escuela.	Jorge and Inés are **the smartest** students **in** the school.

2 We use *menos* in the same way that we use *más.*

El Sr. Brujo es **muy** tacaño.	Mr. Brujo is **very** stingy.
Nadie es **menos** generoso que él.	No one's **less** generous than he (is).
Es la persona **menos generosa de** la ciudad.	He's **the least generous** person **in** town.

3 The adjectives *bueno, malo, viejo,* and *joven* have irregular comparative and superlative forms.

ADJETIVO		COMPARATIVO	ADJETIVO		COMPARATIVO
bueno	→	**mejor**	viejo	→	**mayor**
malo	→	**peor**	joven	→	**menor**

Note that their masculine and feminine forms are the same, and they all add *-es* to form the plural.

Esta fruta es **buena (mala).**   *This fruit is **good (bad).***
La naranja es **mejor (peor).**   *The orange is **better (worse).***
Las manzanas son **las mejores**   *The apples are **the best***
(peores).   *(the worst).*

El Sr. Díaz es **viejo (joven).**   *Mr. Díaz is **old (young).***
Su hermano es **mayor (menor).**   *His brother is **older (younger).***
Su hermana es **la mayor**   *His sister is **the oldest***
(menor).   *(the youngest).*

4 When we use *más* or *menos* with numbers, we use *de* to mean "than".

La película dura **más de tres**   *The film lasts **more than three***
horas.   *hours.*
Tengo **menos de 50** centavos.   *I have **less than 50** cents.*

PRÁCTICA

A Más o menos.   Contesta las preguntas según los dibujos. Usa frases completas.

1. ¿Cuál es el animal más pequeño?
2. ¿Cuál es el animal más alto?
3. ¿Cuál es el animal más gordo?

4. ¿Cuál es el programa más triste?
5. ¿Cuál es el programa más aburrido?
6. ¿Cuál es el programa menos serio?

Tomás   Pedro   Carlos

Práctica B

1. Guillermo es más pesimista que Lola. ...Yo creo que es menos pesimista.
2. El Sr. García es más amable que el Sr. Fuentes. ...Yo creo que es menos amable.
3. El café Roma es más caro que el café París. ...Yo creo que es menos caro.
4. Este programa es más importante que las noticias. ...Yo creo que es menos importante.
5. Carlota es más seria que yo. ...Yo creo que es menos seria.
6. Las muchachas son más inteligentes que los muchachos. ...Yo creo que son menos inteligentes.
7. Esperanza es más generosa que su hermana. ...Yo creo que es menos generosa.
8. Los tigres son más bonitos que los leopardos. ...Yo creo que son menos bonitos.
9. El béisbol es más divertido que el fútbol. ...Yo creo que es menos divertido.
10. Los hijos son más optimistas que sus padres. ...Yo creo que son menos optimistas.

Práctica C
Answers will vary but should follow the model.

Enrichment: Have students work in pairs or small groups to make additional comparisons using the adjectives listed in Ex. C.

7. ¿Quién es el chico más bajo?
8. ¿Quién es el chico más delgado?
9. ¿Quién es el chico más alto?

B Opiniones diferentes. Hay personas que nunca están de acuerdo *(in agreement).* Sigue el modelo.

Las películas románticas / divertido / las películas del oeste
ESTUDIANTE A *Las películas románticas son más divertidas que las películas del oeste.*
ESTUDIANTE B *Al contrario. Yo creo que son menos divertidas.*

1. Guillermo / pesimista / Lola
2. el Sr. García / amable / el Sr. Fuentes
3. el café Roma / caro / el café París
4. este programa / importante / las noticias
5. Carlota / serio / yo
6. las muchachas / inteligente / los muchachos
7. Esperanza / generoso / su hermana
8. los tigres / bonito / los leopardos
9. el béisbol / divertido / el fútbol
10. los hijos / optimista / sus padres

C ¿Qué crees tú? Escoge adjetivos de la lista a la derecha para hacer comparaciones con *más* y *menos.* Sigue el modelo.

autobuses/taxis
Creo que los autobuses son más lentos (menos cómodos) que los taxis.

1. barcos / aviones
2. cerdos / gatos
3. muchachos / muchachas
4. revistas / libros
5. caballos / cebras
6. ajedrez / damas
7. biología / química
8. campo / ciudad
9. dibujos animados / películas policíacas
10. noticias / anuncios comerciales
11. coches grandes / coches pequeños

aburrido   hermoso
agradable   incómodo
cómodo   inteligente
difícil   interesante
divertido   lento
fácil   limpio
gordo   rápido
guapo   sucio

D **¿Cuál es la respuesta?**   El Sr. Montoya quiere ver si sus alumnos son listos, y les da unos acertijos *(riddles)*. Contesta las preguntas.

1. Raúl tiene trece años. Esteban, su hermano mayor, tiene dos años menos que Pablo. ¿Quién es el mayor de los tres? ¿Tiene Pablo más o menos de quince años?
2. Teresa es mayor que María. Si Carlos es mayor que la hermana mayor de Teresa, ¿quién es el menor de los cuatro?
3. Ricardo tiene doce años. Marta tiene tres años más que Pilar. Pilar tiene dos años menos que Ricardo. ¿Quién es el menor? ¿Quién es el mayor? ¿Tiene Pilar más o menos de once años?
4. La Sra. Pereda es menor que su esposo. Si el Sr. Pereda es menor que sus tres hermanos, ¿es la Sra. Pereda mayor que los hermanos de su esposo?

E   **La encuesta.**   Imagina que haces una encuesta *(survey)* en tu clase sobre varias cosas. Pregunta y contesta según el modelo.

> equipo de béisbol
>
> ESTUDIANTE A   *¿Cuál es el mejor equipo de béisbol?*
> ESTUDIANTE B   *Para mí, el mejor equipo es ____.*
> ESTUDIANTE A   *¿Cuál es el peor equipo?*
> ESTUDIANTE B   *Para mí, el peor equipo es ____.*

1. película del año
2. programa de televisión
3. anuncio comercial
4. revista
5. día de la semana
6. grupo de rock
7. canal de televisión
8. estación del año
9. restaurante de la ciudad
10. clase del día

En Barcelona, España

Explicaciones II   **417**

El pretérito de los verbos que terminan en *-ar*: Formas singulares

◆ **OBJECTIVE:**

TO DESCRIBE PURCHASES MADE AND HOW MUCH THEY COST

Until now we have been using most verbs only in the present tense. One of the past tenses in Spanish is called the preterite. We use it to talk about actions or events that occurred at a particular time and have now ended. Here are the singular preterite forms of the verbs *comprar* and *pagar*.

INFINITIVO **comprar**

1	(yo)	compré	*I bought*
2	(tú)	compraste	*you bought*
3	Ud. (él) (ella)	compró	*you (formal) bought* *he bought* *she bought*

INFINITIVO **pagar**

1	(yo)	pagué	*I paid*
2	(tú)	pagaste	*you paid*
3	Ud. (él) (ella)	pagó	*you (formal) paid* *he paid* *she paid*

¿**Compraste** el regalo ayer?   ***Did you buy*** *the gift yesterday?*
Sí. **Pagué** diez dólares.   *Yes. I **paid** $10.00.*

Just as in the present tense, the preterite endings *-é, -aste,* and *-ó* indicate which person has done the action. Notice the written accents on all except the *tú* form. Also notice the difference between the *yo* forms of *comprar* and *pagar*. Verbs whose infinitives end in *-gar* have *-ué* in the *yo* form of the preterite.

Notes: You may want to point out the singular forms of the preterite of *-ar* verbs as presented in mini-dialogue 2, p. 405.

Reteach / Extra Help: Initiate pair work or a chain drill: *¿Qué compraste el sábado? Compré ____. ¿Cuánto pagaste? Pagué ____.*

PRÁCTICA

A Y tú, ¿qué compraste?
Varias personas hablan de cosas que acaban de comprar. Pregunta y contesta según el modelo.

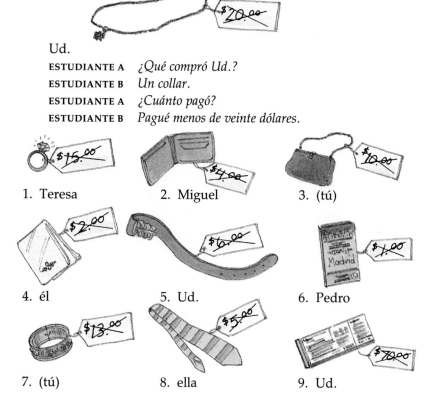

Ud.

ESTUDIANTE A	*¿Qué compró Ud.?*
ESTUDIANTE B	*Un collar.*
ESTUDIANTE A	*¿Cuánto pagó?*
ESTUDIANTE B	*Pagué menos de veinte dólares.*

1. Teresa   2. Miguel   3. (tú)

4. él   5. Ud.   6. Pedro

7. (tú)   8. ella   9. Ud.

B Hablemos de ti.
1. ¿Fuiste de compras el fin de semana pasado? ¿Qué compraste? ¿Cuánto pagaste?
2. ¿Fuiste al cine? ¿Qué película viste? ¿Cuánto pagaste por la entrada?
3. ¿Cuál es el mejor día de la semana para ti? ¿Cuál es el peor día? ¿Por qué?
4. ¿Cuál es el día de fiesta más importante del año para ti? ¿Por qué?
5. ¿Quién es la persona mayor de tu familia? ¿Quién es la persona menor? ¿Cuántos años tienen ellas?
6. ¿Cuáles son las clases más interesantes de tu colegio? ¿Cuáles son las menos interesantes? ¿Por qué?
7. ¿Cuáles son las clases más difíciles? ¿Y las más fáciles? ¿Generalmente sacas buenas notas en las clases fáciles? ¿Son mejores o peores tus notas en las clases más difíciles?

Práctica A
1. ¿Qué compró Teresa? Un anillo. ¿Cuánto pagó? Pagó menos de quince dólares.
2. ¿Qué compró Miguel? Una cartera. ¿Cuánto pagó? Pagó menos de cuatro dólares.
3. ¿Qué compraste? Un bolso. ¿Cuánto pagaste? Pagué menos de diez dólares.
4. ¿Qué compró él? Un pañuelo. ¿Cuánto pagó? Pagó menos de dos dólares.
5. ¿Qué compró Ud.? Un cinturón. ¿Cuánto pagó? Pagué menos de seis dólares.
6. ¿Qué compró Pedro? Una guía (de Madrid). ¿Cuánto pagó? Pagó menos de un dólar.
7. ¿Qué compraste? Una pulsera. ¿Cuánto pagaste? Pagué menos de trece dólares.
8. ¿Qué compró ella? Una corbata. ¿Cuánto pagó? Pagó menos de cinco dólares.
9. ¿Qué compró Ud.? Un boleto. ¿Cuánto pagó? Pagué menos de setenta dólares.

Práctica B
Answers will vary.

Practice Sheet 12–5

Workbook Exs. G–J

Tape Manual Ex. 7 14

Activity Master 12–2

Quiz 12–5

APLICACIONES

Notes: Answers to the **Repaso** and **Tema** appear in the pre-chapter teacher pages.

REPASO

Notes: Review of:
1. *hizo / hiciste*
   adverbs of past time
2. singular preterite of
   comprar + para
   possessive adjectives
3. *creer que*
   comparative of adjectives
4. *e → ie* stem-changing
   verbs + infinitive
5. noun phrases with *de*
   decir que
   superlative of adjectives
   + de

En la Argentina

Look carefully at the model sentences. Then put the English cues into Spanish to form new sentences based on the models.

1. *¿Qué hizo la Srta. Gómez el mes pasado?*
   (What did Carlos do last year?)
   (What did you (fam.) do last winter?)
   (What did you (fam.) do last Thursday?)

2. *Compré un cinturón para mi papá.*
   (I bought a ring for my girlfriend.)
   (You (fam.) bought a handkerchief for your sister.)
   (You (formal) bought a wallet for your grandmother.)

3. *Pero ahora creo que los aretes son más fabulosos que el anillo.*
   (But now they think that Ana is nicer than David.)
   (But today we think that Diego is more pessimistic than Cristina.)
   (But now you (fam.) think that the wallet is better than the purse.)

4. *Piensan abrir esa caja.*
   (I plan to change ten dollars.)
   (We want to close our books.)
   (They want to leave their suitcases.)

5. *El auxiliar de vuelo dice que es el asiento más cómodo del avión.*
   (The plane's pilot says it's the highest mountain in Colombia.)
   (The travel agents say they're the stingiest tourists in the city.)
   (The flight attendant (fem.) says it's the fastest plane in the country.)

Put the English captions into Spanish.

1. What did Mr. Ruiz do last week?

2. He bought a bracelet for his wife.

3. But today he thinks that the necklace is more beautiful than the bracelet.

4. He intends to buy another present.

5. Mrs. Ruiz says he's the most generous man in town (in the city).

REDACCIÓN

Enrichment: You may want to ask students to share what they have written for the **Redacción** with the class, either by reading aloud or by putting their work up on the bulletin board.

Now you are ready to write your own dialogue or paragraph. Choose one of the following topics.

1. Expand the story in the *Tema* by writing a paragraph about Mr. and Mrs. Ruiz. What are they like? How old are they? Are they rich or poor? Generous or stingy? Does Mrs. Ruiz want to get a lot of expensive presents? What kinds of presents does she give to her husband? What does she plan to give him for his next birthday? What did she give him for his last birthday?

2. Create a thought ballon to show what Mr. Ruiz is thinking in each picture. Write one or two sentences for each balloon.

3. Write a paragraph about a shopping trip you went on. Say whether you went to a small store or a large one. Describe what you bought. Did you buy it for yourself or did you give it to someone? How much did you pay?

COMPRUEBA TU PROGRESO   CAPÍTULO 12   Discretionary

Notes: Answers to the **Comprueba** appear in the pre-chapter teacher pages.

A   Lo contrario
Rewrite each sentence, replacing the word in italics with a word that means the opposite.

1. El avión *aterriza* a las nueve.
2. ¿A qué hora *termina* el programa?
3. El Sr. Torres es una persona muy *pesimista*.
4. ¿Me esperas cerca de la *salida*?
5. ¿Puede Ud. *abrir* la ventana, por favor?
6. Yo soy *mayor* que mi hermano.
7. La familia de Ernesto es muy *pobre*.
8. La Srta. Rosario es la cliente más *generosa* de esta tienda.
9. ¿Quién es el *mejor* piloto?

B   Completa las frases
Complete each sentence with the correct form of the verb in parentheses.

1. ¿Qué vuelo ＿＿＿ los turistas?   *(preferir)*
2. Ellos ＿＿＿ las puertas a las cinco.   *(cerrar)*
3. Papá, ¿cuándo ＿＿＿ hacer las maletas?   *(pensar)*
4. (Nosotros) ＿＿＿ hablar con la agente de viajes.   *(querer)*
5. ¿En qué ＿＿＿ Uds.?   *(pensar)*
6. ¿A qué hora ＿＿＿ la película?   *(empezar)*
7. Ud. ＿＿＿ pronto la tienda, ¿verdad?   *(cerrar)*
8. (Nosotros) ＿＿＿ dejar a los perros en casa.   *(preferir)*

C   Más que
Compare the following using the adjectives given. Follow the model.

> este collar y esa pulsera / bello
> *Este collar es más bello que esa pulsera.*

1. esta corbata y ese cinturón / barato
2. la auxiliar de vuelo y el piloto / amable
3. el vuelo 807 y el vuelo 813 / rápido
4. la Argentina y el Uruguay / grande
5. Graciela y Elisa / tacaño
6. el asiento 22C y el asiento 25A / cómodo

7. esta cartera y ese bolso / caro
8. el fútbol y el béisbol / divertido

D   ¿Cuál es tu opinión?
Use the cue in parentheses to answer each question. Follow the model.

> El Alto es un aeropuerto muy alto, ¿verdad? (América del Sur)
> *Sí, es el aeropuerto más alto de la América del Sur.*

1. El Rialto es un cine caro, ¿verdad? (barrio)
2. El desayuno es una comida importante, ¿verdad? (día)
3. Beatriz es una alumna inteligente, ¿verdad? (clase)
4. Los tigres son animales hermosos, ¿verdad? (zoológico)
5. La Sra. Clemente es una profesora muy seria, ¿verdad? (escuela)
6. El Sr. Guillén es una persona amable, ¿verdad? (agencia de viajes)
7. Madrid es una ciudad grande, ¿verdad? (España)
8. Juan Galán es un buen actor, ¿verdad? (televisión)
9. *Mi cerdo y yo* es una película muy mala, ¿verdad? (año)
10. Rosa es una niña muy joven, ¿verdad? (escuela)

E   ¡Qué caro!
Complete the dialogue with the preterite form of the verb in parentheses.

SUSANA   Ayer (yo) *(comprar)* una cartera.
LUIS   ¿Dónde la *(comprar)* (tú)?
SUSANA   En la tienda "Regalos para todos."
LUIS   ¿Ah, sí? Mi mamá *(comprar)* un bolso allí. ¿Cuánto *(pagar)* (tú)?
SUSANA   (Yo) *(pagar)* más de veinte dólares.
LUIS   Creo que (tú) *(pagar)* demasiado. Mi mamá sólo *(pagar)* 18 dólares por un bolso muy hermoso.

Chapter 12 Test   Listening Comprehension Test

Workbook Review: Chapters 9–12   Cumulative Test: Chapters 9–12

VOCABULARIO DEL CAPÍTULO 12

Sustantivos
la agencia de viajes
el/la agente de viajes
el anillo
el arete
el asiento
el/la auxiliar de vuelo
el boleto
el bolso
la caja
la cartera
el centavo
el cinturón, *pl.* los cinturones
el/la cliente
el collar
la corbata
el dólar
la entrada *(entrance)*
la guía
las joyas
la maleta
la montaña
el pañuelo
el pasaporte
el/la piloto
la pulsera
el regalo
la salida
el tiempo *(time)*
el/la turista
las vacaciones
la ventanilla
el viaje
el vuelo

Adjetivos
abierto, -a
amable
bellísimo, -a
bello, -a
bienvenido, -a
carísimo, -a
cerrado, -a
generoso, -a
mejor
optimista
peor
pesimista
pobre
rico, -a
serio, -a
tacaño, -a

Verbos
abrir
aterrizar
bajar (de)
cambiar
cerrar (e → ie)
dejar
despegar
empezar (a + *inf.*) (e → ie)
pensar (+ *inf.* / en / de) (e → ie)
preferir (e → ie)
querer (e → ie)
subir (a)

Adverbio
demasiado *(too much)*

Expresiones
a tiempo
¿cuánto tiempo?
el / la / los / las más + *adj.*
el / la / los / las menos + *adj.*
hacer la maleta
más + *adj.* + que
más de (+ *número*)
menos + *adj.* + que
menos de (+ *número*)
no hay de qué
¿qué hiciste?
¿qué hizo?

CAPÍTULO 13

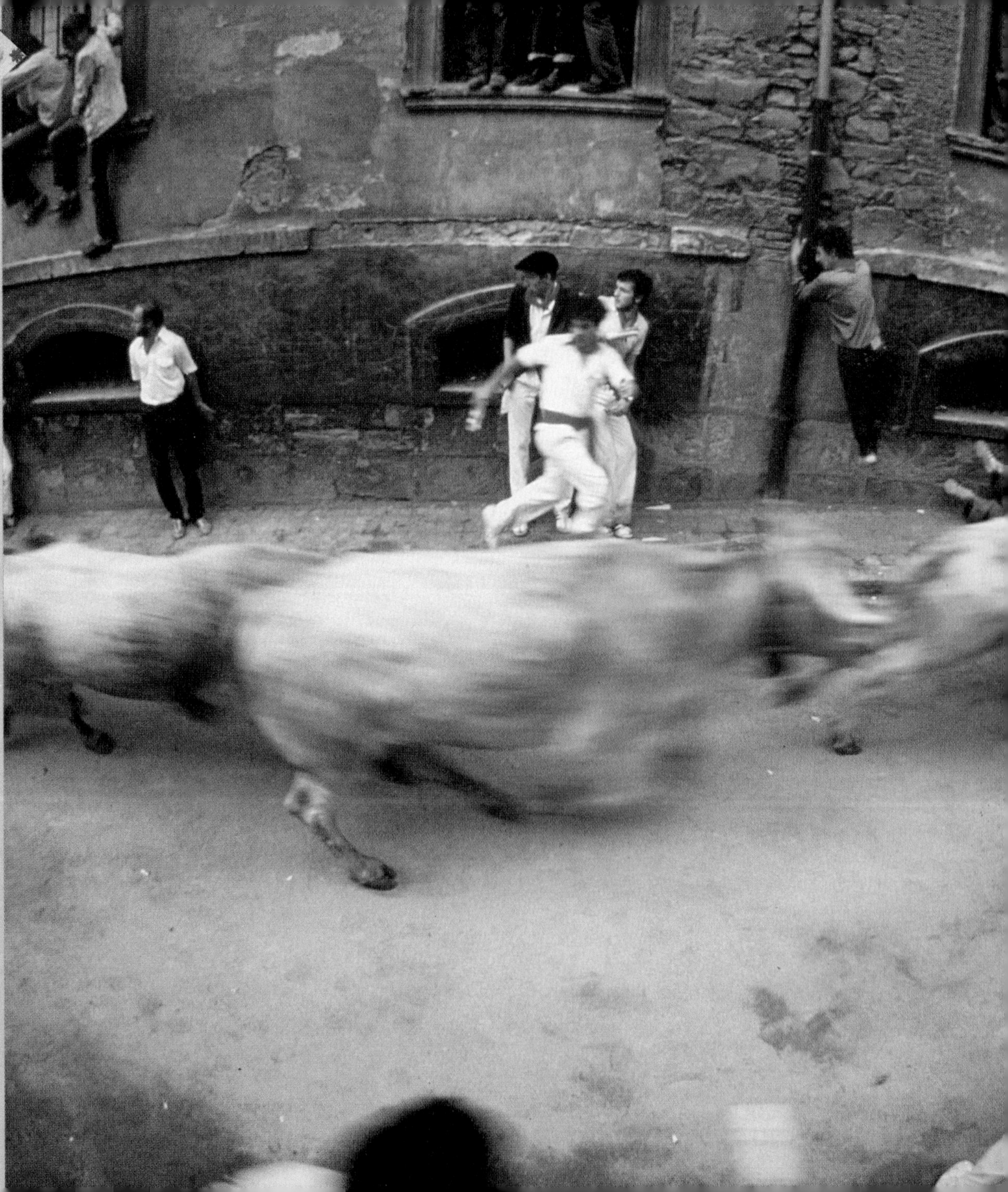

LAS FIESTAS DE SAN FERMÍN

Do you like fireworks, parades, amusement-park rides? All of these are part of the celebration of *las fiestas de San Fermín*. In Pamplona, Spain, exactly at midnight on July 7, fireworks explode high above the crowded central plaza, and the week-long festival in honor of the city's patron saint begins.

At seven o'clock every morning, six bulls are released on the narrow main street. Many young people who dream of becoming *toreros* (bullfighters)—and others who simply enjoy the thrill—have their chance to be chased by the bulls. They must also run for their lives, of course. These are the bulls that will appear in that day's *corridas* (bullfights), and they are on their way to the *plaza de toros* (bullring), a half mile away.

Every morning thousands of men and women dressed in white and wearing red berets and sashes dance in the streets to the music of flutes and drums. On San Fermín Day, a long religious procession begins at the cathedral, winds slowly among the dancers, and then returns to its starting point.

Villagers and tourists participate in contests of strength, watch a parade of costumed figures on stilts, attend outdoor concerts, or dance *la jota*, the traditional folk dance of northern Spain. Crowds are everywhere, but especially at the late afternoon *corridas*. After the last *corrida*, about 7:30 P.M., the crowds spill out into the streets. The evening celebrations reach their peak at midnight with a burst of fireworks, but a noisy amusement park with dozens of rides stays open until three or four o'clock every morning.

After the week's final bullfight, the musicians pass through the streets playing dirges to signal the end of the festival. The celebration is over, and normal life returns to Pamplona for another year.

425

PALABRAS NUEVAS I

En el restaurante

1

Transparency 53
**CONTEXTO
VISUAL**

If students ask: Other related words you may want to present: *la comida típica*, typical food; *el entremés / aperitivo*, appetizer; *la entrada*, entrée.

- el arroz
- el pescado
- el camarero
- el bistec
- la chuleta de cerdo
- la chuleta de cordero
- la camarera
- el vino
- el menú
- la tortilla española
- el pastel
- la naranjada
- la empanada
- la paella
- la sopa
- el flan
- el gazpacho

[1]*Gazpacho* is a cold Spanish soup made with tomatoes, cucumbers, sweet peppers, onion, garlic, and olive oil.

[2]*Pescado* refers to fish that has been caught; *pez* refers only to live fish.

[3]*Paella* is a Spanish dish that includes rice, vegetables, chicken, seafood, sausage, and spices.

[4]A *tortilla española* is made with eggs, potatoes, onions, and olive oil.

[5]*Flan* is baked caramel custard and is a very popular dessert in Spanish-speaking countries.

caliente

frío, -a

el chile

el chile relleno

lleno, -a

vacío, -a

la cuenta

CONTEXTO COMUNICATIVO 2

Reteach / Review: You may want to ask students to expand mini-dialogue 1 by adding two final lines for Ester and Oscar about what to order for dessert.

1 ÓSCAR En este restaurante **sirven** un gazpacho **delicioso.**

ESTER ¡Qué bueno! Entonces voy a **pedir*** gazpacho y un bistec con una ensalada de tomates. ¿Y tú?

ÓSCAR Yo voy a pedir chuletas de cerdo con arroz. Aquí las **preparan** muy bien.

Variaciones:
- un bistec → pescado **frito**
- de tomates → de lechuga
- de cerdo → de cordero

servir (e → i) (yo sirvo, tú sirves) *to serve*

delicioso, -a *delicious*

pedir (e → i) (yo pido, tú pides) *to ask for, to order*

preparar *to prepare*

frito, -a *fried*

2 ALBERTO Camarero, ¿me puede traer un vaso de agua fría, por favor? ¡Este chile está muy **picante**!

CAMARERO ¡Cómo no, señor!

- un vaso de agua fría → una botella de agua mineral
- este chile → esta sopa

picante *spicy, hot (highly spiced)*

Notes: Make sure students understand the difference between *caliente* and *picante.*

3 ÓSCAR ¿Qué vas a beber? ¿Un refresco?

ESTER No, no quiero **ningún** refresco ahora. Y tú, ¿qué pides?

ÓSCAR Una naranjada fría.

- ningún refresco → ninguna **bebida**

ningún, ninguna *no, not any* (adj.)

la bebida *drink, beverage*

* Note that *pedir* means ''to ask for'' or ''to order'' something. *Preguntar* means ''to ask'' (a question) or ''to inquire'' about something.

4 CAMARERO ¿Qué desea Ud. **de postre,** señorita?

RITA Por favor, ¿me puede decir otra vez qué postres hay?

CAMARERO Hay helado y flan.

RITA No quiero **ninguno,** gracias.

CAMARERO ¿Le sirvo el café entonces?

RITA Sí, por favor.

- decir otra vez → **repetir**
- helado y flan → frutas y queso

el postre *dessert*
de postre *for dessert*

ninguno, -a *none, (not) any*
(pron.)

repetir (e → i) (yo repito, tú repites) *to repeat*

5 ALICIA ¿Cuánto es la cuenta?

RICARDO Cuarenta dólares.

ALICIA Más seis **de propina,** ¿no?

RICARDO Voy a dejarle ocho.

- voy a → quiero

Enrichment: Ask students to expand Ricardo's last line in mini-dialogue 5, explaining why he is going to leave a larger tip. For example: *La comida fue deliciosa* or *El camarero fue muy bueno.*

la propina *tip*
de propina *for a tip*

Culture: You may want to ask students to do research and give brief oral reports on typical foods from Spanish-speaking countries.

If there is an inexpensive restaurant in your city that serves food typical of that eaten in Spanish-speaking countries, you may want to take your students there on a field trip.

EN OTRAS PARTES

En España se dice *la carta, la minuta* y *la lista de platos.*

En la América Latina se dice también *el mesero, la mesera.* También se dice *el mozo, la moza.*

En la Argentina se dice *el bife.* También se dice *el bisté* y *el biftec.*

También se dice *la chuleta de puerco.*

También se dice *el ají.*

También se dice *la torta* y *el bizcocho.*

PRÁCTICA

A En un restaurante. A menudo el camarero te pregunta cómo está la comida. ¿Qué le contestas? Pregunta y contesta según el modelo. Escoge (*choose*) tus respuestas de la lista.

ESTUDIANTE A   *¿Cómo están los burritos?*
ESTUDIANTE B   *Bastante buenos.*

muy   ⎫   delicioso
bastante ⎬   bueno

demasiado ⎫
muy   ⎬   ⎧ caliente
bastante ⎪   ⎨ frío
un poco   ⎭   ⎩ picante

1.

2.

3.

4.

5.

6.

7.

8.

9.

10.

11.

12.

Práctica A
Responses to questions will vary but adjectival agreement must be made.
1. ¿Cómo está la sopa?
2. ¿Cómo están los chiles rellenos?
3. ¿Cómo está el pescado?
4. ¿Cómo está la paella?
5. ¿Cómo está el pollo?
6. ¿Cómo están las empanadas?
7. ¿Cómo está el pastel?
8. ¿Cómo está la tortilla española?
9. ¿Cómo está el arroz?
10. ¿Cómo está la chuleta de cordero?
11. ¿Cómo está el bistec?
12. ¿Cómo están las chuletas de cerdo?

En Galicia, España

LA PIZZA

Nuestra famosa pizza es más que una pizza ordinaria. Nosotros fuimos los primeros en introducir esta pizza en Inglaterra en 1977. Desde entonces nuestro menú y comida han sido copiados por muchos imitadores. Nosotros creemos que somos los mejores. Por favor permítanos de 20 a 30 minutos para preparar su pizza. Se necesita algo de tiempo para preparar esta maravilla, pero creemos que Ud. estará de acuerdo en que vale la pena esperar por ella. Una pizza mediana es suficiente para dos personas. Una grande sirve de 3 a 4 personas.
No se preocupe si no se la puede terminar le proveeremos de una bolsa para que se la pueda llevar a casa.

	Individual	Mediana 2 Personas	Grande 3-4 Personas
Queso	400 Pts.	795 Pts.	1.275 Pts.
Queso y Champiñones	475 Pts.	895 Pts.	1.410 Pts.
Queso y Salchicha (nuestra especialidad)			
Queso y Chorizo	495 Pts.	980 Pts.	1.550 Pts.
Salchicha o Chorizo	490 Pts.	980 Pts.	1.550 Pts.
CADA PORCION EXTRA DE:			
o Anchoas	100 Pts.	185 Pts.	275 Pts.
Pimiento verde o Champiñones o Cebolla o Queso 75 Pts.	100 Pts.	135 Pts.	

Servicios e impuestos incluidos

Práctica B
Answers will vary.

Práctica C
Answers will vary.

En un restaurante
en Madrid

B   En el restaurante y en casa.   Dos amigos hablan de la comida que
piden en un restaurante y de la clase de comida que sirven en casa.
Pregunta y contesta según los modelos.

	EN UN RESTAURANTE	EN CASA
ESTUDIANTE A	¿Qué pides en un restaurante?	¿Generalmente qué sirves en casa?
ESTUDIANTE B	A menudo pido _____.	A menudo sirvo _____.
ESTUDIANTE A	¿Qué bebida pides?	¿Qué bebida sirves?
ESTUDIANTE B	Pido _____.	Sirvo _____.
ESTUDIANTE A	¿Y qué pides de postre?	¿Y qué sirves de postre?
ESTUDIANTE B	Pido _____.	Sirvo _____.

agua mineral	flan	pasteles
bistec con papas fritas	frutas y queso	pavo
café	gazpacho	pescado frito
carne con guisantes	hamburguesas	pollo frito
chile con carne	helado	sopa de cebolla
chiles rellenos	jugo de manzana	sopa de tomate
chuletas de cerdo	jugo de tomate	sopa de pollo
chuletas de cordero	leche	tacos
empanadas	naranjada	té
ensalada de lechuga	paella	yogur

Reteach / Review: You may want to change *en un restaurante* to *en _____* using the names of fast-food restaurants popular among your students.

C   Hablemos de ti.

1. ¿A veces comes comida mexicana o española? ¿En tu casa o en un restaurante? ¿Te gusta mucho? ¿Por qué?
2. ¿Qué te gusta más, el bistec o las chuletas de cordero? ¿O prefieres las hamburguesas? ¿Qué pones en las hamburguesas?
3. ¿Cuál es tu bebida fría favorita? ¿Y tu bebida caliente favorita?
4. ¿Te gusta la sopa? ¿Qué clase de sopa prefieres? ¿La sopa de tomate? ¿La sopa de cebolla? ¿De verduras? ¿De pollo?
5. Cuando comes en un restaurante, ¿qué pides de postre? ¿A veces preparas postres? ¿Qué postres preparas?
6. En un restaurante, si recibes una cuenta de diez dólares, ¿cuánto debes dejar de propina? ¿Cuánto dejas si la cuenta es de cinco dólares?

Enrichment: Additional questions for Ex. C: *¿Dónde te gusta comer con tus amigos? ¿Por qué? ¿Dónde te gusta comer con tu familia? ¿Por qué?*

ACTIVIDAD

Tu restaurante. Pretend that you and a partner are opening your own restaurant. Think of a name for it, and plan the menu. Include two or three soups, some meat and fish dishes, several salads and vegetables, desserts, and beverages. Be sure to include the prices (in dollars and cents). Keep your menu. You will be using it again later.

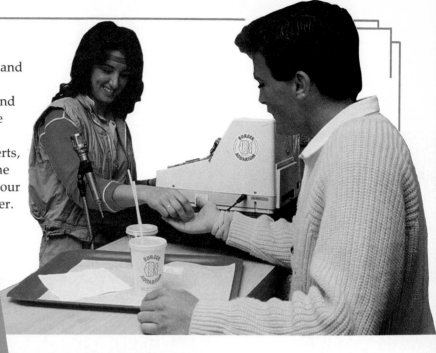

(arriba, izquierda) En Puerto Rico; (abajo, derecha) Un restaurante en Barcelona, España

Enrichment: You may want students to prepare posters and TV commercials to advertise their imaginary restaurants from the **Actividad.**

Palabras Nuevas I   431

APLICACIONES

Discretionary

En "La China Cubana" 6

Estamos en Nueva York. Dos amigos, uno latinoamericano y la otra norteamericana, leen el menú del restaurante "La China Cubana."

     LUISA   ¡Qué hambre tengo!

5   GABRIEL   ¿Qué clase de comida sirven aquí, china[1] o cubana?

     LUISA   Es un restaurante chino cubano. Muchos chinos cubanos de La Habana tienen ahora restaurantes en Nueva York. Aquí podemos comer comida china o cubana.

10   GABRIEL   Entonces, voy a pedir ropa vieja.[2] Me encanta.

  (Llega el camarero.)

  CAMARERO   Buenas noches. ¿Qué van a pedir?

     LUISA   Yo, boliche mechado[3] con arroz blanco, y un té. De postre, flan.

15   GABRIEL   Para mí, ropa vieja, por favor.

  CAMARERO   Hoy no hay ropa vieja. Hay chuletas de cerdo, bistec, pescado frito, . . .

  GABRIEL   Entonces, un bistec con arroz amarillo, frijoles negros y plátanos con mucho ajo.[4] Otro día pido comida
20   china.

---

[1]**chino, -a** *Chinese*   [2]**ropa vieja** *shredded beef with tomatoes, onions, and peppers*   [3]**boliche mechado** *Cuban pot roast*   [4]**el ajo** *garlic*

Preguntas

Contesta según el diálogo.
1. ¿Dónde están los amigos? ¿En qué ciudad?   2. ¿Qué clase de restaurante es?   3. ¿Qué hacen Gabriel y Luisa?   4. ¿Qué pide Luisa? ¿Qué pide de postre? ¿Qué quiere beber?   5. ¿Qué pide Gabriel primero?   6. ¿Qué pide después?   7. ¿Qué es la ropa vieja?   8. ¿Te gusta la comida china? Cuando vas a un restaurante chino, ¿qué pides generalmente?

Una familia cubana en Miami

Diálogo
1. En un restaurante / en Nueva York.
2. Chino cubano.
3. Leen el menú / piden comida.
4. Boliche mechado con arroz blanco / flan / un té.
5. Ropa vieja.
6. Bistec con arroz amarillo, frijoles negros y plátanos.
7. Es carne con tomates, cebollas y chiles.
8. Answers will vary.

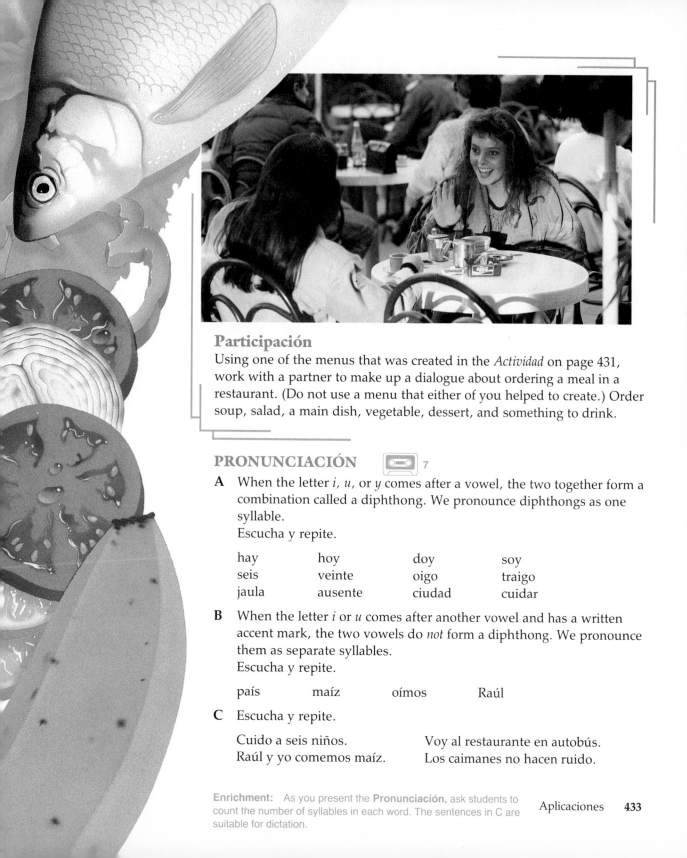

Participación

Using one of the menus that was created in the *Actividad* on page 431, work with a partner to make up a dialogue about ordering a meal in a restaurant. (Do not use a menu that either of you helped to create.) Order soup, salad, a main dish, vegetable, dessert, and something to drink.

PRONUNCIACIÓN 　7

A When the letter *i*, *u*, or *y* comes after a vowel, the two together form a combination called a diphthong. We pronounce diphthongs as one syllable.
Escucha y repite.

hay	hoy	doy	soy
seis	veinte	oigo	traigo
jaula	ausente	ciudad	cuidar

B When the letter *i* or *u* comes after another vowel and has a written accent mark, the two vowels do *not* form a diphthong. We pronounce them as separate syllables.
Escucha y repite.

país	maíz	oímos	Raúl

C Escucha y repite.

Cuido a seis niños.　　　　Voy al restaurante en autobús.
Raúl y yo comemos maíz.　　Los caimanes no hacen ruido.

Aplicaciones　**433**

PALABRAS NUEVAS II

No hay fiesta sin disfraz

los fuegos artificiales

los dulces

el rey   la reina

la máscara

el diablo

el fantasma

**CONTEXTO
COMUNICATIVO**   9

1   Para mí **la celebración** más **emocionante** es **el carnaval.**
Cada año lo **celebramos** con **fiestas de disfraces,** desfiles y
fuegos artificiales. En las plazas y en los parques hay grupos
que tocan música **folklórica** y **gente** que baila y canta toda la
noche.

Variaciones:
■ la celebración → la fiesta
■ emocionante → divertida
■ desfiles → conciertos
■ folklórica → popular

la celebración, pl. **las
   celebraciones**   *celebration*
emocionante   *exciting, thrilling*
el carnaval   *carnival, Mardi Gras*
cada   *each, every*
celebrar   *to celebrate*
la fiesta de disfraces   *costume
   party*
el disfraz, pl. **los disfraces**
   costume, disguise
folklórico, -a   *folk*
la gente   *people*

434   Capítulo 13

If students ask: Other related words
you may want to present: *el trono,*
throne; *la carroza,* float; *la banda,* band.

el desfile

el torero

la torera

la corrida (de toros)

la piñata

decorar

la decoración
pl. las decoraciones

romper

2 RAÚL   Hoy es un día **perfecto** para el desfile. ¿Quieres ir
        conmigo?

  ROSA   No sé . . . las calles ya están **llenas de gente,** y
        creo que va a **llover.**

  RAÚL   ¡Ay, chica, qué pesimista eres!

- perfecto → magnífico
- perfecto → estupendo
- el desfile → la celebración
- llover → **nevar**

perfecto, -a *perfect*

lleno, -a de gente *crowded*
llover (o → ue) *to rain*

nevar (e → ie) *to snow*

Enrichment: In connection with mini-dialogue 2, you may want to ask students
to expand Raúl's last line by having him try to convince Rosa to go with him.

Palabras Nuevas II   **435**

3 **MÓNICA**   ¿Qué disfraz vas a llevar para carnaval?

    NORMA   Voy **vestida de** reina.

    MÓNICA   ¡No me digas! ¡Yo también!

- carnaval → el desfile
- reina → torera
- ¡no me digas! → ¡caramba!

4 **PAPÁ**   Gabi, ¿cuándo **llegaste** a casa?

    GABRIELA   A las cinco.

    PAPÁ   Pues, yo llegué a las cinco también y no te vi.

    GABRIELA   Tal vez porque **luego** fui al mercado. Compré unos comestibles para la cena.

- cuándo → a qué hora
- luego → después
- mercado → supermercado
- comestibles → pasteles

vestido, -a de *dressed as*

Notes: Make sure students omit the indefinite article with the expression *vestido, -a de*: *vestida de torera.*

(yo) llegué, (tú) llegaste, (Ud., él, ella) llegó (from **llegar**) *arrived*

luego *then, later*

EN OTRAS PARTES

También se dice *los carnavales.*

PRÁCTICA

A **¿De qué vas vestido?** Imagina que vas a una fiesta de disfraces. ¿De qué vas vestido(a)? Sigue el modelo.

Práctica A
1. Voy vestida de torera.
2. Voy vestido(a) de fantasma.
3. Voy vestido de rey.
4. Voy vestida de reina.
5. Voy vestido(a) de diablo.
6. Voy vestido de camarero.

 Voy vestido(a) de toro.

1.

2.

3.

4.

5.

6.

Carnaval en Corrientes, Argentina

Práctica B
1. romper / dulces
2. pastel
3. fantasmas
4. decoraciones
5. fuegos artificiales
6. disfraz
7. corrida
8. decorar

Práctica C
1. ... a las siete ...
   ... a las ocho.
2. ... a las siete y media ... .
   ... a las diez.
3. ... a las nueve menos
   cuarto ...
   ... a las nueve.
4. ... a las ocho menos
   cuarto ...
   ... a las ocho.
5. ... a las diez ...
   ... a las once.

Práctica D
Answers will vary.

El desfile de la Revolución
Mexicana, México

B Celebraciones. Completa cada frase con la palabra correcta.

1. Vamos a ver si los niños pueden *(romper / servir)* la piñata. Está llena de *(dulces / gente)*.
2. De postre voy a pedir *(una propina / un pastel)*.
3. ¿Por qué tienes miedo de los *(fantasmas / pañuelos)*?
4. Los niños ponen *(decoraciones / desfiles)* en el árbol de Navidad.
5. ¿Viste los *(fuegos artificiales / ruidos)* anoche?
6. ¿Qué *(desfile / disfraz)* vas a llevar para este carnaval?
7. El torero no está preparado todavía para la *(corrida / máscara)*.
8. Cada persona trae flores para *(decorar / limpiar)* la plaza.

C ¿A qué hora? Imagina que tienes un trabajo nuevo y que tu jefe *(boss)* dice que llegas tarde a veces. ¿Qué le dices? Sigue el modelo.

ESTUDIANTE A *Llego a las ocho, generalmente.*
ESTUDIANTE B *No es verdad. Ayer llegaste a las ocho y cuarto.*
ESTUDIANTE A *Pues, hoy llegué a tiempo.*

1. 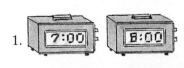 2.

3.  4.

5.

D Hablemos de ti.

1. ¿Cuáles son tus días de fiesta favoritos? ¿Por qué? ¿Cómo celebras esos días?
2. ¿Qué hacen los niños en "Halloween"? ¿Llevas tú disfraz en "Halloween"? ¿De qué vas vestido(a)? ¿Viste disfraces interesantes el "Halloween" pasado? ¿Cuáles?
3. ¿A veces vas a fiestas de disfraces? ¿Qué llevas?
4. ¿A qué hora llegaste a la escuela ayer? ¿Y esta mañana? ¿Generalmente llegas a tiempo?

ESTUDIO DE PALABRAS

Have you noticed that some nouns that end in *-ción* are closely related to certain verbs? For example:

celebrar   la celebración
decorar   la decoración

Two other verbs in this chapter are related to nouns ending in *-ción:*

preparar   la preparación
repetir   la repetición

Can you make nouns ending in *-ción* from these verbs?

continuar   durar   invitar   presentar

What verbs do you think are related to these nouns?

conversación   educación   participación   pronunciación

Estudio de palabras
continuación, duración, invitación, presentación; conversar, educar, participar, pronunciar

PROG

Lejos de nosotros aquella Villa que allá por el siglo XI conociera el pocero y labrador Isidro donde laborara, ayudado por algún que otro angel entre fuentes, huertas y sembrados.

La gran urbe que es hoy la Villa del Oso y el Madroño, se prepara una vez más para conmemorar las fiestas en honor a su santo patrón y protector Isidro.

Las fiestas son ante todo un acontecimiento colectivo y popular. No hay fiestas sin pueblos ni pueblos sin fiestas y los madrileños saben echar el resto de modo singular y personal cuando llegan las suyas.

Estos últimos años de transformación y cambio Madrid ganó las calles y las plazas y supo transformarse en una ciudad en la que tradición y modernismo se dan la mano para ser lo que fue una Villa hospitalaria, fraternal y pacífica con un pie en el pasado, otro en el futuro y el corazón abierto sin reservas a un presente rico en novedades.

Que este Madrid festivo sea una vez más ejemplo de sana alegría, exponte diversión, asombro de propios y extraños y espejo donde se miren otros pueblos deseosos de ser protagonistas como el nuestro.

Que estas Fiestas que publicamos sean motivo de franca colaboración y hermanamiento entre vecinos, muestra de vitalidad entusiasmo y amor a la ciudad.

Con los mejores deseos de que el humor no falte y de que tengamos la fiesta en paz un cariñoso saludo de este vecino y Alcalde.

ALCALDE DE MADRID

JUAN A. BARRANCO GALLARDO

Plaza Mayor

9-18 de Mayo San Isidr

Teatro Real

Martes, día 13
22,30 h. - **VICTORIA DE LOS ANGELES**
Miercoles, día 14
22,30 h. - **NARCISO YEPES**
Jueves, día 15
19,00 h. - **NICANOR ZABALETA**
Viernes, día 16
22,30 h. - **ENRIQUE MORENTE Y ANTONIO ROBLEDO: "FANTASIA DE CANTE JONDO PARA VOZ FLAMENCA Y ORQUESTA".**

PATROCINADO POR:
HIDROELECTRICA ESPAÑOLA
IBERDUERO

Auditorio de la C. de Campo

Sábado, día 10
22,30 h. - **THE KINKS**

Domingo, día 11
21,00 h. - **BARRICADA ROSENDO BURNING**
Lunes, día 12
21,00 h. - **LA POLLA RECOR BELLA BESTIA OBUS**

(arriba, derecha) Un desfile puertorriqueño en Nueva York; (derecha) Fiestas de abril en Sevilla

Enrichment: Additional verbs you may want to present: *declarar, contaminar, imitar.*

Notes: Mini-dialogue 3 on
p. 427 gives an example of a
present-tense form of *pedir;*
1 on p. 427 and 4 on p. 428
illustrate *servir; repetir* appears
in mini-dialogue 4 on p. 428.

EXPLICACIONES I

Verbos con el cambio *e → i*

◆ **OBJECTIVES:**

   **TO ORDER
   DESSERT IN A
   RESTAURANT**

   **TO CONVINCE
   OTHERS**

   TO GIVE REASONS

   **TO MAKE SMALL
   TALK WHILE
   EATING OUT**

Enrichment: Reinforce the
present-tense forms of *pedir,
servir,* and *repetir* by asking
these questions: *¿Qué pides
para el desayuno? ¿Qué sirves
en las fiestas? ¿Repites mucho
en esta clase?* Answers will
vary.

You have already learned two types of stem-changing verbs. One type is like *contar (o → ue)*. Another type is like *pensar (e → ie)*. There is a third type in which the *e* in the stem changes to *i* in all of the present-tense forms except *nosotros* and *vosotros. Pedir* ("to ask for") is an example of this type.

INFINITIVO	**pedir**		
	SINGULAR	PLURAL	
1	(yo) pido	(nosotros) (nosotras) } pedimos	
2	(tú) pides	(vosotros) (vosotras) } pedís	
3	Ud. (él) } pide (ella)	Uds. (ellos) } piden (ellas)	

The infinitives of all *e → i* verbs end in *-ir*. Two verbs of this type that you know are *servir* ("to serve") and *repetir* ("to repeat"). Watch out with *repetir!* It is the second *e* that changes: *(yo) repito.*

Piden huevos fritos con jamón.	*They're ordering fried eggs with ham.*
El Burrito Loco **sirve** comida mexicana.	*El Burrito Loco serves Mexican food.*
El profesor **repite** cada pregunta.	*The teacher repeats every question.*

PRÁCTICA

A ¿Qué piden de postre? Escoge *(choose)* un postre para cada persona y pregunta y contesta según el modelo.

> Jorge y tú
> **ESTUDIANTE A** *¿Qué piden Jorge y tú?*
> **ESTUDIANTE B** *Siempre pedimos naranjas.*

1. Mario y Yolanda
2. Ester
3. Alicia
4. (tú)
5. Catalina y tú
6. la profesora
7. Uds.
8. Miguel y Silvia

Menú de Postres

Manzanas
Plátanos
Naranjas
Ensalada de frutas
Pastel de limón
Pastel de chocolate
Pastel de zanahoria
Pastel de queso
Flan
Yogur con fruta
Helado de chocolate

B Y tú, ¿qué sirves? Imagina que los profesores y estudiantes hacen una feria *(fair)* de comida internacional. En cada puesto *(booth)* hay una clase de comida diferente. Escoge elementos de cada lista para preguntar y contestar.

> Ud.
> **ESTUDIANTE A** *¿Qué sirve Ud.?*
> **ESTUDIANTE B** *Sirvo gazpacho.*
> **ESTUDIANTE A** *¿Cómo está?*
> **ESTUDIANTE B** *Delicioso.*

1. Pilar	chile con carne	delicioso
2. Roberto y Alicia	chiles rellenos	estupendo
3. Pepe y tú	chocolate con churros	fabuloso
4. (tú)	chuletas de cordero	muy bueno
5. Andrés	empanadas argentinas	un poco picante
6. Carolina	frijoles negros con arroz	
7. Luis y Pilar	gazpacho	
8. Uds.	paella	
9. Juan y Ana	pasteles de maíz	
	pescado frito	
	pollo con cebolla	
	tortillas de maíz y frijoles	

Reteach / Extra Help: After students do Ex. A, you may want to expand the practice by asking students to use the subjects in the exercise to ask questions *(¿Piden Jorge y tú naranjas?)* and answer negatively *(No, nunca pedimos naranjas).*

Práctica A
1. ¿Qué piden Mario y Yolanda? Piden…
2. ¿Qué pide Ester? Pide…
3. ¿Qué pide Alicia? Pide…
4. ¿Qué pides (tú)? Pido…
5. ¿Qué piden Catalina y tú? Pedimos…
6. ¿Qué pide la profesora? Pide…
7. ¿Qué piden Uds.? Pedimos…
8. ¿Qué piden Miguel y Silvia? Piden…

Práctica B
1. ¿Qué sirve…? Sirve…
2. ¿Qué sirven…? Sirven…
3. ¿Qué sirven…? Servimos…
4. ¿Qué sirves…? Sirvo…
5. ¿Qué sirve…? Sirve…
6. ¿Qué sirve…? Sirve…
7. ¿Qué sirven…? Sirven…
8. ¿Qué sirven…? Servimos…
9. ¿Qué sirven…? Sirven…

C Repite, por favor. Escoge la frase correcta de la columna de la derecha para hacer diálogos como el modelo.

¿(tú) / la respuesta?

ESTUDIANTE A *¿Por qué repites la respuesta?*

ESTUDIANTE B *Porque los otros no pueden oírme.*

¿POR QUÉ?	PORQUE
1. ¿Víctor / el cuento?	a. los chicos quieren oírlo otra vez
2. ¿(tú) / todo?	b. tienen que estudiarlos
3. ¿ellos / los verbos?	c. nadie los comprende
4. ¿Uds. / las palabras?	d. debemos aprenderlas
5. ¿Felipe / los chistes?	e. los otros no pueden oírme
6. ¿Carolina / la canción?	f. no está en la guía telefónica
7 ¿Ud. / la dirección?	g. nadie me escucha
8. ¿(tú) / el poema?	h. todos quieren escucharla otra vez
	i. tengo que aprenderlo de memoria

D ¿Pedir o preguntar? Gustavo y su familia están en un café. ¿Qué piden? ¿Qué preguntan? Completa las frases con la forma correcta de *pedir* o *preguntar*.

1. Julia _____ una botella de agua mineral.
2. Mi hermanita _____ dónde está el baño.
3. Mamá y yo _____ refrescos de limón.
4. Papá _____ pan con mantequilla.
5. Georgina _____ dónde están las servilletas.
6. Yo _____ si hay pastel de manzana.
7. Mi tío _____ qué sopa sirven hoy.
8. Nosotros le _____ la cuenta al camarero.
9. Mamá _____ cuánto tenemos que dejar de propina.
10. Mi hermano _____ un tenedor y un cuchillo.

Reteach / Review: In preparation for Ex. D, refer students to the note on p. 427. You may want to ask volunteers to model the first few items and explain their answers.

Un restaurante en Torremolinos, España

Palabras negativas

You know how to make negative sentences. You just put *no* in front of the verb.

> **No quiero** preparar sopa.   *I **don't want** to prepare soup.*
> Mario **no pide** el menú.   *Mario **doesn't ask for** the menu.*

♦ **OBJECTIVES:**
TO DENY
TO EXPRESS NEGATIVE REACTIONS
TO COMPLAIN

There are other negative words that you know: *nada* ("nothing"), *nunca* ("never"), *nadie* ("nobody"), *ningún, ninguna* ("not any"), and *tampoco* ("neither"). Notice how we use them:

> **No** bailo **nunca.** ⎫
> **Nunca bailo.**   ⎬   *I **never** dance.*
> **No** tengo **nada.**   *I **don't** have **anything.***
> **Nadie** llega a tiempo.   ***No one** arrives on time.*
> Yo **no** lo comprendo **tampoco.**   *I **don't** understand it **either.***

Sometimes we can put the negative word before the verb and leave out the *no*. But if the negative word comes after the verb, we must use *no* or another negative word before the verb.

> **Nunca** habla con **nadie.**   *He **never** speaks to **anyone.***
> **No** compra **nada.**   *He **doesn't** buy **anything.***

1 *Ningún, ninguna* is an adjective, so it must agree with the noun it modifies.

> **No** hay **ninguna** bebida en el menú.   *There are **no** drinks on the menu.*
>
> **No** tengo **ningún** anillo.   *I **don't** have **any** rings.*

We usually use *ningún, ninguna* in the singular, even when in English we would use the plural.

2 *Ninguno, -a* is a pronoun meaning "none" or "not any." It always agrees with the noun to which it refers.

> **Ninguno** de los niños duerme.   ***None** of the children is sleeping.*
> **No** comprendo **ninguna** de las respuestas.   *I **don't** understand **any** of the answers.*

Notes: Refer to mini-dialogue 3 on p. 427 for an example of the adjective *ningún*; 4 on p. 428 illustrates the pronoun *ninguno*.

3 When *nadie* is the direct object of a verb, we use the personal *a*. When *ninguno(a)* refers to people and is used as a direct object, we also use the personal *a*.

No veo **a nadie.** *I don't see **anyone.***
No veo **a ninguno** de los camareros. *I don't see **any** of the waiters.*

PRÁCTICA

A ¡Nada! Héctor siempre contesta negativamente. Ahora está con un amigo en un restaurante. Contesta con la palabra negativa correcta: *nunca, nadie, nada, ninguno o ninguna.* Sigue el modelo.

ESTUDIANTE A *¿Qué haces?*
ESTUDIANTE B *Nada.*

1. ¿Qué pides?
2. ¿Quién sirve aquí?
3. ¿Cuándo vuelve el camarero?
4. ¿Qué celebras hoy?
5. ¿Cuántos menús tienes?
6. ¿Cuándo vas a empezar?
7. ¿Qué bebidas te gustan?
8. ¿Quién paga la cuenta?
9. ¿Qué traen los camareros?
10. ¿Qué postre vas a pedir?
11. ¿Cuánto dejas de propina?
12. ¿Cuándo vas a volver aquí?

B ¡No hago nada! Ahora contesta las preguntas en Práctica A con *no* y la palabra negativa correcta. Sigue el modelo.

ESTUDIANTE A *¿Qué haces?*
ESTUDIANTE B *No hago nada.*

C Una celebración importante. Elena y sus amigos celebran el carnaval con una fiesta de disfraces. Completa cada frase con *ningún, ninguna o ninguno.*

1. _____ de estos disfraces es perfecto.
2. Mamá llegó pero no trae _____ disfraz de fantasma.
3. La sala está demasiado vacía, no tiene _____ decoración.
4. No hay _____ problema. Voy a comprar decoraciones de carnaval.
5. Luego voy a comprar naranjada. No hay _____ bebida.
6. ¡Cuidado! No queremos romper _____ de los vasos.
7. No tenemos _____ máscara de diablo.
8. No tengo _____ disco de bailes folklóricos.
9. Creo que _____ de los estudiantes viene vestido de rey.
10. No llegó _____ invitado todavía.

Práctica A
1. Nada.
2. Nadie.
3. Nunca.
4. Nada.
5. Ninguno.
6. Nunca.
7. Ninguna.
8. Nadie.
9. Nada.
10. Ninguno.
11. Nada.
12. Nunca.

Práctica B
1. No pido nada.
2. No sirve nadie (*or:* Nadie sirve).
3. No vuelve nunca.
4. No celebro nada.
5. No tengo ninguno (ningún menú).
6. No empiezo (*or:* No voy a empezar) nunca.
7. No me gusta ninguna (bebida).
8. No la paga nadie (*or:* Nadie la paga).
9. No traen nada.
10. No voy a pedir ninguno (ningún postre).
11. No dejo nada.
12. No voy a volver (*or:* No vuelvo) nunca.

Práctica C
1. Ninguno
2. ningún
3. ninguna
4. ningún
5. ninguna
6. ninguno
7. ninguna
8. ningún
9. ninguno
10. ningún

D Hablemos de ti.

1. ¿Cuándo estás aburrido(a)? ¿Duermes en tus clases a veces?
2. ¿Qué te gusta comer cuando vuelves a casa después de la escuela? ¿Qué haces cuando no hay nada en el refrigerador?
3. ¿Cocinas a veces? ¿Qué cocinas? ¿Te gusta también quitar los platos y lavarlos?
4. ¿A quiénes piensas llamar por teléfono esta noche? ¿Con quiénes piensas salir? ¿Qué piensas hacer?

Práctica D
Answers will vary.

Practice Sheet 13–4

Workbook Exs. E–F

Tape Manual Ex. 6   12

Refrán   13

Activity Master 13–1

Quiz 13–4

ACTIVIDAD

Nadie y nunca   Working with a partner, make a list of five things you never do and five things no one does. Take turns asking each other *¿Qué cosas no haces nunca?* and *¿Qué cosas no hace nadie?* For example:

> ¿Qué cosas no haces nunca? Nunca duermo en la clase.
> ¿Qué cosas no hace nadie? Nadie come sombreros.

Then join another pair of students and take turns sharing the answers you have come up with.

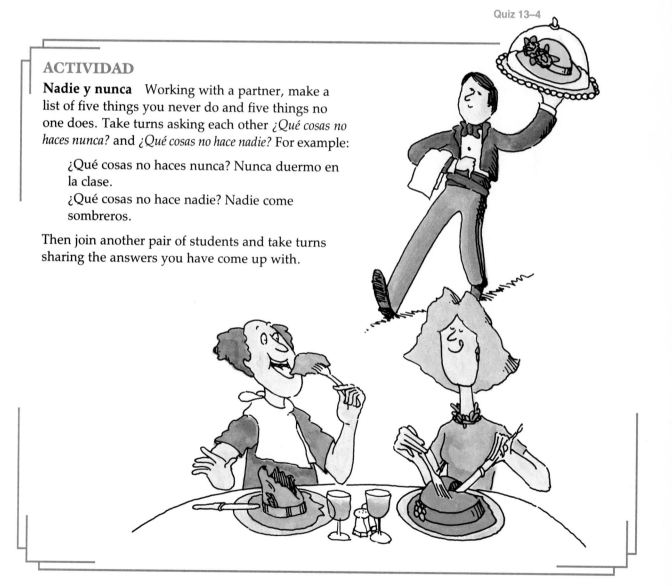

APLICACIONES Discretionary

Notes: Sample dialogues for the **¿Qué pasa?** appear in the pre-chapter teacher pages.

El desfile   Transparency 55

La calle está llena de gente. Hay un gran desfile. ¿Qué clase de disfraces hay? ¿Cuál es la fecha? ¿A qué hora empieza la corrida?

Andrea has just found David. Make up a dialogue in which she asks him what time he got to the parade, which costume he likes best, and whether he plans to go to the bullfight afterward. You may want to use these words or phrases:

celebración	emocionante	luego
fuegos artificiales	vestido(a) de	llegué / llegaste

EXPLICACIONES II

El pretérito de *comer* y *salir*

Notes: Before presenting the singular preterite forms of *comer* and *salir*, you may want to review the preterite forms of *-ar* verbs introduced on p. 418.

You have learned the singular forms of regular *-ar* verbs in the preterite tense: *(yo) compré, (tú) compraste, Ud. (él, ella) compró.* Here are the singular preterite forms of *comer* and *salir*.

◆ **OBJECTIVES:**

TO TELL WHAT YOU ATE

TO FIND OUT AND RELATE ARRIVAL AND DEPARTURE TIMES

TO ACCOUNT FOR YOUR WHEREABOUTS

TO RELATE WHAT HAPPENED AT A SPECIFIC TIME

INFINITIVO	**comer**	
1 (yo)	**comí**	*I ate*
2 (tú)	**comiste**	*you ate*
3 Ud. (él) (ella)	**comió**	*you (formal) ate* / *he ate* / *she ate*

INFINITIVO	**salir**	
1 (yo)	**salí**	*I left*
2 (tú)	**saliste**	*you left*
3 Ud. (él) (ella)	**salió**	*you (formal) left* / *he left* / *she left*

-Er and *-ir* verbs that are regular in the preterite take the same set of endings. Like *-ar* verbs, they have a written accent on all singular forms except the *tú* form.

¿**Comiste** el pescado?   *Did you eat the fish?*
Ricardo **salió** con ella.   *Ricardo went out with her.*

Although *salir* has an irregular *yo* form in the present tense *(salgo),* it is regular in the preterite *(salí).*

PRÁCTICA

A ¿**Qué comiste?** ¿Qué comió cada chico(a) para el desayuno? Pregunta y contesta según el modelo.

Práctica A
All answers will follow the model exactly.

> queso
> ESTUDIANTE A   *¿Qué comiste?*
> ESTUDIANTE B   *Comí queso.*

1. yogur
2. bistec
3. churros
4. huevos fritos
5. ensalada de fruta
6. huevos con jamón
7. jamón
8. una manzana con queso
9. pan tostado con mermelada

Práctica B
Answers will follow the model with final phrase varying.

Práctica C
1. ...salió a las once menos cuarto.
2. ...salió a las once y diez.
3. ...salió un poco después.
4. ...saliste a medianoche.
5. ...salió unos minutos después.
6. ...salió después de ti.
7. ...salí a las doce y media.
8. ...salió más tarde que yo.

Práctica D
1. Fui al hospital...salí a las dos... Llegué a las dos y media.
2. Fui al correo...salí a las diez... Llegué a las diez y media.
3. Fui al almacén...salí a las cuatro... Llegué a las cuatro y media.
4. Fui al aeropuerto...salí a las siete... Llegué a las siete y media.
5. Fui al mercado...salí a las nueve y cuarto... Llegué a las diez menos cuarto.
6. Fui a la panadería...salí a las ocho y cuarto... Llegué a las nueve menos cuarto.

B **¿Qué comió Ud.?** Ahora imagina que le preguntas a tu profesor(a) qué comió para el desayuno. Usa las frases de la Práctica A y escoge de la lista para completar cada respuesta. Sigue el modelo.

> queso
> ESTUDIANTE A   *¿Qué comió Ud.?*
> ESTUDIANTE B   *Comí queso con un vaso de leche.*

jugo de manzana	café con leche
jugo de naranja	chocolate
un vaso de leche	fruta
una naranja	papas fritas
un plátano	mantequilla y mermelada
café sin azúcar	té con limón

C **¿Cuándo salió?** Imagina que le cuentas a un(a) amigo(a) a qué hora salió cada persona de una fiesta de disfraces anoche. Sigue el modelo.

> Marta / 10:30
> *Marta salió a las diez y media.*

1. mi tío Francisco / 10:45
2. mi prima Ángela / 11:10
3. el Sr. Girón / un poco después
4. (tú) / a medianoche
5. José / unos minutos después
6. Luz / después de ti
7. (yo) / 12:30
8. nadie / más tarde que yo

D **Detective.** Imagina que eres un(a) detective. Investigas a varios sospechosos (*suspects*) de un robo (*robbery*). Prepara diálogos según el modelo.

> el parque / 1:00 / 1:30
>
> ESTUDIANTE A   *¿Adónde fuiste ayer?*
> ESTUDIANTE B   *Fui al parque.*
> ESTUDIANTE A   *¿A qué hora saliste de tu casa?*
> ESTUDIANTE B   *Creo que salí a la una.*
> ESTUDIANTE A   *¿Y cuándo llegaste allí?*
> ESTUDIANTE B   *Media hora después. Llegué a la una y media.*

1. el hospital / 2:00 / 2:30
2. el correo / 10:00 / 10:30
3. el almacén / 4:00 / 4:30
4. el aeropuerto / 7:00 / 7:30
5. el mercado / 9:15 / 9:45
6. la panadería / 8:15 / 8:45

E ¿Qué pasó? Cambia del presente al pretérito todos los verbos de este cuento. Aquí están las formas del pretérito que ya sabes *(you already know).*

IR	(yo) fui, (tú) fuiste, Ud. (él / ella) fue
DAR	(yo) di, (tú) diste, Ud. (él / ella) dio
VER	(yo) vi, (tú) viste, Ud. (él / ella) vio
COMPRAR	(yo) compré, (tú) compraste, Ud. (él, ella) compró
PAGAR	(yo) pagué, (tú) pagaste, Ud. (él / ella) pagó
LLEGAR	(yo) llegué, (tú) llegaste, Ud. (él / ella) llegó
COMER	(yo) comí, (tú) comiste, Ud. (él / ella) comió
SALIR	(yo) salí, (tú) saliste, Ud. (él / ella) salió

El día del santo de Paco, su mamá le da dinero para comprar un nuevo radio o una grabadora. El sábado (yo) llego a su casa temprano y luego voy con él al almacén más grande de la ciudad. Paco ve muchos radios, grabadoras y tocadiscos. Después de mucho tiempo,
5 compra la grabadora más cara de la tienda. ¡Paga ochenta dólares! Yo también veo unas grabadoras muy buenas pero no compro ninguna. Sólo compro unas cintas y le doy una a Paco para su santo. Salgo del almacén con Paco. Luego yo voy a un restaurante donde como una hamburguesa, pero él no va conmigo. Él va a su casa muy contento
10 con sus regalos.

F Hablemos de ti.

1. ¿Qué comiste anoche? ¿Comiste carne o pescado? ¿Verduras y ensalada? ¿Qué clase de verduras? ¿Qué clase de ensalada? ¿Qué comiste de postre?

2. ¿A qué hora saliste de casa esta mañana? ¿Cuándo llegaste a la escuela? ¿Llegaste a tiempo?

Una tienda en Caracas, Venezuela

Explicaciones II **449**

APLICACIONES

REPASO

Look carefully at the model sentences. Then put the English cues into Spanish to form new sentences based on the models.

1. *Carolina llegó a la playa a las nueve de la mañana.*
   (*I arrived at the exit at 11:00 A.M.*)
   (*You (fam.) arrived at the parade at 4:00 P.M.*)
   (*You (formal) arrived at the entrance at 10:00 A.M.*)

2. *Comí una ensalada de lechuga y paella.*
   (*She ate a stuffed pepper and soup.*)
   (*You (formal) ate a lamb chop and beans.*)
   (*You (fam.) ate a cheese sandwich and potatoes.*)

3. *Ahora pido un café y flan.*
   (*Now you (fam.) are ordering an orangeade and dessert.*)
   (*Then we order some pastries and tea.*)
   (*Then you (formal) ask for a banana and chocolate.*)

4. *"Nunca sirven comida después de las diez y media," digo yo. "¡Nunca!" repito.*
   (*"We never serve wine before 5:30," we say. "Never!" we repeat.*)
   (*"I never serve paella after 11:45," says Mr. Pérez. "Never?" I ask.*)
   (*"The waiters never serve food before 8:15," they say. "Never!" they repeat.*)

5. *Ves que no hay nada en el vaso.*
   (*I see that there's no one in the dining room.*)
   (*They see that there aren't any forks on the table.*)
   (*We see that there aren't any napkins on the plates.*)

El desfile de los gigantes
en Toledo, España

TEMA

Transparency 56

Enrichment: In connection with the **Tema,** you may want to ask students to create their own cartoon strips and write talk balloons about the different situations. For example: Elena and Celia go to a restaurant and, while looking at the menu, discuss the choices and order the food; or Carlos invites María to a costume party and they discuss what they will wear.

Put the English captions into Spanish.

1. Miguel arrived at the cafeteria at 1:00 P.M.

2. He ate a pork chop and rice.

3. Now he's asking for an apple and milk.

4. "We never serve anything after 1:30," says Mr. Pérez. "Never!" he repeats.

5. Miguel sees that there's no one in the cafeteria!

REDACCIÓN

Enrichment: You may want to add this topic to the **Redacción:** Write a letter inviting a friend to a *desfile de disfraces* or to see *Las fiestas de San Fermín* (see **Prólogo cultural** on p. 425). The letter should describe something typical of the celebration.

Now you are ready to write your own dialogue or paragraph. Choose one of the following topics.

1. Expand the *Tema.* Why did Miguel arrive late in the cafeteria? What is he reading? Is Miguel still hungry? Where are the other students? What is Miguel going to do now? Where can he go to buy more food?

2. Write a dialogue between a waiter and someone visiting a Mexican restaurant for the first time.

3. Write a paragraph about a holiday you like to celebrate. Describe how you celebrate it. Do you give and receive presents? Are there parties? What do you serve? Do you have decorations? Are there fireworks or parades? Do you wear a costume? Do you eat a lot?

Notes: Answers to the **Comprueba** appear in the pre-chapter teacher pages.

A   La comida

Match each word or phrase in the left-hand column with a word or phrase in the right-hand column.

1. el flan	a. arroz con pollo
2. el gazpacho	y pescado
3. una naranjada	b. una sopa
4. una chuleta de cerdo	c. una carne
5. la paella	d. un postre
6. un camarero	e. huevos, papas
7. una tortilla española	y cebolla
8. el carnaval	f. una bebida
9. la reina	g. una persona
10. la gente	h. dulces
11. la corrida	i. toros y toreros
12. el azúcar	j. desfiles y
	disfraces
	k. esposa del rey
	l. unas personas

B   Los verbos *e → i*

Complete each sentence with the correct present-tense form of the verb in parentheses.

1. Mi padre _____ el menú. *(pedir)*
2. (Nosotros) no _____ las palabras. *(repetir)*
3. Eduardo y Marta _____ el postre. *(servir)*
4. ¿Por qué _____ (tú) la respuesta? *(repetir)*
5. Yo _____ paella y flan. *(pedir)*
6. ¿Cuándo _____ Ud. el té? *(servir)*
7. (Nosotros) _____ más dinero. *(pedir)*
8. (Yo) siempre _____ la sopa primero. *(servir)*

C   *Pedir* o *preguntar*

Complete each sentence with the correct present-tense form of *pedir* or *preguntar*.

1. Elena nos _____ un televisor.
2. Él les _____ a sus padres si van al desfile.
3. (Yo) le _____ a Carlos si tiene un disfraz.
4. (Ellas) le _____ una naranjada a su madre.
5. Debes _____ a Laura de quién es la máscara.
6. (Nosotros) le _____ más postre a papá.

D   Los negativos

Complete each sentence with the correct negative word: *ningún, ninguna, ninguno(a), nadie, nada,* or *nunca*.

1. Elena _____ quiere jugar a los naipes.
2. Voy sola porque _____ puede ir conmigo.
3. _____ muchacho quiere bailar.
4. _____ es fácil en esa clase.
5. ¡Qué bueno! No tengo _____ tarea hoy.
6. Paco nunca habla con _____.
7. No hay _____ en el vaso. Está vacío.
8. _____ de los discos es bueno.
9. _____ pongo azúcar en la comida.
10. No cantan _____ canción folklórica.

E   Comer o salir

Complete the sentences with the correct preterite form of *comer* or *salir*.

El martes pasado fui a la casa de mi abuela para celebrar el carnaval. _____ de casa temprano y llegué a su casa antes del almuerzo. Mi hermana llegó un poco después.

5   Mi abuela preparó un almuerzo delicioso, pero yo sólo _____ una chuleta de cordero con papas fritas. Raquel, mi hermana, _____ tres chuletas, papas fritas y una ensalada muy grande. "¿Qué hay de postre?" preguntó ella. "Un pastel de
10 manzana," contestó la abuela, "pero vamos a esperar a tu mamá antes de comerlo."

Mucho más tarde llegó mamá. "Nunca llegas tarde, María. ¿Cuándo _____ de casa?" le preguntó la abuela. "_____ a tiempo," contestó
15 mamá, "pero todas las calles ya están llenas de gente. El desfile empieza muy pronto." "¿Ya _____ el almuerzo?" le pregunté a ella. "¿No, y tengo mucha hambre," contestó mamá.

Sustantivos
el arroz
la bebiba
el bistec
el camarero, la camarera
el carnaval
la celebración, *pl.* las celebraciones
la corrida (de toros)
la cuenta
el chile
el chile relleno
la chuleta de cerdo
la chuleta de cordero
la decoración, *pl.* las decoraciones
el desfile
el diablo
el disfraz, *pl.* los disfraces
los dulces
la empanada
el fantasma
la fiesta de disfraces
el flan
los fuegos artificiales
el gazpacho
la gente

la máscara
el menú
la naranjada
la paella
el pastel
el pescado
la piñata
el postre
la propina
la reina
el rey
la sopa
el torero, la torera
la tortilla española
el vino

Pronombre
ninguno, -a

Adjetivos
cada
caliente
delicioso, -a
emocionante
folklórico, -a
frío, -a
frito, -a
lleno, -a
ningún, ninguna
perfecto, -a
picante
vacío, -a

Verbos
celebrar
decorar
llover (o → ue)
nevar (e → ie)
pedir (e → i)
preparar
repetir (e → i)
romper
servir (e → i)

Adverbio
luego

Expresiones
de postre
de propina
lleno, -a de gente
vestido, -a de

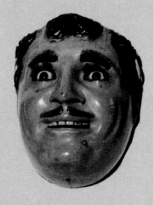

DEPORTES POPULARES

In Latin America and Europe, the most popular sport by far is *fútbol*, and it is followed with intense interest by its fans. Stars like Argentina's Diego Maradona and Paraguay's Julio César Romero are more popular in their own countries than any movie actor.

Soccer may be king, but many other sports, such as basketball, boxing, tennis, and auto racing also have their loyal *aficionados* (fans) in Latin America. Baseball is extremely popular in the Caribbean, Venezuela, Mexico, and some Central American countries. Many major league stars have come from Latin America—Mexico's Fernando Valenzuela, the Dominican Republic's Tony Armas, Panama's Rod Carew, and Puerto Rico's Roberto Clemente, to name just a few.

While we are watching baseball, skiing is the rage during the winter months (July–September) in the southern part of the Andes. Among the most popular ski resorts are Portillo (Chile), Chacaltayo (Bolivia), and the "Switzerland of South America," Argentina's Bariloche. Across the ocean, in the Sierra Nevada, just south of Granada, Spain, every spring skiers can hit the slopes in the morning and then drive a short distance to the Costa del Sol to spend the afternoon swimming and sunbathing.

With so much sports activity, it is not surprising that Spain and Latin America have produced their share of international stars and world champions. In the early 1980s Mexico had five boxers who held world titles. Argentina, Cuba, and Mexico have each won several Olympic gold medals in track and field, and Spain has a gold medal in yachting. But every four years, when soccer's World Cup competition is on, all other sports are forgotten, and *fútbol* rules absolutely in the Spanish-speaking world.

PALABRAS NUEVAS I

Cosas de todos los días

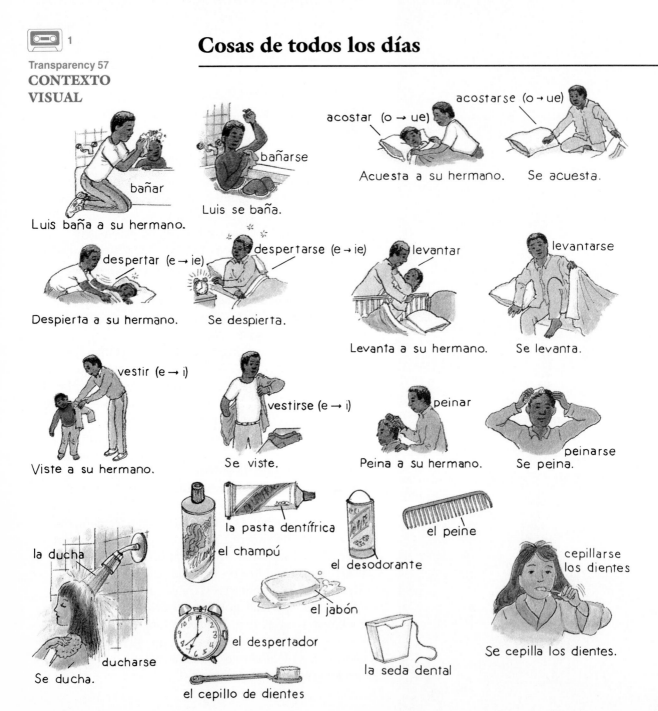

bañar

Luis baña a su hermano.

bañarse

Luis se baña.

acostar (o → ue)

acostarse (o → ue)

Acuesta a su hermano.   Se acuesta.

despertar (e → ie)

Despierta a su hermano.

despertarse (e → ie)

Se despierta.

levantar

Levanta a su hermano.

levantarse

Se levanta.

vestir (e → i)

Viste a su hermano.

vestirse (e → i)

Se viste.

peinar

Peina a su hermano.

peinarse

Se peina.

la pasta dentífrica

el champú

el peine

el desodorante

la ducha

el jabón

cepillarse
los dientes

el despertador

la seda dental

Se cepilla los dientes.

Se ducha.

ducharse

el cepillo de dientes

456   Capítulo 14

la cara — lavarse la cara

Se lava la cara.

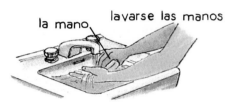

la mano — lavarse las manos

Se lava las manos.

lavarse el pelo

el pelo

Se lava el pelo.

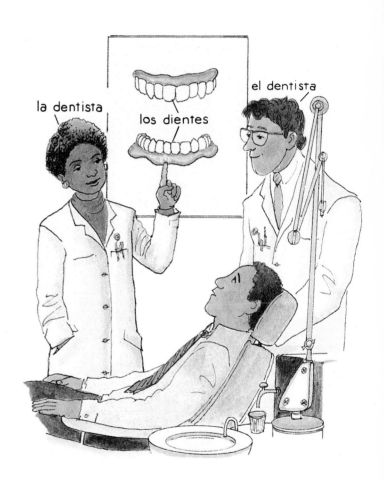

la dentista

los dientes

el dentista

1 MAMÁ   Mario, ¿por qué **te quitas** el suéter? **Hay que** salir
ahora.

MARIO   **¿Me pongo** también una chaqueta?

MAMÁ   No. Volvemos pronto.

Variaciones:
- hay que → tenemos que
- ahora → **de prisa**

2 HORACIO   Me levanto todas las mañanas a las 5:30.

BÁRBARA   ¿Y a qué hora te acuestas?

HORACIO   A las diez.

- todas las mañanas → todos los días
- 5:30 → 6:15

3 LEONOR   Siempre **me duermo** cuando viajo en tren o en
avión.

MÓNICA   ¿No te duermes cuando viajas en coche?

LEONOR   A veces sí, a veces no.

- a veces sí, a veces no → generalmente no

**quitarse (yo me quito, tú te
quitas)** *to take off*

hay que + inf. *we (you, one)
must, it's necessary (to do
something)*

**ponerse (yo me pongo, tú te
pones)** *to put on*

de prisa *in a hurry, quickly, fast*

Enrichment: Other
Variaciones you may want to
suggest in mini-dialogue 1: *No.
Volvemos pronto. → No. No
hace mucho frío*; in 2: *a las
5:30 → a las 7:30; a las
diez → a las once.*

**dormirse (o → ue) (yo me
duermo, tú te duermes)**
to go to sleep, to fall asleep

EN OTRAS PARTES

En muchos países se dice *lavarse los dientes*. En España se dice *lavarse la boca*.

En México se dice *la regadera*.

También se dice *la pasta de dientes*.

También se dice *el hilo dental*.

También se dice *lavarse la cabeza*.

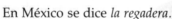

Este anuncio no huele

El desodorante stick CREMA DE LA TOJA elimina con suavidad y eficacia el olor corporal.

No se evapora

Al no contener alcohol, este desodorante no se evapora. Y al tener mayor cantidad de producto, su duración es mucho mayor.

Desodorante sin alcohol

crema de La Toja

no irrita la piel

Sin alcohol.

Mayor duración.

El desodorante stick CREMA DE LA TOJA es cómodo y agradable

EL DESODORANTE DE MODA.

PRÁCTICA

Práctica A
1. pasta dentífrica
2. seda dental
3. dentista
4. de prisa
5. el pelo
6. ponerse
7. lavarse

Reteach / Extra Help: After students do Ex. A in class, you may want to ask them to write five health rules at home using *hay que*. Encourage students to use the vocabulary presented on pp. 456–457.

Práctica B
1. Necesitas el despertador, ¿verdad?
2. el jabón
3. el desodorante
4. la seda dental
5. el cepillo de dientes
6. el champú
7. el peine
8. la pasta dentífrica
9. la toalla

Reteach / Review: You may want to expand Ex. B by asking students to add a response to *mamá's* question. Students should use direct object pronouns. For example: *Necesitas los aretes, ¿verdad? (Ya los tengo.)*

A **Hay que . . .**   Cecilia le dice a su hermanito varias cosas que hay que hacer. Busca las palabras correctas de la derecha para completar las frases.

1. Hay que cepillarse los dientes con _____.   de prisa
2. Hay que usar la _____ también.   dentista
3. Hay que ir al _____ cada seis meses.   desodorante
4. Cuando es tarde, hay que vestirse _____.   lavarse
5. Hay que lavarse _____ con champú, no con jabón.   pasta dentífrica
6. Hay que _____ ropa limpia después de bañarse.   el pelo
7. Siempre hay que _____ las manos antes de comer.   ponerse
                                                      seda dental

B **¿Qué necesito?**   Raquel va a pasar el fin de semana en la casa de una amiga. ¿Qué necesita poner en su maleta? Sigue el modelo.

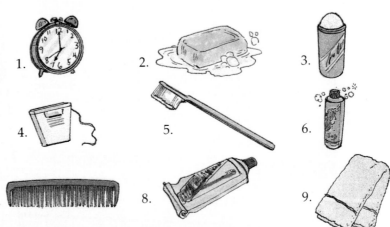

ESTUDIANTE A   *Mamá, ¿qué más necesito?*
ESTUDIANTE B   *Necesitas los aretes, ¿verdad?*

C **Por la mañana.**   ¿Qué haces por la mañana? Sigue el modelo.

Me despierto.

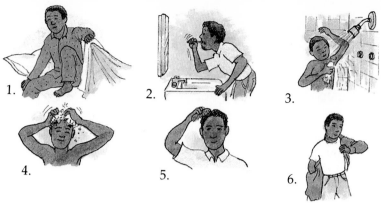

1.
2.
3.
4.
5.
6.

Práctica C
1. Me levanto.
2. Me cepillo los dientes.
3. Me ducho.
4. Me lavo el pelo.
5. Me peino.
6. Me visto.

D Hablemos de ti.

1. ¿A qué hora te levantas cuando tienes que ir a la escuela? ¿Necesitas un despertador? ¿A qué hora te levantas los sábados? ¿Los domingos?
2. Cuando te cepillas los dientes, ¿usas la seda dental también? ¿La usas todos los días? ¿Qué dicen los dentistas sobre la seda dental?
3. ¿Qué te gusta más, el pelo corto o el pelo largo? ¿Por qué?
4. ¿A qué hora te acuestas?

Práctica D
Answers will vary.

Practice Sheet 14–1

Workbook Exs. A–B

Tape Manual Exs. 1–2 3

Quiz 14–1

ACTIVIDAD

Ud. no puede vivir sin . . .   Work in small groups to create a television commercial or a magazine ad for a deodorant, toothpaste, soap, or shampoo. Here are some advertising phrases you might want to use:

Huele bien. (It smells good.)
¡Descubra algo nuevo! (Discover something new!)
¡Qué sabor! (What a taste!)
Es el (la) mejor de todos (todas). (It's the best of all.)
Sus problemas se acabaron. (Your troubles are over.)
¡Cómprelo (cómprela) hoy! (Buy it today!)

Give your product a Spanish name, and when your ad or commercial is finished, share it with the class.

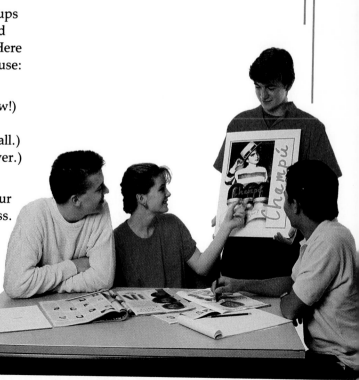

APLICACIONES
Discretionary

La nueva alumna 4

Norma, una muchacha de catorce años, acaba de llegar al internado.[1] Es la primera vez[2] que vive lejos de su familia, y le pregunta a otra alumna qué tiene que hacer.

    NORMA ¿Puedo acostarme y levantarme cuando quiero?

5 DIANA Sólo los domingos. Durante la semana tienes que acostarte a las diez y levantarte a las seis.

    NORMA ¿Y los sábados?

    DIANA También a las seis, porque los sábados hay clases por la mañana. Y hay que ducharse, cepillarse los dientes, peinarse y ponerse el uniforme, todo antes de las siete.

10   Tienes sólo una hora porque sirven el desayuno a las siete en punto.[3]

    NORMA Es suficiente tiempo.

    DIANA Al contrario, no es mucho, porque hay sólo un baño para diez chicas.

15 NORMA ¿Cómo pueden ducharse diez chicas en tan poco tiempo?[4]

    DIANA Lo hacemos de prisa.

---

[1]**el internado** *boarding school (where students live away from home)*
[2]**la vez** *time*   [3]**en punto** *on the dot*   [4]**tan poco tiempo** *such a short time*

Notes: Make sure students understand these cognates that have not been glossed: *el uniforme*, uniform; *suficiente*, sufficient.

Preguntas
Contesta según el diálogo.

1. ¿Quién es Norma? ¿Con quién habla ella?   2. ¿Cuál es el único día libre que tienen en el internado?   3. ¿A qué hora tienen que levantarse durante la semana?   4. ¿Qué tienen que hacer entre las seis y las siete?   5. ¿A qué hora sirven el desayuno?   6. ¿Por qué tienen que hacer todo de prisa?   7. ¿Crees que te gustaría (*you'd like*) asistir a un internado? ¿Por qué?   8. Por la mañana, ¿cuánto tiempo tienes tú entre la hora de levantarte y la hora de salir para la escuela? ¿Tienes que hacer todo de prisa?

Diálogo
1. Una muchacha de catorce años (*or*: una nueva alumna del internado). Con otra alumna del internado.
2. El domingo.
3. A las seis.
4. Ducharse, cepillarse los dientes, peinarse y ponerse el uniforme.
5. A las siete en punto.
6. Porque sólo hay un baño para diez chicas, y sólo tienen una hora (para hacer todo).
7. Answers will vary.
8. Answers will vary.

Enrichment: Additional questions you may want to ask: *¿Cuántos años tiene Norma? (Tiene catorce años.) ¿Acaba de llegar Diana al internado? (No.) ¿Cuántos baños hay para diez chicas? (Hay sólo un baño para diez chicas.) ¿Es un problema? (Sí.)*

Participación

Work with a partner to make up a dialogue. Imagine that you are asking a friend from another town what his or her routine is like in the morning. Start by asking at what time your friend gets up, and finish by asking at what time he or she has to be at school.

PRONUNCIACIÓN 5

A When the letter *i* or *u* comes before another vowel, the two together form a diphthong and are pronounced as one syllable. Escucha y repite.

demasiado	diente	junio	ciudad
estudiante	viernes	delicioso	invierno
cuando	juego	cuenta	cuidado
continuar	abuela	fuiste	puerta

B When the letter *i* or *u* has a written accent, it does not form a diphthong with the vowel that follows it. The two vowels are pronounced as separate syllables.
Escucha y repite.

frío	tío	día	todavía	continúo

C Escucha y repite.

Estudio ciencias y geometría.
Todavía hace frío, Luisa.
Mis abuelos pueden ir a Colombia en julio.
Continúo mi viaje el jueves o el viernes.

PALABRAS NUEVAS II

Deportes y más deportes

el balón
pl. los balones

la pelota

el equipo

el aficionado

la aficionada

* We say *ser aficionado(a) a* to mean "to be a fan of": *Soy aficionado al fútbol americano.*

perder (e → ie)

LOS LEONES 15

LOS CORDEROS 2

ganar

el golf

el volibol

débil

fuerte

correr

perder (e → ie)

1 MATEO ¿Crees que vas a ganar el partido mañana?

PABLO **Espero** ganarlo.

Variaciones:

■ espero ganarlo → **¡espero que sí!**

■ espero ganarlo → **¡por supuesto!**

esperar here: *to hope, to expect*

¡espero que sí! *I hope so*

2 ARMANDO ¡Qué **atlética** es tu hermana!

BEATRIZ Sí, es una **atleta** muy buena.

ARMANDO ¿Corre todos los días?

BEATRIZ Sí, cada mañana.

ARMANDO ¿Y no corres con ella?

BEATRIZ ¿Yo? No. Soy demasiado **perezosa.**

Notes: Make sure students understand that *atleta* in mini-dialogue 2 is both the masculine and feminine form.

■ atlética → **enérgica**

■ soy demasiado perezosa → corro muy **despacio**

■ soy demasiado perezosa → ella corre muy **rápidamente**

atlético, -a *athletic*
el / la atleta *athlete*

perezoso, -a *lazy*

enérgico, -a *energetic*
despacio *slowly*
rápidamente *fast, rapidly*

3 JAIME Este verano fui a la playa sólo **una vez.**

ELISA Yo fui **dos veces.**

JAIME El año próximo espero ir allí en julio y no **regresar** antes de septiembre.

ELISA ¡Ojalá!

■ espero → quiero

■ regresar → volver

■ ¡ojalá! → ¡espero que sí!

la vez, pl. **las veces** *time*
una vez *once*
dos veces *twice*
regresar *to return*

Enrichment: After mini-dialogue 4, ask ¿*Quién es el (la) mejor jugador(a) del equipo de los / las ___?* substituting the names of school or local teams.

4 MARIANA Julia es la mejor **jugadora.** Creo que va a ganar el partido.

CLAUDIA ¡Espero que sí! No **me divierto** cuando pierde.

■ mejor → peor

ganar → perder

¡espero que sí! → **¡espero que no!**

el jugador, la jugadora *player*
divertirse (e → ie) (yo me divierto, tú te diviertes) *to have fun, to have a good time*

¡espero que no! *I hope not*

Reteach / Extra Help: Reinforce some of the new and old vocabulary used in mini-dialogues 1–4 by writing these words on the board or calling them out: *ganar, enérgico, rápidamente, peor, espero que sí.* Then ask for antonyms (*perder, perezoso, despacio, mejor, espero que no*).

5 LUISA   ¿Qué piensas de la lección de inglés?

OSCAR   Bueno, comprendo **lo que** dice la profesora.

LUISA   Yo también, pero no comprendo lo que dicen en las cintas. Y **trato de** hablar inglés, pero es muy difícil.

lo que   *what (that which)*

tratar de + inf.   *to try (to)*

■ lección → clase
■ dice la profesora → leo

(izquierda) Unos estudiantes corren en Barcelona, España.

(arriba) En la playa en Málaga, España; (izquierda) Fútbol en Yucatán, México

Un jugador de fútbol en El Tajín, México

A Deportes favoritos.

Escoge (*Choose*) la palabra correcta para completar cada frase.

1. Margarita tiene mala suerte. Nunca (*gana / pierde*) cuando juega al tenis.
2. Pedro corre muy despacio. Es demasiado (*perezoso / atlético*).
3. Las hermanas Benítez siempre ganan. Son buenas (*aficionadas / atletas*).
4. Necesitamos más (*pelotas / balones*) de golf.
5. Espero llegar a tiempo. (*Trato de / Acabo de*) regresar antes del partido de béisbol.
6. (*El equipo / El aficionado*) gana el partido.
7. Te voy a enseñar (*cuando / lo que*) hacemos en el gimnasio.
8. Gustavo es fuerte y atlético. Nada (*despacio / rápidamente*).
9. Cuando estoy cansado después de un partido (*me acuesto / me despierto*).
10. Siempre trato de ganar, pero (*a veces / dos veces*) hay que perder.

B Lo que esperan hacer.

Varias personas hablan de lo que quieren hacer. Busca las palabras correctas para completar las frases.

balón	despacio	fuerte	no
correr	dormir	golf	regresar
débil	dos veces	jugadora	sí

1. Fui a México el año pasado. Espero _____ allí este verano.
2. Por la mañana, espero jugar al _____.
3. El sábado, hay que comprar un _____ nuevo.
4. Mañana espero _____ más rápidamente.
5. ¿Mi equipo favorito pierde el partido? Espero que _____.
6. Creo que Patricia va a ganar, porque la otra _____ es muy lenta.
7. Tomás es más _____ que yo, porque juega a la pelota todos los días. Yo no practico ningún deporte.
8. Voy a decir cada frase sólo una vez, pero voy a hablar muy _____.
9. ¿No te levantas? ¿Piensas _____ todo el día?

C Hablemos de ti.

1. ¿Eres aficionado(a) a los deportes? ¿A cuáles?
2. ¿Cuál es tu equipo favorito de béisbol? ¿De fútbol americano? ¿De básquetbol? ¿Por qué? ¿Quién es el (la) mejor jugador(a) del equipo?

3. ¿Van a ganar tus equipos favoritos este año o el próximo año? ¿Por qué?
4. ¿Juegas al golf? ¿Al volibol? ¿Cuándo? ¿Dónde juegas al volibol? ¿Con quiénes? ¿Cuántas veces practicas un deporte cada semana?
5. ¿Te gusta correr? ¿Dónde corres? ¿Cuándo? ¿Corres solo(a)?
6. ¿Eres perezoso(a) o enérgico(a)? ¿Qué hacen las personas perezosas? ¿Las personas enérgicas?
7. ¿Qué cosas tratas de hacer todos los días?

ESTUDIO DE PALABRAS

Many nouns in Spanish that refer to people have a masculine form ending in *-o* and a feminine form ending in *-a*. For example: *el veterinario/ la veterinaria*. But nouns ending in *-e* or *-a* have the same masculine and feminine form. You have already learned several words like this.

el / la agente de viajes   el / la cliente
el / la turista   el / la policía

Most masculine nouns referring to people that end in *-dor* have feminine forms ending in *-dora*. For example: *el vendedor / la vendedora*. What are some other nouns referring to people that have the same masculine and feminine forms? Name some that have different forms.

Estudio de palabras
Same form:
  atleta
  auxiliar de vuelo
  dentista
  estudiante
  piloto
Different form:
  actor / actriz
  aficionado(a)
  camarero(a)
  fotógrafo(a)
  granjero(a)
  guardián(ana) de zoológico
  invitado(a)
  profesor(a)
  torero(a)
  plus all family members,
  words for boys / girls, etc.

Practice Sheet 14–2

Workbook Exs. C–D

Tape Manual Exs. 3–4 8

Quiz 14–2

Carteles de fútbol y de carreras de bicicletas, Alcobendas, España

EXPLICACIONES I

Los verbos reflexivos

Notes: Mini-dialogues 1–3 on p. 458 and 4 on p. 466 illustrate various present-tense forms of reflexive verbs.

◆ **OBJECTIVES:**
TO DESCRIBE AND COMPARE DAILY ROUTINES

Enrichment: You may want to prepare flashcards to reinforce the meaning and use of reflexive verbs. Write the reflexive infinitive on one side of an index card, the nonreflexive infinitive on the other. Prepare a card for each of the verbs listed on p. 472; you may want to omit *divertirse.*

Ask volunteers to pick a card and act out the verb in both its reflexive and nonreflexive meanings. Can the rest of the class guess which verb students are performing? Is the distinction between reflexive and nonreflexive clear?

Look at the following sentences.

Rosa tiene un coche.

Lo lava.

Luego **se** lava.

Tiene dos perros.

Los baña.

Luego **se** baña.

Tiene una hija.

La acuesta.

Luego **se** acuesta.

In the middle column, Rosa is performing an action on or for someone or something else: *su coche (lo), sus perros (los), su hija (la)*. In the right-hand column, she is doing something to or for herself *(se)*. The verbs on the right are called reflexive verbs.

El primer *ACEITE LAVANTE* de Tratamiento:
una revolución en el tratamiento específico de los cabellos s

ACEITE LAVANTE DE TRATAMIENTO

DOBLE ACCION

Trata y lava al mismo tiempo

Tiene usted los cabellos secos, frágiles y quebradizos. He
aquí una forma diferente de tratarlos; un nuevo producto
que va a cambiar sus costumbres y cuyos resultados le
asombrarán. Por primera vez, el Aceite Lavante de
Tratamiento Doble Acción DERCOS, reúne las cualidades
tratantes de los aceites vegetales naturales con la eficacia
lavante de un champú.
¡ES REALMENTE UNA INNOVACION!

ceite, nutre, suaviza y refuerza la protección natural de los cabellos contra
antes (sol, agua de mar, tratamientos capilares mal adaptados...).
nte los cabellos gracias a su base lavante muy suave, siendo fácil

e sus cabellos, usted puede utilizarlo regularmente o alternándolo con s
habitual.
SON ESPECTACULARES.
erán limpios, brillantes, con
ra inhabituales.

L LABORATORIOS DERCOS
La innovación capilar en la farmacia.

(arriba) Una joven se cepilla
los dientes en Santander,
España; (abajo) Un
estudiante se peina y otro
se cepilla los dientes en
España.

1 A reflexive verb has two parts—a reflexive pronoun and a verb form. The reflexive pronoun refers to the subject of the sentence (Rosa). Here are all of the present-tense forms of the reflexive verb *lavarse*, "to wash oneself."

INFINITIVO **lavarse**

	SINGULAR		PLURAL	
1	(yo)	**me** lavo	(nosotros) (nosotras)	**nos** lavamos
2	(tú)	**te** lavas	(vosotros) (vosotras)	**os** laváis
3	Ud. (él) (ella)	**se** lava	Uds. (ellos) (ellas)	**se** lavan

Except for *se*, the reflexive pronouns have the same forms as the indirect and direct object pronouns.

2 Like other object pronouns, reflexive pronouns generally come before the verb, or they may be attached to an infinitive.

Me quiero duchar ahora. ⎱
Quiero duchar**me** ahora. ⎰ *I want to take a shower now.*

3 Here is a list of the reflexive verbs you know.

acostarse (o → ue)	dormirse (o → ue)	peinarse
bañarse	ducharse	ponerse
cepillarse	lavarse	quitarse
despertarse (e → ie)	levantarse	vestirse (e → i)
divertirse (e → ie)	llamarse	

Now you know that *¿Cómo te llamas?* and *me llamo*, which you learned on your first day, are forms of the reflexive verb *llamarse:* "my name is" = "I call myself." The only form you have not yet seen is the *nosotros* form:

Nos llamamos López. *Our name is López.*

4 When we use reflexive verbs with parts of the body or articles of clothing, we usually use the definite article.

¿**Te** cepillas **los dientes**?	*Are you brushing **your teeth**?*
Me lavo **la cara**.	*I'm washing **my face**.*
Te puedes quitar **el sombrero**.	*You can take off **your hat**.*
Me pongo **los zapatos**.	*I'm putting on **my shoes**.*

Even when the subject is plural, we generally use the singular form for parts of the body and articles of clothing. We use the plural form only if they come in pairs *(calcetines, manos)* or are logically plural *(pantalones, dientes)*.

Nos lavamos **la cara**.	*We're washing **our faces**.*
Se ponen **el sombrero**.	*They're putting on **their hats**.*
Se quitan **los zapatos**.	*They're taking off **their shoes**.*

PRÁCTICA

A ¿Cuándo? El Sr. Díaz nunca les dice a sus hijos lo que deben hacer. Les pregunta cuándo van a hacer las cosas. Pregunta y contesta según el modelo.

> levantarse
>
> ESTUDIANTE A   *¿Cuándo van Uds. a levantarse?*
> ESTUDIANTE B   *Nos levantamos ahora.*

1. ducharse
2. peinarse
3. lavarse la cara
4. cepillarse los dientes
5. vestirse
6. ponerse los zapatos
7. acostarse
8. dormirse

Reteach / Review: Reinforce the use of the definite article with parts of the body or articles of clothing by asking these questions: *¿Te lavas la cara con jabón? Nos quitamos el sombrero cuando entramos en la escuela, ¿verdad? ¿Siempre se quitan Uds. los zapatos cuando llegan a casa? Tengo frío. Debo ponerme el abrigo, ¿no?* (Answers will vary.)

Práctica A
1. ¿Cuándo van Uds. a ducharse? Nos duchamos…
2. ¿…a peinarse? Nos peinamos…
3. ¿…a lavarse la cara? Nos lavamos…
4. ¿…a cepillarse los dientes? Nos cepillamos…
5. ¿…a vestirse? Nos vestimos…
6. ¿…a ponerse los zapatos? Nos ponemos…
7. ¿…a acostarse? Nos acostamos…
8. ¿…a dormirse? Nos dormimos…

Una muchacha se peina.

Explicaciones I   473

B   Tú sí, pero yo no.   Imagina que le preguntas a un(a) amigo(a) qué
hace. Pero su hermano(a) nunca está de acuerdo *(in agreement)* con lo
que contesta. Pregunta y contesta según el modelo.

> acostarse ahora
> **ESTUDIANTE A**   *¿Te acuestas ahora?*
> **ESTUDIANTE B**   *Sí, me acuesto ahora.*
> **ESTUDIANTE C**   *No, no nos acostamos ahora.*

1. despertarse a las seis
2. divertirse en la playa
3. dormirse por la tarde
4. acostarse temprano
5. vestirse antes del desayuno
6. despertarse tarde los sábados
7. dormirse rápidamente
8. vestirse antes de las ocho

C   La familia Jiménez.   Son las 7:30 de la mañana y todo el mundo
está ocupado. Usa las formas correctas reflexivas y no reflexivas para
describir lo que hacen.

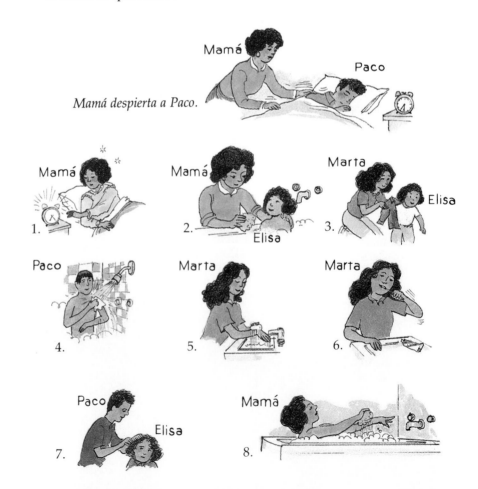

Mamá despierta a Paco.

D No tengo ganas. Algunos días Emilia no quiere hacer nada. Pregunta y contesta según el modelo.

> levantarse
> **ESTUDIANTE A** *¿Por qué no te levantas?*
> **ESTUDIANTE B** *No me quiero levantar.*
> o: *No tengo ganas de levantarme.*

1. bañarse
2. ducharse
3. lavarse el pelo
4. peinarse
5. cepillarse los dientes
6. vestirse
7. ponerse el abrigo
8. acostarse

E Aquí es diferente. Gustavo acaba de llegar a una escuela militar *(military)* y habla con otro alumno sobre lo que hacen allí. Pregunta y contesta según el modelo.

> ducharse cuando quiero / dos veces todos los días
> **ESTUDIANTE A** *En casa me ducho cuando quiero.*
> **ESTUDIANTE B** *Pues aquí tienes que ducharte dos veces todos los días.*

1. vestirse despacio / de prisa
2. cepillarse los dientes por la mañana y por la noche / después de cada comida
3. acostarse a las 11:30 / a las 9:30
4. despertarse a las 8:00 / a las 6:15
5. levantarse tarde / muy temprano
6. lavarse las manos cada mañana / muchas veces cada día
7. divertirse mucho todos los días / los sábados por la tarde

F Hablemos de ti.

1. ¿Quién se despierta primero en tu familia? ¿A qué hora se despierta? ¿A qué hora te despiertas tú? ¿Te despierta un despertador, o puedes despertarte sin uno?
2. ¿Te diviertes cuando sales con tus amigos? ¿Qué hacen Uds. para divertirse?
3. ¿Qué te pones cuando vas a una fiesta? ¿Y a una fiesta de disfraces? ¿Qué te pones cuando hace mucho frío? ¿Qué te pones cuando vas a la playa o a la piscina?

Enrichment: Additional questions for Ex. F: *¿Con qué clase de jabón te lavas la cara? ¿Con qué clase de champú te lavas el pelo? ¿Qué clase de pasta dentífrica usas cuando te cepillas los dientes?*

Práctica D
1. ¿Por qué no te bañas? No me quiero bañar. No tengo ganas de bañarme.
2. ¿Por qué no te duchas? No me quiero duchar. No tengo ganas de ducharme.
3. ¿... te lavas el pelo? No me quiero lavar el pelo. No ... lavarme el pelo.
4. ¿... te peinas? No me quiero peinar. No ... peinarme.
5. ¿... te cepillas los dientes? No me quiero cepillar los dientes. No ... cepillarme los dientes.
6. ¿... te vistes? No me quiero vestir. No ... vestirme.
7. ¿... te pones el abrigo? No me quiero poner el abrigo. No ... ponerme el abrigo.
8. ¿... te acuestas? No me quiero acostar. No ... acostarme.

Práctica E
1. En casa me visto despacio. / Pues aquí tienes que vestirte de prisa.
2. En casa me cepillo los dientes por la mañana y por la noche. / Pues aquí tienes que cepillarte los dientes después de cada comida.
3. ... me acuesto ... / ... acostarte ...
4. ... me despierto ... / despertarte ...
5. ... me levanto ... / ... levantarte ...
6. ...me lavo ... / ... lavarte ...
7. ... me divierto ... / ... divertirte ...

Práctica F
Answers will vary.

Practice Sheets 14–3, 14–4

Workbook Exs. E–F

Tape Manual Exs. 5–6 9

Refrán 10

Activity Master 14–1

Quiz 14–3

APLICACIONES Discretionary

El deporte también es trabajo 11

ANTES DE LEER
What do you think the
answers to these questions
might be?
1. ¿Qué cosas hay que
   hacer para ser atleta?
2. Si su trabajo es el
   deporte, ¿qué hace un(a)
   atleta para divertirse?
3. ¿Es más difícil ser atleta
   o, por ejemplo,
   médico(a)? ¿Por qué?

¡Qué fabulosa es la vida¹ de los atletas! Viajar por todos los países del mundo,² ganar³ mucho dinero y ser muy popular. ¡Qué divertido! Es lo que muchas personas creen.

5 Pero la vida de los atletas no es fácil. Todos los días se levantan muy temprano para correr. Después practican su deporte de dos a cuatro horas. ¡Dos veces todos los días! Y para estar en excelentes condiciones físicas tienen que hacer ejercicio⁴ y comer bien. Hay que ser fuerte y muy enérgico.

En la Argentina, la tenista Gabriela Sabatini es un ídolo nacional. Es 10 muy joven, pero ya es una de las mejores tenistas del mundo.

Gabriela juega al tenis en muchas ciudades y muchos países. Viaja durante seis semanas y después regresa a su casa—pero no puede descansar⁵ porque tiene que practicar cada día. Para divertirse, Gabriela monta en su moto. También le gustan⁶ los juegos electrónicos y la música 15 de Lionel Richie. Gabriela canta muy bien.

Gabriela Sabatini todavía no es la jugadora de tenis número uno del mundo, pero, ¿en el futuro? ¡Tal vez! Por el momento, está contenta porque cada día juega un poco mejor.

---

¹**la vida**   *life*   ²**el mundo**   *world*   ³**ganar**   here: *to earn*   ⁴**hacer ejercicio**   *to exercise*   ⁵**descansar**   *to rest*   ⁶**le gustan**   *she likes*

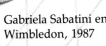

Gabriela Sabatini en
Wimbledon, 1987

Preguntas

Match the sentence beginning on the left with the appropriate ending on the right. Then put the sentences in the proper sequence.

1. Gabriela practica el tenis
2. Para divertirse, Gabriela
3. La vida de un atleta
4. También escucha
5. Gabriela está contenta
6. Es muy joven, pero ya
7. En su país, Gabriela es
8. Una tenista tiene que ser
9. Los atletas se levantan

a. monta en su moto.
b. es una de las mejores tenistas del mundo.
c. fuerte y enérgica.
d. dos veces todos los días.
e. muy temprano.
f. es bastante difícil.
g. la música de Lionel Richie.
h. un ídolo nacional.
i. perezosa.
j. porque cada día juega mejor.
k. muy tarde.

(arriba, izquierda) Tony Armas; (arriba, derecha) Diego Maradona; (abajo) Roberto Clemente

EXPLICACIONES II

El infinitivo con preposiciones

◆ **OBJECTIVES:**

**TO GIVE AND
FOLLOW
DIRECTIONS OR
INSTRUCTIONS**

**TO EXPLAIN AND
UNDERSTAND
CORRECT
SEQUENCE IN
DOING
SOMETHING**

**TO EXPLAIN
PURPOSES OR
INTENTIONS**

In Spanish, we often use the infinitive after prepositions such as *antes de* ("before"), *después de* ("after"), *para* ("to, in order to"), and *sin* ("without").

Me lavo las manos **antes de comer.**   *I wash my hands before* { *eating* / *I eat.*

Después de estudiar, miro la tele.   *After I study* / *After studying* } *I watch TV.*

Practico **para ganar.**   *I practice (in order) to win.*

Salió **sin ponerse** los zapatos.   *He left without putting on his shoes.*

PRÁCTICA

A ¿Antes o después? ¿Hay que hacer la segunda acción antes o después de la primera? Sigue el modelo.

> comer / lavarse las manos
> *Antes de comer hay que lavarse las manos.*
> comer / quitar los platos
> *Después de comer hay que quitar los platos.*

1. cocinar / servir la comida
2. hablar / pensar
3. levantarse / despertarse
4. cepillarse los dientes / acostarse
5. vestirse / levantarse
6. bañarse / quitarse la ropa
7. ver la película / volver a casa
8. jugar al fútbol / ducharse

Práctica A
1. Después de cocinar hay que servir la comida. (*or:* Antes de servir … hay que cocinar.)
2. Antes de hablar hay que pensar.
3. Antes de levantarse hay que despertarse.
4. Después de cepillarse los dientes hay que acostarse. (*or:* Antes de acostarse hay que cepillarse …)
5. Antes de vestirse hay que levantarse. (*or:* Después de levantarse hay que vestirse …)
6. Antes de bañarse hay que quitarse la ropa.
7. Después de ver la película hay que volver a casa.
8. Después de jugar al fútbol hay que ducharse.

Una esquiadora en Sierra Nevada, España.

B ¿Para qué? ¿Para qué usamos estas cosas? Usa palabras de la izquierda y de la derecha para formar frases. Sigue el modelo.

> anteojos
> *Usamos anteojos para ver bien.*
> pasta dentífrica
> *Usamos pasta dentífrica para cepillarnos los dientes.*

1. un balón
2. un tenedor
3. una pelota
4. un despertador
5. champú
6. dinero
7. un peine
8. jabón y agua
9. un bolígrafo
10. un reloj
11. la biblioteca

a. bañarse
b. comer
c. escribir
d. estudiar
e. jugar al golf
f. jugar al volibol
g. lavarse el pelo
h. ver la hora
i. pagar lo que compramos
j. peinarse
k. despertarse
l. ver bien
m. cepillarse los dientes

Práctica B
1. f
2. b
3. e
4. k (despertarnos)
5. g (lavarnos el pelo)
6. i
7. j (peinarnos)
8. a (bañarnos)
9. c
10. h
11. d

C ¡Nunca! Hay cosas que nunca hacemos sin hacer otra cosa antes. Escoge *(Choose)* la expresión apropiada de la derecha para completar cada frase. Sigue el modelo.

> ir afuera cuando llueve
> *Nunca voy afuera cuando llueve sin ponerme un impermeable.*

1. acostarse
2. pedir nada
3. empezar un trabajo
4. regresar de un viaje
5. salir de casa
6. subir a un avión
7. salir de un restaurante
8. pagar la cuenta

a. dejar una propina
b. cepillarse los dientes
c. buscar las salidas
d. ponerse un impermeable
e. comprender lo que debo hacer
f. traer un regalo para mi novio(a)
g. leer todo el menú
h. peinarse y ponerse un sombrero
i. repasarla

Práctica C
1. b
2. g
3. e
4. f
5. h (peinarme / ponerme)
6. c
7. a
8. i

D El horario Imagina que tienes que hacer todas estas cosas hoy. Usa *antes de* y *después de* para preguntar y contestar. Sigue el modelo.

7:30 levantarme
7:40 ducharme
7:50 vestirme
8:00 tomar el desayuno
8:20 ir a la escuela
12:00 comer en la cafetería
3:00 regresar a casa
3:30 dar de comer al gato
4:00 ir al dentista
5:30 mirar la tele
6:30 ayudar a cocinar
7:30 comer en casa
8:00 estudiar
10:30 acostarme

ESTUDIANTE A *¿Qué haces antes de tomar el desayuno?*
ESTUDIANTE B *Antes de tomar el desayuno, me visto.*
ESTUDIANTE A *¿Qué haces después de tomar el desayuno?*
ESTUDIANTE B *Después de tomar el desayuno, voy a la escuela.*

Reteach / Review: After students do Ex. D in class, you may want to ask them to write five sentences at home about their own routines, using *antes de* and *después de*.
  If students wrote sentences about their families' routines for p. 474, ask them to edit those sentences by adding *antes de* and *después de*.

E Hablemos de ti.

1. ¿Puedes decirle a la clase qué haces todos los días por la mañana? Oyes el despertador y luego . . .
2. ¿Qué haces después de regresar a casa por la tarde?
3. ¿Qué haces entre las cinco y las siete de la tarde?
4. ¿Miras la tele por la noche? ¿Lo haces antes o después de hacer la tarea? ¿Qué vas a mirar esta noche?
5. ¿A qué hora te acuestas? ¿Quién se acuesta primero en tu casa?
6. ¿Hay cosas que tú no haces sin hacer otra cosa antes? ¿Cuáles son?

Practice Sheet 14–5   Workbook Exs. G–J

 12 Tape Manual Exs. 7–8   Activity Master 14–2   Quiz 14–4

Práctica E
Answers will vary.

Enrichment: Additional questions for Ex. E: *¿Adónde vas después de salir de la escuela? ¿A qué clase vas después de comer el almuerzo? ¿Vienes a la escuela a veces sin peinarte?*

ACTIVIDAD

Antes y después   Work in groups of three. One person begins by making up a sentence telling something that he or she does. The second person then makes up a sentence about what the first person does next. The third person makes up a sentence about what the first person does before doing either of those two things. For example:

ESTUDIANTE A   Hago la maleta.
ESTUDIANTE B   Después de hacer la maleta, va al aeropuerto.
ESTUDIANTE C   Antes de hacer la maleta, busca su ropa.

APLICACIONES

Notes: Answers to the **Repaso** and **Tema** appear in the pre-chapter teacher pages.

REPASO

Look carefully at the model sentences. Then put the English cues into Spanish to form new sentences based on the models.

1. *Tomás es un piloto alto y delgado.*
   (Ana is a strong but pessimistic player.)
   (We are good but lazy players (m. pl.).)
   (You (pl.) are nice and generous fans (f. pl.).)

2. *Se baña a las ocho.*
   (He goes to bed at 10:00.)
   (I go to sleep at 9:00.)
   (We wake up at 6:00.)

3. *Después de peinarte, te vistes. Te pones el vestido y las sandalias.*
   (After waking up, I get dressed. I put on my suit and tie.)
   (After getting up, we get dressed. We wash our face and hands.)
   (After taking a bath, you (pl.) get dressed. You put on your necklace and earrings.)

4. *Es tarde y hay que trabajar de prisa.*
   (It's late but they must sing twice.)
   (It's late and we must return in a hurry.)
   (It's late but he must walk slowly.)

5. *Te diviertes mucho en el partido de béisbol.*
   (I have a lot of fun in the chemistry lab.)
   (We have a lot of fun in Spanish class.)
   (They have a lot of fun at the golf match.)

En Puerto Rico

Notes: Review of:
1. adjective agreement
   ser + modified noun
2. reflexive verbs
   time telling
3. *después de* + infinitive
   reflexive verbs
   definite article
      with clothing and
      parts of the body
4. *hay que*
   adverbs
5. reflexive verbs
   noun phrases with *de*

En México

TEMA

Transparency 59

Notes: You may want to assign the **Tema** as written homework.

Put the English captions into Spanish.

1. Graciela is a strong and energetic athlete.

2. She gets up at 7:00.

3. After taking a bath, she gets dressed. She puts on her T-shirt and pants.

4. It's late and she must leave quickly.

5. Graciela has a lot of fun at the volleyball game.

REDACCIÓN

Notes: Students may work in pairs to complete their **Redacción** dialogues and paragraphs. Time allowing, ask volunteers to read their work aloud.

Now you are ready to write your own dialogue or paragraph. Choose one of the following topics.

1. Expand the *Tema* by describing what else Graciela does before going to the volleyball game. What sports is she a fan of? Which ones does she play? Who's her favorite player? Do you think she prefers watching or playing sports?

2. Write a paragraph about a sport that you enjoy. Which sport? Are you a player? How often do you play? If you are a fan, who's your favorite player? Which is your favorite team? Describe the kind of player you are. Do you always try to win? Do you usually win?

3. Write a thought (or dream) balloon for each picture in the *Tema*.

COMPRUEBA TU PROGRESO   CAPÍTULO 14   Discretionary

Notes: Answers to the **Comprueba** appear in the pre-chapter teacher pages.

A   ¿Cuál de los dos?
Choose the correct verb form to complete each sentence.

1. María ____ el coche.
   a. lava   b. se lava
2. Yo ____ los zapatos.
   a. pongo   b. me pongo
3. Pilar ____ a su hermana.
   a. peina   b. se peina
4. Ellos ____ por la mañana.
   a. bañan   b. se bañan
5. Jorge y yo ____ los platos.
   a. quitamos   b. nos quitamos
6. Teresa ____ a sus padres todos los días.
   a. despierta   b. se despierta
7. Tú ____ a tu hermanita.
   a. vistes   b. te vistes
8. Uds. ____ a sus hijos cada noche.
   a. acuestan   b. se acuestan

B   Lo que hacen
Complete each sentence with the correct reflexive form.

1. (Nosotros) ____ la cara.   *(lavarse)*
2. Ella nunca ____.   *(divertirse)*
3. Ud. ____ el suéter rojo.   *(ponerse)*
4. Tengo que ____ los dientes.   *(cepillarse)*
5. ¿Por qué no ____ (nosotros) el sombrero?   *(quitarse)*
6. Los niños ____.   *(dormirse)*
7. ¿Vas a ____ ahora?   *(levantarse)*
8. ¿Por qué no ____ (tú) ahora?   *(vestirse)*
9. (Yo) ____ por la noche.   *(bañarse)*

C   ¿Sí o no?
Answer each question according to the model.

   ¿Se lava el pelo con jabón tu amigo?
   (no / champú)
   No, se lava el pelo con champú.

1. ¿Se bañan con agua fría tus hermanos?
   (no / caliente)

2. ¿Te levantas a las siete? (no / seis)
3. ¿Se despiertan temprano Uds.? (no / tarde)
4. ¿Te duchas por la mañana? (no / por la noche)
5. ¿Se cepillan Uds. los dientes antes de comer? (no /después)
6. ¿Te acuestas después de la cena? (no / más tarde)

D   ¿Qué usas para . . . ?
Create a sentence like the one in the model.

   el lápiz
   Uso el lápiz para escribir.

1. el balón   5. la pasta dentífrica
2. el peine   6. el jabón
3. el tenedor   7. el despertador
4. el champú

E   ¿Cómo y cuándo?
Form sentences according to the model.

   Me acuesto. Leo un poco. (antes de)
   Antes de acostarme leo un poco.

1. Nos levantamos. Comemos el desayuno. (después de)
2. Se despiertan. Mis padres necesitan un despertador. (para)
3. Me duermo. Bebo chocolate caliente. (para)
4. Me baño. Me quito la ropa. (antes de)
5. Se divierte. Hace la tarea. (antes de)
6. Me peino. Voy a salir. (después de)

F   Un chico muy malo
Form sentences according to the model.

   Sale del café. No paga.
   Sale del café sin pagar.

1. Se acuesta. No dice buenas noches.
2. Recibe los regalos. No dice gracias.
3. Sube al autobús. No hace cola.
4. Va a la escuela. No se peina.
5. Sale del cuarto. No presenta a los invitados.
6. Empieza a comer. No espera a nadie.

   Chapter 14 Test   Listening Comprehension Test

VOCABULARIO DEL CAPÍTULO 14

Sustantivos
el aficionado, la aficionada
el/la atleta
el balón, *pl.* los balones
la cara
el cepillo de dientes
el champú
el/la dentista
el desodorante
el despertador
los dientes
la ducha
el equipo
el golf
el jabón, *pl.* los jabones
el jugador, la jugadora
la mano
la pasta dentífrica
el peine
el pelo
la pelota
la seda dental
la vez, *pl.* las veces
el volibol

Pronombres Reflexivos
nos
se

Adjetivos
atlético, -a
débil
enérgico, -a
fuerte
perezoso, -a

Verbos
acostar(se) (o → ue)
bañar(se)
cepillar(se) (los dientes, el pelo)
correr
despertar(se) (e → ie)
divertirse (e → ie)
dormirse (o → ue)
ducharse
esperar *(to hope, to expect)*
ganar
lavarse
levantar(se)
peinar(se)
perder (e → ie)
ponerse
quitarse
regresar
tratar de (+ *inf.*)
vestir(se) (e → i)

Adverbios
despacio
rápidamente

Expresiones
de prisa
dos veces
¡espero que sí / no!
hay que
lo que
una vez

MADRID

LOS ESPAÑOLES PREFIEREN EL TREN

Aquí *viene el tren de la Fresa.* "Here comes the Strawberry Train!" As the ancient steam locomotive chugs and puffs its way into the station in Aranjuez, the town band strikes up a lively march. Not every train in Spain gets this kind of reception, but then none of the others has antique cars that are pulled by a real steam engine. *El tren de la Fresa* is a nostalgia special that travels only on summer weekends and holidays.

Originally a private train, it was built to carry the royal family back and forth between Madrid and their summer palace in Aranjuez, about 30 miles away. Later, when the train was opened to the public, the trip became a popular outing for crowds of people who climbed aboard with their picnic baskets. And every night the train brought a freight car full of fresh strawberries back to Madrid.

Even in the age of jet planes, traveling by train is still very popular in Spain. The reason might be found in the trains themselves. Passenger cars usually have a series of compartments along a passageway. In each compartment people sit facing each other, four to a side, and so they have a chance to get acquainted. Even before a train leaves the station, a compartment full of strangers has already begun to look and sound like a gathering of friends in a living room.

Spain also has modern trains, of course, with well-padded seats set in neat pairs, air-conditioning, and little overhead reading lights. But these trains are not nearly as popular as the traditional ones. Most Spaniards would much rather travel in a way that offers congenial conversation in a relaxing, comfortable atmosphere.

PALABRAS NUEVAS I

Transparency 60
CONTEXTO
VISUAL

Un viaje por Europa

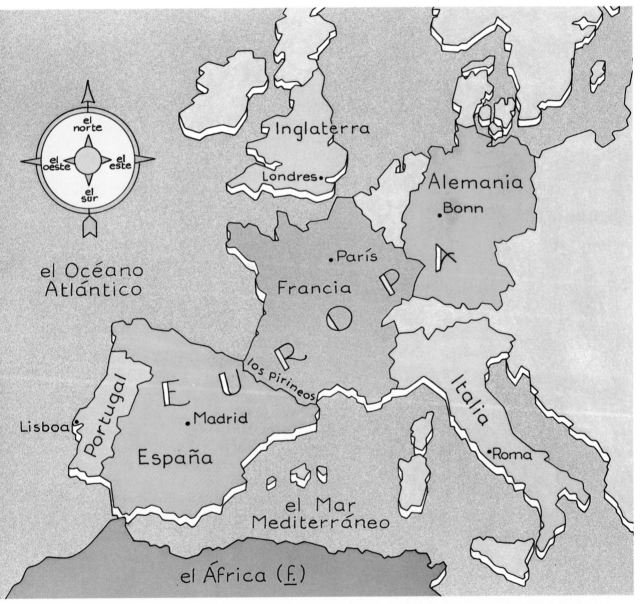

If students ask: Other related words you may want to present: *Irlanda*, Ireland; *Escocia*,
Scotland; *el compás / la brújula*, compass; *nordeste*, northeast; *noroeste*, northwest; *sudeste*,
southeast; *suroeste*, southwest.

los recuerdos

la tarjeta postal

CONTEXTO COMUNICATIVO 2

1 SONIA   ¿De dónde eres, Armando?

ARMANDO   Del Paraguay.

SONIA   ¡Ah! Del Paraguay. ¿Y **cuánto tiempo hace que** estás aquí?

ARMANDO   **Hace** tres años.

Variaciones:
- del Paraguay → **del Brasil**
- estás → vives

¿cuánto tiempo hace que (+ present tense)? *how long has (someone) been (doing something)?*

hace (+ time)   *for* (+ time)

el Brasil   *Brazil*

2 JAIME   Vas a divertirte mucho en tu viaje **por** Europa. ¿**Sabes** hablar francés?

ANDREA   **Más o menos.** Sé también un poco de **alemán** e **italiano.**

JAIME   ¡Qué bueno!

- alemán → **portugués**
- ¡qué bueno! → ¡qué suerte!

por   *through, across*

saber (yo sé, tú sabes)   *to know;* (+ infinitive) *to know how*

más o menos   *more or less*

el alemán   *German (language)*

el italiano   *Italian (language)*

el portugués   *Portuguese (language)*

3 ARTURO   Si **haces un viaje,** vas a necesitar un **guía,** ¿no?

MARÍA   ¡Claro que no! Sólo voy al norte de Italia para visitar a mis abuelos. Y hablo italiano bastante bien.

- al norte → al sur
- al norte → al oeste

hacer un viaje   *to take a trip*

el / la guía   *guide*

4 LOLA   Hace dos años que vivo en Europa. Pero acabo de llegar a Barcelona.

DIEGO   **¿Conoces** a muchos españoles?*

LOLA   ¡Ah, sí! Y conozco a muchos ingleses y franceses también.

DIEGO   Sí. Europa es bastante pequeña, pero hay muchos países.

LOLA   ¡Y docenas de **lenguas**!

- dos años que vivo en → dos meses que viajo por
- ingleses → portugueses
- ingleses y franceses → alemanes e italianos

conocer (yo conozco, tú conoces)   *to know, to be acquainted with*

la lengua   *language*

Notes: Point out the omission of the accent mark in the plural forms of *inglés, portugués, francés,* and *alemán* in minidialogue 4.

5 PABLO   ¿Sabes en qué hotel está Luis? Quiero **mandarle** una carta.

EMILIA   No, **no lo sé.**† Tal vez papá puede darte la dirección.

- mandarle → escribirle
- una carta → una tarjeta postal
- no, no lo sé → sí, **lo sé**
  tal vez papá puede darte → pero no tengo

mandar   *to send*

(yo) no lo sé   *I don't know (that)*

(yo) lo sé   *I know (that)*

PRÁCTICA

Reteach / Extra Help: In preparation for Ex. A, you may want to ask these questions: *¿Cuál es la capital de Alemania? (Bonn.) ¿Y de Francia? (París.) ¿Y de Inglaterra? (Londres.) ¿Y cuál es la capital de Italia? (Roma.) ¿Y de Portugal? (Lisboa.) ¿Y de España? (Madrid.)*

A   **Tarjetas postales.**   Imagina que un(a) amigo(a) viaja por Europa y te manda tarjetas postales de cada país que visita. Describe las tarjetas que recibes. Usa frases de la lista para terminar la conversación.

ESTUDIANTE A   *Está en Italia.*

ESTUDIANTE B   *¿Habla italiano?*

ESTUDIANTE A   *Creo que no.*

o: *Creo que sí.*

ESTUDIANTE B   *¡Qué lástima!*

o: *¡Qué bueno!*

| ¡caramba! | ¡ojalá! | ¡qué lástima! | ¡qué mala suerte! |
| ¡no me digas! | ¡qué bueno! | ¡qué suerte! | ¡espero que sí! |

---

* Adjectives formed from the names of countries can also be used as nouns to refer to people who come from that country: *Una española viene de España, los ingleses vienen de Inglaterra, un alemán viene de Alemania,* etc. Remember that we do not capitalize them.

† In expressions such as *lo sé* and *no lo sé,* the pronoun *lo* refers to a phrase rather than to a specific noun. In this case, *lo = en qué hotel está Luis.* So even if it were a feminine noun—say, *en qué oficina*—we would still use *lo,* not *la.*

B **¿Cuántas lenguas hablas?** Imagina que tienes muchos amigos que hablan otras lenguas o que conocen a gente que habla otras lenguas. Pregunta y contesta *sí* o *no* según los modelos.

> francés / unos muchachos
> ESTUDIANTE A   *¿Sabes hablar francés?*
> ESTUDIANTE B   *No, pero conozco a unos muchachos franceses.*
> o: *Sí, y conozco a unos muchachos franceses.*

1. inglés / unas chicas
2. italiano / una actriz
3. alemán / una guía
4. francés / unas muchachas
5. portugués / unos chicos
6. inglés / una profesora
7. alemán / unos atletas
8. italiano / un fotógrafo
9. español / unos estudiantes
10. portugués / una dentista

C **Hablemos de ti.**
1. ¿Cuánto tiempo hace que estudias español? ¿Qué otras lenguas sabes hablar? ¿Qué otras lenguas quieres aprender a hablar?
2. ¿A veces vas de vacaciones con tu familia? ¿Adónde viajan Uds.? ¿Te gusta hacer viajes?
3. ¿Recibes tarjetas postales de tus amigos cuando viajan? ¿Les mandas tarjetas a ellos cuando tú viajas? ¿Qué escribes en una tarjeta postal?
4. ¿Qué país está al norte de los Estados Unidos? ¿Está Francia al este o al oeste de Alemania? ¿Qué país está más cerca de España, Portugal o Italia?
5. ¿Esperas viajar por Europa? ¿Por qué países piensas viajar? ¿Por qué? ¿Qué quieres ver y hacer allí? ¿Qué sabes del país o de los países que quieres visitar?

Práctica A
Second pair of interchanges will vary.
1. Está en Alemania.
   ¿Habla alemán?
2. Está en Francia.
   ¿Habla francés?
3. Está en Inglaterra.
   ¿Habla inglés?
4. Está en Italia.
   ¿Habla italiano?
5. Está en Portugal.
   ¿Habla portugués?
6. Está en España.
   ¿Habla español?

Práctica B
1. ¿Sabes hablar inglés?
   No, pero (*or:* Sí, y) conozco a unas chicas inglesas.
2. italiano
   una actriz italiana
3. alemán
   una guía alemana
4. francés
   unas muchachas francesas
5. portugués
   unos chicos portugueses
6. inglés
   una profesora inglesa
7. alemán
   unos atletas alemanes
8. italiano
   un fotógrafo italiano
9. español
   unos estudiantes españoles
10. portugués
   una dentista portuguesa

Práctica C
Answers will vary.

APLICACIONES Discretionary

La Carrera[1] Internacional 5

Hugo Molina, un locutor[2] del canal 11, habla con Pedro Colón sobre la Carrera Internacional del ciclismo.[3]

SR. MOLINA	¡Qué suerte para todos los aficionados al ciclismo poder hablar con Pedro Colón!
5 SR. COLÓN	Gracias, Hugo.
SR. MOLINA	El año pasado saliste muy bien en la Tour de France, la gran carrera por Francia. Cada año hay más y más gente de otros países en esa carrera, ¿no?
SR. COLÓN	Por supuesto. Es la carrera más importante del año. 10 ¡Y la más larga! Dura más o menos tres semanas. Hay ciclistas italianos, ingleses, españoles, colombianos y, por supuesto, franceses. Ahora vienen varios norteamericanos también.
SR. MOLINA	¿Qué nos puedes decir sobre la Carrera 15 Internacional?
SR. COLÓN	Va a ser fantástica. Vamos por el norte de España a través de[4] los Pirineos. El viaje dura tres días, más o menos.
SR. MOLINA	Todos tus amigos te desean[5] buena suerte, Pedro.
20 SR. COLÓN	Muchas gracias, Hugo. ¡Y saludos a todos!

Ciclistas cerca de Mar del Plata, Argentina

---

[1]**la carrera** *race*   [2]**el locutor** *announcer*   [3]**el ciclismo** *cycling*
[4]**a través de** *across*   [5]**desear** *to wish*

Preguntas

Contesta según el diálogo.
1. ¿Qué deporte practica Pedro Colón?   2. ¿En qué carrera salió Pedro muy bien el año pasado?   3. Según Pedro, ¿cómo es la Tour de France?   4. En la Tour de France hay ciclistas de muchos países. ¿Cuáles?   5. ¿Cuánto tiempo dura la Carrera Internacional?   6. ¿Crees que es una carrera fácil o no? ¿Por qué?

Notes: Students who do not play any sport or game may talk about a hobby or favorite pastime in their **Participación** dialogues.

Participación

Work with a partner to make up a dialogue about a sport or game you play. How long have you been playing it? When do you practice or play? How long does a game last? Do you have a lot of fun?

Enrichment: Write these unknown words on the board and ask students to pronounce them: *ley, loro, maldad, gemelo, huipil.* The sentences in B are suitable for dictation.

PRONUNCIACIÓN 6

A The letter *l* in Spanish has a sound similar to that of the *l* in the English word "leap." The tip of your tongue touches the ridge right behind your front teeth. Escucha y repite.

león	lago	limón	lugar	lengua
Italia	alemán	elefante	hablar	alumno
capital	árbol	cuál	animal	sol

B Escucha y repite.

Los alumnos hablan alemán.   ¿Cuál es la capital de Italia?
Hay limones en ese árbol.   Luis y Elena salen de la sala.

Aplicaciones   **493**

PALABRAS NUEVAS II

Quiero hacer una reservación

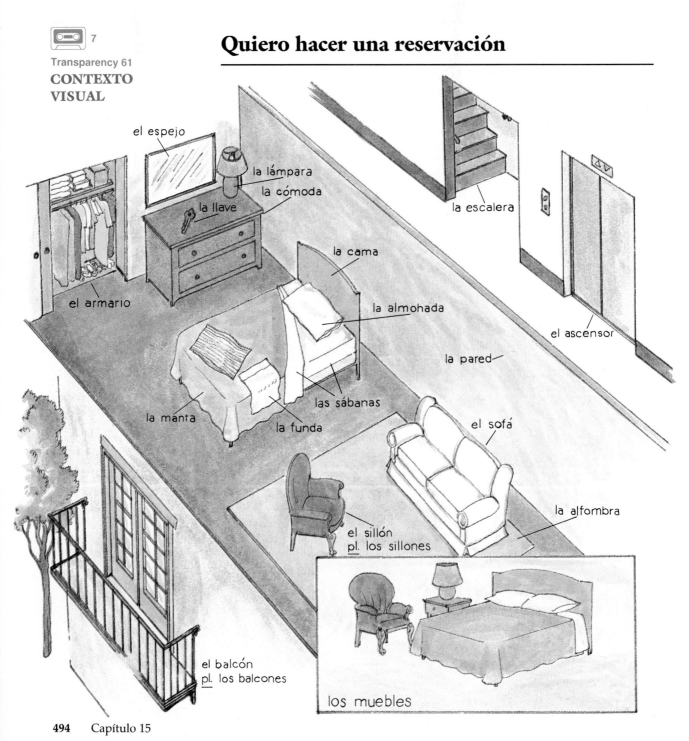

el espejo

la lámpara

la cómoda

la llave

el armario

la escalera

la cama

la almohada

el ascensor

la pared

las sábanas

la manta

la funda

el sofá

el sillón
pl. los sillones

la alfombra

el balcón
pl. los balcones

los muebles

Notes: You may want to point out that *la guía* in mini-dialogue 1 is a guidebook. Note the difference between *el / la guía* (mini-dialogue 3, p. 389) and *la guía*.

Enrichment: Suggest these additional **Variaciones** for mini-dialogue 1: *este año → el año próximo; España → la Argentina.*

CONTEXTO COMUNICATIVO 8

1 FELIPE   Este año quiero hacer un viaje a España.
                 ¿Conoces un buen hotel en Madrid?

   INÉS   Esta guía de viajes **describe** varios hoteles
                 buenos y baratos, pero es **necesario** hacer
                 reservaciones.

                          describir *to describe*
                          necesario, -a *necessary*
                          la reservación, pl. **las reservaciones** *reservation*

Variaciones:
- hacer un viaje a → viajar por
- es necesario → hay que

2 SRA. RUIZ   **Discúlpeme,** ¿puedo hablar con **el gerente**?
   LA GERENTE   Yo soy la gerente, señora. ¿Puedo ayudarla?
   SRA. RUIZ   **Quisiera un cuarto* con vista al** mar.
   LA GERENTE   ¿Y cuánto tiempo piensa Ud. **quedarse**?
   SRA. RUIZ   Tres días.

discúlpeme = (formal) *excuse me, pardon me, I beg your pardon*
el / la gerente *manager*
quisiera *I'd like*
el cuarto *room*
con vista a(l) *with a view of*
quedarse *to stay, to remain*
privado, -a *private*

- discúlpeme → perdón
- con vista al mar → con baño **privado**

3 LA GERENTE   Yolanda, es necesario cambiar las sábanas del
                    cuarto 512.
   YOLANDA   Sí, señora. Vuelvo **en seguida** con sábanas
                    limpias.

en seguida *right away, immediately*

- es necesario → tienes que
- con sábanas → con sábanas y fundas

4 ANDRÉS   **¿Disfrutaste de** tus vacaciones?
   MÓNICA   Sí, me quedé en un hotel cerca de la playa y nadé
                  todos los días.

disfrutar de *to enjoy*

- cerca de la playa → cerca del lago
- cerca de la playa → con vista al río
- nadé → tomé el sol

* We use *el cuarto* to mean any room in a house or hotel. Just as in English, we can use it to mean bedroom: *mi cuarto = mi dormitorio.*

5 MARIO   **Con permiso,*** señor. ¿Me puede Ud. decir dónde está el restaurante del hotel?

GERENTE   Sí, **con mucho gusto.** Está en el primer piso, al lado del ascensor.

MARIO   Muchas gracias. Ud. es muy amable.

- el restaurante → la piscina
- el primer piso → la planta baja
- al lado → enfrente

6 CLARA   ¿Conoces al grupo de rock "Las Sillas"?

RAFAEL   Por supuesto. Son **fantásticos.**

CLARA   Pues, esta noche van a tocar en el Roxi.

RAFAEL   **¿De veras?**

CLARA   Claro.

- fantásticos → fabulosos
- ¿de veras? → ¿estás **segura**?
- ¿de veras? → ¡no me digas!
- claro → sí, ¡de veras!

EN OTRAS PARTES

En México se dice *la cobija*. En el Caribe y la Argentina se dice *la frazada*.

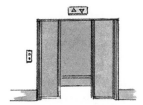

También se dice *el elevador*.

En México se dice *el closet*. También se dice *el guardarropa* y *el ropero*.

En Cuba y en Puerto Rico se dice *la butaca*.

* We use *con permiso* to ask permission to leave or to ask someone to let us pass by. In other situations we usually use *discúlpeme* or *perdón*.

PRÁCTICA

A **¿Dónde está todo?** Imagina que siempre pierdes tus cosas y que un(a) amigo(a) te ayuda a buscarlas. Pregunta y contesta según el modelo.

ESTUDIANTE A *¿Dónde están mis aretes?*
ESTUDIANTE B *Voy a buscarlos. Tal vez los dejaste en el sofá.*

Práctica A

1. ¿Dónde está mi cinturón? Voy a buscarlo. Tal vez lo dejaste en la cómoda.
2. ¿Dónde está mi boleto? Voy a buscarlo. Tal vez lo dejaste en la mesa.
3. ¿... mi cámara? Voy a buscarla. Tal vez la dejaste en el armario.
4. ¿... mi pasaporte? Voy a buscarlo. Tal vez lo dejaste en la cama.
5. ¿... mi pañuelo? Voy a buscarlo. Tal vez lo dejaste en el sillón.
6. ¿... mi anillo? Voy a buscarlo. Tal vez lo dejaste en el baño.
7. ¿... mis llaves? Voy a buscarlas. Tal vez las dejaste en el ascensor.
8. ¿... mi maleta? Voy a buscarla. Tal vez la dejaste en la escalera.

1.

2.

3.

4.

5.

6.

7.

8.

Palabras Nuevas II   **497**

Práctica B
1. quisiera tener un cuarto …
   es necesario hacer …
2. quisiera ir a pie … es
   necesario llevar …
3. quisiera disfrutar de … es
   necesario hacer …
4. quisiera sacar fotos … es
   necesario saber usar …
5. quisiera conocer bien a …
   es necesario caminar …
6. quisiera comprar … es
   necesario llevar …
7. quisiera viajar solo(a) … es
   necesario tener …
8. quisiera ir al norte … es
   necesario llevar …
9. quisiera no estar cansado(a)
   … es necesario tratar de
   acostarse …

B   Querida Abby.   Imagina que tú eres la "Dear Abby" para el periódico de la escuela. Esta semana escribes consejos *(advice)* para turistas. Sigue el modelo.

> viajar a Inglaterra / tener un pasaporte
> **ESTUDIANTE A**   *Querida Abby, quisiera viajar a Inglaterra. ¿Qué tengo que hacer?*
> **ESTUDIANTE B**   *Para viajar a Inglaterra es necesario tener un pasaporte.*

1. tener un cuarto con baño privado / hacer una reservación de prisa
2. ir a pie por la ciudad / llevar zapatos cómodos
3. disfrutar de mi viaje / hacer buenos planes en seguida
4. sacar fotos perfectas / saber usar bien la cámara
5. conocer bien a la ciudad / caminar por las calles
6. comprar muchos recuerdos / llevar bastante dinero
7. viajar solo(a) por el país / tener un buen mapa
8. ir al norte de Europa / llevar un suéter
9. no estar cansado(a) todos los días / tratar de acostarse temprano

Práctica C
1. … no tiene baño privado
2. … no sube hasta el tercer
   piso
3. … no cierra bien
4. … está demasiado fría
5. … no están limpias
6. … no son amables
7. … son viejos e incómodos
8. … no es Morales
9. … no tiene vista al océano

C   De viaje.   El Sr. Romero nunca está contento. ¿Qué le dice el gerente? Escoge *(Choose)* la mejor expresión de la derecha para completar cada frase. Sigue el modelo.

> la cama
> *La cama no es cómoda.*

1. el cuarto	estar demasiado fría
2. el ascensor	no cerrar bien
3. la puerta del baño	no tener baño privado
4. el agua de la piscina	no estar limpias
5. las sábanas	no subir hasta el tercer piso
6. los guías	no ser Morales
7. los sillones	no ser amables
8. mi apellido	no tener vista al océano
9. el balcón	ser viejos e incómodos
	no ser cómoda

Práctica D
1. No estoy seguro.
2. Sí, ¡cuidado!
3. En seguida.

D   ¿Qué dices?   Escoge la respuesta correcta para cada pregunta.

1. ¿Puede Ud. decirme dónde está nuestro guía?
   (¡Fantástico! / No estoy seguro. / Con permiso.)
2. ¿Qué hay en el camino? ¿Es un perro?
   (Sí, ¡cuidado! / Sí, hasta pronto. / ¡Saludos!)
3. ¿Cuándo empieza el partido de fútbol?
   (En el estadio. / No hay de qué. / En seguida.)

4. ¿Te gusta la alfombra de este cuarto?
   (*¡Caramba! / Más o menos. / Espero que sí.*)
5. ¿Vas a viajar en barco por el río Amazonas?
   (*No lo sé. / Ya lo sé. / Con permiso.*)
6. Dices que nuestro cuarto tiene vista al océano. ¿Estás segura?
   (*Sí, ¡de veras! / Sí, hasta luego. / No hay de qué.*)
7. ¿Puede Ud. traer las maletas a nuestro cuarto?
   (*¡No hay de qué! / ¿Qué importa? / Con mucho gusto.*)
8. ¿Es necesario cerrar la puerta con llave?
   (*No lo sé. / ¡De veras! / Yo tampoco.*)

E Hablemos de ti.
1. ¿Puedes describir tu cuarto? ¿Qué muebles hay allí? ¿De qué color son las paredes? ¿Tienes alfombra? ¿De qué color es?
2. ¿Cuál es el edificio más grande de tu ciudad? ¿Tiene ascensores? ¿Hay escaleras en tu casa? ¿Cuántos pisos tiene tu casa?
3. ¿Vives cerca de un río? ¿Cómo se llama? ¿Hay lagos cerca de tu ciudad? ¿Está tu ciudad cerca del océano?
4. Si viajas, ¿compras recuerdos? ¿Qué clase de recuerdos te gusta comprar? ¿Coleccionas recuerdos de otros países? ¿Les mandas recuerdos a tus amigos? ¿Qué les mandas a ellos? ¿Te mandan recuerdos a ti cuando hacen viajes?

4. Más o menos.
5. No lo sé.
6. Sí, ¡de veras!
7. Con mucho gusto.
8. No lo sé.

Práctica E
Answers will vary.

Enrichment: Additional questions for Ex. E: *¿Cómo es tu sala? ¿Tiene sofá? ¿Cuántos sillones hay? ¿Vives en el norte, el sur, el este o el oeste del país?*

Practice Sheet 15–2

Workbook Exs. C–D

Tape Manual Exs. 3–4 9

Quiz 15–2

Iglesia de la Virgen del Pilar en Zaragoza, España

ACTIVIDAD

¿Cómo es tu cuarto?   Get together with a partner
to find out what each other's room is like. You can
describe your room accurately or describe your
dream room. Here are some questions to get you
started:

> ¿Qué muebles hay en tu cuarto? ¿De qué
> colores son?
> ¿Qué vista tiene? ¿Tiene vista a la calle?
> ¿Hay decoraciones en las paredes?

Take turns asking questions until each of you can
describe the other person's room.

ESTUDIO DE PALABRAS

Did you know that many Spanish words originally came from Arabic?
Arabic was the language of the Moors of northern Africa, who invaded
Spain in 711 and remained there for almost eight hundred years. Because
they occupied Spain for so long, the Moors had a great influence on
Spanish culture and language. You can identify some words that came
from Arabic because they begin with *al-*. For example, *álgebra*, *almacén*,
alfombra, and *almohada*.

Here are some other Spanish words you know that came from Arabic:

azúcar   azul   cero   sofá   ojalá

Dos vistas de la Alhambra
en Granada, España

EXPLICACIONES I

Los verbos *saber* y *conocer*

In Spanish the verbs *saber* and *conocer* both mean "to know," but we use them very differently.

1 We use *saber* to talk about knowing *facts* or *information*. Here are all of the present-tense forms of *saber*.

INFINITIVO **saber**

	SINGULAR		PLURAL
1	(yo) **sé**	(nosotros) (nosotras)	**sabemos**
2	(tú) **sabes**	(vosotros) (vosotras)	**sabéis**
3	Ud. (él) **sabe** (ella)	Uds. (ellos) **saben** (ellas)	

¿Sabes dónde vive Javier?	*Do you **know** where Javier lives?*
¿Quién **sabe** la respuesta?	*Who **knows** the answer?*
Yo **sé** que tienes catorce años.	*I **know** (that) you're 14 years old.*

Remember that we can often omit the word "that" in English, but in Spanish we must use *que*.

2 *Saber* followed by an infinitive means to know *how* to do something.

Yo **sé** hacer una reservación.	*I **know how** to make a reservation.*
¿Sabes nadar?	*Do you **know how** to swim?*

◆ **OBJECTIVES:**

TO TELL WHAT AND WHOM YOU KNOW

TO MAKE SMALL TALK

TO BRAG

Notes: Various present-tense forms of *saber* appear in mini-dialogues 2 on p. 489 and 5 on p. 490. Mini-dialogues 4 on p. 490, 1 on p. 495, and 6 on p. 496 illustrate *conocer*.

Reteach / Review: Remind students that they have been using the expression *no sé* since the beginning of the course (**En camino B**).
  Point out the accent mark on *sé*. You may want to remind them that the accent is needed to distinguish *sé* from the pronoun *se*.

3 *Conocer* means "to know" in the sense of being *acquainted* or *familiar with* a person, place, or thing. Here are its present-tense forms.

INFINITIVO **conocer**

	SINGULAR		PLURAL
1	(yo) **conozco**	(nosotros) (nosotras)	**conocemos**
2	(tú) **conoces**	(vosotros) (vosotras)	**conocéis**
3	Ud. (él) **conoce** (ella)	Uds. (ellos) **conocen** (ellas)	

Conozco a Manuel.   *I **know** Manuel.*
¿Conoces esa canción?   *Do you **know** that song?*
¿Conoces a Barcelona?* *Are you **familiar with** Barcelona?*

4 Except for the *yo* forms, *saber* and *conocer* take the regular *-er* verb endings in the present tense.

PRÁCTICA

A **¿Qué saben hacer?** Sigue el modelo para decir lo que saben hacer estas personas.

> Juan / jugar a las damas
> *Juan sabe jugar a las damas.*

1. María / divertirse
2. (tú) / jugar al ajedrez
3. Juana y tú / sacar fotos
4. José / decorar pasteles
5. Ester y Mario / tocar el piano
6. Uds. / dibujar bien
7. (nosotros) / preparar paella
8. Ud. / contar chistes
9. (nosotras) / arreglar lámparas
10. Y tú, ¿qué sabes hacer?

* Many Spanish speakers use the personal *a* with the names of cities and countries after *conocer*.

B ¿Qué conocen? ¿Y a quiénes?   Describe a la gente, los lugares (*places*) y las cosas que conocen estas personas. Usa la *a* personal si es necesario.

> Raúl / Josefina
> *Raúl conoce a Josefina.*

1. Ud. / la gerente
2. Ester y yo / ese hombre
3. Julia / este edificio
5. Javier y tú / esos anuncios

5. (tú) / esas jugadoras
6. (yo) / todos los invitados
7. mis padres / esa guía
8. la tía Gloria / ese almacén

C ¿Lo conoce?   Ahora usa las frases de la Práctica B para preguntar y contestar. Sigue el modelo.

> ESTUDIANTE A   *¿Conoce Raúl a Josefina?*
> ESTUDIANTE B   *Sí, la conoce.*

D ¿Quién es Carlos?   Completa el párrafo (*paragraph*) con las formas correctas de *saber* o *conocer*.

(Yo) _____ a Carlos. Y (yo) _____ que tú lo _____ también. ¡De veras! Vamos a describirlo. Carlos _____ muchas cosas. _____ a qué hora nos despertamos. Y _____ muy bien dónde está la cocina. Él nos _____ y a todos nuestros amigos también. Pero nosotros nunca _____ lo que él
5 piensa, porque él no _____ hablar español, y nosotros no _____ su lengua. ¿Ahora crees que (tú) _____ quién es Carlos? Por supuesto, tú ya _____ a Carlos. Es mi gato.

Un baile folklórico en Barcelona, España

Práctica B
1. Ud. conoce a la gerente.
2. Ester y yo conocemos a ese hombre.
3. Julia conoce este edificio.
4. Javier y tú conocen esos anuncios.
5. Conoces a esas jugadoras.
6. Conozco a todos los invitados.
7. Mis padres conocen (a) esa guía.
8. La tía Gloria conoce ese almacén.

Práctica C
1. ¿Conoce Ud. a la gerente? Sí, la conozco.
2. ¿Conocemos Ester y yo a ese hombre? Sí, lo conocen.
3. ¿Conoce Julia este edificio? Sí, lo conoce.
4. ¿Conocen Javier y tú esos anuncios? Sí, los conocemos.
5. ¿Conoces a esas jugadoras? Sí, las conozco.
6. ¿Conozco a todos los invitados? Sí, los conoces.
7. ¿Conocen mis padres (a) esa guía? Sí, la conocen.
8. ¿Conoce la tía Gloria ese almacén? Sí, lo conoce.

Práctica D
conozco / sé / conoces
sabe / Sabe
sabe / conoce
sabemos
sabe / conocemos (*or:* sabemos)
sabes
conoces

Practice Sheet 15–3

Tape Manual Ex. 5 10

Quiz 15–3

Explicaciones I   **503**

La expresión *hace . . . que*

◆ OBJECTIVES:

**TO FIND OUT HOW
LONG SOMETHING
HAS BEEN GOING
ON**

**TO TELL WHAT
YOU HAVE BEEN
DOING**

To tell how long something that began in the past has been going on, we use this construction:

Hace + period of time + **que** + present-tense verb

Notes: Mini-dialogues 1 on p. 489 and 4 on p. 490 illustrate the *hace ... que* construction.

Hace mucho tiempo **que** Juana **estudia** italiano.
Hace dos horas **que limpias** tu cuarto.
Hace tres semanas **que estoy** aquí.

*Juana **has been studying** Italian **for** a long time.*
***You've been cleaning** your room **for** two hours.*
***I've been** here **for** three weeks.*

Here is how we form questions using *hace . . . que:*

¿**Cuánto tiempo**
¿**Cuántos años** (meses, etc.)   } **hace que** + present-tense verb?
¿**Cuántas semanas** (horas, etc.)

¿**Cuánto tiempo hace que viven** en el África?

How long have they been living in Africa?

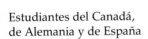

Estudiantes del Canadá, de Alemania y de España

PRÁCTICA

A Hace mucho tiempo.
Di *(Tell)* cuánto tiempo hace que estas personas hacen estas cosas.

15 minutos / Elena / jugar al golf
Hace quince minutos que Elena juega al golf.

1. 20 minutos / Guillermo / cepillarse los dientes
2. 2 años / Pilar / hacer máscaras de carnaval
3. varios meses / Cristina / coleccionar botellas vacías
4. 5 años / Alicia / jugar en el equipo de volibol
5. 4 años / Gregorio / ser aficionado al fútbol americano
6. 6 meses / Rafael / conocer a Norma
7. mucho tiempo / Andrés / disfrutar de la música clásica
8. una semana / Laura / trabajar con el veterinario
9. más o menos media hora / Marcos / buscar la pelota
10. muchos años / la familia Durán / pasar sus vacaciones en este hotel

B ¿Cuánto tiempo hace que . . . ?
Imagina que hay un estudiante alemán en tu clase. Tú no hablas alemán y él no habla mucho inglés. Hay sólo una lengua que Uds. pueden hablar juntos. Pregunta y contesta según el modelo.

estudiar español / 8 meses
ESTUDIANTE A *¿Cuánto tiempo hace que estudias español?*
ESTUDIANTE B *Hace ocho meses que estudio español.*

1. vivir aquí / casi 2 meses
2. sacar fotos de flores / 5 años
3. estudiar francés / 3 años
4. tocar la guitarra / 10 años
5. saber esquiar / mucho tiempo
6. coleccionar sellos / muchos años
7. conocer a tu novia / un mes
8. asistir a esta escuela / un mes

C Hablemos de ti.
1. ¿Cuánto tiempo hace que conoces a tu mejor amigo(a)? ¿Vive cerca de ti? ¿Dónde vive? ¿Sabes su dirección? ¿Cuál es? ¿Sabes su número de teléfono? ¿Cuál es?
2. ¿A qué deportes sabes jugar? ¿Los juegas bien o mal? ¿Generalmente ganas o pierdes? ¿Cuántas veces ganaste el año pasado?
3. ¿Sabes tocar el piano o la guitarra? ¿Cuánto tiempo hace que lo (la) tocas? ¿Tocas bien o mal? ¿Cuántas veces lo (la) tocas cada semana?
4. ¿Cuánto tiempo hace que vives en tu casa?

Práctica A
1. Hace veinte minutos que Guillermo se cepilla los dientes.
2. Hace dos años que Pilar hace …
3. Hace varios meses que Cristina colecciona …
4. Hace cinco años que Alicia juega …
5. Hace cuatro años que Gregorio es …
6. Hace seis meses que Rafael conoce …
7. Hace mucho tiempo que Andrés disfruta …
8. Hace una semana que Laura trabaja …
9. Hace más o menos media hora que Marcos busca …
10. Hace muchos años que la familia Durán pasa …

Práctica B
1. ¿Cuánto tiempo hace que vives aquí? Hace casi dos meses que vivo aquí.
2. ¿… que sacas fotos de flores? … cinco años que saco fotos de flores.
3. ¿… que estudias francés? … tres años que estudio francés.
4. ¿… que tocas la guitarra? … diez años que toco la guitarra.
5. ¿… que sabes esquiar? … mucho tiempo que sé esquiar.
6. ¿… que coleccionas sellos? … muchos años que colecciono …
7. ¿… que conoces a tu novia? … un mes que conozco a mi novia
8. ¿… que asistes a esta escuela? … un mes que asisto a …

Práctica C
Answers will vary.

APLICACIONES Discretionary

Notes: Sample dialogues for the **¿Qué pasa?** appear in the pre-chapter teacher pages.

Necesitan un cuarto   Transparency 62

Los Girondo no tienen reservación y necesitan un cuarto en el hotel. ¿Acaban de llegar a la ciudad? ¿Cuántas maletas tienen? ¿Crees que hace mucho tiempo que viajan por Europa? ¿Cómo lo sabes?

Make up a dialogue between Mrs. Girondo and the hotel manager. Here are some words and phrases you may wish to use:

describir	con vista a(l)	baño privado	de veras
balcón	ducha	es necesario	en seguida

EXPLICACIONES II

El pretérito: Verbos que terminan en *-ar*

You know the singular forms of regular *-ar* verbs in the preterite. Here are all of the forms, both singular and plural.

INFINITIVO   **comprar**

SINGULAR			PLURAL		
1 (yo)	compr**é**	*I bought*	(nosotros) (nosotras) }	compr**amos**	*we bought*
2 (tú)	compr**aste**	*you bought*	(vosotros) (vosotras) }	compr**asteis**	*you bought*
3 Ud. (él) (ella) }	compr**ó**	*you he she* } *bought*	Uds. (ellos) (ellas) }	compr**aron**	*you they* } *bought*

Notice that the *nosotros* form is the same in the preterite as in the present.

1 The *-ar* verbs that have a stem change in the present do *not* have a stem change in the preterite.

contar (o → ue)   **pensar (e → ie)**

PRESENT	PRETERITE	PRESENT	PRETERITE
(yo) cuento	(yo) **conté**	(yo) pienso	(yo) **pensé**

2 Remember that verbs ending in *-gar* have a spelling change in the *yo* form of the preterite in order to keep the hard *g* sound. The *g* becomes *gu* and the *é* is added: *(yo) ju**gué**, (yo) lle**gué**, (yo) pa**gué**.* Otherwise their forms are regular.

3 Verbs ending in *-car* also have a spelling change in the *yo* form of the preterite in order to keep the hard *c* sound. The *c* becomes *qu* and the *é* is added: *(yo) to**qué**, (yo) practi**qué**, (yo) bus**qué**.*

◆ **OBJECTIVES:**

TO FIND OUT OR RELATE WHAT HAS HAPPENED

TO TELL WHAT YOU HAVE DONE

TO EXPLAIN WHY YOU DID OR DID NOT DO SOMETHING

TO BRAG

Notes: The singular preterite forms of *-ar* verbs were presented in Chap. 12, p. 418; mini-dialogue 4 on p. 495 provides additional examples.

You may want to note other *-ar* verbs that have a stem change in the present but not in the preterite: *acostar, encontrar, costar, mostrar, cerrar.*

4   Verbs ending in *-zar* also have a spelling change in the *yo* form of the preterite. The *z* becomes *c* and the *é* is added: *(yo) empecé.*

5   The preterite of *-ar* reflexive verbs is the same as the preterite of *-ar* nonreflexive verbs.

Se levantaron a las ocho.	*They **got up** at 8:00.*
Me acosté temprano anoche.	*I **went to bed** early last night.*

PRÁCTICA

A   ¿Y los amigos?   Hace un año que Pilar no ve a sus amigos y quiere saber qué les pasó. Pregunta y contesta según el modelo.

> ¿Mario y Enrique? / viajar por Francia
> **ESTUDIANTE A**   *¿Mario y Enrique?*
> **ESTUDIANTE B**   *Viajaron por Francia.*

1. ¿Raquel y Virginia? / cantar en la televisión
2. ¿Victoria y Margarita? / celebrar sus quince años juntas
3. ¿Ester y su familia? / pasar dos semanas en París
4. ¿Las novias de Mario y Mateo? / regresar de San Juan
5. ¿Los hermanos de Lucía? / disfrutar de sus vacaciones en Lisboa
6. ¿Los alumnos del Sr. Miranda? / viajar a Londres
7. ¿Roberto y Carlos? / trabajar en un hospital para animales
8. ¿Tus sobrinas? / quedarse un mes con nosotros

B   El primer día de clase.   El profesor Hernández quiere saber cómo los estudiantes pasaron las vacaciones de verano. Pregunta y contesta según el modelo.

> ayudar en casa / todos
> **ESTUDIANTE A**   *¿Ayudaron todos en casa?*
> **ESTUDIANTE B**   *Sí, ayudamos en casa.*
> o: *No, no ayudamos en casa.*

1. nadar en el río / Uds.
2. levantarse temprano / todos
3. pasar mucho tiempo en la playa / tú y tus amigos
4. viajar por el África / Uds.
5. disfrutar del tiempo libre / tú y tus amigos
6. visitar los Pirineos / Uds.
7. ganar muchos partidos de béisbol / Uds.
8. jugar mucho al volibol / tú y tus amigos
9. trabajar en el centro / Uds.
10. regresar contentos / todos

C El primero. Rodolfo siempre quiere ser el primero. Si tú le dices que vas a hacer algo *(something)* él siempre te dice que acaba de hacerlo. Sigue el modelo.

arreglar la moto
ESTUDIANTE A *Quisiera arreglar la moto.*
ESTUDIANTE B *Ya la arreglé.*

1. cambiar las sábanas
2. preparar la naranjada
3. cerrar el armario
4. dejar la propina
5. mandar las tarjetas postales
6. pagar las entradas
7. encontrar la llave
8. limpiar el espejo
9. buscar la manta
10. decorar las paredes

D ¿Qué pasó ayer? Mira los dibujos y forma frases en el pretérito. Sigue el modelo.

despertarse a las seis
Ellos se despertaron a las seis.

1. escuchar la radio

2. jugar a las damas

3. lavarse el pelo

4. viajar al sur de la ciudad

5. acostarse más o menos
temprano

6. empezar a trabajar

7. pagar los muebles

8. caminar por el puente viejo

9. llegar tarde al baile

10. cantar canciones folklóricas

Práctica C
1. Quisiera cambiar las sábanas. Ya las cambié.
2. Quisiera preparar la naranjada. Ya la preparé.
3. Quisiera cerrar el armario. Ya lo cerré.
4. Quisiera dejar la propina. Ya la dejé.
5. Quisiera mandar las tarjetas postales. Ya las mandé.
6. Quisiera pagar las entradas. Ya las pagué.
7. Quisiera encontrar la llave. Ya la encontré.
8. Quisiera limpiar el espejo. Ya lo limpié.
9. Quisiera buscar la manta. Ya la busqué.
10. Quisiera decorar las paredes. Ya las decoré.

Reteach / Extra Help: After students do Ex. C, you may want to expand the practice by asking students to change the subject in the responses from *yo* to *Leo y Lidia*. For example: *Ya la arreglaron Leo y Lidia.*

Práctica D
1. Uds. escucharon la radio.
2. Jugamos a las damas.
3. Me lavé el pelo.
4. Ellas viajaron al sur de la ciudad.
5. Te acostaste más o menos temprano.
6. Empecé a trabajar.
7. Pagué los muebles.
8. Uds. caminaron por el puente viejo.
9. Llegamos tarde al baile.
10. Cantó canciones folklóricas.

Práctica E

1. ¿Por qué no llegaron Clara y Elena temprano?
   Porque terminaron su trabajo tarde.
2. ¿Por qué no sacamos buenas notas?
   Porque no estudiaron (or: estudiamos) para el examen.
3. ¿Por qué no llevaste …?
   Porque no la encontré.
4. ¿Por qué no preparó …?
   Porque se levantó …
5. ¿Por qué no compró Ud. …?
   Porque no entré …
6. ¿Por qué no cocinaron …?
   Porque no compraron …
7. ¿Por qué no se levantó …?
   Porque no se acostó …
8. ¿Por qué no se quedaron …?
   Porque necesitamos divertirnos …

Práctica F

viajé / preparé / Llamé
compré / ayudaron
Estudié
empecé
llegó / me levanté / tomé
bajé / ayudó
di / empezó
miré / dio / Traté
terminé / duró
despegó / aterrizó
llegué / busqué / llevaron
jugué / ayudé
pasamos

E **¿Por qué no lo hiciste?** ¿Por qué no hacen estas personas lo que quieren hacer? Pregunta y contesta según el modelo.

> (tú) / no comprar ese disco / dejar el dinero en casa
> ESTUDIANTE A   *¿Por qué no compraste ese disco?*
> ESTUDIANTE B   *Porque dejé el dinero en casa.*

1. Clara y Elena / no llegar temprano / terminar su trabajo tarde
2. (nosotros) / no sacar buenas notas / no estudiar para el examen
3. (tú) / no llevar esa camiseta nueva / no encontrarla
4. Rogelio / no preparar el desayuno / levantarse tarde
5. Ud. / no comprar nada / no entrar en ninguna tienda
6. (ellos) / no cocinar chiles rellenos / no comprar carne
7. Laura / no levantarse a las seis / no acostarse hasta medianoche
8. Uds. / no quedarse en casa el sábado / necesitar divertirnos un poco

Notes: Ex. F is also suitable for written work.

F **Mi viaje a México.**   Lee el párrafo (*paragraph*) y cambia los verbos al pretérito.

Cuando viajo a México, preparo todo de prisa. Llamo al agente de viajes y compro mi boleto de avión. Luego, mis hermanas me ayudan a comprar regalos para mis tíos y mis amigos mexicanos. Estudio el mapa y también las palabras para las comidas, frutas, bebidas y
5 postres en español. Luego empiezo a contar los días hasta la fecha del viaje. Cuando llega el día del viaje, me levanto temprano y tomo un taxi al aeropuerto. Cuando bajo del taxi el taxista me ayuda con las maletas y yo le doy una buena propina. Cuando empieza el vuelo, miro por la ventanilla. La auxiliar de vuelo me da unas revistas. Trato
10 de leerlas pero no las termino. El vuelo dura casi dos horas. El avión despega a las 10:15 y aterriza en Acapulco un poco después del mediodía.

   Cuando llego, busco mis maletas, y luego mis tíos me llevan a su casa. Por la noche, juego con mis primos y luego ayudo a mi tía a
15 preparar una cena fantástica. Todos pasamos el día muy contentos.

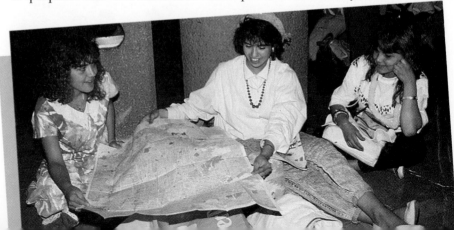

G Hablemos de ti.

Práctica G
Answers will vary.

1. ¿Qué hiciste esta mañana antes de venir a la escuela? ¿A qué hora te despertaste? ¿Te levantaste en seguida? ¿Qué hiciste luego?

2. ¿A qué hora llegaste a la escuela esta mañana? ¿Cuántas personas en tu clase llegaron tarde?

3. ¿A qué hora terminaste la tarea anoche? ¿A qué hora te acostaste? ¿Cuántas personas en tu clase se acostaron después de las once? No se acostó nadie después de la medianoche, ¿verdad?

4. ¿Qué programas de televisión miraste anoche? ¿Disfrutaste de ellos? ¿Viste las noticias? ¿En qué canal? ¿Qué pasó ayer? ¿Cuántas personas en tu clase no miraron la tele?

5. ¿Quién preparó la cena en tu casa anoche? ¿Qué cocinó? ¿Quién quitó los platos y los lavó? ¿Ayudaste en la cocina?

Practice Sheets 15–5, 15–6   Workbook Exs. G–J   12 Tape Manual Exs. 7–8

 13 Refrán   Activity Master 15–2   Quiz 15–5

ACTIVIDAD

¿Qué hiciste el año pasado?   Work in groups of four. On separate slips of paper, each person writes three things he or she did last year: *Compré muebles nuevos. Arreglé una lámpara. Visité a mis abuelos.* Here are some verbs you might use:

arreglar	comprar	jugar	prestar
ayudar	decorar	llevar	quedarse
caminar	empezar	mostrar	terminar
cantar	encontrar	nadar	tomar
celebrar	esquiar	pasar *(tiempo)*	usar
cocinar	estudiar	practicar	viajar
coleccionar	ganar	preparar	visitar

Put all the slips together. Then take turns drawing slips and asking who did what: *¿Quién compró muebles nuevos? ¿Quién arregló una bicicleta?*, etc. Find out how many people did that particular thing and keep a group tally: *¿Cuántas personas compraron muebles nuevos?* Then get together with the whole class and make a class tally. What things were done by the largest number of people?

Notes: You may want to ask students to write their three sentences for the **Actividad** at home.

APLICACIONES Discretionary

Notes: Answers to the **Repaso** and **Tema** appear in the pre-chapter teacher pages.

REPASO

Look carefully at the model sentences. Then put the English cues into Spanish to form new sentences based on the models.

1. *Yo sé hablar portugués muy bien.*
   (You (fam.) *know how to tell jokes rather well.*)
   (We know how to take pictures very well.)
   (They know how to decorate apartments rather well.)

2. *Hace una semana que trabaja en el África.*
   (I've been living in Europe for a month.)
   (It's been raining in Germany for ten days.)
   (We've been studying in England for two weeks.)

3. *Ayer practicamos el piano.*
   (Last night I sent a gift.)
   (Yesterday you (pl.) washed the windows.)
   (Last week you (fam.) paid for the beverages.)

4. *Disfruté mucho de mis vacaciones.*
   (Carmen enjoyed her visit very much.)
   (They enjoyed our concert very much.)
   (We enjoyed your (fam.) dinner very much.)

5. *Creemos que conocemos muy bien a Bogotá.*
   (He thinks I know Bárbara very well.)
   (She thinks that you (formal) know the story very well.)
   (I think we know the answers rather well.)

Notes: Review of:
1. *saber* + infinitive
2. *hace ... que*
   geographical terms
   word order
3. preterite of -*ar* verbs
4. *disfrutar de*
   preterite of -*ar* verbs
   position of adverbs
5. *creer que*
   conocer
   position of adverbs

Una calle en Barcelona, España

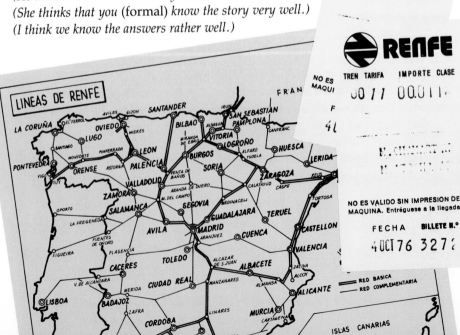

Put the English captions into Spanish.

1. Jim and Bob know how to speak Spanish very well.

2. They've been traveling in Spain for two months.

3. Yesterday they visited Granada.

4. They enjoyed their trip very much.

5. They think they know Spain very well.

REDACCIÓN

Enrichment: In connection with the **Redacción**, encourage students to look for magazine cutouts to accompany their ''postcards'' or ideal-room descriptions.

Now you are ready to write your own paragraph. Choose one of the following topics.

1. Expand the *Tema* by writing something more about Jim and Bob. Where are they from? How old are they? Are they students? Give some additional details about their trip. Did they visit many Spanish towns and cities? Did they buy any post cards and souvenirs? Are they going to come back next summer?

2. Pretend that you are Jim and Bob, and write three post cards to friends at home to tell them about your trip.

3. Write a description of an ideal room in a house or apartment.

COMPRUEBA TU PROGRESO   CAPÍTULO 15   Discretionary

Notes: Answers to the **Comprueba** appear in the pre-chapter teacher pages.

A   El cuarto
Complete the sentences according to the picture.

Hay un _____ sobre la cómoda. El

_____ está al lado del sofá. Las _____

_____ las _____

y la _____ están en la cama, pero las _____

están en la silla. Al lado de la cama hay una

_____

Hay una _____ azul. Fuera del cuarto, el _____

está a la izquierda de la puerta y, a la derecha, está

la _____ El _____ está cerca de la ventana y

por la ventana puedes ver el _____ con vista

al mar.

B   *Saber* y *conocer*
Complete the questions using the correct form of
saber or *conocer*.

1. ¿_____ ella a María Luisa?
2. ¿_____ tus padres bailar?
3. ¿_____ Jorge cantar en francés?
4. ¿_____ Uds. el sur de Italia?
5. ¿_____ (tú) arreglar el coche?

6. ¿_____ nosotros a la gerente?
7. ¿_____ (yo) a esa señora?
8. ¿_____ Uds. contestar en español?

C   El viaje de Alicia
Complete the sentences with the correct form of
saber or *conocer*.

Mañana Alicia va a hacer su primer viaje a
Portugal. Alicia _____ un poco de portugués, pero
no _____ el país. (Ella) no _____ a mucha gente
allá tampoco. (Yo) _____ que ella va a divertirse
mucho, porque (yo) la _____ muy bien. ¿_____
(tú) a qué hora ella tiene que despertarse? (Yo) no
lo _____. Pero (yo) _____ que el avión despega
muy temprano. Nosotros _____ dónde ella va a
quedarse, pero no _____ cuándo va a regresar.

D   ¿Cuánto tiempo hace?
Use the cues to form questions and answers, as in
the model.

(tú) / estudiar español / tres meses
¿Cuánto tiempo hace que estudias español?
Hace tres meses que estudio español.

1. Ud. / conocer a ese guía / diez años
2. (tú) / mirar la televisión / dos horas y media
3. Felipe / estar enfermo / una semana
4. Mariana / saber dibujar / varios años
5. Uds. / quedarse en este hotel / cinco días
6. los niños / vivir en Inglaterra / cuatro meses

E   El pretérito
Complete the sentences using the preterite of the
verbs in parentheses.

Ayer yo *(llegar)* a casa temprano, *(estudiar)* por la
tarde y luego *(ayudar)* a preparar la cena. Mi
hermana y yo *(lavar)* los platos. Después, (yo)
(jugar) al ajedrez con mi hermano. Él *(ganar)*.
Luego él y mi hermana *(jugar)* a las damas. Ellos
(acostarse) temprano, pero mi papá y yo *(mirar)* la
televisión hasta las once. El programa *(terminar)*
entonces, y yo *(acostarse)* en seguida.

Chapter 15 Test   Listening Comprehension Test

VOCABULARIO DEL CAPÍTULO 15

Sustantivos

el África (*f.*)
el alemán
Alemania
la alfombra
la almohada
el armario
el ascensor
el balcón, *pl.* los balcones
el Brasil
la cama
la cómoda
el cuarto
el edificio
la escalera
el espejo
el este
Europa
Francia
la funda
el / la gerente
el / la guía
Inglaterra
Italia
el italiano
la lámpara
la lengua
la llave
la manta
los muebles
el norte
el océano
el oeste
la pared
los Pirineos
Portugal
el portugués
el puente
el recuerdo

la reservación, *pl.* las
  reservaciones
el río
la sábana
el sillón, *pl.* los sillones
el sofá
el sur
la tarjeta postal

Adjetivos

alemán (*pl.* alemanes), alemana
fantástico, -a
francés (*pl.* franceses), francesa
inglés (*pl.* ingleses), inglesa
italiano, -a
necesario, -a
portugués (*pl.* portugueses),
  portuguesa
privado, -a
seguro, -a

Verbos

conocer
describir
disfrutar de
mandar
quedarse
saber

Preposición

por

Expresiones

con mucho gusto
con permiso
con vista a(l)
¿cuánto tiempo hace que?
de veras
discúlpeme
en seguida
hace + *time* + que + *present
  tense*
hacer un viaje
más o menos
(no) lo sé
quisiera
¡saludos!

ESCRIBIR CON DIBUJOS

T hey go *¡Plaf! ¡Cataplún! ¡Raas! ¡Boum! ¡Clonc! ¡Moc! ¡Flup! ¡Driiing!* It's just another scene in a Spanish-language comic book as things fall, bounce, jump, explode, ring, and generally react in the stories of those colorful characters.

The comic book has many names in Spanish. In Spain it's a *tebeo*—in honor of *TBO*, a comic book that has been around since 1917. In Argentina comics are called *historietas* and in Mexico, *cuentos*. They are similar to the comic books you know. In fact, some are translations of North American comic books. The books usually also contain such features as puzzles, jokes, essays, and movie gossip.

Most characters in these comics are humans. Mischievous children like Spain's *Zipe y Zape* and Argentina's famous *Mafalda* are very popular. For every talking animal like *Super Pumby*, a supercat who flies with the help of a portable nuclear reactor, there are half a dozen heroes like *Capitán Trueno*, who battles evil in medieval Europe. War stories and westerns are also popular.

For adults there are *fotonovelas*—stories told entirely with photographs and speech balloons like those in comics. *Fotonovelas* are usually serious, romantic, and moralistic, like Mexico's *El aventurero del amor* and *Traumas psicológicos*. One of the world's best-selling authors is a Spanish woman named Corín Tellado, who has written hundreds of romantic stories that have been made into *fotonovelas*.

The *fotonovela* is the ancestor of the *telenovela* (soap opera). But until television sets become as portable as magazines, these books that tell their stories mostly with pictures will continue to entertain millions every day.

PALABRAS NUEVAS I

El cuerpo

If students ask: Other related words you may want to present: *la lengua*, tongue; *los labios*, lips; *las cejas*, eyebrows; *las pestañas*, eyelashes; *la rodilla*, knee; *el / la paciente*, patient.

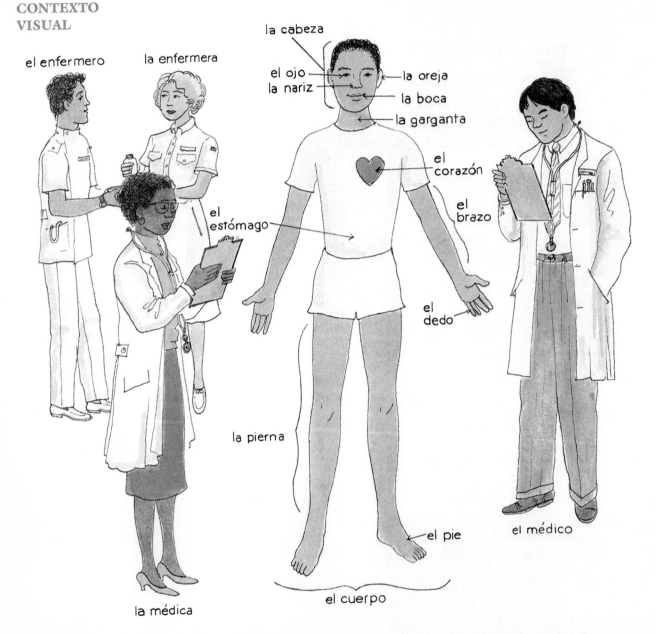

el enfermero

la enfermera

la cabeza

el ojo
la nariz

la oreja

la boca

la garganta

el corazón

el brazo

el estómago

el dedo

la pierna

el pie

el médico

la médica

el cuerpo

CONTEXTO COMUNICATIVO

 2

Notes: In connection with mini-dialogue 1, make sure students understand that *médico / médica* and *doctor / doctora* are wynonyms but that *doctor(a)* is a title used when referring to or addressing a specific doctor.

1 SRA. RUIZ   ¿Qué pasa, Carlitos? **¿Te duele algo?**

CARLOS   Me duele la garganta, mamá.

SRA. RUIZ   **¡Pobrecito! Tienes fiebre** también. Voy a llamar a la médica.

Variaciones:

■ la garganta → **el oído***
■ me duele la garganta → me duelen la cabeza y la garganta
■ tienes fiebre → creo que tienes **gripe**
■ a la médica → a **la doctora** Arias

doler (o → ue) (me duele(n), te duele(n))   *to hurt, to ache*
algo   *something, anything*
pobrecito, -a   *poor thing*
la fiebre   *fever*
tener fiebre   *to have a fever*
el oído   *(inner) ear*
la gripe   *flu*
el doctor, la doctora   *doctor (as title)*

2 SRA. RUIZ   Hace una semana que mi hijo Carlitos tiene un **resfriado.** ¿Puede verlo la médica esta tarde?

ENFERMERA   Va a **examinar** a **alguien** ahora, pero puede ver a Carlitos en media hora.

SRA. RUIZ   Muchas gracias.

■ un resfriado → gripe
■ a alguien → a otro niño

el resfriado   *cold*
examinar   *to examine*
alguien   *someone, somebody, anyone*

3 CARLITOS   ¿Me va a **poner una inyección**?

DRA. ARIAS   Hoy no, Carlitos. Sólo necesitas **descansar.**

■ poner una inyección → dar una **receta**
■ descansar → quedarte en cama

poner una inyección (a)   *to give a shot (to)*
descansar   *to rest*
la receta   *prescription*

4 DRA. ARIAS   ¿Sabes, Carlitos, que a los médicos no **nos gustⱥn** las inyecciones?

CARLITOS   ¿Tampoco **le gustan** a Ud.?

DRA. ARIAS   No, no le gustan a nadie.

■ le gustan a Ud. → **les gustan** a las enfermeras

nos gusta(n)   *we like*

le gusta(n)   *he / she / it / you (formal) like(s)*

les gusta(n)   *they / you (pl.) / like*

* In Spanish we use *el oído* to mean the inner ear and *la oreja* to mean the outer ear. It is usually the inner ear that hurts.

5 EUGENIO El Dr. Suárez es una persona muy amable y un médico buenísimo. **Algún** día espero ser médico como él.

LEONOR Pues yo no quiero ser médica. Quisiera ser piloto.

- algún día → **por eso**
- ser médica → cuidar a las personas enfermas
- piloto → fotógrafa

algún, alguna *a, any, some* (adj.)

por eso *that's why*

6 PROFESORA ¿Por qué no escribes las frases, Miguel?

MIGUEL Porque **me falta** un bolígrafo.

PROFESORA No es una buena **excusa**. Clase, ¿**alguno** de Uds. tiene un bolígrafo para Miguel?

- las frases → las palabras
- me falta → **me olvidé de** traer
- alguno de Uds. → alguien

faltar (me falta(n), te falta(n)) *to need, to be missing (something)*

la excusa *excuse*

alguno(s), alguna(s) *some, any, one (pron.)*

olvidarse (de) + inf. *to forget (to do something)*

7 GRACIELA A mí no **me importa** el dinero, ¿y a ti?

MARCOS Pues a mí me importa mucho.

- el dinero → ser rica

importar (me importa(n), te importa(n)) *to matter (to), to be important (to), to mind*

EN OTRAS PARTES

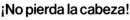

En México se dice *la gripa*.

También se dice *el catarro, el resfrío* y *el constipado*.

HOSPITAL BRITANICO DE BUENOS AIRES
— Fundado en 1844 —
Perdriel 74 - Tel. 23-1081
1280 Buenos Aires

CONSULTORIO MEDICO

Rp.

HOSPITAL BRITANICO DE BUENOS AIRES
— Fundado en 1844 —
Perdriel 74 - Tel. 23-1081
1280 Buenos Aires

CONSULTORIO MEDICO

Rp.

PRÁCTICA

A **¿Qué te duele?** Imagina que te duele algo y la enfermera de la escuela te examina. Pregunta y contesta según el modelo y los dibujos.

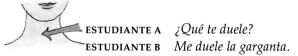

ESTUDIANTE A   *¿Qué te duele?*
ESTUDIANTE B   *Me duele la garganta.*

Práctica A
1. Me duele el ojo.
2. Me duelen las piernas.
3. Me duele la mano.
4. Me duelen los brazos.
5. Me duele el estómago.
6. Me duele la cabeza.
7. Me duele el dedo.
8. Me duele el pie.
9. Me duele la nariz.

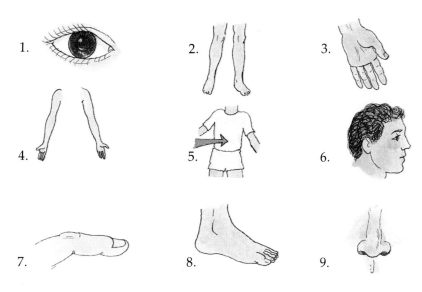

Enrichment: After students have completed Ex. A, you may want to expand the practice by asking students to change 1, 3, 7, and 8 to plural and 2 and 4 to singular.

B **¿Qué hacemos con este muchacho enfermo?** Completa cada frase con la palabra correcta.

1. Me duele el estómago. Tengo (*hambre / sueño / razón*).
2. Tengo fiebre. El médico me va a dar (*un pastel / la gripe / una receta*).
3. Si tienes algo en el ojo, debes ir (*al enfermero / al pobrecito / al colegio*).
4. Una enfermera es una mujer que (*tiene fiebre / cuida a las personas enfermas / está enferma*).
5. Estoy enfermo. El médico me va a (*examinar / dibujar / buscar*).
6. Tengo fiebre y me duele (*la cabeza / la receta / la excusa*).
7. La médica dice que debo (*abrir la boca / examinar los dedos / poner una inyección a alguien*).
8. Si estás cansada, debes (*levantarte / descansar / olvidarte*).
9. Si te duele la garganta, creo que tienes (*un cuerpo / una inyección / gripe*).
10. No puedo oír bien, doctor. ¿Puede darme (*algo / algunas / alguien*) para el oído?

Práctica B
1. hambre
2. una receta
3. al enfermero
4. cuida a las personas enfermas
5. examinar
6. la cabeza
7. abrir la boca
8. descansar
9. gripe
10. algo

Práctica C
1. los pies (o las piernas)
2. la boca y la garganta
3. los pies (o las piernas y/o todo el cuerpo)
4. las manos
5. las manos y la boca
6. los ojos
7. los oídos
8. los pies (o las piernas y/o todo el cuerpo)
9. los ojos

Práctica D
Answers will vary.

C ¿Qué uso? ¿Qué usas para hacer estas actividades? Pregunta y contesta según el modelo.

> para tocar el piano
> ESTUDIANTE A *¿Qué usas para tocar el piano?*
> ESTUDIANTE B *Uso las manos (o los dedos) y los pies.*

1. para caminar
2. para cantar
3. para correr
4. para escribir
5. para comer
6. para ver
7. para oír
8. para bailar
9. para leer

D Hablemos de ti.

1. ¿Cuántas veces vas al médico cada año? ¿A veces te pone inyecciones o te da una receta? Cuando el médico te da una receta, ¿adónde la llevas?
2. ¿Qué haces cuando tienes un resfriado? ¿Dura mucho tiempo, generalmente?
3. ¿Cómo estás hoy? ¿Te duele algo? ¿Qué te duele?
4. ¿Te olvidas de hacer cosas a menudo? ¿De qué te olvidas? ¿Te olvidaste de algo ayer u hoy?
5. ¿Qué te importa? ¿Qué no te importa?

Practice Sheet 16–1   Workbook Exs. A–B

 3 Tape Manual Exs. 1–2   4 Refrán   Quiz 16–1

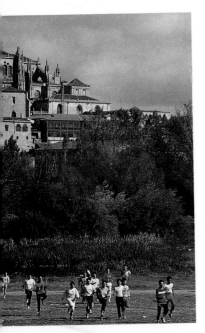

(arriba) Una clase de gimnasia en Salamanca, España; (derecha) Con la médica en España

Enrichment: Additional questions for Ex. D: *¿Te dan miedo las inyecciones? ¿Cuántas veces vas al dentista cada año? ¿Es tu dentista hombre o mujer? ¿Te gusta visitar a tu dentista? ¿Por qué?*

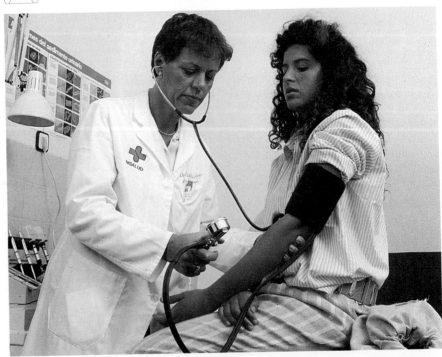

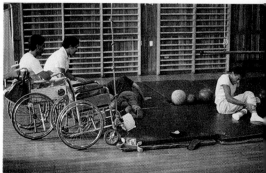

(abajo) Gimnasia en el Hospital Pérez Carreño de Caracas, Venezuela; (abajo, izquierda) Gimnasia en una universidad de Santiago, Chile

APLICACIONES

Discretionary

No puedo ir a la escuela 🔲 5

Consuelo tiene mil excusas para no ir a la escuela.

MAMÁ	¡Levántate,[1] niña! Ya es tarde.
CONSUELO	No puedo ir hoy a la escuela, mamá. Estoy enferma.
MAMÁ	¿Qué tienes,[2] hija?
5 CONSUELO	Me duele todo el cuerpo: la cabeza, la garganta, el estómago . . .
MAMÁ	Hmm . . . No tienes fiebre.
CONSUELO	No, pero tengo mucho frío. Es peor que tener fiebre, ¿no?
10 MAMÁ	A veces sí, a veces no.
CONSUELO	Si tengo frío, entonces tengo un resfriado, ¿no?
MAMÁ	¿O no te gusta ir a la escuela, tal vez?
CONSUELO	¿Qué dices, mamá? Tú sabes cómo me encanta ir a la escuela.
15 MAMÁ	¡Levántate entonces! No tengo tiempo para escuchar excusas. Si no asistes a clase, no vas al cine esta noche.
CONSUELO	¡Mamá! ¡Ya no tengo frío!
MAMÁ	¡Ya lo sabía![3] El cine es la mejor receta que conozco.

---

[1]¡levántate! *get up!*   [2]¿qué tienes? *what's the matter?*   [3]¡ya lo sabía! *I knew it!*

ESCUELA SAN MARTÍN
excusa por ausencia

Nombre del alumno (a) _____
Margarita Cecilia Botero

Motivo de ausencia _____
La niña tuvo gripe y
se sentía mal.

Fecha *27 de marzo*

Firma de los padres o responsables
Patricia de Botero

Diálogo
1. Porque está enferma.
2. Todo el cuerpo: la cabeza, la garganta, el estómago …
3. No, no tiene fiebre.
4. Answers will vary.
5. No.
6. Tiene ganas de quedarse en casa; quedarse en casa.
7. Porque quiere ir al cine.
8. Answers will vary.

Preguntas

Contesta según el diálogo.

1. ¿Por qué Consuelo no puede ir a la escuela?   2. ¿Qué le duele?
3. ¿Tiene mucha fiebre?   4. ¿Qué te duele a ti cuando tienes un resfriado?   5. Según su mamá, ¿está enferma Consuelo?   6. ¿Qué tiene ganas de hacer Consuelo? ¿Prefiere ir a la escuela o quedarse en casa?
7. ¿Por qué no tiene frío Consuelo después?   8. ¿Qué haces tú cuando te quedas en casa y tus compañeros asisten a la escuela? ¿Qué haces cuando tienes que quedarte en cama todo el día?

Enrichment: Additional questions you may want to ask: *Según Consuelo, ¿qué es peor que tener fiebre? (Tener frío.) Según la mamá de Consuelo, ¿cuál es la mejor receta? (El cine.) ¿Cuál es la mejor receta para ti?* (Answers will vary.)

Participación

With a partner, create a dialogue about making excuses. Take turns playing the role of a person who is asking for a date and a person who is trying to avoid going out.

PRONUNCIACIÓN 6

You have probably noticed that when people speak Spanish, they often run words together without pausing in between. For example, the phrase *a la derecha de la casa* may sound more like two words than six. You don't think about it, of course, but we do the same thing in English. When you say "I'm going to go," it will probably sound like "I'm gonna go" or even "Ahmana go!" This combining of sounds is called linking. The following examples show basic patterns of linking in Spanish.

A When the last sound of a word is the same as the first sound of the next word, we usually pronounce them as one sound.
Escucha y repite.

al lado de Elena   los cerdos son negros   va a hacerlo

B We usually run two vowels together.
Escucha y repite.

la ensalada   su esposo   le hablo a ella   su amigo enfermo

C We often pronounce a final consonant as if it were the first letter of the following word.
Escucha y repite.

el amigo   el agua   los actores   el aficionado   los animales

D Escucha y repite.
Ella enseña español.   Ese actor italiano es amigo de Eva.
Mi hijo Enrique no quiere agua.   El león está al lado de las serpientes.

PALABRAS NUEVAS II

La librería

If students ask: Other related words you may want to present:
el libro de bolsillo, paperback; *la portada*, book cover; *el éxito de
librería*, best seller.

la librería

la escritora

el escritor

el título

CONTEXTO COMUNICATIVO

 8

1 MARIO   Quisiera comprar el nuevo libro de poemas de
            Luis Palacios. ¿Todavía lo tienen **en venta**?

en venta	*for sale*

VENDEDORA   Un momento. Voy a buscarlo adentro. (*Sale y
            regresa después de varios minutos.*) No, **lo siento**,
            señor, pero ya los **vendí** todos.

lo siento *I'm sorry*
(yo) vendí, (tú) vendiste
    (preterite of **vender**)   *sold*

MARIO   ¡Qué lástima! Es mi poeta favorito.

Variaciones:
■ quisiera → quiero
■ poeta → escritor
■ favorito → **preferido**

preferido, -a = favorito, -a

526   Capítulo 16

2 TOMÁS   ¿Compraste ya **la novela** de Lola Castillos?

MARTA   No. Pienso **sacarla** de la biblioteca. ¿Por qué?

TOMÁS   Porque no la encuentro en ninguna librería.

MARTA   No debe ser **tan** difícil encontrarla. La vi ayer en la librería Saavedra.

- compraste →**recibiste**
- sacarla de la biblioteca → **pedirla prestada a** alguien

3 RICARDO   **¿Qué te parece** esta novela de **aventuras**?

CLAUDIA   **Me parece excelente.**

RICARDO   No **estoy de acuerdo.** A mí no me gustó.

CLAUDIA   Pues yo disfruté mucho de ella.

- qué te parece → qué piensas de
- excelente → **formidable**

la novela   *novel*

sacar   *to take out, to remove*

tan   *so, as*

(yo) recibí, (tú) recibiste (preterite of **recibir**)   *got, received*

pedir prestado, -a (a)   *to borrow (from)*

¿qué te parece ____?   *how do you like ____?, what do you think of ____?*

la aventura   *adventure*

parecer (me parece, te parece) *to seem (to someone)*

excelente   *excellent*

estar de acuerdo   *to agree*

formidable   *terrific*

A ¡Es formidable! Guillermo y un(a) amigo(a) visitan varias librerías de la ciudad. Pregunta y contesta según el modelo.

> este libro de historia / muy interesante
>
> ESTUDIANTE A ¿*Qué piensas de este libro de historia?*
> ESTUDIANTE B *Me parece muy interesante.*

1. la poeta Julia de Burgos / formidable
2. la librería Saavedra / excelente
3. la venta en la librería Bolívar / magnífico
4. ese escritor alemán / muy serio
5. el cuento *El corazón del poeta* / bastante tonto
6. esta novela nueva / fabuloso
7. ese título / perfecto
8. el libro del Dr. Avellaneda / demasiado largo

B Me falta algo. Eva y sus amigos pasan unos días en el campo, pero les faltan varias cosas. Pregunta y contesta según el modelo.

ESTUDIANTE A *Tengo ganas de leer. Pero me falta un libro.*
ESTUDIANTE B *¿Por qué no pides prestado uno?*

leer

ESTUDIANTE A *Tengo ganas de jugar al béisbol. Pero me falta una pelota.*
ESTUDIANTE B *¿Por qué no pides prestada una?*

jugar al béisbol

1. nadar

2. escribir a mi familia

3. sacar fotos

4. dormir afuera

5. jugar al fútbol

6. descansar

7. mandar unas tarjetas postales

8. tocar cintas

9. levantarme temprano

C   Hablemos de ti.

1. ¿Sacas muchos libros de la biblioteca? ¿Hay una buena biblioteca en tu colegio? ¿Más o menos cuántos libros tiene? ¿Tienes tú muchos libros? ¿Cuántos?
2. ¿Qué clase de libros prefieres? ¿Quién es tu escritor(a) preferido(a)? ¿Por qué disfrutas de sus libros?
3. ¿Te gusta leer poemas? ¿Quién es tu poeta preferido(a)? ¿Aprendiste algunos poemas de memoria este año? ¿Poemas en inglés o en español? ¿Cuáles son los títulos de esos poemas?
4. ¿A veces les pides prestado algo a tus amigos? ¿Qué les pides prestado? ¿Les prestas tú cosas a ellos? ¿Qué te piden prestado a ti?

Práctica C
Answers will vary.

Practice Sheet 16–2

Workbook Exs. C–D

Tape Manual Exs. 3–4 9

Quiz 16–2

ACTIVIDAD

Busco un libro.   Work in groups of three. Take turns playing the role of a clerk in a bookstore while the other two play customers shopping for gifts. First, each of you should make up a list of titles, one book title for each of the following categories. They can be translations of English titles you know or invented titles.

libros de aventura	libros de poemas
libros de arte	novelas de ciencia ficción
libros de cuentos	novelas policíacas
libros de historia	novelas románticas
libros del oeste	obras de teatro

The customers take turns describing the people they want to give books to. The clerk asks for information about the person who is going to receive the gift. Questions might include:

¿Cuántos años tiene?	¿Qué le gusta leer?
¿Es estudiante?	¿Qué le gusta hacer?
¿Qué hace?	

The clerk must then recommend a title to the customer.

Enrichment: You may want to ask students to prepare their title lists for the **Actividad** at home. Point out the capitalization rule for titles in Spanish: Capitalize the first word of a title and any proper nouns that appear in it.

  Students may create book covers with each of their titles, using drawings or magazine cutouts to illustrate them.

Estudio de palabras

1. necesitas (*or:* hay que / es necesario / debes)
2. preferido
3. Prefiero
4. volver
5. decir
6. quiero
7. tomar

1. la salida
2. frío / adentro
3. abren
4. vacía
5. con
6. pedir prestado
7. la pregunta

(abajo, izquierda) Plaza del Zócalo en México; (abajo, derecha) Playa Luquillo en Puerto Rico

ESTUDIO DE PALABRAS

During the year you have learned many words that have the same general meaning. These words are called *synonyms*. Here are some that you have learned.

bello, -a = hermoso, -a   alumno, -a = estudiante
muchacho, -a = chico, -a   formidable = estupendo, -a

You have also learned *antonyms,* words that are opposite in meaning.

alto, -a ≠ bajo, -a   mayor ≠ menor
grande ≠ pequeño, -a   subir ≠ bajar

Can you think of a *synonym* for each italicized word in these sentences?

1. Mamá dice que *tienes que* limpiar los estantes.
2. ¿Quién es tu escritor *favorito?*
3. *Me gustan más* las novelas policíacas.
4. Voy a *regresar* a casa.
5. ¿Me quieres *contar* lo que pasó?
6. No *tengo ganas de* leer esa novela.
7. ¿Quieres *beber* algo?

Now give an *antonym* for each italicized word.

1. Te esperamos en *la entrada* del cine.
2. Hace *calor.* ¿Vamos *afuera*?
3. ¿A qué hora *cierran* la biblioteca?
4. Me parece que esa taza está *llena.*
5. Prefiero ir al médico *sin* mi mamá.
6. No le debes *prestar* nada a él.
7. No comprendo *la respuesta.*

EXPLICACIONES I

Los verbos *doler, encantar, faltar, gustar, importar, parecer*

Notes: Refer to the following mini-dialogues for examples of the verbs discussed on pp. 531-532: *gustar:* 4 on p. 519, 3 on p. 527; *faltar:* 6 on p. 520; *importar:* 7 on p. 520; *parecer:* 3 on p. 527; *doler:* 1 on p. 519.

◆ **OBJECTIVES:**

TO COMPARE LIKES AND DISLIKES

TO ORDER IN A RESTAURANT

TO EMPHASIZE

TO CLARIFY

TO TELL WHAT DOES AND DOESN'T MATTER TO YOU

TO TELL WHERE SOMETHING HURTS

TO TELL OR ASK FOR WHAT YOU NEED

TO ACT AS SPOKES-PERSON FOR A GROUP

To say that we like something, we use the verb *gustar*, which actually means "to be pleasing." In Spanish, whatever is pleasing is the subject of the sentence.

Me gustan las novelas.	*I like novels. (Novels are pleasing to me.)*
Nos gusta la novela.	*We like the novel. (The novel is pleasing to us.)*

Gustar agrees with the subject—*novela(s)*. The person who likes them is the indirect object, *me* or *nos*. We use *gustar* with all of the indirect object pronouns:

me			nos	
te	} gusta(n)		os	} gusta(n)
le			les	

1 Remember that *le* and *les* can have several meanings. To make the meaning clear or for emphasis we can add *a* + a noun or prepositional pronoun.

A él le gusta descansar.	*He likes to rest.*
A Ud. no **le** gustan las inyecciones.	*You don't like shots.*
A nosotros nos gustan los libros de aventuras. Y **a ti**, ¿qué **te** gusta?	*We like adventure books. And what do **you** like?*

If we use a person's name, of course, we also use *a*:

A Juana siempre **le** gusta ganar.	***Juana*** *always likes to win.*

2 The verbs *encantar* "to love," *faltar*, "to need" or "to be missing (something)," *importar*, "to matter, to be important (to)," and *parecer*, "to seem," follow the same pattern.

¿Qué **te falta?** { *What **do you need**?*
{ *What **are you missing**?*

A ellos no **les importa** el dinero.	*Money doesn't **matter to them**.*
Ese libro **me parece** interesante.	*That book **seems** interesting **to me**.*
Me encanta el Dr. Lotito.	*I **love** Dr. Lotito.*

3 The verb *doler,* "to hurt," is a stem-changing verb (*o → ue*). It follows the same pattern.

¿**A Ud. le duele** la cabeza?	Does **your** head **hurt?**
No, **me duele** el oído.	No, **my** ear **hurts.**

Remember that we usually use the definite article with parts of the body.

PRÁCTICA

A **¿Le gusta la comida?** El profesor Guerrero y su clase van a un restaurante español. Escoge *(Choose)* algo del menú para cada persona. Pregunta y contesta según el modelo.

> a Ud.
>
> ESTUDIANTE A *¿Qué le gusta a Ud.?*
> ESTUDIANTE B *A mí me gustan las chuletas de cerdo y una naranjada.*

menú

SOPAS

sopa de verduras   gazpacho   sopa de pollo

COMIDAS DEL DÍA

huevos fritos con papas fritas	ensalada de lechuga y tomate
tortilla española	chiles rellenos
paella	empanadas
chuletas de cerdo	arroz con pollo
chuletas de cordero	bistec

POSTRES	**BEBIDAS**
frutas con queso	té
helado	café
flan	chocolate
pasteles	agua mineral
	naranjada

1. a ti	3. a Uds.	5. a Raúl y a ti
2. a Ud.	4. a ella	6. a Gloria y a Victoria

Reteach / Extra Help: You may want to reinforce the forms of *doler, faltar, gustar, importar,* and *parecer* by asking these questions: *¿Qué te duele después de correr mucho? ¿Le falta dinero a Gabriela Sabatini? ¿Les gusta a Uds. leer poemas en español? ¿Nos importa mucho el dinero? ¿Qué les parece el rock a tus amigos?* (Answers will vary.)

Práctica A

1. ¿Qué te gusta a ti?
   A mí me gusta(n) …
2. ¿Qué le gusta a Ud.?
   A mí me gusta(n) …
3. ¿Qué les gusta a Uds.?
   A nosotros nos gusta(n) …
4. ¿Qué le gusta a ella?
   A ella le gusta(n) …
5. ¿Qué les gusta a Raúl y a ti?
   A Raúl y a mí (*or:* a nosotros) nos gusta(n) …
6. ¿Qué les gusta a Gloria y a Victoria?
   A Gloria y a Victoria (*or:* a ellas) les gusta(n) …

Práctica B

1. A mí no me importa levantarme temprano. ¿Y a él?
   A él no le importa tampoco.
2. A mí no me importa llevar las cajas de libros. ¿Y a Uds.?
   A nosotros no nos importa tampoco.

B ¿Te importa? Imagina que el sábado hay una venta de libros viejos en la biblioteca de la escuela y que tú y unos compañeros van a ayudar. Pregunta y contesta según el modelo.

> trabajar el sábado / a ti
> ESTUDIANTE A *A mí no me importa trabajar el sábado. ¿Y a ti?*
> ESTUDIANTE B *A mí no me importa tampoco.*

1. levantarse temprano / a él
2. llevar las cajas de libros / a Uds.
3. sacar los libros de los estantes / a ellas
4. limpiar los estantes / a ti
5. contar el dinero / Paco
6. vender libros viejos / a la profesora
7. pasar el sábado en la biblioteca / a Jorge y a ti
8. quedarse hasta tarde / a los otros

C ¿Qué te duele? Después del gran partido de volibol, a todos les duele algo. Pregunta y contesta según el modelo.

> a Juan y a ti / las manos
> ESTUDIANTE A *¿Qué les duele a Juan y a ti?*
> ESTUDIANTE B *Nos duelen las manos.*

1. a ellos / la cabeza
2. a él / el oído
3. a Carlota / la boca
4. a Ud. / la nariz
5. a ti / el pie
6. a Uds. / los brazos
7. a Jorge y a Esteban / las piernas
8. a ellas / todo el cuerpo

D En el restaurante. Olga y Leonardo acaban de abrir su primer restaurante. ¿Qué le falta a cada cliente?

a Lorenzo   *A Lorenzo le falta un plato.*

1. a Carolina   2. a ti   3. a Uds.

4. a mí   5. a nosotros   6. a nosotras

7. a ellos   8. a Ud.   9. a Elena y a Marta

3. A mí no me importa sacar los libros de los estantes. ¿Y a ellas?
   A ellas no les importa tampoco.
4. A mí no me importa limpiar …
   A mí no me importa tampoco.
5. A mí no me importa contar …
   A Paco no le importa tampoco.
6. A mí no me importa vender …
   A la profesora no le importa tampoco.
7. A mí no me importa pasar …
   A nosotros no nos importa tampoco.
8. A mí no me importa quedarme …
   A los otros no les importa tampoco.

Práctica C
1. ¿Qué les duele a ellos?
   Les duele la cabeza.
2. ¿Qué le duele a él?
   Le duele el oído.
3. ¿Qué le duele a Carlota?
   Le duele la boca.
4. ¿Qué le duele a Ud.?
   Me duele la nariz.
5. ¿Qué te duele a ti?
   Me duele el pie.
6. ¿Qué les duele a Uds.?
   Nos duelen los brazos.
7. ¿Qué les duele a Jorge y a Esteban?
   Les duelen las piernas.
8. ¿Qué les duele a ellas?
   Les duele todo el cuerpo.

Práctica D
1. A Carolina le falta una cuchara.
2. A ti te falta un tenedor.
3. A Uds. les faltan vasos.
4. A mí me falta un menú.
5. A nosotros nos faltan cuchillos.
6. A nosotras nos faltan sillas.
7. A ellos les faltan servilletas.
8. A Ud. le falta una taza y un platillo.
9. A Elena y a Marta les falta (el) pan.

All will follow the model but
choice of adjectives will vary.
1. parecen / fem. pl. adj.
2. parecen / fem. pl. adj.
3. parecen / masc. pl. adj.
4. parecen / fem. pl. adj.
5. parecen / masc. pl. adj.
6. parecen / masc. pl. adj.
7. parecen / masc. pl. adj.
8. parece / masc. or fem.
   sing. adj.
9. parece / fem. sing. adj.
10. parece / masc. sing. adj.
11. parece / masc. sing. adj.
12. parece / fem. sing. adj.

E ¿Qué les parece . . . ? Imagina que alguien te pregunta qué piensan tus compañeros de clase de varias cosas. Escoge un adjetivo para contestar. Sigue el modelo.

las novelas que leen en su clase de inglés

ESTUDIANTE A *¿Qué les parecen las novelas que leen en su clase de inglés?*

ESTUDIANTE B *Nos parecen aburridas.*

1. las películas románticas
2. las películas cómicas
3. los programas en el canal *(número)*
4. las noticias en el canal *(número)*
5. los anuncios comerciales para *(producto)*
6. los desfiles
7. los fuegos artificiales
8. su profesor(a) de *(materia)*
9. la enfermera de la escuela
10. el título de este libro
11. este libro
12. la lengua española

aburrido
amable
antipático
difícil
divertido
emocionante
estupendo
excelente
fabuloso
fácil
formidable
hermoso
listo
simpático
tonto

Practice Sheet 16–3

10 Tape Manual Exs. 5–6   Quiz 16–3

(izquierda) Estudiantes en Panamá; (derecha) Cartel de un cine en Palma de Mallorca, España

Palabras afirmativas

You know how to use the negative words that are listed below. Here are
the affirmative words that are their antonyms.

◆ OBJECTIVES:

TO CALM
SOMEONE

TO MAKE EXCUSES

TO DISAGREE

TO ASK FOR
SOMETHING IN A
STORE

AFFIRMATIVE WORDS		NEGATIVE WORDS	
alguien	*someone, somebody, anyone*	**nadie**	*no one, nobody, not anybody*
algo	*something, anything*	**nada**	*nothing, not anything*
algún, alguna	*a, any, some* (adj.)	**ningún, ninguna**	*no, not any* (adj.)
alguno, alguna	*some, any, one* (pron.)	**ninguno, ninguna**	*none, no one, (not) any* (pron.)
siempre	*always*	**nunca**	*never*
también	*too, also*	**tampoco**	*neither, not either*

¿Vas al cine con **alguien**?	No, **no** voy con **nadie**.
¿Me compraste **algo**?	No, **no** te compré **nada**.
¿Tienes **alguna** excusa?	No, **no** tengo **ninguna**.
¿**Siempre** los llamas por teléfono?	No, **no** los llamo **nunca**.

Like *ninguno, alguno* agrees with the noun it describes. Before a masculine
singular noun, we use *algún*.

Voy a leerlo **algún** día.	*I'm going to read it **some**day.*
Tengo **algunas** amigas en Colombia.	*I have **some** friends in Colombia.*
Algunas de mis blusas son viejas.	***Some** of my blouses are old.*

Notes: Refer to mini-
dialogues 1 and 2 on p. 519
and 5 and 6 on p. 520 for
examples of affirmative words.
Negative words were explained
in Chap. 13.

Reteach / Extra Help: To
reinforce affirmative words and
review negative words, ask
students to work in pairs to ask
and answer the example
sentences. Elicit or suggest
variations on these questions
and responses.

Práctica A
1. ¿Camina alguien por la
    sala?
    No, no camina nadie.
2. ¿Duerme alguien en el
    dormitorio?
    No, no duerme nadie.
3. ¿Corre alguien por el patio?
    No, no corre nadie.
4. ¿Entra alguien …?
    No, no entra nadie.
5. ¿Baja alguien …?
    No, no baja nadie.
6. ¿Canta alguien …?
    No, no canta nadie.
7. ¿Escribe alguien …?
    No, no escribe nadie.
8. ¿Sube alguien …?
    No, no sube nadie.

PRÁCTICA

A   ¿Hay fantasmas?   Dos niños están en una casa vieja donde no vive
nadie. Tienen un poco de miedo porque creen que ven y oyen cosas
muy extrañas (*strange*). Pregunta y contesta según el modelo.

> venir por el jardín
> ESTUDIANTE A   *¿Viene alguien por el jardín?*
> ESTUDIANTE B   *No, no viene nadie.*

1. caminar por la sala	5. bajar la escalera
2. dormir en el dormitorio	6. cantar en el baño
3. correr por el patio	7. escribir en la pared
4. entrar por el balcón	8. subir a nuestro piso

1. ¿Viste algo interesante en la tele?
   No, no vi nada.
2. ¿Dibujaste algo nuevo para la clase de arte?
   No, no dibujé nada.
3. ¿Encontraste algo interesante …?
   No, no encontré nada.
4. ¿Preparaste algo divertido …?
   No, no preparé nada.
5. ¿Diste algo viejo …?
   No, no di nada.
6. ¿Compraste algo bonito …?
   No, no compré nada.
7. ¿Sacaste algo bueno …?
   No, no saqué nada.
8. ¿Tomaste algo caliente …?
   No, no tomé nada.
9. ¿Te olvidaste de algo importante?
   No, no me olvidé de nada.

Práctica C

1. Siempre estoy contento(a).
   Pues yo nunca …
2. Siempre duermo ocho horas.
   Pues yo nunca …
3. Siempre canto en la ducha.
   Pues yo nunca …
4. Siempre digo la verdad.
   Pues yo nunca …
5. Siempre me baño por la mañana.
   Pues yo nunca …
6. Siempre me olvido de cerrar el armario.
   Pues yo nunca …
7. Siempre me divierto en las ventas de ropa.
   Pues yo nunca …
8. Siempre estoy de acuerdo con mis padres.
   Pues yo nunca …
9. Siempre pido prestado dinero.
   Pues yo nunca …
10. Siempre descanso después del almuerzo.
    Pues yo nunca …

B **¿Qué hiciste anoche?** Imagina que un(a) amigo(a) te pregunta qué hiciste anoche. No hiciste nada. Sigue el modelo.

> cocinar / delicioso para la cena
> ESTUDIANTE A *¿Cocinaste algo delicioso para la cena?*
> ESTUDIANTE B *No, no cociné nada.*

1. ver / interesante en la tele
2. dibujar / nuevo para la clase de arte
3. encontrar / interesante en la cómoda
4. preparar / divertido para el baile de disfraces
5. dar / viejo a la venta de ropa
6. comprar / bonito para María
7. sacar / bueno de la biblioteca
8. tomar / caliente después de la cena
9. olvidarse de / importante

C **Dos hermanos diferentes.** Carmen y Diego son hermanos, pero son muy diferentes en todo. Pregunta y contesta según el modelo.

> estudiar por la noche
> ESTUDIANTE A *Siempre estudio por la noche.*
> ESTUDIANTE B *Pues yo nunca estudio por la noche.*

1. estar contento(a)
2. dormir ocho horas
3. cantar en la ducha
4. decir la verdad
5. bañarse por la mañana
6. olvidarse de cerrar el armario
7. divertirse en las ventas de ropa
8. estar de acuerdo con mis padres
9. pedir prestado dinero
10. descansar después del almuerzo

D **Quisiera comprar . . .** Imagina que viajas por Europa y quieres comprar recuerdos para tu familia. Pregunta y contesta según el modelo.

> manteles portugueses
> ESTUDIANTE A *Discúlpeme, señor(a). Quisiera comprar algunos manteles portugueses.*
> ESTUDIANTE B *Lo siento. No tenemos ninguno.*
> o: *Aquí tiene Ud. algunos.*

1. cintas de música folklórica
2. máscaras de carnaval
3. libros sobre las corridas de toros
4. tarjetas postales de los Pirineos
5. guías de Inglaterra
6. jabones franceses
7. carteles de Italia
8. dulces alemanes

E **Siempre hay alguien.** A Marta le encanta ir a la playa. Completa las frases con las palabras correctas: *algo, alguien, algún, alguno(s), alguna(s).*

Vivo cerca del mar. Siempre voy a la playa con _____ porque no me gusta ir sola. A veces voy con mis padres pero prefiero ir con mis amigas. Llevamos _____ para comer y _____ refrescos. Durante la semana, no hay mucha gente en la playa, pero generalmente hay
5 _____ a quien conozco. Pero los fines de semana siempre hay _____ turistas. _____ de mis amigas nadan muy bien. Yo no. _____ días las olas son enormes y no puedo nadar. Entonces llevo una novela para leer o hablo con _____. _____ día, tú puedes ir conmigo.

F **Hablemos de ti.**
1. ¿Qué haces cuando quieres comprar algo y te falta dinero?
2. ¿Piensas hacer algo interesante o divertido este fin de semana? ¿Qué vas a hacer?
3. ¿Esperas viajar algún día a la América Central? ¿A México? ¿Qué hay que hacer antes de viajar allí?
4. ¿Hay algunos estudiantes centroamericanos o sudamericanos en tu escuela? ¿Hablas español con ellos? ¿A veces te ayudan a hacer tu tarea de español?
5. ¿Qué cosas no haces nunca? ¿Cuáles son algunas de las cosas que no hace nadie en tu escuela?

Practice Sheet 16–4   Workbook Exs. E–F

 11 Tape Manual Ex. 7   Activity Master 16–1   Quiz 16–4

ACTIVIDAD

¿Cuántas veces? How often do you do things? With a partner, make up ten questions about everyday activities. For example:

¿Te acuestas antes de las siete?
¿Les pides prestado dinero a tus amigos?
¿Estás de acuerdo con tus padres?

Then get together with two other pairs of students and take a poll. Take turns asking each other questions and tallying responses on this scale: *siempre / a menudo / a veces / nunca.*

APLICACIONES Discretionary

Los regalos de Quetzalcóatl 12

¿Sabes quién era[1] Quetzalcóatl? Era un dios[2] muy importante para algunos grupos de indios de México. Mucho de lo que sabemos de él viene de la mitología de los aztecas.

¿Te parece difícil pronunciar Quetzalcóatl? Pues su nombre viene de
5   dos palabras aztecas: *quetzal,* que quiere decir pájaro de[3] plumas[4] hermosas, y *cóatl,* que quiere decir serpiente. Quetzalcóatl, pluma-serpiente o serpiente de plumas.

Quetzalcóatl era un dios amable y bueno. Ayudó mucho a los indios. Les dio el maíz y les enseñó la agricultura. Les mostró también cómo
10   hacer ropa y construir templos y casas. También inventó el calendario para enseñar a la gente los secretos de las estrellas y de los planetas.

El buen dios pasó muchos años con la gente de México. Pero un día, otro dios, Tezcatlipoca, salió del oeste y trató de destruir a Quetzalcóatl. Quetzalcóatl fue al este, y cuando llegó al mar se escapó de prisa en un
15   barco.

Muchos años después, el conquistador español Hernán Cortés llegó a México. Cortés le dio mucho miedo a Moctezuma, el emperador de los aztecas. "Este hombre tiene que ser Quetzalcóatl que regresa," pensó Moctezuma. Por eso los indios no atacaron a Cortés, y los españoles
20   conquistaron[5] a México. ¡Y Quetzalcóatl nunca regresó!

---

[1]**era** *(from ser)   he was*   [2]**el dios**   *god*   [3]**de** here: *with*   [4]**la pluma**   *feather*
[5]**conquistar**   *to conquer*

Enrichment: Tell students that Quetzalcóatl is commonly referred to as *la serpiente emplumada.*

Preguntas

Contesta según la lectura.

1. ¿De dónde viene lo que sabemos de Quetzalcóatl?
2. ¿Puedes describir a Quetzalcóatl?
3. ¿Qué hizo para la gente?
4. ¿Qué hizo Tezcatlipoca?
5. ¿Cómo se escapó Quetzalcóatl? ¿Qué está al oeste de México? ¿Al este? (Si es necesario, mira un mapa.)
6. ¿Quién era Cortés?
7. ¿Quién era Moctezuma?
8. ¿Qué pensó Moctezuma cuando vio a Cortés?

EXPLICACIONES II

El pretérito: Verbos que terminan en -er e -ir

You already know the singular forms of *comer* and *salir* in the preterite tense. Here are all of the preterite endings for regular -*er* and -*ir* verbs. They are the same for both types of verbs.

INFINITIVO **comer**

	SINGULAR		PLURAL
1	(yo) comí	(nosotros) (nosotras)	comimos
2	(tú) comiste	(vosotros) (vosotras)	comisteis
3	Ud. (él) (ella) comió	Uds. (ellos) (ellas)	comieron

INFINITIVO **salir**

	SINGULAR		PLURAL
1	(yo) salí	(nosotros) (nosotras)	salimos
2	(tú) saliste	(vosotros) (vosotras)	salisteis
3	Ud. (él) (ella) salió	Uds. (ellos) (ellas)	salieron

Notes: Mini-dialogues 1 on p. 526 and 2 on p. 527 contain examples of preterite forms of -*er* and -*ir* verbs.

◆ **OBJECTIVES:**

TO FIND OUT OR RELATE WHAT HAS HAPPENED

TO TELL WHAT YOU HAVE DONE

TO APOLOGIZE

TO BLAME OTHERS

Reteach / Extra Help: You may want to reinforce the preterite forms by asking these questions. Change verb forms and point to yourself, a girl, two boys, and so on according to the form you are eliciting. *¿Comiste una hamburguesa ayer? ¿A qué hora saliste de casa esta mañana? ¿Comprendiste la lección ayer? ¿Viste una buena película el sábado pasado? ¿Perdiste algo esta semana? ¿Recibiste una tarjeta postal ayer? ¿Escribiste bien las palabras afirmativas?* (Answers will vary.)

Práctica A

1. ¿Saliste …?
   Sí, (No, no) salí con mis …
2. ¿Asististe …?
   Sí, (No, no) asistí a
   (ninguna) …
3. ¿Viste …?
   Sí, (No, no) vi (nada) …
4. ¿Escribiste …?
   Sí, (No, no) escribí (ningún)
   …
5. ¿Perdiste …?
   Sí, (No, no) perdí (ningún) …
6. ¿Aprendiste …?
   Sí, (No, no) aprendí (nada)
   …
7. ¿Recibiste …?
   Sí, (No, no) recibí (ninguna)
   …
8. ¿Rompiste …?
   Sí, (No, no) rompí (nada) …

Práctica B

1. ¿Recibieron Uds. …?
   No, no recibimos ninguna.
2. ¿Abrieron Uds. …?
   No, no abrimos nada.
3. ¿Perdieron Uds. …?
   No, no perdimos nada.
4. ¿Salieron Uds. …?
   No, nunca salimos del
   barrio.
5. Volvieron Uds. …?
   No, no volvimos hasta tarde.
6. ¿Vieron Uds. …?
   No, no vimos a nadie.
7. ¿Rompieron Uds. …?
   No, no rompimos nada.
8. ¿Comprendieron Uds. …?
   No, no comprendimos
   ninguna de ellas.

1 Here are all of the *-er* and *-ir* verbs that you know that follow this pattern.

aprender	correr	perder	abrir	salir
beber	deber	romper	asistir	subir
comer	doler	vender	describir	vivir
comprender	llover*	ver	escribir	
conocer	parecer	volver	recibir	

2 *Ver* does not have an accent mark on any of its preterite forms.

vi	**vimos**
viste	**visteis**
vio	**vieron**

PRÁCTICA

A ¿Qué hiciste la semana pasada? ¿Hiciste algunas de estas cosas la semana pasada? Pregunta y contesta según el modelo.

comer comida mexicana

ESTUDIANTE A *¿Comiste comida mexicana?*
ESTUDIANTE B *Sí, comí comida mexicana.*
o: *No, no comí comida mexicana.*

1. salir con tus amigos el sábado
2. asistir a alguna obra de teatro
3. ver algo bueno en el cine
4. escribir algunos poemas románticos
5. perder algún partido
6. aprender algo nuevo
7. recibir buenas noticias
8. romper algo

B Detective. Imagina que eres detective y que investigas un robo (*robbery*) en tu barrio. Les preguntas a todos qué pasó. ¡Pero nadie sabe nada! Sigue el modelo.

ver a alguien en el balcón del tercer piso / no . . . nadie
ESTUDIANTE A *¿Vieron Uds. a alguien en el balcón del tercer piso?*
ESTUDIANTE B *No, no vimos a nadie.*

1. recibir algunas cartas chistosas / no . . . ninguna
2. abrir algunas cajas grandes / no . . . nada
3. perder las llaves de la casa / no . . . nada
4. salir del barrio hoy / no, nunca . . .
5. volver a casa temprano / no . . . hasta tarde
6. ver a un hombre alto en la esquina / no . . . nadie
7. romper las ventanas de la planta baja / no . . . nada
8. comprender todas mis preguntas / no . . . ninguna de ellas

* *Llover*, of course, has only one preterite form: *llovió*.

C ¿Cuánto dinero? Imagina que tú y varias otras personas vendieron estas cosas el sábado pasado. ¿Qué vendió cada persona y cuánto dinero recibió? Sigue el modelo.

Marta vendió una cámara. Recibió cinco dólares.

Marta

 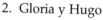   

1. Ricardo y yo   2. Gloria y Hugo   3. (tú)

4. Anita   5. Uds.   6. (yo)

7. Graciela   8. Pedro y Andrés   9. Carlos

(arriba) En un mercado en Cartagena, Colombia; (abajo) Una vendedora en Arcos de la Frontera, España

Práctica C

1. Ricardo y yo vendimos un sillón. Recibimos doce dólares.
2. Gloria y Hugo vendieron una maleta. Recibieron tres dólares.
3. Vendiste una pulsera. Recibiste dos dólares.
4. Anita vendió un pañuelo. Recibió veinticinco centavos.
5. Uds. vendieron (unos / algunos) sellos. Recibieron siete dólares.
6. Vendí una máscara. Recibí setenta y cinco centavos.
7. Graciela vendió un anillo. Recibió cuatro dólares.
8. Pedro y Andrés vendieron cuatro corbatas. Recibieron cuatro dólares.
9. Carlos vendió (unas / algunas) tarjetas postales. Recibió un dólar y cincuenta centavos.

Explicaciones II   541

Práctica D
1. ¿Quién bebió toda la limonada?
   Vicente la bebió.
2. ¿Quién comió todo mi chocolate?
   Nosotros lo comimos.
3. ¿Quién rompió …?
   El perro la rompió.
4. ¿Quién escribió …?
   Juanito las escribió.
5. ¿Quien abrió …?
   Dolores y Juanito las abrieron.
6. ¿Quién rompió …?
   Yo lo rompí.
7. ¿Quién comió …?
   Vicente y yo lo comimos.

Práctica E
volví
abrí / entré
corrió / miré / vi
Subí / escuché / pasaron
caminé
abrió / dio
encontré
preguntó / me quité
contesté / diste / pregunté
miró / salió / se acostó

D **¿Qué pasó aquí?** La Sra. Peña regresó a casa y encontró todo en desorden (*mess*). Le preguntó a su hijo mayor lo que pasó. Sigue el modelo.

> abrir la puerta de mi armario / Dolores
> ESTUDIANTE A *¿Quién abrió la puerta de mi armario?*
> ESTUDIANTE B *Dolores la abrió.*

1. beber toda la limonada / Vicente
2. comer todo mi chocolate / nosotros
3. romper mi taza preferida / el perro
4. escribir esas palabras en mi libro / Juanito
5. abrir mis cartas / Dolores y Juanito
6. romper este espejo / yo
7. comer todo el pastel / Vicente y yo

E **Un cuento de terror.** Un viejo amigo nos contó este cuento. Cambia cada verbo al pretérito.

Una noche sin luna, todavía vestido de fantasma, yo (*volver*) muy tarde de una fiesta de disfraces. (*Abrir*) la puerta y (*entrar*) en la sala. En seguida algo (*correr*) por la escalera, pero cuando (*mirar*), no (*ver*) nada. (*Subir*) al primer piso y (*escuchar*). Unos segundos (*pasar*) . . .
5 y luego, ¡un pequeño ruido en el baño! (*Caminar*) despacio, muy despacio. Alguien (*abrir*) la puerta del baño. Me (*dar*) mucho miedo . . . ¿Pero sabes a quién (yo) (*encontrar*)? ¡A mi hermanito! "¿Q-q-q-quién eres?" me (*preguntar*). Yo (*quitarse*) la sábana blanca. "¡Soy yo, tonto!" (*contestar*). "¿Por qué me (*dar*) un miedo tan grande?" yo (*preguntar*).
10 Él me (*mirar*), (*salir*) del baño sin decir nada más y (*acostarse*).
Dos semanas más tarde todavía no habla conmigo.

F Hablemos de ti.

1. ¿Aprendiste mucho este año? ¿Qué aprendiste?
2. ¿Saliste bien en los exámenes durante el año? ¿Sacaste buenas notas? ¿Te importan mucho las notas? ¿Por qué?
3. ¿Te gustó esta clase? ¡Esperamos que sí!

Práctica F
Answers will vary.

ACTIVIDAD

Opiniones Take a class poll about what you learned this year. As a class, make up a series of questions such as these.

¿Aprendieron Uds. a pedir comida en un restaurante?

¿Aprendieron Uds. a contestar rápidamente qué hora es?

¿Aprendieron Uds. a hablar de actividades que les gustan?

While one person asks the class your questions, another should keep a record of the responses. Afterward, discuss why everyone responded as they did:

¿Están todos de acuerdo?

¿Qué les gustó y no les gustó? ¿Por qué?

Practice Sheets 16–5, 16–6

Workbook Exs. G–J

Canción: 13

Tape Manual Exs. 8–9 14

Activity Master 16–2

Quiz 16–5

APLICACIONES

Notes: Answers to the **Repaso** and **Tema** appear in the pre-chapter teacher pages.

REPASO

Notes: Review of:
1. preterite of -er /
   -ir verbs
   noun phrases with *de*
   algunos, -as
2. emphatic indirect
   object pronoun
   gustar
   personal *a*
   superlative of adjec-
   tives + *de*
3. preterite
   doler
   definite article
   with parts of the
   body
   exclamations
4. preterite
   direct vs. indirect
   object pronouns
   dio
5. preterite
   compound subject
   algunos, -as

Look carefully at the model sentences. Then put the English cues into Spanish to form new sentences based on the models.

1. *Hoy asistí a una clase de computadoras con algunos amigos.*
   (Tonight my sister attended a volleyball game with several friends.)
   (That night they drank a bottle of milk with their friends.)
   (Last night Marcos and I ate lamb chops with our girlfriends.)

2. *A mí me gusta llamar a Anita, la atleta más formidable del equipo.*
   (She likes to watch Ricardo, the youngest person on the team.)
   (They like to listen to Luz, the most intelligent girl in the class.)
   (We like to invite Pilar and Raúl, the funniest students in the school.)

3. *Estudiaron la lección, y ahora les duele la cabeza. ¡Pobrecitos!*
   (We lost the game, and now our legs hurt. What bad luck!)
   (She wrote the letters, and now her hand hurts. What a shame!)
   (I saw the movie, and now my eyes hurt. What a problem!)

4. *La médica la examinó y le dio una receta.*
   (Dr. Jiménez (m.) listened to us and gave us an excuse.)
   (The dentist (m.) examined me and gave me a toothbrush.)
   (The nurse (f.) saw them (f.) and gave them towels.)

5. *Ana caminó un poco. Luego, ella y algunas amigas estudiaron adentro.*
   (Pablo wrote a little. Then he and some friends played inside.)
   (The women cooked a lot. Then they and some guests (f.) ate outside.)
   (I slept too much. Later some boys and I ran outside.)

Put the English captions into Spanish.

1. Yesterday Rosa attended a soccer game with some friends.

2. Rosa likes to watch Antonio, the fastest player on the team.

3. Antonio won the game, and now his legs hurt. Poor thing!

4. The doctor examined him, but he didn't give him anything.

5. Antonio rested a little. Then he, Rosa, and some friends celebrated outside.

REDACCIÓN

Now you are ready to write your own dialogue or paragraph. Choose one of the following topics.

1. Expand the *Tema* by describing Rosa and Antonio. How does she know him? How many boys are there in the locker room? What are they doing? What is the doctor like? Where did Rosa go after the game? What did Antonio and his friends do to celebrate?

2. Write a conversation between Antonio and the doctor. Include the following: The doctor asks Antonio what is wrong. Antonio tells him that his head and legs hurt. The doctor tells Antonio that he is going to examine him. He says he isn't going to give Antonio anything but that Antonio must rest. Antonio thanks the doctor and asks him whether he must return. The doctor says that Antonio should return to his office in one week.

3. For each picture write a sentence that Rosa might write in a letter to a friend describing what happened that day.

LOS NÚMEROS, LOS DÍAS, LOS MESES Y LA HORA

Cardinal Numbers

0	cero	30	treinta
1	uno	40	cuarenta
2	dos	50	cincuenta
3	tres	60	sesenta
4	cuatro	70	setenta
5	cinco	80	ochenta
6	seis	90	noventa
7	siete	100	ciento
8	ocho	200	doscientos
9	nueve	300	trescientos
10	diez	400	cuatrocientos
11	once	500	quinientos
12	doce	600	seiscientos
13	trece	700	setecientos
14	catorce	800	ochocientos
15	quince	900	novecientos
16	dieciséis	1000	mil
17	diecisiete		
18	dieciocho		
19	diecinueve		
20	veinte		
21	veintiuno		
22	veintidós		
23	veintitrés		
24	veinticuatro		
25	veinticinco		
26	veintiséis		
27	veintisiete		
28	veintiocho		
29	veintinueve		

Days of the Week

lunes	*Monday*
martes	*Tuesday*
miércoles	*Wednesday*
jueves	*Thursday*
viernes	*Friday*
sábado	*Saturday*
domingo	*Sunday*

Months

enero	*January*
febrero	*February*
marzo	*March*
abril	*April*
mayo	*May*
junio	*June*
julio	*July*
agosto	*August*
septiembre	*September*
octubre	*October*
noviembre	*November*
diciembre	*December*

Time

¿Qué hora es?   *What time is it?*
Es la una.   *It's 1:00.*
Son las dos.   *It's 2:00.*
Son las dos y cuarto.   *It's 2:15.*
Son las dos y media.   *It's 2:30.*
Son las tres menos cuarto.   *It's 2:45.*
Son las tres.   *It's 3:00.*

VERBOS

INFINITIVE	PRESENT		PRETERITE	

Regular Verbs

cantar

canto	cantamos	canté	cantamos
cantas	cantáis	cantaste	cantasteis
canta	cantan	cantó	cantaron

aprender

aprendo	aprendemos	aprendí	aprendimos
aprendes	aprendéis	aprendiste	aprendisteis
aprende	aprenden	aprendió	aprendieron

vivir

vivo	vivimos	viví	vivimos
vives	vivís	viviste	vivisteis
vive	viven	vivió	vivieron

Reflexive Verbs

lavarse

me lavo	nos lavamos	me lavé	nos lavamos
te lavas	os laváis	te lavaste	os lavasteis
se lava	se lavan	se lavó	se lavaron

Stem-changing Verbs

acostar (o → ue)   See *contar*.

acostarse (o → ue)   See *contar* and Reflexive Verbs.

cerrar (e → ie)

cierro	cerramos	cerré	cerramos
cierras	cerráis	cerraste	cerrasteis
cierra	cierran	cerró	cerraron

contar (o → ue)

cuento	contamos	conté	contamos
cuentas	contáis	contaste	contasteis
cuenta	cuentan	contó	contaron

costar (o → ue)   See *contar*.

despertar (e → ie)   See *cerrar*.

despertarse (e → ie)   See *cerrar* and Reflexive Verbs.

INFINITIVE	PRESENT	PRETERITE

divertirse (e → ie) — See *cerrar* and Reflexive Verbs.

me divertí	nos divertimos
te divertiste	os divertisteis
se divirtió	se divirtieron

doler (o → ue) — See *contar*.

dormir (o → ue) — See *contar*.

dormí	dormimos
dormiste	dormisteis
durmió	durmieron

dormirse (o → ue) — See *contar* and Reflexive Verbs.

me dormí	nos dormimos
te dormiste	os dormisteis
se durmió	se durmieron

empezar (e → ie) — See *cerrar*.

empecé	empezamos
empezaste	empezasteis
empezó	empezaron

encontrar (o → ue) — See *contar*.

jugar (u → ue)

PRESENT		PRETERITE	
juego	jugamos	jugué	jugamos
juegas	jugáis	jugaste	jugasteis
juega	juegan	jugó	jugaron

llover (o → ue) — (llueve) / (llovió)

mostrar (o → ue) — See *contar*.

nevar (e → ie) — (nieva) / (nevó)

pedir (e → i)

PRESENT		PRETERITE	
pido	pedimos	pedí	pedimos
pides	pedís	pediste	pedisteis
pide	piden	pidió	pidieron

pensar (e → ie) — See *cerrar*.

perder (e → ie) — See *cerrar*.

poder (o → ue) — See Irregular Verbs.

preferir (e → ie) — See *cerrar*.

preferí	preferimos
preferiste	preferisteis
prefirió	prefirieron

querer (e → ie) — See Irregular Verbs.

repetir (e → i) — See *pedir*.

repetí	repetimos
repetiste	repetisteis
repitió	repitieron

servir (e → i) — See *pedir*.

serví	servimos
serviste	servisteis
sirvió	sirvieron

INFINITIVE	PRESENT		PRETERITE	
vestir (e → i)	See *pedir*.		vestí	vestimos
			vestiste	vestisteis
			vistió	vistieron
vestirse (e → i)	See *pedir* and Reflexive Verbs.		me vestí	nos vestimos
			te vestiste	os vestisteis
			se vistió	se vistieron
volver (o → ue)	See *contar*.			

Verbs with Spelling Changes

aterrizar	aterrizo	aterrizamos	aterricé	aterrizamos
	aterrizas	aterrizáis	aterrizaste	aterrizasteis
	aterriza	aterrizan	aterrizó	aterrizaron
buscar	busco	buscamos	busqué	buscamos
	buscas	buscáis	buscaste	buscasteis
	busca	buscan	buscó	buscaron
conocer	conozco	conocemos	conocí	conocimos
	conoces	conocéis	conociste	conocisteis
	conoce	conocen	conoció	conocieron
continuar	continúo	continuamos	continué	continuamos
	continúas	continuáis	continuaste	continuasteis
	continúa	continúan	continuó	continuaron
creer	creo	creemos	creí	creímos
	crees	creéis	creíste	creísteis
	cree	creen	creyó	creyeron
despegar	See *llegar*.			
empezar	See Stem-changing Verbs.			
esquiar	esquío	esquiamos	esquié	esquiamos
	esquías	esquiáis	esquiaste	esquiasteis
	esquía	esquían	esquió	esquiaron
jugar	See Stem-changing Verbs.			
leer	See *creer*.			
llegar	llego	llegamos	llegué	llegamos
	llegas	llegáis	llegaste	llegasteis
	llega	llegan	llegó	llegaron
pagar	See *llegar*.			
practicar	See *buscar*.			

INFINITIVE	PRESENT		PRETERITE	
sacar	See *buscar*.			
tocar	See *buscar*.			

Irregular Verbs

INFINITIVE	PRESENT		PRETERITE	
dar	doy	damos	di	dimos
	das	dais	diste	disteis
	da	dan	dio	dieron
decir	digo	decimos	dije	dijimos
	dices	decís	dijiste	dijisteis
	dice	dicen	dijo	dijeron
estar	estoy	estamos	estuve	estuvimos
	estás	estáis	estuviste	estuvisteis
	está	están	estuvo	estuvieron
hacer	hago	hacemos	hice	hicimos
	haces	hacéis	hiciste	hicisteis
	hace	hacen	hizo	hicieron
ir	voy	vamos	fui	fuimos
	vas	vais	fuiste	fuisteis
	va	van	fue	fueron
oír	oigo	oímos	oí	oímos
	oyes	oís	oíste	oísteis
	oye	oyen	oyó	oyeron
poder	puedo	podemos	pude	pudimos
	puedes	podéis	pudiste	pudisteis
	puede	pueden	pudo	pudieron
poner	pongo	ponemos	puse	pusimos
	pones	ponéis	pusiste	pusisteis
	pone	ponen	puso	pusieron
ponerse	See *poner* and Reflexive Verbs.			
querer	quiero	queremos	quise	quisimos
	quieres	queréis	quisiste	quisisteis
	quiere	quieren	quiso	quisieron
saber	sé	sabemos	supe	supimos
	sabes	sabéis	supiste	supisteis
	sabe	saben	supo	supieron

INFINITIVE	PRESENT		PRETERITE	
salir	salgo	salimos	salí	salimos
	sales	salís	saliste	salisteis
	sale	salen	salió	salieron
ser	soy	somos	fui	fuimos
	eres	sois	fuiste	fuisteis
	es	son	fue	fueron
tener	tengo	tenemos	tuve	tuvimos
	tienes	tenéis	tuviste	tuvisteis
	tiene	tienen	tuvo	tuvieron
traer	traigo	traemos	traje	trajimos
	traes	traéis	trajiste	trajisteis
	trae	traen	trajo	trajeron
venir	vengo	venimos	vine	vinimos
	vienes	venís	viniste	vinisteis
	viene	vienen	vino	vinieron
ver	veo	vemos	vi	vimos
	ves	veis	viste	visteis
	ve	ven	vio	vieron

VOCABULARIO ESPAÑOL-INGLÉS

The *Vocabulario español-inglés* contains all active vocabulary from the text.

A dash (**—**) represents the main entry word. For example, **el — mineral** following **el agua** means **el agua mineral.**

The number following each entry indicates the chapter in which the word or expression is first introduced. Two numbers indicate that it is introduced in one chapter and elaborated upon in a later chapter. A letter following an entry refers to the *En Camino* sections.

The following abbreviations are used: *adj.* (adjective), *dir. obj.* (direct object), *f.* (feminine), *fam.* (familiar), *ind. obj.* (indirect object), *inf.* (infinitive), *m.* (masculine), *prep.* (preposition), *pl.* (plural), *pron.* (pronoun), *sing.* (singular).

a, al at (D); to (E, 4); *as sign of dir. obj.* (7)
— menudo often (3)
— pie on foot (4)
— tiempo on time (12)
— veces sometimes (3)
abierto, -a open (12)
el abrigo overcoat (3)
abril April (C)
abrir to open (12)
el abuelo, la abuela grandfather, grandmother (6)
los abuelos grandfathers; grandparents (6)
aburrido, -a bored; boring (5)
acabar de + *inf.* to have just *(done something)* (9)
el acento accent mark (7)
acostar (o → ue) to put *(someone)* to bed (14)
—se to go to bed (14)
el actor, la actriz *(f.pl.* **actrices)** actor, actress (9)
acuerdo: estar de — to agree (16)
adentro inside (16)
adiós good-by (A)
¿adónde? (to) where? (4)
el aeropuerto airport (4)
el aficionado, la aficionada (a) fan (of) (14)

el África *f.* Africa (15)
afuera outside (16)
la agencia de viajes travel agency (12)
el/la agente de viajes travel agent (12)
agosto August (C)
agradable pleasant (10)
el agua *f.* water (8)
el — mineral mineral water (8)
¡ah, sí! oh, yes! (1)
ahora now (D)
el ajedrez chess (11)
alemán *(pl.* **alemanes),** **alemana** German (15)
el alemán German *(language)* (15)
Alemania Germany (15)
la alfombra rug (15)
el álgebra algebra (7)
algo something, anything (16)
tomar — to have something to drink (11)
alguien someone, somebody, anyone (16)
algún, alguna some, any, a (16)
alguno, -a, -os, -as *pron.* some, any, one (16)

el almacén, *pl.* **almacenes** department store (5)
la almohada pillow (15)
el almuerzo lunch (8)
¿aló? hello? *(on phone)* (5)
alto, -a tall (2)
el alumno, la alumna pupil (2)
allá (over) there (5)
allí there (5)
amable kind, nice (12)
amarillo, -a yellow (3)
la América Central Central America (2)
la América del Norte North America (2)
la América del Sur South America (2)
la América Latina Latin America (2)
americano, -a American (E)
el amigo, la amiga friend (2)
anaranjado, -a orange (3)
el anillo ring (12)
animados: los dibujos — movie cartoons (9)
el animal animal (10)
el — doméstico pet (10)
anoche last night (8)
los anteojos eyeglasses (9)
los — de sol sunglasses (9)
antes de before (9)

— + *inf.* before *(doing something)* (9)

antipático, -a unpleasant, not nice (5)

el anuncio comercial commercial (9)

el año year (C)

  ¿cuántos —s tienes? how old are you? (6)

  el día de fin de — New Year's Eve (C)

  los quince —s fifteenth birthday (party) (6)

  tener . . . —s to be . . . years old (6)

el Año Nuevo New Year's Day (C)

el apartamento apartment (6)

el apellido last name, surname (6)

  aprender to learn (7)

   — a + *inf.* to learn how (to) (7)

   — de memoria to memorize (7)

  aquí here (3)

   — lo (la / los / las) tiene(s) here it is, here they are (11)

   — tienes / tiene Ud. here is, here are (11)

el árbol tree (10)

el arete earring (12)

la Argentina Argentina (B)

el armario closet (15)

  arreglar to fix, to repair (9)

el arroz rice (13)

el arte art (7)

el ascensor elevator (15)

  así, así, so-so (A)

el asiento seat (12)

  asistir a to attend (7)

  aterrizar to land (12)

el/la atleta athlete (14)

  atlético, -a athletic (14)

  ausente absent (7)

el autobús, *pl.* **autobuses** bus (4)

el/la auxiliar de vuelo flight attendant (12)

la avenida avenue (5)

la aventura adventure (16)

el avión, *pl.* **aviones** plane (4)

  ayer yesterday (8)

  ayudar (a + *inf.)* to help (1, 6)

el azúcar sugar (8)

  azul blue (3)

  bailar to dance (E)

el baile dance (11)

  bajar to come down, to go down (12)

   — de to get off or out of *(vehicles)* (12)

  bajo, -a short (2)

   la planta —a ground floor (6)

el balcón, *pl.* **balcones** balcony (15)

el balón, *pl.* **balones** ball (14)

el banco bank (4)

la bandera flag (1)

  bañar to bathe *(someone)* (14)

   —se to take a bath (14)

el baño bathroom (6)

  el traje de — bathing suit (3)

  barato, -a cheap, inexpensive (3)

el barco boat (4)

el barrio neighborhood (8)

el básquetbol basketball (E)

  bastante rather, fairly, kind of (2)

  beber to drink (8)

la bebida drink, beverage (13)

el béisbol baseball (E)

  bellísimo, -a very beautiful (12)

  bello, -a beautiful (12)

la biblioteca library (4)

la bicicleta bicycle (E)

  montar en — to ride a bicycle (E)

  bien well, good (A)

  está — okay, all right (11)

  bienvenido, -a welcome (12)

  bilingüe bilingual (7)

la biología biology (7)

el bistec steak (13)

  blanco, -a white (3)

la blusa blouse (3)

la boca mouth (15)

el boleto ticket (12)

el bolígrafo (ballpoint) pen (B)

  Bolivia Bolivia (B)

el bolso purse (12)

  bonito, -a pretty, good-looking (2)

el borrador (blackboard) eraser (7)

  borrar to erase (7)

la bota boot (3)

la botella bottle (8)

el Brasil Brazil (15)

el brazo arm (15)

  bueno (buen), -a good (4)

  —as noches good evening, good night (A)

  —as tardes good afternoon, good evening (A)

  bueno, . . . well, . . . (9)

  ¡bueno! okay, fine (4)

  —os días good morning (A)

  hace buen tiempo it's nice (out) (3)

  ¡qué —! great! (9)

la bufanda scarf, muffler (3)

el burrito burrito (1)

  buscar to look for (3)

el caballo horse (10)

la cabeza head (16)

la cabina telefónica phone booth (5)

  cada each, every (13)

el café café (5); coffee (8)

  el — con leche coffee with cream (8)

la cafetería cafeteria (7)

el caimán, *pl.* **caimanes** alligator (10)

la caja box (12)

el calcetín, *pl.* **calcetines** sock (3)

el calendario calendar (C)

  caliente hot (13)

el calor:
    hace — it's hot (out) (3)
    tener — to be hot *(person)* (9)
la calle street (5)
la cama bed (15)
la cámara camera (11)
el camarero, la camarera waiter, waitress (13)
  cambiar to change, to exchange (12)
  caminar to walk (10)
el camino road (10)
el camión, *pl.* **camiones** truck (4)
la camisa shirt (3)
la camiseta t-shirt (3)
el campo country, countryside (4)
el Canadá Canada (2)
  canadiense Canadian (2)
el canal TV channel (9)
la canción, *pl.* **canciones** song (11)
  cansado, -a tired (5)
  cantar to sing (E)
la capital capital (2)
el capítulo chapter (7)
la cara face (14)
  ¡caramba! gosh! gee! (9)
el Caribe Caribbean (2)
  carísimo, -a very expensive (12)
el carnaval carnival, Mardi Gras (13)
la carne meat (8)
la carnicería butcher shop (8)
  caro, -a expensive (3)
la carta letter (7)
el cartel poster (1)
la cartera wallet (12)
la casa house (4)
  a — *(to one's)* home (4)
  en — at home (1)
  casi almost (9)
  catorce fourteen (C)
la cebolla onion (8)
la cebra zebra (10)
la celebración, *pl.* **celebraciones** celebration (13)

celebrar to celebrate (13)
la cena dinner, supper, evening meal (8)
el centavo cent (12)
el centro downtown (4)
  centroamericano, -a Central American (2)
  cepillar (el pelo) to brush (someone's hair) (14)
  —se (los dientes, el pelo) to brush one's (teeth, hair) (14)
el cepillo de dientes toothbrush (14)
  cerca de near, close to (5)
el cerdo pig (10)
  la chuleta de — pork chop (13)
  cero zero (C)
  cerrado, -a closed (12)
  cerrar (e → ie) to close (12)
el cielo sky (10)
  cien one hundred (D)
  ciencia ficción: de — *adj.* science fiction (9)
las ciencias science (7)
  ciento uno, -a; ciento dos; etc. 101; 102; etc. (8)
  cinco five (C)
  cincuenta fifty (D)
el cine movie theater (E)
la cinta tape (E)
el cinturón, *pl.* **cinturones** belt (12)
la ciudad city (4)
  claro (que sí) of course (10)
  — que no of course not (10)
la clase (de) class (A); kind, type (9)
  el compañero, la compañera de — classmate (2)
  clásico, -a classical (1)
el/la cliente customer (12)
la cocina kitchen (6)
  cocinar to cook (E)
el coche car (4)
  cola: hacer — to stand in line (11)
  coleccionar to collect (11)

el colegio high school (7)
Colombia Colombia (B)
el color color (3)
  ¿de qué —? what color? (3)
  en —es in color (9)
el collar necklace (12)
el comedor dining room (6)
  comer to eat (E)
  dar de —a to feed (6)
  comercial *see* **anuncio**
los comestibles groceries (8)
  cómico, -a comic (9)
la comida food (E); meal (8)
  cómo:
    ¿— es . . . ? what's . . . like? (2)
    ¿— estás? how are you? *fam.* (A)
    ¿— está Ud.? how are you? *formal* (A)
    ¡— no! of course! (1)
    ¿— se dice . . . ? how do you say . . . ? (B)
    ¿— se escribe . . . ? how do you spell . . . ? (B)
    ¿— te llamas? what's your name? (A)
la cómoda dresser (15)
  cómodo, -a comfortable (6)
el compañero, la compañera de clase classmate (2)
  comprar to buy (3)
  compras: de — shopping (8)
  comprender to understand (7)
  no comprendo I don't understand (B)
la computadora computer (7)
  con with (1)
  — mucho gusto gladly, with pleasure (15)
  — permiso excuse me (15)
el concierto concert (11)
  conmigo with me (7)
  conocer to know, to be acquainted with (15)
  conocido, -a: muy — well-known (9)
  contar (o → ue) to count; to tell (11)

contento, -a happy (5)
contestar to answer (3)
contigo with you *fam.* (7)
continuar to continue (9)
contrario: al — on the contrary (2)
el corazón heart (16)
la corbata tie (12)
el cordero lamb (10)
    la chuleta de — lamb chop (13)
correcto, -a correct (7)
el correo post office (4)
correr to run (14)
la corrida (de toros) bullfight (13)
corto, -a short (2)
la cosa thing (8)
costar (o → ue) to cost (11)
    ¿cuánto cuesta(n) . . . ? how much does / do . . . cost? (3)
Costa Rica Costa Rica (B)
creer to think, to believe (10)
    creo que no I don't think so (10)
    creo que sí I think so (10)
el cuaderno notebook (B)
¿cuál, -es? what? (D); which one(s)? (3)
    ¿— es la fecha de hoy? what's the date today? (C)
cuando when (3)
¿cuándo? when? (D)
¿cuánto? how much? (3)
    ¿— cuesta(n) . . . ? how much does / do . . . cost? (3)
    ¿— dura? how long does *(something)* last? (9)
    ¿— tiempo? how long? (12)
¿cuántos, -as? how many? (C)
    ¿— años tienes? how old are you? (6)
cuarenta forty (D)
cuarto:
    menos — quarter to (D)
    y — quarter after, quarter past (D)

el cuarto room (15)
cuatro four (C)
cuatrocientos, -as four hundred (8)
Cuba Cuba (B)
cubano, -a Cuban (2)
la cuchara spoon (8)
el cuchillo knife (8)
la cuenta check *(in restaurant)* (13)
el cuento story (11)
el cuerpo body (16)
cuesta(n) *see* **costar**
cuidado:
    ¡—! watch out! be careful! (9)
    tener — to be careful (9)
cuidar a los niños to baby-sit (6)
el cumpleaños birthday (C)

el champú shampoo (14)
la chaqueta jacket (3)
el chico, la chica boy, girl (6)
Chile Chile (B)
el chile chili pepper (13)
    el — con carne chili con carne (1)
    el — relleno stuffed pepper (13)
el chiste joke (11)
chistoso, -a funny (11)
el chocolate chocolate, hot chocolate (8)
la chuleta de cerdo / cordero pork / lamb chop (13)
los churros churros (8)

las damas checkers (11)
dar to give (9)
    — de comer a to feed (6)
    — miedo a to frighten, to scare (9)
    — una película / un programa to show a movie / a program (9)

de (del) from (B, 5); of (C); *possessive* **—'s, —s'** (5); about (11)
    antes — before (9)
    — compras shopping (8)
    ¿— dónde? from where? (B)
    — nada you're welcome (B)
    — origen . . . of . . . origin (2)
    — postre for dessert (13)
    — prisa in a hurry, quickly, fast (14)
    — propina for a tip (13)
    ¿— qué color? what color? (3)
    ¿— quién? whose? (5)
    — vacaciones on vacation (3)
    — veras really (15)
debajo de under (8)
deber should, ought to (9)
débil weak (14)
decir to say, to tell (10)
    ¿cómo se dice . . . ? how do you say . . . ? (B)
    — que sí / no to say yes / no (10)
    ¡no me digas! you don't say! (5)
    ¿qué quiere — . . . ? what does . . . mean? (B)
la decoración, *pl.* **decoraciones** decoration (13)
decorar to decorate (13)
el dedo finger (16)
dejar to leave (behind) (12)
delante de in front of (5)
delgado, -a thin (2)
delicioso, -a delicious (13)
demasiado too (2); too much (12)
dentífrica: la pasta — toothpaste (14)
el/la dentista dentist (14)
dentro de inside (of) (9)
el deporte sport (1)
derecha: a la — (de) to the right (of) (5)
el desayuno breakfast (8)

el granjero, la granjera farmer (10)

la gripe flu (16)

gris, *pl.* **grises** gray (3)

el grupo group (11)

el guante glove (3)

guapo, -a handsome, good-looking (2)

el guardián, la guardiana (de zoológico) (zoo)keeper (10)

Guatemala Guatemala (B)

la guía guidebook (12)

   la — telefónica phone book (5)

el/la guía guide (15)

los guisantes peas (8)

la guitarra guitar (E)

gustar to like (16)

   me / te gusta(n) I / you *fam.* like (E, 1)

gusto:

   con mucho — gladly, with pleasure (15)

   mucho — pleased to meet you (A)

hablar to speak, to talk (E)

   — por teléfono to talk on the phone (E)

hace:

   — + *time* **+ que** for + *time* (15)

   See also **calor, fresco, frío, sol, tiempo, viento**

hacer to do (E); to make (8)

   — cola to stand in line (11)

   —la maleta to pack a suitcase (12)

   — un viaje to take a trip (15)

   (tú) haces you do (3)

   (yo) hago I do (3)

hambre: tener — to be hungry (9)

la hamburguesa hamburger (1)

hasta until (9)

   — la vista see you later (11)

   — luego see you later (A)

   — mañana see you tomorrow (A)

   — pronto see you soon (11)

hay there is, there are (C)

   — que + *inf.* we (you, one) must, it's necessary (14)

   no — de qué you're welcome (12)

el helado ice cream (1)

el hermanito, la hermanita little brother, little sister (6)

el hermano, la hermana brother, sister (6)

los hermanos brothers; brother(s) and sister(s) (6)

hermoso, -a beautiful (10)

hiciste: ¿qué —? what did you *fam.* do? (12)

la hierba grass (10)

el hijo, la hija son, daughter (6)

los hijos sons; son(s) and daughter(s) (6)

el hipopótamo hippopotamus (10)

la historia history (7)

hizo: ¿qué —? what did he / she / you *formal* do? (12)

la hoja leaf (10)

   la — de papel, *pl.* **—s de papel** piece of paper (B)

hola hello, hi (A)

el hombre man (2)

Honduras Honduras (B)

la hora hour (D)

   ¿a qué —? (at) what time? (D)

   la media — half an hour (9)

   ¿qué — es? what time is it? (D)

el horario schedule (7)

el hospital hospital (4)

el hotel hotel (4)

hoy today (C)

   — no not today (9)

el huevo egg (8)

la iglesia church (4)

la iguana iguana (10)

¡imagínate! imagine! (9)

el impermeable raincoat (3)

importante important (6)

importar to matter to, to be important to, to mind (16)

   ¿qué importa? so what? (9)

incómodo, -a uncomfortable (6)

Inglaterra England (15)

inglés (*pl.* **ingleses), inglesa** English (15)

el inglés English (*language*) (7)

inteligente intelligent (5)

interesante interesting (5)

el invierno winter (3)

la invitación, *pl.* **invitaciones** invitation (11)

el invitado, la invitada guest (11)

invitar to invite (11)

la inyección, *pl.* **inyecciones** shot (16)

   poner una — to give a shot (16)

ir to go (E)

   ir a + *inf.* going to + *verb* (4)

Italia Italy (15)

italiano, -a Italian (15)

el italiano Italian (*language*) (15)

izquierda: a la — de to the left of (5)

el jabón, *pl.* **jabones** soap (14)

el jamón ham (1)

el jardín, *pl.* **jardines** garden (6)

la jaula cage (10)

los jeans jeans (3)

la jirafa giraffe (10)

joven, *pl.* **jóvenes** young (2)

las joyas jewels, jewelry (12)

el juego game (11)

jueves Thursday (C)

    el — on Thursday (C)

el jugador, la jugadora player (14)

jugar (u → ue) to play (E, 11)

    — a(l) to play *(sports or games)* (E)

el jugo (de) juice (8)

julio July (C)

junio June (C)

juntos, -as together (4)

el kilo kilo (8)

la the *f. sing.* (C); you *f. formal,* her, it *dir. obj.* (8)

el laboratorio laboratory (7)

lado: al — de next to, beside (5)

el lago lake (10)

la lámpara lamp (15)

el lápiz, *pl.* **lápices** pencil (B)

largo, -a long (2)

las the *f. pl.* (C); you *f. pl.,* them *f. dir. obj.* (8)

lástima: ¡qué —! that's too bad, that's a shame (5)

latinoamericano, -a Latin American (2)

lavar to wash (1)

    —se (la cara, las manos, el pelo) to wash (one's face, hands, hair) (14)

le (to / for) you *formal,* him, her *ind. obj.* (9)

la lección, *pl.* **lecciones** lesson (7)

la leche milk (1)

    el café con — coffee with cream (8)

la lechuga lettuce (8)

leer to read (E)

lejos de far from (5)

la lengua language (15)

lento, -a slow (4)

el león, *pl.* **leones** lion (10)

el leopardo leopard (10)

les (to / for) you *pl.,* them *ind. obj.* (9)

levantar to lift, to raise (14)

    —se to get up (14)

libre free, not busy (11)

la librería bookstore (16)

el libro book (B)

el limón, *pl.* **limones** lemon (8)

la limonada lemonade (1)

limpiar to clean (6)

limpio, -a clean (6)

la línea line (5)

listo, -a smart, clever (7)

el litro liter (8)

lo you *m. formal,* him, it *dir. obj.* (8)

    — que what (14)

    — siento I'm sorry (16)

loco, -a crazy (5)

los the *m. pl.* (C); you, them *dir obj.* (8)

luego then, later (13)

    hasta — see you later (A)

la luna moon (10)

lunes Monday (C)

    el — on Monday (C)

la llama llama (10)

llamar to call (7)

    ¿cómo te llamas? what's your name? (A)

    — por teléfono to phone (11)

    —se to be called, to be named (14)

    me llamo my name is (A)

la llave key (15)

llegar to arrive (8)

lleno, -a full (13)

    — de gente crowded (13)

llevar to wear; to carry (3)

llover (o → ue) to rain (13)

    llueve it's raining (3)

la lluvia rain (10)

la madre mother (6)

magnífico, -a magnificent (10)

el maíz corn (8)

mal not well, badly (5)

la maleta suitcase (12)

    hacer la — to pack a suitcase (12)

malo (mal), -a bad (4)

la mamá mom (6)

mandar to send (15)

la mano hand (14)

la manta blanket (15)

el mantel tablecloth (8)

la mantequilla butter (1)

la manzana apple (8)

mañana tomorrow (C)

    hasta — see you tomorrow (A)

la mañana morning (D)

    de la — in the morning; A.M. (D)

    por la — in the morning (7)

el mapa map (1)

el mar sea (9)

marrón, *pl.* **marrones** brown (3)

martes Tuesday (C)

    el — on Tuesday (C)

marzo March (C)

más plus (C); more (1)

    el / la / los / las — + *adj.* the most + *adj.,* the + *adj.* + -est (12)

    — + *adj.* + que more + *adj.* + than, *adj.* + -er + than (12)

    — de + *number* more than (12)

    — o menos more or less (15)

    — tarde later (D)

    me / te gusta(n) — I / you prefer, like *(something)* more (1)

la máscara mask (13)

las matemáticas mathematics (7)

la materia (school) subject (7)

mayo May (C)

mayor older (6)

me me *dir. obj.,* (to / for) me *ind. obj.* (11); myself (14); *see also* **encantar, gustar, llamar**

media:

  la — hora half an hour (9)

  y — half-past (D); and a half (9)

la medianoche midnight (D)

el médico, la médica doctor (16)

el mediodía noon (D)

  al — at noon (8)

mejor better (12)

  el/la — the best (12)

memoria: aprender de — to memorize (7)

menor younger (6)

menos minus (C); + *number (in time telling)* (minutes) to (D)

  el/la/los/las — + *adj.* the least + *adj.* (12)

  más o — more or less (15)

  — + *adj.* + **que** less + *adj.* + than (12)

  — de + *number* less than (12)

el menú menu (13)

menudo: a — often (3)

el mercado market (8)

la mermelada jelly, preserves (8)

el mes month (C)

la mesa table (1)

  poner la — to set the table (8)

el metro subway (4)

mexicano, -a Mexican (E, 2)

México Mexico (B)

mi, mis my (C, 4)

mí me *after prep.* (7)

miedo:

  dar — a to frighten, to scare (9)

  tener — (de) to be afraid (of) (9)

miércoles Wednesday (C)

  el — on Wednesday (C)

mil one thousand (8)

el minuto minute (D)

mirar to look (at), to watch (E)

la mochila knapsack, backpack (10)

un momento just a moment (5)

la moneda coin (11)

el mono monkey (10)

la montaña mountain (12)

montar en bicicleta to ride a bicycle (E)

morado, -a purple (3)

moreno, -a dark, brunette (2)

mostrar (o → ue) to show (11)

la moto motorcycle (4)

el muchacho, la muchacha boy, girl (2)

mucho a lot, much (1)

mucho, -a, -os, -as much, many, a lot of (1); very (9)

  — gusto pleased to meet you (A)

los muebles furniture (15)

la mujer woman (2)

el mundo: todo el — everybody, everyone (9)

el museo museum (5)

la música music (1)

musical *adj.* musical (9)

muy very (A)

nada nothing, not anything (3)

  de — you're welcome (D)

nadar to swim (E)

nadie no one, nobody, not anyone (7)

los naipes cards (11)

la naranja orange (8)

la naranjada orangeade (13)

la nariz nose (16)

la Navidad Christmas (C)

necesario, -a necessary (15)

necesitar to need (8)

negro, -a black (3)

nevar (e → ie) to snow (13)

  nieva it's snowing (3)

Nicaragua Nicaragua (B)

la nieve snow (10)

ningún, ninguna *adj.* no, not any (13)

ninguno, -a *pron.* none, (not) any (13)

el niño, la niña little boy, little girl (6)

los niños little boys; boys and girls; children (6)

  cuidar a los — to baby-sit (6)

no no (A); not (E)

  ¡cómo —! of course (1)

  ¿—? don't you? aren't I? etc. (E)

la noche night (D)

  de la — at night, in the evening; P.M. (D)

  esta — tonight (4)

  por la — in the evening, at night (7)

el nombre name (B)

el norte north (15)

norteamericano, -a North American (2)

nos us *dir. obj.,* (to / for) us *ind. obj.* (11); ourselves (14)

nosotros, -as we (2); us *after prep.* (7)

la nota grade (7)

las noticias news (9)

novecientos, -as nine hundred (8)

la novela novel (16)

noventa ninety (D)

noviembre November (C)

el novio, la novia boyfriend, girlfriend (5)

la nube cloud (9)

nublado: está — it's cloudy (9)

nuestro, -a our (6)

nueve nine (C)

nuevo, -a new (2)

el número number (C)

  el — de teléfono phone number (D)

nunca never (4)

o or (1)
la obra de teatro play (5)
el océano ocean (15)
octubre October (C)
ocupado, -a busy (5)
ochenta eighty (D)
ocho eight (C)
ochocientos, -as eight hundred (8)
el oeste west (15)
  del — western (9)
la oficina office (5)
el oído (inner) ear (16)
oír to hear (10)
¡ojalá! I hope so! let's hope so! (7)
el ojo eye (16)
la ola wave (9)
olvidarse (de + *inf.)* to forget (to) (16)
once eleven (C)
optimista optimistic (12)
la oreja ear (16)
origen: de — of . . . origin (2)
el oso bear (10)
el otoño autumn, fall (3)
otro, -a other, another (11)
  otra vez again (11)
la oveja sheep (10)
¡oye! listen! hey! (11)

el padre father (6)
los padres parents, mother and father (6)
la paella paella (13)
pagar to pay (for) (11)
  — + *sum of money* + **por** to pay + *sum of money* + for (11)
la página page (7)
el país country (2)
el pájaro bird (2)
la palabra word (7)
el pan bread (1)
  el — tostado toast (8)
la panadería bakery (8)
Panamá Panama (B)
los pantalones pants (3)

las pantimedias pantyhose (3)
el pañuelo handkerchief (12)
el papá dad (6)
la papa potato (8)
  las —s fritas French fries (1)
el papel: la hoja de — piece of paper (B)
la papelera wastebasket (7)
para for (1)
  — + *inf.* to, in order to (8)
el paraguas umbrella (3)
el Paraguay Paraguay (B)
parecer to seem *(to someone)* (16)
  ¿qué te parece . . . ? how do you like . . . ? what do you think of . . . ? (16)
la pared wall (15)
el parque park (5)
el partido (de + *sport)* game, match (5)
pasa: ¿qué —? what's going on? what's happening? (5)
pasado, -a last; past (11)
el pasaporte passport (12)
pasar to spend *(time)* (11)
el pasatiempo pastime, hobby (11)
la pasta dentífrica toothpaste (14)
el pastel cake, pastry (13)
el patio courtyard (6)
el pato duck (10)
el pavo turkey (8)
pedir (e → i) to ask for, to order (13)
  — prestado, -a (a) to borrow (from) (16)
peinar to comb someone's hair (14)
  —se to comb one's hair (14)
el peine comb (14)
la película movie, film (9)
pelirrojo, -a red-haired (2)
el pelo hair (14)
la pelota ball (14)
pensar (e → ie) to think (12)

  — + *inf.* to plan, to intend (12)
  — de to think of, to have an opinion about (12)
  — en to think about (12)
peor worse (12)
  el/la — the worst (12)
pequeño, -a small, little (2)
perder (e → ie) to lose (14)
¡perdón! pardon me (5)
perezoso, -a lazy (14)
perfecto, -a perfect (13)
el periódico newspaper (1)
permiso: con — excuse me (15)
pero but (E)
el perro dog (2)
la persona person (10)
el Perú Peru (B)
el pescado fish *(cooked)* (13)
la peseta peseta (8)
pesimista pessimistic (12)
el peso peso (3)
el pez, *pl.* **peces** fish *(live)* (2)
el piano piano (11)
picante spicy, hot (13)
el pie foot (16)
  a — on foot (4)
la pierna leg (16)
el/la piloto pilot (12)
la piñata pinata (13)
los Pirineos Pyrenees Mts. (15)
la piscina swimming pool (4)
el piso floor, story (6)
  el primer (segundo, tercer) — second (third, fourth) floor (6)
la pizarra chalkboard (B)
el plan plan (11)
la planta baja ground floor (6)
el plátano banana (8)
el platillo saucer (8)
el plato dish (1); plate (8)
  quitar los — to clear the table (8)
la playa beach (9)
la plaza town square, plaza (4)
pobre poor (12)
¡pobrecito, -a! poor thing! (16)

un **poco** a little (5)
    un — de a little (8)
    pocos, -as a few, not many (1)
poder (o → ue) can, to be able to (11)
    (tú) puedes you can (6)
    (yo) puedo I can (6)
el **poema** poem (7)
el/la **poeta** poet (16)
el/la **policía** police officer (5)
    policíaco, -a adj. detective, mystery (9)
el **pollo** chicken (8)
poner to put, to place (8)
    — la mesa to set the table (8)
    —se to put on (clothes) (14)
    — una inyección to give a shot (16)
popular popular (1)
por through, across (15)
    — eso that's why (16)
    — favor please (B)
    — la mañana in the morning (7)
    — la noche in the evening, at night (7)
    — la tarde in the afternoon (7)
    ¿— qué? why? (1)
    ¡— supuesto! of course (5)
    — teléfono on the phone (E)
porque because (1)
Portugal Portugal (15)
portugués (pl. **portugueses**), **portuguesa** Portuguese (15)
el **portugués** Portuguese (language) (15)
el **postre** dessert (13)
    de — for dessert (13)
practicar to practice (1)
preferido, -a favorite (16)
preferir (e → ie) to prefer (12)
    (tú) prefieres you prefer (3)
    (yo) prefiero I prefer (3)
la **pregunta** question (3)
preguntar to ask (3)

preocupado, -a worried (5)
preparado, -a prepared, ready (7)
preparar to prepare (13)
presentar to introduce (11)
presente adj. present (7)
prestado, -a: pedir — (a) to borrow (from) (16)
prestar to lend (11)
la **primavera** spring (3)
    primero (primer), -a first (4)
    el — piso second floor (6)
el **primero** the first (C)
el **primo**, la **prima** cousin (6)
    prisa: de — in a hurry, quickly, fast (14)
privado, -a private (15)
el **problema** problem (11)
el **profesor**, la **profesora** teacher (A)
el **programa** program (9)
pronto soon (8)
    hasta — see you soon (11)
la **propina** tip (13)
    de — for a tip (13)
próximo, -a next (4)
la **prueba** test (7)
puedo, puedes see **poder**
el **puente** bridge (15)
la **puerta** door (B)
    Puerto Rico Puerto Rico (B)
puertorriqueño, -a Puerto Rican (2)
pues well (1)
la **pulsera** bracelet (12)
el **pupitre** student desk (1)

que that; who (10); than (12); see also **hay, tener**
    lo — what (14)
qué what (C)
    no hay de — you're welcome (12)
    ¿por —? why? (1)
    ¡— + adj.! how + adj.! (2)
    ¡— + noun! what a(n) + noun! (11)
    ¡— bueno! great! (9)

    ¿— desea Ud.? can I help you? (3)
    ¿— importa? so what? (9)
    ¡— lástima! that's too bad! that's a shame! (5)
    ¡— (mala) suerte! what (bad) luck! (5)
    ¿— tal? how's it going? (A)
quedarse to stay, to remain (15)
querer (e → ie) to want (12)
    ¿qué quiere decir . . . ? what does . . . mean? (B)
    (tú) quieres you want (4)
    (yo) quiero I want (4)
    quisiera I'd like (15)
el **queso** cheese (1)
¿quién, -es? who? (1, 3)
    ¿a —? whom? to whom? (7)
    ¿con —? with whom? (1)
    ¿de —? whose? (5)
    ¿para —? for whom? (7)
la **química** chemistry (7)
quince fifteen (C)
la **quinceañera** fifteen-year-old girl (6)
los **quince años** fifteenth birthday (party) (6)
quinientos, -as five hundred (8)
quisiera see **querer**
quitar:
    — los platos to clear the table (8)
    —se to take off (clothes) (14)

la **radio** radio (broadcast) (E)
el **radio** radio (set) (11)
rápidamente fast, rapidly (14)
rápido, -a fast (4)
razón:
    no tener — to be wrong (9)
    tener — to be right (9)
la **receta** prescription (16)
recibir to receive, to get (7)
el **recuerdo** souvenir (15)
el **refresco** soda, pop (1)

el refrigerador refrigerator (6)
el regalo present, gift (12)
regresar to return, to go back, to come back (14)
la reina queen (13)
el reloj clock (D)
relleno: el chile — stuffed pepper (13)
repasar to review (7)
repetir (e → i) to repeat (13)
la República Dominicana Dominican Republic (B)
la reservación, *pl.* **reservaciones** reservation (15)
el resfriado cold (16)
la respuesta answer (7)
el restaurante restaurant (5)
la revista magazine (11)
el rey king (13)
rico, -a rich (12)
el rinoceronte rhinoceros (10)
el río river (15)
el rock rock *(music)* (11)
rojo, -a red (3)
romántico, -a romantic (9)
romper to break (13)
la ropa clothing, clothes (3)
rubio, -a blond (2)
el ruido noise (10)

sábado Saturday (C)
el — on Saturday (C)
la sábana sheet (15)
saber to know (15)
— + *inf.* to know how to (15)
(no) lo sé I (don't) know that (15)
no sé I don't know (B)
sacar to take out, to remove (16)
— fotos to take pictures (11)
— una buena / mala nota to get a good / bad grade (7)
la sala living room (6)
la salida exit (12)

salir (de) to leave, to go out, to come out (8)
— bien / mal en to do well / badly on *(tests)* (7)
¡saludos! greetings! (15)
las sandalias sandals (9)
el sandwich sandwich (1)
el — de jamón / de queso ham / cheese sandwich (1)
el santo saint's day (C)
se yourself *formal,* himself, herself, itself, yourselves, themselves (14)
sé *see* **saber**
sed: tener — to be thirsty (9)
la seda dental dental floss (14)
seguida: en — right away, immediately (15)
según according to (7)
segundo: el — piso third floor (6)
el segundo second (D)
seguro, -a sure (15)
seis six (C)
seiscientos, -as six hundred (8)
el sello stamp (11)
la semana week (C)
el fin de — weekend (4)
el señor (Sr.) Mr.; sir (A)
la señora (Sra.) Mrs.; ma'am (A)
la señorita (Srta.) Miss; ma'am (A)
septiembre September (C)
ser to be (2)
serio, -a serious (12)
la serpiente snake (10)
la servilleta napkin (8)
servir (e → i) to serve (13)
sesenta sixty (D)
setecientos, -as seven hundred (8)
setenta seventy (D)
si if (9)
sí yes (A)
siempre always (4)
siento: lo — I'm sorry (16)
siete seven (C)

la silla chair (1)
el sillón, *pl.* **sillones** armchair (15)
simpático, -a nice, pleasant (5)
sin without (1)
sobre on (8); about (9)
el sobrino, la sobrina nephew, niece (6)
los sobrinos nephews; niece(s) and nephew(s) (6)
el sofá sofa (15)
el sol sun (10)
hace — it's sunny (3)
los anteojos de — sunglasses (9)
tomar el — to sunbathe (3)
solo, -a alone (4)
sólo only (C)
el sombrero hat (3)
la sombrilla beach umbrella (9)
son (they) are (C)
— las + *number* it's . . . o'clock (D)
la sopa soup (13)
soy I am (B)
su, sus his, her, your *formal,* their (6)
subir to go up, to come up (12)
— a to get on or in *(vehicles)* (12)
sucio, -a dirty (6)
sudamericano, -a South American (2)
sueño: tener — to be sleepy (9)
suerte:
¡qué (mala) —! what (bad) luck! (5)
tener (mala) — to be (un)lucky (9)
el suéter sweater (3)
el supermercado supermarket (8)
supuesto: por — of course (5)
el sur south (15)

tacaño, -a stingy (12)

el taco taco (1)

tal:
    ¿qué —? how's it going? (A)
    — vez maybe, perhaps (11)

también too, also (E)

tampoco neither, not either (6)

tan so, as (16)

tarde late (D)
    más — later (D)

la tarde afternoon (D)
    de la — in the afternoon or early evening; P.M. (D)
    por la — in the afternoon (7)

la tarea homework (1)

la tarjeta postal post card (15)

el taxi taxi (4)

la taza cup (8)

te you *fam. dir. obj.*, (to / for) you *fam. ind. obj.* (11); *see also* **gustar, llamar**

el té tea (8)

el teatro theater (5)
    la obra de — play (5)

telefónico, -a:
    la cabina —a phone booth (5)
    la guía —a phone book (5)

el teléfono telephone (D)
    el número de — phone number (D)
    hablar por — to talk on the phone (E)
    llamar por — to phone (11)

la televisión (tele) television (TV) (E)

el televisor TV set (9)

temprano early (D)

el tenedor fork (8)

tener to have (6)
    — fiebre / gripe to have a fever / the flu (16)
    — ganas de + *inf.* to feel like *(doing something)* (6)
    — que + *inf.* to have to (6)
    See also **año, calor, cuidado,**

frío, hambre, miedo, razón, sed, sueño, suerte

el tenis tennis (E)

tercer: el — piso fourth floor (6)

terminar to end, to finish (7)

terror: de — *adj.* horror (9)

ti you *fam. after prep.* (7)

la tía aunt (6)

el tiempo weather (3); time (12)
    a — on time (12)
    ¿cuánto —? how long? (12)
    hace buen / mal — it's nice / bad (out) (3)
    ¿qué — hace? what's the weather like? what's it like out? (3)

la tienda store (3)
    la — de (ropa, discos) (clothing, record) store (3)

la tierra earth, soil (10)

el tigre tiger (10)

el tío, la tía uncle, aunt (6)

los tíos uncles; aunt(s) and uncle(s) (6)

el título title (16)

la tiza chalk (1)

la toalla towel (9)

el tocadiscos, *pl.* **tocadiscos** record player (11)

tocar to play *(musical instruments / records)* (E, 11)

todavía still (5)

todo *pron.* everything (8)

todo, -a, -os, -as every; all; the whole (7)
    todo el mundo everybody, everyone (9)
    todos los días every day (7)

tomar to take (4); to drink (11)
    — algo to have something to drink (11)
    — el sol to sunbathe (3)

el tomate tomato (8)

tonto, -a dumb, foolish (5)

el torero, la torera bullfighter (13)

el toro bull (10)

la tortilla española Spanish omelet (13)

tostado: el pan — toast (8)

trabajar to work (E)

el trabajo job; work (10)

traer to bring (10)

el traje suit (3)
    el — de baño bathing suit (3)

tratar de + *inf.* to try (to) (14)

trece thirteen (C)

treinta thirty (C)
    — y uno (un); — y dos; etc. 31; 32; etc. (C)

el tren train (4)

tres three (C)

trescientos, -as three hundred (8)

triste unhappy, sad (5)

tu, tus your (B; 4)

tú you *fam.* (A)

el/la turista tourist (12)

u or (11)

¡uf! ugh! phew! (D)

un, una a, an, one (C)
    a la una at 1:00 (D)
    una vez once (14)

único, -a only (16)
    el hijo —, la hija — only child (6)

uno one (C)

unos, -as some, a few (4)

el Uruguay Uruguay (B)

usar to use (7)

usted (Ud.) you *formal sing.* (A)

ustedes (Uds.) you *pl.* (2)

la vaca cow (10)

las vacaciones vacation (12)
    de — on vacation (3)

vacío, -a empty (13)

vámonos let's leave, let's go (11)

vamos: — a + *inf.* let's + *verb* (4)

varios, -as several (10)

el **vaso** glass (8)

veces *see* **vez**

veinte twenty (C)

veintiuno (veintiún); veintidós; etc. 21; 22; etc. (C)

el **vendedor,** la **vendedora** salesperson (3)

vender to sell (8)

— **a** + *amount of money* to sell for . . . (8)

Venezuela Venezuela (B)

venir to come (6)

la **venta** sale (16)

en — for sale (16)

la **ventana** window (B)

la **ventanilla** little window (12)

ver to see (9)

el **verano** summer (3)

veras: de — really (15)

la **verdad** truth (10)

¿—? isn't that so? right? (1)

verde green (3)

la **verdura** vegetable (8)

el **vestido** dress (3)

vestido, -a de dressed as (13)

vestir (e → i) to dress *(someone)* (14)

—se to get dressed (14)

el **veterinario,** la **veterinaria** veterinarian (10)

la **vez,** *pl.* **veces** time (14)

a veces sometimes (3)

dos veces twice (14)

otra — again (11)

tal — maybe, perhaps (11)

una — once (14)

vi I saw (11)

viajar to travel (4)

el **viaje** trip (12)

la agencia de —s travel agency (12)

el/la agente de —s travel agent (12)

hacer un — to take a trip (15)

viejo, -a old (2)

el **viento: hace —** it's windy (3)

viernes Friday (C)

el — on Friday (C)

el **vino** wine (13)

vio he / she / you *formal* saw (11)

la **visita** visit (10)

visitar to visit (10)

vista:

con — a(l) with a view of (15)

hasta la — see you later (11)

viste you *fam.* saw (11)

vivir to live (7)

el **volibol** volleyball (14)

volver (o → ue) to return, to go back, to come back (11)

el **vuelo** flight (12)

el/la auxiliar de — flight attendant (11)

vuelta: a la — de la esquina around the corner (5)

y and (A)

— + *number (in time telling)* (minutes) past (D)

— media half-past (D); and a half (9)

ya already (8)

— no not anymore (9)

yo I (B)

el **yogur** yogurt (1)

la **zanahoria** carrot (8)

el **zapato** shoe (3)

el **zoológico** zoo (10)

el guardián, la **guardiana de —** zookeeper (10)

ENGLISH-SPANISH VOCABULARY

The *English-Spanish Vocabulary* contains all active vocabulary from the text.

A dash (—) represents the main entry word. For example, **— from** following **across** means **across from.**

The number following each entry indicates the chapter in which the word or expression is first introduced. Two numbers indicate that it is introduced in one chapter and elaborated upon in a later chapter. A letter following an entry refers to the *En camino* sections.

a, an un, una (C); algún, alguna (16)

able: to be — poder (o → ue) (11)

about sobre (9); de (11)

absent ausente (7)

accent mark el acento (7)

according to según (7)

to **ache** doler (o → ue) (16)

acquainted: to be — with conocer (15)

across por (15)

  — from enfrente de (5)

actor, actress el actor, la actriz, *f.pl.* actrices (9)

address la dirección, *pl.* direcciones (5)

adventure la aventura (16)

afraid: to be — (of) tener miedo (de) (9)

Africa el África (15)

after después de (+ *noun / inf.*) (7)

afternoon la tarde (D)

  good — buenas tardes (A)

  in the — de la tarde (D); por la tarde (7)

afterwards después (4)

again otra vez (11)

agency: travel — la agencia de viajes (12)

agent: travel — el / la agente de viajes (12)

to **agree** estar de acuerdo (16)

airplane el avión, *pl.* aviones (4)

airport el aeropuerto (4)

alarm clock el despertador (14)

algebra el álgebra (7)

all todo, -a (7)

alligator el caimán, *pl.* caimanes (10)

all right está bien (11)

almost casi (9)

alone solo, -a (4)

already ya (8)

also también (E)

always siempre (4)

A.M. de la mañana (D)

American americano, -a (E)

amusing divertido, -a (5)

and y (A); e (11)

animal el animal (10)

another otro, -a (11)

answer la respuesta (7)

to **answer** contestar (3)

any *adj.* algún, alguna (16); *pron.* alguno, -a, -os, -as (16)

  not — *adj.* (no . . .) ningún, ninguna (13); *pron.* (no . . .) ninguno, -a (13)

anymore: not — ya no (9)

anyone alguien (16)

  not — (no . . .) nadie (7)

anything algo (16)

  not — (no . . .) nada (3, 13)

apartment el apartamento (6)

apple la manzana (8)

  — juice el jugo de manzana (8)

April abril (C)

Argentina la Argentina (B)

arm el brazo (16)

armchair el sillón, *pl.* sillones (15)

around the corner a la vuelta de la esquina (5)

to **arrive** llegar (8)

art el arte (7)

as tan (16)

to **ask** preguntar (3)

  to — for pedir (e → i) (13)

asleep: to fall — dormirse (o → ue) (14)

at a(l) (D)

  — home en casa (1)

athlete el / la atleta (14)

athletic atlético, -a (14)

to **attend** asistir a (7)

attendant *see* **flight attendant**

August agosto (C)

aunt la tía (6)

  —(s) and uncle(s) los tíos (6)

author el escritor, la escritora (16)

autumn el otoño (3)
avenue la avenida (5)

to **baby-sit** cuidar a los niños (6)
back: to come / go — volver
(o → ue) (11); regresar (14)
backpack la mochila (10)
bad malo (mal), -a (4)
—ly mal (5)
it's — out hace mal tiempo (3)
that's too — ¡qué lástima! (5)
bakery la panadería (8)
balcony el balcón, *pl.* balcones
(15)
ball la pelota (14); el balón, *pl.*
balones (14)
banana el plátano (8)
bank el banco (4)
baseball el béisbol (E)
basketball el básquetbol (E)
bath: to take a — bañarse (14)
to **bathe (someone)** bañar (14)
bathing suit el traje de baño (3)
bathroom el baño (6)
to **be** ser (2); estar (5)
beach la playa (9)
— umbrella la sombrilla (9)
beans los frijoles (8)
bear el oso (10)
beautiful hermoso, -a (10);
bello, -a (12)
very — bellísimo, -a (12)
because porque (1)
bed la cama (15)
to go to — acostarse (o → ue)
(14)
to put (someone) to — acostar (o → ue) (14)
bedroom el dormitorio (6)
before antes de (+ *noun / inf.*)
(9)
to **begin** empezar (e → ie) (a +
inf.) (12)
behind detrás de (5)
to **believe** creer (10)
belt el cinturón, *pl.* cinturones
(12)
beside al lado de (5)

best: the — + *noun* + **in** el / la
mejor + *noun* + de(l) (12)
better mejor (12)
between entre (5)
beverage la bebida (13)
bicycle la bicicleta (E)
to ride a — montar en bicicleta (E)
big grande (2)
bilingual bilingüe (7)
biology la biología (7)
bird el pájaro (2)
birthday el cumpleaños (C)
fifteenth — los quince años
(6)
black negro, -a (3)
blanket la manta (15)
blond rubio, -a (2)
blouse la blusa (3)
blue azul (3)
boat el barco (4)
body el cuerpo (16)
Bolivia Bolivia (B)
book el libro (B)
bookstore la librería (16)
boot la bota (3)
booth: phone — la cabina telefónica (5)
bored aburrido, -a *(estar)* (5)
boring aburrido, -a *(ser)* (5)
to **borrow (from)** pedir prestado,
-a (a) (16)
bottle la botella (8)
box la caja (12)
boy el muchacho (2); el chico (6)
little — el niño (6)
boyfriend el novio (5)
bracelet la pulsera (12)
Brazil el Brasil (15)
bread el pan (1)
to **break** romper (13)
breakfast el desayuno (8)
bridge el puente (15)
to **bring** traer (10)
brother el hermano (6)
—(s) and sister(s) los hermanos (6)
little — el hermanito (6)
brown marrón, *pl.* marrones (3)
brunette moreno, -a (2)

to **brush (someone's hair)** cepillar
(el pelo) (14)
— (one's teeth / hair) cepillarse (los dientes / el pelo) (14)
building el edificio (15)
bull el toro (10)
bullfight la corrida (de toros)
(13)
bullfighter el torero, la torera
(13)
burrito el burrito (1)
bus el autobús, *pl.* autobuses (4)
busy ocupado, -a (5)
not — libre (11)
but pero (E)
butcher shop la carnicería (8)
butter la mantequilla (1)
to **buy** comprar (3)
by en + *vehicle* (4)

café el café (5)
cafeteria la cafetería (7)
cage la jaula (10)
cake el pastel (13)
calendar el calendario (C)
to **call** llamar (7)
to — on the phone llamar por
teléfono (11)
called: to be — llamarse (14)
camera la cámara (11)
can poder (o → ue) (11)
— I help you? ¿qué desea
Ud.? (3)
I / you — (yo) puedo / (tú)
puedes (6)
Canada el Canadá (2)
Canadian canadiense (2)
candy los dulces (13)
capital la capital (2)
car el coche (4)
cards los naipes (11)
careful:
be —! ¡cuidado! (9)
to be — tener cuidado (9)
Caribbean el Caribe (2)
carnival el carnaval (13)
carrot la zanahoria (8)
to **carry** llevar (3)

cartoons los dibujos animados (9)

cat el gato (2)

to celebrate celebrar (13)

celebration la celebración, *pl.* celebraciones (13)

cent(avo) el centavo (12)

Central America la América Central (2)

Central American centroamericano, -a (2)

chair la silla (1)

chalk la tiza (1)

chalkboard la pizarra (B)

to change cambiar (12)

channel el canal (9)

chapter el capítulo (7)

cheap barato, -a (3)

check *(in restaurant)* la cuenta (13)

checkers las damas (11)

cheese el queso (1)

chemistry la química (7)

chess el ajedrez (11)

chicken el pollo (8)

child el niño, la niña (6)

children *(boys and girls)* los niños (6); *(sons and daughters)* los hijos (6)

Chile Chile (B)

chili (pepper) el chile (13)

chili con carne el chile con carne (1)

chocolate el chocolate (8)

hot — el chocolate (8)

chop la chuleta (13)

lamb / pork — la chuleta de cordero / cerdo (13)

Christmas la Navidad (C)

church la iglesia (4)

churros los churros (8)

city la ciudad (4)

class la clase (de) (A)

classical clásico, -a (1)

classmate el compañero, la compañera de clase (2)

clean limpio, -a (6)

to clean limpiar (6)

to clear the table quitar los platos (8)

clever listo, -a (7)

clock el reloj (D)

alarm — el despertador (14)

to close cerrar (e → ie) (12)

close to cerca de (5)

closed cerrado, -a (12)

closet el armario (15)

clothes, clothing la ropa (3)

cloud la nube (9)

cloudy: it's — está nublado (9)

coat el abrigo (3); la chaqueta (3)

coffee el café (8)

— with cream el café con leche (8)

coin la moneda (11)

cold frío, -a (13)

it's — (out) hace frío (3)

to be — *(people)* tener frío (9)

cold el resfriado (16)

to collect coleccionar (11)

Colombia Colombia (B)

color el color (3)

in — en colores (9)

what —? ¿de qué color? (3)

comb el peine (14)

to comb someone's hair peinar (14)

to — one's hair peinarse (14)

to come venir (6)

to — back volver (o → ue) (11); regresar (14)

to — down bajar (12)

to — in entrar (en) (3)

to — out salir (de) (8)

to — up subir (12)

comedy *(film)* la película cómica (9)

comfortable cómodo, -a (6)

comic *adj.* cómico, -a (9)

commercial el anuncio comercial (9)

computer la computadora (7)

concert el concierto (11)

congratulations! ¡felicidades! (C); ¡felicitaciones! (6)

to continue continuar (9)

contrary: on the — al contrario (2)

to cook cocinar (E)

cool: it's — (out) hace fresco (3)

corn el maíz (8)

corner la esquina (5)

around the — a la vuelta de la esquina (5)

correct correcto, -a (7)

to cost costar (o → ue) (11)

how much does / do . . . —? ¿cuánto cuesta(n) . . .? (3)

Costa Rica Costa Rica (B)

costume el disfraz, *pl.* disfraces (13)

— party la fiesta de disfraces (13)

to count contar (o → ue) (11)

country el país (2)

country(side) el campo (4)

courtyard el patio (6)

cousin el primo, la prima (6)

cow la vaca (10)

crazy loco, -a (5)

cream: coffee with — el café con leche (8)

crowded lleno, -a de gente (13)

Cuba Cuba (B)

Cuban cubano, -a (2)

cup la taza (8)

custard el flan (13)

customer el / la cliente (12)

dad el papá (6)

dance el baile (11)

to dance bailar (E)

dark(-haired) moreno, -a (2)

date la fecha (C)

what's the — today? ¿cuál es la fecha de hoy? (C)

daughter la hija (6)

day el día (C)

every — todos los días (7)

December diciembre (C)

to decorate decorar (13)

decoration la decoración, *pl.* decoraciones (13)

delicious delicioso, -a (13)

dental floss la seda dental (14)

dentist el / la dentista (14)

deodorant el desodorante (14)

department store el almacén, *pl.* almacenes (5)

to describe describir (15)
desk el escritorio (1)
  student — el pupitre (1)
dessert el postre (13)
  for — de postre (13)
detective *adj.* policíaco, -a (9)
devil el diablo (13)
difficult difícil (7)
dining room el comedor (6)
dinner la cena (8)
dirty sucio, -a (6)
disguise el disfraz, *pl.* disfraces
  (13)
dish el plato (1)
to do hacer (E)
  to — well / badly on *(tests)*
    salir bien / mal en (7)
doctor el médico, la médica (16);
  el doctor (Dr.), la doctora
  (Dra.) *(as title)* (16)
dog el perro (2)
dollar el dólar (12)
Dominican Republic la República Dominicana (B)
door la puerta (B)
down: to come / go — bajar (12)
downtown el centro (4)
dozen la docena (de) (8)
to draw dibujar (7)
drawing el dibujo (B)
dress el vestido (3)
to dress (someone) vestir (e → i)
  (14)
  to get —ed vestirse (e → i)
    (14)
dressed as vestido, -a de (13)
dresser la cómoda (15)
drink la bebida (13)
to drink beber (8); tomar (11)
  to have something to —
    tomar algo (11)
drugstore la farmacia (4)
duck el pato (10)
dumb tonto, -a (5)
during durante (4)

each cada (13)
ear la oreja (16)
  (inner) — el oído (16)

early temprano (D)
earring el arete (12)
earth la tierra (10)
east el este (15)
easy fácil (7)
to eat comer (E)
Ecuador el Ecuador (B)
egg el huevo (8)
eight ocho (C)
eighteen dieciocho (C)
eight hundred ochocientos, -as
  (8)
eighty ochenta (D)
either: not — (no . . .) tampoco
  (6, 16)
elephant el elefante (10)
elevator el ascensor (15)
eleven once (C)
El Salvador El Salvador (B)
empty vacío, -a (13)
to end terminar (7)
energetic enérgico, -a (14)
England Inglaterra (15)
English inglés (*pl.* ingleses),
  inglesa (15)
English *(language)* el inglés (7)
to enjoy disfrutar de (15)
enormous enorme (2)
to enter entrar (en) (3)
entertaining divertido, -a (5)
entrance la entrada (12)
to erase borrar (7)
eraser el borrador (7)
Europe Europa (15)
evening: good — buenas tardes /
  buenas noches (4)
every todo, -a (7); cada (13)
  — day todos los días (7)
everybody / everyone todo el
  mundo (9)
everything todo (8)
exam el examen, *pl.* exámenes
  (1)
to examine examinar (16)
excellent excelente (16)
to exchange cambiar (12)
exciting emocionante (13)
excuse la excusa (16)
excuse me con permiso (15);
  discúlpeme (15)

exit la salida (12)
to expect esperar (14)
expensive caro, -a (3)
  very — carísimo, -a (12)
eye el ojo (16)
eyeglasses los anteojos (9)

fabulous fabuloso, -a (11)
face la cara (14)
fairly bastante (2)
fall el otoño (3)
to fall asleep dormirse (o → ue)
  (14)
family la familia (6)
fan (of) el aficionado, la aficionada (a) (14)
fantastic estupendo, -a (9); fantástico, -a (15)
far from lejos de (5)
farm la granja (10)
farmer el granjero, la granjera
  (10)
fast *adj.* rápido, -a (4); *adv.* rápidamente (14); *adv.* de prisa
  (14)
fat gordo, -a (2)
father el padre (6)
favorite favorito, -a (7); preferido, -a (16)
February febrero (C)
to feed dar de comer a(l) (6)
to feel like *(doing something)* tener
  ganas de + *inf.* (6)
  to have a — tener fiebre (16)
fever la fiebre (16)
few: a — pocos, -as (1); unos,
  -as (4)
fifteen quince (C)
fifteenth birthday los quince
  años (6)
fifteen-year-old girl la quinceañera (6)
fifty cincuenta (D)
film la película (9)
to find encontrar (o → ue) (11)
fine ¡bueno! (4)
finger el dedo (16)
to finish terminar (7)

fireworks los fuegos artificiales (13)

first el primero *in dates* (C); primero (primer), -a (4)

  — **floor** la planta baja (6)

fish (*live*) el pez, *pl.* peces (2); (*cooked*) el pescado (13)

five cinco (C)

  — **hundred** quinientos, -as (8)

to **fix** arreglar (9)

flag la bandera (1)

flan el flan (13)

flight el vuelo (12)

  — **attendant** el / la auxiliar de vuelo (12)

floor el piso (6)

  ground — la planta baja (6)

  second (third / fourth) — el primer (segundo / tercer) piso (6)

flower la flor (10)

flu la gripe (16)

  to have the — tener gripe (16)

folk *adj.* folklórico, -a (13)

food la comida (E)

foolish tonto, -a (5)

foot el pie (16)

  on — a pie (4)

football el fútbol americano (E)

for para (1)

  — **sale** en venta (16)

to **forget (to)** olvidarse (de + *inf.*) (14)

fork el tenedor (8)

forty cuarenta (D)

fountain la fuente (5)

four cuatro (C)

  — **hundred** cuatrocientos, -as (8)

fourteen catorce (C)

fourth floor el tercer piso (6)

France Francia (15)

free libre (11)

French francés (*pl.* franceses), francesa (15)

French (*language*) el francés (7)

French fries las papas fritas (1)

Friday viernes (C)

  on — el viernes (C)

fried frito, -a (13)

friend el amigo, la amiga (2)

to **frighten** dar miedo a (9)

from de(l) (B); desde (9)

  — **what country?** ¿de qué país? (2)

  — **where?** ¿de dónde? (B)

front: in — **of** delante de (5)

fruit la fruta (8)

full lleno, -a (13)

fun: to have — divertirse (e → ie) (14)

funny chistoso, -a (11)

furniture los muebles (15)

game el partido (de + *sport*) (5); el juego (11)

garage el garaje (6)

garden el jardín, *pl.* jardines (6)

gave di / diste / dio (11)

gazpacho el gazpacho (13)

gee! ¡caramba! (9)

generally generalmente (10)

generous generoso, -a (12)

geometry la geometría (7)

German alemán (*pl.* alemanes), alemana (15)

German (*language*) el alemán (15)

Germany Alemania (15)

to **get** recibir (7)

  to — **a good / bad grade** sacar una buena / mala nota (7)

  to — **dressed** vestirse (e → i) (14)

  to — **off / out of** (*vehicles*) bajar de (12)

  to — **on / in** (*vehicles*) subir a (12)

  to — **up** levantarse (14)

ghost el fantasma (13)

gift el regalo (12)

giraffe la jirafa (10)

girl la muchacha (2); la chica (6)

  little — la niña (6)

girlfriend la novia (5)

to **give** dar (9)

  to — **someone a shot** poner una inyección (16)

gladly con mucho gusto (15)

glass el vaso (8)

glasses los anteojos (9)

  dark —**es** los anteojos de sol (9)

glove el guante (3)

to **go** ir (E)

  —**ing to** + *verb* ir a + *inf.* (4)

  how's it —**ing?** ¿qué tal? (A)

  to — **back** volver (o → ue) (11); regresar (14)

  to — **down** bajar (12)

  to — **in(to)** entrar (en) (3)

  to — **out** salir (de) (8)

  to — **to bed** acostarse (o → ue) (14)

  to — **to sleep** dormirse (o → ue) (14)

  to — **up** subir (12)

  what's —**ing on?** ¿qué pasa? (5)

golf el golf (14)

good bien (A); bueno (buen), -a (4)

  — **afternoon** buenas tardes (A)

  — **evening** buenas tardes / buenas noches (A)

  — **morning** buenos días (A)

  — **night** buenas noches (A)

  to be — **in** estar fuerte en (7)

  to have a — **time** divertirse (e → ie) (14)

good-by adiós (A)

good-looking bonito, -a (2); guapo, -a (2)

gosh! ¡caramba! (9)

grade la nota (7)

  to get a good / bad — sacar una buena / mala nota (7)

gram el gramo (8)

grandfather el abuelo (6)

grandmother la abuela (6)

grandparents los abuelos (6)

grass la hierba (10)

gray gris, *pl.* grises (3)

great gran (4); fantástico (9)

  —**!** ¡qué bueno! (9)

green verde (3)

greetings! ¡saludos! (15)

groceries los comestibles (8)
ground floor la planta baja (6)
group el grupo (11)
Guatemala Guatemala (B)
guest el invitado, la invitada (11)
guide el / la guía (15)
guidebook la guía (12)
guitar la guitarra (E)
Gulf of Mexico el Golfo de México (2)
gym(nasium) el gimnasio (7)

hair el pelo (14)
  to brush one's — cepillarse (el pelo) (14)
  to brush someone's — cepillar (el pelo) (14)
  to comb one's — peinarse (14)
  to comb someone's — peinar (14)
half:
  and a — y media (9)
  — an hour la media hora (9)
  — -past y media (D)
ham el jamón (1)
hamburger la hamburguesa (1)
hand la mano (14)
handkerchief el pañuelo (12)
handsome guapo, -a (2)
happening: what's —? ¿qué pasa? (5)
happy contento, -a (5)
hard difícil (7)
hat el sombrero (3)
to have tener (6)
  to — a good time / fun divertirse (e → ie) (14)
  to — a fever / the flu tener fiebre / gripe (16)
  to — just *(done something)* acabar de + *inf.* (9)
  to — something to drink tomar algo (11)
  to — to tener que + *inf.* (6)
he él (B)
head la cabeza (16)

to hear oír (10)
heart el corazón (16)
hello ¡hola! (A); ¿aló? *(on phone)* (5)
to help ayudar (a + *inf.*) (1, 6)
  may I — you? ¿qué desea Ud.? (3)
hen la gallina (10)
her su, sus *poss. adj.* (6); ella *after prep.* (7); la *dir. obj.* (8)
  to / for — le (9)
here aquí (3)
  — is / — are aquí tienes / tiene Ud. (11)
  — it is / — they are aquí lo (la, los, las) tiene(s) (11)
herself se (14)
hey! ¡oye! (11)
hi ¡hola! (A)
high school el colegio (7)
him él *after prep.* (7); lo *dir. obj.* (8)
  to / for — le (9)
himself se (14)
hippopotamus el hipopótamo (10)
his su, sus (6)
history la historia (7)
hobby el pasatiempo (11)
holiday la fiesta (C); el día de fiesta, *pl.* días de fiesta (C)
home la casa (1)
  at — en casa (1)
  (to one's) — a casa (4)
homework la tarea (1)
Honduras Honduras (B)
to hope esperar (14)
  I — not espero que no (14)
  I — so ¡ojalá! (7); espero que sí (14)
  let's — so ¡ojalá! (7)
horror *adj.* de terror (9)
horse el caballo (10)
hospital el hospital (4)
hot caliente (13); *(spicy)* picante (13)
  it's — (out) hace calor (3)
  to be — *(people)* tener calor (9)
hotel el hotel (4)
hour la hora (D)

half an — la media hora (9)
house la casa (4)
how? ¿cómo? (A, B)
  — + *adj.*! ¡qué + *adj.*! (2)
  — are you? ¿cómo estás / está Ud.? (A)
  — do you like . . .? ¿qué te parece . . .? (16)
  — long? ¿cuánto tiempo? (12)
  — long does (something) last? ¿cuánto dura? (9)
  — many? ¿cuántos, -as? (C)
  — much? ¿cuánto? (3)
  — old are you? ¿cuántos años tienes? (6)
  —'s it going? ¿qué tal? (A)
  to know — (to) saber + *inf.* (15)
  to learn — (to) aprender a + *inf.* (7)
huge enorme (2)
hundred cien (D); *see also* **two, three,** etc.
  101; 102; etc. ciento uno, -a; ciento dos; etc. (8)
hungry: to be — tener hambre (9)
hurry: in a — de prisa (14)
to hurt doler (o → ue) (16)
husband el esposo (6)

I yo (B)
ice cream el helado (1)
if si (9)
iguana la iguana (10)
imagine! ¡imagínate! (9)
immediately en seguida (15)
important importante (6)
  to be — to importar (16)
in en (C)
  — order to para + *inf.* (8)
inexpensive barato, -a (3)
inside adentro (16)
  — (of) dentro de (9)
intelligent inteligente (5)
to intend to pensar (e → ie) + *inf.* (12)
interesting interesante (5)

into en (3)
to introduce presentar (11)
invitation la invitación, *pl.* invitaciones (11)
to invite invitar (11)
it lo, la *dir. obj.* (8)
Italian italiano, -a (15)
Italian (*language*) el italiano (15)
Italy Italia (15)
itself se (14)

jacket la chaqueta (3)
January enero (C)
jeans los jeans (3)
jelly la mermelada (8)
jewels, jewelry las joyas (12)
job el trabajo (10)
joke el chiste (11)
juice el jugo (de) (8)
July julio (C)
June junio (C)
just: to have — (*done something*) acabar de + *inf.* (9)

key la llave (15)
kilo el kilo (8)
kind *adj.* amable (12)
kind la clase (de) (9)
kind of *adv.* bastante (2)
king el rey (13)
kitchen la cocina (6)
knapsack la mochila (10)
knife el cuchillo (8)
to know saber (15); conocer (15)
  I don't — no sé (B)
  I (don't) — that (no) lo sé (15)
  to — how (to) saber + *inf.* (15)

laboratory el laboratorio (7)
lake el lago (10)
lamb el cordero (10)
  — chop la chuleta de cordero (13)

lamp la lámpara (15)
to land aterrizar (12)
language la lengua (15)
large grande (2)
last pasado, -a (11)
  — name el apellido (6)
  — night anoche (8)
to last durar (9)
late tarde (D)
later más tarde (D); después (4); luego (13)
  see you — hasta luego (A); hasta la vista (11)
Latin America la América Latina (2)
Latin American latinoamericano, -a (2)
lazy perezoso, -a (14)
leaf la hoja (10)
to learn aprender (7)
  to — how (to) aprender a + *inf.* (7)
least: the — + *adj.* el / la / los / las menos + *adj.* (12)
to leave salir (de) (8)
  to — (behind) dejar (12)
left: to the — of a la izquierda de (5)
leg la pierna (16)
lemon el limón, *pl.* limones (8)
lemonade la limonada (1)
to lend prestar (11)
leopard el leopardo (10)
less:
  — + *adj.* + **than** menos + *adj.* + que (12)
  — than + *number* menos de + *number* (12)
  more or — más o menos (15)
lesson la lección, *pl.* lecciones (7)
let's vamos a + *inf.* (4)
  — leave! ¡vámonos! (11)
letter la carta (7)
lettuce la lechuga (8)
library la biblioteca (4)
to lift levantar (14)
like:
  to feel — (*doing something*) tener ganas de + *inf.* (6)

what's (*someone / something*) **—?** ¿cómo es . . .? (2)
what's the weather —? ¿qué tiempo hace? (3)
to like gustar (16)
  how do you — . . .? ¿qué te parece . . .? (16)
  I / you — me / te gusta(n) (E, 1)
  I'd — quisiera (15)
line la línea (5)
  to stand in — hacer cola (11)
lion el león, *pl.* leones (10)
to listen (to) escuchar (E)
  —! ¡oye! (11)
liter el litro (8)
little pequeño, -a (2)
  a — un poco (5); un poco de (8)
to live vivir (7)
living room la sala (6)
llama la llama (10)
long largo, -a (2)
  how —? ¿cuánto tiempo? (12)
to look (at) mirar (E)
  to — for buscar (3)
to lose perder (e → ie) (14)
lot:
  a — mucho (1)
  a — of muchos, -as (1)
to love encantar (16)
  I — me encanta(n) (E, 1)
lucky: to be — tener suerte (9)
lunch el almuerzo (8)

ma'am señora / señorita (A)
magazine la revista (11)
magnificent magnífico, -a (10)
to make hacer (8)
man el hombre (2)
manager el / la gerente (15)
many muchos, -as (1)
  how —? ¿cuántos, -as? (1)
  not — pocos, -as (1)
map el mapa (1)
March marzo (C)
Mardi Gras el carnaval (13)
market el mercado (8)

mask la máscara (13)
match el partido (de + *sport*) (5)
mathematics las matemáticas (7)
to matter to importar (16)
May mayo (C)
may I help you? ¿qué desea
   Ud.? (3)
maybe tal vez (11)
me mi *after prep.* (7); me (11)
   to / for — me (11)
   with — conmigo (7)
meal la comida (8)
mean: what does . . . —? ¿qué
   quiere decir . . .? (B)
meat la carne (8)
   — pie la empanada (3)
meet: pleased to — you mucho
   gusto (A)
to memorize aprender de memoria
   (7)
menu el menú (13)
Mexican mexicano, -a (2)
Mexico México (B)
midnight la medianoche (D)
milk la leche (1)
to mind importar (16)
mineral water el agua mineral (8)
minus menos (C)
minute el minuto (D)
mirror el espejo (15)
Miss (la) señorita (Srta.) (A)
missing: to be — something
   faltar (16)
mom la mamá (6)
Monday lunes (C)
   on — el lunes (C)
money el dinero (11)
monkey el mono (10)
month el mes (C)
moon la luna (10)
more más (1)
   — or less más o menos (15)
   — + *adj.* + than más + *adj.*
    + que (12)
   — than + *number* más de +
    number (12)
morning la mañana (D)
   good — buenos días (A)
   in the — de la mañana (D);
    por la mañana (7)

yesterday — ayer por la mañana (8)
most: the — + *adj.* el / la / los /
   las más + *adj.* (12)
mother la madre (6)
— and father los padres (6)
motorcycle la moto (4)
mountain la montaña (12)
mouth la boca (16)
movie la película (9)
   —s el cine (E)
   — theater el cine (E)
Mr. (el) señor (Sr.) (A)
Mrs. (la) señora (Sra.) (A)
much mucho (1)
   how —? ¿cuánto? (3)
   too — demasiado (12)
muffler la bufanda (3)
museum el museo (5)
music la música (1)
musical *adj.* musical (9)
must: we / you / one — hay
   que + *inf.* (14)
my mi, mis (C, 4)
myself me (14)

name el nombre (B)
   last — el apellido (6)
   my — is me llamo (A)
   what's your —? ¿cómo te
    llamas? (A)
named: to be — llamarse (14)
napkin la servilleta (8)
near cerca de (5)
necessary necesario, -a (15)
   it's — (to) hay que + *inf.* (14);
    es necesario (15)
necklace el collar (12)
to need necesitar (8); faltar (16)
neighborhood el barrio (8)
neither (no . . .) tampoco (6, 16)
nephew el sobrino (6)
never (no . . .) nunca (4, 13)
new nuevo, -a (2)
New Year's Day el Año Nuevo
   (C)
New Year's Eve el día de fin de
   año (C)

news las noticias (9)
newspaper el periódico (1)
next próximo, -a (4)
   — to al lado de (5)
Nicaragua Nicaragua (B)
nice simpático, -a (5); amable
   (12)
   it's — out hace buen tiempo
    (3)
   not — antipático, -a (5)
niece la sobrina (6)
   —(s) and nephew(s) los
    sobrinos (6)
night la noche (D)
   at — de la noche (D); por la
    noche (7)
   good — buenas noches (A)
   last — anoche (8)
nine nueve (C)
   — hundred novecientos, -as
    (8)
nineteen diecinueve (C)
ninety noventa (D)
no no (A); *adj.* (no . . .) ningún,
   ninguna (13)
   — one (no . . .) nadie (7, 13)
nobody (no . . .) nadie (7, 13)
noise el ruido (10)
none (no . . .) ninguno, -a (13)
noon el mediodía (D)
   at — al mediodía (8)
north el norte (15)
North America la América del
   Norte (2)
North American norteamericano, -a (2)
nose la nariz (16)
not no (E)
   — any *adj.* (no . . .) ningún,
    ninguna (13); *pron.* (no . . .)
    ninguno, -a (13)
   — anyone (no . . .) nadie (7)
   — many pocos, -as (1)
   — well mal (5)
notebook el cuaderno (B)
nothing (no . . .) nada (3, 13)
novel la novela (16)
November noviembre (C)
now ahora (D)
number el número (C)

nurse el enfermero, la enfermera (16)

ocean el océano (15)
o'clock:
    it's 1 — es la una (D)
    it's 2 —, 3 —, etc. son las dos, tres, etc. (D)
October octubre (C)
of de(l) (D)
of course ¡cómo no! (1); ¡por supuesto! (5); ¡claro (que sí)! (10)
    — not ¡claro que no! (10)
off:
    to get — *(vehicles)* bajar de (12)
    to take — *(planes)* despegar (12); *(clothes)* quitarse (14)
office la oficina (5)
often a menudo (3)
oh! ¡ah! (1)
    —, yes ¡ah, sí! (1)
okay ¡bueno! (11); está bien (11)
old viejo, -a (2)
    how — are you? ¿cuántos años tienes? (6)
older mayor (6)
omelet: Spanish — la tortilla española (13)
on en (5); sobre (8)
    — foot a pie (4)
    — the phone por teléfono (E)
    — time a tiempo (12)
    — vacation de vacaciones (3)
once una vez (14)
one uno (C); *pron.* alguno, -a (16)
    at — o'clock a la una (D)
    — hundred cien (D)
    — thousand mil (8)
    which —(s)? ¿cuál(es)? (3)
onion la cebolla (8)
only sólo *adv.* (C); único, -a *adj.* (6)
open abierto, -a (12)
to open abrir (12)
    opinion: to have an — about pensar (e → ie) de (12)

opposite enfrente de (5)
optimistic optimista (12)
or o (1); u (11)
orange *adj.* anaranjado, -a (3)
orange la naranja (8)
    — juice el jugo de naranja (8)
orangeade la naranjada (13)
order: in — to para + *inf.* (8)
to order pedir (e → i) (13)
origin: of . . . — de origen . . . (2)
other otro, -a (11)
ought to deber + *inf.* (9)
our nuestro, -a (6)
out:
    it's cool (cold / hot) — hace fresco (frío / calor) (3)
    it's nice (bad) — hace buen (mal) tiempo (3)
    to come / go — salir (de) (8)
    to get — of *(vehicles)* bajar de (12)
outside afuera (16)
    — (of) fuera de (9)
overcoat el abrigo (3)
over there allá (5)

to pack a suitcase hacer la maleta (12)
paella la paella (13)
page la página (7)
Panama Panamá (B)
pants los pantalones (3)
pantyhose las pantimedias (3)
paper: piece of — la hoja de papel, *pl.* hojas de papel (B)
parade el desfile (13)
Paraguay el Paraguay (B)
pardon me perdón (5); discúlpeme (15)
parents los padres (6)
park el parque (5)
party la fiesta (D)
passport el pasaporte (12)
past pasado, -a (11)
pastime el pasatiempo (11)
pastry el pastel (13)
to pay (for) pagar (11)

to — + *sum of money* + **for** pagar + *sum of money* + por (11)
peas los guisantes (8)
pen el bolígrafo (B)
pencil el lápiz, *pl.* lápices (B)
people la gente (13)
pepper:
    chili — el chile (13)
    stuffed — el chile relleno (13)
perfect perfecto, -a (13)
perhaps tal vez (11)
person la persona (10)
Peru el Perú (B)
peseta la peseta (8)
peso el peso (3)
pessimistic pesimista (12)
pet el animal doméstico (10)
pharmacy la farmacia (4)
phew! ¡uf! (D)
phone el teléfono (D)
    on the — por teléfono (E)
    — book la guía telefónica (5)
    — booth la cabina telefónica (5)
    — number el número de teléfono (D)
to phone llamar por teléfono (11)
photo la foto (11)
photographer el fotógrafo, la fotógrafa (11)
physical education la educación física (7)
physics la física (7)
piano el piano (11)
picture: to take —s sacar fotos (11)
piece of paper la hoja de papel, *pl.* hojas de papel (B)
pig el cerdo (10)
pillow la almohada (15)
pillowcase la funda (15)
pilot el / la piloto (12)
piñata la piñata (13)
to place poner (8)
plan el plan (11)
to plan to pensar (e → ie) + *inf.* (12)
plane el avión, *pl.* aviones (4)
plate el plato (8)

play la obra de teatro (5)
to play jugar (u → ue) (E, 11); tocar (*musical instruments, records*) (E, 11)
  to — (*sports, games*) jugar a(l) (E)
player el jugador, la jugadora (14)
plaza la plaza (4)
pleasant simpático, -a (5); agradable (10)
please por favor (B)
pleased to meet you mucho gusto (A)
pleasure: with — con mucho gusto (15)
plus más (C)
P.M. de la tarde / de la noche (D)
poem el poema (7)
poet el / la poeta (16)
police officer el / la policía (5)
poor pobre (12)
  — thing! ¡pobrecito, -a! (16)
  to be — in estar flojo, -a en (7)
pop el refresco (1)
popular popular (1)
pork chop la chuleta de cerdo (13)
Portugal Portugal (15)
Portuguese portugués (*pl.* portugueses), portuguesa (15)
Portuguese (*language*) el portugués (15)
post card la tarjeta postal (15)
post office el correo (4)
poster el cartel (1)
potato la papa (8)
to practice practicar (1)
to prefer preferir (e →ie) (12)
  I / you — (yo) prefiero / (tú) prefieres (3)
to prepare preparar (13)
prepared preparado, -a (7)
prescription la receta (16)
present *adj.* presente (7)
present el regalo (12)
preserves la mermelada (8)
pretty bonito, -a (2)

private privado, -a (15)
problem el problema (11)
program el programa (9)
Puerto Rican puertorriqueño, -a (2)
Puerto Rico Puerto Rico (B)
pupil el alumno, la alumna (2)
purple morado, -a (3)
purse el bolso (12)
to put poner (8)
  to — on (*clothes*) ponerse (14)
  to — (someone) to bed acostar (o → ue) (14)
Pyrenees Mts. los Pirineos (15)

quarter:
  — after / past y cuarto (D)
  — to menos cuarto (D)
queen la reina (13)
question la pregunta (3)
quickly de prisa (14)

radio (*broadcast*) la radio (E); (*set*) el radio (11)
rain la lluvia (10)
to rain llover (o → ue) (13)
  it's —ing llueve (3)
raincoat el impermeable (3)
to raise levantar (14)
rapidly rápidamente (14)
rather bastante (2)
to read leer (E)
ready preparado, -a (7)
really de veras (15)
to receive recibir (7)
record el disco (E)
  — player el tocadiscos, *pl.* tocadiscos (11)
red rojo, -a (3)
  —-haired pelirrojo, -a (2)
refrigerator el refrigerador (6)
to remain quedarse (15)
to remove sacar (16)
to repair arreglar (9)
to repeat repetir (e → i) (13)
reservation la reservación, *pl.* reservaciones (15)

to rest descansar (16)
restaurant el restaurante (5)
to return volver (o → ue) (11); regresar (14)
to review repasar (7)
rhinoceros el rinoceronte (10)
rice el arroz (13)
rich rico, -a (12)
to ride a bicycle montar en bicicleta (E)
right:
  all — está bien (11)
  —? ¿verdad? (1)
  — away en seguida (15)
  to be — tener razón (9)
  to the — (of) a la derecha (de) (5)
ring el anillo (12)
river el río (15)
road el camino (10)
rock (*music*) el rock (11)
romantic romántico, -a (9)
room el cuarto (15)
rooster el gallo (10)
rug la alfombra (15)
to run correr (14)

sad triste (5)
saint's day el santo (C)
salad la ensalada (1)
sale la venta (16)
  for — en venta (16)
salesperson el vendedor, la vendedora (3)
sandals las sandalias (9)
sandwich el sandwich (1)
  ham (cheese) — el sandwich de jamón (queso) (1)
Saturday sábado (C)
  on — el sábado (C)
saucer el platillo (8)
to say decir (10)
  how do you — . . .? ¿cómo se dice . . . ? (B)
  to — yes / no decir que sí / no (10)
  you don't — ¡no me digas! (5)
to scare dar miedo a (9)

scared: to be — (of) tener miedo (de) (9)

scarf la bufanda (3)

schedule el horario (7)

school la escuela (E)

    high — el colegio (7)

science las ciencias (7)

    — fiction *adj.* de ciencia ficción (9)

sea el mar (9)

season la estación, *pl.* estaciones (3)

seat el asiento (12)

second el segundo (D)

    — floor el primer piso (6)

to see ver (9)

    — you later hasta luego (A); hasta la vista (11)

    — you soon hasta pronto (11)

    — you tomorrow hasta mañana (A)

to seem *(to someone)* parecer (16)

to sell vender (8)

    to — for + *sum of money* vender a + *sum of money* (8)

to send mandar (15)

sentence la frase (7)

September septiembre (C)

serious serio, -a (12)

to serve servir (e → i) (13)

to set the table poner la mesa (8)

seven siete (C)

    — hundred setecientos, -as (8)

seventeen diecisiete (C)

seventy setenta (D)

several varios, -as (10)

shame: that's a — ¡qué lástima! (5)

shampoo el champú (14)

she ella (B)

sheep la oveja (10)

sheet la sábana (15)

shelf el estante (16)

shirt la camisa (3)

shoe el zapato (3)

shopping de compras (8)

short bajo, -a (2); corto, -a (2)

shot la inyección, *pl.* inyecciones (16)

to give someone a — poner una inyección (16)

should deber + *inf.* (9)

to show mostrar (o → ue) (11)

    to — a movie / a program dar una película / un programa (9)

shower la ducha (14)

    to take a — ducharse (14)

sick enfermo, -a (5)

to sing cantar (E)

sir señor (A)

sister la hermana (6)

    little — la hermanita (6)

six seis (C)

    — hundred seiscientos, -as (8)

sixteen dieciséis (C)

sixty sesenta (D)

to ski esquiar (E)

skirt la falda (3)

sky el cielo (10)

to sleep dormir (o → ue) (11)

    to go to — dormirse (o → ue) (14)

sleepy: to be — tener sueño (0)

slow lento, -a (4)

    —ly despacio (14)

small pequeño, -a (2)

smart listo, -a (7)

snake la serpiente (10)

snow la nieve (10)

to snow nevar (e → ie) (13)

    it's —ing nieva (3)

so entonces (1); tan (16)

    I don't think — creo que no (10)

    I hope — ¡ojalá! (7); espero que sí (14)

    I think — creo que sí (10)

    let's hope — ¡ojalá! (7)

    — what? ¿qué importa? (9)

soap el jabón, *pl.* jabones (14)

soccer el fútbol (E)

sock el calcetín, *pl.* calcetines (3)

soda el refresco (1)

sofa el sofá (15)

soil la tierra (10)

some unos, -as (4); algún, alguna (16); *pron.* alguno, -a, -os, -as (16)

somebody / someone alguien (16)

something algo (16)

    to have — to drink tomar algo (11)

sometimes a veces (3)

son el hijo (6)

    —(s) and daughter(s) los hijos (6)

song la canción, *pl.* canciones (11)

soon pronto (8)

    see you — hasta pronto (11)

sorry: I'm — lo siento (16)

so-so así, así (A)

soup la sopa (13)

south el sur (15)

South America la América del Sur (2)

South American sudamericano, -a (2)

souvenir el recuerdo (15)

Spain España (B)

Spanish español, -a (B)

Spanish *(language)* el español (E)

to speak hablar (E)

special especial (6)

spell: how do you spell . . .? ¿cómo se escribe . . .? (B)

to spend *(time)* pasar (11)

spicy picante (13)

spoon la cuchara (8)

sport el deporte (1)

spring la primavera (3)

stadium el estadio (5)

stairs la escalera (15)

stamp el sello (11)

to stand in line hacer cola (11)

star la estrella (10)

to star empezar (e → ie) (a + *inf.*) (12)

station la estación, *pl.* estaciones (4)

to stay quedarse (15)

steak el bistec (13)

still todavía (5)

stingy tacaño, -a (12)

stomach el estómago (16)

store la tienda (de) (3)

    department — el almacén, *pl.* almacenes (5)

story el piso (6); el cuento (11)
stove la estufa (6)
street la calle (5)
   — corner la esquina (5)
strong fuerte (14)
student el / la estudiante (A)
to study estudiar (1)
   stuffed pepper el chile relleno (13)
stupid tonto, -a (5)
subject (*in school*) la materia (7)
subway el metro (4)
sugar el azúcar (8)
suit el traje (3)
   bathing — el traje de baño (3)
suitcase la maleta (12)
   to pack a — hacer la maleta (12)
summer el verano (3)
sun el sol (10)
to sunbathe tomar el sol (3)
Sunday domingo (C)
   on — el domingo (C)
sunglasses los anteojos de sol (9)
sunny: it's — hace sol (3)
supermarket el supermercado (8)
supper la cena (8)
sure seguro, -a (15)
sweater el suéter (3)
to swim nadar (E)
   swimming pool la piscina (4)

table la mesa (1)
   to clear the — quitar los platos (8)
   to set the — poner la mesa (8)
tablecloth el mantel (8)
taco el taco (1)
to take tomar (4)
   to — a bath bañarse (14)
   to — a shower ducharse (14)
   to — a trip hacer un viaje (15)
   to — off (*planes*) despegar (12); (*clothes*) quitarse (14)
   to — out sacar (16)
   to — pictures sacar fotos (11)

to talk hablar (E)
tall alto, -a (2)
tape la cinta (E)
   — recorder la grabadora (11)
taxi el taxi (4)
tea el té (8)
to teach enseñar (7)
teacher el profesor, la profesora (A)
team el equipo (14)
teeth los dientes (14)
   to brush one's — cepillarse los dientes (14)
telephone *see* **phone**
television la televisión (tele) (E)
   — channel el canal (9)
   — set el televisor (9)
to tell decir (10); contar (o → ue) (11)
ten diez (C)
tennis el tenis (E)
terrific formidable (16)
test el examen, *pl.* exámenes (1); la prueba (7)
than que (12)
thanks, thank you gracias (A)
   — a lot muchas gracias (B)
that ese, -a (10); que (10)
   —'s why por eso (16)
the el, la, los, las (C)
theater el teatro (5)
   movie — el cine (E)
their su, sus (6)
them ellos, ellas *after prep.* (7); los, las *dir. obj.* (8)
   to / for — les (9)
themselves se (14)
then entonces (1); luego (13)
there allí (5)
   over — allá (5)
   — is / — are hay (C)
these estos, -as (10)
they ellos, ellas (2)
thin delgado, -a (2)
thing la cosa (8)
to think creer (10); pensar (e → ie) (12)
   I don't — so creo que no (10)
   I — so creo que sí (10)
   to — about pensar en (12)

   to — of pensar de (12)
   what do you — of . . .? ¿qué te parece . . .? (16)
third floor el segundo piso (6)
thirsty: to be — tener sed (9)
thirteen trece (C)
thirty treinta (C)
   31; 32; etc. treinta y uno (un); treinta y dos; etc. (C)
this este, -a (10)
those esos, -as (10)
thousand mil (8)
three tres (C)
   — hundred trescientos, -as (8)
thrilling emocionante (13)
throat la garganta (16)
through por (15)
Thursday jueves (C)
   on — el jueves (C)
ticket la entrada (*entrance*) (11); el boleto (*travel*) (12)
tie la corbata (12)
tiger el tigre (10)
time el tiempo (12); la vez, *pl.* veces (14)
   (at) what time? ¿a qué hora? (D)
   on — a tiempo (12)
   to have a good — divertirse (e → ie) (14)
   what — is it? ¿qué hora es? (D)
tip la propina (13)
   for a — de propina (13)
tired cansado, -a (5)
title el título (16)
to a(l) (E)
   (in order) — para + *inf.* (8)
   minutes — (*in time-telling*) menos + *number* (D)
   — where? ¿adónde? (4)
toast el pan tostado (8)
today hoy (C)
   not — hoy no (9)
together juntos, -as (4)
tomato el tomate (8)
tomorrow mañana (C)
   see you — hasta mañana (A)
tonight esta noche (4)

too también (E); demasiado (2)
— **much** demasiado (12)
toothbrush el cepillo de dientes (14)
toothpaste la pasta dentífrica (14)
tourist el / la turista (12)
towel la toalla (9)
town square la plaza (4)
train el tren (4)
to **travel** viajar (4)
travel agency la agencia de viajes (12)
travel agent el / la agente de viajes (12)
tree el árbol (10)
trip el viaje (12)
to take a — hacer un viaje (15)
truck el camión, *pl.* camiones (4)
truth la verdad (10)
to **try (to)** tratar (de + *inf.*) (14)
t-shirt la camiseta (3)
Tuesday martes (C)
on — el martes (C)
turkey el pavo (8)
TV la tele (E)
twelve doce (C)
twenty veinte (C)
21; 22; etc. veintiuno (veintiún); veintidós; etc. (C)
twice dos veces (14)
two dos (C)
— **hundred** doscientos, -as (8)
type la clase (de) (9)

ugh! ¡uf! (D)
ugly feo, -a (2)
umbrella el paraguas (3)
beach — la sombrilla (9)
uncle el tío (6)
uncomfortable incómodo, -a (6)
under debajo de (8)
to **understand** comprender (7)
I don't — no comprendo (B)
United States los Estados Unidos (2)

unlucky: to be — tener mala suerte (9)
unpleasant antipático, -a (5)
until hasta (9)
up:
to come / go — subir (12)
to get — levantarse (14)
Uruguay el Uruguay (B)
us nosotros, -as *after prep.* (7); nos (11)
to / for — nos (11)
to **use** usar (7)
usually generalmente (10)

vacation las vacaciones (12)
on — de vacaciones (3)
vegetable la verdura (8)
Venezuela Venezuela (B)
very muy (A); mucho, -a (9)
veterinarian el veterinario, la veterinaria (10)
view: with a — **of** con vista a(l) (15)
visit la visita (10)
to **visit** visitar (10)
volleyball el volibol (14)

to **wait (for)** esperar (4)
waiter, waitress el camarero, la camarera (13)
to **wake up** despertarse (e → ie) (14)
to — **(someone)** despertar (e → ie) (14)
to **walk** ir a pie (4); caminar (10)
wall la pared (15)
wallet la cartera (12)
to **want** querer (e → ie) (12)
I / you — (yo) quiero / (tú) quieres (4)
to **wash** lavar (1)
to — **(one's face, hands, hair)** lavarse (la cara, las manos, el pelo) (14)
wastebasket la papelera (7)
to **watch** mirar (E)
— **out!** ¡cuidado! (9)

water el agua *f.* (8)
wave la ola (9)
we nosotros, -as (2)
weak débil (14)
to **wear** llevar (3)
weather el tiempo (3)
what's the — **like?** ¿qué tiempo hace? (3)
Wednesday miércoles (C)
on — el miércoles (C)
week la semana (C)
weekend el fin de semana, *pl.* fines de semana (4)
welcome bienvenido, -a (12)
you're — de nada (B); no hay de qué (12)
well bien (A); pues (1); bueno (9)
not — mal (5)
— **known** muy conocido, -a (9)
went fui / fuiste / fue (8)
west el oeste (15)
western *adj.* del oeste (9)
what lo que (14)
so —¿ ¿qué importa? (9)
—**?** ¿qué? (C); ¿cuál? (D)
—**a(n)** + *noun!* ¡que + *noun!* (2)
—**'s (someone / something) like?** ¿cómo es . . .? (2)
—**'s your name?** ¿cómo te llamas? (A)
when ¿cuándo? (C); cuando (C)
where? ¿dónde? (5)
from —**?** ¿de dónde? (B)
(to) —**?** ¿adónde? (4)
which, which one(s)? ¿cuál(es)? (3)
white blanco, -a (3)
who que (10)
—**?** ¿quién(es)? (1, 3)
whole: the — todo, -a (7)
whom? ¿a quién(es)? (7)
for —**?** ¿para quién(es)? (7)
to —**?** ¿a quién(es)? (7)
with —**?** ¿con quién(es)? (1)
whose? ¿de quién(es)? (5)
why? ¿por qué? (1)
that's — por eso (16)

wife la esposa (6)
to win ganar (14)
window la ventana (B); la ventanilla (12)
windy: it's — hace viento (3)
wine el vino (13)
winter el invierno (3)
with con (1)
   — me conmigo (7)
   — you *fam.* contigo (7)
without sin (1)
woman la mujer (2)
word la palabra (7)
work el trabajo (10)
to work trabajar (E)
worried preocupado, -a (5)
worse peor (12)
worst: the — + *noun* + **in** el / la peor + *noun* + de(l) (12)
to write escribir (7)

writer el escritor, la escritora (16)
wrong: to be — no tener razón (9)

year el año (C)
   to be . . . —s old tener . . . años (6)
yellow amarillo, -a (3)
yes sí (A)
yesterday ayer (8)
   — morning ayer por la mañana (8)
yogurt el yogur (1)
you *fam.* tú (A); *formal* usted (Ud.) (A); *pl.* ustedes (Uds.) (2); ti, ustedes *after prep.* (7); lo, la *sing. formal dir. obj.* (8); los, las *pl. dir.*

obj. (8); te *fam. dir. obj.* (11).
   to / for — le *sing. formal* (9); les *pl.* (9); te *fam.* (11)
   with — *fam.* contigo (7)
young joven, *pl.* jóvenes (2)
younger menor (6)
your tu, tus *fam.* (B, 4); su, sus *formal & pl.* (6)
you're welcome *see* **welcome**
yourself te *fam.* (14); se *formal* (14)
yourselves se (14)

zebra la cebra (10)
zero cero (C)
zoo el zoológico (10)
zookeeper el guardián, la guardiana (de zoológico) (10)

INDEX

Most structures are first presented in conversational contexts and explained later. Bold-face numbers refer to pages where structures are explained or highlighted. Light-face numbers refer to pages where they are initially presented or, after explanation, where they are elaborated upon.

reflexive verbs 456–58, *470–73*, 508

saber 489, *501*
salir 274, *287–88*
ser *97, 188*
   vs. **estar** *196*
   singular forms 11
spelling-changing verbs *see* verbs
stem-changing verbs *see* verbs
stress 57
subject pronouns *see* pronouns
superlative 405, 409, *414–15*

tener 207, *221*

expressions with 207, 216, *221, 312–14*
   with **que** + infinitive 207, *221, 379*
   in telling age 216
time telling *33–34,* 188
traer 336, *347*
tú vs. **usted** *2*

venir 207, *223*
ver 305, *317*
   preterite 371, *540*
verbs
   irregular *see individual listings*
   reflexive 456–58, *470–73,* 508

regular **-ar** *126–27*
regular **-er** / **-ir** *252–53*
spelling-changing *418,* 436, *507–8*
stem-changing:
   e → **i** 427, *440*
   e → **ie** 114, 147, 396, *410,* 507
   o → **ue** 207, 363–64, 371–72, *374,* 507
   u → **ue** *377*
   see also infinitive, preterite
vowels *see* pronunciation

weather expressions *120–22*

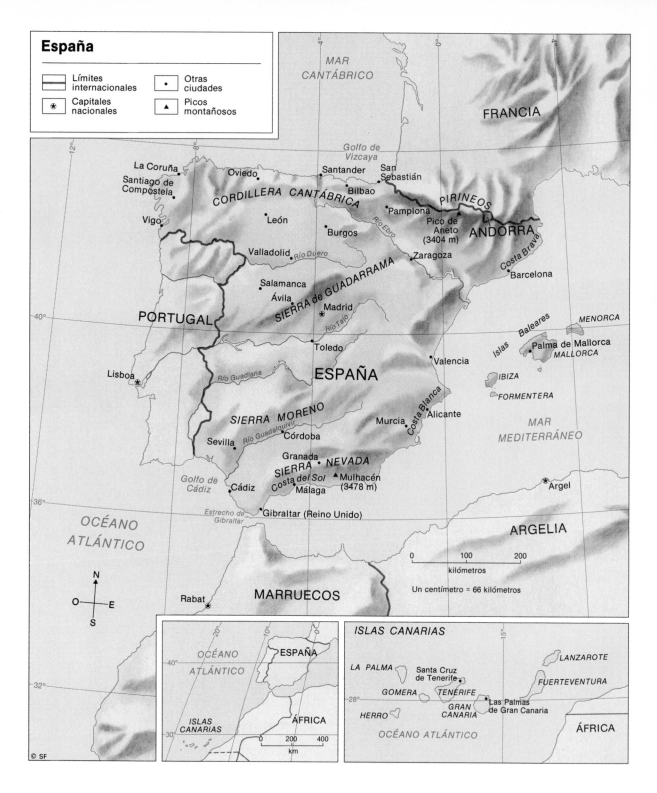

España

España

- Límites internacionales
- Capitales nacionales
- Otras ciudades
- Picos montañosos

MAR CANTÁBRICO

FRANCIA

Golfo de Vizcaya

La Coruña
Santiago de Compostela
Vigo

Oviedo
Santander
San Sebastián
Bilbao
Pamplona

CORDILLERA CANTÁBRICA

PIRINEOS

Pico de Aneto (3404 m)

ANDORRA

León
Burgos
Río Ebro
Zaragoza

Costa Brava

Barcelona

Valladolid
Río Duero

Salamanca
Ávila

SIERRA de GUADARRAMA

Madrid
Río Tajo

PORTUGAL

ESPAÑA

Toledo

Valencia

Islas Baleares

MENORCA

Palma de Mallorca
MALLORCA

IBIZA

FORMENTERA

Lisboa

Río Guadiana

SIERRA MORENO

Río Guadalquivir

Sevilla
Córdoba

Granada
SIERRA NEVADA
Costa del Sol
Cádiz
Málaga
Mulhacén (3478 m)

Golfo de Cádiz

Gibraltar (Reino Unido)

Estrecho de Gibraltar

Murcia
Alicante

Costa Blanca

MAR MEDITERRÁNEO

Argel

ARGELIA

OCÉANO ATLÁNTICO

N
O   E
S

Rabat

MARRUECOS

0   100   200
kilómetros

Un centímetro = 66 kilómetros

OCÉANO ATLÁNTICO

ESPAÑA

ÁFRICA

ISLAS CANARIAS

0   200   400
km

ISLAS CANARIAS

LA PALMA
GOMERA
HERRO

Santa Cruz de Tenerife
TENERIFE

GRAN CANARIA

Las Palmas de Gran Canaria

LANZAROTE

FUERTEVENTURA

OCÉANO ATLÁNTICO

ÁFRICA

© SF

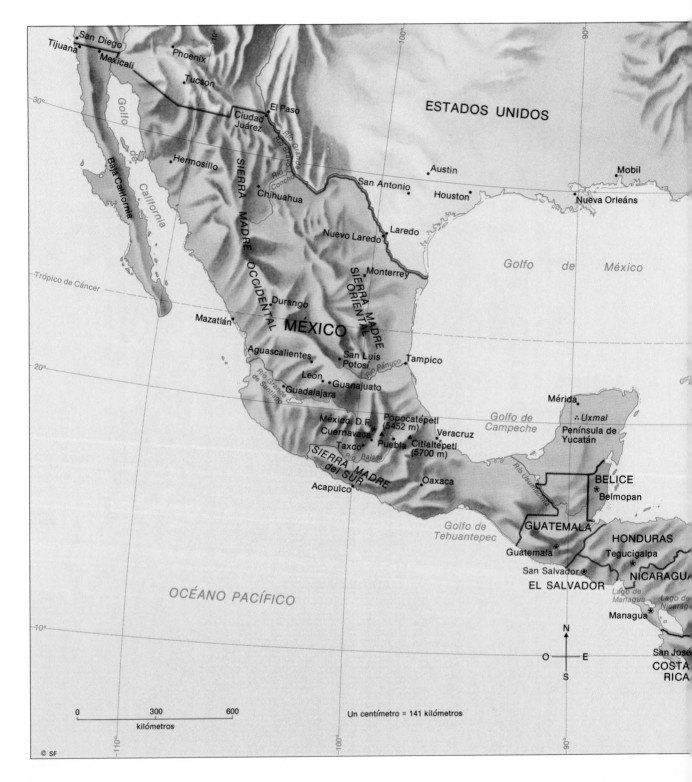

San Diego
Tijuana
Mexicali
Phoenix
Tucson
Hermosillo
El Paso
Ciudad
Juárez
ESTADOS UNIDOS
Austin
Mobil
San Antonio
Houston
Nueva Orleáns
Chihuahua
SIERRA MADRE OCCIDENTAL
Nuevo Laredo
Laredo
Golfo de México
Baja California
Golfo de California
Trópico de Cáncer
Monterrey
SIERRA MADRE ORIENTAL
Durango
Mazatlán
MÉXICO
Aguascalientes
San Luis
Potosí
Tampico
León
Guanajuato
Guadalajara
Río Pánuco
Río Grande de Santiago
Mérida
Uxmal
Golfo de
Campeche
México, D.F.
Popocatépetl
(5452 m)
Veracruz
Península de
Yucatán
Cuernavaca
Puebla
Citlaltépetl
(5700 m)
Taxco
Río Balsas
SIERRA MADRE del SUR
Oaxaca
Río Usumacinta
BELICE
Belmopan
Acapulco
GUATEMALA
HONDURAS
Golfo de
Tehuantepec
Guatemala
Tegucigalpa
San Salvador
NICARAGUA
EL SALVADOR
OCÉANO PACÍFICO
Lago de
Managua
Lago de
Nicaragua
Managua
N
O   E
S
San José
COSTA
RICA
0   300   600
kilómetros
Un centímetro = 141 kilómetros
© SF

586   Mapas

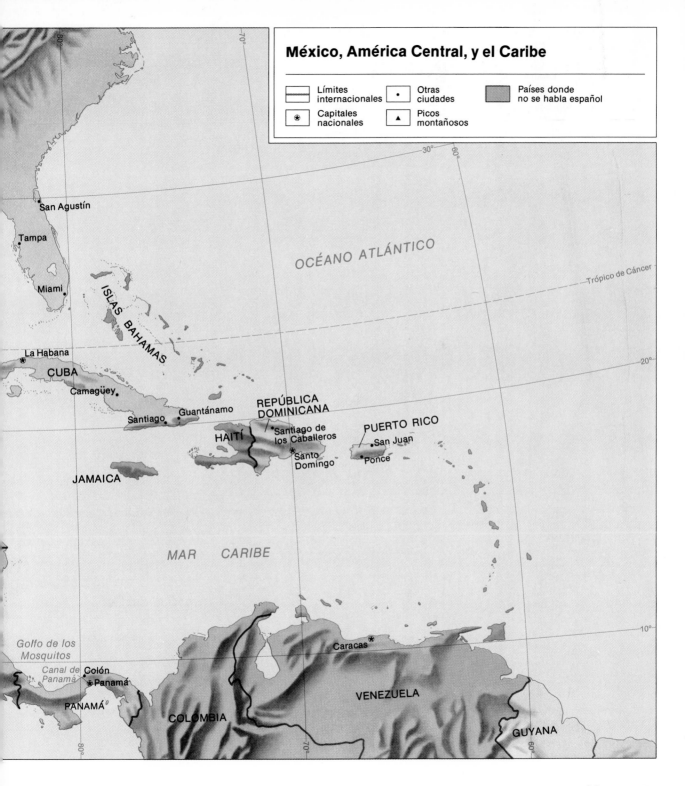

México, América Central, y el Caribe

Límites internacionales	●	Otras ciudades		Países donde no se habla español
⊛ Capitales nacionales	▲	Picos montañosos		

OCÉANO ATLÁNTICO

San Agustín

Tampa

Miami

ISLAS BAHAMAS

Trópico de Cáncer

La Habana

CUBA

Camagüey

Santiago Guantánamo

REPÚBLICA DOMINICANA

HAITÍ

Santiago de los Caballeros

PUERTO RICO

San Juan

Santo Domingo

Ponce

JAMAICA

MAR CARIBE

Golfo de los Mosquitos

Caracas

Canal de Panamá

Colón

Panamá

PANAMÁ

COLOMBIA

VENEZUELA

GUYANA

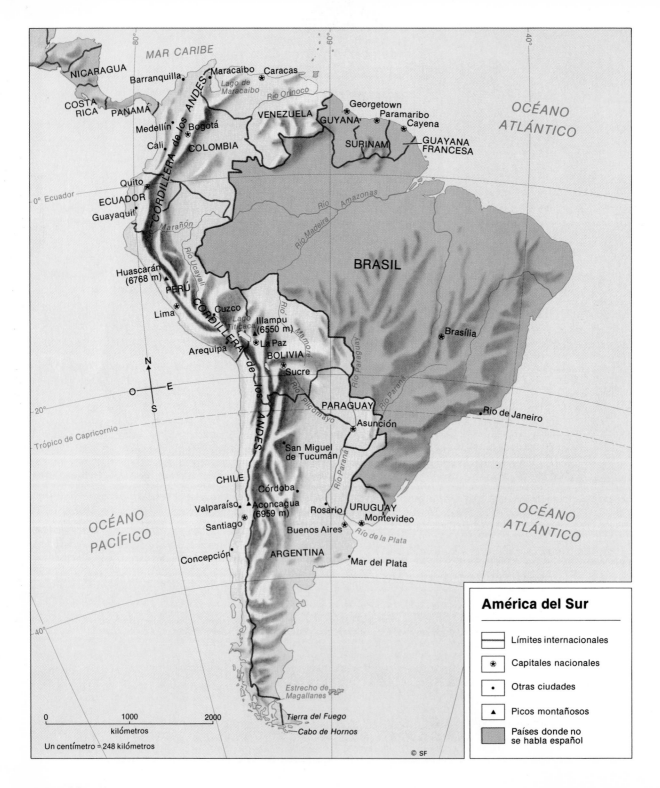

América del Sur

Límites internacionales

Capitales nacionales

Otras ciudades

Picos montañosos

Países donde no
se habla español

MAR CARIBE

NICARAGUA

COSTA
RICA   PANAMÁ

Barranquilla   Maracaibo   Caracas

Lago de
Maracaibo

Río Orinoco

VENEZUELA   Georgetown
                 GUYANA   Paramaribo
Medellín   Bogotá   Cayena
Cali   GUAYANA
       COLOMBIA   SURINAM   FRANCESA

Quito

ECUADOR

Guayaquil

Río   Amazonas

Río Marañón

CORDILLERA de los ANDES

Río Ucayali

Río Madeira

BRASIL

Huascarán
(6768 m)

PERÚ

Lima   Cuzco

Lago
Titicaca   Illampu
            (6550 m)

Arequipa   La Paz

BOLIVIA

Sucre

CORDILLERA de los ANDES

Río Mamoré

Río Paraguay

Brasília

PARAGUAY

Río Pilcomayo

Asunción

Río de Janeiro

San Miguel
de Tucumán

Río Paraná

CHILE

Córdoba

Valparaíso   Aconcagua
              (6959 m)   Rosario   URUGUAY

Santiago   Montevideo

            Buenos Aires

Concepción   Mar del Plata

            ARGENTINA

OCÉANO
PACÍFICO

OCÉANO
ATLÁNTICO

OCÉANO
ATLÁNTICO

Trópico de Capricornio

Río de la Plata

N
O   E
S

Estrecho de
Magallanes

Tierra del Fuego

Cabo de Hornos

0   1000   2000

kilómetros

Un centímetro = 248 kilómetros

© SF

0° Ecuador

20°

40°

80°   60°   40°

ACKNOWLEDGMENTS

Illustrations

Palabras Nuevas and *Práctica* illustrations by Steven Schindler and Don Wilson. All other illustrations by Steve Boswick, Aldo Castillo, Linda Kelen, Bob Masheris, Rob Porazinski, Steven Schindler, Ed Tabor, John Walter & Associates, Don Wilson, and John Youssi.

Photos

Positions of photographs are shown in abbreviated form as follows: top (t), bottom (b), center (c), left (l), right (r), insert (INS). Unless otherwise acknowledged, all photos are the property of Scott, Foresman and Company. **Cover,** Robert Frerck/Odyssey Productions, Chicago; ii–iii, Robert Frerck/Odyssey Productions, Chicago; iv–v, Ian Lea; vi–vii, Stuart Cohen; viii, Bob Glaze/ Artstreet; ix, Peter Menzel; x & xi(t), Gary Braasch; xi(b), Stuart Cohen; xii(t), Norman Perman, Inc.; xii(b), Peter Menzel; xiii, Arte Gallery, Chicago, Illinois; xiv, Robert Frerck/Odyssey Productions, Chicago; xvi, Eugenia Fawcett; xvii, Loren McIntyre; 1, Robert Frerck/Odyssey Productions, Chicago; 4, David R. Frazier Photolibrary; 5 & 9, Robert Frerck/Odyssey Productions, Chicago; 17, David R. Frazier Photolibrary; 22, Norman Prince; 24(t), Robert Frerck/Odyssey Productions, Chicago; 24(bl & br), Joseph F. Viesti; 25(l), Charmayne McGee; 25(r), Robert Frerck/Odyssey Productions, Chicago; 34 & 37, David Phillips; 40(t), Stuart Cohen; 40(b) & 44, Robert Frerck/Odyssey Productions, Chicago; 45, Stuart Cohen; 47, Joseph F. Viesti; 48–49, Peter Menzel; 55 & 56, Robert Frerck/Odyssey Productions, Chicago; 57, Norman Prince; 63, Beryl Goldberg; 63(INS) & 66, Stuart Cohen; 68, Robert Frerck/Odyssey Productions, Chicago; 76(l), Joseph F. Viesti; 76(r), Robert Frerck/Odyssey Productions, Chicago; 79, Eugenia Fawcett; 80–81, Victor Englebert/Scott, Foresman; 85(l), Joseph F. Viesti; 85(c), Lee Foster; 85(r), Robert Frerck/Odyssey Productions, Chicago; 87, David Phillips; 92(r), Stuart Cohen; 94, David R. Frazier Photolibrary; 95(l & r), Peter Menzel; 100, Beryl Goldberg; 100(INS), Robert Frerck/Odyssey Productions, Chicago; 105, Rice Sumner Wagner; 106, 110–111, 114(l), Robert Frerck/Odyssey Productions, Chicago; 109, Eugenia Fawcett; 114(r), Milt & Joan Mann/Cameramann International, Ltd.; 118 & 119, Stuart Cohen; 126, Paul Conklin; 127 & 130, Owen Franken; 131, Stuart Cohen; 137, Milt & Joan Mann/ Cameramann International, Ltd.; 140(l), Stuart Cohen; 140(r), Owen Franken; 143, Eugenia Fawcett; 144–145 & 150, Peter Menzel; 151, Stuart Cohen; 154 & 163(t), Robert Frerck/Odyssey Productions, Chicago; 163(b), Stuart Cohen; 166, © 1985 Robert Fried/D. Donne Bryant; 168, Beryl Goldberg; 171, Eugenia Fawcett; 172–173, Steve Vidler/Leo de Wys; 177, Joseph F. Viesti; 179(t), Artstreet; 179(bl), D. Donne Bryant; 179(bc), Charmayne McGee; 179(br), D. Donne Bryant; 180 & 181, Artstreet; 186(l), Milt & Joan Mann/Cameramann International, Ltd.; 186(r), Stuart Cohen; 194, Milt & Joan Mann/Cameramann International, Ltd.; 197, Robert Frerck/Odyssey Productions, Chicago; 198(tl) & 198(br), Milt & Joan Mann/Cameramann International, Ltd.; 199(b), Beryl Goldberg; 200(t), D. Donne Bryant; 200(bl), Robert Frerck/Odyssey Productions, Chicago; 200(br), D. Donne Bryant; 203, Museum of the American Indian, The Heye Foundation; 204–205, Joseph F. Viesti; 212 & 213, Robert Frerck/ Odyssey Productions, Chicago; 217(tl), Milt & Joan Mann/Cameramann International, Ltd.; 217(tr), Chip & Rosa Maria Peterson; 217(c & b), Joseph F. Viesti; 219, Robert Frerck/Odyssey Productions, Chicago; 220(t), Collection: Guadalupe López; 220(bl), Julio S. Simons; 220(br), Emilio Rosa Negrón; 225, David R. Frazier Photolibrary; 227, Milt & Joan Mann/Cameramann International, Ltd.; 232, Joseph F. Viesti; 235, Eugenia Fawcett; 236–237, Owen Franken; 241, 244, 245, 249, Robert Frerck/Odyssey Productions, Chicago; 251, David R. Frazier Photolibrary; 255, Milt & Joan Mann/Cameramann International, Ltd.; 256, Robert Frerck/Odyssey Productions, Chicago; 263, Stuart Cohen; 265, Chip & Rosa Maria Peterson; 266, Owen Franken; 269, Eugenia Fawcett; 270–271, Milt & Joan Mann/Cameramann International, Ltd.; 274(l), Stuart Cohen; 279, Robert Frerck/Odyssey Productions, Chicago; 284(l & r), Stuart Cohen; 285, Chip & Rosa Maria Peterson; 286 (Counter-clockwise from top), Robert Frerck/Odyssey Productions, Chicago, Robert Frerck/Odyssey Productions, Chicago, Beryl Goldberg, Stuart Cohen, Beryl Goldberg; 288, Stuart Cohen; 290(l), Robert Frerck/Odyssey Productions, Chicago; 290(r), Joseph F. Viesti; 291(r), Robert Frerck/ Odyssey Productions, Chicago; 292, Vautier/Click/Chicago Ltd.; 297, Joseph F. Viesti; 298(t) & 306, Robert Frerck/Odyssey Productions, Chicago; 301, Private Collection; 308, Stuart Cohen; 309, Owen Franken; 310(all), Stuart Cohen; 311, Joseph F. Viesti; 314, Robert Frerck/Odyssey Productions, Chicago; 315, D. Donne Bryant; 319, Robert Frerck/Odyssey Productions,